D0557633

Memory Observed

"I apologise for the non-arrival of the guest speaker —— who I'm almost sure I invited!"

Memory Observed

Remembering in Natural Contexts

SECOND EDITION

Selections and Commentary by
Ulric Neisser
Cornell University
Ira E. Hyman, Jr.
Western Washington University

WORTH PUBLISHERS

Memory Observed, second edition

Copyright © 2000, 1982 by Worth Publishers and W.H. Freeman and Company

Printed in the United States of America.

ISBN: 0-7167-3319-6

Printing: 5 4 3 2 1

Year: 04 03 02 01 00

Library of Congress Cataloging-in-Publication Data.

Memory observed: remembering in natural contexts / selections and commentary
by Ulric Neisser, Ira E. Hyman, Jr.—2nd ed.
    p. cm.
  Includes bibliographical references and index.
  1. Memory. 2. Memory—Research—Field work.   I. Neisser, Ulric. II. Hyman,
    Ira E.

BF371.M455 2000
153.1'2—dc21   99-049080

Sponsoring editor: Jessica Bayne
Senior marketing manager: Renee Ortbals
Designer: Cambraia (Magalháes) Fernandes
Production editor: Tracey Kuehn
Production manager: Sarah Segal
Composition: Compset, Inc.
Printing and binding: R.R. Donnelley & Sons

Worth Publishers
41 Madison Avenue
New York, New York 10010
www.worthpublishers.com

For Mark and Julie and Philip and Toby,
Jenny and Katherine and Joe,
and for Thomas and Alex

Contents

Preface to the First Edition

Psychology has followed two routes in the study of memory. Travelers on the high road hope to find basic mental mechanisms that can be demonstrated in well-controlled experiments; those on the low road want to understand the specific manifestations of memory in ordinary human experience. *Memory Observed* is a kind of guidebook to the lower road. Like any guidebook, it acquaints the reader with the major landmarks, the significant and famous observations of memory that everyone should know. In addition, I hope it will be helpful to those travelers and explorers who are seeking remote areas and untrodden paths. The lower terrain has not been well mapped as yet, and much remains to be discovered.

The high road in the study of memory has been popular since Ebbinghaus opened it a century ago by memorizing long lists of nonsense syllables. He argued that the laws of association would be best revealed by the study of rote learning, using meaningless material that was indifferent to the vagaries of individual experience. His argument prevailed. The study of rote memory has had an established place in experimental psychology since Ebbinghaus's time, even during the long decades when behaviorism virtually outlawed the investigation of the human mind. When modern cognitive psychology began to appear, based on the new conceptions of information and coding that had emerged after World War II, memory was among its central concerns. Cognition includes (as I once put it) "all the processes by which the sensory input is transformed, reduced, elaborated, stored, recovered, and used." At least half of those hypothetical processes involve memory; hundreds of models of memory were soon proposed and tested in thousands of experiments. As I will argue at greater length in Selection 1, the upshot of so much effort has been disappointing. There is little sense of progress; genuinely important questions are rarely addressed; most research focuses on questions that are essentially methodological. It has taken me a long time to understand why.

At first, it seemed that we just had too many facts and not enough theory. There have been more memory experiments than anyone can count, enough to discourage even the most intrepid maker of systems. Yet without a theoretical framework all facts remain uncoordinated and uninteresting. Eventually, I realized that no theory can be expected to integrate an essentially arbitrary set of data. We have been accumulating the wrong *kind* of knowledge. Although we have found out a lot about performance in specific laboratory tasks, we do not know nearly enough about the phenomena that motivate the study of memory in the first place. Consequently, theories of memory are either so closely bound to particular experiments that they are uninteresting, or so vague that they are intellectually unsatisfying.

I believe that a similar state of affairs prevails in many areas of psychology. Perception, too, is studied mostly in laboratory settings that lack ecological validity (that is, settings that are not representative of the environment in which perception usually occurs). As a result, the prevailing theories of perception are inadequate in many ways, too numerous to list here. In 1976 I tried to present an alternative approach to perception in a book called *Cognition and Reality* (W. H. Freeman and Company), which stressed the need for a more ecological orientation throughout cognitive psychology.

Cognition and Reality had little to say about memory. By 1976 I had formed the opinion that there were too few facts in hand rather than too many: "We have almost no systematic knowledge about memory as it occurs in the course of everyday life." As it turns out, this assessment was overly pessimistic. Quite a few travelers have already taken the lower road. They include some distinguished company: Sigmund Freud and William Stern, Gregory Bateson and Alexander Luria, the United States Supreme Court and the Senate Watergate Investigating Committee. There are many others, whose names are less familiar but whose work is no less important. It is a privilege to present their observations in this book. Since the publication of *Cognition and Reality* I have often been asked to make suggestions for research. If the standard paradigms of cognitive psychology are inadequate, what is to be done? Here, at least, are some interesting things that have been done already.

I am grateful for all the help I have had in assembling *Memory Observed*: To the authors who wrote the selections and the publishers who have allowed me to reprint them; to my own publisher, who has put up with repeated delays and changes of plan; to the Psychology Department of the University of Pennsylvania, whose hospitality allowed me to spend a sabbatical putting things together; to all the students, undergraduate and graduate, who have helped me to think about memory in natural contexts. Students are far more generous with their professors than most people understand; they give time and energy, ideas and hypotheses, references and corrections, and endless valuable argument. Most of all, I am grateful to Arden Neisser, who has not only helped me to think about memories but given me so many that I cherish.

Ulric Neisser
October 1981

Preface to the Second Edition

These days, both of the two routes described in the 1982 preface are carrying a lot of traffic. The high road—the laboratory study of memory—is no longer the narrow and pedestrian enterprise described so critically in Selection 1. An impressive array of new laboratory memory paradigms has been developed in recent years, some with promising links to new methods in neuroscience. But what was then the low road—the study of memory in natural contexts—has changed even more. Once a marginal enterprise with few systematic studies and little recognition in major psychology journals, it has now become an influential and widely accepted research tradition. The International Conference on Practical Aspects of Memory, so radical a venture when it first met in 1978, is almost an institution by this time: two more conferences have already been held and a fourth is planned for 2001. The recently established Society for Applied Research in Memory and Cognition (SARMAC) *is* an institution, and so is its journal, *Applied Cognitive Psychology*. A new generation of naturalistic memory researchers has been trained, and examples of their work are routinely described in standard textbooks.

This dramatic shift in the status of the ecological study of memory has significantly changed the task of editing *Memory Observed*. The chief problem in putting the first edition together was finding enough papers to include. In contrast, the problem this time was how to select among a wealth of attractive and interesting possibilities. The choices have not been easy. It seemed important to keep many selections from the first edition—some that are obvious classics, others that are our own particular favorites. In many cases, however, those selections are no longer at the cutting edge of research; recent developments have shed new light on the phenomena they describe. This has driven us to include many new selections on such established topics as flashbulb memory, childhood amnesia, eyewitness testimony, and recall of daily events. We have also introduced several new topics of current interest, especially memory for real and imagined trauma. Even so, much has been left out: we apologize to the many researchers whose work might well have found its way into these pages if our space limitations had been less strict.

We have had a lot of help in putting this book together. To begin with, we are grateful to the authors of all these selections and to their publishers: thanks for allowing us to use your material! We also appreciate the careful work of the editorial staff at Worth Publishing, particularly Michael Kimball, Jessica Bayne, and Tracey Kuehn. Moreover, it is important to acknowledge the three universities that have generously supported our research: not only Cornell and Western Washington where we (Neisser and Hyman, respectively) now teach but also Emory University in Atlanta, where we met when Hyman was a graduate student and Neisser was his advisor. We owe a significant debt to the many students and colleagues at those institutions who have helped us in our research, our thinking, and our writing. Like all sciences, the study of memory is a collaborative process that depends heavily on the work of enthusiastic and hard-working students. Special thanks go to the students in Hyman's seminars at Western Washington University, who read many candidate articles for this volume: your feedback is much appreciated. Another special vote of thanks goes to Eugene Winograd, our valued friend and colleague at Emory, who has contributed so much to our thinking and to this field. We also wish to knowledge the work and friendship of Steen Folke Larsen, whose recent untimely death deprived the ecological study of memory of one of its most creative researchers.

Finally we thank Angela Harwood and Arden Neisser, not only for their help with this project but for providing so many great memories for us to observe. Arden, whose love was Ulric Neisser's inspiration for thirty-five years, will unfortunately provide no more.

Ulric Neisser, Ithaca, New York
Ira E. Hyman Jr., Bellingham, Washington
August 1999

Part I

<u>THE ARGUMENT</u>

In which the argument for the study of memory in natural settings
is presented, disputed, and reaffirmed.

1 | Memory: What Are the Important Questions?

Ulric Neisser

These remarks were made rather a long time ago, at the 1978 conference on "Practical Aspects of Memory," which also inspired the frontispiece of this volume. They present a straightforward argument: The orthodox psychology of memory has very little to show for a hundred years of effort, in part because it systematically avoids the most interesting issues. Just as the naturalistic, ethological study of animal behavior turned out to be much more interesting than traditional studies of "animal learning," so a naturalistic study of memory might prove more productive than its laboratory counterpart.

It is a distinct honor to open a conference on "Practical Aspects of Memory," and an unusual one. So far as I know, there has never been such a conference before. Perhaps it seems especially remarkable to me because I am an American, and therefore have relatively little experience of fruitful interchange between theoretical and applied psychology. British experimental psychologists have a long tradition of benefiting from that interchange, but we are less used to it in the United States. Unfortunately, the naturalistic tradition has been weaker in the study of memory than in many other areas, even in Britain. Nevertheless, it has not been entirely lacking: it was from Cambridge that Bartlett launched his quixotic challenge to the memory establishment of the 1920s and 1930s. He was convinced that his contemporaries understood neither the purpose nor the nature of memory, and that standard laboratory procedures just obscure its

※ From U. Neisser (1978). Memory: What are the important questions? In M. M. Gruneberg, P. E. Morris, & R. N. Sykes (Eds.), *Practical Aspects of Memory*. London: Academic Press, 3–24.

real characteristics. His challenge went almost unheard for 40 years, from the publication of *Remembering* (1932) until this decade, but it is unheard no longer. There is suddenly a host of theorists talking about "schemata" (e.g., Anderson, 1977; Rumelhart, 1975) and a host of experimenters studying memory for stories (e.g., Bransford & Johnson, 1973; Mandler & Johnson, 1977). In my view this work is still somewhat deficient in ecological validity—hardly anyone memorizes one-page stories except in the course of psychological experiments—but it is still a great step forward. Perhaps, as someone once said of something else, the naturalistic study of memory is an idea whose time has come.

I am slightly embarrassed that I cannot remember the source of that particular expression, but not surprised. It is a frequent experience for me. I am often unable to recall the authors of phrases that I would like to quote, and have equal difficulty in remembering who told me things. These retrieval failures pose some interesting questions. Why do they occur? Do other people have less trouble recalling sources than I do? Is my difficulty in remembering the source of a written quotation related to other types of memory failure, or are they independent? In fact, how does one go about remembering sources, or arguments, or material appropriate to one's train of thought? What makes for skill in such activities?

These questions may not be the "important" ones that my title has promised, but they are interesting nevertheless. They involve real uses of memory in humanly understandable situations. It is therefore discouraging to find that nothing in the extensive literature of the psychology of memory sheds much light on them, so that anyone who wishes to study such problems must start from scratch. Unfortunately, this is not an isolated instance. It is an example of a principle that is nearly as valid in 1978 as it was in 1878: If X is an interesting or socially significant aspect of memory, then psychologists have hardly ever studied X.

Let me give another example of that principle, again drawn from my own immediate experience. In giving this address, I naturally hope that I will make some impression on you—that you will remember at least part of what I say. But what *do* people remember of speeches that they hear, or arguments made to them? Who remembers what, and why? The social psychologists have touched lightly on these issues in their examination of persuasion, but they have been interested in opinion change rather than in memory. Apart from their work, the effect of lectures on listeners has hardly been studied at all. A couple of recent exploratory experiments—one by Kintsch and Bates (1977) and the other by Keenan, MacWhinney and Mayhew (1977) suggest that such studies might yield intriguing results: listeners seem to remember the lecturer's irrelevant asides better than his text, for example.

This is part of a larger question. Most experimental psychologists of memory are also teachers. We earn our living by presenting information to students, often by lecturing, and at the end of the term we set examinations to see if they remember any of it. But what happens after that? Students attend universities partly because they hope to acquire knowledge that will be valuable to them afterwards; that is, they expect to remember some of it. We certainly share their hope. Despite the old saying that "Education is what is left over when you have forgotten what you learned" (which I also cannot reference properly), we would be dismayed if a kind of educational Korsakov amnesia regularly wiped out all trace of our teachings. How much, then, do students retain? This really *is* an important question. Higher education has become a central feature of Western culture, involving millions of people every year, and it depends heavily on the assumption that students remember something valuable from their educational experience. One might expect psychologists to leap at the opportunity to study a critical memory problem so close at hand, but they never do. It is difficult to find even a single study, ancient or modern, of what is retained from academic instruction. Given our expertise and the way we earn our livings, this omission can only be described as scandalous.

Other illustrations of the general principle are readily available. You need only tell any friend, not himself a psychologist, that you study memory. Given even a little encouragement, your friend will describe all kinds of interesting phenomena: the limitations of his memory for early childhood, his inability to remember appointments, his aunt who could recite poems from memory by the hour, the regrettable recent decline in his ability to recall people's names, how well he could find his way around his home town after a thirty years' absence, the differences between his memory and someone else's. Our research, of course, has virtually nothing to say about any of these topics.

Psychology's thundering silence on such questions might be excused if the study of memory had only just begun. One cannot do everything right away. The fact is, however, that we have been studying memory, and doing memory experiments, for nearly a hundred years. Research on the topic went on continuously even during the dreary decades of behaviorist domination, and has recently reached almost frenzied proportions. This research was not carried out by uneducated or incompetent people; some of the best minds in psychology have worked, and are presently working, in the area of memory. Why, then, have they not turned their attention to practical problems and natural settings?

The answer is not far to seek. Psychologists are not interested in such questions primarily because they believe they are doing something more important. They are working toward a general theory of memory, a scientific understanding of its underlying mechanisms, more fundamental and far-reaching than any research on worldly questions could possibly be. They can claim that their work has already established broad generalizations and led to new discoveries; it is even now converging on specific and powerful theories. If these claims were valid, they might justify neglecting problems that seem more obvious and interesting to our nonpsychologist friends. Therefore I will examine each of them briefly: the established principles, the new discoveries, and the theories themselves. As you may already suspect, the results of my survey will not be encouraging.

Let us take the empirical generalizations first. No one could deny that many of them are solid and well-established; so solid that occasional exceptions may be intriguing but cannot undermine their validity. Consider, for example, mnemonic interference and its dependence on similarity, the superiority of meaningful material (stories) over meaningless material (lists), the positive effect of increasing study time, or the savings that appear when once-familiar material is relearned. Such enduring principles comfort those of us who teach courses in memory, because they provide a refuge from the undecided quarrels of the theoreticians. Besides, they are true. Unfortunately, they rarely make much impression on our students, perhaps because they are so unsurprising. Students know them long before they hear our lectures. This has been made embarrassingly obvious by the results of Kreutzer, Leonard, and Flavell's (1975) interview study of children's knowledge about memory. Every one of the generalizations I have mentioned is familiar to the average middle-class third-grader in America from his own experience! Indeed, most of them are known to kindergarteners. If the psychology of memory must rest its case on accomplishments like these, it has little to boast of.

In teaching these familiar generalizations, of course, we do not confine ourselves to simply stating the naked facts. We emphasize method as well as content: appropriate experimental conditions, suitable control groups, well-defined terms, limiting cases. Most of all we emphasize theoretical explanations, of which there are never less than two for any phenomenon. In this way we always have a good deal to talk about, and there are many fine points by which the better students can be separated from the poorer ones. It is doubtful, however, whether the experimental details add anything to the power of the principles themselves. The opposite is more often the case. When a particular experimental result seems to contradict an established principle, a dozen psychologists leap into the breach to restore it. A case in point occurred when Tulving (1966) apparently showed that prior study of a list of words does not improve performance if that list appears later as part of a longer one. Tulving's finding seemed to undermine one of the commonplace principles, but it was an empty threat. The flaws in the experiment were soon revealed (e.g., Novinski, 1969; Slamecka, Moore, & Carey, 1972) and the status quo restored. The only long-run effect of the controversy was to provide another theoretical complication that students can be required to master.

Let me leave the familiar generalizations now and turn to the genuine discoveries. There certainly have been some, although perhaps no list of them could command universal agreement. One important cluster of discoveries concerns the various kinds of immediate and short-term memories. We *do* know more about these now than third-graders, and for that matter more than William James or Ebbinghaus did. Although we are not yet entirely clear about the details of the iconic and posticonic mechanisms in vision, for example, a good deal of progress has been made. Similarly, we have begun to unravel the tangle of echoic stores, articulatory loops, and working memories that are related to hearing and to speech. This is an important area, and I would not deny that the work has added to our understanding of cognition. Nevertheless, it stretches a point to call such mechanisms "memories." They fit the formal definition, but what most people mean by "memory" is quite different. It is disconcerting to find that contemporary textbooks of memory devote a quarter or a third of their pages to "memories" that last less than a minute. Shouldn't memory have something to do with the past?

If the work on short-term memory seems to be leading to significant progress, other discoveries have fared less well. A particularly discouraging example is Sternberg's (1966) discovery that what may be called "memory search time" increases linearly with the number of alternatives that must be searched, at least in many situations. This phenomenon seemed important when it was first reported, but by now it has almost become a bore. It has been so thoroughly investigated and described that everything is known except what it means. We have found out too much about it, and yet not enough. Psychology seems to exploit its experimental effects somewhat in the way that the mass media exploit public figures. It is as difficult for a phenomenon to remain interesting as for a statesman to remain impressive and admirable, given the relentless scrutiny of television and the press. In that case, too, the details with which we are bombarded never add up to a genuine understanding of the subject himself. Instead, we are presented with a continuous stream of reactions, elaborations, and details that ends by putting us to sleep. The linear search function has suffered a similar fate. It may even be at a greater disadvantage than the politicians, whose power over us makes them intrinsically interesting. We return to the television set again and again in the faint hope of understanding the people whose decisions are significant for us. Once we have become disenchanted with Sternberg's linear function, however, why should we ever go back to it?

Another important discovery on my short list is the possibility of deliberately rotating mental images, established by Roger Shepard and his colleagues (Shepard & Metzler, 1971; Cooper & Shepard, 1973, etc.). It has not yet been overexploited, and there are tantalizing promises of more discoveries to come. Recent work by Lynn Cooper (1976), for example, suggests that there may be fundamental individual differences in how people make the visual comparisons that such experiments require. Unfortunately, little work is being done to follow up her finding. Instead, every-one's attention is riveted on much weightier theoretical issues. Does the existence of mental rotation force us to assume that there are "analogue" representations in memory, or can the phenomenon be reconciled with the hypothesis that all mental structures are "propositional"? This is just the sort of question that psychologists love—the kind that has kept us busy for a hundred years. After an overall theory of forgetting or storage or remem-bering is established, the effort to bring every new experimental result un-der its umbrella can occupy an army of researchers for a decade at a time. Has it been an effective way to study memory? Let's look at the record.

Before the current crop of theories—EPAM, HAM, ACT, ELINOR, and their highly capitalized competitors—there were others. For example, there was the interference theory of forgetting (McGeoch, 1942; Postman & Underwood, 1973). Interference theorists believed (some still believe) that all forgetting is due to interference from irrelevant associations, and have occasionally tried to demonstrate it directly. More often, they have tried to settle questions about the nature and origin of the interference: re-sponse competition, unlearning, intraexperimental interference, extraex-perimental interference, and so on. Like almost all theorists, they took cer-tain assumptions for granted (motives as drives, spontaneous recovery of extinction over time) while they treated others as taboo (repression, decay of memories). Now that their approach has gone out of fashion, we can see that this selection of assumptions was questionable. Why should we take some motivational effects as fundamental and treat others as epiphenom-ena, or accept time as an independent variable for spontaneous recovery but not for spontaneous decay? That particular pattern of assumptions ap-peared because interference theory was an offshoot of a more general stimulus–response psychology, or "learning theory," of whose decline and fall I shall have more to say shortly. With learning theory out of fashion, the experiments of the interference theorists seem like empty exercises to most of us. Were they ever anything else?

To me, the very notion of uncovering the "cause of forgetting" seems rather strange. It is a little like trying to establish the cause of juvenile delinquency or crime. Such studies are no longer popular, because both "crime" and "cause" turned out to be much richer notions than had been supposed. There are white-collar crimes and violent crimes, premeditated crimes and crimes of passion, crimes committed by the poor and by the rich, undiscovered crimes and crimes leading to conviction, crimes that are part of an accepted cultural pattern and crimes committed by lonely and desperate individuals. There are causes of crime like racism and capi-talism, like ignorance and folly, like opportunity and lack of opportunity, like an impoverished childhood or a spoiled one, like inadequate law en-forcement or the enactment of absurd laws, like criminal organizations, like lust and greed and the other five sins but also like the demands of conscience and the clear-eyed perception of all the alternatives. Most of all, there is the complexly intertwined history of a particular individual who encounters particular situations. How, then, can one hope to discover the cause of crime?

Forgetting is an equally incoherent notion. Perhaps you fail to retrieve a piece of information that, by some standard, should have been available: you can't think of my name. At the same time, though, there is a lot that you *are* thinking of. What you do and what you think in every human situation has many causes at many levels, ranging from social convention to unconscious drive. What you do *not* do (i.e., think of my name) is an aspect of what you are doing, and has just as many causes. A great deal is going on. To point this out is not to argue that forgetting is due only to interference and not to decay. The matter is equally complex if the necessary information has decayed simply because you and I were introduced too long ago. Even then, its nonexistence would be a cause of remembering just as much as of forgetting—of what you do as well as of what you don't do. What is needed to understand such failures is a detailed examination of what actually happens in them, rather than the theoretical manipulation of abstract and a priori concepts. But I am getting ahead of my story.

Today the interference theory of forgetting has few supporters. It has been replaced by new theories, mostly models of information storage and retrieval systems with various subdivisions and properties. Before considering their importance and probable fate, I would like to review another part of the history of psychology. It offers an analogy that can teach us a great deal, and perhaps help us to avoid some unnecessary labor. As someone (whom I again cannot remember) once put it, those who do not study history are condemned to repeat it. The history I have in mind is that of learning theory and behaviorism.

Not long ago, learning theory dominated almost the whole of experimental psychology (at least in America). It set the problems, prescribed the methods, defined the range of permissible hypotheses, and seemed generalizable to every aspect of life. Its intellectual leaders wrote books with titles like *Principles of Behavior* and *The Behavior of Organisms,* and their broad claims were backed up by hundreds of experiments. To be sure, the experimental subjects were almost always white rats; a few skeptics wondered whether it was quite safe to generalize from "animals" to humans, but hardly anyone doubted that at least animal behavior was being investigated in a scientifically fruitful way. The most influential philosophers of the time produced accounts of scientific method—hypothesis testing, manipulation of variables, and the like—that justified the learning theorists at every step. There was dispute about whether Hull, Spence, Skinner, or (as an outside possibility) Tolman was closest to ultimate truth, but not much about the merit of their common enterprise.

Today, learning theory has been almost completely swept away. Not entirely, perhaps: with the mainland of animal behavior lost to their foes, a behaviorist remnant is holding out on well-defended islands like "behavior modification" or "behavior therapy." They still sound confident, but they are watching the straits with an anxious eye. There are even a few stalwarts fighting rearguard actions in the rat laboratories, putting out research reports that the triumphant majority don't bother to read. Nevertheless, the battle is essentially over, and it was surprisingly brief. What happened?

The fundamental blow was struck by a small group of scientists who called themselves "ethologists," not psychologists, and who were not concerned with learning theory at all. They wanted to know how animals really behaved in natural environments. They were not so much interested in hypotheses as in the animals themselves. Wasps, herring gulls, ducklings, and jackdaws are a curious base on which to build a scientific revolution, but one occurred. The work of the ethologists showed that the concepts and methods of learning theory were simply irrelevant to the understanding of natural behavior. Every species seems to have a different set of learning abilities, and to respond to different sorts of variables. Even in a single species or a single organism, patterns of behavior vary drastically with changes in the gross environment, with fluctuations in hormone levels, with stages of maturation. Given these facts, notions like "conditioning," "reinforcement," "extinction," and "generalization" require constant reinterpretation if they are to survive at all. The very distinction between what is learned and what is innate has become uncertain. Even the laboratory rat has turned on his old friends (rats are apparently treacherous after all) by exhibiting a kind of learning that none of the old models could accommodate: a food aversion acquired on a single trial with a reinforcement delay of many hours.

This new wave of research has not resulted in universal agreement on theoretical issues. The disputes among "behavioral biologists," as these investigators are now often called, are just as vigorous as the arguments between learning theorists once were. Many of them will surely seem just as pointless to the eye of the historian. But whatever the ultimate fate of the theories may be, the observations of animal behavior that are now being made can never become irrelevant or uninteresting. We are finding out what really happens in the world around us, and that will be worth knowing in any imaginable future.

I have dwelt on this bit of psychological history at some length because I believe it has a clear application to the subject at hand. Theories of memory are invariably based on the performance of experimental subjects in specialized laboratory tasks. So, too, were the learning theories of the 1930s and 1940s. The tasks themselves are ingeniously designed to shed light on the experimenter's hypothesis, or to decide among competing theories. So, too, were the procedures of the behaviorists. The most widely acclaimed memory theories are those which seem most far-reaching and which explain many experimental results on the basis of relatively few assumptions. This, too, characterized the glory days of stimulus–response psychology. A plausible and explicit set of methodological assumptions justifies current research practices. The same thing was true in the case of learning theory, although the old reliance on the hypothetico-deductive method has been replaced by a new attachment to computer simulation. Finally, modern theories of memory have as little relevance to everyday memory as learning theory had to what is usually called "learning." The sentences and brief "stories" that are popular in research laboratories today are an improvement on the nonsense syllable, but they are far from representative of what ordinary people remember and forget.

In short, the results of a hundred years of the psychological study of memory are somewhat discouraging. We have established firm empirical generalizations, but most of them are so obvious that every ten-year-old knows them anyway. We have made discoveries, but they are only marginally about memory; in many cases we don't know what to do with them, and wear them out with endless experimental variations. We have an intellectually impressive group of theories, but history offers little confidence that they will provide any meaningful insight into natural behavior. Of course, I could be wrong: perhaps this is the exceptional case where the lessons of history do not apply, and the new theories will stand the test of time better than the old ones did. Let me be frank: I have not pinpointed any fatal flaw in Hunt's distributed memory model (Hunt, 1971), Tulving's conception of encoding specificity (Tulving, 1974), Anderson's ACT (1976), or the others. I cannot prove that they are misguided. But because they say so little about the everyday uses of memory, they seem ripe for the same fate that overtook learning theory not long ago.

The psychologists who have spent a century studying esoteric forms of memory in the laboratory are not really uninterested in its more ordinary manifestations, and have always hoped that their work would have wide applicability sooner or later. Their preference for artificial tasks has a rational basis: one can control variables and manipulate conditions more easily in the lab than in natural settings. Why not work under the best possible conditions? Memory is memory, or so it would seem. This methodological assumption resembles the assumptions made by the learning theorists in their study of "learning." Unfortunately, it turned out that "learning" in general does not exist: wasps and songbirds and rats integrate past experiences into their lives in very different ways. I think that "memory" in general does not exist either. It is a concept left over from a medieval psychology that partitioned the mind into independent faculties: "thought" and "will" and "emotion" and many others, with "memory" among them. Let's give it up, and begin to ask our questions in different ways. Those questions need not be uninformed by theory, or by a vision of human nature, but perhaps they can be more closely driven by the characteristics of ordinary human experience.

What we want to know, I think, is how people use their own past experiences in meeting the present and the future. We would like to understand how this happens under natural conditions: the circumstances in which it occurs, the forms it takes, the variables on which it depends, the differences between individuals in their uses of the past. "Natural conditions" does not mean in the jungle or on the desert, unless that happens to be where our subjects live. It means in school and at home, on the job and in the course of thought, as carefree children and as reflective old men and women. Because changes in the social and cultural environment can change the uses of the past, we will have to study many settings. The psychological laboratory is the easiest of these settings in which to work, but it is also among the least interesting; we ourselves are the only people who spend much time there voluntarily.

The task before us is much harder than that which confronted the ethologists. They had several great advantages. For one thing, it is easier to observe animals than people. Animals don't mind it as much (if you are quiet) and are not so aware of what you are up to. Their habitats are more limited, in many cases, and their behaviors more stereotyped. Moreover, the time-dependence of their behavior is much shorter: you rarely have to consider events of twenty years ago to understand what an animal is doing today. They do not have language to help them control the application of the past to the present, and seem to spend more of their time in action as opposed to thought.

One difference between our task and that of the ethologists deserves special mention. They began with a ready-made categorization of their subject matter, whereas we have none. It is obvious that there are many different kinds of animals—species—which can be studied separately. In setting out to do a field study of animal behavior, one usually need not worry about how to distinguish the robins from the herring gulls. In studying memory, however, we do not know how to separate different kinds of cases. Indeed, we cannot even be sure whether any natural lines of demarcation exist. This is a genuinely important question, and one of the first things we should be trying to find out. Are there functionally different types of memory in everyday life? If so, what are they?

Although I am far from sure how to classify the phenomena of memory, I must put them in some kind of order to discuss them at all. Science cannot proceed without some way of defining things so we can set out to study them. The organization I will use is based on the functions of memory. What do we use the past *for?* Happily, when the question is put in this way, it turns out that the sum total of relevant psychological work is not zero after all. There has been some valuable research and thinking about the natural uses of memory, usually by individuals outside the mainstream of contemporary theory. These beginnings offer promising leads for further work; I will mention some of them below.

First of all, everyone uses the past to define themselves. Who am I? I have a name, a family, a home, a job. I know a great deal about myself: what I have done, how I have felt, where I have been, whom I have known, how I have been treated. My past defines me, together with my present and the future that the past leads me to expect. What would I be without it? Much of that formative past is now tacit rather than explicit knowledge: I do not dwell on it, and I cannot recall it as such. The specifics are beyond recall, although their resultant is here in person. Some things, however, I can remember very explicitly when I choose. I think back on my childhood, or my youth, or on something that happened this morning. Typically I do this alone, silently, without telling anybody. I often do it deliberately and voluntarily, but memories may also come un-bidden—"involuntary memories," as Salaman (1970) [see Selection 5] calls them—either in waking life or in sleep. All these are cases where the past becomes present to me, and to me alone.

Many questions suggest themselves about such personal evocations. Some were asked long ago by Freud and the psychoanalysts. Why do just these memories come, and not others? When are they trustworthy, and when fabricated? Why do I have so few from my very early childhood? Do some people have more of them than others, and if so why? What function do they serve? How does the nature and incidence of personal recollection vary with age, culture, sex, and situation? What happens when whole sections of the past become inaccessible, as in functional amnesias?

Work has been done on some of these questions, but not much. Freud (1905) drew attention to the phenomenon of infantile amnesia and tried to explain it by repression; Schachtel (1947) [see Selection 27] later proposed a cognitive account which seems more plausible (cf. Neisser, 1962). Freud also wrote two papers on early memories (1899, 1917) [see Selection 26], a topic which has been studied sporadically over the years by many psychologists (Dudycha & Dudycha, 1941) recently including Douglas Herrmann and me. Our questionnaire study (Herrmann & Neisser, 1978) suggests that women college students may have slightly better memory of childhood experiences than men do. Others have noticed the same sex difference in early memories; I wish I understood it. We still know very little about these questions, and what we do know mostly concerns deliberate, voluntary remembering. Spontaneous recall may be quite a different matter. Esther Salaman's fascinating autobiographical book *A Collection of Moments* (1970) [see Selection 5], which describes many images of early childhood that came to her unbidden and unexpected, may be a useful source of hypotheses about spontaneous memory.

One frequently recalls past experiences in search of some sort of self-improvement. Where did I go wrong? Could I have done things differently?

What were my alternatives? How did all this start? These questions can be asked privately or with a listener. "Going public," even to a single individual, makes a difference. Both private and shared recollection can have profound consequences for that sense of self which is so dependent on what one remembers. Psychoanalysis and psychotherapy are obvious examples of this use of the past, but they are by no means the only ones. Something similar probably happens in the Catholic confessional, of which I know very little. Some Communist countries have institutionalized confession as a way of strengthening social unity and reforming individual behavior. To be sure, those who confess in political settings must be quite careful about what they say. Is that selectivity exhibited only in their public statements, or does it extend to what they remember privately? According to recent experimental evidence, people's memory of their own prior attitudes can change dramatically when the attitudes themselves have shifted (Goethals & Reckman, 1973).

There are other occasions when one's personal memories achieve a kind of public importance. A familiar example occurs in legal testimony, where an exact account of the past can be critical in determining a defendant's future. Psychologists have been interested in this issue for many years. At the beginning of the century William Stern published several volumes of a scholarly journal devoted exclusively to the psychology of testimony (*Beiträge zur Psychologie der Aussage*) [*see Selection 20*] and Münsterburg wrote a widely cited book about it called *On the Witness Stand* (1909). Unfortunately, this early work produced few insights except that the testimony of eyewitnesses is often inaccurate. A series of ingenious experiments by Elizabeth Loftus (e.g., Loftus & Palmer, 1974; Loftus, 1975) has revived interest in the problem, and begun to define the kinds of distortions that can occur as well as their sources.

One does not remember only events that one has personally experienced, but also those known at secondhand—things that have happened to other people. We learn from the experiences of our friends and acquaintances, and also from historical figures whose lives are somehow relevant to our own. In a literate society, we do not often think of history as something remembered; it is usually something written down. In many parts of the world, however, history has long been the responsibility of memory specialists, or oral historians, whose knowledge of ancient deeds and agreements exerts a controlling influence on contemporary events. D'Azevedo (1962) [*see Selection 39*] has described the role of oral historians among one African tribe, the Gola; it seems clear that this cultural practice is widespread in Africa and elsewhere. The history that is passed on through generations in this way is surprisingly accurate. The historians do not learn it by rote, but in an integrated and intelligent way. Whether this requires special gifts and special training, or whether anyone could remember any amount of oral history if it were appropriate to do so, is an open question.

In general, the relation between literacy and memory is poorly understood. It is one of those issues where every possible position can be and has been plausibly argued. Perhaps unschooled individuals from traditional societies have particularly *good* memories, because they must rely on those memories so heavily where nothing can be written down (Riesman, 1956). Perhaps, however, they have relatively *poor* memories because they lack the general mnemonic skills and strategies that come with literacy and schooling (Scribner & Cole, 1973). Certainly they perform badly in standard psychological memory experiments (Cole, Gay, Glick, & Sharp, 1971). Or maybe they are just like us: good at remembering what interests them. That is what Bartlett (1932) thought, though he could not resist endowing nonliterate Africans with a special facility for low-level "rote recapitulation" as well. In my own view, it may be a mistake to treat culture and literacy as overriding variables: individual differences and individual experience are more important. If the experimental task is remembering oral stories, then experience in listening to stories will make a big difference. That is probably why E. F. Dube (1977) [*see Selection 41*] recently found that both schooled and unschooled young people from Botswana were far better at story recall than American school children of the same age. However, he also found enormous individual differences correlated with estimates of the subjects' intelligence, made by tribal elders for the nonliterate children and on the basis of school grades for the others. The best of the unschooled subjects exhibited remarkably high levels of recall.

Memory is also involved in many activities of daily life. We make a plan and have to remember to carry it out, put something down and have to recall where it is, are given directions and must remember them if we are to reach our destination, encounter a prior acquaintance and want to pick up the relationship where it left off. Our access to the past is probably better when remembering is embedded in these natural activities than when it occurs in isolation. At least this is true for young children, as Istomina (1975) has shown in an elegant series of experiments. Different individuals are unequally skilled in different kinds of everyday memory, according to questionnaire data that Herrmann and I have recently collected (Herrmann & Neisser, 1978). But we still know almost nothing about these practical uses of memory, important as they are.

In most instances of daily remembering, it is meanings and not surface details that we must recall. Just as the oral historian remembers what happened instead of memorizing some formula of words that describes it, so too we recall the substance of what we heard or read rather than its verbatim form. This is now generally acknowledged, even in laboratory research. The new wave of enthusiasm for Bartlett's ideas and for the use of stories as memory materials has led us to devalue the study of rote rememorization almost completely. This is entirely appropriate, if "rote memory" means the learning of arbitrary lists of words or syllables for experimental purposes. The fact is, however, that many cultural institutions depend heavily on exact and literal recall. When we speak of remembering a song or a poem, for example, we do not mean that we have the gist of it but that we know the words. Rubin (1977) [*see Selection 36*] has recently shown that literal memory for the National Anthem, the Lord's Prayer, and similar texts is widespread among Americans. Verbatim memory is even more important in other societies, I think; some memorize the Koran where others study the Bible and still others learn long speeches from Shakespeare. This happens whenever it is the text itself, and not just its meaning, that is important. A text can be important for many reasons: patriotic, religious, esthetic, or personal. For singers and actors, the reason can even be professional. Whatever the reason, people's ability to recite appropriate texts verbatim at appropriate times ought to be deeply interesting to the psychology of memory. The fact that we have not studied it is another particularly striking example of my original proposition: If X is an interesting memory phenomenon, psychologists avoid it like the plague. Hundreds of experimentalists have spent their lives working on rote memory, without ever examining the rote memorization that goes on around them every day.

The last use of the past that I will discuss concerns intellectual activity itself. Although I have little talent for recalling the sources of quotations, I am not too bad at remembering experiments; if it were otherwise, I could not have prepared this address. However, this ability certainly does not make me unique. Everybody who is skilled at anything necessarily has a good memory for whatever information that activity demands. Physicists can remember what they need to know to do physics, and fishermen what they need for fishing; musicians remember music, art critics recall paintings, historians know history. Every person is a prodigy to his neighbors, remembering so much that other people do not know. We should be careful in what we say about memory in general until we know more about these many memories in particular.

These are some of the important questions, and we must seek the answers as best we can. Our search need not be entirely haphazard; I am not recommending an aimless accumulation of ecological minutiae. We will surely be guided by our general conceptions of human nature and human social life, as well as by more particular hypotheses about the phenomena we study. Without such conceptions and hypotheses, we can make little progress. The challenge will be to shift from testing hypotheses for their own sake to using them as tools for the exploration of reality.

It is a challenge that will not be easy to meet. The realistic study of memory is much harder than the work we have been accustomed to—so much harder that one can easily forgive those who have been reluctant to undertake it. After all, we bear no malice toward that legendary drunk who kept looking for his money under the streetlamp although he had dropped it ten yards away in the dark. As he correctly pointed out, the light was better where he was looking. But what we want to find *is* in the dark, out there where real people make use of their pasts in complicated ways. If we are to find it, we must look there. The convening of this conference may suggest that we are finally heading in that direction.

REFERENCES

Anderson J. R. (1976). *Language, memory, and thought.* Hillsdale, N.J.: Lawrence Erlbaum.

Anderson, R. C. (1977). The notion of schemata and the educational enterprise. In R. C. Anderson, R. T. Spiro, & W. E. Montague (Eds.), *Schooling and the acquisition of knowledge.* Hillsdale, N.J.: Erlbaum.

Bartlett, F. C. (1932). *Remembering.* Cambridge: Cambridge University Press.

Bransford, J. D., & Johnson, M. K. (1973). Consideration of some problems of comprehension. In W. G. Chase (Ed.), *Visual information processing.* New York: Academic Press.

Cole, M., Gay, J., Glick, J. A., & Sharp, D. W. (1971). *The cultural context of learning and thinking.* New York: Basic Books.

Cooper, L. A. (1976). Individual differences in visual comparison processes. *Perception and Psychophysics, 19,* 433–444.

Cooper, L. A., & Shepard, R. N. (1973). Chronometric studies of the rotation of mental images. In W. G. Chase (Ed.), *Visual information processing.* New York: Academic Press.

D'Azevedo, W. L. (1962). Uses of the past in Gola discourse. *Journal of African history, 3,* 11–34.

Dube, E. F. (1977). *A cross-cultural study of the relationship between "intelligence" level and story recall.* Doctoral Dissertation, Cornell University, Ithaca, N.Y.

Dudycha, G., & Dudycha, M. (1941). Childhood memories: A review of the literature. *Psychological Bulletin, 38,* 668–682.

Freud, S. (1905). Three contributions to the theory of sex. In A. A. Brill (Ed.), *The basic writings of Sigmund Freud.* New York: Random House; republished 1938.

Freud, S. (1899). Screen memories. In J. Strachey (Ed.), *Collected papers of Sigmund Freud* (Vol. 5). London: Hogarth Press; republished 1956.

Freud, S. (1917). Eine Kindheitserinnerung aus 'Dichtung und Wahrheit'. *Imago, 5.*

Goethals, G. R., & Reckman, R. F. (1973). The perception of consistency in attitudes. *Journal of Experimental Social Psychology, 9,* 491–501.

Herrmann, D. J., & Neisser, U. (1978). An inventory of everyday memory experiences. In M. M. Gruneberg, P. E. Morris, & R. N. Sykes (Eds.), *Practical aspects of memory.* London: Academic Press.

Hunt, E. (1971). What kind of a computer is man? *Cognitive Psychology, 2,* 57–98.

Istomina, Z. M. (1975). The development of voluntary memory in preschool-age children. *Soviet Psychology, 13,* 5–64.

Keenan, J. M., MacWhinney, B., & Mayhew, D. (1977). Pragmatics in memory: A study of natural conversation. *Journal of Verbal Learning and Verbal Behavior,* *16,* 549–560.

Kintsch, W., & Bates, E. (1977). Recognition memory for statements from a classroom lecture. *Journal of Experimental Psychology: Human Learning and Memory, 3,* 150–159.

Kreutzer, M. A., Leonard, C., & Flavell, J. H. (1975). An interview study of children's knowledge about memory. *Monographs of the Society for Research in Child Development, 40,* Serial No. 159.

Loftus, E. G. (1975). Leading questions and the eye-witness report. *Cognitive Psychology, 7,* 560–572.

Loftus, E. G., & Palmer, J. C. (1974). Reconstruction of automobile destruction: An example of the interaction between language and memory. *Journal of Verbal Learning and Verbal Behavior, 13,* 585–589.

Mandler, J. M., & Johnson, N. S. (1977). Remembrance of things parsed: Story structure and recall. *Cognitive Psychology, 9,* 111–151.

McGeoch, J. A. (1942). *The psychology of human learning.* New York: Longmans, Green.

Münsterburg, H. (1909). *On the witness stand.* New York: Doubleday.

Neisser, U. (1962). Cultural and cognitive discontinuity. In T. E. Gladwin & W. Sturtevant (Eds.), *Anthropology and human behavior.* Washington, D.C.: Anthropological Society of Washington, D.C.

Neisser, U., & Hupcey, J. (1974). A Sherlockian experiment. *Cognition, 3,* 307–311.

Novinski, L. S. (1969). Part–whole and whole–part free recall learning. *Journal of Verbal Learning and Verbal Behavior, 8,* 152–154.

Postman, L., & Underwood, B. J. (1973). Critical issues in interference theory. *Memory and Cognition, 1,* 19–40.

Riesman, D. (1956). *The oral tradition, the written word, the screen image.* Yellow Springs, Ohio: Antioch Press.

Rubin, D. C. (1977). Very long-term memory for prose and verse. *Journal of Verbal Learning and Verbal Behavior, 16,* 611–622.

Rumelhart, D. E. (1975). Notes on a schema for stories. In D. G. Bobrow & A. Collins (Eds.), *Representation and understanding.* New York: Academic Press.

Salaman, E. (1970). *A collection of moments.* London: Longman Group.

Schachtel, E. G. (1947). On memory and childhood amnesia. *Psychiatry, 10,* 1–26.

Scribner, S., & Cole, M. (1973). Cognitive consequences of formal and informal education. *Science, 182,* 553–559.

Shepard, R. N., & Metzler, J. (1971). Mental rotation of three-dimensional objects. *Science, 171,* 701–703.

Slamecka, N. J., Moore, T., & Carey, S. (1972). Part-to-whole transfer and its relation to organization theory. *Journal of Verbal Learning and Verbal Behavior, 11,* 73–82.

Sternberg, S. (1966). High-speed scanning in human memory. *Science, 153,* 652–654.

Tulving, E. (1966). Subjective organization and effects of repetition in multi-trial free-recall learning. *Journal of Verbal Learning and Verbal Behavior, 5,* 193–197.

Tulving, E. (1974). Recall and recognition of semantically encoded words. *Journal of Experimental Psychology, 102,* 778–787.

2 | The Bankruptcy of Everyday Memory

Mahzarin R. Banaji and Robert G. Crowder

My complaint that psychologists had neglected the study of memory in natural contexts was soon out of date. A short decade later, its popularity had skyrocketed; I even found myself saying that "If X is an interesting or socially important memory phenomenon, the chances are good . . . that quite a few people are [now] trying to study it" (Neisser, 1988, p. 546). When this trend became obvious, it began to attract critical attention. As one might expect, researchers with a commitment to standard laboratory methods were often less than enthusiastic. The most outspoken of those researchers were Banaji and Crowder, who regarded the whole enterprise as "bankrupt." Here is their argument.

Once upon a time, when chemistry was young, questions of ecological validity were earnestly raised by well-respected chemists and were debated at scientific meetings and in scholarly journals. We understand from a colleague (who is a distinguished historian of science but modestly asked not to be named) that partisans of one point of view called themselves the "everyday chemistry movement." They pointed out that the world offered many vivid examples of chemical principles at work in our daily lives—the rising of pastry dough, the curdling of sauces (the great chef Brillat-Savarin was then laying the foundation for the principles of applied chemistry thereafter called French cuisine), the smelting of metal alloys, the rusting of armor, and the combustion of gunpowder. Why not, they asked, study chemical principles in these ecologically faithful settings

From *American Psychologist*, 1989, 44, 1185–1193.

rather than in tiresome laboratories with their unnatural test tubes, burners, and finicky rules of measurement? The normal world around us, they said, has no end of interesting and virtually unstudied manifestations of chemistry. One scholar, who was famous for his contributions to the new science, even commented that he thought one thing was certain: "If X is an interesting or socially significant aspect of chemistry, then chemists have hardly ever studied X." (Some advocates were actually abusive in their statements; we cite one of the nicer ones).

Of course this parable is apocryphal. Its purpose is to make the point that the other sciences would have been hopelessly paralyzed if they had been deprived of the methods of science during their evolution. Imagine astronomy being conducted with only the naked eye, biology without tissue cultures, physics without vacuums, or chemistry without test tubes! The everyday world is full of principles from these sciences in action, but do we really think their data bases should have been those everyday applications? Of course not. Should the psychology of memory be any different? We think not.

There has been more than a decade of passionate rhetoric claiming that important questions about memory could be tackled if only researchers looked to the "real world" for hypothesis validation. Yet, no delivery has been made on these claims: No theories that have unprecedented explanatory power have been produced; no new principles of memory have been discovered; and no methods of data collection have been developed that add sophistication or precision. In this article, we argue that the movement to develop an ecologically valid psychology of memory has proven itself largely bankrupt and, moreover, that it carries the potential danger of compromising genuine accomplishments of our young endeavor.

...

A CHALLENGE TO THE EXPERIMENTAL
SCIENCE OF MEMORY

We proceed by presenting some issues raised by Neisser (1978) in a chapter that is widely cited as the vision of an ecological approach to the study of memory, assuming for now that such a goal is possible in psychology, unlike astronomy, for example. (We take it to be beyond question, here and elsewhere, that we do not mean to personalize the controversy by citing Neisser repeatedly. Some of his pronouncements, besides being influential, are especially articulate and thus are inviting pegs on which to hang our arguments. Indeed, his most recent statement [Neisser, 1988] is considerably less severe in its indictment of laboratory techniques in the study of memory.)

The Thundering Silence

The first conference on practical aspects of memory (Gruneberg et al., 1978) began with a talk titled "Memory: What Are the Important Questions?" in which Neisser rebuked psychology's "thundering silence" about questions of great interest, such as how one remembers sources of information, arguments, or material that is relevant to one's current thought. He also pointed to the embarrassment of discovering that we psychologists have no answers for our layperson friend who eagerly poses innocent questions such as the following: Why are there limitations on memories for early childhood? Why is it difficult to remember appointments? Why is it easy to find one's way around one's hometown after a 30-year absence? Why did I forget what I had for breakfast this morning?

Neisser's (1978) lament was that psychologists are not interested in such questions because they do not believe them to be truly important. This allegation has at least two answers: First, it is a misrepresentation. Psychologists have no delusions that laboratory techniques are their own justification. Rather, many of us believe that the way in which questions about memory can best be answered is through the empirical discovery of facts about memory that have *generalizability,* and not by the use of tasks that carry an illusion of ecological validity by testing memory in everyday contexts. By analogy, our apocryphal chemist might well retain an interest in why cake dough rises during baking but decide that controlled experimentation on yeast or the reactions of moist baking powder to heat would pay off more than loitering in professional bakeries and taking careful notes. (This issue will receive fuller discussion in a later section.)

Second, no embarrassment is in order when a psychologist is confronted with a layperson asking so-called interesting questions about memory. Science is an acquired taste, and scientific priorities may or may not continue to respect the mundane definition of what is "interesting." What other science, we ask, has established that its students should decide on the importance of questions by checking first with Aunt Martha or the expressway toll-taker? Why, and with what value, should the science of memory be singled out among the other sciences and burdened with this absurd criterion of legitimacy? If one wished to maintain that psychology has an inherently different responsibility from those of the other sciences, namely, the responsibility to provide the everyday public with everyday explanations, then one would need to explain why this peculiar demand is attached to psychology. That philosophical analysis is missing from the literature in our judgment, but to refute it here would take us far afield of our agenda.

Counterintuition as a Criterion of Good Science

Another issue in research on memory concerns the findings themselves. Neisser pointed out that enduring principles of memory, such as the effects of meaningfulness, practice, savings at relearning, and so on, are painfully obvious to students (and even to kindergartners!). According to Neisser, this should be yet another embarrassment to psychologists, who discover that the pinnacle of 100 years of slaving in the laboratory is a string of simplistic, intuitive effects. Again, there are several answers to the accusation.

It is our experience that students in introductory courses are often surprised and intrigued when they are introduced to experimental findings about memory, one example being the serial position curve. In fact, one of us has routinely asked her introductory psychology class a question before conducting the well-known classroom demonstration: "I am going to read a list of words to you, such as Apple, Mug, Square, etc. At the end of reading that list, I will ask you to write down as many of the words as you can remember. Before I do that, however, can you tell me which of these words you think you will remember?" Of the many and interesting hypotheses students have generated, rarely has one borne resemblance to the correct answer. Contrary to Neisser's claim, students do not always know these findings before they hear our lectures.

However, even if laypersons do find out that our experimental data only reaffirm their preconceived theories about how memory works, that confirmation should not be a source of embarrassment to us as Neisser has proclaimed. The belief that objects that are thrown up will fall down also corresponds to intuition and everyday observation. Needless to say, if the principle of counterintuition were applied to decisions of scientific worth, Isaac Newton might easily have ignored inventing the calculus. Risking the embarrassment of stating the obvious and intuitive, we say that the question to the scientist is not only that an effect occurs, but why it occurs. That a wise undergraduate can predict that a recency effect will be obtained unless the subject is assigned to an immediate distractor condition cannot belittle the efforts of a scientist interested in the nature of short-term memory.

Myths About Memory

Our students and laypersons in general "know" many things about memory that are complete nonsense. One is that slow learners show less forgetting than faster learners (Underwood, 1964). Another is that rote repetition increases the probability of later recall (Craik & Watkins, 1973; Rundus, 1977). A third is that some lucky adults have photographic memories (see Klatzky, 1984, Chap. 6, for other examples of "commonsense" principles of memory that are just silly in light of evidence that we have).

As with intuitive physics (McCloskey, 1983), a systematic body of knowledge is needed for people to sort out which of their many beliefs are worth holding on to and which are worthless.

Intuitive psychology, below the surface, is just as fraught with ignorance as intuitive physics (McCloskey, 1983). If the growth of memory performance with repeated practice is a boring, Ebbinghausian platitude, painfully obvious to the laity, then so is the growth of recall under conditions of maintenance rehearsal. The latter belief, however, is dead wrong. Folk wisdom embraces many correct intuitions, but it also embraces many ideas that are utter nonsense. Our great grandparents knew for sure that mushrooms were poisonous, but they also "knew" that tomatoes were poisonous. A systematic body of knowledge about memory needs to be accumulated in order to separate the myths from the facts, and our experimental techniques will serve well to accomplish this goal.

A TWO-BY-TWO ARRAY OF APPROACHES

The attitude reflected in Neisser's (1978) commentary is based on at least one fundamental confusion, that the use of lifelike methods guarantees generality of conclusions to real-life situations. We argue that ecological validity of the methods as such is unimportant and can even work against generalizability.

This theme can be clarified by the construction of a two-dimensional array of scientific approaches. One dimension is the ecological validity of the methodology. The other is the external generalizability of the conclusions permitted by the research. For simplicity, these may be imagined as a two-by-two array (Figure 2-1), although in reality we think of them as dimensions. Now, nobody would deny that, other things being equal, the cell in which ecologically valid methods are used to achieve generalizable results is the best situation in which to find oneself. Nor could it possibly be denied that the combination of contrived, artificial methods and conclusions with no external validity produces a sorry state. The only real debates

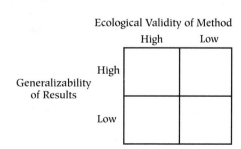

Figure 2-1 *A two-by-two array of approaches to science.*

focus on the other two cells, where a cost-benefit analysis must be applied, and it is these two cells that we scrutinize in the rest of the article.

We come down solidly in favor of accepting contrived methods as long as the payoff in generality of conclusions is great enough. Gathering from a survey of the sources cited, we conclude that others of our colleagues in the study of memory would opt for the other cell, lifelike methods at all costs. That strategy, we fear, would lead the psychology of memory into the same stultification as studying backyard astronomy with the naked eye, chemistry in the kitchen, and biology with a walk through the forest. We have nothing against backyards, kitchens, or forests, but they are not ideal settings for the practice of science, and neither is everyday memory. We question whether the principles of learning discovered in the animal laboratory (see Rescorla, 1988) would have emerged if behaviorists had been dedicated to following rats around their natural urban habitats, craning their necks peering into upturned manhole covers.

Of course, some sciences absolutely require naturalistic observation and description in order to define the phenomena under study. Certain areas of ethology, and perhaps primate social behavior, are good examples of areas that depend on naturalistic observation, but we deny that a case has been made for this approach in the study of memory. The method of naturalistic observation can succeed in a science that has developed precise techniques for translating observations into a formal language such that the operations of invariant mechanisms can be shown obviously. For example, even before the theory of problem solving embodied in General Problem Solver (Newell & Simon, 1972) was developed, Duncker (1945) had used verbal protocol data to study problem solving. The difference, besides the availability of tape-recording equipment, was that Newell and Simon were able to cast their "naturalistic" observations into a formal language (i.e., IPL-V, LISP) allowing the construction of formal theories of cognitive processes.

...

We are not surprised that field investigations of everyday memory . . . succeed occasionally in turning up instances of well-known principles of memory. After all, we retain our faith that laboratory abstractions are controlled by the same laws as mundane phenomena, in psychology just as in chemistry. However, we have not been able to see any new principles of memory emerging from the everyday memory studies. Again and again, what seem at first like new, dramatic, emergent principles turn out to be everyday manifestations of laboratory wisdom. For example, early reports of flashbulb memories (Brown & Kulik, 1977) prove, on close inspection, to present nothing unexpected to conventional laboratory work on memory (McCloskey, Wible, & Cohen, 1988). Similarly, research on the role of the self in memory has shown that superior memory for self-referent information can be explained in terms of ordinary principles of memory (Greenwald & Banaji, 1989; Klein & Kihlstrom, 1987).

Principles of memory that cannot be discovered using the scientific method may indeed exist, and emergent principles may someday be discovered using everyday memory methods. One such argument, presented by Erdelyi and Goldberg (1979), was that the lack of experimental confirmation for the phenomenon of repression could not be a criterion for rejecting the idea of motivated forgetting ("existence arguments can hardly be settled on the basis of laboratory failures in creating the phenomenon—whether we are concerned with the existence of Mt. Everest, the rings of Saturn, or, for that matter, the white rat," pp. 359–360). However, as Erdelyi's more recent writing indicates, Ebbinghaus may have provided the first experimental evidence for repression, which indicates that the mechanisms by which "repression" is accomplished are the same as those employed in everyday types of forgetting, such as lack of rehearsal (Erdelyi, in press). Thus although we must reserve the possibility that everyday memory research may yield emergent principles of memory that have not and cannot be discovered in the laboratory, that supposition is, at present, a pure matter of faith.

Low Ecological Validity of Method but High Generalizability of Results

Perhaps we can reinforce our case with examples of research findings we believe to be low in the ecological validity of method, although high in external validity as defined by the generality of conclusions. Landauer and Bjork (1978) reported such a finding. They had people memorize briefly presented paired associate items on a CRT and later tested them after measured delays. Surely Ebbinghaus himself would have been gratified by this methodology (though perhaps disapproving of the stimuli). The main manipulation was the schedule of presenting items that were exposed more than once. Departing from the distribution-of-practice literature, these authors contrived some conditions with wide spacing, some with narrow, and two new conditions with irregular spacing, one with increasing lags and the other with decreasing lags. Their main result was that increasing lag had an impressive beneficial effect on subsequent recall comparable in size to some of the classic mnemonic techniques. As an empirical rule, the generalization seems to be that a repetition will help most if the material has been in storage long enough as to be just on the verge of being forgotten. Because repetition is known to reduce the slope of the forgetting curve, this means that successive repetitions should be scheduled with expanding lags.

Leaving aside the issue of whether this finding is painfully obvious to the undergraduate student (which it is not), we note that Landauer and

Bjork could never have stumbled on this finding without using tightly controlled laboratory methods. The 50-trial sessions in which their subjects participated, sitting before the CRT, memorizing artificial first and last names, are no more ecologically representative than experiments in a bubble chamber or gas chromatography. Yet, Landauer and Bjork, as they commented, have turned in a finding that can readily be applied to one's daily life. The technique is easily explained and can be exploited whenever one can choose the interval after which some piece of information can be rehearsed or self-tested.

...

CONCLUSION

In summary, we students of memory are just as interested as anybody else in why we forget where we left the car in the morning or in who was sitting across the table at yesterday's meeting. Precisely for this reason we are driven to laboratory experimentation and away from naturalistic observation. If the former method has been disappointing to some after about 100 years, so should the latter approach be disappointing after about 2,000. Above all, the superficial glitter of everyday methods should not be allowed to replace the quest for truly generalizable principles.

REFERENCES

Brown, R., & Kulik, J. (1977). Flashbulb memories. *Cognition, 5,* 99.

Craik, F. I. M., & Watkins, M. J. (1973). The role of rehearsal in short-term memory. *Journal of Verbal Learning and Verbal Behavior,* 599–607.

Duncker, K. (1945). On problem-solving. *Psychological Monographs, 58,* 5, (whole no. 270).

Erdelyi, M.H. (in press). Repression, reconstruction, and defense: Integration of the psychoanalytic and experimental frameworks. In J. Singer (Ed.), *Repression: Defense mechanism and cognitive style.* Chicago: University of Chicago Press.

Erdelyi, M. H., & Goldberg, B. (1979). Let's not sweep repression under the rug: Toward a cognitive psychology of repression. In J. F. Kihlstrom & F. J. Evans (Eds.), *Functional disorders of memory.* Hillsdale, NJ: Erlbaum, 355–402.

Greenwald, A. G., & Banaji, M. R. (1989). An experimental analog of the self as a memory system: Powerful, but ordinary. *Journal of Personality and Social Psychology, 57,* 41–54.

Gruneberg, M. M., Morris, P. E., & Sykes, R. N. (1978). *Practical aspects of memory.* London: Academic Press.

Klatzky, R. L. (1984). *Memory and awareness: An information processing perspective.* New York: Freeman.

Klein, S., & Kihlstrom, J. (1987). Elaboration, organization, and the self-reference effect in memory. *Journal of Experimental Psychology: General, 115,* 26–38.

Landauer, T. K., & Bjork, R. A. (1978). Optimum rehearsal patterns and name learning. In M. M. Gruneberg, P. E. Morris, & R. N. Sykes (Eds.), *Practical aspects of memory.* New York: Academic Press.

McCloskey, M. (1983). Intuitive physics. *Scientific American, 248,* 122–130.

McCloskey, M., Wible, C. G., & Cohen, N. J. (1988). Is there a special flashbulb-memory mechanism? *Journal of Experimental Psychology: General, 117,* 171–181.

Neisser, U. (1978). Memory: What are the important questions? In M. M. Gruneberg, P. E. Morris, & R. N. Sykes (Eds.), *Practical aspects of memory.* London: Academic Press, 3–24.

Neisser, U. (1988). New vistas in the study of memory. In U. Neisser & E. Winograd (Eds.), *Remembering reconsidered: Ecological and traditional approaches to the study of memory.* Cambridge, England: Cambridge University Press, 1–10.

Newell, A., & Simon, H. A. (1972). *Human problem solving.* Englewood Cliffs, NJ: Prentice-Hall.

Rescorla, R. A. (1988). Pavlovian conditioning: It's not what you think it is. *American Psychologist, 43,* 151–160.

Rundus, D. (1977). Maintenance rehearsal and single-level processing. *Journal of Verbal Learning and Verbal Behavior, 16,* 665–681.

Underwood, B. J. (1964). Degree of learning and the measurement of forgetting. *Journal of Verbal Learning and Verbal Behavior, 3,* 112–129.

3 | A Case of Misplaced Nostalgia

Ulric Neisser

I welcomed Banaji and Crowder's critique. The fact that they took the trouble to write it—and that it appeared in such a widely-read journal—must mean that the naturalistic study of memory was beginning to attract some interest! The obvious next step was to write a reply.

I have bad news for Banaji and Crowder (September 1989). It's too late: The good old days are gone, the genie is out of the bottle. The situation I described and deplored in 1978 ("If X is an interesting or socially significant aspect of memory, then psychologists have hardly ever studied X," Neisser, 1978, p. 4) will never return, however much they may long for it. The present state of affairs is nearly the opposite. Nowadays, if X is an ecologically common or socially significant domain of memory, somebody is probably studying it intensively. Estimates of one's own traits at earlier points in time, memory in young children (and recollections of childhood), retrieval of material learned in school, recall of unusual or emotional experiences—these are only a few of the naturalistic domains in which important findings have recently appeared. The psychologists who made those findings will surely go on with their work; no amount of nostalgic grumbling about the proper methods of science is likely to deter them. This being rather obviously the case, two questions present themselves: (a) Why does it bother Banaji and Crowder so much? (b) How does it fit into the study of memory as a whole?

But perhaps it is not the case. Banaji and Crowder (1989) simply denied it. According to them, the study of *everyday memory* (an awkward phrase, I think) has not produced any important results at all. That claim

From *American Psychologist*, 1991, 46, 34–36.

must be refuted before we proceed; otherwise, my argument would rest on shaky ground. Luckily, Banaji and Crowder phrased it so sweepingly that refutation is easy:

> No *delivery has been made on these claims:* No *theories that have unprecedented explanatory power have been produced;* no *new principles of memory have been discovered; and* no *methods of data collection have been developed that add sophistication or precision. (p. 1185; all emphasis added)*

A single counterexample would suffice to refute null hypotheses like these: I will list four for good measure. To be sure, there is something arbitrary about any such list; other students of memory in natural contexts have their own favorite studies, and I do not claim any unique privilege for mine. Some of the studies mentioned here combine theory and data in a way that should appeal even to Banaji and Crowder; others have produced results that would never have emerged from standard laboratory studies. One (which, of course, I like especially) is partly my own work. Four should be enough.

1. People often have occasion to recall what they were like at some earlier point in time. How bad were my headaches last week? How fast did I read before I took this study-skills course? Was I happy in my college days? Michael Ross (1989) developed a systematic theory of such estimates. In his view they are largely derived from the trait's *present* value (my pain today, my reading speed now, my current happiness), taken together with an implicit hypothesis about its stability or change over time. If I have no reason to believe that my headaches have changed, for example, then recall of last week's pain will be biased toward today's level. If I have just been through a treatment program, however, recall of pain levels before it began will be biased upward from today's level—after all, the program must have done some good! In a recent issue of *Psychological Review,* Ross (1989) reported about a dozen studies, covering a wide range of personally significant traits, that support his theory. (An independent measure of the original trait was available in each case.) This work, which offers unexpected and yet systematic insights into a commonplace use of memory, meets every standard methodological criterion.

2. The use of everyday events as targets may be optional in studying adult memory, but it is essential with young children. Using naturalistic methods, Katherine Nelson (1986) and her associates showed that recall of familiar routines as well as of specific

episodes can be elicited from two-year-olds, and perhaps even (Nelson, 1988) from one-year-olds. Such recall is quite sketchy at first, but interestingly, it is rarely wrong. It takes an increasingly rich narrative form during development, as parents instruct their children in the social uses of memory (Hudson, 1990). Some characteristics of young children's memory—its dependence on external cueing; its focus on things that adults would take for granted—may help to explain the "childhood amnesia" that will overtake their recall later (Fivush & Hamond, 1990).

3. Harry Bahrick's (1984) studies of memory for school-learned material are now well-known. By locating people who had studied Spanish at various times in the past (and controlling other variables with covariance techniques), Bahrick was able to trace out 50-year forgetting functions. Although some aspects of those functions were predictable from traditional theories of memory (e.g., effects of the level of original learning), others were not: The rate of forgetting dropped to zero after 5 years or so, producing a 25-year plateau in performance. These data, which could not have been obtained by standard laboratory methods, have obvious theoretical and practical significance.

4. Banaji and Crowder (1989) believe that so-called *flashbulb memories*, such as recalling how one first heard the news of the explosion of the space shuttle *Challenger*, "present nothing unexpected to conventional laboratory work on memory" (p. 1190). They probably mean that although such memories are roughly accurate, no special memory mechanism is involved. That is the view of McCloskey, Wible, and Cohen (1988), whose study they cited. But recent work suggests that the real puzzle about flashbulb memories is quite different: Why do people so often have vivid recollections that are entirely incorrect? Nicole Harsch and I asked Emory University freshmen, on the morning after the *Challenger* disaster, how they had heard the news the day before (Harsch & Neisser, 1989; Neisser & Harsch, 1992). Three years later, 44 of them were asked to recall it again. Most gave very plausible and confident accounts, but about one third of those accounts were dead wrong. Although errors do often occur in eyewitness testimony (Loftus, 1979), neither folk psychology nor conventional theories of memory had led us to expect so many utterly false reports. Not all forms of everyday memory are prone to such errors. For example, they do not occur in recall of randomly selected events (Brewer, 1988). Clarification of these issues will probably require continued naturalistic research: The strong emotions and long retention intervals characteristic of

flashbulb memories are not easily established under laboratory conditions.

...

WHERE DOES IT FIT?

The ecological approach is not the only source of new ideas about remembering. The "traditional" study of memory itself has undergone radical changes since I characterized it so harshly in 1978. At that time it was chiefly focused on explicit recognition or recall of isolated items from lists. Today, a glance at the *Journal of Experimental Psychology: Learning, Memory, and Cognition* shows that such research has become almost an endangered species. Currently popular topics include implicit memory, mental imagery, motor skills, story schemata, social scripts, object recognition, and cognitive maps—many of them appreciably closer (than the old methods were) to the sorts of things people do everyday. Whether laboratory study of such problems will produce what Banaji and Crowder (1989) called "truly generalizable principles" (p. 1192) remains to be seen—or rather, to be tested across the relevant ecological settings. (Taken by themselves, encapsulated laboratory experiments can never ensure true generalizability.) But even without such tests, some of these studies clearly meet what Eugene Winograd (1988) has called "the one requirement for scientific research we all implicitly follow: our understanding of memory is enhanced" (p. 18).

Much ecologically oriented work on memory also meets that test. The research described here is only a sample. There is not enough space to describe the many excellent studies of oral tradition, prospective remembering, conversational use of the past, personal recall, and eyewitness testimony that have also enhanced our understanding in the last few years. Far from "compromising genuine accomplishments of our young endeavor" (Banaji & Crowder, 1989, p. 1185), this work is an integral part of those accomplishments. No serious student of memory can afford to ignore it.

For more discussion of the value of naturalistic memory research, see the January 1991 issue of American Psychologist; *it is largely devoted to commentary on Banaji and Crowder's paper. In addition to Neisser's critique (reproduced in this selection) there are comments by Elizabeth Loftus, Martin Conway, Stephen Ceci and Urie Bronfenbrenner, John Morton, Henry Roediger, Endel Tulving, Roberta Klatzky, and Darryl Bruce. While the discussion focuses on the study of memory, many of the papers also discuss the nature of scientific inquiry more generally.*

REFERENCES

Bahrick, H. P. (1984). Semantic memory content in permastore: Fifty years of memory for Spanish learned in school. *Journal of Experimental Psychology: General, 113*, 1–29.

Banaji, M. R., & Crowder, R. G. (1989). The bankruptcy of everyday memory. *American Psychologist, 44*, 1185–1193.

Brewer, W. F. (1988). Memory for randomly sampled autobiographical events. In U. Neisser & E. Winograd (Eds.), *Remembering reconsidered: Ecological and traditional approaches to the study of memory*. New York: Cambridge University Press, 21–90.

Fivush, R., & Hamond, N. R. (1990). Autobiographical memory across the preschool years: Toward reconceptualizing childhood amnesia. In R. Fivush & J. A. Hudson (Eds.), *Knowing and remembering in young children*. New York: Cambridge University Press.

Harsch, N., & Neisser, U. (1989, November). *Substantial and irreversible errors in flashbulb memories of the* Challenger *explosion*. Poster presented at the meeting of the Psychonomic Society, Atlanta, GA.

Hudson, J. A. (1990). The emergence of autobiographic memory in mother–child conversation. In R. Fivush & J. A. Hudson (Eds.), *Knowing and remembering in young children*. New York: Cambridge University Press.

Loftus, E. (1979). *Eyewitness testimony*. Cambridge, MA: Harvard University Press.

McCloskey, M., Wible, C. G., & Cohen, N. J. (1988). Is there a special flashbulb memory mechanism? *Journal of Experimental Psychology: General, 117*, 171–181.

Neisser, U. (1978). Memory: What are the important questions? In M. M. Gruneberg, P. E. Morris, & R. N. Sykes (Eds.), *Practical aspects of memory*. London: Academic Press, 3–24.

Neisser, U., & Harsch, N. (1992). Phantom flashbulbs: False recollections of hearing the news about Challenger. In E. Winograd & U. Neisser (Eds.), *Affect and accuracy in recall: Studies of "flashbulb" memories*. New York: Cambridge University Press.

Nelson, K. (1986). *Event knowledge: Structure and function in development*. Hillsdale, NJ: Erlbaum.

Nelson, K. (1988). The ontogeny of memory for real events. In U. Neisser & E. Winograd (Eds.), *Remembering reconsidered: Ecological and traditional approaches to the study of memory*. New York: Cambridge University Press, 244–276.

Ross, M. (1989). Relation of implicit theories to the construction of personal histories. *Psychological Review, 96*, 341–357.

Winograd, E. (1988). Continuities between ecological and laboratory approaches to memory. In U. Neisser & E. Winograd (Eds.), *Remembering reconsidered: Ecological and traditional approaches to the study of memory*. New York: Cambridge University Press, 11–20.

Part II

SPECIAL OCCASIONS

In which we consider the sort of memories that people often describe as "unforgettable." Are they really?

4 | Personal Event Memories

David B. Pillemer

Let's begin with some examples of genuinely memorable events—dangerous war experiences, self-defining moments, first encounters with a future spouse. We certainly remember such occasions, and should acknowledge their existence before we begin to ask more detailed and critical questions.

A human life is composed of an unending stream of particular instances. As I write this sentence, my behavior and thoughts are influenced by attitudes and skills that grew out of an accumulation of countless past learning experiences, experiences that are for the most part no longer identifiable as individual lived episodes. But *right now*, the writing is taking place in a particular location (my office), at a particular time (2:30 in the afternoon), accompanied by a particular set of feelings, perceptions, and bodily sensations (blue sky and sun visible from my window, sore jaw from recent surgery). Will this singular moment, marking the beginning of writing the first chapter of a book, be preserved in memory, or will it suffer the fate of most experiences and drift from consciousness into oblivion? More generally, what determines whether a pinpointed life event will persist in memory, will remain accessible to conscious awareness, and will continue to influence the life course days, months, or years after its initial occurrence?

For truly momentous events, memory longevity is expected. A person is likely to remember, for example, an episode in which his or her life was in danger, even if the event occurred long ago. Howard Hoffman's oral

※ From D. B. Pillemer (1998). *Momentous events, vivid memories.* Cambridge, MA: Harvard University Press, 1–3, 50–52.

history of his experiences as a soldier in World War II included a life-threatening encounter that happened 35 years earlier:

> I was in a truck and I was sitting in the cab of the truck, and we were driving along a road, our whole convoy, when I looked straight in front of me, and I see a plane coming down to make a strafing run, and it's a German plane, and it's coming down very, very low, just exactly like what you always see in the movies . . . It made two runs, and between the first and the second run a lot of the guys ran into a house that was right by the side of the road. I was planning to run to the house, but for some reason I didn't, and the plane made a second run and this time I just maybe took one shot at it when it was pretty far in front of me and then I could see the bullets coming down . . . I saw a puff of smoke six inches from my foot . . . It made that run and then disappeared, and I went on into the house and the guys in there had been watching through the window, and they said, "Jesus Christ, I thought you were hit. I saw those shells coming down right next to you and I thought I saw one hit you." That's how close it was, but I hadn't been hit. (Hoffman & Hoffman, 1990, pp. 113–114)

When extraordinary danger or death strikes a loved one rather than oneself, memories can be similarly vivid and long-lasting. Henri Benchoan traveled to Auschwitz, the Nazi concentration camp, some 50 years after his mother was sent to her death there. He was 8 years old when he saw his mother for the last time: "We were at the police station all morning. There was lots of confusion. Suddenly my mother, sensing the danger, said to me, 'Take your brother and get out fast.' [From a nearby doorway, Henri and his brother watched his mother board a bus that took her to the train to Auschwitz.] She saw us and waved. I will never forget the look on her face" ("French Jews' Kin Retrace Rail Journey to Auschwitz," 1992, p. 12; no author).

Just as one would expect to be revisited by vivid mental images of a direct threat to one's own life or the life of a significant other, it is commonplace to remember the death of a beloved public figure. The assassination of President John F. Kennedy in 1963 is the most celebrated example, but it is by no means unique. The renowned social reformer Jane Addams recounted how as a young child she heard the news of Lincoln's assassination:

> Although I was but four and a half years old when Lincoln died, I distinctly remember the day when I found on our two white gate posts American flags companioned with black. I tumbled down on the harsh gravel walk in my eager rush into the house to inquire what they were "there for." To my amazement I found my father in tears, something that

I had never seen before, having assumed, as all children do, that grown-up people never cried. The two flags, my father's tears and his impressive statement that the greatest man in the world had died, constituted my initiation, my baptism, as it were, into the thrilling and solemn interests of a world lying quite outside the two white gate posts. (Addams, 1992, pp. 507–508)

Not all vivid and persistent memories involve intense shock, danger, or death. Most graduates can recall specific influential episodes from their college years (Pillemer, Picariello, Law, & Reichman, 1996), most women can recall the details of their first menstrual period (Pillemer, Koff, Rhinehart, & Rierdan, 1987), and most married couples can recount the moment when they first met (Belove, 1980). At an interview for a special tribute to Benny Goodman, Helen Ward, a vocalist with the famous swing band led by Goodman, reported a vivid memory of a marriage proposal she had received decades earlier:

I remember my date taking me to the Brown Derby and we're sitting there talking and Benny [Goodman] leans over to Bill—that was my date's name—and says, "You know I'm going to marry that girl." And I'm sitting there like this. And my friend looks at me—What the heck's going on there? Bill took me home. Before I knew it, there's a ring at the doorbell. And it's Benny. And I let him in. And I'll never forget this. I'm, I'm sitting on the couch and Benny's standing in front of me and he's saying, "I want to marry you." And now no prelude, no inkling, no, out of left field, "Want to marry you." He convinced me to go East with him. (O. Jacoby, 1986)

Still other memories record personal milestones or turning points. A select few episodes come to be perceived as "originating events" (Pillemer et al., 1996) or "self-defining memories" (Singer & Salovey, 1993), moments that are believed to have profoundly influenced the life course. Photographer Margaret Bourke-White experienced such a moment in childhood:

Now and then Father put the drafting tools aside and took me with him on trips to factories where he was supervising the setting up of his presses. One day, in the plant in Dunellen, New Jersey . . . I saw a foundry for the first time. I remember climbing with him to a sooty balcony and looking down into the mysterious depths below. "Wait," Father said, and then in a rush the blackness was broken by a sudden magic of flowing metal and flying sparks. I can hardly describe my joy. To me at that age, a foundry represented the beginning and end of all beauty. Later when I became a photographer, with that instinctive de-

sire that photographers have to show their world to others, this memory was so vivid and so alive that it shaped the whole course of my career. (Bourke-White, 1992, p. 425)

Although the topics represented in this sample of memories are diverse, the narratives share several basic characteristics: they each describe a circumscribed, one-moment-in-time event rather than an extended time period or series of repeated experiences; they focus on the rememberer's personal circumstances at the time of the event, including what was seen, heard, thought, and felt; they contain many specific details, such as direct quotations and descriptions of physical surroundings; and they have retained their vivid, life-like quality through the years. The term *personal event memory* captures these general characteristics.

...

The defining characteristics of personal event memories are as follows:

- The memory represents a *specific* event that took place at a particular time and place, rather than a general event or an extended series of related happenings.

- The memory contains a *detailed* account of the rememberer's *own personal circumstances* at the time of the event.

- The verbal narrative account of the event is accompanied by *sensory images*, including visual, auditory, olfactory images or bodily sensations, that contribute to the feeling of "reexperiencing" or "reliving."

- Memory details and sensory images correspond to a particular *moment* or moments of phenomenal experience.

- The rememberer *believes* that the memory is a truthful representation of what transpired.

...

The definition of personal event memories may seem at first glance to apply to a narrow set of vividly remembered events, but in fact the five qualities are defining characteristics of what is usually meant by "remembering" any particular episode. Consider the question, "Do you remember any specific events that occurred during your college years?" Respondents will know where and when they attended college, what courses they took, who their friends were, what the campus and familiar faculty members looked like, and other general information. But to give a convincing response to a question about specific college episodes, one must remember and recount a detailed memory of personal circumstances at the crucial moment: where and when the event occurred, what was seen, heard, and felt, and so forth.

An experience recounted by a Wellesley College alumna provides a vivid illustration of the core qualities of personal event memories:

> *I remember sitting in X's class on the day that a midterm . . . was handed back. I was a freshman and felt that I was in over my head. The professor gave a stern lecture on the value of good writing before she handed back the papers. As she reproached us, my terror grew because her remarks seemed to be personally directed at me. I was from a small town, did not have the same background as anyone in my class, and had immediately felt my inadequacies when class began in September. Suddenly she turned and looked directly at me—I thought I would die of humiliation. Then she said, "But Y has answered the question well and has an unusual lyrical and personal style that enhanced her answer." I couldn't believe that she was talking about my paper, but she was. I can still envision that dimly lit little room in the bottom of Z and smell its peculiar musty odor. I can still picture her stern but kind face and feel the relief and pride that I felt at that moment. (Pillemer, 1992b, p. 252)*

Not all personal event memories are as detailed and fully elaborated as in this example. Nevertheless, the basic characteristics of personal event memories are still identifiable. The description of personal circumstances may be highly selective, and the imagery (accounts of what was seen, heard, smelled, or felt) may focus on one sensory modality only, "but remembering some fragment of personal experience is probably necessary to feel and believe with conviction that 'I was there' " (Pillemer, 1992b, p. 239). In order to qualify as a personal event memory, it must be clear that the memory represents the phenomenal experience of a specific, one-moment-in-time event, even if that moment is embedded in a more general description of related experiences. Distinguishing between specific personal event memories and more general autobiographical memories is in most cases relatively straightforward: when independent raters are asked to divide personal memories into specific and general categories, they can do so at an acceptable level of agreement (Pillemer et al., 1986; Pillemer et al., 1988; Williams & Broadbent, 1986).

REFERENCES

Addams, J. M. (1992). Captive memories. In J. K. Conway (Ed.), *Written by herself.* New York: Vintage, 506–525.

Belove, L. (1980). First encounters of the close kind (FECK): The use of the story of the first interaction as an early recollection of a marriage. *Journal of Individual Psychology, 36*, 191–208.

Bourke-White, M. (1992). Portrait of myself. In J. K. Conway (Ed.), *Written by herself.* New York: Vintage, 425–453.

French jews' kin retrace rail journey to Auschwitz (1992. April 7). *The Boston Globe*, p. 12.

Hoffman, A. M., & Hoffman, H. S. (1990). *Archives of memory: A soldier recalls World War II*. Lexington, KY: The University Press of Kentucky.

Jacoby, O. (Producer and Director) (1986). *Benny Goodman: Adventures in the Kingdom of Swing* (film).

Pillemer, D. B. (1992). Remembering personal circumstances: A functional analysis. In E. Winograd & U. Neisser (Eds.), *Affect and accuracy in recall: Studies of "flashbulb" memories*. New York: Cambridge University Press.

Pillemer, D. B., Goldsmith, L. R., Panter, A. T., & White, S. H. (1988). Very long-term memories of the first year in college. *Journal of Experimental Psychology: Learning, Memory and Cognition, 14*, 709–715.

Pillemer, D. B., Koff, E., Rhinehart, E. D., & Rierdan, J. (1987). Flashbulb memories of menarche and adult menstrual distress. *Journal of Adolescence, 10*, 187–199.

Pillemer, D. B., Piciarello, M. L., Law, A. B., & Reichman, J. S. (1996). Memories of college: The importance of specific educational episodes. In D. C. Rubin (Ed.), *Remembering our past: Studies in autobiographical memory*. New York: Cambridge University Press, 318–337.

Pillemer, D. B., Rhinehart, E. D., & White, S. H. (1986). Memories of life transitions: The first year in college. *Human Learning, 5*, 109–123.

Singer, J. A., & Salovey, P. (1993). *The remembered self: Emotion and memory in personality*. New York: Free Press.

Williams, J. M. G., & Broadbent, K. (1986). Autobiographical memory in suicide attempters. *Journal of Abnormal Psychology, 95*, 144–149.

5 | A Collection of Moments

Esther Salaman

In this selection Esther Salaman, a Russian novelist, describes a kind of memory that psychologists have almost completely ignored. "Involuntary memories" are those that come "unexpectedly, suddenly, and bring back a past moment accompanied by strong emotions, so that a 'then' becomes a 'now'." She presents us with many beautiful examples, from her own experience as well as from others' autobiographies; she tries to analyze the conditions that give rise to such memories, the degree to which they are reliable, and their relationship to more conscious and deliberate kinds of remembering.

Writing about memories, towards the end of his life, Dostoyevsky says that a man could not go on living without them, especially the sacred and precious memories of childhood. "Some people appear not to think of their memories of childhood, but all the same preserve such memories unconsciously. They may be grave, bitter, but the suffering we have lived through may turn in the end into sacred things for the soul."

This is an obvious truth, recognizable by anyone who has recollected childhood, and it makes the lack of knowledge of the nature of memories quite unbelievable. There is widespread and dense ignorance. How, for instance, is it possible for serious students of Proust to describe his involuntary memories as a discovery, a revelation, a miracle, when so many others have had these experiences? Harriet Martineau, De Quincey, Aksakov, Rousseau, Edwin Muir, Dostoyevsky, to mention but a few. Why, there can be hardly a person who has fully recollected his childhood who has not experienced involuntary memories!

※ From E. Salaman, *A Collection of Moments: A Study of Involuntary Memories*. London: Longman, 1970, 1–3, 11–17, 32–33, 45.

Subjectively the feeling is miraculous, miraculous as a moment of love, the first sight of a newborn healthy baby to a mother, the sudden light of understanding of your idea in another person's eyes, or a moment of recognition of beauty in a work of art or a scientific theory.

Where would you expect a knowledge about memories in general, and of this particular phenomenon, involuntary memories? Among poets, novelists, autobiographers: all those to whom memories are their quarry. Years ago, while I was a student of physics and mathematics, walking occasionally into a lecture on psychology I had the impression that writers knew things about memories and their relation to the creative process of which the psychologists knew next to nothing. The distinguished psychoanalyst Anton Ehrenzweig writes: "Psychoanalysis knows as yet little about the lower levels of perception that become activated during creative work. So far it has been concerned with the content of the unconscious and its fantastic symbolism. The study of creative work requires more" (*Nature*, 16 June 1962).

Why so little of what writers knew about memories was available to others I realized only after writing some autobiographical novels. I made extensive use of memories, but like other writers, I used them as a means to an end, and made only passing observations about their general nature.

For many years my experience of involuntary memories was unpredictable, sporadic, and elusive. Only in maturity, when a large number came back within a comparatively short period of time, did a pattern of their general nature begin to appear. But I was then too preoccupied by the submerged ship of childhood, adolescence, and early youth, which was rising to the surface, to concentrate on the nature of memories as an end in itself. It was not until some years later that I began to decipher my own observations about memories, and to understand other writers' passing remarks. It was then that I became certain that one can gather much knowledge about the nature of memories from writers.

I shall deal with many aspects of involuntary memories, and try to make it clear how they differ from the conscious memories which are available to us. A number of conclusions are confirmed by psychoanalysis. I. M. L. Hunter, professor of psychology at Keele University, who has done important work on the nature of memory, read an early version of the book, and by his appreciation and comments did me great service. Commenting on my involuntary memories he said: "These remarkably fresh memories concern somewhat traumatic experiences which are, therefore, important to the person but have now lost their trauma for the current way of life. . . . Psychoanalytic thought holds a similar notion of repressed memories once they are 'allowed to appear'." This was new to me. He went on: "In all honesty I have never been impressed by this notion as a generality but have always tended to think of the phenomena the other way round, i.e., the person is now able to construct remembering which formerly he was not interested in constructing. But perhaps these seemingly opposed views are merely matters of taste rather than fact."

I found this comment most stimulating. The two views are not opposed. The memories which came back involuntarily in maturity (I was in my early fifties), when I was writing about childhood, adolescence, and youth, added many new memories of moments to my old conscious memories. It was then that their traumatic origin became apparent, though by that time the fear, shame, and guilt had faded. But if I had not had the urge to write a book they would not have come back, certainly not in such large numbers. The autobiographer is not trying to get rid of a neurosis, is not even in pursuit of self-knowledge, as Stendhal believed he was—self-knowledge is a by-product: his primary purpose is the same as that of the artist.

Why are so many autobiographies of childhood written late in life? De Quincey and Aksakov both found that childhood was dead to them in their middle age. De Quincey believed that there was no such thing as forgetting, but that our memories, or as he calls them "the secret inscriptions," are "waiting to be revealed when the obscuring daylight shall have withdrawn." Proust expressed the same idea, using a different image. Marcel says that the echo of his tears, in his traumatic memory of demanding his mother's kiss, never ceased, but was not audible until life grew quiet, like those convent bells which are drowned in the noise of daytime, and sound out again in the silence of the evening.

...

A vast amount of information is stowed away in our brain; that much we know for certain. There is a great variety in the faculty of memory: verbal, musical, mathematical, sculptural, a memory for chess configurations, for faces, names, habits, customs, and so on. Very often a person excels in one and not in the others. From observation alone we can tell that children of very similar IQ have very different kinds of memory. The memory for experiences is as common as any of the other kinds, but varies from person to person. Let anyone confine himself to a particular period, preferably to one before he settled down, in youth, adolescence, or childhood, and he will find a number of memories available to him. If he concentrates he will find that many more come back, and even make him wonder how he could have forgotten them.

There is another kind of memory of experience, which comes unexpectedly, suddenly, and brings back a past moment accompanied by strong emotions, so that a "then" becomes a "now." Proust was not the first to describe such memories. Some have called such memories "spontaneous," others, "revived"; they have also been called "unconscious" or "involuntary." Of all these names, none of which is perfect, I choose "involuntary." I believe that the experience of involuntary memories is not uncommon, and hope to make it clear why many people are not aware of having experienced them. But to begin with, here are a few typical examples.

The first is from Chateaubriand's *Memoires d'Outre-Tombe*. Walking alone in the evening, "I was drawn from my reflections by the warbling of a thrush perched upon the highest branch of a birch tree. At that instant the magical sound brought my paternal estate before my eyes; I forgot the catastrophes of which I had been a witness and, transported suddenly into the past, I saw again that country where I had so often heard the thrush sing."

There are a number of distinct features in this involuntary memory. He is walking alone in a disturbed state of mind; he suddenly hears a thrush, and it is "magical" to him; but the magic is not in the immediate impression but in his memory. Immediately it brings back his home, the country where he had often heard a thrush sing, and he forgets the painful present and lives in the past. Many involuntary memories have a similar pattern. Proust quotes this memory of Chateaubriand's in *A la Recherche du Temps Perdu;* Marcel says that he was reassured to discover that his involuntary memories were "fundamentally analogous to experiences of other writers." But we cannot take Marcel's experiences at face value: they are not always Marcel Proust's. Proust used involuntary memories for a purpose: to make his ingenious plot. So I will take an example of a real memory of Proust's, analogous to Chateaubriand's, from *Jean Santeuil,* an autobiographical novel, which Proust abandoned and never revised. Jean (who, by the way, sometimes becomes "I") had started out on his way to the Lake of Geneva in a low mood, but when the sight of it suddenly brought him back the memory of Begmeil his disappointment vanished. He had often made an effort to bring back his memories of Brittany, but they seemed dead. Now, "In a flash that life in Brittany, which he had thought useless and unusable, appeared before his eyes in all its charm and beauty, and his heart swelled within him as he thought of his walks at Begmeil when the sun was setting and the sea stretched out before him." The analogy to Chateaubriand's experience is pretty close. Proust had also set out in a depressed state of mind, and the sight of the lake was "magical" to him because it brought back a memory of the sea at Begmeil.

Another example is De Quincey's memory of Altrincham Market Place. It comes in the revised version of the *Confessions of an English Opium-Eater.* When De Quincey was seventeen he ran away from school. He set out that morning on foot for Altrincham in a disturbed state of mind and full of misgivings. It was a heavenly early morning in July, and when he reached the town a memory of just such a dazzling morning when he had stayed at Altrincham with his nurse when he was three years old came back to him. He had waked early and woken up the nurse, and when she lifted him in her arms and threw open the window, he saw the gayest scene he had ever seen: the market-place at Altrincham at eight o'clock in the morning. It was market day: "fruit, such as can be had in July, and flowers were scattered about in profusion: even the stalls of the butchers, from their brilliant cleanliness, appeared attractive: and the bonny young women of Altrincham were tripping about in caps and aprons coquetishly disposed. . . ."

Just as to Chateaubriand there was magic in the song of a thrush, to Proust in the sight of the Lake of Geneva, so there was to De Quincey in the sight of the marketplace at that early hour; and in every case it is made clear that it was not the impression itself which took them out of their despondency but a memory of a similar impression. De Quincey becomes the child of three: "perhaps the window of my bedroom was still open, only my nurse and I were not looking out: for alas! on recollection, fourteen years had passed since then." He was refreshed by the walk and the memory, and after a rest and breakfast "all my gloom and despondency were already retiring to the rear." Such a memory, as Proust said, overthrows the order of time and makes one live in another period. Had more people recognized these experiences there would not have been so much nonsense talked about Proust's involuntary memories in *A la Recherche du Temps Perdu*. Why did they not? What Chateaubriand, Proust, and De Quincey had in common was a long experience of recapturing memories.

To show how elusive involuntary memories are, I will go for further examples to my own experience of them in youth, when they were comparatively frequent. They puzzled me then, but later they afforded me material to work on. I left Russia in 1920, and a couple of years later, when I was a student in Berlin, I began to suffer homesickness: to be exact I was visited by it. But there was no longer any home in Russia: my father had died of typhus and the rest of the family had left the country.

I had known homesickness as a child. I remember it coming over me at twilight when I was staying with an aunt. The house was very quiet. I felt that I was in a mist—she never lit the lamps until it was quite dark—the sunlit hours had vanished as if they had never existed, and the *now* felt endless in memory. I pined for home, as if stretching out towards it.

My new homesickness, in Berlin, did not resemble the old one in the least: it did not come at twilight, or at any definite time; I did not pine: on the contrary it was as if something came to me, bringing a sense of mystery, magic, and loss. For years I did not know how to describe this kind of homesickness.

The next thing I noticed (there seems an infinity of time between the two observations, as there must seem to the baby between rolling over and crawling) was that my homesickness did not come when I might well have expected it: sitting with Russians round the samovar, reminiscing nostalgically about lilac and syringa, school outings in May and wild strawberries and cream, teachers of literature and essays on Turgenev's women, or moved to tears by a line in a Russian song. Such purposeful journeys in chosen company were not at all like my unpredictable, sudden homesickness, my feelings of something precious in the past, reassuring by its mere existence, a fleeting joy, not to be held even for a moment in the mind. It was then that I used to say, being still in my early twenties, that I would give ten years of my life to revisit Russia. In time it dawned on me that some of the Russian emigres I met, whose childhood had been a paradise, did not seem to know my kind of homesickness. So why did I, whose childhood had been full of darkness as well as light, have these intimations of a paradise lost?

I never knew when this homesickness would come or why, nor what started it, and though it was usually gone before my conscious mind seized anything, I sometimes caught an aspect of a street, the hour of the day, a colour, a face: unmistakable fragments of Russian memories. One day I was walking in the Tiergarten when my homesickness touched me: at once I found myself turning my head in the direction it seemed to have come from. That the magic feeling was in a memory of Russia I was certain from the start, but the memory itself eluded me. It did not occur to me that I may have turned towards a sound or a scent similar to one in which the memory was preserved. In fact, I remember thinking that I had turned east, in the direction of Russia.

Another time was when I was coming out of the University, one fine afternoon in summer, in a troubled mood. All my friends had arranged to start their work for the Ph.D. degree, and that afternoon they had asked me why I was so dilatory about it. I had said without thinking: "If I stay another three years I shall never leave Germany. I'll become a German." A friend had comforted me, laughing affectionately: "You'll never become a German." But a mood of anxiety had persisted through the next lecture. As I reached the gateway on to the Unter-den-Linden, I halted. I looked up, and saw a small white cloud slightly to my right: at once I was transported home, to the street in which we lived, on just such a summer afternoon, but with a sky unmistakably stretching over my native town. In memory I am still standing in the gateway aware of the statues of the brothers Humboldt on either side.

To sum up my experiences of involuntary memories in Berlin: they always came suddenly, they brought me great joy, and more often than not I lived in the "then" and forgot the "now." In Contre Sainte-Beuve, where Proust described his real experience of involuntary memories, he says that it happens that we come upon an object and a lost sensation thrills in us, but we cannot give it a name. Still more elusive was an element of fear and it was years before I found this confirmed in Proust's experience recorded in Jean Santeuil.

So elusive are these experiences of involuntary memories that Aksakov goes so far as to say that when involuntary memories came back to him in childhood the moment was "imperceptible to consciousness."

Often one notices nothing more than a change of mood. If I had not been the kind of person who is drawn to his memories like a musical person to sounds, and had not re-created many of them in words, nothing more than fragments would have been left of my experience of involuntary memories in youth. One thing I remember clearly: saying to myself that they helped me to live; yes, they sustained me and gave me courage, which I needed in the utter insecurity in which I, like so many emigres and refugees, found myself.

It was years before I realized that my homesickness in Berlin had been for the past, that people who have never left their country have similar experiences: we are all exiles from our past. It was then that I was surprised, indeed amazed, that my involuntary memories in Berlin had not reminded me of similar experiences which I had had before I left home: memories of a pale blue figured-velvet outfit, a little yellow magic stick, colors changing in the neck of a drake, for these and other fragments had brought me indescribable joys when I was still a schoolgirl.

Looking back I can see now what made confusion worse confounded. As well as being unpredictable, elusive, and desultory, my involuntary memories did not always bring me joy: some brought only great distress. Some had the glory and freshness of a dream, but others were nightmares. I had a memory of my sister who died before she was four of diphtheria. I was nine years old, the eldest, and she the fourth. I had memories of her, playing with Father, unafraid of him, and delighting me as she did him. But the memory of her dying, which came back to me while I was still a child suddenly and unexpectedly, did something terrible to me. I am standing in the doorway, she is lying on her back on the bed, and her face in agony is in a pool of morning sunlight coming from the window opposite. My father on one side, my mother on the other, are desperately trying to help her. Death was not new to me: my grandfather died in our house not many months earlier, neighbors' children had died. I cannot separate the components in my unmitigated horror when this memory suddenly hit me, and I know for certain it happened more than once, but I do remember trying to shake off the memory as one tries to wake from a nightmare.

···

One day, while working on some early memories, and living in one of the 1905 Revolution when I was five, I was terribly taken aback. I was looking out of the window, with my eyes on two women running past, just underneath, each frightened in her own way. They had neither hats nor kerchiefs and their hair was bobbed. "The Revolutionaries," Mother said, close behind me: I turned my head to her. To my amazement I realized that the room I was looking at was the sitting-room of the house to which we moved when I was thirteen! I looked again at my other early memories and now realized that I was using the background of the later house. Let me say straight away that this house, unlike the houses where we lived between 1908 and 1913, was on the same side of the road as the first house, not far from it, and not unlike it to look at. The parlor in both houses had two windows which looked out on the street.

I had a number of memories of events in the early house. In some the table in the center of the parlor figured, in others the stove, and in yet another the door in the wall opposite to the windows. I have a memory of the door being open and my standing and looking in amazement at the enormous red sun, low down, behind the trees. I have vivid memories of my paternal grandmother lying on the sofa which stood against the right wall when she had sprained her ankle. It is easy to date this, since she died before I was six. But what stood against the opposite wall? I could not see that wall at all; and then one day I discovered that it had a door in it.

Of the many early memories which came back to me towards the end of working on childhood, one was of my maternal grandmother, standing between the foot of the bed and the shuttered window, dressing in the faint light which came through the chinks round the shutters. I discover that her hair is brown (it was usually hidden in daytime under a kerchief, and at night under a cap); she is not as composed as I knew her, and what greatly amuses and surprises me is that she is trying to be very quiet, not realizing that I am watching her. I have not another memory of being in that room, where I know I slept with her when I was little. In my memory she turns to the right and I see the door which leads into the parlor. It is my first and only memory of that door. I try in imagination to go through the door into the parlor, but I cannot. What I see is the parlor of the 1913 house, but in that house the door did not exist, nor was there a bedroom on that side, for the parlor adjoined our neighbor's house, and a sofa stood along that wall. But in the first house, according to my memories, the sofa stood against the opposite wall, and indeed it could not have stood by the left wall for there was a door there.

Every early memory was an island without a background; the intrinsic objects in such a memory seemed not merely indispensable but immovable, and invariably precious. It struck me that such a memory was like a scene in a play which one can move as a whole, from one theater to another, from one period to another, changing the scenery. But I did not change the position of objects within my island memories: I did not move furniture about, and I did not duplicate objects. If we had not left the first house when I was eight but had stayed there a few more years, and I had acquired a knowledge of the background and had used it for my island memories, I should never have known that they were originally without a background.

...

To summarize the argument so far: I have shown that memories of events are easily distinguishable from memories of the background; that only memories of events come back involuntarily, bring with them strong emotions, and give a sensation of living in a past moment; that memories of events are of two kinds: whole memories, which always contain a disturbance or a shock, and fragment memories which do not; that because both of these bring back emotions of the same kind and intensity, and both give us the feeling of living in the past, they are probably basically similar, and therefore that the fragments were originally associated with a shock or disturbance which has been lost. I also pointed out that we all carry innumerable other floating fragment-memories—of faces, names, numbers—which are easily distinguishable from the kind of "precious fragments" I have been considering by the fact that they carry no strong emotions, do not give the feeling of living in the past, and never come back involuntarily.

For a thoughtful theoretical analysis of involuntary memories, see Donald Spence's chapter "Passive Remembering" in U. Neisser and E. Winograd (Eds.), Remembering Reconsidered *(Cambridge University Press, 1988). For some empirical data, see two recent papers by Dorthe Berntsen:*

- *(1996). Involuntary autobiographical memories,* Applied Cognitive Psychology, *10, 435–454.*

- *(1998). Voluntary and involuntary access to autobiographical memory,* Memory, *6, 113–141.*

6 | Flashbulb Memories

Roger Brown and James Kulik

Even today, many Americans remember how they heard the news that President Kennedy had been shot. Brown and Kulik elicited reports of such "flashbulb memories" by asking eighty subjects if they recalled hearing the news of nine noteworthy events (assassinations, etc.), and of a single self-selected personally relevant event as well. "Flashbulbs" were more likely for events that subjects rated as more "consequential," and differences between black and white subjects in the consequentiality of certain events were reflected in different likelihoods for certain flashbulbs. Reports of rehearsals were also obtained.

The phenomenon is a robust one: Yarmey and Bull (1978) found that Canadians recall John Kennedy's assassination in much the same way, and Colegrove's subjects (Selection 7) had equally vivid memories of the day they heard about Lincoln. Why are these memories so durable? Brown and Kulik suggest a physiological hypothesis; I offer a different interpretation in Selection 8.

"**H**ardly a man is now alive" who cannot recall the circumstances in which he first heard that John Kennedy had been shot in Dallas. Not just the *fact* that John Kennedy was shot and died; we remember that too, of course, but we really do not need to since it is recorded in countless places and in many forms. It is not the memory of the tragic news that invites inquiry, but the memory of one's own circumstances on first hearing the news. There is no obvious utility in such memories.

The second author recalls: "I was seated in a sixth-grade music class, and over the intercom I was told that the president had been shot. At first, everyone just looked at each other. Then the class started yelling, and the music teacher tried to calm everyone down. About ten minutes later I

From *Cognition*, 1977, 5, 73–99.

heard over the intercom that Kennedy had died and that everyone should return to their homeroom. I remember that when I got to my homeroom my teacher was crying and everyone was standing in a state of shock. They told us to go home."

The first author recalls: "I was on the telephone with Miss Johnson, the Dean's secretary, about some departmental business. Suddenly, she broke in with: 'Excuse me a moment; everyone is excited about something. What? Mr. Kennedy has been shot!' We hung up, I opened my door to hear further news as it came in, and then resumed my work on some forgotten business that 'had to be finished' that day."

Ten years after the assassination, the always-enterprising *Esquire* magazine (Berendt, 1973) asked a number of famous people a question similar to ours: "Where were you?" Julia Child was in the kitchen eating soupe de poisson. Billy Graham was on the golf course, but he felt a presentiment of tragedy. Philip Berrigan was driving to a rally; Julian Bond was in a restaurant; Tony Randall was in the bathtub. The subtitle of the 1973 *Esquire* article could, we are sure, be used again today: "Nobody Forgets."

Probably everyone who has read until this point is primed with an account of his own, which he would rather like to tell, perhaps because there is something strange about this recall. John Kennedy was shot thirteen years ago. What else can one remember from 1963? Almost everyone testifies that his recall of his circumstances is not an inference from a regular routine. It was a primary, "live" quality that is almost perceptual. Indeed, it is very like a photograph that indiscriminately preserves the scene in which each of us found himself when the flashbulb was fired. But why should the human species have such a flashbulb potentiality? Where is the use in carrying certain scenes in permanent store?

"Flashbulb memory" (FB) is a good name for the phenomenon inasmuch as it suggests surprise, an indiscriminate illumination, and brevity. But the name is inappropriate in one respect that had better be brought forward at once. An actual photograph, taken by flashbulb, preserves everything within its scope; it is *altogether* indiscriminate. Our flashbulb memories are not. The second author's crying teacher had a hairdo and a dress that are missing from his memory. The first author faced a desk with many objects on it, and some kind of weather was visible through the window, but none of this is in his memory picture. In short, a flashbulb memory is only somewhat indiscriminate and is very far from complete. In these respects, it is unlike a photograph.

Is it only the news of John Kennedy's assassination that has ever set off the flashbulb registration of each person's circumstances on first hearing the news? Anticipating our data, it seems to have precipitated the effect in greater strength, and for a larger number of persons, than any other event of recent history. However, it is not the only event that has fired flashbulbs. There are, in the first place, other events in our recent national history that have had this effect for some: the assassinations of Robert

Kennedy and of Martin Luther King and the attempted assassinations of George Wallace and Gerald Ford, as well as the startling Chappaquiddick episode involving Ted Kennedy.

But unexpected events that involve nationally prominent persons simply constitute a class of events for which one may reasonably hope to uncover a good number of flashbulb memories. There are also the sundry private shocks in each person's life. Some of our older informants had, prior to 1963, been jolted by midnight phone calls bringing the sad news of the unexpected death of a parent. And slightly younger subjects heard, out of the blue, that a friend had been killed in an accident or by an overdose of heroin. Such personal jolts also cause flashbulb memories; that is, memories not just of the crucial event, but of the circumstances in which one first learned of them. What chiefly differentiates them from presidential assassinations and the like is the absence of a very large population of like-minded people. Only a few feel the shock of a family death or are interested in how you felt when you heard. There is, therefore, no named central event that one can use to retrieve possible flashbulb memories. The best one can do is to ask each informant to search his memory for events of this order.

We began with a familiar phenomenon which, however, does not follow from such well-established determinants of memory as primacy or recency or repetition, even though the data one can collect are a variety of verbal free recall. We had definite intuitions about the variables that might be important and also a large quantity of general curiosity which guided us in the construction of a very long and difficult questionnaire. When about half the data had been collected, we came upon a neurophysiological theory that paralleled our intuitions in its own terms and we decided to bring out the parallels in our exposition. The theory is Robert B. Livingston's (1967a,b), and it is called by the evocative name: "Now Print!"[1]

The steps are postulated to occur as follows: (1) Reticular recognition of novelty; (2) Limbic discrimination of biological meaning for that indi-

---

[1]Some friends, among physiological psychologists, have advised us that the "Now Print!" theory is, as we had guessed, entirely speculative. Furthermore, and this we did not know, it has inspired little or no direct psychophysiological research. There is apparently no clear reason why the theory could not be correct, but it has not had heuristic value in psychophysiology and so there is really nothing clearly pro or con. We were sorry to learn that the "Now Print!" theory has been of such slight consequence in physiological psychology and, of course, we could not very well provide any direct evidence as to its truth value with a paper-and-pencil study. In actual fact, as you will see, all of our own measures and concepts are behavioral, and our theory is completely independent of Livingston's. Nevertheless, at the considerable risk of seeming naive or willful, we have elected to build Livingston's theory into our exposition because his speculations did interest us and we see no harm in stretching an arm (or is it a neck?) in the direction of ultimate synthesis.

vidual at that moment; (3) Limbic discharge into the reticular forma-
tion; (4) A diffusely projecting reticular formation discharge distributed
throughout both hemispheres, a discharge conceived to be a 'Now
print!' order for memory; and finally (5) All recent brain events, all re-
cent conduction activities will be 'printed.' . . . (1967b, p. 576)

Without the neurology one may say: First comes the recognition of high novelty or unexpectedness; then comes a test for biological meaning for the individual; if this second test is met, there follows the permanent registration not only of the significant novelty, but of all recent brain events. What confirmed our interest in this theory was Livingston's first application of it: "I suggest that almost all of you will remember exactly where you were on November 22, 1963, when you heard the news that President Kennedy had been assassinated. You can probably tell us where you were, with whom, and very likely whether you were sitting, standing, or walking—almost which foot was forward when your awareness became manifest" (1967b, p. 576).

METHOD

We had two major intuitions about the determinant of FBs when we designed our study and before we knew of their neurological parallels in Livingston's theory. Perhaps the most obvious property of President Kennedy's assassination was its extreme unexpectedness; in most of our lives no other major political figure had been assassinated. And, in selecting events to use in prospecting for FBs, we generalized this property and so chose ten very unexpected or novel events, among which assassinations loom large. As a consequence, one can reasonably say that for all the events we chose, the first operation in Livingston's theory was satisfied: the registration of novelty. However, we know that the level of novelty varied a good deal, and there is some reason to suppose that the only full-fledged FB effects we obtained were for John Kennedy and for the personal shock described by each person.

The second intuition we luckily had was that, among national events like assassinations, there might well be a difference between white Americans and black Americans, in the public figures who set off FBs.[2] How

---

[2]Nowadays, it is perhaps the case that any study comparing black Americans and white Americans on any sort of cognitive task risks suspicion of seeking tendentious or even downright invidious comparisons. Nothing of the sort is true in the present study. We worked with black Americans and white Americans, only because there have been a number of assassinations in America in recent years which might reasonably be expected to differ in importance or emotional significance for these two demographic populations. We would expect the same kinds of differences for any two groups, such as two ethnic minorities, two professions, the two sexes or, for that

many white Americans, for instance, could say just where they were and what they were doing when they first heard that Martin Luther King had been shot? Not many, we suspected, but probably quite a few black Americans would be able to do so. What should account for a difference of this kind if it were, indeed, attained? We guessed that what would matter would be the comparative *consequentiality* for the black and white individual of each national event. And so we composed a five-point scale for the rating of consequentiality which, as we shall see, we defined in a way that makes it a plausible parallel to Livingston's "biological significance."

Our behavioral data were more fine-grained than the parallel concepts in Livingston's theory. By eliciting spontaneous accounts of whatever length and by conceiving of consequentiality as a five-point scale, we obtained data clearly important to the further development of a behavioral theory. Livingston does not attempt to account for the length or elaborateness of the memory, but our data presented us with wide variation in this respect, and we thought it possible that the rated degree of consequentiality (interpreted as biological significance) would be one of the determinants.

Subjects

Forty white Americans and forty black Americans filled out our questionnaire. The age range was 20–54 for whites with a median age of 27; for blacks the range was 20–60 with a median of 25. We had to tolerate these small differences of age distribution because the length of the questionnaire made it somewhat difficult to recruit enough informants. We used several means to attract informants, including newspaper advertisements and posters in Harvard University buildings. Our collection of informants cannot be considered a random sample of any definable population. We, ourselves, think that the population for which the major results, in abstract form, hold true, may be the human species.

The Questionnaire

The heart of the questionnaire is the set of persons set down in Table 6-1. We used a little over two pages to describe the exact nature of the flash-bulb effect—a vivid recall of the circumstances in which one first learned of some important event. Since almost everyone had such recall in connection with the assassination of John Kennedy, it was possible to illustrate

---

matter, two individuals, providing there were highly publicized and surprising events known to both, but differing in significance. In fact, however, only recent assassinations in America and their effects on blacks and whites meet the requisite criteria and exist in some substantial number of instances for large populations. As we shall see, when the data are reported, our black subjects and our white subjects followed the same principles of human memory, and there is nothing at all suggestive of, or relevant to, differences in any intellectual capacity.

the mental state we hoped to evoke with the two examples provided by the memories of the authors. All informants but two (whom we have excluded from the analysis) correctly understood what we meant. The two who misunderstood reported various facts about the events as they have been described in the press, rather than their personal circumstances on hearing the news. Essentially, the questionnaire was composed by using each of the person-event pairs of Table 6-1 to form the nucleus of a set of similar inquiries. We will describe here only those that are directly relevant to the argument we want to make.

Initial Free Accounts

In the case of each person-event listed in Table 6-1 informants were first asked: "Do you recall the circumstances in which you first heard that . . . ?" In the event that he did not, the informant checked "no" and was directed to turn four pages or so to the next person-event. Whenever he checked "yes," he was asked to write a free recall of the circumstances in any form or order and at any length he liked.

The first set of inquiries offered three possible criteria of a flashbulb effect: (a) the subject's simple response "yes" or "no"; (b) some number of words that we might arbitrarily require for an account to be considered a genuine flashbulb; (c) a content coding of the circumstances reported in terms of such prevalent categories as "Place," "Ongoing Event," "Informant," and so on. Of course, these potential criteria were all closely intercorrelated. However, in spite of that fact, there were reasons to prefer one possible criterion over another.

Simple reliance on the informant's "yes" and "no" would only dichotomize responses into those that are flashbulbs and those that are not, whereas many things indicated that the division was not so absolute and, more importantly, that within the accounts themselves there was much to interest us. Adding up the number of words (or any other objective index of length of account) would enable us to represent the fact that flashbulbs varied in degree, but did not represent variations as well as constancies evident to us in the content of the reports. It is possible reliably to report our conclusions about content, using content analysis, but these conclusions cannot be proved to be necessary emanations of the data. Still, they are too suggestive and, in our eyes, obvious to go unreported.

The first author read 20 FB accounts of the assassination of President John Kennedy, and to him it seemed that there were only six classes of information reported in 50 percent or more of the accounts. An informant was most likely to report the "Place" in which he learned of the assassination, the "Ongoing Event" that was interrupted by the news, the "Informant" who brought him the news, "Affect in Others" upon hearing the news, as well as "Own Affect," and finally some immediate "After-

TABLE 6-1

Chronological order of events used to search for flashbulb memories

Name	Race	Event	Date	Place
1. Medgar Evers	Black	Shot to death	June 12, 1963	Mississippi
2. John F. Kennedy	White	Shot to death	Nov. 22, 1963	Dallas
3. Malcolm X	Black	Shot to death	Feb. 21, 1965	Harlem
4. Martin Luther King	Black	Shot to death	April 1, 1968	Memphis
5. Robert F. Kennedy	White	Shot to death	June 6, 1968	Los Angeles
6. Ted Kennedy	White	Drowning involvement	July 19, 1969	Chappaquiddick
7. George Wallace	White	Shot, but not killed	May 15, 1972	Laurel, Md.
8. Gerald Ford	White	Failed attempt at assassination	Sept. 5, 1975	San Francisco
9. Gen. Francisco Franco	White	Died of natural causes	Nov. 20, 1975	Madrid
10. A personal, unexpected shock, such as death of a friend or relative, serious accident, diagnosis of a deadly disease, etc.				

math" for himself on hearing the news. Sampling the flashbulb accounts for all nine historical events, it appeared that the six categories listed were a kind of "canonical" form for the historical FB memory in the sense that they were more likely to be recalled than any other content though, of course, no informant always used all six.

It is important to bear in mind that the canonical categories listed are abstractions. Each informant's "Place" of hearing the news and "Ongoing Activity" and so on, was, of course, unique. The variation is dramatic: ". . . conversation with a classmate at Shaw University in North Carolina"; ". . . engaging in a game of softball"; ". . . talking to a woman friend on the telephone"; ". . . working for a market research organization"; ". . . I was having dinner in a French restaurant"; etc. For an instant, the entire nation and perhaps much of the world stopped still to have its picture taken.

In addition to the variation within each canonical category, there was, in many records, a sentence or so that fit none of the abstract categories, but was as idiosyncratic on the abstract level as on the concrete: "The weather was cloudy and gray"; "She said, 'Oh, God! I knew they would kill him'"; ". . . We all had on our little blue uniforms"; ". . . I was carrying a carton of Viceroy cigarettes which I dropped. . . ." Responses like these fell outside the canonical categories and also were so unlike one another as to resist grouping in some new category. Is it possible that so endlessly diverse a collage satisfies one law? Both facts about the content are important: the existence of six abstract canonical categories into which most of the, always unique, content could be easily and naturally placed; the existence in some accounts, but not all, of completely idiosyncratic content that the first author could not subsume under any recurrent categories. [*Methodological details omitted.*]

...

A "yes" answer to our initial question and a canonical content score of 1 or more defined the flashbulb (FB) effect in this study. Of course, the higher the content score, the more elaborated the account. However, since the coding is ultimately not an "objective" feature of the data, we shall also sometimes cite number of words, an objective index of the degree of elaboration.

Consequentiality

For each of the ten persons referred to in Table 6-1, there was a 5-point Consequentiality Scale, labeled "Little or no consequentiality for me" at 1 and "Very high consequentiality for me" at 5. The scale came at the end of the questionnaire to minimize the likelihood of disclosing the point of the inquiry.

We spilled a lot of ink in our questionnaire trying precisely to define consequentiality and beseeching our informants to keep the exact sense always in mind, answering as painstakingly as possible. To quote our own efforts at defining the concept: "In order to rate the consequentiality in your life of the death of someone, let us say President John F. Kennedy, you must try to imagine the things that might have gone differently had President Kennedy lived." We pointed out that not only world figures had consequentiality for oneself, but also, obviously, relatives, friends, admired persons, and others could be very consequential. To quote again: "Probably the best single question to ask yourself in rating consequentiality is, 'What consequences for my life, both direct and indirect, has this event had?'" While no one could possibly tote up all the consequences for himself of any particular event, the judgment proved to be one informants could make and, in the data, there are several indications that they followed our directions. It is certain that they did not simply report attitudes or historical prominence.

Rehearsal

For the purposes of this paper, it remains only to describe several items included in the set of questions asked concerning each figure in Table 6-1. To investigate the role of rehearsal as a determinant of flashbulb memories, we asked each informant to indicate, if he gave a flashbulb account at all, how often he had related that account:

". . . never told anyone."

". . . gave the same account roughly 1–5 times."

". . . gave the same account roughly 6–10 times."

". . . gave the same account more than 10 times."

[*Some speculative discussion omitted here.*]

. . .

We propose that higher consequentiality of an event for an individual works both to make more elaborate flashbulb memories and also to compel more frequent rehearsal of that which is all or part of the FB memory. An event which has great consequentiality for an individual is more likely both to be "on the mind" of the person (covert rehearsal) and to be worked into conversation (overt rehearsal). However, we doubt that this rehearsal of the memory is a simple reproduction of the brain events constituting the memory, but think it must also be a constructive process, especially when it is an overt account. Probably, the rehearsal process, set off by high consequentiality, draws its content from the unchanging FB memory, but, in rehearsal, a verbal narrative is likely to be created.

We propose that rehearsals build up associative strength between the verbal narrative created and the (retrieval) cues used in the various settings. It seems likely that the sort of cue that elicited overt rehearsals in our subjects in the past would have been similar to our cue in the present study. A typical cue in our experience has not been "Do you remember the facts of John Kennedy's assassination?" but rather one more along the lines of "Do you remember what you were doing when you heard that John Kennedy had been assassinated?" If such is the case for our informants, we might expect informants who report more frequent rehearsals to have easier access to their verbal accounts by virtue of having relatively greater associations between cue and verbal narrative. In addition, the fact that qualitatively different cues are also likely to have been used would build additional associations between those cases and different aspects of the FB memory. Subjects who have rehearsed their accounts should thus be more likely to give more extensive verbal accounts in the present scheme. It is our assumption then that the FB memory is always there, unchanging as the slumbering Rhinegold, and serving by means of rehearsal to generate some variety of accounts.

Of course, rehearsal need not be either overt or verbal. Bellugi, Klima, and Siple (1975) have given evidence that, in the deaf, rehearsal is manual, at least as reflected on the periphery. But that is still a semantic sort of rehearsal. We believe, with Norman, that: "When the items to be rehearsed are not words but are actions, sounds, visual scenes, tastes, or smells, then the rehearsal tends to mimic the properties of these sensory modalities. Almost nothing is known about rehearsal for nonverbal items, but almost everyone has experienced it" (1976, p. 101). Certainly we have, since we started to attend to the process. Following a sudden consequential automobile accident, one of us finds his covert rehearsal of the circumstances as uncontrollable as the tongue that seeks an aching tooth. Of course, one of the principal things we should like to know about nonverbal rehearsal is whether it tends to build into narrative accounts. Our introspection suggests that it somehow operates on the materials from the FB memory so that a narrative is promptly produced when an audience exists that cares about the story.

Our abstract speculation may be made clear with an example. The shooting of President Kennedy was, we know, much the most surprising of all our historical events. It "bowled over" just about everybody. The rated consequentiality of the event was, for whites, also highest in the historical list and only slightly edged out by the category of "Personal Shocks." For blacks, Kennedy was also rated very high on consequentiality. On the evidence, John Kennedy rated as a member of almost everyone's immediate family. In these circumstances, we expect Livingston's "Now Print!" mechanism to operate and to record permanently all immediately previous and contemporaneous brain events above some level of organization. We further believe that this inaccessible memory will be more elaborated (in canonical content forms or words) than any other historical memory in spite of the fact that it occurred thirteen years ago before all assassinations but that of Medgar Evers. It was so, for blacks as well as whites.

Of course, the memory is not directly accessible and what we have, in fact, is 79 FB accounts, similar in their references to "Place," "Ongoing Event," and the other canonical categories but, in some irrelevant detail, always unique. These accounts are by far the most elaborated in content or in words of any historical event; in content they are slightly less so than the "Personal Shocks." How should it happen that the accounts reflect the high degree of elaboration we attribute to the memories? We have data on overt rehearsals though not on covert. Overt rehearsal would be expected to be especially frequent relative to covert in just this case because there existed a national, indeed an international, highly interested audience. The overt rehearsals reported were far higher than those for any other event; 73 percent of whites and 90 percent of blacks reported telling their personal tales more than once and generally between 1–5 or 5–10 times. Those who did not report overt rehearsals, but nevertheless gave FB accounts, must either be assumed to have forgotten past rehearsals and/or to have rehearsed covertly. It is of some importance that no one reported an overt rehearsal within the past year. In short, we propose that frequent rehearsals, covert and overt, made accessible elaborate FB accounts because of the high consequentiality posited to produce both an elaborate memory and many rehearsals.

...

RESULTS

Race Membership and Frequency of FB Memories

Our advance prediction was that the 40 black informants would be most likely to register biological significance in the case of those national leaders who were most involved with American civil rights, whether the leader be black or white, a friend or an enemy of the black minority. Our intuitive guess was that three such leaders in our set were black and were clear champions of the civil rights of black Americans: Medgar Evers, Malcolm X, and Martin Luther King. These men could truly be said to have attempted to advance the position of American blacks in a way that was ultimately biological since their immediate concerns with education, employment opportunities, and income must ultimately translate into improved opportunities for blacks to survive and contribute to the American gene pool. The fourth leader closely identified with civil rights is former Governor George Wallace, a white man. Whatever George Wallace may have intended his rhetoric to suggest, it was clear to our black informants that he was an enemy (they rated their attitude to him as "extremely unfavorable"). Wallace seemed interested in preserving the disadvantage of the black minority. The other national leaders—Franco, Ford, and the Kennedys—seemed to us not so strongly concerned with civil rights.

In Table 6-2 we have the absolute frequencies of FB memories (really, of course, FB accounts) for each racial group and the nine political leaders. It is possible to use frequencies rather than percentages because the numbers were the same for both groups. Perhaps the easiest way to absorb the information in this table is to look first at the four leaders we have identified as strongly concerned with civil rights and so most likely to elicit FB memories from blacks. For Malcolm X and Martin Luther King, the difference in frequency of FBs is in the predicted direction (blacks greater

TABLE 6-2

Numbers of white and black subjects reporting flashbulb memories for various events

Event	FB Whites (N = 40)	FB Blacks (N = 40)
*1. Medgar Evers	0	5
2. John F. Kennedy	39	40
***3. Malcolm X	1	14
***4. Martin Luther King	13	30
5. Robert F. Kennedy	25	20
6. Ted Kennedy	13	10
**7. George Wallace	11	20
8. Gerald Ford	23	16
9. Gen. Francisco Franco	17	13
10. A personal, unexpected shock	37	32 (36)[a]

By chi square analysis:
***$p < 0.001$
**p between 0.05 and 0.02
*p with Yates's correction between 0.10 and 0.05
[a]Four informants said they had an FB memory for a personal shock but that it was too personal to relate, and so these four did not fully satisfy the definition for an FB account which includes at least one canonical content category.

than whites) and is very highly significant. For Wallace, the difference is again as predicted (nearly twice as many FBs for blacks as for whites), but the significance level is lower. For Medgar Evers, only five informants of all 80 had a FB memory, but all five were blacks, and so the difference approaches significance.

After the fact, it is clear why the Evers' FBs were so few. Medgar Evers was assassinated in June of 1963; 24 of our informants were, in 1976, between 20 and 24 years of age and so, in 1963, would have been between 7 and 11 years old. John Kennedy was also assassinated in 1963, and yet all but one of the full 80 informants, including the youngest, had FB memories of that event. Reading the accounts of their circumstances when they heard the news, it is clear that some, especially the youngest, knew nothing, or next to nothing, of President Kennedy. Had the news (inconceivably) been reported as no more than a routine newspaper headline, the early school-age informants would not have registered surprise, nor probably would they have experienced the event as a consequential one.

In fact, however, they did, most of them, experience surprise and consequentiality. But they experienced them in the microcosms of their own

62 🔲 Roger Brown and James Kulik

lives, usually in school, where the regularities of life were disturbed by reflection from the events in Dallas. Principals made unscheduled announcements over public address systems, teachers or parents burst into tears, and school was dismissed for the day. Events unthinkably surprising and consequential when you are 7 years old. But for Medgar Evers, not a very famous figure, no schools were closed, no announcements were made by principals, some tears were shed but not so many, with blacks still predominantly resigned to injustice.

Looking next, in Table 6-2, at the leaders thought not to be deeply involved in civil rights—John Kennedy, Robert Kennedy, Ted Kennedy, Gerald Ford, and General Franco—we find, as predicted, no significant differences between the groups. The tenth event, a personal unexpected shock, was, of course, entirely different for each informant. The very high levels of personal FBs, almost identical for blacks and whites, simply mean that almost everyone could find in his memory an event answering to our abstract description.

In Table 6-3 we have arrayed the mean consequentiality scores assigned each event by the total groups of blacks and whites. Let us look first at what does not take us by surprise. The mean consequentiality scores for

TABLE 6-3

Mean consequentiality scores for all subjects in two groups

	Whites (N = 40)	Blacks (N = 40)	Significance level of difference by student's t
1. Medgar Evers	1.39[a]	3.00[b]	$p < 0.001$
2. John F. Kennedy	3.39	3.81	$p < 0.10$
3. Malcolm X	1.49[c]	3.40	$p < 0.001$
4. Martin Luther King	2.88	4.34	$p < 0.001$
5. Robert F. Kennedy	3.08	3.56	$p < 0.10$
6. Ted Kennedy	2.07	2.16	
7. George Wallace	1.75	2.23	$p < 0.10$
8. Gerald Ford	1.88	1.63	
9. Gen. Francisco Franco	1.55	1.29	
10. A personal, unexpected shock	3.68[c]	4.22[d]	

[a]Four informants failed to complete this item.
[b]One informant failed to complete this item.
[c]Three informants failed to complete this item.
[d]Seven informants failed to complete this item.

the civil rights leaders—Medgar Evers, Malcolm X, and Martin Luther King—are all very significant and, as anticipated, their consequentiality is greater for blacks. George Wallace's consequentiality is also greater for blacks, but at a borderline level of significance. The simplest way, then, to read Table 6-3 is to say that it provides independent validation of our obvious-enough notion that just these men had greater biological significance or consequentiality for blacks than for whites. Since the notions are obvious, one may also say that the results provide a degree of validation for the consequentiality scale. There is firmer validation in the fact that whites gave a higher consequentiality score to their personal shocks than to any events on the national level, and blacks rated only the consequentiality of the death of Martin Luther King above their personal shocks.

···

DISCUSSION

[*Part of Brown and Kulik's discussion is omitted.*]

The "Now Print!" neurobiological mechanism surely did not evolve in the human species in historical time, that is, in the few thousand years since writing was invented or the few hundred since printing was invented. The mechanism surely evolved much earlier in the (roughly) 1 million years since our species appeared. At the time when the mechanism evolved, there was no actual printing; there was only the human memory. What surely had to be printed neurologically and put in permanent store was not the circumstances of an unexpected and biologically significant event, but the event itself. To survive and leave progeny, the individual human had to keep his expectations of significant events up to date and close to reality. A marked departure from the ordinary in a consequential domain would leave him unprepared to respond adequately and endanger his survival. The "Now Print!" mechanism must have evolved because of the selection value of permanently retaining biologically crucial but unexpected events. It seems to be an irony of evolution that it is just the central newsworthy events that no longer need to be retained because cultural devices have taken over the job. And today the automatic recording of the circumstances, concomitant to the main event, is what captures our interest and calls for explanation.

But the explanation has not been given. Certainly the surprising and consequential had to be permanently remembered, but why should man ever have developed a mechanism for storing his concomitant circumstances? When—ever—would such memories have had survival value?

Suppose we imagine a state of life for primitive man. We are not now at a time when presidential assassinations are the critical events to evoke. They would be something more like the appearance in one's territory of a new dangerous carnivore or the sight of a serious injury to a dominant male of the same species or the moving on, of a troop of baboons, to a new and remote range. These things have to be stored in memory promptly and enduringly and are most closely similar to the "Person" and "Event" categories which in our "Personal Shock" cases were never, literally never, omitted from the account. What might the concomitant circumstances have been like, and would there have been any reason to remember them?

Place, after all, is important almost always. Where was the primitive man when he saw the new carnivore or the baboon troop on the march? The significance of the main event is, in great degree, defined by its locus. Nothing is always to be feared or always to be welcomed. It depends. In part on place. What about ongoing activity? Well, perhaps it is the nature of that activity that has attracted an animal or enraged him or allowed him to draw near without being noticed. Affect in others may well be a clue from more experienced conspecifics of the character of an intruder or the quality of some prey or some sheltering space. So it is not really difficult to conceive of reasons for permanently remembering the circumstances in which something novel and consequential occurred. But we have not yet quite unraveled the mystery of these memories.

The canonical category called "Informant" was the category most often specified in FB accounts and, in that fact, we find the reason why these enduring memories for personal circumstances struck us as mysterious in the first place. All of the ten events we used to search for FB memories were events like John Kennedy's assassination, in which there was a sharp separation between the time and place of the significant event and the circumstances in which each of many millions first heard of that event. An informant was essential for all who were not on the scene, and that informant was usually radio or television. Primitive man, lacking such instruments of telecommunication, would not so regularly register an informant. Sometimes, of course, he would, at least for separations of moderate length since spoken and gestural language may be as old as the species.

But what if there were no informant, then or now, no separation between the event and the circumstances in which one learned of it? You are in a startling and serious automobile accident, or you narrowly miss being struck by lightning. There is novelty and biological significance, and also a FB memory. But what now are the preceding and concomitant circumstances? Still, perhaps, place and maybe time and ongoing activity and affect with only informant missing. But what a difference it makes! The place of an automobile accident, the ongoing activity, the affect are no longer circumstances attendant upon hearing the news. In a way, they are the news, at least parts of it or dimensions of it. The precise intersection, the make of the car, the signal unobserved all together define the event. And so it makes sense that all of these brain patterns should have to be permanently stored and that a "Now Print!" mechanism for doing it would have evolved. What is relatively new is telecommunication which makes an informant a necessity and creates the sharp separation between news and circumstances of hearing the news, and that is what first made us think we were on the trail of a mystery. Probably the same "Now Print!" mechanism accounts both for the enduring significant memories in which one has played the role of protagonist and those in which one has only been a member of an interested audience of millions.

REFERENCES

Bellugi, U., Klima, E. S., & Siple, P. (1975). Remembering in signs. *Cognition, 3,* 93–125.

Berendt, J. (1973, November). Where were you? *Esquire.*

Livingston, R. B. (1967a). Brain circuitry relating to complex behavior. In G. C. Quarton, T. Melnechuck, & F. O. Schmitt (Eds.), *The neurosciences: A study program.* New York: Rockefeller University Press, 499–514.

Livingston, R. B. (1967b). Reinforcement. In G. C. Quarton, T. Melnechuck, & F. O. Schmitt (Eds.), *The neurosciences: A study program.* New York: Rockefeller University Press, 568–576.

Norman, D. A. (1976). *Memory and Attention,* 2nd ed. New York: Wiley.

ADDITIONAL REFERENCES

Yarmey, A. D., & Bull, M. P. (1978). Where were you when President Kennedy was assassinated? *Bulletin of the Psychonomic Society, 11,* 133–135.

7 | The Day They Heard About Lincoln

F. W. Colegrove

Whatever the correct explanation of "flashbulb memories" may be, the phenomenon is at least a robust one. Kennedy, King, and Evers were not the first American political leaders to be assassinated, and Brown and Kulik were not the first psychologists to ask Americans to recall how they heard such news. Colegrove's nineteenth-century report, like Jane Addams' memory cited in Selection 4, shows that the apparent vividness of such memories is not a product of modern sensibilities or modern media of communication.

. . . A well-known pedagogical principle is that vivid impressions are easily recalled. With frequency, recency, and emotional congruity, vividness plays an important role in association. In order to test the abiding character of a vivid experience, 179 middle-aged and aged people were asked in personal interviews the following question: "Do you recall where you were when you heard that Lincoln was shot?" An affirmative answer required the exact location, an example of which is the following reply: "My father and I were on the road to A—in the State of Maine to purchase the 'fixings' needed for my graduation. When we were driving down a steep hill into the city we felt that something was wrong. Everybody looked so sad, and there was such terrible excitement that my father stopped his horse, and leaning from the carriage called: 'What is it, my friends? What has happened?' 'Haven't you heard?' was the reply—'Lincoln has been assassinated.' The lines fell from my father's limp hands, and with tears streaming from his eyes he sat as one bereft of motion. We were far from

※ From F. W. Colegrove (1899). Individual memories, *American Journal of Psychology, 10,* 228–255.

home, and much must be done, so he rallied after a time, and we finished our work as well as our heavy hearts would allow."

Not all the replies were so vivid as this one, but only those were accounted as affirmative which contained facts as to time of day, exact location, and who told them.

J.P., age 76:	I was standing by the stove getting dinner; my husband came in and told me.
M.B., age 79:	I was setting out a rose bush by the door. My husband came in the yard and told me. It was about 11 o'clock A.M.
H.R., age 73:	We were eating dinner. No one ate much after we heard of it.
J.T., age 73:	I was fixing fence, can go within a rod of the place where I stood. Mr. W. came along and told me. It was 9 or 10 o'clock in the morning.
L.B., age 84:	It was in the forenoon; we were at work on the road by K.'s mills; a man driving past told us.

Of the 179 persons interviewed, 127 replied in the affirmative, and were able to give full particulars; 52 replied in the negative. A few who gave a negative reply recalled where they were when they heard of Garfield's death. Inasmuch as 33 years have elapsed since Lincoln's death, the number who made an affirmative reply must be considered large, and bears testimony to the abiding character of vivid experiences.

8 | Snapshots or Benchmarks?

Ulric Neisser

This response to Brown and Kulik was written especially for the first edition of this book. Later selections will provide additional evidence for its conclusions.

A "flashbulb memory" is a subjectively compelling recollection of an occasion when we heard an important piece of news. There is an impressive consistency to the organization of such memories: Colegrove's account of how his subjects remembered hearing about Lincoln is strikingly similar to what Brown and Kulik's subjects say when they recall getting the news about John F. Kennedy. Yet although the phenomenon itself is clear enough, its interpretation is not. At least, it seems to me that the interpretation offered by Brown and Kulik should not go unchallenged.

Why is any interpretation necessary at all? At first glance, flashbulb memories appears to be obvious illustrations of a commonsense principle: people remember what is important. The problem arises only when we realize (with Brown and Kulik) that the actual content of flashbulb memories does not meet that criterion. The fact of John F. Kennedy's death may be important, but what difference does it make who told *me* about it, or where *I* was when I heard the news? None, really. Why, then, do I seem to remember such things? Brown and Kulik think that a special "Now Print" mechanism in my brain is triggered whenever I believe that an important or "consequential" event is taking place. Supposedly this mechanism "prints" the whole event—including many though not all unimportant details—into a permanent record for later recall. This hypothesis implies (a) that flashbulb memories are accurate; (b) that the process by which the memory is created occurs at the time of the event itself; (c) that surprise, emotionality, and similar reactions are closely correlated with the "consequentiality" of an event, and that higher levels of surprise and emotionality lead to good memory; and (d) that the similarities among different flashbulb memories reflect the common characteristics of an underlying neural mechanism. All these implications deserve careful scrutiny.

THE ACCURACY OF FLASHBULB MEMORIES

Brown and Kulik never doubt their informants. They take it for granted that a carton of Viceroy cigarettes *was* dropped, that there *was* a game of softball, that Kulik *was* in his sixth-grade music class, that Berrigan *was* on his way to a rally. They are no more skeptical than Livingston, whom they quote approvingly: "You can probably tell us where you were, with whom, and very likely whether you were sitting, standing, or walking—almost which foot was forward when your awareness became manifest" (1967, p. 576). I find such unquestioning acceptance remarkable: If someone offered to tell me which of his feet had been "forward" at a specific moment in 1963, I would assume he had only a 50-percent chance of being right. Unfortunately, there is ample precedent for this kind of credulity about memory. When hypnotized subjects are "age-regressed," for example, their vivid descriptions of long-past events are often taken at face value even by well-trained scientists. This is a mistake: Careful studies of hypnotic age regression demonstrate that it produces much confabulation and little or no hypermnesia (O'Connell, Shor, & Orne, 1970). In a similar vein, Penfield's (e.g., 1952) accounts of the "recollections" triggered by electrical stimulation of the brains of certain patients are often accepted uncritically even though none of the alleged recollections has ever been verified. (For additional discussion of this issue see Neisser, 1967; Loftus & Loftus, 1980.) By virtue of their vividness and detail, flashbulb memories seem to elicit the same unhesitating assent.

They shouldn't. The psychology of testimony—see Part IV of this book—teaches over and over again that vivid recollection and accurate testimony may be wrong. Indeed, there is at least one documented example of complete fabrication in a flashbulb. Marigold Linton, whose work we shall consider shortly [*see Selection 11*], began her study of memory as Brown and Kulik did: she asked people what they were doing when John Kennedy was assassinated. She abandoned the method abruptly when one of her subjects replied as follows (1975, pp. 386–387):

When I'm reminded of that date, particularly by you, I remember that you were the one who told me about the assassination, or at least that's the way I remember it. . . . I believe that you, I know that you came down and told me about what you . . . had heard on the news. I don't know what time it was. Because down in the hole in F _____ Hall one tended to lose track of time. . . . I had been working for some ex-

tended period of time and I was very much concentrating on what I was doing when I was interrupted by you having heard something about it. You said, I'm sure it was you who said, "The President has been assassinated, or shot—shot." And I probably looked up and said, "What?" and you said, "Kennedy, he's been shot." And I said "What do you mean? Where?" and you said you didn't know. . . .

This recollection is incorrect. Linton has no memory of such an exchange. More significantly, she writes that ". . . Examination of a variety of documentable external events demonstrates that the two of us could not then have been at the same place" (p. 387).

I can supply another counterexample from my own experience. For many years I have remembered how I heard the news of the Japanese attack on Pearl Harbor, which occurred on the day before my thirteenth birthday. I recall sitting in the living room of our house—we only lived in that house for one year, but I remember it well—listening to a baseball game on the radio. The game was interrupted by an announcement of the attack, and I rushed upstairs to tell my mother. This memory has been so clear for so long that I never confronted its inherent absurdity until last year: no one broadcasts baseball games in December! (It can't have been a football game either: professional football barely existed in 1941, and the college season ended by Thanksgiving.) Apparently flashbulbs can be just as wrong as other kinds of memories; they are not produced by a special quasi-photographic mechanism.

WHEN ARE FLASHBULBS ESTABLISHED?

The metaphor of a "flashbulb" suggests that the peculiar strength of these memories is established at the moment of the event itself. Brown and Kulik attribute their creation to the hypothesized special "Now Print" mechanism, while Colegrove gives credit to the more familiar principle that ". . . vivid impressions are easily recalled." I believe, however, that memories become flashbulbs primarily through the significance that is attached to them *afterwards*: later that day, the next day, and in subsequent months and years. What requires explanation, after all, is not the immediate survival of the memory—we can all give good accounts of what happened earlier today—but its long endurance. Moments like these are sure to be pondered, discussed, and redescribed on subsequent occasions: why shouldn't we suppose that their persistence is due to the frequent reconsideration they receive? Brown and Kulik treat rehearsals as mere products of the flashbulb memory, itself "as unchanging as the slumbering Rhinegold," but they may play a more essential role.

If flashbulbs are created after the fact, we can easily understand that they may be inaccurate. A long tradition in psychology teaches us that memories can be altered. The names of Freud and Bartlett come to mind immediately in this context; many later selections in this book make the same point. It also explains how we can have flashbulbs for events whose "consequentiality" was established only later. One informant has told me that she remembers how she heard the news about Kennedy even though she did not believe it at the time; only afterward did she find out that it was true.

"CONSEQUENTIALITY"

It is somewhat surprising that Brown and Kulik asked their subjects to rate the flashbulbed events by their effects: "What consequences for my life, both direct and indirect, has this event had?" Such a question accepts—or asks subjects to accept—the "great man" theory of history. To believe that my life would be different today if one or another of these assassinations had not occurred is to believe that particular political leaders, rather than cultural or economic forces, determine our destinies. Surely this cannot be casually taken for granted. (Moreover, such a criterion contradicts the "Now Print" idea: often, we do not evaluate the significance of an event "now" but only later.) My guess is that the subjects in Brown and Kulik's study were wise enough not to take their instructions too literally: that their ratings were probably based less on "consequences" than on another criterion of importance to be considered below.

Whatever its significance for the subsequent course of events, the first Kennedy assassination was certainly *unexpected*; it took everyone by surprise. Is surprisingness essential for flashbulb formation? Livingston's theory begins with the recognition of novelty, but I doubt that it can be crucial. Long-expected events may also give rise to flashbulbs. The death of General Franco, for example, had been anticipated for weeks in the press. I can offer another relevant case from my own experience. One of my most vivid memories is of a political event that had been eagerly awaited in many quarters: President Nixon's resignation. I vividly recall the circumstances and the company in which I watched the resignation speech, but my memory includes no element of surprise. To be sure it was an emotional occasion, as are many such moments. But emotionality itself is also a poor candidate for the defining characteristic of flashbulbs: the study of testimony does not indicate that emotional experiences are especially well remembered. High levels of arousal are often said to narrow the focus of attention as they energize ongoing activity; it is unlikely that they also promote detailed recall of circumstances.

THE STRUCTURE OF THE MEMORIES

Brown and Kulik are right, I think, to stress the similarities of structure of the many flashbulb memories they collected. Place, ongoing activity, informant, aftermath, one's own affect and that of others: these are important aspects of the memories, and they appear again and again. Nevertheless it may be a mistake to attribute them to "the uniform terms in which the event was experienced," or to "the regnant brain processes at the time." They seem more like narrative conventions to me. News reporters and novelists, mythmakers and autobiographers have a fairly coherent idea of how events should be described, of what readers and listeners want to know. Everyone in our culture is at least roughly aware of these conventions. In effect, we have *schemata* for the arrival of important news as we have for other kinds of social transactions, and we apply these schemata when we try to remember how we heard about President Kennedy's assassination. Traditional advice to newspaper reporters is to include *who, what, when, where,* and *why* in their stories, preferably with a little *human interest* thrown in. *When* and *why* are self-evident for the flashbulbs that an experimenter asks about; *who, what, where* and *human interest* remain, and generate the canonical categories of recall.

In my view, the notion of narrative structure does more than explain the canonical form of flashbulb memories; it accounts for their very existence. The flashbulb recalls an occasion when two narratives that we ordinarily keep separate—the course of history and the course of our own life—were momentarily put into alignment. All of us have a rough narrative conception of public affairs: Time runs on, events unfold, and occasionally there are "historic moments." History has to have such moments, because otherwise it wouldn't be much of a story. The death of a prominent person—or the resignation of a president—is a good place to end a chapter or to highlight a theme. This means that judgments of "importance" are a kind of *metacognition.* They are not so much judgments of the event itself as of how it has been or will be used by the media, by historians, and by ordinary people thinking about their experiences. How dramatic was the event, how central, how "big"? This, I think, is what Brown and Kulik's subjects called its "consequentiality."

In addition to the narrative of public events that we all keep to some extent, everyone elaborates another and more detailed story as well: his own. Our lives are laid out behind us in a richly structured way, full of landmarks and stages and critical moments. I break a leg, I move to a new city, I have a spectacular vacation, I get married—the list stretches distantly into the past and hopefully into the future. (I think it is because young children do not have such a conception of themselves in time that no one has coherent memories of his early childhood; see Selection 27 for

Schachtel's exposition of a similar view.) But this otherwise absorbing story has one disadvantage: it bears little relation to the historical period in which I have actually lived. All those important public events, and where was I? Well, I can tell you *just* where I was: I got the news of President Kennedy's assassination as I. . . .

My suggestion is that we remember the details of a flashbulb occasion because those details are the links between our own histories and "History." We are aware of this link at the time and aware that others are forging similar links. We discuss "how we heard the news" with our friends and listen eagerly to how *they* heard. We rehearse the occasion often in our minds and our conversations, seeking some meaning in it. Indeed, in a good novel there *would* be some meaning to such a sudden eruption of the public into the private; something later in the story would hinge on it. In real life there may be no such meaning, but we cannot help seeking it. The more we seek it, the more compelling our memory of the moment becomes. That memory may be accurate—frequent rehearsal and discussion probably contribute to accuracy—but it need not be. Its purpose is served equally well whether or not the details are correct. It is the very existence of the memory that matters, not its contents. The term "flashbulb" is really misleading: such memories are not so much momentary snapshots as enduring benchmarks. They are the places where we line up our own lives with the course of history itself and say "I was there."

† *For an interesting discussion of Neisser's memory of learning about the attack on Pearl Harbor, see C. P. Thompson and T. Cowan, A nicer interpretation of a Neisser recollection (Cognition, 1985, 22, 199–200). Thompson and Cowan argue that Neisser was probably listening to a* football *game on the radio that Sunday, and that the change from football to baseball amounted to only a small error in what may be an essentially correct memory. In his response Remembering Pearl Harbor (Cognition, 1986, 23, 285–286), Neisser describes the same change as significantly related to his self-schema at the time.*

REFERENCES

Linton, M. (1975). Memory for real-world events. In D. A. Norman & D. E. Rumelhart (Eds.), *Explorations in Cognition*. San Francisco: W. H. Freeman and Company.

Livingston, R. B. (1967). Reinforcement. In G. C. Quarton, T. Menelchuk, & F. O. Schmitt (Eds.), *The neurosciences: A study program.* New York: Rockefeller University Press.

Loftus, E. F., & Loftus, G. R. (1980). On the permanence of stored information in the human brain. *American Psychologist, 35,* 409–420.

Neisser, U. (1967). *Cognitive psychology.* New York: Appleton-Century-Crofts.

O'Connell, D. N., Shor, R. E., & Orne, M. T. (1970). Hypnotic age regression: An empirical and methodological analysis. *Journal of Abnormal Psychology, 76* (Monograph Supplement No. 3), 1–32.

Penfield, W. (1952). Memory mechanisms. *AMA Archives of Neurology and Psychiatry, 67,* 178–191.

9 | Phantom Flashbulbs

Ulric Neisser and Nicole Harsch

Any assessment of the accuracy of memory requires some record of the to-be-remembered events themselves. One way to get those records is to obtain immediate first-hand accounts of experiences that are likely to give rise to vivid recollections later. On the morning after the explosion of the space shuttle Challenger *in 1986, it occurred to me that shock of hearing about this disaster might be just such an experience for many Americans. With this in mind I asked a number of Emory undergraduates to make written records of how they had heard the news on the previous day. Three years later, we compared their still vivid recollections of that experience with those records. I expected to find errors—at least minor ones, comparable to my own transformation of a football into a baseball game (see Selection 8). As you will see, the actual results far exceeded my expectations.*

When I first heard about the explosion I was sitting in my freshman dorm room with my roommate and we were watching TV. It came on a news flash and we were both totally shocked. I was really upset and I went upstairs to talk to a friend of mine and then I called my parents.

I was in my religion class and some people walked in and started talking about [it]. I didn't know any details except that it had exploded and the schoolteacher's students had all been watching which I thought was

From U. Neisser & N. Harsch (1992). Phantom flashbulbs: False recollections of hearing the news about *Challenger*. In E. Winograd & U. Neisser (Eds.) *Affect and accuracy in recall.* New York: Cambridge University Press, 9–31.

so sad. Then after class I went to my room and watched the TV program
talking about it and I got all the details from that.

The two memories above are actually written responses to the question
"How did you first hear the news of the *Challenger* disaster?" The first account was given in the fall of 1988, long after the event, by an Emory senior whom we will call "RT." It was a vivid recollection, which met or exceeded all the standard tests of a "flashbulb memory." Asked for 5-point
confidence ratings of various aspects of the memory, RT hit the top of the
scale: 5 on *How did you hear it?* (television), *Where were you?* (her room),
What were you doing? (watching television), *Who was with you?* (roommate), and *How did you feel?* (shocked and upset). She was slightly less
confident (rating 4) about *What time of day was it?*, answering "2:00 or
3:00 p.m." (In fact, the shuttle exploded shortly after 11:00 in the morning
on January 28, 1986.) But despite her confidence, RT was mistaken. Two
and a half years earlier, she had answered the same question 24 hours after the explosion. The report she gave then is the second response transcribed above. It tells us that RT had originally heard about the disaster in
one of her classes. She did *not* first learn about it from television, as she
later came to believe.

RT is one of 44 subjects whose 1988/1989 recollections of hearing
about *Challenger* are examined in this chapter. These recollections are especially interesting because in each case we also have a report written by
the same subject on the morning after the event. Comparison with these
original reports shows that none of the enduring memories was entirely
correct, and that many were at least as wide of the mark as RT's.

This finding poses a serious challenge to current theories of flashbulb memories. It also raises a number of new questions—at least,
questions that are new in this context. In such cases, has the incorrect
"memory" completely obliterated all tracts of the original event, or could
the earlier memory be retrieved by more adequate cueing? Where do the
incorrect recalls come from? Why are the subjects so confident of them?
Such questions have rarely been asked about flashbulb memories, because we have taken their accuracy more or less for granted. Brown and
Kulik (1977), of course, postulated a special mechanism to explain that
putative accuracy. Other theorists argued that the special mechanism
hypothesis was unnecessary (Neisser, 1982; McCloskey, Wible, &
Cohen, 1988). According to them, ordinary principles of memory—
rehearsal, uniqueness, the schemata provided by narrative conventions—were enough to explain such memories. But in making these arguments, even the critics took the recollections themselves more or less
at face value: It was their accuracy that the "ordinary principles" were
supposed to explain.

...

A questionnaire on which individuals could record how they had first heard the news about *Challenger* was prepared early on the morning following the explosion. The questionnaire was given to 106 Emory students in Psychology 101 ("Personality Development") near the end of the 10:00–11:00 a.m. class hour, that is, less than 24 hours after the event itself. The students filled it out on the spot and returned it as they left the classroom.

The completed questionnaires were left untouched until the fall of 1988. Then, $2^1/_2$ years after the event, we were ready to study the accuracy of flashbulb memories. That fall, a new questionnaire was administered to all the subjects we could still find at Emory, a total of 44. When it became clear that many now had substantially incorrect memories, we decided to examine them further. Forty of the original subjects were interviewed at length in the spring of 1989, using a structured format that was designed to provide numerous recall cues. At the end of the interview we showed them the questionnaires they had filled out 3 years earlier, and recorded their reactions to the discrepancies that thus became apparent.

...

PROCEDURE

The original questionnaire was filled out by 106 students on the morning after the explosion. They began by writing a free description of how they had heard the news, then turned over the page and answered a set of questions based on the "canonical categories" of Brown and Kulik (1977): What time was it, how did you hear about it, where were you, what were you doing, who told you, who else was there, how did you feel about it, how did the person who told you seem to feel about it, what did you do afterward? A final item asked for an estimate of how much time the subject had spent, on the previous day, in talking about the event or following radio/television coverage of it. (It was hoped— perhaps too optimistically—that responses to this item might provide a rough estimate of what the literature on flashbulb memories calls "rehearsal.")

By the fall of 1988, the freshmen of January 1986 had become seniors. The Emory student directory was searched for the names of students who had been in the original sample. Each of them was offered $3 to participate in a brief experiment. (The nature of the experiment was not described. If they asked why they had been selected, the experimenter replied that their names had come from a list of students enrolled in an introductory psychology class several years ago.) Almost all agreed to participate; the sample included 30 women and 14 men. When they came to the lab (either individually or in small groups), the subjects were told for the first time that the study concerned memory for the *Challenger* explosion. They filled out a new questionnaire and left. The study was ostensibly complete at that point; they were not warned that they might be contacted again later.

The 1988 questionnaire closely resembled the one on which the same subjects had recorded the original event, 32–34 months earlier. They first wrote an account of how they had heard the news, then turned the page and answered canonical questions. This time each question was accompanied by a 5-point confidence scale: 1 was defined as "just guessing," 5 as "absolutely certain." As before, they were also asked how much time they had spent (on the day of the explosion) in discussing or following radio/television coverage of the event.

A final item asked whether they had ever filled out a questionnaire on this subject before. Surprisingly, only 11 subjects (25%) answered "yes" to this question; the other 33 were sure that they had not. Compared to other similar studies, this represents rather poor recall of the first questionnaire. The long delay interval (over $2\frac{1}{2}$ years) must be partially responsible for this. In addition, the manner in which the original questionnaire was presented probably minimized its status as a distinct event. It was an easy and undemanding task; all the questions concerned a readily memorable event of the previous day. The participants did not have to sign up or go anywhere; it was just something that filled the last few minutes of an ordinary class, and not worth any subsequent rehearsal or comment.

Some months later, when a preliminary analysis had shown that many of the memories were far off the mark, we decided to interview the subjects more thoroughly. This time they were offered $5 for their help with an experiment. Again, in calling them, NH did not say what the experiment was about. Forty of the original 44 agreed to return; NH interviewed each of them individually (in March/April 1989) for about three-quarters of an hour. During the interviews, she was "blind" with respect to the accuracy of the individual memories. She knew that some subjects' questionnaire responses had been essentially correct and others far off the mark, but with two exceptions she did not know whether any given individual had been accurate or not. The interviews were tape-recorded, and subsequently transcribed.

...

[*Details of the interview procedure are omitted.*]

Finally, at the end of the interview, the subjects were shown their own original 1986 reports in their own handwriting. This often produced considerable surprise, not only for the subject but also for NH, who had not seen the individual questionnaires before. Any discrepancies between the subjects' present recollections and their original records were then discussed: "Why do you suppose you said this here and something different a couple of years ago?" Finally they were asked which version of the event they liked better and believed more. After some concluding discussion of their attitudes toward NASA and the space program, they were dismissed.

CODING

Accuracy is not all-or-none: Many subjects had memories that were partly right and partly wrong. Consider HC, whose overall statement on the 1988 memory questionnaire was:

> "I was returning to my room in Dobbs Hall after a morning class. . . . I heard commotion while I was walking down my hall, and I think somebody must have told me what happened because when I got to my room I turned the television on to see what I knew would be reruns of the explosion." On the backside of the same page, he recalled the time as 11:30, the place as his dorm, and the activity as returning to his room. In response to who told you he gave a specific name, X, presumably the "somebody" in the hall; in response to others present he said "no one."

Compare this recall with HC's morning-after account of the same event in 1986:

> "At about 1 p.m. I was returning from class with a friend of mine who was visiting. Passing through the basement of my dorm, an acquaintance of mine named Y from Switzerland said 'Go turn on the TV.' When I asked why, what happened, he said 'Just go turn it on; it's all over the TV.' I ran up the stairs thinking of presidential assassinations, with my friend muttering something about war in the Middle East. When I entered my room I noticed my TV was already plugged in, telling me that the event happened earlier that morning and my roommate had watched it for a while. Then I turned the TV on." On the backside of that page, in 1986, he had listed time as 1:10, activity as "Worrying about how I was going to get my car started," and others present as "my friend Z" (yet another name).

These two accounts agree on the basic situation: HC was walking through the dorm when he encountered an acquaintance, who told him something that made him turn on his television as soon as he got to his room. But they differ in many details: What time it was, who the acquaintance was, what he said, where the encounter took place, and who else was present. Using the initial account as a standard, the accuracy of the remembered version is somewhere between zero and 100%. But where?

One way to score such responses is just to have judges make global ratings of the similarity between the two accounts. We experimented with several rating scales of this kind, but none had satisfactory reliability. The scheme we eventually selected does not require an overall similarity judgment. Instead, the rater considers five well-defined attributes one at a time. These are, of course, *location, activity, informant, time,* and *others present.* (We did not count *affect;* a separate analysis of affect appears below.) Each of these five attributes can be reliably rated on a 3-point scale. A score of 2 means an essentially correct response (within sight distance of the same location for *place,* the same individual for *informant,* etc.) A zero means that it is obviously wrong (in the dorm rather than in class for *place,* seeing the news on television rather than hearing it from a friend for *informant*). Scores of 1 were given for intermediate cases, like HC's "walking into the dorm hall" for "going through the dorm basement."

These attributes are not all equally important. We defined *location, activity,* and *informant* as "major" attributes because they seem essential to the identity of the event itself. If you misremember where you were or what you were doing or who actually told you about the explosion, you are seriously mistaken. *Time of day* and *others present,* in contrast, are "minor" attributes: You could be wrong on both and still essentially right about what happened. Using this distinction, we defined a *Weighted Attribute Score* (WAS) with a range from 0 to 7. The WAS is the sum of the scores on the three major attributes, plus a bonus point awarded if the subject scores 3 or more (of 4 possible) on the minors. HC has a WAS of four: 2 for *activity* (walking to his room), 1 for the approximately correct *location,* and 1 for an approximately correct *informant.* (He got the wrong person, but at least he remembered that it was a person and not a television set.) This coding system is quite reliable. The two coders who first used it achieved a reliability of .79; after resolving disputed cases, their combined ratings correlated .89 with those of a naive third coder.

Accuracy scores for the fall 1988 recall questionnaires are called "WAS-2/1" because they compare the second reports with the first. Analogous accuracy scores for the spring interviews (again compared with the initial 1986 reports) are called "WAS-3/1"; they had a reliability of .96. We also used this method to measure consistency across the two recall sessions; these scores, called "WAS-3/2," had a reliability of .94.

RESULTS

Accuracy and Confidence

The distribution of accuracies on the fall 1988 questionnaire (WAS-2/1) is shown in Figure 9-1. The mean was 2.95, out of a possible 7. Eleven subjects (25%) were wrong about everything and scored 0. Twenty-two of them (50%) scored 2 or less; this means that if they were right on one major attribute, they were wrong on both of the others. Only three subjects (7%) achieved the maximum possible score of 7; even in these cases there were minor discrepancies (e.g., about the time of the event) between the recall and the original report.

What makes these low scores interesting is the high degree of confidence that accompanied many of them. To quantify this, it was necessary to collapse the several confidence ratings on the fall questionnaire into a single value. We decided to average the ratings for the three major attributes—*place, activity,* and *informant.* This produced a continuous variable (confidence-T2) ranging between 1 to 5, with a mean of 4.17. Its distribution appears in Figure 9-2. To clarify the relation between confidence and

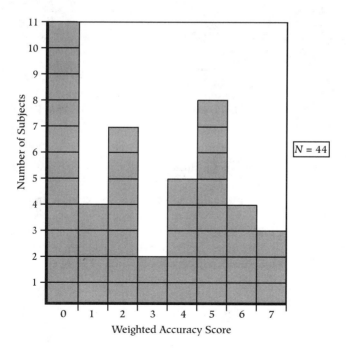

Figure 9-1 *Frequency distribution of accuracy scores on the recall questionnaire, fall 1988 (WAS-2/1).*

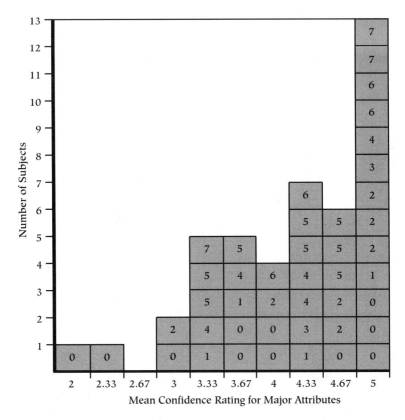

Figure 9-2 *Frequency distribution of confidence ratings on the recall questionnaire, fall 1988. The number inside each cell is the subject's accuracy score, WAS-2/1.*

accuracy, the figure also shows the WAS-2/1 score of each individual subject in the distribution.

The two subjects at the left end of Figure 9-2 exhibit an entirely appropriate relation between confidence and accuracy—they had none of either. These two subjects frankly admitted that they no longer remembered how they had heard the news. In the rest of the group there seems to be no relation between confidence and accuracy at all. (The overall correlation, based on all 44 subjects, was a nonsignificant 0.29.) The 13 subjects at the right side of the figure are particularly interesting: Their mean rating of 5.00 implies that they were maximally confident about all three major attributes. Nevertheless, they were not unusually accurate. The distribution of WAS scores in these 13 was essentially identical to that in the sample as a whole: Again, about 25% were at zero and the median was at 2.

For the most part, our subjects told the same stories in the spring as in the fall: The average consistency (WAS-2/3) was 5.20. This result implies,

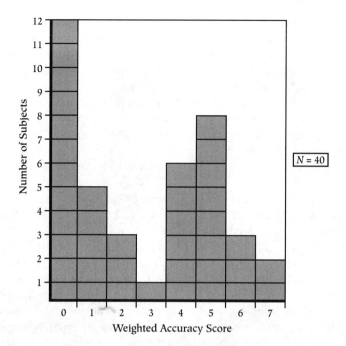

Figure 9-3 *Frequency distribution of accuracy scores on the follow-up interview, spring 1989.*

of course, that the additional cues presented in the spring interviews had little effect on accuracy. Indeed, this was the case. The distribution of accuracy scores (WAS-3/1) for the interviews are shown in Figure 9-3. It is just like the distribution of questionnaire accuracies given in Figure 9-1, or perhaps a bit lower: 12 subjects are at zero rather than 11, and the mean has slipped from 2.95 to 2.75.

Instead of a series of confidence ratings for the various attributes, the interview subjects estimated the "overall quality" of their memories on a 7-point scale. These estimates (which we call "confidence-T3") were still high (mean = 5.28) and still unrelated to accuracy ($r = .30$, ns). They were positively correlated (.565, $p < .001$) with confidence-T2 (average confidence on the fall questionnaires). The most consistent subjects were also the most confident: WAS-2/3 correlated .633 with confidence-T2 and .544 with confidence-T3, both highly significant.

Effects of Additional Retrieval Cues

The accuracy scores in Figure 9-3 are based on the entire interview, up to the time when the subjects were shown their 1986 reports. We had originally intended to develop two such scores, one for the account given at the beginning and another after the presentation of the eight standard recall

cues. This proved entirely unnecessary. Our attempts to enhance retrieval—asking subjects to reinstate the context, having them imagine how
a friend might have heard the news, and the like—made no difference at
all. No subjects changed their minds on any specific point after any of the
eight cognitively designed retrieval cues. No one said, "Oh, now I remember how it really was!" Two subjects' WAS scores went up by a point in the
interview (compared to the fall questionnaire) but six scores went down
by 1 to 3 points; 32 scores were unchanged. The techniques of the "cognitive interview" (Geiselman et al., 1985) may be effective shortly after a
to-be-remembered event, but they are apparently useless after a lapse of
several years.

Perhaps the most interesting outcome of the interviews is what happened—and what did *not* happen—at the end. Many subjects exhibited
great surprise when confronted with their own original reports. They
found it hard to believe that their memories could be so wrong: "Whoa!
That's totally different from how I remember it." We had expected these
exclamations of surprise. But we had also expected something else: that
seeing the original records would at least partially revive the original
memories. If anything can recall a forgotten event to mind, it should be
one's own first-hand report! In initially designing the interviews, we had
anticipated a methodological problem that never materialized. How would
we distinguish between (a) genuine remindings and (b) false impressions
of being reminded that subjects might try to present? We need not have
worried. No one who had given an incorrect account in the interview even
pretended that they now recalled what was stated on the original record.
On the contrary, they kept saying, "I mean, like I told you, I have no recollection of it at all" or "I still think of it as the other way around." As far as
we can tell, the original memories are just gone.

...

[*Various analyses—the role of vividness, reported rehearsal, and emotionality—have been omitted here.*]

TV Priority

Finally, let us look briefly at the errors themselves. When subjects' stories
were wrong, what kind of mistakes did they make? A quick skim through
the protocols suggests that television often played a larger role than that to
which it was rightfully entitled. Recall subject RT's flashbulb account: "We
were watching TV and we saw it." Like many other subjects, RT forgot the
more personal way in which she had actually heard the news (some people had walked into her religion class and talked about it) and came to believe that she saw it first on television. To quantify this effect, we coded
both the original records and the recalls for a binary variable called "TV

TABLE 9-1

TV priority: Numbers of subjects reporting that they first heard the news via TV or otherwise, in 1986 and 1988

	Original 1986 Reports		
1988 Recalls	Yes	No	Totals
Yes	7	12	19 (45%)
No	2	21	23 (55%)
Totals	9 (21%)	33 (79%)	$N = 42$

Priority." Accounts in which the subjects' *first contact* with the news is via television were coded 1. (This includes cases where they were already watching television when the event occurred as well as those where they saw other people watching TV and stopped to look.) All other accounts were coded zero, even if the subject reported watching television later on. As Table 9-1 shows, our subjects' recalls exhibited significantly more TV priority than was justified by their original experiences.

The bottom line of Table 9-1 shows that only 9 of 42 codable subjects (21%) had actually learned about the disaster from television. The right margin shows that by 1988, 45% *believed* they had first heard of it in this manner. Whereas 12 subjects shifted from 0 to 1 (i.e., added TV priority), only two shifted from 1 to 0. The MacNemar Test (essentially a binomial test on the 14 subjects who changed) shows that this is significant at $p < .01$.

DISCUSSION

What are we to make of all this? Two and half years after the original event, many of the flashbulb memories we obtained were quite mistaken. Some subjects were both confident and right, but others—who were just as confident—were dead wrong. When errors did occur, they seemed to be permanent: The subjects pretty much stuck to their stories over the half-year between recalls. Nothing we could think of to do—up to and including showing them their own 1986 questionnaires—brought back the original memories. Where did all the errors come from? Why were the subjects so confident of them? Can these results be reconciled with the emotional strengthening hypothesis?

...

Wrong Time Slices

One possible source of these errors is particularly intriguing: They may represent events that actually happened at another point in time. As in Brewer's (1988) beeper experiment, some recalls may have been based on wrong time slices. The subject remembers a real event, but that event was not the occasion on which he or she first heard about the explosion. RT, with whom this chapter began, is a case in point. She first heard the news when some people walked into her religion class and began talking about the shuttle. Two years later she had forgotten this entirely, but still remembered watching the news on television in her room. Because watching television in her room was the only shuttle explosion event she remembered, RT came to believe that it was the occasion on which she first heard the news. Because her memory of it was so vivid, she gave it a high confidence rating. But because she had really heard the news elsewhere, her accuracy score was zero.

Such "mislocations" are common in autobiographical memory. In his Watergate testimony, for example, John Dean frequently mislocated President Nixon's remarks: Things that had actually been said at Time A were falsely attributed to a different conversation at Time B (Neisser, 1981). Another example: In *A Collection of Moments*, Esther Salaman (1970) documents a clear case of a vivid childhood recollection assigned to the wrong setting. Memories do not carry intrinsic time tags or cross-references. However confidently we may assign them to particular points in our own lives, that assignment must be based on inference from plausible scripted sequences or contextual cues. As details fade with the passage of time, mislocations become increasingly likely.

Reception episodes like hearing the news of a public disaster may be especially vulnerable to internal mislocation. Although they produce strong feelings, those feelings are not intrinsically linked to the personally experienced sequence of events that began on hearing the news. Moreover, that sequence itself may not follow any familiar script. When some fragment of the event later comes to mind, how can the subject tell if it was the beginning of the sequence or occurred only later? This kind of uncertainty is rare with respect to directly experienced events, which usually have a clearer structure. If one narrowly escapes some danger, for example, the sequence "before it happened . . . while it was happening . . . what I did afterwards" is available to guide one's reconstruction and recall. Each phase of the sequence must have included appropriate actions and been accompanied by appropriate emotions. No such script—at least, none that necessarily fits the facts—is available for reception events.

The Bias Toward Television

For our error-prone subjects, the remembered event often involved television although first hearing the news had not. This shift toward "TV priority" is one of the clearest trends in the data. It probably results from the combined effect of several factors. First, most of the subjects did in fact watch a lot of television that night. For them, television coverage of the disaster was an extended, repeated, and easily remembered event. Second, most television channels showed repeated replays of the dramatic explosion itself. Those replays established a vivid and persistent visual image: Many subjects could "still see it" 2 years later. In contrast, the actual occasions of first hearing the news events usually lacked these advantages. They were brief, not visually salient, and perhaps not very interesting. Although a few subjects succeed in making personally significant narratives out of such moments (as suggested elsewhere: Neisser, 1982), many do not. What happens instead is that the original event is simply forgotten, and the more memorable one takes its place.

Another factor may also have played a role in the shift to TV priority. Although we noted above that there is no *necessary* script for hearing disaster news, there does seem to be a culturally familiar one: namely, one sees them on television. In an informal study, we asked a number of younger subjects (who had not been on campus in 1986) to imagine how Emory students *might have first heard* about the space shuttle explosion. Many of them listed "watching television" as the most plausible scenario. If such a schema does exist, subjects who no longer remembered how they actually heard the news may have relied on it in giving their responses.

...

Other Types of Error

Several of our subjects had false recollections that do not easily fit the wrong time slice paradigm. GA, who had actually heard the news in the cafeteria (it made her so sick that she couldn't finish her lunch), later recalled that "I was in my dorm room when some girl came running down the hall screaming, 'The space shuttle just blew up.' " GA went on to say that she "wanted to run after the screaming girl and question her," but instead turned on the television to get more information. This memory probably isn't a wrong time slice: We have no reason to believe that the screaming-girl episode ever took place. It seems more like a fantasy, based on some stereotyped conception of how people react to shocking news. We do not know when GA first had this fantasy; it may even have been very shortly after hearing the news at lunch. (Perhaps she initially imagined *herself* as the girl in question: "I feel like screaming through the dorm . . .") Later, she forgot the original event and remembered only the dramatic fantasy itself.

If this interpretation of GA's report is correct, it was based less on a wrong time slice than on a failure of "reality monitoring" (Johnson & Raye, 1981). Such failures may be rather common. Once the supporting context has been forgotten, it may be genuinely difficult to distinguish memories of events that happened from memories of those we only imagined. (John Dean did not always succeed in making this distinction either.) Another possible example: Subject MS, who had learned about the disaster at Emory like all of our subjects, later recalled being at home with her parents when she first heard the news! Did MS originally *imagine* what it would have been like to share the experience with her parents, and later mistake that imagined scenario for what had really happened? One can only speculate, and we may already have speculated quite enough.

Conclusions

Once again it appears that establishing facts is one thing; interpreting them is quite another. Our data leave no doubt that vivid and confident flashbulb recollections can be mistaken. When this happens, the original memories seem to have disappeared entirely; none of our retrieval cues enabled the subjects to recover them. This finding rules out the simplest form of the emotional strengthening hypothesis, but it does not eliminate more sophisticated versions. Perhaps the strongest feelings took some time to develop, and thus strengthened the memory of later events rather than of the subjects' first contacts with the news. Other theories of flash-bulb memories are also still in the running. The hours of later television watching may have been more strongly rehearsed, more unique, more compatible with a social script than the actual occasions of first contact. Any of these hypotheses might explain the shift to TV priority in our data.

It is not yet clear how far these findings can be generalized to other cases of vivid memory. Reception experiences—hearing the news of some tragic public event—are rather unusual in that they are not constrained by any necessary script or sequence. The emotions produced are not attached to the events that the subject actually experiences; rather, they are directed to the reported disaster itself. Thus the fragments that remain in memory some years later cannot be easily assigned to a coherent narrative—at least, not to the sequence as it actually occurred. We come, at the end, to a rather paradoxical conclusion. Flashbulb memories of reception events, like those originally described and defined by Brown and Kulik (1977), may be appreciably less reliable than other cases of vivid and confident recall.

REFERENCES

Brewer, W. F. (1988). Memory for randomly sampled autobiographical events. In U. Neisser & E. Winograd (Eds.), *Remembering reconsidered: Ecological and traditional approaches to the study of memory.* New York: Cambridge University Press.

Brown, R., & Kulik, J. (1977). Flashbulb memories. *Cognition, 5,* 73–99.

Geiselman, R. E., Fisher, R. P., Mackinnon, D. P., & Holland, H. L. (1985). Eyewitness memory enhancement in the police interview: Cognitive retrieval mnemonics versus hypnosis. *Journal of Applied Psychology, 70,* 401–402.

Johnson, M. K., & Raye, C. L. (1981). Reality monitoring. *Psychological Review, 88,* 67–85.

McCloskey, M., Wible, C. G., & Cohen, N. J. (1988). Is there a special flashbulb memory mechanism? *Journal of Experimental Psychology: General, 117,* 171–181.

Neisser, U. (1981). John Dean's memory: A case study. *Cognition, 9,* 1–22.

Neisser, U. (1982). Snapshots or benchmarks? In U. Neisser (Ed.), *Memory observed: Remembering in natural contexts.* New York: Freeman.

Salaman, E. (1970). *A collection of moments: A study of involuntary memories.* London: Longman.

10 Remembering the Earthquake: Direct Experience vs. Hearing the News

Ulric Neisser, Eugene Winograd, Erik T. Bergman, Charles A. Schreiber, Stephen E. Palmer, and Mary Susan Weldon

People may forget how they heard the news of some remote catastrophe, but would they forget their own experiences of a real disaster if they were personally involved in it? Maybe not: in this study of earthquake memories, recall of personal experience was very good indeed. But why? As we shall see, the theoretical questions raised by Brown and Kulik's initial "flashbulb" study still have not been completely resolved.

Most everyday experiences are soon forgotten, but some give rise to vivid, confident memories that last for years or decades. In many cases, such memories are essentially accurate accounts of the original experience. The present study illustrates this point. As we shall see, individuals who directly experienced the California earthquake in 1989 recalled their experiences confidently and accurately after a delay of a year and a half. But memory is not always so good: the subjects of Neisser and Harsch (1992) *[see Selection 9]*, for example, made gross errors in recalling how they had first heard about the *Challenger* space shuttle disaster. What variables might distinguish experiences that are destined for accurate recall from those doomed to error or oblivion?

※ From *Memory*, 1996, 4, 337–357.

At one level, the present findings simply suggest that experiencing events as a participant (rather than as a mere observer) improves the accuracy of recall. This argument is plausible, and has been made before (e.g., Goodman, Rudy, Bottoms, & Amann, 1990). But . . . most life events involve "participation" and yet are soon forgotten. What was so special about [being] in an earthquake?

. . .

At a first level of analysis, it seems likely that participation is a key variable. Although many of Neisser and Harsch's subjects were genuinely upset by the space shuttle disaster . . . they were still not personally involved in it. To see whether this variable matters, the present study explicitly compares *participants*—individuals who actually experienced an event—with control subjects who only heard about it. The event in question was an important one: the Loma Prieta earthquake of 17 October, 1989. (Non-Californians often call it the "San Francisco earthquake," but the actual epicentre was well to the south of that city.) The recall interval was about a year and a half: from October 1989 to mid-spring of 1991.

There is independent evidence that the Loma Prieta earthquake affected those who experienced it. This evidence comes from a study of nightmare content conducted by Wood, Bootzin, Rosenhan, Nolen-Hoeksema, and Jourden (1992). In a design similar to ours, Wood et al. compared Bay area students who had actually experienced the earthquake with Arizona controls who had not. All subjects kept dream logs for 21 nights, starting one or two weeks after the event. About 40% of the California sample reported at least one "slightly to moderately intense" nightmare about an earthquake, compared to only 5% of the comparison group.

Three coordinated teams of investigators—at the University of California campuses in Berkeley and Santa Cruz, and at Emory University in Atlanta—carried out the present study. Our aim was to contrast the memories of California students, for whom the quake was a personally experienced event, with students at Emory for whom it was a reception event. A within-subject comparison of the same two categories is also available: we will contrast the California informants' recollections of their own earthquake experiences with their recalls of how they first heard about the collapse of the San Francisco Bay Bridge. A number of related variables—especially the subjects' own ratings of their emotional responses—will also be reported.

METHOD

Informants

There were three groups of informants. For most of the Emory students in the Atlanta group ($n = 76$), the earthquake was just something that had happened thousands of miles away. Its major consequence for them may have been the postponement of the baseball World Series between the Oakland As and the San Francisco Giants: the earthquake struck just as the third game of that series was scheduled to begin in San Francisco. The subset of Atlanta subjects who had friends or family in the Bay Area constitutes a special case, to be considered in some detail later.

For the Berkeley informants (n = 41), it was a moderate earthquake experienced at first hand. Berkeley is on the east side of San Francisco Bay, which is some five miles wide at that point. It is connected to San Francisco itself by the Bay Bridge, which was damaged and rendered impassable by the quake. Major damage occurred in San Francisco itself as well as at one freeway at the east shore, but the effects in Berkeley were relatively minor. Although the tremors could be clearly felt, no University buildings were seriously affected. Classes met the next day.

The subjects at the University of California in Santa Cruz (n = 44) experienced much more severe conditions. The epicenter of the earthquake (which registered 7.1 on the Richter Scale) was relatively close to Santa Cruz, a coastal city some 75 miles south of San Francisco. Its impact there was far greater than anything experienced in Berkeley, or indeed in most of San Francisco itself. There was extensive physical damage to buildings, loss of electric power, and a general disruption of everyday activities. Classes at the University were canceled for several days.

The timing of our initial questionnaires was as follows:

At Emory: Questionnaires were given to an introductory psychology class (n = 95) on 19 October, less than 48 hours after the quake. Another introductory class (n = 195) was given the same questionnaire a week later. These groups did not differ significantly on any outcome measure, and have been combined in all analyses reported here.

At Berkeley: A total of 172 questionnaires were given in various undergraduate courses at Berkeley on 18 October, the day after the quake; another 138 were given on 19–20 October.

At Santa Cruz: Logistical factors prevented us from collecting initial accounts at Santa Cruz until the first week in November, a delay of 15–21 days.

Questionnaires were then obtained from 135 upper- and lower-level students in psychology classes.

Questionnaires

After giving their name, sex, and age, the Emory group first described in their own words "how you first learned that such an earthquake had occurred." Then they turned the page and answered a number of specific questions:

- What time of day was it when you first heard the news?

- How did you hear it (TV, radio, someone told you, etc)?

- Where were you at the time?

- What were you doing at the time?

- Who told you? (If TV/radio, what program/newscaster, if person, who?)

- Who else was present?

They then rated their emotional reaction to the news on a 7-point scale ("1 means you have no emotional reaction at all; 7 is the strongest emotion you have ever felt in your life") and answered several further questions: whether there was a family member or friend—someone they felt close to—in the affected area; whether they had ever experienced an earthquake personally; what they did immediately after hearing the news; how much time they had spent talking about the earthquake and following coverage of it, both on the day of the quake and on the following day.

The Berkeley investigators modified the questionnaire in several ways that seemed appropriate to their situation. (For example, the "informant" category is irrelevant for subjects who experienced the earthquake directly.) Their subjects did not begin with an overall free recall of the experience, but were asked a larger number of specific questions. Besides reporting where they were, what they were doing, what time it was, and who they were with when the earthquake struck, they were asked what went through their mind at the time (and afterwards), how they had reacted, how strong they had thought the quake was at the time, and when they had realized how serious it really was.

After these items, the Berkeley informants were asked a further set of questions about how they had learned about the collapse of the upper deck of the Bay Bridge. (This was a major feature of the earthquake for everyone in the Bay Area, widely reported in the news media.) These questions were: When you first heard about the collapse of the upper deck on the Bay Bridge (not to be confused with the Nimitz Freeway), where were you? What time was it? What were you doing? Who were you with? What went through your mind? How did others react?

Three 7-point rating scales concerning reactions to the events concluded the questionnaire:

- How you felt during the earthquake (1 = very calm to 7 = terrified).

- Immediately after the quake, how concerned were you? (1 = not at all concerned to 7 = extremely worried)

- Immediately after you heard the news of the bridge collapse, how concerned were you? (same scale)

The Santa Cruz informants began with a free recall like that of the Emory subjects, but were then asked all the questions used at Berkeley.

Follow-up Survey

The retention interval of a year and a half was dictated by the composition of the California samples, many of whom became graduating seniors during the next academic year. In the spring of 1991, follow-up surveys were administered to all informants who could be reached by telephone and agreed to come to the lab to fill out a questionnaire. (They were not told on the phone that the questionnaire would deal with the earthquake.) These included 76 Emory students (39 from the group that had first responded two days after the quake and 37 from the nine-day group), 41 Berkeley students,[1] and 44 Santa Cruz students. The follow-up questionnaires were essentially identical to the originals except that a confidence rating scale was included with each question: 5-point scales at Emory and Santa Cruz (1 = just guessing, 5 = absolutely certain), 7-point scales at Berkeley. Informants were also asked whether they remembered filling out the earlier questionnaire. In addition, Berkeley subjects were asked how long they had lived in California (75% of the informants indicated 12 years or more of residence), and whether they had ever experienced an earthquake prior to Loma Prieta (of the 39 who answered this question, 36 said "yes").

Scoring

Accuracy was scored with a modified version of the system used by Neisser and Harsch (1992). For the Atlanta subjects, whose recall concerned hearing the news about the earthquake, judges scored five attributes: *place, informant, activity* (what they were doing when they heard the news), *others present,* and *time of day.* To maximize reliability, each attribute was scored on a simple 3-point scale. A score of 2 meant that the first and second reports of the attribute were essentially identical, while 0 meant that they were clearly inconsistent (or that the attribute was not mentioned on the second questionnaire). Intermediate degrees of fit were scored 1. The primary source of information for these judgments was the subject's answer to the specific question about the given attribute. Judges scoring the Emory and Santa Cruz questionnaires were also free to use the subject's initial free recall (or responses to other items) to resolve any ambiguities.

For many purposes it is convenient to have an index of overall accuracy, summed across relevant attributes. Here we report "Combined Accu-

---

[1]Forty-four students were actually tested at Berkeley, but three have been omitted from subsequent analyses because, according to their original reports, they hadn't realised it was an earthquake until subsequently informed by others or the media.

racy Percent" (CAP) scores, based on three attributes common to all groups: *place, activity before,* and *others present.* No other attribute is suitable for such an index: *informant* does not apply to direct experience, *activity during* does not apply to reception events, *time* was not used because information about it was very widely available. (The media in California often used the impact time, 5:04, as a sort of synonym for the quake itself; it even appeared on T-shirts.) These three attribute scores, each ranging from zero to two, were summed and converted to a "Combined Accuracy Percent" (CAP) score.

$$CAP = 100 \times [(place + activity + others)/6].$$

Two separate CAP scores were calculated for the California groups, CAP(DIR) for recall of the direct earthquake experience and CAP(BNEWS) for recall of hearing the news about the Bay Bridge. The score for the Emory group may be called CAP(ENEWS) since it concerns news of the earthquake itself.

RESULTS

Almost all informants gave full and complete initial reports. The only exceptions were three informants at Santa Cruz who did not say how they heard the news of the Bridge collapse, two at Emory who did not answer the question about "others present," and three who did not record a time. Most of those who filled out the second questionnaire still remembered having answered the first one: 66/76 at Emory, 32/44 at Santa Cruz, 29/41 at Berkeley. Because there were no significant sex differences, data for men and women have been combined in all analyses reported here.

Accuracy: Global Measures

There are five major sets of CAP scores: CAP(DIR) at Berkeley and Santa Cruz, CAP(BNEWS) at the same two sites, and CAP(ENEWS) at Emory. These means are shown in Figure 10-1 on page 96. Three comparisons are of primary interest here.

Experiencing the quake vs. hearing about it. As can be seen, both California samples were essentially at ceiling for recall of direct experience (first two bars), with mean CAP(DIR)s of 99 and 96 respectively. These scores were very much higher than those at Emory, where the mean CAP(ENEWS) of 55 was significantly lower than either CAP(DIR) by Mann-Whitney U test. (Non-parametric tests are used throughout this section because of the skewed CAP distributions.)

A few of the Emory subjects made gross recall errors, comparable to those described by Neisser and Harsch (1992). Subject LG, for example, was very confident on the follow-up questionnaire: she had first heard about the earthquake on the following morning, listening to the radio while at work. ". . . sitting on a stool, looking at the radio in amazement at the news." But in fact (according to her own earlier report), her parents had told her about the quake on the telephone on the previous evening: "My dad was going to watch the World Series. The(y) described the destruction of the Bay Bridge for me & the evacuation of the stadium." LG's CAP(ENEWS) score was zero. In contrast, no error of this magnitude was made by any Californian informant in recalling the experience of the earthquake.

Experiencing the quake vs. hearing about the bridge. In both California groups, recall of hearing about the bridge was substantially lower than recall of direct experience. Wilcoxon matched-pair tests show that these differences were significant (for Berkeley $Z = 3.74$, $P < 0.001$; for Santa Cruz

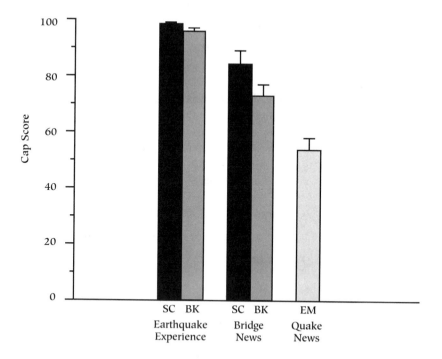

Figure 10-1 *Mean Combined Accuracy Percent (CAP) scores, with standard error bars, for recalls of: earthquake experiences (Santa Cruz and Berkeley informants), hearing about the Bay Bridge (Santa Cruz and Berkeley informants), and hearing the news of the earthquake (Atlanta informants).*

$Z = 2.97$, $P < 0.01$). Being personally involved in an event is evidently more memorable than just hearing the news of one. But although they were weaker than memories of direct experience, the California recalls (both groups combined) of hearing about the bridge were still more accurate than the Atlanta subjects' recollections of hearing about the earthquake itself ($U = 1759$, $Z = 4.68$, $P < 0.0001$).

Santa Cruz vs. Berkeley. In spite of near-ceiling effects, there are significant differences favoring the Santa Cruz group over the Berkeley group on both CAP(DIR) ($U = 766$, $Z = 1.98$, $P < 0.05$), and CAP(BNEWS) ($U = 589$, $Z = 2.56$, $P = 0.01$). These differences may reflect the greater intensity of the earthquake as experienced in Santa Cruz, but they may also have resulted from procedural differences between the two locations. Two such differences seem especially relevant. First, the Santa Cruz informants (like those at Emory but unlike those at Berkeley) were asked to give free-recall accounts of their experiences before answering specific questions. This format may have aided recall; it may also have affected subsequent scoring, because coders could use the free recalls to clarify answers that might otherwise have seemed inconsistent. Second, the baseline Santa Cruz reports were not obtained until 2–3 weeks after the quake and hence may reflect more solidly established initial narratives. Note, however, that a (admittedly smaller) delay in interviewing some of the Berkeley informants did *not* result in more consistent reports. The mean CAP(DIR) and CAP(BNEWS) scores of the Berkeley subjects first seen on 18 October were almost identical to those of others who were not interviewed until 20 October, two days later.

Affect

The subjects' affect ratings can be used to address three distinct issues: the degree of emotional response actually produced by the earthquake, the correlation of reported arousal levels with accuracy of recall, and the subjects' ability to recall their own reported feelings a year and a half later.

Mean reaction ratings. How emotionally disturbing was the earthquake, and how disturbing was the subsequent news about the Bay Bridge? Mean initial ratings on three different scales—reaction during the quake, concern after the quake, concern about the Bay Bridge—appear in the first column of Table 10-1. On all three scales, the mean ratings of the California informants were close to 4.00, the middle of the 7-point scale. (Emory subjects used a differently worded scale and will not be considered here.) On the average, then, the earthquake was *not* a traumatic event. This is congruent with findings of Wood et al. (1992), whose subjects rated their anxiety at only 3.61 (in Stanford) and 3.17 (in San Jose) on a 5-point scale. It is interesting that the Berkeley and Santa Cruz means did not differ significantly on any of these scales, even though Santa Cruz was closer to the epicenter and experienced more damage.

In both cities, the concern engendered by news of the bridge collapse was appreciably *higher* than the concern reported after the earthquake itself. Separate Wilcoxon tests show that the difference was significant in both groups ($Z = 4.38$, $P < 0.0001$ for Berkeley; $Z = 3.45$, $P < 0.0001$ for Santa Cruz). Although the two rating scales were worded somewhat differently, we are inclined to take this result at face value. Most of our subjects were not seriously concerned for themselves because, in fact, their local situations were not dangerous. On the other hand, all of them were exposed to dramatic reports of major catastrophes elsewhere.

Affect as a predictor of recall. Perhaps the most obvious question to ask of these data is whether higher affect is associated with greater recall. The relevant correlations—between initial affect ratings and subsequent CAP scores—are shown in the second column of Table 10-1. The answer is clearly negative: none of them is significant. This may be an artifact of ceiling effects in the case of correlations with CAP(DIR), but even without any such constraint the correlations with CAP(BNEWS) in California or CAP(ENEWS) at Emory were still essentially zero.

TABLE 10-1

Ratings of affect

Group	Mean Initial Rating	Correlation with Accuracy (CAP)	Mean Remembered Rating
Berkeley[a] during quake	3.84	−0.02	4.04
Santa Cruz[a] during quake	4.02	−0.05	4.09
Berkeley[b] after quake	3.89	−0.22	3.73
Santa Cruz[c] after quake	4.03	−0.04	4.07
Berkeley[b] after bridge news	5.28	−0.11	5.63
Santa Cruz[c] after bridge news	5.29	−0.14	5.32
Emory[d] after quake news	3.60	−0.03	3.49

[a]Scale went from 1 = "very calm" to 7 = "terrified"
[b]Scale went from 1 = "not at all concerned" to 7 = "extremely worried and upset"
[c]Scale went from 1 = "not at all concerned" to 7 = "extremely worried"
[d]Scale went from 1 = "no emotional reaction at all" to 7 = "the strongest emotion you have ever felt in your life"

Concern for Friends and Relatives

Individuals who do not experience an event themselves may nevertheless feel concern for others more directly involved. To assess the effect of this concern, we examined the CAP(ENEWS) scores of Emory students who reported having friends or family in the affected area. . . . subjects with friends or family in the Bay Area had significantly higher scores than those without ($U = 3.86$, $Z = 2.08$, $P < 0.05$). The mean CAP(ENEWS) for those involved in this way was 67.46, only slightly below CAP(BNEWS) in Berkeley. Surprisingly, however, this difference was not reflected in mean affect ratings . . . These did not differ significantly; in fact, the mean for informants *without* such involvement was slightly higher. Moreover, there was no significant correlation between rated emotional reaction and accuracy in either group.

...

DISCUSSION

Two independent comparisons in these data show that experiencing the earthquake directly was more memorable than just hearing about it. First, the subjects in Berkeley and Santa Cruz who had experienced the earthquake themselves remembered much more than those in Atlanta for whom it had just been a reception event. Second, both California groups remembered their direct experience of the quake better than they remembered learning about the Bay Bridge collapse. How can these differences be explained? Several alternative hypotheses present themselves.

The Arousal Hypothesis

Perhaps the most obvious possibility is that the difference results from emotional arousal. Is it not reasonable to assume that earthquakes are frightening, and that the heightened arousal level they produce improves memory (Christianson, 1992; Gold, 1992)? Perhaps surprisingly, our data do not support this interpretation. For one thing, most of our California subjects were simply not frightened: their ratings of affect and concern were by no means high. It is important to realize that earth tremors are common in California. As noted earlier, more than 90% of our Berkeley sample had experienced at least one previous earthquake. Two of the present authors, both Californians (ETB & CAS), are sure they have been through more quakes than they can now recall. For such subjects, feeling the earth move is neither frightening nor intrinsically memorable.

Even more important is the absence of correlation between affect ratings and CAP scores in any group. The most concerned or frightened subjects did *not* establish the strongest memories. This negative finding contradicts any simple arousal hypothesis. Moreover, the subgroup of Atlanta subjects with friends or relatives in the Bay Area, who had relatively high CAP scores, rated their feelings as no stronger than did their peers without such attachments.

These data do not make an arousal hypothesis untenable; they just make it more complicated. Perhaps our affect ratings failed to capture some key aspect of emotional response; perhaps arousal itself is unconscious, or at least goes unrecognized. It is also possible that what matters is not the subject's arousal during the quake itself but during some later memory-consolidation phase. At present, however, these hypotheses remain *ad hoc*.

The Consequentiality Hypothesis

Another variable that must be considered is the "consequentiality" of the event, a term first introduced by Brown and Kulik (1977). They asked subjects to assess "what consequences for my life, both direct and indirect, has this event had," and got very high ratings for the John F. Kennedy assassination. In the same vein, Conway et al. (1994) use "consequentiality" to explain why Britons remember how they heard the news of Margaret Thatcher's resignation better than do nationals of other countries. We find this argument unsatisfying, especially where reception events are concerned. Although the fact that an assassination or resignation has occurred may have real consequences for citizens of a given country (though even this is not obvious: cf Neisser, 1982, p. 46), the *occasion on which they heard about it* surely does not. Nevertheless it is just that occasion which they are asked to remember in these experiments. The subjects of our study were not asked to recall facts about the earthquake itself (which indeed had major consequences) but rather to relate their own personal experiences at the time (which probably did not). Why then was their memory so good?

The Distinctiveness Hypothesis

Some experiences are unique and distinctive; others are familiar, commonplace, similar to much that has gone before. In general, the former are remembered better than the latter. In Brewer's (1988) study for randomly sampled personal events, for example, the uniqueness of an event was the best overall predictor of how well it would be recalled later on. Some of our subjects certainly had unique or distinctive experiences during the earthquake, often including a substantial disruption of their ongoing activity. Winograd and Killinger (1983) suggest that such a disruption can be a source of distinctiveness in its own right.

It is possible that recalls of direct experience were more accurate than recalls of hearing about the Bay Bridge simply because subjects' immediate experiences of the quake were more distinctive than the various ways in which they got the Bridge news. (The bridge-news recalls may also have been more vulnerable to what Brewer [1988] has called "wrong time slice" errors: the subject recalls a reception event that really did happen, but was not the occasion on which he or she *first* heard the news.) Unfortunately, this argument depends entirely on post hoc assessments of distinctiveness.

A further issue concerns the scope of the event whose distinctiveness is being assessed. Even when a California subject's momentary experience of the quake was *not* distinctive, the full set of his or her earthquake-related experiences—the first shock, hearing about the Bay Bridge, talking about it all repeatedly, encountering the sequelae of the quake for days afterward—must have been unique indeed. This brings us to the final and (in our view) most persuasive explanation of the findings: subjects remembered their earthquake experience so well because they had talked about them so much.

The Narrative Hypothesis

One's personal experience of a major earthquake is definitely worth talking about. Some of its narrative demands are essentially social: friends and relatives want to know how you survived, acquaintances want to compare your story with their own. Others are more ego-related: one achieves a sort of vicarious importance in recounting one's experience of the big quake, even if that experience was unremarkable. (Consider the three Berkeley informants mentioned in Footnote 1, who did not even notice that an earthquake was happening; later, they nevertheless gave good accounts of what they had been doing at that moment!) In any case, most of our Californian informants surely told their earthquake stories many times.[2] Atlanta subjects, in contrast, had little reason to talk about how they had heard the news of an earthquake on the other side of the continent.

---

[2]In an attempt to get some measure of "rehearsal," the first Berkeley questionnaire asked informants to estimate how much total time they had spent in "talking about the earthquake." As in previous studies (Neisser & Harsch, 1992), these estimates were unrelated to the accuracy of later recall—e.g., the r with CAP(BNEWS) was 0.05. Such estimates are intrinsically flawed: not only is it hard to recall and combine time intervals, but the question did not specifically refer to how long they had spent in relating *their own experiences*. Moreover, an internal contradiction suggests that such estimates cannot be taken at face value: the total times reported by subjects interviewed on 19/20 October were *smaller* (on average) than those from 18 October, although the former had had at least one extra day to talk! This incongruity appeared in two independent groups: (a) 234 informants who completed only the first questionnaire (the 18 October subjects averaged 4.3 hours; the 19/20 October subjects averaged 4.1 hours); (b) 36 informants who—having answered this question initially—later completed the follow-up (4.7 & 3.4 hours respectively). It is easy to think of explanations for this pattern of results; our point is only that such estimates are not valid measures of rehearsal.

Our assumptions about the frequency of narrative rehearsal receive independent support from the data of Pennebaker and Harber (1993), who conducted a telephone interview study of reactions to the same earthquake. Their informants from the San Francisco Bay Area (unlike those from control cities) reported very high rates of "talking about the earthquake" in the first two weeks after the event. In the third week those rates began to diminish, although informants reported that they were still *thinking* about the quake for several weeks more. People eventually got bored: T-shirts reading "Thank you for not sharing your earthquake experience" appeared in the Bay Area after about a month.

The narrative rehearsal hypothesis may also explain another aspect of the data. The collapse of the Bay Bridge was the defining moment of this particular earthquake, the feature that established it as "big." For this reason many individuals may have incorporated the occasion of hearing about the bridge into their narratives, and rehearsed it nearly as often as their direct experiences.

The relation between these two memories is particularly intriguing. We have argued that, in Berkeley at least, most people's direct experience of the earthquake was neither dramatic nor unique. It became memorable only in view of what was learned afterwards, including (but not limited to) the news about the Bay Bridge. Brown and Kulik's (1977) "novelty" and "consequentiality" hypotheses make the wrong prediction here. It was the Bay Bridge news, not their own direct experiences of the earthquake, that was novel and consequential for these subjects. Nevertheless, the direct experiences were remembered much better than the occasions on which they learned about the bridge.

The hypothesis that memory for a given event can be enhanced by later development (in this case, by learning how "big" the quake had been) has been proposed before (e.g., Linton, 1982). A phone call that asks whether you might be interested in a certain job becomes memorable if you accept that job and it changes your life; otherwise, it will probably be forgotten. Your first date with your future spouse may not have been all that remarkable; you still remember it, but only because it later became a turning point in your life narrative. Some years ago one of us gave a similar interpretation of Brown and Kulik's (1977) Kennedy flashbulbs: "[Such experiences] are the places where we line up our own lives with the course of history and say 'I was there'" (Neisser, 1982, p. 48). In the same way, experiencing a relatively modest earth tremor becomes memorable if—and only if—it turns out to be part of an historical disaster.

The Atlanta subjects who had friends or relatives in the Bay Area are a particularly interesting group. Although they did not rate themselves as especially aroused or upset, they had substantially higher CAP scores than those without such links to the event itself. This advantage, too, can be explained in terms of narrative and rehearsal. Most of these subjects had surely called up their California friends after the quake, just to see if they were all right. In most cases the resulting conversation must have included an eager exchange of earthquake narratives, one of which was the Atlanta subject's account of how he or she had first heard the news.

Although we are convinced that it was the subsequently established narratives (rather than the immediate levels of arousal) that made these experiences so memorable, the details of that process are not entirely clear. We do not know whether establishing a narrative strengthens memory because it increases the distinctiveness of the experience as a whole or because it is actually rehearsed on many occasions (or both). Rehearsal and distinctiveness are never easy to separate in naturalistic studies: the distinctive stories are the ones that tend to get rehearsed. Brewer (1992) has recently emphasised the joint roles of rehearsal and distinctiveness while noting the difficulty of teasing them apart.

For more readings on flashbulb memories, see E. Winograd and U. Neisser (Eds.), Affect and accuracy in recall: Studies of "flashbulb" memories *(Cambridge University Press, 1992) and also M. Conway,* Flashbulb memories *(Erlbaum, 1995).*

REFERENCES

Brewer, W. F. (1988). Memory for randomly sampled autobiographical events. In U. Neisser & E. Winograd (Eds.), *Remembering reconsidered: Ecological and traditional approaches to the study of memory.* New York: Cambridge University Press, 21–90.

Brewer, W. F. (1992). The theoretical and empirical status of the flashbulb memory hypothesis. In E. Winograd & U. Neisser (Eds.), *Affect and accuracy in recall: Studies of "flashbulb" memories.* New York: Cambridge University Press, 277–305.

Brown, R., & Kulik, J. (1977). Flashbulb memories. *Cognition, 5,* 73–99.

Christianson, S. A. (Ed.). (1992). *Handbook of emotion and memory: Research and theory.* Hillsdale, NJ: Lawrence Erlbaum Associates Inc.

Conway, M. A., Anderson, S. J., Larsen, S. F., Donnelly, C. M., McDaniel, M. A., McClelland, A. G. R., Rawles, R. E., & Logie, R. H. (1994). The formation of flashbulb memories. *Memory and Cognition, 22,* 326–343.

Gold, P. E. (1992). A proposed neurobiological basis for regulating memory storage for significant events. In E. Winograd & U. Neisser (Eds.), *Affect and accuracy in recall: Studies of "flashbulb" memories.* New York: Cambridge University Press, 141–161.

Goodman, G. S., Rudy, L., Bottoms, B. L., & Aman, C. (1990). Children's concerns and memory: Issues of ecological validity in the study of children's eyewitness testimony. In R. Fivush & J. A. Hudson (Eds.), *Knowing and remembering in young children.* New York: Cambridge University Press, 249–284.

Linton, M. (1982). Transformations of memory in everyday life. In U. Neisser (Ed.), *Memory observed: Remembering in natural contexts.* New York: Freeman, 77–91.

Neisser, U. (1982). Flashbulbs or benchmarks? In U. Neisser (Ed.), *Memory observed: Remembering in natural contexts.* New York: Freeman, 43–48.

Neisser, U., & Harsch, N. (1992). Phantom flashbulbs: False recollections of hearing the news about *Challenger.* In E. Winograd & U. Neisser (Eds.), *Affect and accuracy in recall: Studies of "flashbulb" memories.* New York: Cambridge University Press, 9–31.

Pennebaker, J. W., & Harber, K. D. (1993). A social stage model of collective coping: The Loma Prieta earthquake and the Persian Gulf war. *Journal of Social Issues, 49,* 125–145.

Winograd, E., & Killinger, W. A., Jr. (1983). Relating age at encoding in early childhood to adult recall: Development of flashbulb memories. *Journal of Experimental Psychology: General, 112,* 413–422.

Wood, J. M., Bootzin, R. R., Rosenhan, D., Nolen-Hoeksema, S., & Jourden, F. (1992). Effects of the 1989 San Francisco earthquake on frequency and content of nightmares. *Journal of Abnormal Psychology, 101,* 219–224.

Part III

EVERYDAY EXPERIENCES

In which it appears that people cannot give accurate accounts of coins they handle daily or texts they have read thousands of times; they also forget where they have put their most prized possessions. Several intriguing types of memory distortion are documented, as are certain (real or rumored) gender differences. Nevertheless, studies using daily event diaries show little forgetting and few distortions.

11 | Transformations of Memory in Everyday Life

Marigold Linton

In 1972, Marigold Linton undertook a singular memory experiment. Like Hermann von Ebbinghaus, who had founded the classical psychology of memory about a century earlier, she was her own subject. Every day she recorded at least two events from her own life; every month she tested her ability to remember, order, and date a sample of the events she had previously recorded. Linton has presented the basic results of the study elsewhere; here she reflects on some of its implications. How can we understand the effects of "emotionality" and "importance" on memory? What are the long-run consequences of repetition? What kinds of events will be remembered best? The answers are often surprising.

Some years ago, my curiosity about how memory functions in a naturalistic setting led me to an investigation of my own memory. During the course of this six-year-study, I developed event items based on my own experiences, and later attempted to reconstruct the probable dates of the events' occurrences. (Dating may seem a rather restricted, perhaps even uninteresting behavior, but its quantifiability continues to appeal to me.) Performing a prolonged study on personal life events has, I believe, provided me with a unique perspective on memory functioning; perhaps some of these insights as well as a description of the unforeseen difficulties I encountered in conducting this research may be informative to others. I begin by briefly describing the study (more detailed presentations appear in

※ This selection was written especially for the first edition of *Memory Observed*.

Linton 1975, 1978) and then focus on issues that may be loosely labeled (1) episodic/semantic transformations in memory, and (2) emotion/memory interactions.

A LITTLE ABOUT THE STUDY

The stimuli for this long-term study were brief descriptions of events from my life written each day throughout the study's six-year duration. At first it seemed there might be a set of simple heuristics for describing events, but rather shortly I abandoned the search for simple regularities. So wide a range of content and presentation styles may be employed to specify events that the elements necessary or sufficient to describe "an event" have continued to elude me. To avoid unnecessary narrowness in my event pool I accepted all brief unique descriptions. (No description exceeded 180 letters, and when it was written, every item was discriminable from all other events then accessible in memory.) These criteria were dictated by my major dependent variables: dating accuracy (only unique items can be uniquely dated) and response speed (reading times must be brief/uniform enough not to differentially contribute to memory-search response times). Each newly written item was rated for salience on a number of dimensions. I return to emotionality ratings in a later section.

Memory tests proceeded as follows: Once a month items were drawn semirandomly from the accumulated event pool. After reading a pair of randomly paired event descriptions, I estimated their chronological order and attempted to reconstruct each item's date. Next I briefly classified my memory search (for example, I might "count backwards" through a series of similar events, as school quarters, Psychonomic Society meetings, and the like) and reevaluated each item's salience. After six years the experiment had reached imposing dimensions. I had written more than 5,500 items (a minimum of two times each day) and tested (or retested) 11,000 items (about 150 items each month). Item generation required only a few minutes each day but the monthly test was extremely laborious, lasting 6–12 hours. The time required for individual memory searches varied widely from month to month as well as from item to item in the course of a single day.

MEMORY: SOME CONCEPTUAL ISSUES

The study of autobiographical memory is complicated by the modifications and changes that any newly encoded information undergoes as the result of interactions with information already in memory and through reinterpretations of existing data forced by the acquisition of subsequent knowledge. I'm speaking therefore, not only of the role that semantic memory plays in interpreting new information, but also of progressive changes in interpretation and evaluation that occur as the target information interacts with relevant information, either existing or acquired later, in the knowledge base. In our personal history, as in political or cultural histories, the importance of a singular event may be interpreted in a variety of ways, from differing historical perspectives, and may be reinterpreted repeatedly as its role in different contexts emerges. And in personal, as in many other histories, first or early events in sequences receive royal treatment, with better encoding and associated recall.

Transformation from Episodic to Semantic Memory

The issues to be raised are probably best understood if I first present my conclusion concerning the acquisition of episodic and semantic memories. Figure 11-1, which depicts this conclusion, may be summarized: "Number of trials (or experiences) has contrastive effects on episodic and semantic memories. Increased experience with any particular event class increases semantic (or general) knowledge about the event and its context. Increased experience with similar events, however, makes specific episodic

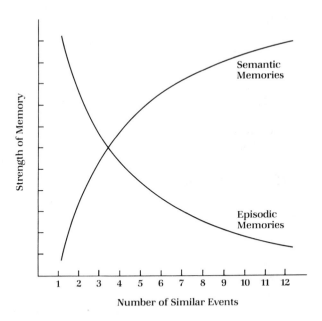

Figure 11-1 *Number of trials (or experiences) has contrastive effects on episodic and semantic memories. Increased experience with any particular event class increases semantic (or general) knowledge about the event and its context. Increased experience with similar events, however, makes specific episodic knowledge increasingly confusable, and ultimately episodes cannot be distinguished.*

knowledge increasingly confusable, and ultimately episodes cannot be distinguished." Examples of this pervasive phenomenon abound in both the laboratory and everyday experience. An event in my file notes that I was invited to serve on a distinguished board that met occasionally in a distant city. I looked forward to the first meeting with trepidation. My arrival in the city confronted me with a new airport, a new system of surface transportation, new hotel. My meeting with the new board provided 25 new names, faces, and intellectual/social styles to be absorbed. Following this unique, attention-compelling experience this trip would be readily recalled as a discrete episode. It was long anticipated and well encoded, and the specific configuration was easily distinguished from other memory compounds. Emphasizing semantic rather than episodic memory would produce a different result (although not one documented in my study). What do I know about the airport layout? How do the ground transportation systems operate and interact? What are the board members' names? What are their relationships with each other? These questions would be vaguely and inadequately answered after only a single contact. I might know (immediately after the trip) that I was on a United flight and caught a Yellow Cab at the airport. I might recall the names of several individuals who had particularly struck me, and might remember some provocative conversational topics but I have poor understanding and poor recall of the complex interrelations among these fragments.

Some years later, after many meetings, I have lost my capacity to reliably pinpoint particular board meetings and I could not describe proceedings of most meetings—except perhaps the first, and (if it were recent) the last. But if required I could map the airport terminal; evaluate the airport to city transportation systems; confidently introduce committee members, and reliably predict board members' interaction styles.

By what mechanism do events or episodes become confusable with repetition? It seems plausible that a fairly small number of general schemes provide the basic framework for storing episodic information. These schemes organize the event in terms of actors, action, location, and the like. These elements that comprise the building blocks of *episodic* memories are themselves information from our semantic store. Furthermore, as with all semantic knowledge, some is well and some is less well learned. A specific event is an unique *configuration* of these elements. As our experience with a particular event type increases, we seem at first to make finer discriminations among related events; we may subdivide elements (for example, by characterizing people, actions, or locations more precisely) and identify more complex configurations of these elements. At some point, however, this expansion of elements and configuration ends. The elements, remember, already comprise part of our semantic knowledge. As similar events are repeated, the specific configurations—the patterns that link familiar elements to form unique episodes—themselves become a well-established potentially confusable part of semantic knowledge. This lack of discriminability may be plausibly attributed to encoding or to memorial difficulties: perhaps discriminations with the required resolution are not routinely made among real-world events, or perhaps desultory memory is capable of handling only relatively short descriptive chains.

The issue of memory transformations is reflected in a number of problems I encountered as I wrote events and in the successful and unsuccessful reinstatement of events in my dating exercises. I turn now to these problems.

Problems from the Study

1. Writing items. When I designed my study I had intended to include in my event pool each day's most salient experiences. As the preceding discussion suggests, it was relatively simple to characterize the "first event" in some on-going life sequence. A large number of cues suffice: "I go to New York for the first time." "I meet with the Carnegie Foundation for the first time." "I meet Clark Kerr for the first time." In fact, "X, for the first time" has unparalleled effectiveness as a cue. (My event writing strategy permitted any particular first item to sometimes include and sometimes omit this unique specification.) As any series of similar or related events in my life became long, the length of the descriptions required to uniquely characterize particular events also increased. Indeed, many events could not be adequately characterized in the space permitted. Thus my file—whose contents are shaped by the requirements of brevity and uniqueness—is silent on whole sets of activities that comprise the warp and woof of my existence. One could scarcely know that I teach, or spend many hours each day in academic activities. A perusal of the file hints only faintly of my passion for racquet sports, my enjoyment of good food, or my pleasure in interacting with loved ones. I simply cannot adequately characterize the year's two-hundredth hour in the classroom, my three-hundredth racquet match, or the one-hundredth dinner with friends. But some items do enter: I teach a new class or perform a novel demonstration; I find a new racquet partner, or we find half a boysenberry pie on the court surface; a new restaurant opens, or a special friend makes a rare visit to town. These minor variations (a la Von Restorff) permit a few such items to gleam distinctively among their blurred and coalesced brethren.

2. Forgetting, failing to discriminate, and related processes. My major experimental task was to order and date items. If I could not recall an item from my description, the task ranged from difficult to nonsensical; consequently I eliminated all "forgotten" items from the event pool. Deciding what was forgotten was more complex than I had anticipated. Early in the study I began to distinguish two kinds of recall failure: (a) the "failure to distinguish" an item from others in memory at test time, and (b) simple "failure to recall" the event. Although it is unremarkable in retrospect, I was surprised to identify loss of item distinctiveness as a major source of "forgetting." I hadn't forgotten items in the sense I had anticipated—instead my written descriptions cued a number of plausible events in memory, or sometimes only a generalized memory; in particular, descriptions that discriminated perfectly among early memories in event sequences did not adequately specify happenings as the sequences lengthened.

Thus, part of my forgetting depended on the episodic to semantic transition I've described. Moreover, the study grossly underestimated transitions as a source of memory loss because items most susceptible to these changes were never written. (Recall that I included only items for which I could formulate descriptions that distinguished them from any other remembered events.) One item from the file poignantly captures the difficulty of creating items impervious to memory changes produced by the occurrence of unanticipated events. In 1972 I wrote an item approximately as follows: "I xerox the final draft of the statistics book and mail it to Brooks/Cole." Some years later after the *third* "final draft" had been submitted this item was singularly nondiscriminating. Which event did I mean? Was the item written when I naively believed that the first draft would be the "final draft"? after the second submission when it was clear that the *final* draft had now been submitted? or was this allusion to the third submission, which historically became the "final draft"? Sometimes, of course, it was possible to guess from the language employed where an event occurred in a sequence. For example, it is most likely that an unqualified statement about "final drafts" refers to the first event in a sequence.

In short, I failed to distinguish events that contained familiar elements and configurations. These configurations pointed not to a single memorial event, but to two or more happenings. Items that I "did not recall" differed somewhat from those that I could "not distinguish." The former items often had lower salience and were more likely to be described in vague terms; in addition, the elements and configurations were sometimes relatively unfamiliar. Such items referred to plausible events that were simply not accessible in memory. Yet another kind of forgetting began to occur late in the study. During the fourth and subsequent years I began to encounter a few old items that simply did not "make sense." Often whole phrases were uninterpretable. Were these items badly written? Successful tests without comprehension problems in earlier years argue against this possibility. Thus, items that I could interpret meaningfully shortly after they were written did not, at the time of the crucial test, permit me to reconstruct a sensible whole. That these nonsense items comprised scraps and fragments from my life made this experience particularly uncomfortable. I could hear my voice describe fragments from my own life that were somehow completely meaningless. Presumably success-ful event descriptions reinstate general memory (semantic) frameworks that permit items to be interpreted and understood. When this cuing fails—when the semantic framework is not reinstated—I cannot reinte-grate the event, and the item seems not to make sense. Total recall failure occurs after much longer delays (after four to six years) than do the other kinds of forgetting (observed as early as the first year) presumably be-cause general semantic frameworks are more robust than specific episodic or semantic information.

3. A forgetting function. I originally expected a rapid loss of to-be-forgot-ten events that would produce a function resembling Ebbinghaus' classic negatively accelerated forgetting curve. Forgetting in my study should, of course, require longer than the days or weeks characteristic of Ebbing-haus' study because: (a) I employed easily encoded, meaningful, and memorable items, and (b) the study's cued-recall task allowed greater ac-cessibility of memories than did Ebbinghaus' free-recall tasks.

These considerations, however, nowhere suggest that the shape of the present more durable curve would not be negatively accelerated. I was surprised, therefore, when several analyses suggested that items were lost from my event memory at a linear rate. Remember that although dating ac-curacy was my major dependent variable, if items were forgotten I re-moved them from my file. Thus, forgetting was a second, almost inadver-tent, dependent variable. I began by considering all items written in any particular year (for example, 1,345 items describe events from 1972) and computed the number of items forgotten during each subsequent year as a percentage of the total number of items written in that target year. Cumu-lative forgetting curves* for each year of the study were similar and a com-posite function (Figure 11-2: Number forgotten/Number written) shows average forgetting for all years of the study. Fewer than 1 percent of the items were forgotten during the calendar year in which they were written (to consider 1972 again, ten items were written and forgotten in that year). After the first year, however, items were forgotten at the relatively even rate of 5–6 percent each year. Thus, while Ebbinghaus found rapid forget-

---

*[That is, curves that show what proportion of the items originating in a given target year T had been tested, found to be forgotten, and removed from the pool by the end of a specified test year $T + k$; they are "cumulative" because they include not only items tested and found to be forgotten in year $T + k$ itself but also in all earlier years $T, T + 1, T + 2, \ldots$. There is a different cumulative curve for each target year (those for the later years of the study having fewer points because there were fewer subsequent test years); corresponding points on these curves were averaged to form the composite "Number forgotten/Number written" function plotted in Fig-ure 11-2.]

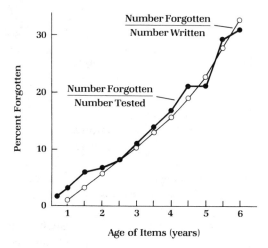

Figure 11-2 *Percent of items forgotten during six years as a function of number of items written or number of items tested. "Number forgotten/Number written" is a cumulative function; "Number forgotten/Number tested" is a noncumulative function. Both are composites over the appropriate years.*

ting followed by slow forgetting, the present function indicates almost linear forgetting after an early period of almost perfect retention.

Two factors make it likely that this function actually underestimates forgetting rate. First, as items are successfully tested, forgotten, and dropped from the pool, the remaining events are increasingly salient and memorable. Second, only a small subset of items of any target age is tested at any time (this is especially significant in the first year when many non-memorable items have never been tested); hence, to consider forgetting against the baseline of all items originally written probably yields an underestimate of forgetting. These considerations suggested that a second function relating the number of forgotten to the *number tested* at a specified test time* (rather than the total number of items written) might provide a more accurate estimate of forgetting rate.† A comparison of the resulting, approximately linear, function (Figure 11-2: Number forgotten/Number tested) with the earlier curve shows that not only have 30 percent of the items been forgotten in six years, but that in the sixth year forgetting is apparent in 30 percent of the items tested from the restricted population

---

*[As noted earlier, about 150 items were tested monthly, 1,800 annually. In 1972, the first year of the study, all tests were necessarily of 1972 items, so the tested subset of those items was very large. (It did not exhaust the pool, however; chance determines which items are selected for test, and many are tested repeatedly.) In later years the tested subsets for various ages became appreciably smaller.]

†[Suppose that m_T items from target year T were selected for test in year $T + k$, and f_T of them turned out to be forgotten. The m_T tested items are a sample of the M_T items from year T that were still in the pool at that time, so the ratio f_T/m_T estimates the fraction of those remaining items that were no longer in a memorable state. This ratio is called "Number forgotten/Number tested" in Figure 11-2, where it has been averaged over target years and plotted as a function of event age.]

that remains. The first (cumulative) and the second (noncumulative) functions differ most in the first year and a half with the latter providing a higher estimate of forgetting in this period than does the earlier one.

"Failure to recall" and "failure to distinguish" contribute unequally to the total forgetting described. Because items are complex, some features of a single item may be forgotten while others are confused—thus both kinds of failure may contribute to an item's being forgotten. While the two kinds of forgetting can be discriminated, the general pattern appears to be that for young items, both failures occur about equally often. After the end of the second year, simple recall failures become increasingly frequent until they occur almost twice as often as confusions.

Thus, real-world episodic memories not only were found to be considerably more durable than laboratory induced memories, but over the six-year study the course of forgetting appeared to be almost linear. There are two ways that this linear forgetting of episodic memories may be viewed. If one assumes that the memories themselves are being lost, it would be plausible to hypothesize that the forgetting curve would become negatively accelerated within a few additional years (if the present rate of forgetting—about 5–6 percent a year—continued, in only a dozen more years all items in the pool would be forgotten). An alternative assumption is that even a real-world study of autobiographical memory is more "contrived" than one would guess. I expect memories to be long-lasting because, like everyone else, I can access a large number of very old memories, some of them from two or three decades past. The memories are "real" but the cues with which I dealt in this study were "real" in that sense only at the time that I wrote them. With the passage of every year the cues become more "contrived" and removed from both my contemporaneous memory organization and from cues that I would spontaneously employ to elicit these memories. If this latter notion were correct, it would be possible for most, if not all, existing cue cards to become inadequate over time; that is, these cues would not elicit personal memories which might, however, remain moderately accessible to cues more suited to my contemporary memory. This decreased accessibility of memories to my cues may be responsible for the differences in kind of forgetting. Confusions may occur when the matches between cues and memories are beginning to break down while simple forgetting and total recall failure would reflect more extreme mismatches between cues and memory organization.

Summary

Some recall difficulties in everyday memory result from episodic to semantic transformations associated with repetitions of the same or similar occurrences in our lives. In representations of personal events a number of basic semantic elements are repeatedly used and eventually configurations of these basic elements are themselves repeated, making it difficult to provide unique event descriptions. Although less significant than simple forgetting, for the present set of everyday materials decreased distinctiveness is responsible for a major memory loss. Somewhat remarkably, overall forgetting for these autobiographical items is almost linear (about 5 percent a year).

In this section I have tried to illustrate difficulties associated with describing events and some of the complexities associated with forgetting them. In the following section I make a tentative effort to describe problems in understanding the relationship between emotionality and recall.

EMOTIONALITY AND RECALL

For more than 75 years psychologists have wrestled with the relationship between materials' emotionality and recall. Although Freud cautioned that negative memories may be forgotten through repression, our common experience is that important emotional events are often easily recalled even after many years. Such a prolonged and frustrating inquiry suggests a complex relationship between emotionality and recall. My experiment, which permitted me to examine changes in recall over many years' time with complex and salient life-related materials, seemed an ideal context in which to examine these variables. In the following I suggest some memorial and other factors that complicate this relationship.

Throughout the study I provided emotionality and importance ratings (among others) for each event item, both at the time it was written and each time its recall was tested. Although analyses of these data are not complete, the correlations between initial salience ratings and the recall measures will almost certainly remain small and unimpressive. (The relationship between current salience ratings and recall is stronger but this correlation cannot be easily interpreted.) What are some of the reasons that initial emotionality ratings are not useful in predicting event recall? A number of variables complicate efforts to deal with emotionality over time. First, the ratings of a single event may change over time. Second, superficially similar events do not receive similar ratings over time. Third, the emotionality of ongoing pieces of life, or of memories, is inherently difficult to judge.

Emotionality: Habituation, Contrast, and Reinterpretation

Why do emotionality ratings of events change? Repetition of events is an important factor in predicting changed emotionality for similar events; most commonly, the emotionality of events appears to habituate. Even event classes that originally produce high levels of emotionality are likely to be judged less emotional with repetition. Thus, (a) repeated events late in a series of similar events are less emotional—at time of occurrence—than early events in the series, and (b) retrospective judgments of an event's emotionality decrease when other similar events follow.

Emotionality of events may also be affected by *changes* in the cognitive surround. The first of these effects may be referred to as *contrast*. Level of expectation may be raised by a single highly emotional event (Brickman, Coates, & Janoff-Bulman, 1978), or by a number of moderately important or emotional events. After the "enrichment" of the emotional environment, any particular event may look less emotional or important than it did before the change.

But other changes remotely or closely associated with the target item may affect the rated emotionality or importance of the target. Just as historians must interpret and rewrite history as time passes, so we all rewrite our own personal histories. Few of us are wise enough to be able to predict at the time of their occurrence how significant events will prove to be. A person inconspicuously enters our life. He later becomes a friend, a lover, or an antagonist. Others appear with grand flourish and then simply vanish. Thus, our salience judgments are erroneous for many events. We are offered a job. If we accept a new job that involves permanent changes in our life, for example, if it is accompanied by a move, and increased responsibility and status, the events surrounding the job offer are likely to continue to be perceived as important and emotional. If exactly the same job is turned down, salience ratings are likely to decrease over time. In general, events that initially are perceived as important and highly emotional may be perceived as less emotional or important later as the result of changes in the real world. Events may similarly increase in importance or emotionality as our perspectives on them are modified. If they come to be less important than anticipated we may simply delete them from memory. If they become more important we link them to the later crucial events—we rewrite this chapter in our lives.

Under some circumstances, the emotions currently associated with past events may be at variance with our memories of the emotions associated with the events at the time. It is often difficult to recall the intensity of past emotion—indeed, to examine a highly emotional event two, five, or ten years later is an informative experience. Sometimes the memory for the emotion is only remotely present (I may wonder *why* I experienced a strong emotion if it is obvious that I did or I may *remember* having had the emotion but be completely removed from it in the present). This discrepancy between memory of the emotion and the presently experienced emotion creates considerable problems when I attempted to rate items years later. What is the proper rating? The emotion I remember having felt when the event occurred, the emotion that is aroused now, and how do I discern the difference? Sometimes, of course, years later events may elicit clear strong emotions congruent with, continuous with, or clearly identifiable as a part of the feeling present when the event occurred.

Finally, aside from issues of instability of ratings, emotions and events are inherently complex. Events may be conceptualized across small or large units of activity, their structure may be simple or complex, and they may come from many thousands of domains. To show the difficulty of making such judgments, let us attempt to answer the question: Which is more important? What is more emotional?—the love of our significant other, or a promotion? Most people probably value ongoing emotional support more than occupational advancement but any specific comparison is likely to be complicated. In most of my ratings important, unique events receive the highest ratings. Thus, receiving an important promotion would be rated higher than, for example, such repetitive events as a loved one's embrace, or a single dinner with my women's group. Part of the ambiguity results from the difficulty in knowing precisely what it is that is being evaluated, that is, the size of the memorial unit. A kiss against a promotion is hardly a fair comparison. A promotion implies a whole range of future activities— and only that kiss similarly filled with meaning should be rated as high. Furthermore, ratings are anomalous precisely because the importance of the love relationship does not inhere in the single embrace, nor the import of having good friends depend upon a single evening spent with them. On the contrary, for many individuals (although surely not all) the feelings of warmth and closeness and the significance of the relationship increase even as the specific details of the interaction begin to be lost in routine. Thus, some aspects of important events may receive relatively low ratings—and indeed these specific subevents may be forgotten relatively rapidly. But while we may forget a birthday or an embrace we are not likely to forget—ever during our lifetimes—a sustained emotional relationship. The sub-elements lack significance but the totality of these memories, laid down—as some artists paint—layer upon layer, create a fabric of such extraordinary durability and richness that it is never forgotten.

...

REFERENCES

Brickman, P., Coates, D., & Janoff-Bulman, R. (1978). Lottery winners and accident victims: Is happiness relative? *Journal of Personality and Social Psychology, 36,* 917–927.

Linton, M. (1975). Memory for real-world events. In D. A. Norman & D. E. Rumelhart (Eds.), *Explorations in cognition.* San Francisco: W. H. Freeman & Company.

Linton, M. (1978). Real-world memory after six years: An in vivo study of very long-term memory. In M. M. Gruneberg, P. E. Morris, & R. N. Sykes (Eds.), *Practical aspects of memory.* London: Academic Press.

12 | Memory Day by Day

Ulric Neisser

Other investigators soon began to keep diaries too, expanding and refining Linton's (1975—see Selection 11) paradigm. Here are some of their surprising findings.

Perhaps the most persistent of all memory diarists is the Dutch psychologist Willem Wagenaar (1986), who kept one-event-per-day records for six full years. Those records were organized in a very useful way: each event was encoded in terms of the four basic attributes *who, what, where,* and *when,* together with a *critical detail.* Those attributes then served as cues in the recall tests, which took place at the end of the first, fifth, and sixth years of the study. Thus the first cue for the recall of a particular event might be *who* had been present. Wagenaar would then try to remember the experience; more specifically, to recall the other three cues and the critical detail. After that another cue would be presented: perhaps *when* (i.e., the date of the event). The third cue might be *what* had happened; if so, the last would be *where* it took place. (The sequence of recall cues, presented in special test booklets prepared by a colleague, varied randomly from one item to the next.) If all four cues together did not enable Wagenaar to recall the critical detail, it too was presented as a sort of fifth recall cue. If even this failed to elicit the memory, the target was scored as "completely forgotten."

Wagenaar's data produced a regular (though rather shallow) forgetting curve: the older an event, the more *who/what/when/where* cues were required to elicit it. Interestingly, however, a full sequence of cues usually enabled him to recall the experience. Even after a delay of five years, fewer than 20% of the tested items were completely forgotten. In a further exploration of the power of cueing, Wagenaar focused on ten events, scored

※ This chapter was written especially for this edition of *Memory Observed.*

"completely forgotten," that had involved other participants. He got in touch with those participants and asked them about the events in question. In every case, the additional details that they provided enabled him to remember the lost event. "In the light of this," says Wagenaar (1986, p. 235), "one cannot say that any event was completely forgotten." This conclusion may be a bit strong, but the data are still impressive: the forgetting of adequately cued life experiences is much slower than laboratory forgetting curves would have led us to expect.

Wagenaar's study also uncovered a surprising relation between the "pleasantness" of experiences and their later recall. (He had rated the pleasantness of each event on a 5-point scale—from *very unpleasant* to *very pleasant*—when he initially recorded it.) A first look at the data (Wagenaar, 1986) suggested that pleasant experiences were remembered better than unpleasant ones, a finding that would easily fit the Freudian concept of repression. In a later analysis, however, he also distinguished between *self-related* and *other-related* emotions (Wagenaar, 1994). Categorizing the 47 *very unpleasant* and the 73 *very pleasant* events in his entire corpus along this dimension established four different categories, which the following examples may serve to illustrate:

> "*Very unpleasant, self-related* ($n = 11$): I complain in a rather impolite manner to a lady who parked her car on the sidewalk in front of our house; it [then] appears that she is an invalid with a special permit, who was visiting the neighbors.
>
> *Very unpleasant, other-related* ($n = 36$): The daughter of a close colleague dies from cancer; I go to her funeral.
>
> *Very pleasant, self-related* ($n = 14$): I have a big success with a magic lantern show at the International Convention of the Magic Lantern Society, in London.
>
> *Very pleasant, other-related* ($n = 59$): I dine with Maya Bar-Hillel and Gideon Keren on the Margareten Island in Budapest, and we laugh ourselves almost to death." (Wagenaar, 1994, p. 197)

Contrary to expectation, the category with the best average recall was *very unpleasant, self-related!* That means that events which contradicted Wagenaar's (generally positive) self-image were enhanced rather than repressed—an interesting finding that surely deserves further research.

Are diary studies really representative of memory in general? One potential problem is that recording an event in a memory diary is itself a form of rehearsal, which might be expected to improve later recall. Surprisingly, data reported by Charles Thompson of Kansas State University and his collaborators suggest that this is not always the case. Thompson asks college students to keep memory diaries for relatively short periods, often just three to six weeks. No specific format is imposed; the subjects simply record a brief description of one event per day. Memory is tested after relatively short delays, usually also just a few weeks. The subjects view their own event descriptions and judge how well they now remember the experiences in questions, using a 7-point rating scale that goes from *not at all* to *perfectly*.

In the first of these studies (Thompson, 1982), the subjects' task was to record one of their own experiences and also one event that their *roommate* had experienced each day. Later, both the subjects and their roommates viewed these records and rated how well they remembered the experiences in question. Although the roommates had made no records and had not even known that a memory experiment was in progress, they remembered their experiences just as well as the subjects (who had made the recordings) remembered theirs! This finding has now been replicated several times (Thompson, Skowronski, Larsen, & Betz, 1996). It seems that record-keeping does *not* improve later memory, at least as measured by rating scales. (Another interesting comparison: the subjects rated their memories of their own events as substantially better than their memories of their roommates' events, although they themselves had originally recorded both; Skowronski, Betz, Thompson & Shannon, 1991.)

Ratings are one thing, accuracy is another. As we have already seen, people's confidence in their own memories is not always justified. This point is further illustrated in the diary studies of Craig Barclay and his associates (Barclay & Wellman, 1986; Barclay & DeCooke, 1988). Their memory test items included not only genuine entries (i.e., records actually made by the subject being tested) but also "lures" in which the original record had been altered in various ways. Would the diarists detect these alterations? As one might expect, the answer depended on the scope and nature of the changes themselves. Even 2½ years later, subjects easily rejected records that had been drawn from other people's experience rather than their own. But when only part of a genuine diary entry had been altered—making plausible changes either in what had happened or how they had evaluated it—false positives were surprisingly frequent (Barclay & Wellman, 1986). We all know what kinds of lives we lead, but we may not remember just what happened on a particular occasion.

In most diary studies, the experiences to be recorded and remembered are selected (by the subjects themselves) as the most important or memorable event of the day. How well would more ordinary experiences be remembered? William Brewer (1988) addressed this question by equipping his subjects with "beepers" that sounded at random intervals. Whenever the beeper went off they were to record where they were, what they were doing, what they were thinking, etc. At the end of the day each subject also recorded one "special" event, comparable to those selected in other diary studies. The recording phase lasted for a week or two, and memory was tested several weeks or months later. Following Wagenaar's general procedure, part of what a subject had recorded on a given occasion (location, time, ongoing thought, etc.) served as a cue to recall the rest.

As one might expect, Brewer's diarists did not recall nearly as many events as Wagenaar had. There are several obvious reasons for this difference: the to-be-remembered events had been selected at random, and the subjects got only one recall cue rather than five. (Also, Wagenaar's single subject—himself—may have had an exceptional memory!) Also as expected, the events selected by the diarists as especially memorable were remembered somewhat better than those selected by the beepers. The single most common response in the cued recall of random events was "nothing": no event came to mind at all. The next most common response was the recall of a different (and hence "wrong") event, not the target. There were also a number of occasions when the right experience did come to mind but the subject recalled a different "time slice" of the event than he or she had originally recorded.

In addition to these various errors, Brewer's diarists produced many full and correct memories. (These were typically accompanied by reports of vivid visual imagery, which was less often the case for recalls of wrong events.) Importantly, there were no major confabulations like those reported by Neisser and Harsch [Selection 9], and indeed very few "constructive" errors of any kind. When the subjects did recall the right event for a given cue, they almost never misremembered or distorted its details. Why were they so much less likely to confabulate than the subjects of the space shuttle study?

To make an adequate comparison between so-called "flashbulb memories" and ordinary recall, we need cases where some extraordinary event makes the news just when some enterprising psychologist is already carrying out a diary study. As it happens, two investigators have experienced this fortunate coincidence. One is the Danish psychologist Steen Folke Larsen, who was conducting a diary study (with himself as subject) in early 1986. Larsen's (1992) goal was to compare memory for "reception events"—occasions when one first learns about some public happening from the media—with memory for more directly personal experiences. With this in view, he recorded one event of each type daily for half a year, and tested his memory after intervals ranging from one to eleven months. His tests included both cued recall (like Wagenaar and Brewer) and recognition—a simple rating of whether the event seemed familiar. The results showed extremely poor recall of the reception events, which for him were always via radio, TV, or newspaper. Even at short delays, Larsen typically failed to remember anything at all about how he had heard or learned of a piece of news. The results leave no doubt that, in general, reception events are much less memorable than special personal experiences.

Taken by itself, this result is hardly surprising. What makes the study interesting is that several genuinely important news events occurred while Larsen was making his records. Two that struck him with particular force were the assassination of Prime Minister Olaf Palme of Sweden (a closely related neighboring country) and the nuclear accident at Chernobyl in the Soviet Union (which sent dangerous clouds of radioactive material drifting toward Denmark). Although he had personally recorded these reception events and had marked them as having a fairly high level of "personal involvement," Larsen made serious errors in recalling both of them a few months later. With considerable confidence, he remembered wrong places and wrong "others present" for the Palme news as well as for the news of Chernobyl. As he himself points out, these confident misrememberings ". . . add two well-controlled episodes to the body of examples of inaccuracies in flashbulbs" (Larsen, 1992, p. 33).

Five years later, in January 1991, Charles Weaver was teaching an undergraduate cognition course at Baylor University. As a class exercise, students were told that the next time they saw their roommate (or a friend, if they lived alone) they should do their best to remember the circumstances surrounding that event; as soon as possible thereafter, they were to record those circumstances on a special questionnaire. By coincidence, the bombing of Iraq—the beginning of the 1991 Gulf War—began that same evening. When the class met again two days later, the students filled out a similar questionnaire about how they had first heard the news of the bombing. Three months later, they were asked to recall both sets of circumstances. The results (Weaver, 1993) were clear. There were no significant differences in the *accuracy* with which Weaver's students recalled the two events (neither was perfect), but they were substantially more *confident* of their memories for hearing the Iraq news than for their roommate encounters. As in Larsen's study, confidence was a poor guide to the accuracy of "flashbulb memories."

No simple summary can do justice to all these studies, but two points deserve special emphasis. First, success in recalling life events depends on the adequacy of the available cues: more and better cues lead to more and better recall (Wagenaar, 1986, especially as compared to Brewer, 1988). This principle also explains why adults who return to their childhood homes after long absences often experience rich flashes of memory (Hall, 1899).

The second conclusion is more complex, and perhaps also more speculative. People are somewhat able to pick out those experiences that will later be memorable—at least, more memorable than run-of-the-mill random events (Brewer, 1988). Randomly selected events are more likely to be forgotten, but there is little evidence that they undergo distortion or misremembering (at least by Brewer's criteria). On the other hand, important-seeming high-profile experiences can lead to later overconfidence and error. This seems especially true for major reception events (Larsen, 1992; Neisser & Harsch, 1992; Weaver, 1993), where the considerable emotion that the individual feels is not directed at any concrete aspect of the local situation, and hence does not raise recall of that situation above its usual low level. Recall of that emotion makes the event seem more memorable than it actually was, and thus leads to overconfidence at the time of recall.

REFERENCES

Barclay, C. R., & DeCooke, P. A. (1988). Ordinary everyday memories: Some of the things of which selves are made. In U. Neisser & E. Winograd (Eds.), *Remembering reconsidered: Ecological and traditional approaches to the study of memory*. New York: Cambridge University Press, 91–125.

Barclay, C. R., & Wellman, H. M. (1986). Accuracies and inaccuracies in autobiographical memories. *Journal of Memory and Language, 25,* 93–103.

Brewer, W. F. (1988). Memory for randomly sampled autobiographical events. In U. Neisser & E. Winograd (Eds.), *Remembering reconsidered: Ecological and traditional approaches to the study of memory*. New York: Cambridge University Press, 21–90.

Hall, G. S. (1899). Note on early memories. *Pedagogical Seminary, 6*(4), 485–512.

Larsen, S. F. (1992). Potential flashbulbs: Memories of ordinary news as the baseline. In E. Winograd & U. Neisser (Eds.), *Affect and accuracy in recall: Studies of "flashbulb" memories*. New York: Cambridge University Press, 32–64.

Linton, M. (1975). Memory for real-world events. In D. A. Norman & D. E. Rumelhart (Eds.), *Explorations in cognition*. San Francisco: Freeman.

Neisser, U., & Harsch, N. (1992). Phantom flashbulbs: False recollections of hearing the news about *Challenger*. In E. Winograd & U. Neisser (Eds.), *Affect and accuracy in recall: Studies of "flashbulb" memories*. New York: Cambridge University Press, 9–31.

Skowronski, J. J., Betz, A. L., Thompson, C. P., & Shannon, L. (1991). Social memory in everyday life: Recall of self-events and other-events. *Journal of Personality and Social Psychology, 60,* 831–843.

Thompson, C. P. (1982). Memory for unique personal events: The roommate study. *Memory and Cognition, 10,* 324–332.

Thompson, C. P., Skowronski, J. J., Larsen, S. F., & Betz, A. L. (1996). *Autobiographical memory: Remembering what and remembering when*. Mahwah, NJ: Erlbaum.

Wagenaar, W. A. (1986). My memory: A study of autobiographical memory over six years. *Cognitive Psychology, 18,* 225–252.

Wagenaar, W. A. (1994). Is memory self-serving? In U. Neisser & R. Fivush (Eds.), *The remembering self*. New York: Cambridge University Press, 191–204.

Weaver, C. A. (1993). Do you need a "flash" to form a flashbulb memory? *Journal of Experimental Psychology: General, 122,* 39–46.

13 | Long-Term Memory for a Common Object

*Raymond S. Nickerson and
Marilyn Jager Adams*

Do you know what a penny looks like? Probably not; almost nobody does, according to the research reported in this selection. Of course, sophisticated psychologists are free to claim that this finding does not surprise them. People probably don't attend to the details on pennies in the first place, and they are not motivated to rehearse or recode those details later on. But be honest: Weren't you inclined to answer "yes" to the question that began this paragraph? Perhaps you are still so inclined. Why not turn to the last figure in this selection and try your luck?

Many things can be recognized on the basis of their visual characteristics. Moreover, laboratory studies have shown that people are quite adept at discriminating between complex pictures they have seen a short time before and those they have not, even when given hundreds (Nickerson, 1965; Shepard, 1967) or thousands (Standing, 1973; Standing, Conezio, & Haber, 1970) of pictures to remember and allowed to inspect each for only a few seconds. Both of these observations are consistent with the idea of a visual memory that readily assimilates and retains an abundance of information about the stimuli to which it is exposed.

In fact, neither introspection nor the results of picture recognition studies tells us how much information regarding any particular visual pattern has been stored. When people demonstrate the ability to recognize something they may be demonstrating only that they can place that thing in an appropriate conceptual category. And the category may be more or

From *Cognitive Psychology*, 1979, *11*, 287–307.

less broadly defined, depending on one's purpose—as when an object is recognized as an automobile, as opposed to being recognized as a Volkswagen, or as the specific Volkswagen that belongs to John Doe. Similarly, when people show that they can distinguish a picture they have seen before from one they are looking at for the first time, they show only that they have retained enough information about the "old" picture to distinguish it from the new one. Given that one typically cannot say how much information *must* be retained in order to permit such categorizations and distinctions, one cannot rule out the possibility that they may be made on the basis of a small portion of the information that the patterns contain.

The experiments reported in this paper are addressed to the question of how accurately and completely the visual details of a common object, a United States penny, are represented in people's memories. We chose to study people's knowledge of a common object rather than of laboratory stimuli because we are interested in the nature of the information that normally accrues in memory. As a stimulus, a penny has the advantage of being complex enough to be interesting but simple enough to be analyzed and manipulated. And it is an object that all of our subjects would have seen frequently.

EXPERIMENT 1

The purpose of the first experiment was to see how accurately people could reproduce a penny through unaided recall.

Method

The subjects were 20 adult United States citizens. Each was given a set of empty circles, 2 in. in diameter, and asked to draw from memory what is on each side of a U.S. penny. Subjects were asked to include all the pictorial and alphanumeric detail they could, and they were allowed to draw as many versions of each side as they wanted.

For purposes of scoring the drawings, we focused on the eight features listed in Table 13-1. Each subject's drawing was scored according to: (a) whether each of these eight features was present; (b) whether each was located on the correct side of the coin; and (c) whether it was drawn in the correct position in the circular area. The head was scored as being in the correct position only if it was drawn as an east-facing profile.

Results

In general, performance was remarkably poor. Figure 13-1 shows some examples of the drawings we obtained. Of the eight critical features, the me-

TABLE 13-1

Features identified for scoring purposes in Experiment I

Top side

Head
"IN GOD WE TRUST"
"LIBERTY"
Date

Bottom side

Building
"UNITED STATES OF AMERICA"
"E PLURIBUS UNUM"
"ONE CENT"

dian number recalled and located correctly was three. Not counting the Lincoln head and the Lincoln Memorial, the median number of recalled and correctly located features was one. Only four of our 20 subjects got as many as half of them. Only one subject (an active penny collector) accurately recalled and located all eight.

Figure 13-2 shows an analysis of the errors with respect to each feature. The overall probability that a feature would be either omitted or mislocated was .61. The probability that a feature would be omitted was .33;

Figure 13-1 *Examples of drawings obtained from people who tried to reproduce a penny from memory.*

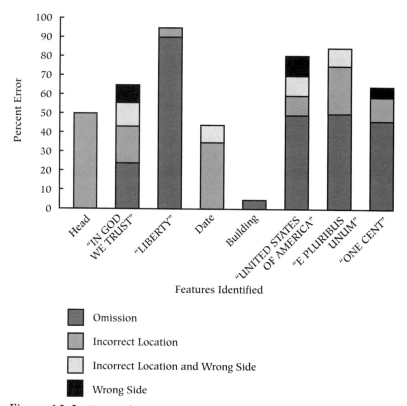

Figure 13-2 *Types of errors produced when subjects attempted to draw a penny from memory.*

excluding the Lincoln head and the Lincoln Memorial, this probability was .43. The only features that all our subjects produced were a head and a date. All but one subject also recalled a building as the central figure on the bottom side. The feature most frequently omitted was LIBERTY: only two of our subjects remembered that this is on the coin, and one of them located it on the wrong side. UNITED STATES OF AMERICA, E PLURIBUS UNUM, and ONE CENT were also omitted by about half of our subjects. It is interesting to note that with the exception of Lincoln's head, the Memorial, and ONE CENT, all of these items occur on every current U.S. coin.

Figure 13-2 also shows that subjects were quite poor at locating those features they did recall. The probability of mislocating a correctly recalled feature was .42. The only feature that was consistently located correctly was the building, which would be difficult to position incorrectly if it were recalled at all. Excluding the building, the probability of mislocating a feature was .50. Exactly half of our subjects faced the Lincoln head in the wrong direction.

[*Experiment II omitted.*]

...

EXPERIMENT III

The results of Experiments I and II indicate that people cannot accurately recall either the features that appear on a penny or how those features are arranged. We reasoned that these data might not reflect people's lack of knowledge of pennies so much as the inappropriateness of recall tasks for purposes of assessing that knowledge. Perhaps performance would be more impressive on a recognition task. Item recognition is often taken to be a more sensitive test of memory than item production (Anisfeld & Knapp, 1968; Kintsch, 1970a, 1970b; Underwood, 1972). Moreover, recognition tasks would seem to be more closely related to what we normally do with pennies. In view of these considerations, Experiments III, IV, and V were done using recognition tasks. Experiment III was designed to assess awareness of the features that are on a penny, independently of awareness of their location or appearance.

Method

Twenty new subjects (adult U.S. citizens) were given a list of 20 features. Their task was to indicate with respect to each feature (a) whether it is on a penny, and (b) their degree of confidence (on a 3-point scale) in their answer. Two answer forms were used, each with ten subjects. The two forms, which are shown in Table 13-2 on page 130, differed only with respect to the "distractor" items.

Results

Subjects used the highest, intermediate, and lowest confidence levels on about 45, 31, and 24 percent of the test items, respectively. We take this as evidence that the task was not perceived as trivially easy.

The overall probability of a correct response in this task was .85. The relationship between confidence and correctness is shown in Figure 13-3 on page 131. In general, the higher the subject's confidence in an answer, the more likely was the answer to be correct. The probability that a response would be correct was somewhat higher for negative than for positive responses at all confidence levels, but this could be an artifact of the greater number of negative than of positive items on the answer sheet. Because of this asymmetry, random negative guesses would have been more likely to be correct than random positive guesses.

TABLE 13-2

**The lists of features that were given to subjects
in Experiment III**

1. The word JUSTICE	1. The words ONE PENNY
2. The words UNITED STATES OF AMERICA	2. The words UNITED STATES OF AMERICA
3. The words LEGAL TENDER	3. The words ONE NATION UNDER GOD
4. The words VERITAS	4. The right side of Washington's face
5. The words ONE CENT	5. The words ONE CENT
6. The date (year) of mint	6. The date (year) of mint
7. The presidential seal	7. The great seal
8. The word COIN	8. The words LINCOLN MEMORIAL
9. The words WASHINGTON, D.C.	9. The number 1 centered
10. The left side of Lincoln's face	10. The full face of Lincoln
11. The right side of Lincoln's face	11. The right side of Lincoln's face
12. The White House	12. A laurel wreath
13. An eagle with spread wings	13. The words MADE IN TAIWAN
14. The Lincoln memorial	14. The Lincoln memorial
15. The words IN GOD WE TRUST	15. The words IN GOD WE TRUST
16. The word LIBERTY	16. The word LIBERTY
17. Sheaves of wheat	17. The words ANNO DOMINI
18. The Roman numeral I	18. The word COPPER
19. The words E PLURIBUS UNUM	19. The words E PLURIBUS UNUM
20. The words MINTED IN USA	20. The Statue of Liberty's torch

Figure 13-4 shows the percentages of correct (positive) and incorrect (negative) responses at each confidence level for those features that are in fact on the penny. The bars representing correct responses (left of each pair) are connected, as are those representing incorrect responses (right of each pair). More often than not subjects tended to believe that these eight features were on a penny, but the response distribution was far from bimodal. The only feature that subjects selected with both consistent accuracy and high confidence was the date. Although several other features were selected by at least 80 percent of the subjects, the degree of confi-

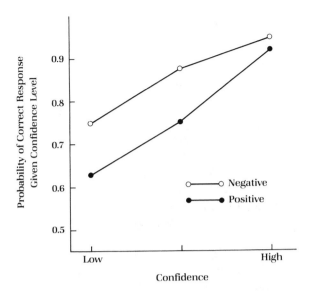

Figure 13-3 *The relationship between the degree of confidence expressed in a response and the probability that the response was correct.*

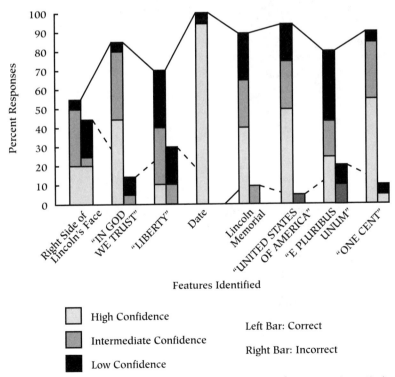

Figure 13-4 *The percentage of correct (positive) and incorrect (negative) responses, and associated confidence levels, for those features that are on a penny.*

dence in the presence of these items was not uniformly high. Again, LIB-
ERTY proved to be difficult; only two of the 20 subjects were certain that it
belonged to the coin. The poor showing with respect to the "right side of
Lincoln's face" must be weighed in light of the fact that of the nine subjects
who rejected this item, six opted for the "left side of Lincoln's face," one for
his full face, and one for the right side of Washington's face.

The distractor features that were judged to be on the penny by at least
two subjects were the left side of Lincoln's face (6), a laurel wreath (6),
sheaves of wheat (4), the words LINCOLN MEMORIAL (3), the number 1
centered (2), the great seal (2), the Roman numeral I (2), and the words
WASHINGTON, D.C. (2). No one voted for MADE IN TAIWAN.

On the whole, the results from Experiment III seem to present a
slightly more positive assessment of memory for visual features than did
those of Experiments I and II. At least with the particular set of distractor
features that was used, subjects were able to distinguish between bona
fide features and distractors with fair accuracy. However, this performance
measure may be somewhat misleading. It may reflect not only what subjects remember about a penny, but what they can infer. Even a subject who
had never seen a penny might accept some of the candidate features on
the grounds that they ought to be on a U.S. penny (e.g., UNITED STATES
OF AMERICA, ONE CENT, a date) and reject others on the grounds that
they ought not to be there (e.g., MADE IN TAIWAN). The possibility that
our subjects may have done some judicious guessing gets some support
from the fact that they often did not report high confidence in their answers even when they were correct.
[*Experiment IV omitted.*]

...

EXPERIMENT V

Rather than concluding that we know so little about the appearance of an
object that is so very familiar, we again considered the possibility that our
tasks had been somewhat inappropriate for tapping that knowledge. We
decided to try one more method: each subject was given all 15 of the drawings in Figure 13-5 and asked to select the most plausible from among
them. We were sure this task would be quite easy. The subjects would
have all 15 versions before them. If the correct version did not just pop out
at them, they could compare and contrast the alternatives in any way they
pleased.

Method

Each of 36 female students from Lesley College (all U.S. citizens) was
given the 15 drawings from Experiment IV, each printed on a separate

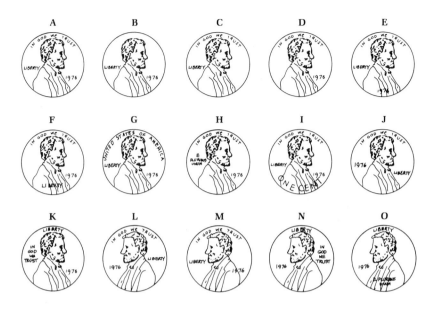

Figure 13-5 *The fifteen drawings of the top side of a penny that were used in Experiments IV and V. A brief characterization of each drawing is given in Table 13-3.*

card. The subjects were told that one of the drawings was correct, whereas each of the others had one or more things wrong with it. The subject's task was to sort the drawings into the following four categories: (1) the one drawing she thought most likely to be correct; (2) drawings she could easily believe to be correct if the one she had chosen as correct proved not to be; (3) drawings that might possibly be correct; and (4) drawings that she felt sure were incorrect. Suitable labels were provided to facilitate the sorting. Subjects were told that they must assign exactly one drawing to the first category, but that they could have as many or as few drawings in each of the other categories as they wished and that it was not necessary to use all categories. They were given as much time as they wanted and were free to move drawings from one category to another until satisfied with their selections.

Results

The last four columns of Table 13-3 on page 134 show the distribution of category placements for each of the 15 drawings. Although the correct drawing was more likely to be judged correct than were any of the counterfeits, it was not recognized as the obvious choice by all, or even by a majority, of our subjects. Somewhat less than half (15 of the 36) of our subjects placed it in Category 1. As in Experiment IV, drawing I proved to be relatively plau-

TABLE 13-3

Characterizations of the drawings shown in Figure 13-5 and results from Experiments IV and V

Drawing	Characteri-zation	No. of Subjects	No. who thought drawing accurate	No. who identified error(s)	Response category 1	2	3	4
			Experiment IV		Experiment V			
A	Correct	8	4	—	15	12	4	5
B	1 omission	9	0	6(2)	0	0	6	30
C	1 omission	9	0	9(1)	0	1	4	31
D	1 omission	8	2	3(1)	1	3	6	26
E	1 mislocation	9	0	8(0)	0	12	9	15
F	1 mislocation	8	0	5(0)	0	5	17	14
G	1 substitution	9	4	1(0)	4	10	10	12
H	1 substitution	8	0	2(0)	2	6	8	20
I	1 addition	9	6	2(1)	7	5	5	19
J	2 features interchanged	8	2	4(2)	2	18	5	11
K	2 features interchanged	8	3	3(1)	0	5	13	18
L	Mirror image	9	0	4(3)	1	8	4	23
M	Reversed face	8	3	3(1)	4	9	5	17
N	Mirror with 2 features interchanged	9	1	1(1)	0	3	5	28
O	Mirror with 1 omission, 1 mislocation, and 1 addition	8	0	0(0)	0	3	4	29

sible, and was selected as the most likely one by seven subjects. Drawings G and M both got four votes, and D, H, J, and L got at least one.

A second general observation that may be made from Table 13-3 is that many of the drawings were considered as possibilities by many of the subjects. In fact, excluding the Category I assignments, about one-quarter of the drawings, on the average, were judged as easily believed to be correct, one-quarter were judged conceivably correct, and one-half were judged as certainly incorrect.

Examination of the response distributions shown in Table 13-3 points out one of the dangers involved in making inferences about the contents of memory on the basis of forced-choice recognition tasks. If our subjects had been asked only to select the one drawing they considered most likely to be correct, we might have concluded that recognition memory was rather good, inasmuch as the correct alternative would have been chosen at least twice as frequently as any other. And had the set of distractors been made smaller by exclusion of some of the more plausible alternatives (e.g., versions G, I, M), performance would have been much more impressive. As is apparent from the table, however, although subjects were more likely to choose the correct drawing than any other, they were not, as a rule, able to reject all the other possibilities with a high degree of confidence. (Only two subjects classified all but one of the drawings as certainly incorrect, and one of these subjects selected an incorrect drawing—version I—as the one most likely to be correct.)

How does the degree of plausibility of a drawing depend upon the relationship between that drawing and the correct one? On the assumption that, at least in a statistical sense, the correct drawing is more plausible than any of the incorrect ones, we might expect the degree of plausibility of the incorrect drawings to drop off as the degree of their similarity to the correct drawing decreased. Unfortunately, we have no measure of between-drawing similarity. However, one thing seems clear in this regard: If similarity were defined as the number of features with respect to which two drawings differed, the relationship between similarity and plausibility would not be simple. Two of the least plausible drawings (B and C) differed from the correct one with respect to only a single feature; the inscription IN GOD WE TRUST was missing from one and the date from the other.

※

CONCLUDING COMMENT

On balance, the results from these experiments demonstrate that frequent exposure to an object and the ability to "recognize" that object for practical purposes do not guarantee that the object is represented accurately in memory in any great detail. To the contrary, they raise the question of whether visual long-term memory is much less rich and elaborate than has often been supposed.

The results also lead us to the following conjecture: Typically, the details of visual stimuli are not retained in memory—or at least they are not available from memory—unless there is some functional reason for them to be. In other words, what one is most likely to remember about the visual properties of objects is what one needs to remember in order to distinguish those objects in everyday life. In general, investigators of human memory have not focused on the question of sufficiency. As one aspect of the study of what is stored in memory, it might be useful to give more thought to the question of what information must be retained in order to permit one to identify common objects or to distinguish them from each other. It may turn out that because of the multiplicity of features with respect to which most objects of interest differ from each other, the constraining effects of the contexts in which objects are typically encountered, and the role of inferential processes, recognition may make much smaller demands on memory than has commonly been believed.

REFERENCES

Anisfeld, M., & Knapp, M. (1968). Association, synonymity, and directionality in false recognition. *Journal of Experimental Psychology, 77,* 171–179.

Kintsch, W. (1970a). *Learning, memory, and conceptual process.* New York: Wiley.

Kintsch, W. (1970b). Models for free recall and recognition. In D. A. Norman (Ed.), *Models of human memory.* New York: Academic Press.

Nickerson, R. S. (1965). Short-term memory for complex meaningful visual configurations: A demonstration of capacity. *Canadian Journal of Psychology, 19,* 155–160.

Shepard, R. N. (1967). Recognition memory for words, sentences, and pictures. *Journal of Verbal Learning and Learning Behavior, 6,* 156–163.

Standing, L. (1973). Learning 10,000 pictures. *Quarterly Journal of Experimental Psychology, 25,* 207–222.

Standing, L., Conezio, J., & Haber, R. N. (1970). Perception and memory for pictures: Single-trial learning of 2500 visual stimuli. *Psychonomic Science, 19,* 73–74.

Underwood, B. J. (1972). Are we overloading memory? In A. W. Melton & E. Martin (Eds.), *Coding processes in human memory.* Washington, D.C.: Winston.

14 | Professor Sanford's Morning Prayer

Edmund Clarke Sanford

Here is another failure of memory, even more surprising than the prevailing ignorance of pennies that was demonstrated in Selection 13. Perhaps most people don't bother to read what is written on their pennies, but Professor Sanford—a distinguished psychologist of an earlier generation—read his morning prayer aloud day after day. After 5,000 trials, he still didn't know it.

The value of distributed repetitions in memory has long been established. It has even been suggested that one repetition a day might show a maximum of economy. This may very well be the case when the repetitions are made with the purpose ... of memorizing, but it is certainly not so when this purpose is absent. A very large number of single repetitions at 24-hour intervals may then have little or no mnemonic result.

It has been my custom for many years to read in my family the form of Morning Prayer provided by the Episcopal Church. The reading has been interrupted at various periods but at a conservative estimate I have read this form of words at least 5,000 times in the last 25 years, usually at 24-hour intervals, often for many weeks in succession, and I am able to read it with a minimum of attention—almost automatically—and yet my memory of it is notably defective, as becomes only too patent when I lose my place in reading or fumble the turning of a page.

In order to obtain a more precise index of my deficiency I have recently made a test of how much I was able to write from memory, starting myself by the sight of a single word and writing as much as I could before

From E. C. Sanford (1917), A letter to Dr. Titchener. In *Studies in psychology contributed by colleagues and former students of Edward Bradford Titchener*. Worcester, Mass.: Louis N. Wilson, 8–10.

being stopped by inability to recall, then uncovering the text until one new word was revealed and again writing as much as I could.

The first of the five prayers composing the group is the Lord's Prayer which I learned as a child, and which I was able to write correctly (71 words) except for the omission of an "and." The group closes with a benediction (25 words) which some years ago I committed to memory intentionally. This I was able to reproduce without error.

The test with the four intermediate prayers gave the following results:

Prayer #1 (124 words) . . . 44 promptings (2.82 words/prompt)

Prayer #2 (73 words) . . . 20 promptings (3.65 words/prompt)

Prayer #3 (146 words) . . . 38 promptings (3.84 words/prompt)

Prayer #4 (158 words) . . . 27 promptings (5.85 words/prompt)

The increasing size of the groups of words recalled probably indicates increasing adaptation to the method of testing, and introspection confirms this interpretation; but that the material was very far short of complete recall is abundantly witnessed by the fact that even in the most favorable case the average word group was less than six words and that many outright blunders—usually the substitution of words of similar import—were made.

Such a result as this emphasizes two things: First, the dominating importance of the mental set or attitude . . . which is now generally recognized; and second, the probability that repetition under the domination of a particular [set] tends toward the formation of habits which are increasingly specialized. This also is not unknown. As long ago as his original experiments on the learning of nonsense syllables Ebbinghaus noticed that increasing the number of repetitions strengthened the bonds of contiguous syllables relatively more than the bonds of widely separated members of the series. . . .

15 | On Forgetting the Locations of Things Stored in Special Places

Eugene Winograd and Robert M. Soloway

OK, so you don't care about pennies and don't say a daily prayer; maybe you've never even lived through an earthquake. Here, at last, is an experience that will sound familiar even to you. Did you ever put something in a very special place—a place where you would surely find it again but no one else would ever think of looking? And then tear up the house looking for it? If not, you've been unusually fortunate—so far. Don't press your luck.

One type of memory failure that is extremely vexing occurs when we are unable to find a needed object even though we took special pains to store it for future use. Reader, do you know where your passport is? Your extra set of car keys? How about copies of your 1982 and 1983 income tax returns? Or the flashlight you put away so it would be readily accessible during power failures? Consider the adventitious finding of an object too late for use, as when a friend of ours reported finally finding his passport in a pouch of a suitcase, a year after having had to replace it.

It should be emphasized at the outset that we are interested in the forgetting of object locations for which special pains have been taken at the time of storage. The loss of misplaced objects as a result of inattentiveness or absentmindedness during storage (Where did I leave my glasses, my pen?) does not concern us here (Tenney, 1984). We are specifically interested in the case where we are our own mnemonic enemy, where the task

※ From *Journal of Experimental Psychology: General*, 1986, *115*, 366–372.

is to find something we know we have purposely put in a special place in order to be able to find it in the future which has, alas, arrived. It is as though an appointment has been made for a future time, the date usually unspecified (we cannot, therefore, write in a calendar, "Get the snorkeling mask from the shelf that has the outdoor stuff"). The appointment is with an object instead of a person; for example, "meet the antique bracelet in the shoe box." Circumstances now require that the object be found, but sometimes the place cannot be recalled.

This article is the report of speculations about and research on the conditions that contribute to this unfortunate memory failure. We say unfortunate for two reasons. First, the object of the search is valuable, either intrinsically, as with jewelry, or because of our own particular needs at the time, as with a passport. Second, there seems to be something peculiarly exasperating about being in the position of a hunter who knows not only that the object of the hunt is close by, but that he or she is the one who put it there. It is relevant here to note that, in a survey of memory aids used in everyday life, all of the subjects polled by Harris (1978) reported putting things in special places.

When are things put in special places? We put things in special places when there is an anticipated future need, but no present need, for them. That is, the object is not in regular use the way a wallet, purse or watch is. We do it for things that are of some importance or value, as with jewelry, passports, keys, bankbooks, photographs, letters, and so on. Sometimes we have two purposes in mind when we put an object in a special place: we want to hide it from others and be able to find it ourselves. Again, these objects may be intrinsically valuable, as in jewelry that we hide from potential burglars, or of only personal importance, as in contraband, pornography, or love letters that we hide from people who have no business knowing about them. It will be argued that circumstances that lead to hiding objects from others increase the probability of hiding them from ourselves.

What are special places? Consider two kinds, likely and unlikely places. A likely place is a place where one might expect an object to be stored by the nature of the object and the nature of the place. Towels and toothbrushes belong in bathrooms in their own special niches; cutlery and crockery belong in the kitchen or dining room. These are obvious places (see Edgar Allan Poe's *The Purloined Letter* for an example of how sometimes the obvious place is the best hiding place), just as the tops of dressers and night tables are obvious places for watches, eyeglasses, and wallets. But these are things used daily.

What about unlikely places? One great advantage of an unlikely place, for instance, a light fixture for your safe-deposit box key, is that it has a low probability of being guessed by somebody else. It seems a fine and private place, as is a vase for love letters. Another possible advantage is its distinctiveness. Of course, it may well be that the low probability of such places being guessed for these objects has a pernicious side in that the person who stores the objects may confound him- or herself and not be able to remember more than that it was put in a very unusual place.

We report here three experiments designed to explore the validity of some of these notions. The first experiment was designed to capture the phenomenon. We started with the assumption that one only stores an object in a place when one is confident that the place will be remembered. There is no point in putting something away if, at the time it is stored, you doubt that you will remember where you put it. Our most important assumption has to do with the kind of place one chooses for storing an object. We assume that people sometimes choose unlikely, rather than likely, places for storing an object. The conditions for not being able to find something that has been put in a special place, then, are the joint judgments, at the time of storage, of high memorability and low likelihood. At the time of storage, the person simultaneously believes that this place will be recalled when the object is needed even though (perhaps we should say *because*) he or she judges that the place generally would be regarded as an unlikely place for this object.

EXPERIMENT 1

Method

Materials. Two sets of 20 sentences were constructed of the form "The (object) is in the (place)." Here are some examples: "The concert tickets are in a book"; "The love letters are under the mattress"; "The lottery ticket is in the sugar bowl"; "The jewelry is in the oven"; "The sales receipt is in the file cabinet." We purposely made up some likely pairings of objects and places and others that seemed unlikely. The alternate set of 20 sentences simply re-paired the objects and places from the first set while trying to retain a balance of likely and unlikely pairings. An additional 6 sentences of the same type served as primacy (3 sentences) and recency (3 sentences) buffers and were not tested.

Subjects. Subjects were 127 undergraduate students of both sexes. All were Emory University students who participated to fulfill a course requirement, and all were tested in small groups.

Procedure. Initially, two sets of instructions were composed for Experiment 1. The 37 subjects in the memorability condition were asked to judge the likelihood that they would remember the location of the object in the indefinite future if they had put it in that particular place. Here is part of the memorability instructions:

> *Imagine that you are about to leave town for about six weeks. One of the problems that people encounter when they go away for a long time is finding needed objects upon their return. This is very much like the problem people often have when Winter comes around of remembering where they stored their gloves last Spring. This practice of hiding things from ourselves can be very annoying. We are trying to find out more about how this happens. On the sheet before you is a list of things we commonly look for, and sometimes misplace, and places where they might be kept. We would like you to judge in each case how confident you would be that you would remember the location when you need the object some time in the future, if you had put it in that particular place.*

The subjects were asked to make their judgments using a 6-point rating scale ranging from 1 (*extremely unlikely to remember*) to 6 (*extremely likely to remember*).

Another group of 42 subjects, the likeliness of place condition group, were asked to rate the same sentences as to how likely it was that somebody would store a given object in a given place. Their instructions, in part, read as follows:

> *We would like you to go through the sentences and rate each one for how likely it would be for someone to keep each object in the particular place described in the sentence. Try going about it this way. Imagine that you are in a friend's house for the first time and you've been asked by him to find and send to him each object. The trouble is that he has neglected to tell you where it is kept. How likely is it in your opinion that each object would be in the location described? Make your judgments on a six point scale with 1 standing for the "least likely" and 6 for the "most likely" place for that object. Here's an example. "The milk is in the refrigerator." I'm sure that this would rate a 6 since that is where milk is ordinarily kept. We have tried to select combinations of things and locations which vary in how likely they are to go together.*

Both sets of sentences were used approximately equally often for each condition. Subjects in neither condition were informed that a memory test would follow. After all the sentences had been rated, a 5-min arithmetic filler test was administered followed by a cued recall test. In the cued recall test, the experimenter read aloud the name of the items one at a time at a 10-s rate and the subjects were asked to recall the location of the objects. The memory question was of the form, "Where is the (object)?" In short, subjects in the memorability condition predicted how well they might remember where they had put something stored in a specific place, whereas subjects in the likeliness of place condition judged the likelihood that somebody would put a specific object in a specific place. Both groups were then administered a cued recall test of their memory for the location of the objects.

After the data for the memorability and likelihood of place conditions had been collected and scored, an additional group of 48 subjects from the same source was tested. Subjects in this condition, the mental imagery condition, were told to imagine placing each object in their own home in the particular location specified and were given intentional memory instructions. The purpose of this manipulation was to come closer to what people presumably do when they store actual objects for a future need. The instructions resemble the method of loci, the ancient mnemonic method in which things are placed in locations in imagination (Yates, 1966). Subjects also rated memorability for each sentence in the same manner as the memorability condition. The instructions for the mental imagery subjects were almost identical to those of the memorability group with the addition of the following:

> *Here's how I would like you to go about remembering where each thing is. First, pick a house which you are familiar with. For many of you this will be your family's home. As you read each sentence, imagine yourself in that house, or around that house, placing the object in that particular location. If the house you imagine is not suitable for a given sentence, because let's say it doesn't have a basement, try to imagine that object being placed in some basement. It is most important that you envision yourself placing these objects. Once you have formed this image, I want you to write down on the line next to each sentence how memorable you think that particular object in that particular location is. In other words, if you had actually stored that object in that location, how confident are you that you would remember where that object was some time in the future. Use the six point scale at the top of the page.*

In all other respects, the procedure was the same as it was for the memorability and likelihood of place conditions.

Results

The mental imagery instructions had the same effect as the instructions read to the memorability rating group. The proportion of locations recalled were .62 and .65 for the memorability and mental imagery conditions, respectively; $t(39) = 1.03$. The .05 significance level was used in all tests reported in this article. This and all subsequent analyses in Experiment 1,

TABLE 15-1

Probability of recall as a function of rating: Experiment 1

	Judgment	
Rating	Memorability	Likeliness of place
1	.42	.54
2	.52	.62
3	.61	.71
4	.69	.79
5	.71	.85
6	.77	.86

unless otherwise stated, were done across the 40 object-location sentences. The correlation between the memorability ratings for these two conditions was .91 and the correlation between the recallability of the locations was .82. In view of these commonalities, the data from subjects who rated memorability were combined across the two conditions yielding 85 subjects for the memorability ratings and 42 subjects who rated likelihood of recall.

The relation between ratings of memorability or likeliness of recall and subsequent recall is shown in Table 15-1. Clearly, the higher the rating of either aspect of the sentences, the higher the probability of recall of the location. An unanticipated outcome was that overall mean recall was higher following ratings of likeliness of place (71%) than ratings of memorability (62%), $t(39) = 3.19$. It is possible that judging how likely a place is for an object leads to more attention to the relational aspects of the pair.

The correlation between rated memorability and recall was .59; the correlation between rated likelihood of recall and recall was .57. The correlation between rated memorability and rated likelihood of recall was .63. These correlations, as well as others, are shown in Table 15-2. All of the first-order correlations shown in Table 15-2 are significant. Because of the high correlation between ratings of memorability and likelihood of place, partial correlations were calculated between the ratings on each of these dimensions and recall, taking out the relation between recall and the other dimension. These partial correlations are shown in parentheses in Table 15-2. The correlations involving rated memorability remain significant but those involving likelihood of place are not.

The conceptual analysis presented in the introduction emphasized that the conditions in ordinary life that combine to produce failure to find objects stored in special locations are high judged memorability and low likelihood of the object being placed in that location. To pursue this analysis empirically, the 40 sentences were ranked according to their ratings of

TABLE 15-2

Correlations: Experiment 1

Variable	Likelihood of place rating	Recall after memorability rating	Recall after likelihood of place rating
Memorability rating	.63*	.59* (.47)*	.57* (.34)*
Likelihood of place rating		.35* (−.20)	.56* (.31)
Recall after memorability rating			.77*

Note. Values in parentheses are partial correlations. See text for explanations.
*p < .05.

likeliness of place and the 10 most likely and the 10 least likely sentences were segregated. Examples of very likely object-location combinations are, "The concert tickets are in the jacket pocket"; "The fever thermometer is in the medicine chest"; "The sales receipt is in your wallet." Examples of unlikely item/location pairs are, "The airplane tickets are in the shoe"; "The jewelry is in the oven"; "The extra set of car keys is in the light fixture."

The central findings of the research are shown in Table 15-3. Table 15-3 shows the proportion not recalled, or "lost," for these two sets of items as a function of their rated memorability. The data in Table 15-3 are derived from the rankings given by the 85 subjects who judged the sentences for memorability on the grounds that one places items in special places in order to remember them. The total number of ratings observations that each proportion is based on is given in each case. The data of

TABLE 15-3

Proportion of failure to recall locations as a function of judged memorability for objects in low versus high likely places: Experiment 1

Object location	Rated memorability					
	1	2	3	4	5	6
10 low-likely places	.60	.48	.44	.36	.33	.33
n	86	93	61	58	83	49
10 high-likely places	.40	.33	.35	.28	.25	.15
n	15	24	26	65	130	165

Table 15-3 show that, at each level of rated memorability, subjects are less likely to recall where items were placed when the items are in unlikely places than when they are in likely places. The extreme right-hand column is the most pertinent case. This column represents only those cases in which subjects indicated that they were extremely likely (rating of 6) to remember where the particular items were. In spite of their certainty, subjects were more than twice as likely to forget the location of the item (33% vs. 15%) when it was independently judged to be in an unlikely place. Even with maximum confidence in the memorability of a particular item in a particular place, it is apparently risky to choose an unlikely place. Apparently, items are best remembered if they are stored where they belong, no matter how confident one might be in the memorability of an unlikely combination.

Another interesting aspect of Table 15-3 is that the distributions of ratings differ for the high-likely and low-likely places. One way to summarize the difference is that there is less agreement about memorability for low-likely places than for high-likely places. For high-likely places, 85% of the total ratings pile up under ratings of high memorability (ratings of 4, 5, and 6), whereas only 56% of the low-likely places are rated as low in memorability (ratings of 1, 2, and 3).

Discussion

Why then do people put things in unlikely locations? One possibility is that they have observed that unusual or uncommon events are remembered better than ordinary events and generalize from this to the belief that unusual locations will be highly memorable. In short, the choice of unlikely places may reflect the belief that distinctiveness confers memorability. In her survey questionnaire of 434 adults, Tenney (1984) asked, "Have you recently found an object that you had misplaced or lost?" Of those who recalled such an episode within 2 weeks prior to the questionnaire, 38% reported that the object was not found in a "logical" place. Although Tenney emphasizes absentmindedness in her analysis, it is likely that a substantial number of these cases represent intentional storage in a special place. At the time of storage, it does not seem that one can forget that the car keys are in the light fixture or that the jewelry is in the oven, yet one does. One of the authors has a friend who, before going abroad, placed her jewelry in the oven to prevent it from being stolen. She thought it unlikely that a burglar would look for valuables in the oven. Upon her return, she found herself hungry as well as tired and put a frozen casserole in the oven to heat while she showered and changed. Her story of the ruined jewelry occasions sympathy or laughter among listeners depending upon a set of social psychological factors we do not propose to analyze here. However, in our terms, she placed valuable items in a place she considered to be both highly unlikely and memorable and lost out to the consequences of putting things in improbable places.

...

[*Experiments 2 and 3, which confirm the findings of Experiment 1, are omitted here.*]

GENERAL DISCUSSION

The research presented in this article attempted, first, to analyze a common type of memory failure and, second, to test some speculations stemming from the analysis. The core of the analysis is that people are most likely to forget where they stored important things when they have elected to store them in an unlikely place. The results of Experiments 1 and 2 show that recall is better for likely than unlikely places. Most important, Experiment 1 showed that this is true even when one is maximally confident that the place will be remembered. In Experiment 3, it was argued that a major disadvantage of unusual locations is that, if forgotten, they have a low probability of being retrieved by an auxiliary generation–recognition strategy.

Why, then, do people often put things in unlikely places? We have already noted two possible reasons for the choice of unlikely storage places, namely, the desire to hide valuables from others and the belief that distinctiveness increases memorability. To hide something means putting it in a place in which others are unlikely to see it. The problem with hiding objects from strangers is that one increases the probability of forgetting where one stored them.

...

Another aspect of choosing places for objects is that there is often a logic involved in the choice of unlikely places. For example, a friend of ours was required by her insurance company to acquire a safe if she wished to insure her valuable gems. Recognizing that she might forget the combination to the safe, she thought carefully about where to keep the combination. Her solution was to write it in her personal phone directory under the letter *S* next to "Mr. and Mrs. Safe," as if it were a telephone number. There is a clear logic here: Store numerical information with other numerical information. She was appalled, however, when she heard a reformed burglar on a daytime television talk show say that, upon encountering a safe, he always headed for the phone directory because many people keep the combination there. Another logical unlikely place, apparently, is the use of the freezer to store cash. What these places have in common seems to be that they engender the false conviction that they are unlikely storage places when, in fact, they are known to professional burglars as likely places (see MacLean, 1983, chap. 5, for an interesting discussion from the perspective of a professional burglar of where to hide valuables). Although they are unusual as far as the user is concerned, the same logic that led to choosing them may be used by other members of the culture. Indeed, some individuals may be experts in this logic. Detectives in the classic mystery story, as in the Poe story mentioned earlier or in the traditional buried treasure story in which the hiding place for a map or treasure must be found, share this expertise with burglars. Of course, one can forget even logical unlikely places, as in the case of the passport stored in the forgotten suitcase.

Fortunately, most people do not regularly store things in unlikely places. Most of us have certain places where things that will be needed in the future are kept, whether it be a favorite drawer or shoe box. For valuable items, safe-deposit boxes are common. The present research commends these as prudent strategies. When it is difficult to implement these strategies, an alternative would be to keep a list of where things have been stored. Then, if one cannot recall where a particular object is when it is needed, one need only consult the list. Of course, it is important to have a good place for the list, but in this case, at least only a single location must be remembered rather than different locations for different things. Still, it would not be a good idea to store the list in an unusual location.

REFERENCES

Harris, J. E. (1978). External memory aids. In M. M. Gruneberg, P. E. Morris, & R. N. Sykes (Eds.), *Practical aspects of memory*. New York: Academic Press, 172–174.

MacLean, J. (1983). *Secrets of a superthief*. New York: Berkley.

Tenney, Y. J. (1984). Ageing and the misplacing of objects. *British Journal of Developmental Psychology, 2*, 43–50.

Yates, F. A. (1966). *The art of memory*. Chicago: University of Chicago Press.

16 | Getting What You Want by Revising What You Had

Michael Conway and Michael Ross

In his widely cited paper "Relation of Implicit Theories to the Construction of Personal Histories," Michael Ross (1989) argues that what we remember is often influenced by what we think "must have" happened. He illustrates that principle with many impressive examples, one of which is described in this selection. Have you ever taken a course that was supposed to improve your study skills? Did it work? How do you know it did? That's easy: by comparing your current level of skill to your skills before you took the course. But can you really recall that earlier level? Of course you can: after all, it must have been lower than your skill level now! But wait a minute . . .

Previous social psychological research tends to portray people as cognitive conservatives who bias their memories so as to deny changes and maintain consistency. For example, in a number of experiments, subjects have been induced to alter their opinions and then asked to report their past attitudes. Subjects recall attitudes that are virtually identical to their new opinions and thus effectively deny that any change has occurred (Bem & McConnell, 1970; Goethals & Reckman, 1973; Ross & Shulman, 1973). Moreover, they revise their memories of past behaviors to bring them in line with their new attitudes (Olson & Cal, 1984; Ross, McFarland, Conway, & Zanna, 1983; Ross, McFarland, & Fletcher, 1981).

From *Journal of Personality and Social Psychology*, 1984, 47, 738–748.

These results suggest that: (a) Recall of personal histories involves an active, reconstructive process (cf. Bartlett, 1932), and (b) the reconstruction is theory driven. In the above studies, subjects presumably did not desire a change in their attitudes or work toward this end in a conscious fashion. Consequently, subjects may have had little reason to assume that change had occurred. In reconstructing their past, they probably used the best available information—their current attitudes—and applied a theory of consistency that in many contexts would be quite appropriate (Mischel & Peake, 1982). In the attitude change studies, this theory happens to be invalid because, unbeknownst to subjects, they have altered their opinions.

How pervasive is the tendency to exaggerate temporal consistency? It should occur primarily when people adhere to a theory that implies stability in a context of actual change. In contrast, if people invoke a theory of change, they may recognize a transformation and, indeed, overestimate the degree to which they have altered. In the current studies, we examine the impact of a potentially invalid theory of change on the reconstruction of personal histories in a socially significant setting.

People are likely to overestimate change when they hold a theory of change in a context of actual stability. One setting in everyday life where this may occur is self-improvement programs. Many different kinds of improvement programs thrive, and there is no shortage of participants who testify to their merits. For example, new diet books are often bestsellers, each promising the achievement of ideal weight via some novel means. Pop therapies and so-called cults, such as est, Scientology, or Silva Mind Control have attracted and seemingly satisfied many with their procedures of complete personal renewal (Henderson, 1975). Although participants often laud them, many of these programs have been judged ineffective or even harmful by expert program evaluators (e.g., Polivy & Herman, 1983).

Assuming the validity of formal evaluation, and that program participants are of normal intelligence and not unusually gullible, we face a dilemma. Participants, as informal program evaluators, judge a program as beneficial. Formal evaluators conclude the opposite.

By what psychological processes can participants convince themselves that their theory of change is valid—that an ineffective program has worked? Let us assume that a program promises more than it delivers with respect to some type of personal improvement. If participants nonetheless believe the promises, they may inadvertently manufacture evidence that supports the claims. One possibility is that they will overestimate their postprogram standing. This is not always feasible, however, as there are frequently reality constraints. For instance, obese people cannot persuade themselves, or a scale, that they are now thin. More often, participants may be able to claim improvement by revising how they were before the program began. In effect, they can say to themselves: "I may not be perfect now, but I was much worse before." Such revision is most likely if objective records either were not taken in the past or have become unavailable.

Our hypothesis is that participants in a self-improvement program may attribute greater gain to themselves than seems warranted, by exaggerating in recall how poorly off they were before the program. A number of conditions seem likely to foster this tendency to rewrite one's past as a consequence of participating in such an intervention program. First, the program must be assumed valid by its participants. This may be facilitated when the program demands the commitment of considerable energy, time, or money (Cooper, 1980). Otherwise, participants may discount the whole exercise and adopt, with a vengeance, a theory of consistency. When participants accept the program's validity, they will anticipate change from the outset and adopt a theory of change as they are going through the program. Second, participants' theories must dictate a greater amount of change than actually occurs. Even if recall is theory driven, it can be accurate. An overestimation of change would be engendered if participants expect change when actual improvement is minimal. Finally, participants should desire improvement; they would then be most susceptible to adopting a theory of change.

THE CURRENT STUDIES

We selected a context in which to test our hypothesis on the basis of our analysis of when exaggeration of change is likely. A study skills program seemed appropriate. As we planned to draw subjects from a university student population, such a program would address issues of concern to them. Moreover, the study skills programs commonly offered in many universities and colleges require a certain amount of effort, if only to attend program meetings. Most important, formal evaluation, typically adopting academic performance as the criterion, suggests that study skills programs are of questionable worth despite their prevalence and face validity. After a review of the literature, Gibbs (1981) concluded that study skills courses have little value. For example, he noted that researchers have found "no difference in academic performance between those who had received guidance and a carefully chosen control group" (p. 69). Moreover, research on one of the most "highly developed and heavily sold courses in Britain" revealed "only *short-term* differences in study habits and even a deterioration in some habits" (italics in original, Gibbs, 1981, p. 69). Main (1980) drew a similar, albeit less extreme, conclusion: "there is already enough disquiet to suggest that courses in methods are not a universal answer to student study difficulties" (p. 65). Finally, in line with our major theme, study skills courses are judged to be beneficial by students who take them (e.g., Chibnall, 1979; Hills & Potter, 1979).

We conducted two studies to examine the impact of a study skills program on subjective and objective indicants of skills. In both studies, subjects evaluated their study skills and reported their amount of study time at a first meeting. They were then randomly assigned to either the skills program or a waiting list control group. After program participants had attended 3 weekly skills sessions, they and the waiting list subjects returned for a final meeting. All were asked to recall their initial evaluations and to rate their skills improvement. We subsequently examined subjects' recall to determine whether, relative to waiting list control subjects, participants in the skills program belittled their prior study skills and amount of study time. In addition, we obtained subjects' grades to compare participants' perceived improvement to their academic performance. This also allowed us to assess the program's impact on an objective measure of performance. We followed this procedure in two independent studies that are described in tandem below. The second study consisted of a replication in which we obtained a different set of measures. In Study 1, we also assessed (6 months after the last meeting) subjects' recall of their academic performance for the term during which the program was conducted. We anticipated that participants might retrospectively exaggerate how well off they were after the program.

METHOD

Subjects

Study 1. Subjects were recruited from an introductory psychology course in which credit was given for participating in the experiment. In class, students completed a questionnaire in which they indicated their interest in participating in 13 different kinds of self-improvement programs (exercise, weight loss, study skills, etc.). The study skills program was most popular. Sixty-nine students who indicated interest in participating in this program were contacted by telephone to determine times available for skills sessions; all but 5 could make one of the available sessions. Students were told that random assignment either to the program or to a waiting list control group was required because the program was being conducted to assess the aspects of self-improvement programs that participants find helpful. Students assigned to the waiting list would be able to participate in the program at a later time.

Of the 64 interested students we could accommodate, 59 (92%) attended their first meeting. Eighteen males and 21 females were randomly assigned to the program, and 5 males and 15 females to the waiting list. The only subsequent attrition resulted from 1 female program participant quitting the program, due to illness, after having attended two meetings.

Study 2. Subjects were recruited from two introductory psychology courses and an introductory social psychology course. Subjects did not receive course credit for participating. The study skills program was described in class. Students were also told that random assignment to either the program or a waiting list was required both to evaluate the program and to keep skills groups small. Interested students were later scheduled over the telephone for an organizational meeting.

Fifteen males and 10 females of the 30 (83%) subjects who were randomly assigned to the program completed it. Two subjects dropped out before attending any program sessions; the remaining 3 quit after two sessions. Ten males and 13 females of the 25 subjects (92%) on the waiting list attended both waiting list meetings.

Procedure

The study skills program. Our skills program was modeled on one offered by a counseling center of a local university. This program is advertised regularly and is administered to about 250 students each semester. The general areas covered by our program over 3 weekly sessions were: (a) course requirements, scheduling, and task definition, (b) effective listening and note taking, and (c) overviewing, skimming, and reading. The first author was trained by a study skills counselor to lead the skills sessions. During the 1½-hr sessions, he discussed issues and prompted participants to share their relevant thoughts and experiences. To best accommodate subjects, we conducted 3 weekly sessions in Study 1, and 4 in Study 2. In Study 1, participants attended the sessions in groups varying in size from 8 to 14; in Study 2, the groups ranged in size from 3 to 10. After each study, waiting list subjects were offered the skills program. In Study 1, no waiting list subjects opted for the program presumably because it was then near the end of the semester. Study 2 was conducted early in a semester, and most waiting list subjects opted for a skills program that began the week after the second study.

Experimental Procedure

Study 1. We began the initial meeting by obtaining the measures we would later ask subjects to recall; they evaluated their study skills and reported their study time. First, subjects recorded all of their activities of the prior week, including study time, in a diary divided into ½-hr units. Next, they rated their study skills in response to the questions listed in Table 16-1. Each question was followed by a 121 mm line with endpoints labeled appropriately. For example, the labels for the first question in Table 16-1 were *very little time well spent* and *almost all the time well spent*, for question 3, *very frequently distracted* and *rarely distracted*, and for question 5, *not at all satisfactory* and *very satisfactory*. Subjects responded

TABLE 16-1

Study skills evaluations

1. Consider the number of hours spent studying. How much of your study time was well spent?
2. Are you pleased with how much of your study time was well spent?
3. When you study for a set period of time, are you often distracted from your work?
4. Once you sit down to study, how long does it usually take you to concentrate well on your work?
5. How satisfactory are your listening and note taking skills (in class)?
6. How satisfactory is your ability to concentrate on your studies when you want to?
7. How satisfactory are your reading and study skills (for textbooks)?
8. How satisfactory is your ability to draw up and work from a schedule for your studies?

Note. These questions were used for initial, recall, postprogram, and improvement skills evaluation in both Studies 1 and 2. In Study 2, these questions were supplemented by those of Table 16-2 for all skills evaluations except for improvement.

by putting a slash through each line. After subjects completed the ratings, the experimenter described the procedure and purpose of random assignment. Subjects then drew lots. Those assigned to the waiting list were reminded of their second meeting and excused. The experimental subjects then began the study skills program.

The skills program continued for 2 more weeks. During the 4th week, waiting list subjects attended meetings that were expected by program participants to be their 4th and last skills sessions. The principal dependent measures were collected at these final meetings. All subjects were asked to remember their responses to the questionnaire completed at the first meeting. Thus, subjects recalled both their diary records of the activities of the week prior to the initial meeting and their responses to the skills evaluation questions. The importance of accuracy was stressed; the experimenter stated that he was interested in how well they could remember their prior diary entries and skills evaluations. Subjects were asked to answer the skills questions by putting a slash through the line "where you think you did three weeks ago." Subjects then described their current study habits by completing a diary for the immediately preceding week and responding to skills evaluation questions. The diary was of the same format as the first diary. The skills evaluation questions referred to current skills but were otherwise identical to those presented in Table 16-1. Finally, all subjects were asked to indicate whether their study skills had improved since the first meeting. Prefixed by "As compared to before the program" and referring to current levels, each of the skills questions (see Table 16-1) was followed by a 171 mm anchored line on which subjects indicated change, if any, in their skills (e.g., *much less satisfactory* to *much more satisfactory*). Instructions deemphasized the skills program's impact and suggested to program participants that "you may feel that it [the program] has either helped to improve your skills or not."

Subjects' psychology grades for their midterm and final exams were obtained from the course instructor. The midterm preceded and the final exam followed the study. In addition, subjects' term averages were obtained from registrar records at the end of the semester. Six months after the last meeting, subjects were telephoned concerning their grades under the guise of a survey of university undergraduates. We reached 28 (74%) of the 38 program participants, and 14 (70%) of the 20 waiting list control subjects. Respondents were asked to estimate their average in their major and their overall average for the semester during which they had participated in the study. The survey allegedly had no connection to the experiment. No mention was made of the study skills program during the telephone call; moreover, the interviewer had not participated earlier in the study and was blind to subjects' experimental condition. Subjects were later sent a letter in which the full details of the study were described.

Study 2. Measures of amount of study time and of skills evaluation were obtained at the beginning of the first meeting just as in Study 1, except in reverse order. Time spent studying was again obtained from a diary and the evaluation of skills was in response to the questions listed in Table 16-1. The latter were supplemented by questions that address the same skill domains but require numerical answers. We thought these responses would be more memorable, thus providing a stronger test of our hypothesis. The skills questions appropriate to a numerical response format, questions 3 through 7 of Table 16-1, were translated into the questions listed in Table 16-2. The session ended after subjects completed the skills evaluation and diary.

As subjects were a diverse lot, ranging from full-time students to students taking only one course, we assigned them to treatment by matching pairs sampling, with study time reported in the initial diary as the matching characteristic. From the study time ranking, one subject from each contiguous pair was randomly assigned to the program, the other to the waiting list. Because we expected greater attrition in the program group, we randomly selected one waiting list subject from each third of the study

TABLE 16-2

Numerical study skills evaluations used in Study 2

1. Once you sit down to study, how long does it usually take you to concentrate well on your work? (4)
2. Usually, for how long can you concentrate on your studies at one time? (6)
3. Usually, when you study for 1 hour, how many times do you get distracted? (3)
4. Usually, during a 1 hour lecture, how often do you get distracted away from the lecture? (5)
5. What percentage of a typical 1 hour lecture do you think you actually pay attention to? (5)
6. Thinking of your psychology textbook, how long do you think it has taken you or will take you to read the chapter being covered this week in your psychology course? (7)

Note. These questions were used for initial, recall, and postprogram skills evaluation in Study 2, in addition to those skills evaluation questions listed in Table 16-1. For each question, subjects were required to respond in specified units (e.g., min, frequency in 1 hr). The parenthesized number following each question indicates the question of Table 16-1 to which it corresponds.

time ranking and reassigned him or her to the program. Subjects were then telephoned and informed of their assignment to condition. Experimental subjects were scheduled for the skills program over the next 3 weeks.

Both waiting list subjects and program participants returned for the final meetings. The experimenter followed the procedure of Study 1. Under demands of accuracy, subjects first recalled their responses to the initial skills questions (Tables 16-1 and 16-2) and diary. Reports of current study habits followed recall; subjects completed the skills questions and diary for the immediately preceding week. Subjects then assessed their skills improvement in response to questions identical to those in Study 1. Finally, subjects indicated the average grades they expected to obtain on their end of semester exams.

Subjects from one psychology course had their midterm exam the week after the study ended, and their marks were obtained from the instructor. Apart from this exam, an effective comparison between program participants and waiting list subjects on term grade point averages or other grades was precluded because most waiting list subjects began a study skills program one week after Study 2 ended, before the end of term.

RESULTS

Recall: Study Time

In both studies, all subjects recalled their initial study time diary at the final meeting. Our hypothesis was that program participants would exaggerate how poorly off they were before the program began by remembering having studied less, whereas control subjects would exhibit no systematic bias. Statistically, this translates into a significant interaction between time of measurement (initial vs. recall) and experimental condition. This interaction did not approach significance on the study time measure in either experiment, $Fs < 1$. The only effect that approached significance is a tendency for subjects in both conditions of Study 1 to recall studying less than they initially reported, $F(1, 56) = 2.58$, $p = .11$. The mean number of hours recorded in the initial and recall diaries are reported in the third and fourth columns of Table 16-3.

TABLE 16-3

Mean initial skills evaluation, study time, and recall of each

Groups	Skills evaluation[a]		Study time[b]	
	Initial	Recall	Initial	Recall
Study 1				
Experimental				
$n = 38$	0.020	−0.265	25.57	23.16
Control				
$n = 20$	0.264	0.193	29.78	27.93
Study 2				
Experimental				
$n = 25$	0.109	−0.186	19.11	18.68
Control				
$n = 23$	0.013	0.098	18.00	19.13

[a]Larger positive numbers indicate a more favorable skills evaluation. For Study 1, scores are averages of the standardized responses to the questions in Table 16-1. The effective range is −1.985 to 1.536. For Study 2, scores are the sum of the averages of the standardized responses to the questions in Tables 16-1 and 16-2. The effective range is −2.449 to 2.783.
[b]Initial and recall study time are, respectively, the number of hours of study time recorded in the diary completed at the initial meeting for the immediately preceding week, and in the diary completed at the last meeting for that same 1 week period.

Recall: Skills Evaluation

Study 1. Initial and recall measures were obtained on eight skills evaluation questions. The overall means are reported in the first and second columns of Table 16-3. The ANOVA revealed a marginally significant Time × Condition interaction, $F(1, 56) = 3.34$, $p < .07$. Two planned comparisons are particularly relevant to our hypothesis. As anticipated, program participants remembered being worse than they had actually reported at the initial meeting, $F(1, 56) = 17.07$, $p < .001$. In contrast, waiting list subjects exhibited no systematic bias in recall, $F < 1$.

Study 2. The repeated measures ANOVA on the skills evaluation questions revealed the expected Time × Condition interaction, $F(1, 45) = 4.43$, $p < .04$ (see Table 16-3 for means collapsed across the scale and numerical measures). This interaction was not qualified by the type of skills evaluation question (scale vs. numerical). Thus, the Type of Question × Experimental Treatment interaction was nonsignificant, $F < 1$, as was the Type of Question × Experimental Treatment × Time interaction, $F < 1$. Most important, as in Experiment 1, two planned comparisons provide strong support for the major experimental hypothesis. Program participants recalled their study skills as significantly worse than they initially reported, $F(1, 45) = 11.39$, $p < .005$. Waiting list subjects recalled their study skills as being nonsignificantly better than they reported initially, $F < 1$.

In both studies, then, program participants exaggerated in recall how poor their study skills were before the program began. In contrast, waiting list subjects did not exhibit a systematic bias in recall.

Self-Evaluation of Postprogram Standing

Study time. At the last meetings of both studies, we assessed subjects' perceptions of their postprogram standing. An examination of the number of hours of study time derived from the diary yielded no significant differences between program participants and waiting list subjects in Study 1, $M = 27.9$ versus $M = 32.7$, $t(56) = 1.69$, $p = .10$, or in Study 2, $M = 21.9$ versus $M = 22.0$, $t < 1$. If anything, program participants in Study 1 were studying less after the program than were waiting list subjects.

Study skills. In Study 1, program participants reported a postprogram skills level, $M = .012$, that was nonsignificantly higher than waiting list subjects' self-evaluations, $M = -.031$, $t < 1$. In Study 2, program participants rated their study skills significantly higher after the program, $M = .213$, than did waiting list subjects, $M = -.233$, $t(46) = 2.76$, $p < 0.008$.

Thus, in Study 1, program participants did not differ from waiting list subjects on their postprogram study time or skills evaluation. In Study 2, although program participants did not differ from waiting list subjects on study time, they evaluated their skills more favorably after the program than did waiting list subjects.

Subjective Improvement

At the last meetings of both studies, all subjects evaluated the change in their study skills since their first meeting. In Study 1, program participants reported greater skills improvement during the period of the program than did waiting list subjects, $M = 0.202$ versus $M = -0.383$, $t(56) = 3.58$, $p < .0005$. In Study 2, program participants similarly judged themselves to have improved more during the period of the program than did waiting list subjects, $M = 0.402$ versus $M = -0.437$, $t(46) = 4.38$, $p < .0005$. Consistent with their perceptions of improvement, program participants in Study 2 expected higher final exam grades for their current courses, $M = 76.6\%$, than did waiting list subjects, $M = 71.8\%$, $t(45) = 2.11$, $p < 0.04$.

The major hypothesis underlying the current studies is that people can exaggerate improvement by retrospectively derogating their initial status. This can be examined at the individual level by correlating subjective improvement with recall of initial skills evaluation, controlling for actual initial skills evaluation. However, all of these measures are positively correlated with subjects' evaluations of their current, postprogram, skills, $ps < .05$. To assess the improvement–recall relation in an uncontaminated fashion, it is therefore necessary to partial out both current skills evaluation and initial skills evaluation. The resulting average, within cell, partial correlation was $-.32$ in Study 1 and $-.45$ in Study 2, $ps < .05$. As anticipated, the greater the perceived improvement, the lower the recalled initial skills levels.

In both studies, then, participants reported greater improvement in study skills than did waiting list subjects. In Study 2, program participants also expected better exam grades (a measure not obtained in Study 1). The negative correlation between recall of initial skills levels and perceived improvement, with initial and final skills evaluations controlled for, is consistent with the hypothesis that people may exaggerate improvement by retrospectively downgrading their earlier skills.

Postprogram Academic Performance

Study 1. No significant differences emerged on final psychology exam or term average grades between program participants and waiting list subjects. If anything, program participants had somewhat lower psychology exam grades, $M = 61\%$, than did waiting list subjects, $M = 63.3\%$, $t < 1$. In addition, program participants' overall and major term averages did not differ significantly from those of waiting list subjects, $M = 67.1\%$ versus $M = 71.6\%$, and $M = 69.1\%$ versus $M = 71.1\%$, $ts < 1$.

Study 2. A comparison of semester grade point averages between program participants and waiting list subjects was precluded because most waiting list subjects subsequently enrolled in the skills program. In one of the psychology courses, an exam was held after the study and before waiting list subjects took their skills program. Eleven program participants and eight waiting list subjects wrote this exam. Program participants obtained somewhat higher marks, $M = 71.9\%$, than did waiting list subjects, $M = 69.7\%$, but the difference was not significant, $t < 1$.

In both studies, the comparison of program participants' grades with those of waiting list subjects suggests that the study skills program did not have a significant impact on academic performance.

Recall of Postprogram Performance

Subjects' overall and major grades for the term during which the study was conducted provided both the authors and subjects with objective criteria of postprogram standing. Reports in hand, subjects would presumably be very accurate in assessing their academic performance for the term. When the reports are put away and time has passed, subjects must rely on their memories. Perceptions of postprogram standing may then become distorted. We tested for this possibility 6 months after the end of the study; we asked subjects in Experiment 1 about their academic performance for the term during which the study occurred. For courses in their major, a repeated measures ANOVA, with experimental condition (program vs. waiting list) as the between factor and grade report (actual vs. recall) as the within factor, revealed the expected, albeit marginally significant, Condition × Grade Report interaction, $F(1, 39) = 3.49$, $p < .07$ (other $Fs < 1$). Program participants remembered doing significantly better, $M = 73.3\%$, than they actually did, $M = 72.0\%$, $F(1, 39) = 4.47$, $p < .05$, whereas waiting list subjects remembered doing slightly worse, $M = 70.6\%$, than they did, $M = 71.3\%$, $F < 1$. The increase program participants allotted themselves is small, but effectively raised their major average from B− to B. The hypothesized interaction for overall average was not significant, $F(1, 40) = 1.92$, $p = .17$. A similar test of differential recall was not possible in Experiment 2 because most waiting list subjects went on to take the program after the study.

DISCUSSION

The two experiments provide support for the major experimental hypothesis. Program participants retrospectively disparaged their prior study skills; waiting list control subjects did not. Program participants also reported significantly greater improvement in their study skills and expected better grades (Experiment 2) than did waiting list subjects. Participants' high expectations were unwarranted. Academic grades were not affected by the program in either study. Interestingly, this did not prevent program participants from later recalling their performance as superior (Experiment 1). When contacted 6 months later, program participants reported better grades than they had actually obtained in their major for the term during which the program was conducted. In contrast, waiting list subjects did not exhibit a systematic bias in recall.

Our results do not imply that people's recollections are always biased following participation in self-improvement programs. Program participants did not differ from waiting list subjects in their recall of the initial study time diary. Diary events are concrete and part of a daily routine. Perhaps, subjects can retrieve them by reconstructing this routine. It would then be unnecessary and inefficient to base recall on a more general theory of change. Moreover, even when theories of change are invoked, recall may be valid. Recall is inaccurate if a theory dictates greater or lesser change than has actually occurred.

The major finding in the present studies is that program participants retrospectively belittled their initial study skills. This memory bias occurred in the face of experimental procedures that might be expected to militate against it. At the first session, subjects explicitly evaluated and recorded their preprogram status, rendering it relatively salient, memorable, and presumably less susceptible to later bias. As such extensive initial records would not be made in most real-life settings, even larger effects might be anticipated. In addition, subjects were subsequently asked to recall their preprogram responses, knowing full well that the experimenter would compare their recall with their prior reports. This knowledge may have increased the accuracy of their recall. Nonevaluative settings might allow people to work less hard at remembering and to claim greater support for their theories of change.

...

There are several applied implications of the reconstructions obtained in the current studies. First, the research reveals once again the potential invalidity of self-reports and the need for formal evaluation to assess improvement programs. This lesson is not new, but is easy to forget. Even informed observers sometimes base their analyses of the effectiveness of therapeutic approaches on self-reports (e.g., Schachter, 1982).

Second, in a pluralistic society in which many self-improvement programs are authoritatively offered to an often naive public, an ability to exaggerate personal change becomes a liability. There may well be validity to the alarms sounded by some analysts of pop therapies and so-called cults (Conway & Siegelman, 1979). People who join and participate in self-improvement programs may, at times, be deceived, both by the agency that offers the program and by themselves.

Third, those who conduct worthless programs are often lambasted by the press and the public. These "helpers" may simply be too credulous. Doubts they may have as to their programs' effectiveness may be assuaged by participants' glowing reports. Sophisticated observers have long questioned the value of such self-reports on the grounds that they might represent efforts at self-presentation. Health professionals, for example, often realize that patients may feel compelled to report that a treatment is helpful even when they know it is not (Ross & Olson, 1982). We are saying something different, however. Patients may well believe their reports of self-improvement, yet be wrong. The best reminder of this is the history of medicine, as it is replete with examples of miracle cures that turn out to be nothing more than placebo effects (Ross & Olson, 1981, 1982). Many of these cures were evaluated solely on the basis of patients' self-reports. When self-reports are a primary indicant of improvement, a conspiracy of ignorance may emerge in which the helper and helped each erroneously believe in the achievement of their common goal.

Finally, there are situations in which exaggeration of change is advantageous. For instance, consider a self-improvement program that is effective but whose benefits take a relatively long time to accrue. Participants may better persist in their efforts if they adopt a theory of short-term change and exaggerate their progress. Other examples of adaptive theories of change may be found in how people cope with personal crises. Psychological reactions to breast cancer and spinal cord injury often include the perception that one is now a "better person." This perceived improvement gives meaning to the illness and contributes to psychological adjustment (Bulman & Wortman, 1977; Taylor, 1983). Conceivably, victims exaggerate improvement by overestimating how petty, misguided, or maladjusted they were before their misfortune. In this way, theories of personal improvement contribute to the illusions that facilitate coping with undesirable life events.

REFERENCES

Bartlett, F. C. (1932). *Remembering: A study in experimental and social psychology.* London: Cambridge University Press.

Bem, D. J., & McConnell, H. K. (1970). Testing the self-perception explanation of dissonance phenomena: On the salience of premanipulation attitudes. *Journal of Personality and Social Psychology, 14*, 23–31.

Bulman, R. J., & Wortman, C. B. (1977). Attributions of blame and coping in the "real world": Severe accident victims react to their lot. *Journal of Personality and Social Psychology, 35*, 351–363.

Chibnall, B. (1979). The Sussex experience. In P. J. Hills (Ed.), *Study courses and counselling: Problems and possibilities.* Surrey, England: Society for Research into Higher Education, Guilford, 37–46.

Conway, F., & Siegelman, J. (1979). *Snapping.* New York: Delta.

Cooper, J. (1980). Reducing fears and increasing assertiveness: The role of dissonance reduction. *Journal of Experimental Social Psychology, 16,* 199–213.

Gibbs, G. (1981). *Teaching students to learn.* Milton Keynes, England: Open University Press.

Goethals, G. R., & Reckman, R. F. (1973). The perception of consistency in attitudes. *Journal of Experimental Social Psychology, 9,* 491–501.

Henderson, C. W. (1975). *Awakening: Ways to psychospiritual growth.* Englewood Cliffs, NJ: Prentice-Hall.

Hills, P. J., & Potter, F. W. (1979). Group counselling and study skills. In P. J. Hills (Ed.), *Study courses and counselling: Problems and possibilities.* Surrey, England: Society for Research into Higher Education, Guilford, 13–22.

Main, A. (1980). *Encouraging effective learning.* Edinburgh: Scottish Academic Press.

Mischel, W., & Peake, P. K. (1982). Beyond déjà vu in the search for cross-situational consistency. *Psychological Review, 89,* 730–755.

Olson, J. M., & Cal, A. V. (1984). Source credibility, attitude, and the recall of past behaviours. *European Journal of Social Psychology, 14,* 203–210.

Polivy, J., & Herman, C. P. (1983). *Breaking the diet habit.* New York: Basic Books.

Ross, M. (1989). Relation of implicit theories to the construction of personal histories. *Psychological Review, 96,* 341–357.

Ross, M., McFarland, C., Conway, M., & Zanna, M. P. (1983). Reciprocal relation between attitudes and behavior recall: Committing people to newly formed attitudes. *Journal of Personality and Social Psychology, 45,* 257–267.

Ross, M., McFarland, C., & Fletcher, G. J. O. (1981). The effect of attitude on the recall of personal histories. *Journal of Personality and Social Psychology, 40,* 627–634.

Ross, M., & Olson, J. M. (1981). An expectancy-attribution model of the effects of placebos. *Psychological Review, 88,* 408–437.

Ross, M., & Olson, J. M. (1982). Placebo effects in medical research and practice. In Eiser, J. R. (Ed.), *Social psychology and behavioral medicine* (pp. 441–458). New York: Wiley.

Ross, M., & Shulman, R. F. (1973). Increasing the salience of initial attitudes: Dissonance versus self-perception theory. *Journal of Personality and Social Psychology, 28,* 138–144.

Schachter, S. (1982). Recidivism and self-cure of smoking and obesity. *American Psychologist, 37,* 436–444.

Taylor, S. E. (1983). Adjustment to threatening events: A theory of cognitive adaptation. *American Psychologist, 38,* 1161–1173.

17 Accuracy and Distortion in Memory for High School Grades

Harry P. Bahrick, Lynda K. Hall,
and Stephanie A. Berger

Bahrick and his associates asked college students to re-
call their high school grades, and then checked the re-
sponses against actual transcripts. No less than 29 per-
cent of the recalled grades proved to be incorrect!
What's more, the errors were not neutral: far more
grades were shifted up (recalling an A instead of a B, a
B instead of a C) than down. As the authors note, this
asymmetry is at least partly due to what Michael Ross
(Selection 16) would call an "implicit theory." Students
who are accustomed to getting good grades will suppose
that the grades they can't remember were probably also
good, and recall accordingly.

  This is not the whole story. A similar (but smaller)
upward bias appeared even in the recalls of low-GPA
students, whose implicit theories would not have been so
positive. Bahrick et al. regard this finding as support for
the widely held assumption that people reconstruct their
memories in positive, self-flattering ways over time. But
they also note something else: The actual number of er-
rors made by each subject was not significantly corre-
lated with that subject's degree of asymmetry (i.e., the
extent to which those very errors were biased upward).
This suggests that the factors which produce the bias
are not the same as those that cause the original forget-
ting. "Distortion [of memory] reflects bias in reconstruc-
tive inferences that occur after the veridical content has

✸ From *Psychological Science*, 1996, 7, 265–271.

been forgotten for other reasons" (Bahrick, Hall, & Berger, 1996, p. 265).

During the past century, memory research focused primarily on the loss of memory content over time. Systematic modifications of memory content were also investigated, but methodological problems made this research more difficult and less popular. Gestalt theorists were the first to investigate distortions of content (Wulf, 1922/1938), and the classic research of Bartlett (1932) inspired current reconstructive views of memory (Bransford & Franks, 1972; Neisser, 1981), including accounts of reconstructive bias (Ross, 1989).

There is now abundant evidence that memory content can undergo systematic changes. Diverse paradigms have been developed to investigate changes that are either induced by experimental interventions, such as Loftus's (1975) modifications of eyewitness reports and Fischoff's (1975) hindsight effect, or induced by the subject, reflecting reconstructions of the autobiographical past in accord with current self-perceptions (Ross, 1989). However, integrative accounts of the circumstances that produce systematic distortion instead of unbiased forgetting and of the direction and degree of distortion associated with various situational and individual difference variables are still lacking.

Koriat and Goldsmith (1994) advocate research emphasizing the differences between quantity-oriented (number correct) and accuracy-oriented (fidelity) approaches to memory assessment. The former approach characterizes traditional laboratory research on the amount of retention; the latter characterizes naturalistic investigations concerned with the degree of fidelity of the recalled content relative to the objective content. The present investigation describes a framework to promote research related to this distinction. We wanted to obtain measures of both aspects of retention in the same investigation so that the interrelations between the amount forgotten and the degree of distortion of forgotten content could be examined.

Grades received in school are a very suitable content for examining accuracy and distortion of autobiographical memory. The data are plentiful because most adults have received a large number of course grades in their secondary education. Encoding conditions for the data are fairly similar, and the data are usually comparably scaled so that direction and magnitude of errors of recall can be determined. The degree of retention is typically within a sensitive range that avoids floor or ceiling effects and, finally, the accuracy of recall can usually be verified on the basis of archival records.

METHOD

Forty male and 59 female Ohio Wesleyan University freshmen and sophomores fulfilled a research requirement in an introductory psychology course by participating. Prior to completing a questionnaire about their high school grades, all participants gave written permission for the registrar to release their high school transcripts to the investigator in order to verify the recalled grades. We believe that this requirement controlled deliberate falsifications of recalled grades.

The questionnaire required participants to recall grades from all 4 years of high school in the following five content areas: mathematics, science, history, foreign language, and English. For each recalled grade, students rated their degree of confidence that the recall was accurate (on a 3-point scale) and their degree of present satisfaction with the grade (on a 5-point scale). If students did not recall having taken a particular course, they were instructed to mark an X instead of a grade.

We subsequently verified 3,220 grades from the registrar's records. Numerical grades were transformed into corresponding letter grades, and pluses and minuses were ignored in our verification.

RESULTS AND DISCUSSION

Accuracy of Recall

Table 17-1 shows frequencies of recalled grades as a function of the verified letter grades. We discuss first the frequencies that indicate accurate recall, that is, correspondence between recalled grade and verified grade. The relevant frequencies are those in the diagonal cells (top left to bottom right) of Table 17-1. All other cell frequencies represent various kinds of errors of recall that we examine later.

Overall, 71% of grades (i.e., 2,271 of the 3,220 grades) were recalled correctly. To determine the extent of forgetting during the 4 high school years, we calculated the mean percentage of course grades correctly recalled for courses taken in 9th, 10th, 11th, and 12th grades, respectively. These data are shown in the first two columns of Table 17-2 on page 168. Fewer grades were reported from the 12th grade than from the 3 earlier years because a number of students did not take mathematics or science courses during the last year in high school. Recall accuracy is slightly higher for grades

TABLE 17-1

Frequency of recalled grades by actual grades

Recalled grade	Actual grade					Total
	A	B	C	D	F	
A	1,110	357	35	1	—	1,503
B	127	843	230	20	—	1,220
C	3	108	296	28	1	436
D	1	8	24	21	3	57
F	—	—	—	3	1	4
Total	1,241	1,316	585	73	5	3,220

from the last year of high school than for the preceding 3 years. Assuming that virtually all grades would be correctly recalled immediately after being received, we can conclude that most forgetting occurs during the 1st year of the retention interval.

Our data are in accord with classical retention functions and with our earlier findings (Bahrick, Hall, & Dunlosky, 1993). In another recent investigation of the accuracy of recalled grades, Schmela (1993) reported that German students in their 12th or 13th school year correctly recalled 57% of their grades from their 6th and 9th years of school. Recall from the 9th grade was 4% more accurate than recall from the 6th grade. Thus, the German students were somewhat less accurate than the students in our investigation, probably because of the larger variance of German grades. Almost none of our participants had poor high school records. Another reason for the difference may be that the transition to U.S. high schools is marked by context changes of buildings, curriculum, and peer group. These changes may render high school grades more discriminable from grades obtained in earlier years of school.

The percentage of accurately recalled grades as a function of the verified letter grade, the confidence rating, and the satisfaction rating is also shown in Table 17-2. The relation between the degree of confidence and correct recall is in the expected direction, but modest. The same is true of the relation between expressed satisfaction with the grade and accuracy. Greater confidence and more satisfaction are associated with somewhat higher percentages of correct recall.

The most startling finding pertains to differences in the accuracy of retention of high versus low letter grades. Disregarding the data for grades of F ($N = 5$), recall accuracy monotonically declines from 89% for grades of A to 29% for grades of D. Past research (Koch, 1930; Thompson, 1985; Waters & Leeper, 1936) has generally shown that retention is best for experi-

TABLE 17-2

Proportion of accurately recalled grades as a function of year in high school, letter grade, satisfaction, and confidence

Year in high school		Letter grade		Satisfaction rating[a]		Confidence rating[b]	
Year	Proportion recalled	Grade	Proportion recalled	Rating	Proportion recalled	Rating	Proportion recalled
12	.73 (634)	A	.89 (1.241)	5	.75 (1.412)	3	.74 (2.052)
11	.70 (863)	B	.64 (1,316)	4	.67 (871)	2	.63 (893)
10	.70 (865)	C	.51 (585)	3	.68 (558)	1	.67 (213)
9	.70 (858)	D	.29 (73)	2/1	.65 (370)		

Note. The number of responses is in parentheses; discrepancies reflect missing data.
[a]Satisfaction was rated on a scale from 1 (*not very satisfied*) to 5 (*very satisfied*).
[b]Confidence was rated on a scale from 1 (*not very confident*) to 3 (*very confident*).

ences that are affectively pleasant, intermediate for experiences that are unpleasant, and worst for experiences that are neutral. The present findings are distinctive in that the order of recall accuracy monotonically reflects the degree of pleasantness associated with higher achievement. We believe that previous investigations may have confounded the degree or intensity of affect with the degree of importance, or the significance of the experience to the life of the individual. The confounding of emotionality and consequentiality of events has also been pointed out by Neisser (1982) in his critique of flashbulb memory research. Rubin and Kozin (1984) have shown that the most memorable autobiographical experiences are almost always rated high in personal importance or significance. Neutral autobiographical experiences not only lack affective attributes, but also generally lack significance. They have little impact on the quality of life and may therefore be less well encoded. In contrast, grades, regardless of their level, have equal significance. Each grade contributes equally to the overall record of achievement and, in turn, to future opportunities. The descending level of accuracy as a function of grade therefore reflects a descending degree of pleasantness, unconfounded by systematic covariance with significance.

...

Two factors can account for the results pertaining to accuracy of recalled grades. One factor reflects the influence of affect. Higher grades are affectively pleasant: they are associated with the satisfaction of achievement motives. This condition reinforces rehearsals of the memory content and thus enhances retention of that content (Jersild, 1931). The rehearsal hypothesis is also supported by Rubin and Kozin (1984), whose subjects reported 6.7, 4.1, and 3.7 rehearsals, respectively, for the first, second, and third most memorable autobiographical experiences.

The second factor involves reconstructive inferences. Students who have earned mostly As will infer that grades they cannot specifically recall are As, and their inferences are more likely to be correct than the inferences of students who have earned an equal number of As, Bs, and Cs. Larger variance in past performance reduces the accuracy of inferences based on overall past performance.

The result of the interaction of these two factors is that higher grades are remembered more accurately than lower grades by all students, but the effect is enhanced for students who have earned mostly As. Our sample included no students whose academic records were uniformly poor, so our data cannot confirm the related prediction that poorer students have greater recall accuracy for low grades than do better students.

In addition, accuracy of recalling grades of A is enhanced by a ceiling effect, which precludes errors in an upward direction. However, this artifact does not apply to other grades and therefore accounts for only a small portion of the very large overall effect of grade level on recall accuracy.

Distortion of Recall

The preceding analyses have been limited to variations in accuracy of recall, as reflected in the diagonal cell frequencies of Table 17-1. We now turn to analyses of distortion of recall based on the error frequencies reported in the remaining cells of Table 17-1.

We define memory distortion as systematic changes of reported content with respect to verified content. Thus, memory of grades is distorted to the extent that reported grades are systematically higher or lower than verified grades. We calculated overall distortion scores and distortion scores for each participant based on the ratio of asymmetry of the error distribution. The numerator of the ratio was the number of recalled grades that were higher than verified grades. The denominator was the total number of errors in both directions. The ratio can vary from 0 to 1.0. An asymmetry ratio of .50 indicates no distortion; the number of incorrectly recalled grades that are higher than actual grades equals the number that are lower than actual grades. Ratios larger than .50 indicate systematic upward distortion, and a ratio of 1.0 indicates total distortion with all errors in the upward direction. Ratios smaller than .50 indicate downward distortion. Only errors in reporting grades of B, C, and D were included in calculating the ratio because grades of A and F can be distorted in only one direction and are therefore not suitable for calculating asymmetry of errors.

The cell frequencies in Table 17-1 show that of 814 errors in recalling grades B, C, and D, 671 are in the upward direction and 143 are in the downward direction, for an overall asymmetry ratio of .82. Separate asymmetry ratios calculated for recall of individual letter grades are .75 for grades of B, .92 for grades of C, and .94 for grades of D. In the following analyses of the influence of individual difference variables on distortion, we first present asymmetry ratios based on errors in reporting verified grades of B only. The reasons for this limitation are that grades of C and D were nearly always distorted in the upward direction, so that asymmetry ratios based on these grades exhibit ceiling effects that render them insensitive to the effects of other variables.

Overall, 79 of the 99 subjects inflated their grades (ratios > .50), 13 subjects recalled all of their grades correctly, 1 subject had a symmetrical error distribution (ratio = .50), and 6 subjects deflated their grades (ratios < .50). Too few students deflated their grades to permit generalizations about characteristics associated with the direction of distortion, and all subsequent analyses focus on variations in the degree of distortion among the 80 subjects with distortion ratios equal to or greater than .50.

TABLE 17-3

Asymmetry ratios for actual grades of B as a function of individual difference variables

Satisfaction		Confidence		Grade point average	
Tercile	Asymmetry ratio	Tercile	Asymmetry ratio	Quartile	Asymmetry ratio
3 (4.7)	.95	3 (3.0)	.87	4 (3.8)	.98
2 (4.0)	.80	2 (2.7)	.75	3 (3.4)	.91
1 (3.2)	.57	1 (2.1)	.65	2 (2.9)	.75
				1 (2.4)	.46

Note. Values in parentheses are tercile or quartile means of individual difference variables.

Table 17-3 relates the degree of asymmetry of errors in the recall of grades of B to individual difference variables. It is evident that the degree of asymmetry increases with confidence, with degree of grade satisfaction, and with academic achievement.

...

We interpret individual differences in distortion on the basis of two factors, the first of which also applied to our interpretation of the results on accuracy of retention. Participants reconstruct or infer grades they cannot specifically recall in accord with relevant, generic memories, or what Flavell (1979) has called metacognitive knowledge. This assumption leads to the prediction that students with an outstanding academic record will infer a grade of A when a B has been forgotten. Students whose overall academic record is mediocre will be less likely to infer high grades on this basis. This differential effect on the asymmetry of errors of students with high versus low past achievement is in accord with the position of Ross (1989).

Although the data for recall of grades of A and F are not suitable for an asymmetry analysis, the frequency with which grades of A were recalled as Bs also exhibits this differential effect. For example, participants in the highest quartile of the GPA distribution recalled only 5% of their As as Bs, compared with 23% for participants in the lowest GPA quartile.

Beyond this differential effect, there is a second general effect that favors reconstructions in a positive, emotionally gratifying direction. Loftus (1982) has described this effect: "Memory naturally shifts in a positive or prestige-enhancing direction, perhaps for the purpose of allowing us to have

TABLE 17-4

Intercorrelations among individual difference variables

Variable	Distortion	Accuracy	Satisfaction	Confidence
Distortion	—			
Accuracy	.156	—		
Satisfaction	.375*	.370*	—	
Confidence	.160	.158	.325*	—
Grade point average	.450*	.687*	.705*	.189

*$p < .01$.

a more comfortable recollection of the past" (p. 146). It has been methodologically difficult to quantify this positive reconstruction effect. In our data, the effect accounts for the overall asymmetry ratio of .82. It is important to note that 6 subjects distorted in the opposite direction and that conclusions regarding this subpopulation require a much larger sample.

Table 17-4 shows the intercorrelations among the following individual difference variables: degree of asymmetry of the error distribution (based on grades of B, C, and D), percentage of correct recall, mean confidence, mean grade satisfaction, and GPA. The table shows that degree of memory distortion is positively correlated with academic achievement and with grade satisfaction. The correlation between GPA and mean grade satisfaction is in the expected direction: that is, students who had higher grades were more satisfied with their grades, and our rationale relating higher GPA to greater accuracy and to more distortion therefore also applies to the effects of mean grade satisfaction shown in Tables 17-2 and 17-3. The correlation of GPA with grade satisfaction is attenuated because grade satisfaction does not accurately reflect the level of achievement. Grade satisfaction reflects the remembered grade, rather than the actual grade, and this fact explains the interaction between grade satisfaction and accuracy reported earlier. High satisfaction with grades that were actually B or C, but were recalled as A, attenuates the relationship between satisfaction and accuracy of recall.

The correlation between recall accuracy and degree of distortion is not statistically significant ($p > .05$), and this finding requires further discussion.

Relation Between Accuracy and Distortion

Our hypothesis was that distortion of memory content is an important cause of forgetting, that is, that systematic changes of the remembered content block access to the objective content. Our data do not support this conclusion. If distortions cause failures to recall the objective content, then individuals who showed the greatest degree of distortion (highest asymmetry ratios) should also show the lowest recall accuracy. This is not the case. Even when GPA is held constant, the partial correlation between accuracy and degree of distortion of recall remains a low $-.23$.

The independence of degree of distortion from the amount of accurate retention is further illustrated by comparing the percentage of accurate recall and the asymmetry ratios for subjects in the highest and the lowest GPA quartiles. The data based on grades of B are most revealing. The percentage of recall accuracy was .57 for the high achievers and .62 for the low achievers, and the distortion ratio was .98 for the high achievers and .46 for the low achievers. Thus, the two groups were very similar in accuracy, but extremely different in degree of distortion. If distortion of the objective content is a primary cause of failures to recall the objective content, then two groups extremely different in the degree of distortion should also differ in the percentage of accurate recall.

These data suggest that loss of objective memory content and distortion of that content are largely independent processes. Distortion does not cause forgetting in this situation, but generally occurs after the objective content has been lost for other reasons.

The investigation supports the conclusion that affective attributes associated with academic achievement have strong effects on the long-term retention of autobiographical content. High grades are recalled with much greater accuracy than low grades. Once the specific grade in a course has been forgotten, recall appears to be based on reconstructive inferences. Such inferences reflect relevant, metacognitive knowledge of past high or low academic achievements and a strong tendency to generate emotionally gratifying content (higher grades). As a result, correct recall of grades is based on specific memories and on successful inferences. Errors of recall are based on unsuccessful inferences, and these reflect the bias of positive reconstruction.

Our findings support the view that recall of autobiographical content reflects a combination of specific and generic memories. Generic memories provide the basis for inferences that can bring about distortions of content. Barring systematic interventions, such distortions do not appear to displace specific memories; rather, they supplement them and fill in the gaps when specific memories are lost.

REFERENCES

Bahrick, H. P., Hall, L. K., & Dunlosky, J. (1993). Reconstructive processing of memory content for high versus low test scores and grades. *Applied Cognitive Psychology, 7,* 1–10.

Bartlett, F. C. (1932). *Remembering.* Cambridge, England: Cambridge University Press.

Bransford, J. D., & Franks, J. J. (1972). The abstraction of linguistic ideas: A review. *Cognition, 1,* 211–249.

Fischoff, B. (1975). Hindsight ≠ foresight: The effect of outcome knowledge on judgement under uncertainty. *Journal of Experimental Psychology: Human Perception and Performance, 1,* 288–299.

Flavell, J. H. (1979). Metacognition and cognitive monitoring: A new area of cognitive-developmental inquiry. *American Psychologist, 34,* 906–911.

Jersild, A. (1931). Memory for the pleasant as compared with the unpleasant. *Journal of Experimental Psychology, 14,* 284–288.

Koch, H. (1930). The influence of some affective factors upon recall. *Journal of Genetic Psychology, 4,* 171–190.

Koriat, A., & Goldsmith, M. (1994). Memory in naturalistic and laboratory contexts: Distinguishing the accuracy-oriented and quantity-oriented approaches to memory assessment. *Journal of Experimental Psychology: General, 123,* 297–315.

Loftus, E. F. (1975). Leading questions and the eyewitness report. *Cognitive Psychology, 7,* 560–572.

Loftus, E. F. (1982). Memory and its distortions. In A. G. Kraut (Ed.), *G. Stanley Hall Lectures.* Washington, DC: American Psychological Association, 119–154.

Neisser, U. (1981). John Dean's memory: A case study. *Cognition, 9,* 1–22.

Neisser, U. (1982). Snapshots or benchmarks? In U. Neisser (Ed.), *Memory observed: Remembering in natural contexts.* San Francisco: Freeman, 43–48.

Ross, M. (1989). Relation of implicit theories to the construction of personal histories. *Psychological Review, 96,* 341–357.

Rubin, D. C., & Kozin, M. (1984). Vivid memories. *Cognition, 16,* 81–95.

Schmela, M. (1993). Abiturienten erinnern sich an ihre alten Zeugnisnoten—Zur Qualitaet leistungsbezogener autobiographischer Erinnerungen [Pupils remember their former final grades: About the quality of achievement-related autobiographical memories]. *Zeitschrift für Paedogogische Psychologie, 7*(1), 475–478.

Thompson, C. (1985). Memory for unique personal events: Effects of pleasantness. *Motivation and Emotion, 9,* 277–289.

Waters, R., & Leeper, R. (1936). The relation of affective tone to the retention of experiences of daily life. *Journal of Experimental Psychology, 19,* 203–215.

Wulf, F. (1938). Tendencies in figural variation. In W. D. Ellis (Ed. and Trans.), *A source book of gestalt psychology.* New York: Harcourt, Brace & World, 136–148. (Reprinted from *Psychologische Forschung,* 1922, *1,* 333–373.)

18 | Parental Recall of Child-Rearing Practices

The last two selections focused on memory errors made by students; to keep things in perspective, this one is about parents. It seems that by the time their babies are three years old, both mothers and fathers are likely to misremember their own child-rearing practices. The methods they recall using have moved closer to expert opinion about what parents should do; the course of baby's development is remembered as easier and smoother than it really was. Implicit theories ride again!

T he accuracy with which parents can recall and report, after a period of years, details of the early functioning of their children and of their own child-care practices is a significant issue in view of the large number of investigations which have used retrospective parental reports as their primary data. Tests of theories of personality development, and discussions of similarities and differences in the child rearing patterns of various class and color groups (see, e.g., Davis & Havighurst, 1946; Miller & Swanson, 1958; Sears, Maccoby, & Levin, 1957), have been based on such data, often without sufficient regard for possible factual errors.

...

The present study endeavors to examine accuracy of recall by comparing retrospective accounts of child rearing obtained from parents of 3-year-olds with reports they previously gave in the course of a longitudinal study begun with the birth of the child (Thomas & Chess, 1957). It differs from other appraisals of parental accuracy by focusing on objective, nonattitu-

⬛ From L. C. Robbins (1963). The accuracy of parental recall of aspects of child development and of child rearing practices. _Journal of Abnormal and Social Psychology, 66,_ 261–270.

dinal, yet long-term aspects of child development, such as the onset of toilet training and the duration of weaning—items which form the basis for most descriptive and comparative studies of child rearing patterns. Since it is not feasible to have an observer live with families for prolonged periods of time, there can only be assessment of the consistency of parental reports for material of this sort, and not of its validity.

The sample used is particularly favorable for maximizing the accuracy of recall since continued participation in the longitudinal study ensured parents' original awareness of the information sought. In addition, this is a middle-class group, whose practices are predominantly child centered, with the mothers accepting care of the baby as their prime responsibility, so that it can be presumed that maximum attention has been paid to details of the child's functioning.

This report will deal with two aspects of parental recall: the accuracy of retrospective parental reports, and the relationship between errors in retrospective parental reports and recommendations made by authorities in the child rearing field.

METHOD

Subjects

The broader longitudinal study, in progress since March 1956, has been mainly directed at exploring the relationship between initial patterns of reactivity in infants, and subsequent personality development (Chess, Thomas, & Birch, 1959; Chess, Thomas, Birch, & Hertzig, 1960; Thomas, Birch, Chess, & Robbins, 1961; Thomas & Chess, 1957; Thomas, Chess, Birch, & Hertzig, 1960). Parents have been seen at frequent intervals and their participation in the study has been extensive. Interviews have been held, usually with both mother and father present, every three months during the child's first year, and at six-month intervals thereafter. Questions were designed to elicit objective and specific description of the child's behavior during the normal routines of daily living, with items of a type which parents can usually answer easily and without defensiveness. Parents were used as the observers since their intimate contact with the child serves to make them the best reporters of consistent patterns and long-range activities. Other procedures have included independent observations of the children in order to check the validity of concurrent parental reports, the Stanford–Binet at three years, and direct observations in nursery school.

When the retrospective interviews were conducted, in the spring of 1959, 49 children of the families under study were approximately 3 years old. Recurrent illness and a recent divorce made scheduling impossible in two cases, so that only 47 families could be interviewed. Six fathers were not seen: four were no longer living with their wives, who had custody of the child; no appointment could be made with another because of the pressures of his business; and one family had moved to the midwest so that only the mother could be interviewed on one of her visits to New York.

In order to make this study more directly comparable to others, the data for three nonwhite families, among them one of the divorced couples, have not been included. As a result, the sample consists of 44 mothers and 39 fathers. All but five of the mothers have attended college, and many have advanced degrees in medicine, law, or psychology. The majority of the men work in a professional or executive capacity, and, with the exception of five, have gone to college. Most hold advanced degrees. The group is predominantly Jewish and is located in the greater New York area. Its socioeconomic status is uniformly high, with the two men who have had no schooling beyond high school at the upper extreme. The median age of the children at the time of interview was 37.0 months, with a range of 29–45 months.

Procedure

Appointments were arranged through the project secretary, who had a long-standing acquaintance with the parents in the study. On the night of the interview, the author and her husband, a psychiatrist, arrived at the parents' home and introduced themselves. Arrangements were made so that interviews could simultaneously be held in two different rooms. This technique made possible the assessment of individual attitudes and recall in a way that joint interviews with both parents could not achieve. At the same time, it eliminated the contamination which might ensue if parents were interviewed one after the other.

...

The effect of experts' recommendations on parental recall was evaluated by comparing the kinds of errors made with the advice of authorities. For example, if a mother who had originally described feeding "on schedule" stated in the retrospective interview that she had fed her baby "on demand," this was scored as an error in the direction of the experts' recommendations. Spock (1957) was used as the basis of comparison since all the parents in the present group were more or less familiar with his work. However, his recommendations are so similar to those in other common sources of child rearing advice, such as *Infant Care* (United States Department of Health, Education, and Welfare, 1955), and women's magazines, that it was felt that parental agreement with experts in general, rather than with Spock alone, was being tested.

RESULTS

Question 1

How accurate are retrospective parental reports of child rearing practices?

...

Table 18-1 (on page 180)... demonstrates that parental recall tends to be inaccurate. On four of the 13 quantitative items—those dealing with the age of weaning, beginning of bowel and bladder training, and the stopping of the 2 A.M. feeding—mean retrospective reports by both mothers and fathers differed significantly from the original records. Fathers' reports were also significantly inaccurate on the items dealing with the introduction of cereal, the introduction of the cup, and the child's age when he first stood alone. For two of the six qualitative items—those dealing with feeding on schedule versus demand, and thumbsucking—retrospective reports by both parents differed significantly from the original records.

For certain of the quantitative items, the mean discrepancy scores showed extreme distortion in recall. For instance, with regard to the onset of bowel training, mothers erred by an average of +14.2 weeks and fathers by an average of +22.7 weeks, both recalling the event as occurring later than was originally reported. As for bladder training, the average discrepancies were +22.3 and +25.5 weeks, respectively. These discrepancies of 3–6 months seem especially large when one considers that they are for behaviors that typically do not begin much before the end of the first year (Thomas et al., 1961), so that they are relative to a maximum time span of approximately two years.

The age of first standing was recalled correctly by a far smaller percentage of parents than the onset of walking. Furthermore, the mean discrepancy scores were opposite in sign, with both mothers and fathers tending to recall standing as having occurred later than it did and walking as having started earlier. The parents considerably shortened the time required for the progression from one stage to the next, with the fathers believing that it took 14.8 weeks on the average and the mothers, 16.8 weeks. The average interval between standing and walking was actually 21.8 weeks.

In the case of weaning, the same tendency to shorten the learning process was found, with the age of introducing the cup recalled as having been later than was really the case, while the age of completion of weaning was placed significantly earlier. The former discrepancy was significant for the fathers only (at the .05 level); the latter for fathers and mothers alike (at the .001 and .01 levels, respectively).

With regard to bowel and bladder functions, the initiation of training was also recalled as significantly later by both sets of parents. Since a majority of the children had not yet been fully trained at the time of the retrospective interviews, information concerning the date of completion was not sought. However, in those families where training was complete, the parents tended to describe its accomplishment as taking place virtually overnight, and to gloss over the lengthy process of acquisition.

···

Question 2

Is there any relationship between the recommendations of experts in child rearing and retrospective parental reports of their own practices?

···

Although no cause and effect relationship can positively be established, the parallelism between experts' advice and prevailing direction of distortion is suggestive. . . . Mothers tended to be inaccurate in the direction of the recommendations on every one of the nine items for which suggestions were clearly made in the child rearing literature. For instance, of the 20 mothers who gave inaccurate responses regarding the mode of infant feeding they employ, 65 percent shifted in the direction of more demand feeding and only 35 percent toward less. This discrepancy suggests that mothers were desirous of appearing to have fed on demand even when they had not actually engaged in the practice. The age of weaning was markedly reduced in the retrospective reports, while the onset of toilet training was recalled as later than was really the case. In both instances, the shifts paralleled the recommendations of Spock (1957; see Table 18-1) regarding the ideal timing of these practices. Finally, with regard to thumbsucking, of which Spock disapproves, and the pacifier, whose use he favors, errors again reflected the recommendations. All seven of the mothers who were inaccurate in their reports of thumbsucking denied that their child had ever sucked his thumb. The original records showed not only that thumbsucking had occurred, in three cases for as long as a year, but also that several of these mothers had expressed concern about it at the time. In contrast, of five mothers who erred in their recall of the use of the pacifier, four stated that their child had used one when, according to the longitudinal records, he had not.

On items for which expert advice was relatively less specific or irrelevant, maternal errors were random in direction. Thus, with respect to the introduction of cereal, 17 mothers recalled the date of onset as later and 18 as earlier, while the birth weight was understated by eight and overstated by six.

. . . The fathers tended to be less affected by expert advice than the mothers. While they all reported some acquaintance with Spock (1957), the fathers felt they were less thorough in their reading than their wives, and that he influenced them little.

···

TABLE 18-1

Accuracy of parental recall

Parental recall	N_a	Mothers' mean discrepancy	t	N_a	Fathers' mean discrepancy	t
Quantitative items						
C4b. If breast—how long?	20	+.4[b]	<1	16	−.4[b]	<1
C5. Cereal—when introduced?	41	−.3	<1	29	+7.3	3.09**
D1. Cup—when introduced?	26	+7.7	<1	21	+12.7	2.48
D2a. Bottle—when stopped?	25	−13.6	3.52**	19	−18.2	4.7***
F1a. Bowel training—when begun?	44	+14.2	3.49***	38	+22.7	4.92***
F1a. Bladder training—when begun?	42	+22.3	5.23***	36	+25.5	4.86***
G5a. 2 a.m. feeding—when stopped?	34	+2.8	2.13*	25	+5.5	2.15*
G5b. 10 p.m. feeding—when stopped?	28	+2.3	<1	16	−5.9	1.23
I1. When first stood alone?	35	+1.9	1.31	31	+9.1	3.08**
I1a. When first walked alone?	43	−1.1	1.36	32	−1.1	1.08
L2. First injection—when?	27	−1.6	1.55	22	+4.0	<1
L4. Birth weight?	43	+.02	<1	37	−1.1 oz	<1
L4a. Birth length?	19	+.1 in.	1.56	10	+.2 in.	<1

Qualitative items	N	% Accurate	Significance[c]	N	% Accurate	Significance[c]
C3. Schedule vs. demand?	43	53	.05[d]	38	37	.05[d]
C4. Breast vs. bottle?	44	95	—	39	97	—
D2b. If stop bottle—transition?	23	61	—	19	74	—
D3. Ever suck thumb?	44	84	.01[e]	39	78	.05[e]
D4. Ever suck pacifier?	43	88	—	38	87	—
G5c. How well sleep at 6 months?	42	79	—	38	66	—

[a] Ns vary because of ODM (Original Data Missing), DK (Don't Know), or DNA (Does Not Apply) responses.

[b] In weeks except Items L4 and L4a.

[c] Significance depends upon the direction of errors, rather than the percentage of accurate responses. Thus, seven mothers denied thumbsucking and none erroneously added it in the retrospective reports, so that the responses on original and retrospective interviews significantly differ from one another. For item G5c, where the percentage accuracy is actually lower, change was not significant since four mothers said the child had slept well when he had slept poorly and three erred in the opposite direction.

[d] Significantly more modified demand and less schedule than had occurred were mentioned in the retrospective interview than in the original reports.

[e] Significantly less thumbsucking than had occurred was reported in the retrospective interview.

$*p \leq .05$, $**p \leq .01$, $***p \leq .0001$.

REFERENCES

Chess, S., Thomas, A., & Birch, H. G. (1959). Characteristics of the individual child's behavioral responses to the environment. *American Journal of Orthopsychiatry, 29,* 791–802.

Chess, S., Thomas, A., Birch, H. G., & Hertzig, M. (1960). Implications of a longitudinal study of child development for child psychiatry. *American Journal of Psychiatry, 117,* 434–441.

Davis, A., & Havighurst, R. J. (1946). Social class and color differences in child rearing. *American Social Review, 11,* 698–710.

Miller, D. R., & Swanson, G. E. (1958). *The changing American parent.* New York: Wiley.

Sears, R. R., Maccoby, E. E., & Levin, H. (1957). *Patterns of child rearing.* Evanston, Ill.: Row, Peterson.

Spock, B. (1957). *Baby and child care* (rev. ed.). New York: Pocket Books.

Thomas, A., Birch, H. G., Chess, S., & Robbins, L. C. (1961). Individuality in responses of children to similar environmental situations. *American Journal of Psychiatry, 177,* 798–803.

Thomas, A., & Chess, S. (1957). An approach to the study of sources of individual differences in child behavior. *Journal of Clinical and Experimental Psychopathology, 18,* 347–357.

Thomas, A., Chess, S., Birch, H. G., & Hertzig, M. (1960). A longitudinal study of primary reaction patterns in children. *Comprehensive Psychiatry, 1,* 103–112.

United States Department of Health, Education and Welfare, Children's Bureau. (1955). *Infant care.* Washington, D.C.: United States Government Printing Office (Children's Bureau Publ. No. 8).

19 Gender Differences in the Recall of a Close Relationship

Michael Ross and Diane Holmberg

Art—even musical comedy—is often a step ahead of psychology. Consider this wonderful song by Lerner and Loewe, called I Remember It Well:

> HE: *I can remember everything as if it were yesterday. We met at nine.*
> SHE: *We met at eight.*
> HE: *I was on time.*
> SHE: *No, you were late.*
> HE: *Ah yes, I remember it well. We dined with friends.*
> SHE: *We dined alone.*
> HE: *A tenor sang.*
> SHE: *A baritone . . .*

The full text is in this selection, along with some data to show that Lerner and Loewe probably got it right.

F rancis Galton is generally recognized as one of the great, albeit misguided, geniuses of the last century (misguided because he expressed an enthusiasm for eugenics that offends our modern sensibilities). He is also known for his outstanding memory. Galton was a child prodigy who memorized, at an early age, a great deal of Scott, Milton, and of the *Iliad* and the *Odyssey*. In this context, it is interesting to note that he begins his

※ From M. Ross & D. Holmberg (1990). Recounting the past: Gender differences in the recall of events in the history of a close relationship. In M. P. Zanna & J. M. Olson (Eds.), *Self-inference processes*. Hillsdale, NJ: Erlbaum, 135–152.

memoirs by bemoaning the death of his latest surviving sisters (Galton, 1908/1974). According to Galton, the "minds [of these sisters] were sure storehouses of family events" (p. 1). He observes that he depended on his sisters when he wanted a "date or particulars of a long-past fact" (p. 1).

Galton's comments intrigued us because they were consistent with data emerging from research in which we examined married couples' recall of events in their relationship. Our interest in studying the stories people tell about their pasts stemmed from a general concern with self and social perception. People's accounts of their personal histories may help us understand how they view themselves and others. Recall of shared events in a close relationship may be particularly informative. These accounts may both reflect and influence people's views of themselves, their partner, and their relationship.

In presenting our study, we begin with the procedure and data, and subsequently attempt to place the findings in a broader context. The results that we describe were largely unanticipated; our reversal of the typical ordering of theory and data is intended to emphasize the post hoc nature of our theorizing.

During the spring and summer of 1988, we asked married couples to participate in a study of autobiographical memory. Participants were selected from a list of couples who had applied for a marriage license in the city of Waterloo in 1984 and 1985. Of the 624 couples who applied for licenses in those 2 years, we found current local addresses for 236. These couples were sent an initial letter describing the study and asking them to consider participating. We contacted 173 of the couples with a follow-up phone call and 43% of those eligible for the study agreed to participate (5 couples were now separated, divorced, or widowed). We were unable to schedule 7 couples at a mutually convenient time and another 5 couples were assigned to a pretest. Sixty couples participated in the experiment. Some of the characteristics of this sample are shown in Table 19-1.

Each couple was asked to recall three incidents from their past: their first date together, their last vacation together, and a recent argument between the two of them. The events were presented in counterbalanced order. We selected these particular events for several reasons: they involved both participants, they varied in importance and affect, and they were at least somewhat memorable and meaningful for the relationship. Participants' estimates of the length of time that had elapsed since the target events averaged 6.8 years for the first date (range: 2.3–15.4 years), 9.4 months for the argument (range: less than a day–7.8 years), and 10.0 months for the vacation (range: 4 days–3.9 years).

The participants were asked to recall each event in detail, speaking into a tape recorder for up to 10 minutes per episode. The study included two between-group, experimental manipulations. First, participants were either alone or together with their spouses when they tape-recorded their recall. In the together condition, spouses discussed their memories with each other during the recall period. The together-alone manipulation allowed us to evaluate the impact of differing perspectives on recall and to observe how idiosyncratic memories are merged to form a common story. In both conditions, the experimenter asked participants to come to an agreement on the particular event to be recalled (e.g., which argument or vacation) before beginning the tape recording. The experimenter then retired to another room, leaving the participants on their own during the recording periods.

In addition to the open-ended recall, participants completed questionnaires individually in which they reported their impressions of each event. The second experimental manipulation involved the timing of these questionnaires. Participants answered the questionnaires either immediately *before* they tape-recorded their recall of each event, or immediately *after* their recording. The timing manipulation enabled us to assess whether participants' private impressions of the events were influenced by their tape-recorded recall.

Finally, participants completed a brief questionnaire at the conclusion of the study in which they were asked general questions about the accuracy of their memory and about the effects of social context on recall. Participants' responses to all of the questionnaires were private and were not shown to their spouses.

In this chapter, we focus on participants' questionnaire responses. In the questionnaires associated with each event, six items were designed to assess respondents' impressions of the clarity and vividness of their recall. Several of these questions are modified versions of items used by Johnson in her research on the clarity of memories for perceived and imagined events (e.g.,

TABLE 19-1

Characteristics of sample

		Husbands	Wives
Age	Mean:	32.3	30.1
	Range:	22–76	23–70
Years of education	Mean:	13.6	13.0
	Range:	9–20	9–21
Percentage employed		95	80

1. Participants were employed in a broad range of jobs. Examples include floor installer and principal (for men), and custodian and university professor (for women).
2. The mean number of children per couple was 1.12, with a range of 0–5 (including children from previous marriages).

TABLE 19-2

Items assessing clarity of memory

1. How clear is your memory of your first date with your spouse?
   vague   1 2 3 4 5 6 7   clear/distinct
2. Is your memory of this first date sketchy or highly detailed?
   (i.e., Can you remember only bits and pieces, or can you recall the entire sequence of events?)
   sketchy   1 2 3 4 5 6 7   highly detailed
3. Overall, how well do you remember your first date with your spouse?
   hardly   1 2 3 4 5 6 7   very well
4. Do you have any doubts about the accuracy of your memory for the date?
   a great deal
   of doubt   1 2 3 4 5 6 7   no doubt whatsoever
5. Do you remember what you thought during the course of the date?
   not at all 1 2 3 4 5 6 7   clearly
6. How clearly or vividly can you recall the emotions you experienced during the course of your first date?
   not at all
   clearly   1 2 3 4 5 6 7   very clearly

Johnson, Foley, Suengas, & Raye, 1988; Suengas & Johnson, 1988). Table 19-2 shows the questions we asked respondents about their first date. Similar items appeared on the argument and vacation questionnaires.

As well as obtaining this subjective measure of clarity of memory, we obtained more objective evidence. Two research assistants examined typed transcripts of the tape-recorded recall. For each couple, the assistants completed the same clarity and vividness of memory questions as did the participants. In addition, the assistants recorded the number of times in each transcript that respondents explicitly stated an inability to recall an aspect of the target event.

CLARITY OF MEMORY

Participants' responses to the six clarity questions were all highly inter-correlated. Consequently, we created an index of clarity by averaging the six responses. Means and significance levels are shown in Table 19-3. The data were analyzed treating gender (husbands vs. wives) as a within-subjects factor and the experimental manipulations as between-subjects factors.

The results are easy to summarize: Females reported more detailed and vivid memories of all three events than did males. The two experimental manipulations failed to influence the strength of this effect. Females reported more vivid memories than did males whether the clarity measure was assessed before or after the tape-recorded recall, and whether participants recalled the events alone or together with their spouses.

The gender effect is not simply in the minds of our subjects. Averaging across all three of the events, our research assistants rated typed transcripts of the women's memories as more vivid and detailed, $M = 5.63$, than their spouses' memories for the same events, $M = 5.26$, $p < .01$. In addition, we examined observers' ratings of each event separately. Females' memories of the date and the argument were rated as significantly more vivid than those of their spouses. No gender difference was obtained for memories of the vacation.

The assistants also counted the number of times that each respondent explicitly stated that he or she could not recall a particular detail (e.g., "I forget what day it was," or "I can't remember whose house we went to"). An analysis of these data revealed a significant main effect for experimental condition. Spouses were more likely to report forgetting aspects of the events when they recalled the events together, $M = 4.99$, than when they recalled the events alone, $M = 2.58$. In addition, a significant interaction was found between experimental condition and gender. When spouses recalled the events together, a gender effect was obtained that paralleled the results found on the vividness ratings. Males reported a significantly greater number of memory failures, $M = 6.26$, than did females, $M = 3.71$. When spouses recalled the events alone, the gender difference was nonsignificant (male $M = 2.31$; female $M = 2.86$).

The increase in reports of forgetting in the together condition appears to reflect, in part, efforts to elicit information from one's spouse, a process that Wegner (1986) has labeled "transactive retrieval" (p. 190). In the alone condition, there is no possibility of help, and reports of forgetting

TABLE 19-3

Mean clarity of recall

Event Recalled	Husbands' Ratings	Wives' Ratings	$p <$
Argument	4.69	5.37	.01
First date	4.32	5.00	.001
Vacation	5.52	5.86	.01
All 3 events	4.84	5.44	.0001

Higher numbers indicate greater clarity of memory. Possible range is 1–7.

TABLE 19-4

Evaluation of own and partner's memory for details from the past

		Rater	
		Husband	Wife
Target	Husband	4.05	4.33
	Wife	5.12	4.98

Higher numbers indicate better memory on a 7-point scale. Both partners agreed that the wife has the better memory, $F = 16.4$, $p < .001$.

are relatively infrequent. Furthermore, in the together condition males were more likely than females to report forgetting details of the events. Presumably, males, with their less vivid memories, felt a greater need to call on their spouses for aid.

After recalling all three of the events, respondents independently completed a final questionnaire in which they were asked to assess their own and their spouse's overall memory for "details from the past." Both spouses rated the female partner's memory as superior (Table 19-4). This result is worthy of comment. Available research indicates that males and females expect women to perform less well than men on a wide variety of tasks (e.g., Bem & Bem, 1970; Feldman–Summers & Kiesler, 1974). The present finding that both sexes praised females' memories suggests that males have convincing evidence of their inferiority on this dimension and females of their superiority.

To indicate how the discussions proceeded in the together condition, we present excerpts from one couple's recall of their first date together:

Wife: Here's your memory test. When was our first date?
Husband: When? Do we have to know dates?
Wife: No, not when exactly.
Husband: I thought it was in wintertime.
Wife: Good, yes. . . . We met in January.
Husband: Ya, I remember that. January 8th.
Wife: On the 8th. And our first date was about the 16th or 17th.
Husband: Oh, I don't remember the first.

. . . .

Wife: Do you remember how you asked me out?
Husband: No, I don't remember that.

Wife:	You said "Gee, I really like the way you dress. You want to take me shopping for clothes?" . . . Ok, so we went shopping.
Husband:	Ya, we went to Conestoga Mall. I remember that.
Wife:	And Fairview Mall too, I think.
Husband:	Fairview too?
Wife:	I think so.
Husband:	I don't remember going to Fair . . . wait a minute. Ya, I do remember going to Fairview because . . .
Wife:	We went to Star's Men's Shop. That's where you bought . . .
Husband:	you commented, you commented twice . . .
Wife:	your leather tie.
Husband:	ya, you commented twice when we were in Conestoga. You said "everybody's staring at me" and then we went to Fairview and you said the same thing. I remember.

. . . .

Wife:	Do you remember how the evening ended?
Husband:	No.
Wife:	It didn't. It lasted until the next morning. You fell asleep on the couch.
Husband:	Oh that's right. Ya, we . . . that's right.

This exchange between a couple in our sample may sound familiar to readers who are fans of Broadway musicals. Below are the words of the song *I Remember It Well,* as we transcribed them from the 1958 film of Lerner and Loewe's *Gigi.* The song records an exchange between two former lovers, Maurice Chevalier, who plays an aging roué, and Hermione Gingold, who plays Gigi's grandmother. They recall their final date together, many years earlier.

He:	I can remember everything, as if it were yesterday. We met at nine.
She:	We met at eight.
He:	I was on time.
She:	No, you were late.
He:	Ah yes, I remember it well. We dined with friends.
She:	We dined alone.
He:	A tenor sang.
She:	A baritone.
He:	Ah yes, I remember it well. That dazzling April moon. . . .

She:	There was none that night
	And the month was June.
He:	That's right, that's right.
She:	It warms my heart to know that you
	Remember still the way you do.
He:	Ah yes, I remember it well.
	How often I've thought of that Friday . . .
She:	Monday.
He:	Night when we had our last rendezvous.
	And somehow I foolishly wondered if you might
	By some chance be thinking of it too.
	That carriage ride . . .
She:	You walked me home.
He:	You lost a glove.
She:	I lost a comb.
He:	Ah yes, I remember it well.
	That brilliant sky . . .
She:	We had some rain.
He:	Those Russian songs . . .
She:	From sunny Spain.
He:	Ah yes, I remember it well.
	You wore a gown of gold.
She:	I was all in blue.
He:	Am I getting old?
She:	Oh no, not you.
	How strong you were,
	How young and gay
	A prince of love in every way.
He:	Ah yes, I remember it well.

WHY ARE FEMALES' MEMORIES MORE VIVID?

Both song and data indicate that women possess more detailed and vivid memories of interactions within intimate relationships than do men. The evidence suggests that women tend to be the interpersonal historians in our culture. Why might this be the case?

There have been many studies examining cultural stereotypes of males and females in North American society. Generally, men are described as independent, rational, and competent; in contrast, women are seen as dependent and emotional. Women are also depicted as more concerned with interpersonal relationships, more aware of the feelings of others, and more expressive of their own feelings (e.g., Deaux, 1976; Parsons & Bales, 1955). The evidence does not necessarily indicate that men and women possess different values; it does suggest that the sexes are socialized to assume somewhat different roles in the pursuit of common values within the family (Parsons & Bales, 1955).

If women are socialized to be more concerned with interpersonal relationships, they may attend more closely to an ongoing social interaction and/or think about it more afterwards than do men. Women may then possess a more vivid memory of the interaction than males.

Additional items on our questionnaires asked respondents how often they had thought and how often they had talked about each event (with their spouse or with others) since it had occurred. The responses to the thought and talk questions were highly correlated; we combined them into a single measure of reminiscence. Participants were also asked to assess the personal importance of each event at the time it had occurred. The means shown in Table 19-5 reveal a gender difference. In comparison with their husbands, wives tended to report that they were more likely to reminisce about the events. Women also rated the events as more important.

A closer scrutiny of the results suggests that differential rehearsal and importance may not account for the gender effect on vividness of recall.

TABLE 19-5

Reminiscence and personal importance

Event Recalled	Mean Frequency of Reminiscence		$p <$
	Husbands' Ratings	Wives' Ratings	
Argument	2.46	2.84	n.s.[a]
First date	3.95	4.57	.05
Vacation	4.20	4.76	.01
All 3 events	3.54	4.06	.01

Event Recalled	Mean Personal Importance		$p <$
	Husbands' Ratings	Wives' Ratings	
Argument	4.40	5.56	.01
First date	5.10	5.23	n.s.[b]
Vacation	5.40	5.91	.05
All 3 events	4.96	5.57	.05

1. [a]$F = 1.34$; [b]$F < 1$
2. Frequency of reminiscence could range from 1 (not at all) to 7 (many times).
3. Ratings of personal importance could range from 1 (not at all important) to 7 (very important).

Ratings of personal importance did not correlate significantly with ratings of vividness for any of the recalled events; averaging across the three events, $r = .18$, p = n.s. Ratings of frequency of reminiscence were correlated with ratings of vividness for each event, $ps < .01$; averaging across the three events, $r = .47$. However, the impact of gender on vividness of recall remained strong when ratings of frequency of reminiscence were entered into the analyses as a covariate. Thus, we suspect that these two variables do not fully explain the vividness effect. Our conclusions remain tentative, however, because the reliability and validity of our measures of importance and frequency of reminiscence are unknown.

A second possible explanation for the vividness effect can be dismissed with greater confidence. The males in our sample were somewhat older than the females (see Table 19-1). Conceivably, vividness of recall decreases with age. The effect of gender on vividness did not decline in strength, though, when age of subject was entered as a covariate in the analyses. Evidently, age does not account for the gender difference in vividness.

A third and more interesting possibility is that women may be relationship experts (Parsons & Bales, 1955). Experts in domains such as chess, physics, and soccer possess detailed cognitive schemata that facilitate fast, accurate judgments and superior memory in their area of expertise (Charness, 1988; Morris, 1988). Similarly, women may develop a more articulated and complex understanding of relationships than do men. Observations that can be related to such a well-differentiated memory structure are more likely to be recalled.

Conceivably women become relationship experts as a result of culturally mediated gender differences in social roles and power. In our culture, women have been traditionally assigned to the roles of caring for the family and social functions (Kidder, Fagan, & Cohn, 1981). The degree of task specialization should not be exaggerated. Couples share responsibilities in many areas (Aronoff & Crano, 1975; Davis, 1976) and there is no doubt a good deal of variability across families. Nonetheless, women may be socialized to accept somewhat more responsibility for social and family activities, and thus develop a greater degree of expertise in the interpersonal domain. In addition, women have tended to be the less powerful member of the marital relationship, in both physical and economic terms (Frieze, Parsons, Johnson, Ruble, & Zellman, 1978; Turner, 1970). It is important for less powerful members of a relationship to become knowledgeable about their partner's feelings and behaviors (Thibaut & Kelley, 1959; Turner, 1970). They must learn how to influence and not to offend their high power partner.

We have suggested that women possess more vivid memories of events in a relationship because of culturally mediated sex differences in roles and power. Another possibility must be addressed. Perhaps women simply have better memories than men. The evidence does not seem to support this interpretation. Maccoby and Jacklin's (1974) review indicates that traditional tests of memory have generally failed to show systematic sex differences.

The possibility that women possess superior memories cannot be totally discounted, however. The Maccoby and Jacklin review suggested that verbal memory may be better in females than in males. Furthermore, the research summarized by Maccoby and Jacklin was conducted primarily with children.

Evidence from the adult memory literature is sparse. Tests for sex differences are typically not reported in published studies of memory. We recently examined the journal entitled *Memory and Cognition*. Many researchers simply noted that their subjects were undergraduates; the researchers failed to indicate the ratio of males to females in their sample. Not a single study of the more than 100 that we scanned reported a significance test for gender. Similarly, Johnson (personal communication) has not tested for sex differences in her research on the vividness of people's memories for perceived and imagined events.

Researchers in the gerontology area have been somewhat more interested in gender differences in accuracy of recall (e.g., Botwinick & Storandt, 1974; Storandt, Grant, & Gordon, 1978). The data are mixed. In one study (Storandt et al., 1978), for example, adult males of all ages remembered historical events more accurately than their female counterparts (e.g., the date of Pearl Harbor and the name of the ship that hit an iceberg and sank on its maiden voyage in 1912). In contrast, there was no gender difference in recall of people or events from the entertainment industry (e.g., the names of the author of *Gone With the Wind* and of the actress who played the wife of Jackie Gleason in the "Honeymooners"). Botwinick and Storandt (1980) attribute the gender difference in recall of historical events to differential encoding. They infer that females probably pay less attention to historical events than do males.

Finally, consider the self-reports of the participants in our study. Spouses were asked to evaluate the accuracy of each other's memory for "details from the past" on the final questionnaire. Both spouses rated the female's memory as superior (Table 19-4). The item was posed as a general memory question; it did not specify memory for interpersonal episodes. Nonetheless, the question was asked in a context in which participants had recently been required to describe and evaluate their memories of interpersonal events. It is likely that spouses' responses to the general memory question were influenced by the vividness of their recall of these target events.

We conclude that a gender effect in vividness of recall probably reflects a difference in process, rather than faculty. Vividness will vary with expertise, interest, rehearsal, and other variables that will sometimes, but not always, be associated with gender. This conclusion remains tentative, however, because of a lack of available data.

It is important to emphasize that the findings that we have reported concern the vividness of recall, rather than its accuracy. We have no basis for concluding that women's memories of the events are more accurate than those of their husbands. Women report a greater tendency to reminisce about the events, but such rehearsal may lead to increased amounts of fabrication, as well as to the preservation of the original information (Johnson, 1988). In addition, past research on flashbulb memories (Neisser, 1982b) and eyewitness testimony (Wells & Loftus, 1984) reveals that it can be a mistake to equate detailed and vivid recall with accuracy.

In everyday life, this caveat may often be ignored. Vivid memories are likely to be accepted as genuine, unless other evidence casts doubt upon them. However, autobiographical memories are typically not open to objective forms of verification. For example, the married couples in our study probably cannot obtain a documentary record of their first date. Consensual verification is more readily available, but we suspect that people rarely seek it. Research on the false consensus effect suggests that individuals commonly assume that their own view of reality would be shared by others (Ross, Greene, & House, 1977). Therefore, people may rarely feel a need to verify their memories. It is evident from transcripts of discussions in the together condition that our experiment was the first occasion on which some of the couples had discussed and become aware of their differing perspectives on the events in question.

Cognitive psychologists who study recall are perhaps more skeptical than most people about the veracity of memory. Yet even they were slow to doubt the validity of highly detailed, flashbulb memories (Neisser, 1982b, 1986). Vivid memories often assume a reality of their own.

▩

FACT OR FICTION?

We began with quotes from Galton's autobiography. In the middle of the chapter we burst into song. It seems fitting to close with the words of a contemporary novelist who specializes in stories of marital relationships. In Updike's (1963) short story entitled *Walter Briggs*, a husband and wife engage in a competitive memory game to enliven a boring car trip. They try to recall a summer, 5 years earlier. The husband observes that his wife "danced ahead, calling into color vast faded tracts of that distant experience. . . . It made him jealous, her store of explicit memories. . . . Their past was so much more vivid to her presumably because it was more precious" (pp. 15–16).

REFERENCES

Aronoff, J., & Crano, W. D. (1975). A re-examination of the cross-cultural princi-ples of task segregation and sex role differentiation in the family. *American Sociological Review, 40,* 12–20.

Bem, S. L., & Bem, D. J. (1970). Case study of a non-conscious ideology: Training the woman to know her place. In D. J. Bem (Ed.), *Beliefs, attitudes, and hu-man affairs.* Monterey, CA: Brooks/Cole, 80–99.

Botwinick, J., & Storandt, M. (1974). *Memory related functions and age.* Spring-field, IL: C. Thomas.

Botwinick, J., & Storandt, M. (1980). Recall and recognition of old information in relation to age and sex. *Journal of Gerontology, 35,* 70–76.

Charness, N. (1988). Expertise in chess, music and physics: A cognitive perspec-tive. In L. Obler & D. Fein (Eds.), *The exceptional brain.* New York: Guilford Press, 399–426.

Davis, H. L. (1976). Decision making within the household. *Journal of Consumer Research, 2,* 241–260.

Deaux, K. (1976). *The behavior of women and men.* Monterey, CA: Brooks/Cole.

Feldman–Summers, S., & Kiesler, S. (1974). Those who are number two try harder: The effects of sex on attributions of causality. *Journal of Personality and Social Psychology, 30,* 846–855.

Frieze, I. H., Parsons, J. E., Johnson, P. B., Ruble, D. N., & Zellman, G. L. (1978). *Women and sex roles: A social psychological perspective.* New York: Norton.

Galton, F. (1974). *Memories of my life.* New York: A.M.S. (Original work published 1908)

Johnson, M. K. (1988). Reality monitoring: An experimental phenomenological approach. *Journal of Experimental Psychology: General, 117,* 390–394.

Johnson, M. K., Foley, M. A., Suengas, A. G., & Raye, C. L. (1988). Phenomenal characteristics of memories for perceived and imagined autobiographical events. *Journal of Experimental Psychology: General, 117,* 371–376.

Kidder, L. H., Fagan, M. A., & Cohn, E. S. (1981). Giving and receiving: Social jus-tice in close relationships. In M. J. Lerner & S. C. Lerner (Eds.), *The justice motive in social behavior.* New York: Plenum, 235–256.

Maccoby, E. E., & Jacklin, C. N. (1974). *The psychology of sex differences.* Stanford, CA: Stanford University Press.

Morris, P. (1988). Expertise and everyday memory. In M. M. Gruneberg, P. M. Morris, & R. N. Sykes (Eds.), *Practical aspects of memory: Current research and issues, 1,* 459–465.

Neisser, U. (1982b). Snapshots or benchmarks? In U. Neisser (Ed.), *Memory ob-served.* San Francisco: Freeman, 43–48.

Neisser, U. (1986). Remembering Pearl Harbor: Reply to Thompson and Cowan. *Cognition, 23,* 285–286.

Parsons, T., & Bales, R. F. (1955). *Family, socialization and interaction process.* Glencoe, IL: Free Press.

Ross, L., Greene, D., & House, P. (1977). The "false consensus effect": An egocen-tric bias in social perception and attribution processes. *Journal of Experimen-tal Social Psychology, 13,* 279–301.

Storandt, M., Grant, E. A., & Gordon, B. C. (1978). Remote memory as a function of age and sex. *Experimental Aging Research, 4,* 365–375.

Suengas, A. G., & Johnson, M. K. (1988). Qualitative effects of rehearsal on memories for perceived and imagined complex events. *Journal of Experimental Psychology, General, 117,* 377–389.

Thibaut, J. W., & Kelley, H. H. (1959). *The social psychology of groups.* New York: Wiley.

Turner, R. H. (1970). *Family interaction.* New York: Wiley.

Updike, J. (1963). *Pigeon feathers and other stories.* New York: Ballantine Books.

Wegner, D. M. (1986). Transactive memory. In B. Mullen & G. R. Goethals (Eds.), *General theories of group behavior.* New York: Springer-Verlag, 185–208.

Wells, G. L., & Loftus, E. F. (1984). *Eyewitness testimony.* Cambridge, England: Cambridge University Press.

Part IV

Under Oath

For nearly a century, experiments using what seem to be "realistic" methods have found that eyewitness testimony is unreliable and that children's recall is vulnerable to suggestion. Courts should not rely on this kind of testimony except when it is absolutely necessary, which of course it usually is. A few studies, like that of Yuille and Cutshall, do paint a more positive picture. And even a witness with fairly poor memory for individual episodes, like John Dean of Watergate fame, may still manage to tell the truth about what matters.

20 | Realistic Experiments

William Stern

There have been many experimental demonstrations of the unreliability of testimony; this paper was among the earliest. The author, William Stern, was a notable German developmental psychologist. (It was he who suggested that a child's "mental age," as established by Binet-type intelligence tests, could be divided by chronological age to obtain a fixed quotient, the IQ.) Around the turn of the century, Stern became convinced that psychological research on memory had important implications for legal procedure. He founded a journal, Contributions to the Psychology of Testimony, *devoted entirely to this possibility. The present study is from Volume 2 of that journal. By modern standards, Stern's analysis of the data leaves much to be desired. There are no tests of null hypotheses, and the percentages of error on which he lays so much stress are rather arbitrary; they depend on the specific questions asked and on the method of scoring. We can be equally critical of some of his interpretations, which he delivers with the assertiveness characteristic of professors in 1904. Still, his basic claims about the unreliability of testimony have stood the test of time.*

Two principal procedures have been developed for the psychological study of testimony: the picture method and the realistic method. In the former case the testimony deals with a pictorial representation, while in the latter it is some object or event of real life. In previously published research I have used pictures; here I report two experiments based on the "realistic" procedure. The first deals with testimony about a real place, the other with an actual event. In both cases I hoped to study impressions that had been

From W. Stern (1904). Wirklichkeitsversuche, *Beitrage zur Psychologie der Aussage, 2*(1), 1–31. Translation by Ulric Neisser.

formed under conditions of less than maximal attention. Almost all previous research has been based on cases of sharply focused attention; it seemed appropriate to raise the practically significant question of the quality and quantity of reports of less attentively observed experiences.

The experiments were conducted during seminars in psychology; the subjects were students and teachers in training. Analysis of the data and discussion of the results were also carried out, in part, in a psychology course.

. . .

[*Stern's account of his first experiment is omitted here. In that experiment, 24 students were asked various questions about a classroom where they had heard a lecture eight days before: how many windows there were, if there was a second exit, the details of the (architecturally interesting) ceiling, etc. After the subjects had written their replies, they were asked to underline those which they would be willing to swear to in court. About 20 percent of the answers were incorrect; even the "sworn" answers were wrong 7 percent of the time. (It is hard to know what to make of these percentages, given the varied nature of the questions.) Some people were much more accurate than others. Students who had been in the lecture room repeatedly were more accurate than those who had been only once, but even they were not perfect. Law students were less accurate than those of other colleges, but Stern does not think this result should be too hastily generalized!*]

EXPERIMENT II

The friendly help of Mr. Lipmann (a graduate student) made it possible to stage a small "event" at the first meeting of my psychology course in the winter term 1903–1904. This experiment, like the preceding one, was intended to elicit testimony about facts that had not been closely attended to. For this reason we selected a rather banal event; one that was not noteworthy in its own right but only because it created a small interruption of an ongoing seminar. Lipmann (the target person, designated *T*) entered, asked to speak to me, handed me a large envelope, asked for permission to examine the books in the bookcase, perused one for about five minutes, and took it with him; as he was leaving, I asked him to wait outside for me until the end of the seminar. A detailed scenario of the event appears in Table 20-1. Every action and every word had been carefully rehearsed, and the words I was to speak were written out on a small card, placed where the students could not see it. The entire event took place exactly according to plan, at least as far as we (*T* and myself) were able to judge.

Figure 20-1 illustrates the situation. My position is marked "Stern"; the positions of the students are indicated by letters of the alphabet, the women with an asterisk. It can be seen that there were six women (mostly teachers) and nine graduate students. [*Throughout the paper, Stern distinguishes between the "students"—males, candidates for the Ph.D.—and the "teachers"—all women—in his seminar. He uses the term "listeners" for the full set, which indicates something of the ambience of a turn-of-the-century German seminar.*]

T entered the room as I was in the middle of a lecture, which I interrupted only long enough to accept the manuscript. I continued to lecture during his presence. As he left, I interrupted myself to say, "Please wait for me outside; I have something to tell you." Thus, the participants in the seminar were given no reason to attend to the detailed course of the event; at most they may have experienced the slight interruption as a nuisance. None suspected that the event had been staged. When I opened the second meeting of the seminar (eight days later) by asking the participants to report the entire event as best they could, the reaction was one of complete astonishment.

As in my earlier experiments with schoolchildren, the required testimony consisted of two parts: a "report" and an "interrogation." The subjects first wrote out an overall report of the event. Then they were asked to "swear" to part or all of their account as follows: "Please underline those parts of your report which you would be willing to swear to, under oath, if you were testifying in court." I then asked them 24 specific questions; each question had to be answered in writing unless the answer had already been included in the report. The questions are listed in Table 20-1 together with the correct answers; 41 specific points altogether. The 24

(*text continues on page 206*)

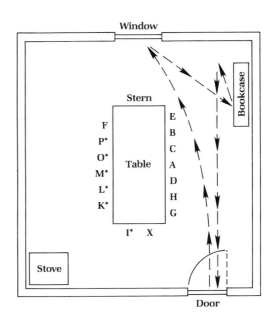

Figure 20-1 *Sketch of the situation. Letters denote the students in the seminar; females are marked with an asterisk (*). T's route is indicated by → → →.*

TABLE 20-1
A protocol from the event experiment

Questions on the interrogation Correct answers (points scorable)	Initial Report	Responses of subject K., a teacher Sworn testimony in *italics* (points awarded)
		Interrogation
I. Time and Duration		
1. When did T come in? At 7:30.	About quarter of eight	—
2. How long did he stay? 5 minutes.	—	2 or 3 minutes
II. Description of T		
3. Describe T's body build Small (1).	*smaller than average* (+1)	—
4. Color of hair? Brown (1).	—	Brown (+1)
5. Had he a beard or moustache? Yes (1).	—	No (−1)
6. Describe it Moustache (1) and Pointed beard (1).	—	—
7. His approximate age? 23 years old.	—	Early twenties
8. A special identifying feature? Hair flecked with white (1).	—	don't know (?)

9. How was he dressed? Grey jacket, buttoned (3); Brown gloves (2); Soft brown hat (3).	Brown overcoat (−2); Round black hard hat (−2, +1)	—
10. Describe his voice Soft, slightly hoarse (1); High rather than low (1).	—	Strong and rather deep voice (−2)

III. The Sequence of Events

11. Did T have anything in his hand when he came in? Yes (1).	Yes (+1)	—
12. What was it? A large envelope (1) and the hat (1).	His hat (see #9)	—
13. What did T say as he entered? "Excuse me" (1). "Could I speak to you for a moment, sir?" (1).	He begged Stern's pardon for the interruption (+1, −1)	—
14. What did Stern reply? To T: "Please come here" (1). To the class: "Excuse me a moment" (1).		don't know (?)
15. Did Stern get up or remain seated? He stood up (1).		Remained seated (−1)
16. What did the two of them do next? Both went over to the alcove by the window (1); T gave Stern the envelope (1), saying "I just wanted to bring you the manuscript" (1).		Stern did not permit any further interruption (−1).

(continued)

TABLE 20-1
(Continued)

Questions on the interrogation Correct answers (points scorable)	Responses of subject *K.*, a teacher Sworn testimony in *italics* (points awarded)
III. The Sequence of Events	
17. What did Stern do with the envelope *T* had given him? He tried vainly to put it into his jacket pocket (1) and then laid it on the window sill (1).	*T* did not give him an envelope (−1).
18. What did *T* do next? *T* asked permission to look at a book (1); took one from the bookcase (1); he then stood by the bookcase (1) reading in the book (1).	*(As soon as he entered T went quickly to the bookcase* (−1, +1)*; after a brief search he took out a book* (+1)*; then he made his way out just as fast* (−1)*.*
19. What happened to the book? *T* took it with him (1).	*T* took it with him (+1).

		Report	Interrogation
20. Did T have anything in his hand as he left? The book and his hat (1).		—	The book and the hat (+1)
21. What did T say as he left? "Thank you sir" (1). "I beg your pardon if I've disturbed you. Goodbye" (1).		—	Nothing (−1)
22. What did Stern say to T as he was leaving? "Please wait for me outside" (1); "I have something to tell you" (1).		"Please wait for me outside" (+1).	—
23. Did T wait outside? No (1).		—	I didn't see him (+1)
24. Where did he wait?		—	—
Total possible score: 41		Report: +7, including +4 sworn; −7, including −2 sworn.	Interrogation: +4, −7, ?2; none sworn.

questions covered all the essential features of the event: questions 1 and 2 dealt with its time and duration, 3–10 concerned the description of *T*, and 11–24 referred to the course of the event itself.

The analysis of the data proceeded as follows. Each subject's responses were arranged into a protocol like that illustrated in Table 20-1. The subject's initial report was first scanned for information bearing on each question (first column at right); then his responses to the specific questions were added (second column at right). Table 20-1 shows these entries for the subject (*K.*) with the poorest performance. (Responses that the subject was willing to answer to are underlined.) The protocols were scored by marking each correct response +1, each false response −1, and each "don't know" with a question mark. Questions 1, 2, and 7 were excluded from this tally since they required a different method of analysis (see below). The protocols were then evaluated in the seminar itself, with each student scoring another student's testimony. Naturally this practice analysis could not be used, and a reanalysis was conducted by a single student, Mr. Zenker. The data presented here are based on my own careful rechecking and partial recalculation of his results.

Results

The numerical results appear in Table 20-2, which gives individual scores as well as means for graduate students, teachers, and the group as a whole. The table shows the absolute numbers of correct, incorrect, and indeterminate responses for each subject, separately for initial reports and interrogations as well as a combined score. These figures have also been converted into accuracy percentages: number correct divided by the sum of correct plus incorrect. "Error percentages" may be obtained by subtracting the given entries from 100.

Testimony can be evaluated in terms of two principal criteria: the amount of recall and its accuracy. Table 20-2 shows that the average amount, in terms of the absolute number of correct responses, is far from negligible. The mean of 13.4 per subject is quite substantial, considering the minimal degree of participation and attention that had been devoted to the event, and considering that eight days had elapsed. Accuracy, in contrast, is poor indeed. On the average a full quarter of the statements in the initial reports are false, and about half of the responses to the interrogation! Overall, about one-third of the subjects' assertions are incorrect.

This level of performance is substantially poorer than was obtained in my picture experiments with schoolchildren, and it is much worse than the outcome of a rather similar experiment with workers recently reported by Lipmann.[1] That study also dealt with a relatively banal event occurring

---

[1]Lipmann, O. (1902). Experimentelle Aussagen über einen Vorgang und eine Lokalität. *Beitrage zur Psychologie der Aussage, 1*, 222–231.

TABLE 20-2

Results of the event experiment

Numbers of correct (C), incorrect (I) and indeterminate (?) responses by each subject in both the report and the interrogation. The subset of "sworn" responses is indicated separately.

Subject	Report			Interrogation				Combined Rep. + Interr.			"Sworn" only		
	C	I	%C	C	I	%C	(?)	C	I	%C	C	I	%C
"Students" (male)													
A	7	5	58	4	4	50	(6)	11	9	55	5	2	71
B	11	3	79	3.5	4.5	44	(2)	14.5	7.5	66	11	2	85
C	4	0	100	0.5	2.5	17	(12)	4.5	2.5	64	4	0	100
D	7	0	100	3	3	50	(5)	10	3	77	7	0	100
E	9	2.5	78	5.5	3	65	(3)	14.5	5.5	73	6	0	100
F	13	1.5	90	3	4	43	(5)	16	5.5	74	11	1	92
G	7	1	88	7.5	0	100	(4)	14.5	1	94	7	1	88
H	9	2.5	78	2.5	3	45	(3)	11.5	5.5	68	9	2.5	78
X	14	5	74	5	3	63	(4)	19	8	70	9	0	100
Mean (males)	9	2.3	80	3.8	3	56	(4.9)	12.8	5.3	71	7.7	0.9	90
"Teachers" (females)													
I	12.5	4	76	3	3	50	(5)	15.5	7	69	8	3	73
K	7	7	50	4	7	36	(2)	11	14	44	4	2	67
L	14.5	3	83	0	5	0	(5)	14.5	8	64	10	2	83
M	8	3	73	3.5	2.5	58	(5)	11.5	5.5	68	5	2	71
O	9	1	90	8	4	67	(6)	17	5	77	6	0	100
P	12.5	3	81	3	5	38	(5)	15.5	8	66	9.5	1	90
Mean (females)	10.6	3.5	75	3.6	4.4	45	(4.7)	14.2	7.9	64	7.1	1.7	81
Grand mean	9.6	2.8	77	3.7	3.6	51	(4.8)	13.4	6.3	68	7.4	1.2	86

during an instructional hour, and with an inquiry taking place several days later. The error percentages in Lipmann's experiment—10 percent in the initial report, 19 percent in the interrogation, 16 percent overall—were only half of those reported here. I would regard it as a mistake to conclude that the memories of uneducated subjects are better than those of educated ones. It is clear that the witnesses of Lipmann's event paid much closer attention than those in the present study; moreover, his inquiry occurred half a week after the event while ours was eight days later. Finally, Lipmann had no female subjects; those in our experiment lowered the average performance.

Nevertheless, our data lead to a conclusion that it is not unimportant. *The consequence of inadequate attention to an event is not that testimony becomes very brief, but that it becomes very prone to error.* This suggests a general principle: as conditions become more difficult, it is not so much the quantity as the quality of performance that decreases. Similar results have been obtained in experimental studies of fatigue. For a wide range of mental processes, fatigue produces a degradation of performance far in excess of any reduction in the total amount. This is a point at which the psychology of memory has important educational implications. One must struggle against the tendency to maintain a constant amount of poorer and poorer output; the cult of quantity must be replaced by a higher respect for quality.

In agreement with many other studies of testimony, we found a much higher error rate (by a factor of two) in the interrogations than in the initial reports. In the present case there were an equal number of right and wrong answers, so the responses to the interrogation have no credibility at all.

[*Omitted here are two pages of discussion of sex differences in accuracy. We have already seen Stern casually dismiss data that seem to show that law students (in the first experiment) have especially poor memories or that uneducated people are better witnesses than educated ones (in the comparison with Lipmann's experiment, above). Unfortunately, his treatment of data on sex differences shows no such restraint. He notes that his female subjects made more errors than the men even though they were better situated to see most of T's movements; that the most reliable witness was a man and the least reliable a woman; that the single nearsighted male subject D. gave relatively few responses while the nearsighted female subject K. made many errors but used her nearsightedness as an excuse. Stern seems to take considerable satisfaction in this "scientific" demonstration that women are fundamentally unreliable. Of course the data prove no such thing; apart from the different populations involved and the statistical difficulty of concluding anything from such small and variable samples, there are obvious differences in the social situations of men and women both in his seminar and during his interrogation.*]

...

The content of the testimony is remarkably varied. For the sake of clarity, we will deal separately with the actual event and with the description of *T*, the target person.

The Event

The event consisted of two main parts: *T*'s delivery of the manuscript to me and his subsequent activity at the bookcase. To show how very differently these stages were understood by the subjects, consider the three following reports (from which descriptions of *T* have been omitted). The first of these is the best report, overall, obtained from any subject; the others are less good.

G., a Ph.D. candidate, reported:

It happened on Monday, November 9, while Dr. Stern was having a seminar with his group in the Psychology Seminar Room, Schmiedebrucke 35. A young man unexpectedly entered the room, went up to Dr. Stern, and asked whether he might look something up in one of the volumes in the bookcase. Dr. Stern naturally granted this request. The man (whom I believe I have never seen before, by the way) left the room again after staying for a total of about three minutes. Dr. Stern called after him just as he was leaving, asking him to wait in the anteroom until the end of the seminar. I would estimate that it was around 7:00 or 7:15 in the evening as he left the room.

In the interrogation G. added the following:

Stern stood up. . . . T handed Stern a letter . . . stood for a little while, reading in the book he had taken from the bookcase. . . . He took the book with him. . . . He thanked Stern for allowing him to look at the book.

C., a doctor of political science, reported:

On Monday, November 9, during Dr. Stern's class, a gentleman entered the Psychology Seminar Room and wished to speak to Dr. Stern. Dr. Stern, although reluctant to interrupt the seminar, did get up and went briefly over to the window with the man who had come in. Then he told him to wait outside. The time was roughly between 7:30 and 7:45.

During his interrogation, C. added these statements:

The whole event took one minute. . . . When Lipmann expressed his wish to speak with Stern, the latter said something to indicate that he regretted the interruption.

L., a teacher, reported:

A gentleman appeared during the lecture, apologizing to Dr. Stern for the interruption that his entrance had created. In addition, he asked whether he might take a book from the library and look something up. Dr. Stern replied, "Please do, and wait outside for me; I have something else to tell you." The man then took one or two volumes from the bookcase and looked into them as he stood there. Then he took his leave and went out of the room. He was in the room for about seven minutes; it was during the second half of the lecture.

During the interrogation, she added that:

Stern remained seated.

When one compares the last two reports, it is hard to believe that they refer to one and the same objective event. All they have in common is that a gentleman entered and exchanged a few words with me, and that I asked him to wait outside for me afterwards. In all other respects they are totally discrepant. According to *C.*, the core of the event was a conversation that *T* and I held by the window; in *L.*'s account everything revolves around his taking out and reading a book, for which I gave him permission without getting up. *C.* reports that I was reluctant to be interrupted and said so explicitly; *L.* noticed nothing of this. The event lasted one minute for *C.*, seven minutes for *L. C.* knows nothing about the book, *L.* knows nothing about the conversation by the window. Finally *L.* is confused about the chronological sequence of events, in that she places my request (that *T* wait outside) near the beginning of the conversation instead of at the end.

C. was the only subject who knew nothing of *T*'s activity at the bookcase. Everyone else mentioned this part of the episode, even in their original reports. The results with respect to the earlier part of the episode are quite different, however. A majority of the initial reports (11 of 15) suggest that *T* asked and received permission to go to the bookcase as soon as he came in; three reports mention that *T* and I held a brief conversation between his first entrance and his taking out the book; only one witness (*J.*, a teacher) mentioned that he gave me a manuscript. The interrogation helped several subjects to recall additional material. *G.*, for example, had failed to mention the envelope affair in his report (see above); the question "What took place between the two of them?" reminded him of it and he corrected his previous testimony. Four of the other male subjects did not recall this episode until question 17, which explicitly mentions the envelope and asks what became of it. Among the women, oddly enough, the interrogation never rectified the omission of this episode in their original reports. One female subject even insisted, in her response to question 17, that "*T* gave no envelope." Thus, the women perform badly in this important respect. Five out of six (83 percent) know nothing of the envelope episode, as compared with four out of nine male subjects (44 percent). Here also we see an effect of lack of attention (or of attention directed elsewhere) whose importance is often underestimated. It is an effect I have pointed out before, one "through which other impressions, although fully present to the senses, can slide by without making the slightest impression on consciousness."

It is important to realize that of the few subjects who knew anything at all about the envelope, three (two men and one woman) maintained that I had put it into my pocket; two other men said I had placed it on the windowsill. Moreover, a third of the males and two-thirds of the females believe I remained seated throughout the entire episode! In short, the testimony about the first phase of the event constituted such a chaotic array of conflicting accounts that it would have been quite impossible for an investigator who had to rely on it to establish the actual facts.

In the second phase of the event, *T* took a book from the bookcase and looked into it. With the exception of a single subject, the witnesses' accounts of these activities were rather consistent. However, their agreement did not extend to his next action, when he left the room and took the book with him. We had deliberately incorporated this action in the scenario in order to present the witnesses with a bit of questionable behavior. Every student is familiar with the strict rule against removing books from the seminar-room shelves, and a notice to that effect is posted on the bookcase itself. Only one subject spontaneously mentioned this "criminal" act in his report, and in his version *T* had asked my permission first! In response to question 19 of the interrogation ("What happened to the book?"), three of the remaining witnesses said they did not know and seven indicated that *T* had put it back in the bookcase. Only four subjects (including one woman) said he had taken it with him.

These results are similar to those obtained by Lipmann in the study mentioned earlier. His experiment also included the unauthorized removal of a book. The question "What happened to the book?" [*Actually, the question was "Did she take anything from the lectern?"*] produced two "don't knows," three wrong answers, and no correct reports. [*There were five subjects.*]

In the present experiment, then, seven accounts indicated that *T* had put the book back in the bookcase—an event that never occurred at all. Indeed, no trace of such a thing had happened; *T* did not even begin to replace the book. These confident answers were given only because the return of the book was taken for granted; it *must* have happened.

We had intended to convey a similarly effective suggestion in the last part of the event, but our procedure was too crude to be very effective. All the subjects heard and reported my parting comment to *T*, asking him to wait outside for me. Only subject X., however, testified that T had actually waited. The others said that they didn't know or hadn't noticed, that T would have had to wait for this or that amount of time, etc. Even X., who did say that he had waited, was unable to say where. Nevertheless even this single case shows how "He was supposed to wait," "He probably waited," and "He did wait" can become interchangeable under certain circumstances.

The Description of T

The typical difference between the sexes, which had appeared in testimony about the event, was not apparent in the descriptions of the target person.

T's height was usually reported correctly as "average." His body build was occasionally described as "slender" although he is in fact somewhat stocky. Similarly, estimates of his age were fairly accurate. Since these data were not included in the overall totals, we present them here. The overall mean of the estimates was 25.4 years; he was actually 23. The men's estimates were further off than the women's: 25.7 versus 24.8. Three estimates were correct; there was only one underestimate (21); the highest estimate, which occurred twice, was 30.

With respect to all other features of T's appearance, the inaccuracy of the testimony is frightening. The greatest number of mistakes occurred in reports of color. His brown hair was described three times as "black," once as "dark blond," and once as "blond" (mostly by men). His gray jacket was called "blue" twice and "brown" four times; his brown hat was termed "black" by one man and three women. These errors take on added significance because the *true* colors of his suit and hat were never mentioned by anyone. The six incorrect reports of the jacket's color are counterbalanced only by five reports that it was "dark." These were counted as correct, but they provide information only about the achromatic lightness of the jacket and not about its actual hue. The hat was always called "black" whenever its appearance was mentioned at all. It must not be supposed that the hat (which T carried in his hand) was of a particularly dark brown that might easily be confused with black; on the contrary, it was of a distinct coffee color.

Accounts of T's face and voice also exhibited numerous errors. In fact, he had a moustache and a small pointed beard. Nevertheless, three descriptions credit him with a full beard and two others with a moustache alone, while two female subjects described him as clean-shaven. His voice is soft, slightly muffled, and relatively high in pitch. The five-and-a-half correct descriptions of it contrast with five-and-a-half others that were wrong. According to the incorrect reports his voice was deep and relatively loud; a pleasant baritone.

Finally, several isolated oddities are worth mentioning. One male and one female subject described *T* as wearing spectacles, although he does not do so and never has. Both of them mentioned the spectacles in their spontaneous reports, and the female subject was willing to swear to their existence. In addition, one subject mentioned a nonexistent cap, and another a brown overcoat.

These points are enough to show how remarkably inaccurate and uncritical the memory of a person's appearance can be. Sometimes the errors of testimony cumulate into a complete confabulation. The description given by subject *K.* (see Table 20-1) is one example of this. For another, consider this description given by *X.*: "round black hat; dark or black shoes; reversed collar." In fact the hat was brown, the shoes red, and the collar completely concealed by the closed jacket.

Descriptions of individuals play an extremely important part in the testimony of witnesses. With respect to such testimony, the outcome of the present experiment leads to a clear conclusion. *Retrospective accounts of people's appearance, especially about hair color, beardedness, and color of clothing, should be given no credit whatsoever unless special attention was directed to these features during observation itself.*

21 | Eyewitness Testimony

Robert Buckhout

Eyewitnesses may be mistaken for many reasons, not all of which involve faulty memory. Here is an overview of some common sources of error.

The woman in the witness box stares at the defendant, points an accusing finger and says, loudly and firmly, "That's the man! That's him! I could never forget his face!" It is impressive testimony. The only eyewitness to a murder has identified the murderer. Or has she?

Perhaps she has, but she may be wrong. Eyewitness testimony is unreliable. Research and courtroom experience provide ample evidence that an eyewitness to a crime is being asked to be something and do something that a normal human being was not created to be or do. Human perception is sloppy and uneven, albeit remarkably effective in serving our need to create structure out of experience. In an investigation or in court, however, a witness is often asked to play the role of a kind of tape recorder on whose tape the events of the crime have left an impression. The prosecution probes for stored facts and scenes and tries to establish that the witness's recording equipment was and still is in perfect running order. The defense cross-examines the witness to show that there are defects in the recorder and gaps in the tape. Both sides, and usually the witness too, succumb to the fallacy that everything was recorded and can be played back later through questioning.

Those of us who have done research in eyewitness identification reject that fallacy. It reflects a nineteenth-century view of man as perceiver, which asserted a parallel between the mechanisms of the physical world and those of the brain. Human perception is a more complex information-processing mechanism. So is memory. The person who sees an accident or witnesses a crime and is then asked to describe what he saw cannot call up an "instant replay." He must depend on his memory, with all its limita-

From *Scientific American*, 1974, *231* (6), 23–31.

tions. The limitations may be unimportant in ordinary daily activities. If someone is a little unreliable, if he trims the truth a bit in describing what he has seen, it ordinarily does not matter too much. When he is a witness, the inaccuracy escalates in importance.

Human perception and memory function effectively by being selective and constructive. As Ulric Neisser of Cornell University has pointed out, "Neither perception nor memory is a copying process." Perception and memory are decision-making processes affected by the totality of a person's abilities, background, attitudes, motives and beliefs, by the environment and by the way his recollection is eventually tested. The observer is an active rather than a passive perceiver and recorder; he reaches conclusions on what he has seen by evaluating fragments of information and reconstructing them. He is motivated by a desire to be accurate as he imposes meaning on the overabundance of information that impinges on his senses, but also by a desire to live up to the expectations of other people and to stay in their good graces. The eye, the ear, and other sense organs are therefore social organs as well as physical ones.

Psychologists studying the capabilities of the sense organs speak of an "ideal observer," one who would respond to lights or tones with unbiased eyes and ears, but we know that the ideal observer does not exist. We speak of an "ideal physical environment," free of distractions and distortions, but we know that such an environment can only be approached, and then only in the laboratory. My colleagues and I at the Brooklyn College of the City University of New York distinguish a number of factors that we believe inherently limit a person's ability to give a complete account of events he once saw or to identify with complete accuracy the people who were involved.

The first sources of unreliability are implicit in the original situation. One is the insignificance—at the time and to the witness—of the events that were observed. In placing someone at or near the scene of a crime, for example, witnesses are often being asked to recall seeing the accused at a time when they were not attaching importance to the event, which was observed in passing, as a part of the normal routine of an ordinary day. As long ago as 1895, J. McKeen Cattell wrote about an experiment in which he asked students to describe the people, places, and events they had encountered walking to school over familiar paths. The reports were incomplete and unreliable; some individuals were very sure of details that had no basis in fact. Insignificant events do not motivate a person to bring fully into play the selective process of attention.

The length of the period of observation obviously limits the number of features a person can attend to. When the tachistoscope, a projector with a variable-speed shutter that controls the length of an image's appearance on a screen, is used in controlled research to test recall, the shorter times produce less reliable identification and recall. Yet fleeting glimpses are common in eyewitness accounts, particularly in fast-moving, threatening situations. In the Sacco–Vanzetti case in the 1920s a witness gave a detailed description of one defendant on the basis of a fraction-of-a-second glance. The description must have been a fabrication.

Less than ideal observation conditions usually apply; crimes seldom occur in a well-controlled laboratory. Often distance, poor lighting, fast movement or the presence of a crowd interferes with the efficient working of the attention process. Well-established thresholds for the eye and the other senses have been established by research, and as those limits are approached eyewitness accounts become quite unreliable. In one case in my experience a police officer testified that he saw the defendant, a black man, shoot a victim as both stood in a doorway 120 feet away. Checking for the defense, we found the scene so poorly lit that we could hardly see a person's silhouette, let alone a face; instrument measurements revealed that the light falling on the eye amounted to less than a fifth of the light from a candle. The defense presented photographs and light readings to demonstrate that a positive identification was not very probable. The members of the jury went to the scene of the crime, had the one black juror stand in the doorway, found they could not identify his features and acquitted the defendant.

The witness himself is a major source of unreliability. To begin with, he may have been observing under stress. When a person's life or well-being is threatened, there is a response that includes an increased heart rate, breathing rate, and blood pressure and a dramatic increase in the flow of adrenalin and of available energy, making the person capable of running fast, fighting, lifting enormous weight—taking the steps necessary to ensure his safety or survival. The point is, however, that a person under extreme stress is also a less than normally reliable witness. In experimental situations an observer is less capable of remembering details, less accurate in reading dials, and less accurate in detecting signals when under stress; he is quite naturally paying more attention to his own well-being and safety than to nonessential elements in the environment. Research I have done with Air Force flight-crew members confirms that even highly trained people become poorer observers under stress. The actual threat that brought on the stress response, having been highly significant at the time, can be remembered; but memory for other details such as clothing and colors is not as clear; time estimates are particularly exaggerated.

The observer's physical condition is often a factor. A person may be too old or too sick or too tired to perceive clearly, or he may simply lack the necessary faculty. In one case I learned that a witness who had testified about shades of red had admitted to the grand jury that he was color-blind. I testified at the trial that he was apparently dichromatic, or red-green color-blind, and that his testimony was probably fabricated on the basis of information other than visual evidence. The prosecution brought on his ophthalmologist, presumably as a rebuttal witness; but the ophthalmologist testified that the witness was actually monochromatic, which meant he could perceive no colors at all. Clearly the witness was "filling in" his testimony. That, after all, is how color-blind people function in daily life, by making inferences about colors they cannot distinguish.

...

The tendency to see what we want or need to see has been demonstrated by numerous experiments in which people report seeing things that in fact are not present. R. Levine, Isador Chein, and Gardner Murphy had volunteers go without food for 24 hours and report what they "saw" in a series of blurred slides presented on a screen. The longer they were deprived of food the more frequently they reported seeing "food" in the blurred pictures. An analysis of the motives of the eyewitness at the time of a crime can be very valuable in determining whether or not the witness is reporting what he wanted to see. In one study I conducted at Washington University, a student dressed in a black bag that covered him completely visited a number of classes. Later the students in those classes were asked to describe the nature of the person in the bag. Most of their reports went far beyond the meager evidence: the bag-covered figure was said to be a black man, "a nut," a symbol of alienation, and so on. Further tests showed that the descriptions were related to the needs and motives of the individual witness.

Journalists and psychologists have noted a tendency for people to maintain they were present when a significant historical event took place near where they live even though they were not there at all; such people want to sound interesting, to be a small part of history. A journalist once fabricated a . . . story about a naked woman stuck to a newly painted toilet seat in a small town and got it distributed by newspaper wire services. He visited the town and interviewed citizens who claimed to have witnessed and even to have played a part in the totally fictitious event. In criminal cases with publicity and a controversial defendant, it is not uncommon for volunteer witnesses to come forward with spurious testimony.

Unreliability stemming from the original situation and from the observer's fallibility is redoubled by the circumstances attending the eventual attempt at information retrieval. First of all there is the obvious fact, supported by a considerable amount of research, that people forget verbal and pictorial information with the passage of time. They are simply too busy coping with daily life to keep paying attention to what they heard or saw; perfect recall of information is basically unnecessary and is rarely if ever displayed. The testing of recognition in a police "lineup" or a set of identification photographs is consequently less reliable the longer the time from the event to the test.

...

In analyses of eyewitness reports in criminal cases we have seen the reports get more accurate, more complete, and less ambiguous as the witness moves from the initial police report through grand-jury questioning to testimony at the trial. The process of filling in is an efficient way to remember but it can lead to unreliable recognition testing: the witness may adjust his memory to fit the available suspects or pictures. The witness need not be lying; he may be unaware he is distorting or reconstructing his memory. In his very effort to be conscientious he may fabricate parts of his recall to make a chaotic memory seem more plausible to the people asking questions. The questions themselves may encourage such fabrication. Elizabeth Loftus of the University of Washington has demonstrated how altering the semantic value of the words in questions about a filmed auto accident causes witnesses to distort their reports. When witnesses were asked a question using the word "smashed" as opposed to "hit" they gave higher estimates of speed and were more likely to report having seen broken glass—although there was no broken glass.

Unfair test construction often encourages error. The lineup or the array of photographs for testing the eyewitness's ability to identify a suspect can be analyzed as fair or unfair on the basis of criteria most psychologists can agree on. A fair test is designed carefully so that all faces have an equal chance of being selected by someone who did not see the suspect; the faces are similar enough to one another and to the original description of the suspect to be confusing to a person who is merely guessing; the test is conducted without leading questions or suggestions. All too frequently lineups or photograph arrays are carelessly assembled or even rigged. If, for example, there are five pictures, the chance should be only one in five that any one picture will be chosen on the basis of guessing.

Frequently, however, one picture—the picture of the suspect—may stand out. In the case of the black activist Angela Davis, one set of nine photographs used to check identification included three pictures of the defendant taken at an outdoor rally, two police "mug shots" of other women with their names displayed, a picture of a 55-year-old woman and so on. It was so easy for a witness to rule out five of the pictures as ridiculous choices that the test was reduced to four photographs, including three of Miss Davis. The probability was therefore 75 percent that a witness would pick out her picture whether he had seen her or not. Such a "test" is meaningless to a psychologist and is probably tainted as evidence in court.

Research on memory has also shown that if one item in the array of photographs is uniquely different—say in dress, race, height, sex, or photographic quality—it is more likely to be picked out. Such an array is simply not confusing enough for it to be called a test. A teacher who makes up a multiple-choice test includes several answers that sound or look alike to make it difficult for a person who does not know the right answer to succeed. Police lineups and picture layouts are multiple-choice tests; if the rules for designing tests are ignored, the tests are unreliable.

No test, with photographs or a lineup, can be completely free of suggestion. When a witness is brought in by the police to attempt an identification, he can safely assume that there is some reason: that the authorities have a suspect in mind or even in custody. He is therefore under pressure to pick someone even if the officer showing the photographs is properly careful not to force the issue. The basic books on eyewitness identification all recommend that no suggestions, hints, or pressure be transmitted to the witness, but my experience with criminal investigation reveals frequent abuse by zealous police officers. Such abuses include making remarks about which pictures to skip, saying, "Are you sure?" when the witness makes an error, giving hints, showing enthusiasm when the "right" picture is picked, and so on. There is one version of the lineup in which five police officers in civilian clothes stand in the line, glancing obviously at the real suspect. Suggestion can be subtler. In some experiments the test giver was merely instructed to smile and be very approving when a certain kind of photograph or statement was picked; such social approval led to an increase in the choosing of just those photographs even though there was no "correct" answer. A test that measures a need for social approval has shown that people who are high in that need (particularly those who enthusiastically volunteer information) are particularly strongly influenced by suggestion and approval coming from the test giver.

Conformity is another troublesome influence. One might expect that two eyewitnesses—or 10 or 100—who agree are better than one. Similarity of judgment is a two-edged sword, however: people can agree in error as easily as in truth. A large body of research results demonstrates that an observer can be persuaded to conform to the majority opinion even when the majority is completely wrong. In one celebrated experiment, first performed in the 1950s by Solomon E. Asch at Swarthmore College, seven observers are shown two lines and asked to say which is the shorter. Six of the people are in the pay of the experimenter; they all say that the objectively longer line is the shorter one. After hearing six people say this, the naive subject is on the spot. Astonishingly, the majority of the naive subjects say that the long line is short—in the face of reality and in spite of the fact that alone they would have no trouble giving the correct answer.

To test the effect of conformity a group of my students at Brooklyn College, led by Andrea Alper, staged a "crime" in a classroom, asked for individual descriptions, and then put the witnesses into groups so as to produce composite descriptions of the suspect. The group descriptions were more complete than the individual reports but gave rise to significantly more errors of commission: an assortment of incorrect and stereotyped details. For example, the groups (but not the individuals) reported incorrectly that the suspect was wearing the standard student attire, blue jeans.

The effects of suggestion increase when figures in obvious authority do the testing. In laboratory research we find more suggestibility and changing of attitudes when the tester is older or of apparently higher status, better dressed or wearing a uniform or a white coat—or is a pretty woman. In court I have noticed that witnesses who work together under a supervisor are hard put to disagree with their boss in testifying or in picking a photograph. The process of filling in details can be exaggerated when the boss and his employee compare their information and the employee feels obligated to back up his boss to remain in his good graces. Legal history is not lacking in anecdotes about convict witnesses who were rewarded by the authorities for their cooperation in making an identification.

In criminal investigations, as in scientific investigations, a theory can be a powerful tool for clarifying confusion, but it can also lead to distortion and unreliability if people attempt, perhaps unconsciously, to make fact fit theory and close their minds to the real meanings of facts. The eyewitness who feels pressed to say something may shape his memory to fit a theory, particularly a highly publicized and seemingly reasonable one. Robert Rosenthal of Harvard studied this effect. He devised a test in which people were supposed to pick out a "successful" face from a set of photographs. There was actually no correct answer, but the experimenter dropped hints to his assistants as to what he thought the results should be. When they subsequently administered the tests the assistants unconsciously signaled the subjects as to which photograph to pick, thus producing results that supported their boss's theory. Any test is a social interaction as well as a test.

There is a nagging gap between data on basic perceptual processes in controlled research settings and important questions about perception in the less well-controlled real world. Inspired by the new approach to perception research exemplified in the work of Neisser and of Ralph Norman Haber of the University of Rochester, my colleagues and I have felt that this gap can only be bridged by conducting empirical research on eyewitness identification in a somewhat real world. In one such experiment we staged an assault on the campus of the California State University at Hayward: a student "attacked" a professor in front of 141 witnesses; another outsider of the same age was on the scene as a bystander. We recorded the entire incident on videotape so that we could compare the true event with the eyewitness reports. After the attack we took sworn statements from each witness, asking them to describe the suspect, his clothes, and whatever they could remember about the incident. We also asked each witness to rate his own confidence in the accuracy of his description.

As we expected, the descriptions were quite inaccurate, as is usually the case in such situations. The passage of time was overestimated by a factor of almost two-and-a-half to one. The average weight estimate for the attacker was 14 percent too high, and his age was underestimated by more than two years. The total accuracy score, with points given for those judgments and for others on appearance and dress, was only 25 percent of the maximum possible score. (Only the height estimate was close. This may be because the suspect was of average height; people often cite known facts about the "average" man when they are uncertain.)

We then waited seven weeks and presented a set of six photographs to each witness individually under four different experimental conditions. There were two kinds of instructions: low-bias, in which witnesses were asked only if they recognized anybody in the photographs, and high-bias, in which witnesses were reminded of the attack incident, told that we had an idea who the suspect was, and asked to find the attacker in one of two arrangements of photographs, all well-lit frontal views of young men including the attacker and the bystander. In the unbiased picture spread, all six portraits were neatly set out with about the same expression on all the faces and with similar clothing. In the biased spread the attacker was shown with a distinctive expression and his portrait was positioned at an angle.

Only 40 percent of the witnesses identified the suspect correctly; 25 percent of them identified the innocent bystander instead; even the professor who was attacked picked out the innocent man. The highest proportion of correct identifications, 61 percent, was achieved with a combination of a biased set of photographs and biased instructions. The degree of confidence in picking suspect No. 5, the attacker, was also significantly higher in that condition. We have subsequently tested the same picture spreads with groups that never saw the original incident. We describe the assault and ask people to pick the most likely perpetrator. Under the biased conditions they too pick No. 5.

In another study undertaken at Brooklyn College, a student team, led by Miriam Slomovits, staged a live purse-snatching incident in a classroom. We gave the witnesses the usual questionnaire and got the usual bad scores. This time, however, we were concerned with a specific dilemma: Why is recognition so much better than recall? In private most lawyers and judges agree that the recall of a crime by a witness is very bad, but they still believe people can successfully identify a suspect. What we had to do was to break away from our demonstrations of how bad witnesses are at recalling details and search for what makes a witness good at recognizing a face. To do so we took the witnesses who had predictably given poor recall data and gave them a difficult recognition test. Our witnesses got not only a lineup with the actual purse-snatcher in the group but also a second lineup that included only a person who looked like the purse-snatcher. The question was: Would the witnesses pick only the real culprit and avoid making a mistaken identification of the person who looked like him?

We videotaped two lineups of five persons each and showed them in counterbalanced order to 52 witnesses of the purse-snatching. Very few witnesses were completely successful in making a positive identification without ambiguity. An equal number of witnesses impeached themselves by picking the man who resembled the culprit after having correctly picked the culprit. Most people simply made a mistaken identification. Our best witnesses had also been among the best performers in the recall test; that is, they had made significantly fewer errors of commission (adding incorrect details). They had not given particularly complete reports, but at least they had not filled in. The good witnesses also expressed less confidence than witnesses who impeached themselves. Finally, when we referred to the earlier written descriptions of the suspect we found our successful witnesses had given significantly higher, and hence more accurate, estimates of weight. People guessing someone's weight often invoke a mental chart of ideal weight for height and err substantially if the person is fat. Our purse-snatcher was unusually heavy, something the successful witnesses managed to observe in spite of his loose-fitting clothing. The others were guessing.

Once again we noted that witnesses tend not to say, "I don't know." Eighty percent of our witnesses tried to pick the suspect even though most of them were mistaken. The social influence of the lineup itself seems to encourage a "yes" response.

...

Psychological research on human perception has advanced from the nineteenth century recording machine analogy to a more complex understanding of selective decision-making processes that are more human and hence more useful. My colleagues and I feel that psychologists can make a needed contribution to the judicial system by directing contemporary research methods to real-world problems and by speaking out in court.

...

It is discouraging to note that the essential findings on the unreliability of eyewitness testimony were made by Hugo Munsterberg nearly 80 years ago, and yet the practice of basing a case on eyewitness testimony and trying to persuade a jury that such testimony is superior to circumstantial evidence continues to this day. The fact is that both types of evidence involve areas of doubt. Circumstantial evidence is tied together with a theory, which is subject to questioning. Eyewitness testimony is also based on a theory, constructed by a human being (often with help from others), about what reality was like in the past; since that theory can be adjusted or changed in accordance with personality, with the situation or with social pressure, it is unwise to accept such testimony without question. It is up to a jury to determine if the doubts about an eyewitness's testimony are reasonable enough for the testimony to be rejected as untrue. Jurors should be reminded that there can be doubt about eyewitness testimony, just as there is about any other kind of evidence.

Memory for Faces and the Circumstances of Encounter

22

Evan Brown, Kenneth Deffenbacher, and William Sturgill

We've all had the experience of being sure that we've seen someone before and yet we are unable to recall just where or when. It's easy to be wrong about what the authors of this selection call the "circumstances of encounter"—so easy that we may be sure of having met the person himself when actually we've only seen his photograph! This suggests that serious errors may occur if eyewitnesses to a crime have been shown police mugshots before they testify.

$\mathbf{R}$ecent research suggests that visual recognition of scenes and faces can be strikingly accurate, at least under optimal conditions. Using self-paced presentations, Shepard's (1967) subjects viewed 612 pictures of "things" and "scenes" in a directed-memory test. Recognition accuracy on an immediate test of 68 "old–new" pairs was about 98 percent. With a one-week delay, accuracy was about 90 percent. In similar tasks but with controlled presentation times, Standing, Conezio, and Haber (1970) and Standing (1973) reported immediate recognition of about 90-percent accuracy on old–new pairs even when several thousand pictures of scenes were presented for only a few seconds each. Accuracy rates for face recognition are somewhat more difficult to compare given procedural variations. However, accuracy here seems generally to be rather good as well, if somewhat below that for scenes. Thus, in a study using procedures similar to Shep-

※ From the *Journal of Applied Psychology*, 1977, *62*, 311–318.

ard's, Hochberg and Galper (1967) showed subjects as many as 60 pictures of college-student faces, testing immediate recognition with 15 old–new pairs. Accuracy was about 90 percent.

Though these studies suggest that recognition memory for faces or scenes can be quite good, it might be misleading to extrapolate from them to witness identifications of criminal suspects. To be accurate, such witnesses must indeed be able to recognize a previously encountered face; in addition, however, they must be able to recall the circumstances in which that face was encountered, whether in fact at the scene of the crime, whether instead in newspaper or television presentations or police mugshots. The possibility that a witness might be able to recognize a face and at the same time be unable to recall correctly the circumstances of encounter has been addressed by the U.S. Supreme Court (*Simmons et al. v. United States,* 1968). In that decision, the Court noted the potentially biasing effects of showing a witness a single mugshot or showing mugshots in which a particular suspect is somehow emphasized (e.g., Buckhout, 1974) [*see Selection 21*]. In addition, however, and most relevant to the present question, they noted that even with best procedures, a witness may be biased by a mugshot if he "obtained only a brief glimpse of a criminal, or may have seen him under poor conditions" (p. 383). In such circumstances, they held, "the witness thereafter is apt to retain in his memory the image of the photograph rather than of the person actually seen" (p. 383). On the other hand, in denying Simmons's appeal, the Court noted that he had apparently been visible to witnesses for up to five minutes during a robbery in a well-lit bank.

Experimental evidence regarding this possibility—that recognition might occur with a failure to recall the circumstances of encounter—seems to be lacking. Studies of memory for picture orientation (e.g., Standing, Conezio, & Haber, 1970) do suggest that recall at least for orientation may be poorer and show more marked decline than visual recognition memory. However, the recall task seems too different from that required of a witness to warrant generalization. Similarly, although several studies of witness memory in situations approximating real life have recently appeared (e.g., Buckhout, 1974; Laughery, Alexander, & Lane, 1971; Loftus, 1975), potential differences between visual recognition memory and memory for the circumstances of encounter have not been to our knowledge among the variables investigated. The present experiments were designed to deal with this question.

EXPERIMENT 1

Experiment 1 was designed to compare the highly accurate recognition memory shown by subjects for pictures of faces in directed memory tasks such as those of Hochberg and Galper (1967) with the same subjects' ability to recall the circumstances in which those faces were encountered.

Method

Subjects. Subjects were 14 introductory psychology students, 13 women (12 white, 1 black), and 1 (white) man, who volunteered in order to receive a minor amount of extra course credit.

Stimulus materials and situations. One hundred 7.62 × 12.70 cm black-and-white photographs of male and female white children ranging in age from 8 to 10 years comprised the stimulus materials. These photographs were from a single suburban school and were originally collected to provide an unselected pool of pictures for facial attractiveness research. The three rooms used for the experiment differed markedly in size and general appearance.

Procedure. Subjects, tested individually, were presented 25 photographs of faces in one room, and 2 hours later, in another room, were presented 25 more such photographs. Two days later, in yet a third room, they were shown 100 pictures of faces in pairs, with one in each pair having been previously presented and the other a new one. The subjects were asked to indicate for each pair the picture previously presented and the room in which it had been presented. In an effort to maximize memory performance, subjects had been warned in advance of the original presentation that they would be asked both these questions and had been given 20 seconds for the study of each picture. Final presentation was self-paced, with no subject taking more than 20 seconds.

Results and Discussion

Recognition accuracy was as previous directed memory studies (e.g., Hochberg & Galper, 1967) would lead one to expect. Across subjects, the mean proportion of photographs correctly identified as old versus new was .96, a proportion far above chance, $z = 24.41$, $p < .01$. Recall of the circumstances of encounter for correctly recognized photographs was much less impressive, however, with a mean proportion of only .58, $z = 5.44$, $p < .01$. Examination of the data from individual subjects showed a similar pattern. Recognition scores ranged from .84 to 1.00, with all scores reliably above chance ($ps < .01$); whereas recall scores ranged from .44 to .68, with only five of the 14 able to recall the circumstances of encounter in a statistically reliable fashion ($ps < .01$). Though picture set and room were confounded in the design of this experiment, no systematic bias toward either combination was observed. For purposes of comparison with later experiments, signal detectability analyses were also performed, yielding group d's of 2.48

(obtained from a table for two-alternative, forced-choice experiments in El-liott, 1964) and .40 (hit proportion = .58; false alarms = .42) for recognition and recall, respectively. Gourevitch and Galanter's (1967) test of signifi-cance between two d's indicated that subjects discriminated among faces better than they discriminated among circumstances of encounter ($p = .01$).

These results clearly support the notion that persons are better able to recognize faces than they are able to remember where they saw them. Fur-ther, these results suggest that witnesses in real-life situations might, if suffi-ciently confused as to whether a suspect's face was seen in mugshots or at the scene of the crime, indict a suspect on the basis of face recognition alone. Given this possibility, Experiment 2 was designed to simulate more closely one possible situation for an actual witness, one somewhat like the *Simmons et al. v. United States* (1968) case, in which a witness knows that a crime is taking place and attempts to remember the participants. As com-pared to Experiment 1, Experiment 2 differs primarily in using actual per-sons rather than pictures of them (where appropriate) and in using a smaller and probably more realistic number of such persons. In addition, Experi-ment 2 does not separate recognition responses from recall. Rather, it mod-els the usual criminal identification procedure with its mugshots and lineups so as to document better any confusions or biases introduced by them.

Experiment 3 was designed instead to simulate less optimal viewing conditions, a situation in which witnesses interact with criminals but do not suspect that a crime is occurring and lack any obvious motivation to remember the criminals, or even to look at them closely. Such a situ-ation is somewhat analogous to laboratory studies of incidental mem-ory. It differs, however, in that it is not of direct concern here whether a given witness may have difficulty for strictly memorial reasons or be-cause of a failure to note the suspect's facial and other characteristics in the first place. In addition to this difference, Experiment 3 involves fewer criminals than in Experiment 2, the rationale being that it would be futile to expect accurate identification of a large number of criminals under these circumstances.

...

[The authors' account of their Experiment 2 is omitted here. In that experi-ment, ten "criminals" briefly appeared before a class that had been fore-warned to observe them carefully. Afterwards the class was shown pictures—"mugshots"—of some of these "criminals" together with other mugshots of people they had not seen. A week later, the same class was presented with sev-eral "lineups" that included some of the original "criminals" whose mugshots had been shown, some who had not appeared in mugshots, some of the non-criminals whose mugshots had been shown, and some new individuals. Be-cause Experiment 3 (below) was very similar in design and somewhat more *realistic in its setting, it seems unnecessary to describe the results of Experiment 2 in detail. The authors' summary of those results follows.]*

Though our subjects did much better than chance at distinguishing criminals from noncriminals, these results would still not be overly confidence inspiring were they to hold in real-life situations. There was some tendency to mistake having seen a mugshot for having seen a person, as shown by the significantly greater indictment of mugshot suspects over lineup-only suspects. Although these tendencies not to recall circumstances in which faces were encountered did not appear to be so important here as in Experiment 1, there was still a one-in-five probability that a mugshot-only suspect would be indicted and a one-in-two probability that a criminal without mugshot would escape indictment by a typical witness. Compounding this from a forensic standpoint, there was as previously no significant relation between subject confidence and accuracy $r(62) = .12$, $p > .05$, whereas there was as before a significant relation between confidence when correct and confidence when incorrect, $r(12) = .70, p < .01$.

EXPERIMENT 3

Method

Subjects. Subjects were 238 male and female students in a large second-semester introductory psychology class, with data from 175 (all white) used for the mugshot phase (35 no shows, 9 knew a criminal, and 19 incomplete protocols) and data from 146 used for the lineup phase (29 additional no shows in this phase). Initially, the witnesses were unaware that they were participating in a research project. However, at the start of the mugshot phase, they were informed of what had occurred and were told that they did not have to participate further unless they so wished. All in attendance agreed to participate.

Stimulus persons and materials. The stimuli were four persons posing as "criminals" and mugshots of 14 persons, including those of the criminals. The criminals were four of the stimulus persons described in Experiment 2 who ranged in height from 1.70 m to 1.76 m. Each criminal was paid $2.50 for each block of activity in which he participated. Mugshots were 20.32 × 25.40 c nonglossy color photographs of the four criminals and of ten other stimulus persons from Experiment 2. Each suspect was represented by one front- and one right-side view, mounted side by side.

Procedure. At the first midterm of the class, the witnesses were given their examination materials by persons who unbeknownst to them were the criminals. The classroom used had two entrance corridors, and two criminals were in each corridor; one handed out test questions and the other, IBM answer sheets. Witnesses entering through a given corridor were unable to see the criminals in the other corridor. Thus, approximately half the class encountered one set of criminals, and the other half encountered the other set. The IBM sheets were unobtrusively coded so that it could be determined which set had been encountered by each witness.

In their discussion sections two or three days later, witnesses were shown a matrix of 12 mugshot pairs of suspects on a display board. For a given witness, one mugshot pair was of a criminal encountered at the midterm, one was of a criminal from the other corridor—a person not previously encountered and therefore for that witness an innocent—and ten were innocent fillers. Witnesses were asked for each suspect to indicate whether or not he had given them test materials at the midterm and, if so, which sort of test materials (answer sheet or questions). They were also asked to indicate their confidence in each judgment in the same manner as in Experiment 2.

Finally, at the next meeting of the whole class, four or five days after the mugshot session, the witnesses were shown a lineup of four persons, the four criminals. For any given witness, one person in the lineup was a criminal whose mugshot had also been seen (criminal with mugshot); one a criminal whose mugshot had not been seen (criminal without a mugshot); one an innocent—a person from the other corridor—whose mugshot had been seen (mugshot only); and one an innocent—the other person from the other corridor—whose mugshot had not been seen (lineup only). The witnesses were asked to answer the same questions regarding each suspect as they had earlier been asked of the mugshots. In addition, however, they were asked to indicate for each whether or not his mugshot had been among the 12 shown in the discussion section. As before, they were also asked to indicate their confidence in each judgment, using the scale described in Experiment 2.

Results and Discussion

In the mugshot phase of the experiment, the mean proportion of innocents falsely indicted was .15 ($d' = .46$, $p < .01$). As compared to Experiment 2, these indictment proportions are lowered in part for procedural reasons having nothing to do with memory performance, namely, the presence of 12 mugshots where witnesses were aware that there were at most two criminals. The d' is unaffected by such considerations of relative frequency, however, and the lowered value presumably reflects differences in instructions regarding subsequent tests of memory together with any effects of the greater retention interval, two or three days in this experiment versus 1½ hours in Experiment 2. As previously, there was no correlation of accuracy and confidence across subjects, $r(173) = .03$, $p < .05$. There was also, as before, a correlation between confidence when correct and confidence when incorrect, $r(173) = .61$, $p < .01$.

When witnesses at the lineup were asked whether the suspects had been involved in the crime, that is, had given them test materials, indictment proportions for the criminals with mugshots, criminals without mugshots, mugshots-only, and lineup-only conditions were .45, .24, .29, and .18, respectively, with a mean of .29. Four of the pairwise comparisons of indictment proportions were statistically significant ($ps < .05$), with the two exceptions being the comparisons of the criminals without mugshots with the mugshot-only condition and also with the lineup-only condition. Signal-detection analyses yielding the same pattern of results are given in Table 22-1. Again, there was no significant correlation between accuracy and confidence, $r(144) = .12$, $p < .05$, but there was a significant relationship between confidence when correct and when incorrect, $r(144) = .60$, $p < .01$.

These results would scarcely be satisfactory were they to hold for real-life situations involving undirected memory. Despite the fact that only two criminals were encountered by each witness, in contrast to the ten of Experiment 2, accuracy was much reduced in this situation. Even the suspects appearing both as criminals and in mugshots were only indicted 2.5 times as often as those not previously encountered at all, and those appearing only in mugshots were at least as likely to be indicted as criminals without mugshots. This latter finding is particularly important from a forensic standpoint. Although mugshots might be useful for investigative purposes, we would tend to distrust indictments in situations such as those where witnesses had previously seen the suspects' mugshots.

TABLE 22-1

Between-conditions d' scores in Experiment 3

Conditions	Score
CMS vs. CNMS	.56**
CMS vs. MS	.40**
CMS vs. LO	.76**
CNMS vs. MS	−.15
CNMS vs. LO	.21
MS vs. LO	.36*

CMS = criminals with mugshots; CNMS = criminals without mugshots; MS = mugshots only; LO = lineup only.
*$p < .05$, **$p < .01$

Witnesses' responses to a further question were even less accurate. They were asked, for each suspect they placed at the crime, about the suspect's actions, that is, whether the suspect had handed them an answer sheet or a test booklet. Even if the analysis was restricted to witnesses who had been correct in their identifications of a criminal, the responses regarding actions were essentially at the chance level. For correctly indicted criminals with mugshots suspects, the proportion of correctly recalled actions was .43, and for correctly indicted criminals without mugshots suspects the proportion of actions correctly recalled was .46; in both cases chance would have been .50.

GENERAL DISCUSSION

The implications of the present experiments for forensic decision making seem fairly straightforward. For this purpose, Experiment 1 is relevant insofar as it clearly demonstrates that face recognition is much better than recall of circumstances of encounter, raising the possibility that on some occasions witnesses might base their indictments on face recognition alone. The results of the other experiments would seem to bear primarily on two questions, the general question of witness accuracy and the question of biases induced by mugshot encounters. With respect to the general question of witness accuracy, the main results of concern are the lack of correlation between accuracy and confidence and the evidence of considerable confusion both in mugshot identifications and in identifications out of lineups. Though real-life situations might produce different hit and false-alarm rates, the differences, or lack thereof, in indictment rates among suspect conditions documented by the d' analyses should be much more generalizable.

More interesting, however, than the general evidence of witness fallibility are the results that relate to mugshot-induced biases, since they could have considerable bearing on questions of legal procedure and admissibility of evidence. Thus, although one cannot abandon the use of witnesses simply because their memories are less than perfect, one can restrict admissibility of testimony in situations where procedures, such as use of mugshots, may most bias such testimony. So far as our present experiments are concerned, the U.S. Supreme Court's strictures would appear to apply to Experiment 3, as involving a brief glimpse under poor conditions; in Experiment 3 the witnesses did appear "to retain . . . the image of the photograph rather than of the person . . . ," since they were at least as likely to indict a suspect on the basis of a single mugshot encounter as compared to a single live encounter. Experiment 2, in contrast, seems somewhat similar to the Simmons case itself in that they both involved more nearly optimal original viewing conditions. The difference in viewing time is probably not terribly critical, given the finding that observers still show about 90-percent recognition accuracy even with as little as 1 second original viewing time (Standing et al., 1970). Certainly, there would be some greater likelihood of confusion induced by mugshot encounters in a case like Experiment 2 because of the greater number of suspects involved. In any event, we are pleased to report empirical support for the Court's distinctions.

REFERENCES

Buckhout, R. (1974). Eyewitness testimony. *Scientific American, 231* (6), 23–31.

Elliott, P. B. (1964). Tables of *d'*. In J. A. Swets (Ed.), *Signal detection and recognition by human observers.* New York: Wiley.

Gourevitch, V., & Galanter, E. (1967). A significance test for one-parameter isosensitivity functions. *Psychometrika, 32,* 25–33.

Hochberg, J., & Galper, R. (1967). Recognition of faces: I. An exploratory study. *Psychonomic Science, 9,* 619–620.

Laughery, K., Alexander, J., & Lane, A. (1971). Recognition of human faces: Effects of target exposure time, target position, pose position, and type of photograph. *Journal of Applied Psychology, 55,* 477–483.

Loftus, E. (1975). Leading questions and the eyewitness report. *Cognitive Psychology, 7,* 560–572.

Shepard, R. (1967). Recognition memory for words, sentences, and pictures. *Journal of Verbal Learning and Verbal Behavior, 6,* 156–163.

Simmons et al. v. United States. 390 U.S. 377 (1968).

Standing, L. (1973). Learning 10,000 pictures. *Quarterly Journal of Experimental Psychology, 25,* 207–222.

Standing, L., Conezio, J., & Haber, R. (1970). Perception and memory for pictures: Single trial learning of 2500 visual stimuli. *Psychonomic Science, 19,* 73–74.

23 | Preschoolers Remember Sam Stone

Michelle D. Leichtman and Stephen J. Ceci

If it is hard to be sure whether we've seen a given person before (or only his photograph), it can also be hard to know whether we're remembering what actually happened or only what's been suggested to us. Such difficulties are even greater for young children, especially if they have been exposed to repeated suggestive questioning by authoritative adults. Unfortunately, this often happens when allegations of child abuse are at issue. In this ingenious study, Leichtman and Ceci examine the consequences of preconceptions and suggestions for children's recall of a real event.

A burgeoning literature on children's suggestibility has appeared over the past decade, spawned by both theoretical issues surrounding memory development and applied issues surrounding children's courtroom testimony. Put simply, the theoretical issues in children's suggestibility concern one or more of a family of cognitive and social developmental factors, whereas the applied issues concern the limits of children's testimonial competence and, particularly, the issue of ecological validity. In the present study, we build on a base of work from both arenas to address the issue of how two critical factors might affect preschool children's reports of an event that centers on the actions of a particular person. These factors are the stereotypes about a person held by children before their witnessing the event of interest and repeated suggestive questioning that occurs during multiple interviews after the event.

To put our work in context, we briefly indicate below the cognitive and social factors that have received the most attention from researchers con-

❋ From M. D. Leichtman & S. J. Ceci (1995). The effects of stereotypes and suggestions on preschoolers' reports. *Developmental Psychology, 31,* 568–578.

cerned with the suggestibility of children's memory and reporting. We then discuss the related testimonial issues.

...

To recap, observed developmental differences in suggestibility may be the result of cognitive factors such as age differences in trace strength and source misattributions, and social factors such as bribes, threats, and expectations. In addition to the basic research conducted on these issues, there are many studies that have been animated by a desire to learn more about how these factors conspire to influence children's statements to forensic interviewers and their testimony in court (e.g., Goodman et al., 1992). We turn to this next, as a means of framing the present experiment.

TESTIMONIAL ISSUES

Despite the widespread empirical evidence of age differences in suggestibility, it remains unclear whether similar levels of suggestibility may be assumed to be present in real-world cases involving the testimony of individuals in the courtroom. The overarching concern here is that many experiments, in particular those from the first half of this century (see Ceci & Bruck, 1993), lack sufficient ecological validity to allow us to confidently extrapolate their findings to the real world. Specifically, the experimental conditions in which participants demonstrate their memorial suggestibility under the watchful eyes of researchers differ in several significant ways from those in which individuals give forensically relevant testimony. The affectively laden nature of the encoding and retrieval contexts in some actual forensic situations, as well as the motivational forces and demand characteristics involved in these situations, is difficult to ethically incorporate into empirical research programs (Ceci, Leichtman, & Bruck, in press). As a result, we still do not know much about the way children respond to them.

The goal of the present study was to evaluate suggestibility under conditions that have not heretofore been investigated, but that nevertheless characterize a large number of situations in which child witnesses eventually appear in court. Because these conditions have gone unexplored, it is not clear whether the suggestibility effects documented in the existing literature underestimate or overestimate the magnitude of children's reported distortion under these real-world forensic conditions. Certain factors that frequently crop up in courtroom testimony, particularly those pertaining to the number and timing of witness interviews, would lead one to suspect that youngsters relating past events are more prone to suggestion in such situations than current research would have us believe. Alternatively, other variables that play a role in the real world, such as the salience of events about which children testify, would lead to the opposite conclusion, namely, that experimental conditions give rise to less optimistic views of children's resistance to suggestion than those reflected by their real-world analogs. In the present work, we considered how a number of contextual factors involved in the experience and reporting of an event might affect the accuracy of preschoolers' reports. Following this, we evaluated the ability of condition-blind adults to assess whether children's reports were factually accurate. We did so because adults' ability to determine the accuracy of children's reports bears heavily on the importance of the issue of suggestibility in legal cases.

STEREOTYPES AS PERSON SCHEMAS

Stereotypes are naive theories about personal characteristics, which function to organize and structure experience by directing individuals to look for expectancies in their environment and advising them on how to interpret such expectancies. Thus, stereotypes are a form of schematic knowledge that help organize memory, by adding thematically congruent information that was not perceived, or sometimes by distorting what is perceived (Martin & Halverson, 1983; Strangor & McMillan, 1992). Before witnessing an event, a child may be provided with a particular stereotype about the person involved, and this may direct the child's attention to expectancy-congruent behaviors (e.g., in court cases, the defendant might be an estranged parent who has been previously criticized by the custodial parent in the child's presence, and the child may even have come to accept these criticisms as stable aspects of the parent's character). Hence, such behaviors may be remembered and reported disproportionately.

REPEATED SUGGESTIONS OVER LONG INTERVALS

It is probably not an exaggeration to say that the presence of multiple repetitive interviews over the course of long retention intervals has become the norm in cases in which children testify (see Ceci & Bruck, 1993, for similar examples from other cases; see Humphrey, 1985). Recent estimates indicate that by the time they get to court, children have been subjected to 4 to 11 forensic interviews, on average, and in most cases they have experienced numerous other bouts of questioning from family members, therapists, social workers, and other interested parties (Gray, 1993; McGough, 1994). Nonetheless, most studies to date have focused on the suggestibility of children after a single suggestive interview, as reflected in Ceci and Bruck's (1993) comprehensive review. (For exceptions, see, for example, Goodman & Clarke-Stewart, 1991; Lepore & Sesco, 1994; Poole & White, 1991, 1993.)

...

The present study was designed to experimentally examine the combined effect of stereotypes and repeated suggestive interviews. We refer to it as the "Sam Stone Study," because the event of interest was the visit of a man named Sam Stone to the day-care centers of our participants.

METHOD

Participants

One hundred and seventy-six preschoolers participated in this experiment. They were enrolled in private day-care centers, and they represented a wide range of social and ethnic groups, with approximately 15% of all participating children coming from families receiving Aid to Families With Dependent Children (AFDC) and the remaining children coming about evenly split between blue-collar/middle-class and white-collar/professional families. The children were divided into two age groups: early preschoolers (3- and 4-year-olds) and older preschoolers (5- and 6-year-olds). Assignment to experimental condition was random, but the unit of assignment was the classroom ($n = 8$) rather than the individual child. (This was done to obviate the potential contaminating effect of classmates sharing with each other the details of their interviews.)

Procedure

Children were assigned to one of four conditions, denoted as follows: (a) control, (b) stereotype, (c) suggestion, and (d) stereotype plus suggestion. The central event of interest was the visit of a stranger named Sam Stone to the preschoolers in all conditions at their day-care centers. In each of the eight day-care classrooms, Sam Stone enacted the same scripted event. First, he entered the classroom and said hello to a teacher or aide who sat amidst the assembled children during a story-telling session, and he was introduced by the teacher or aide to the children. Next, he commented on the story that was being read to the children by the teacher or aide ("I know that story; it's one of my favorites!") and strolled around the perimeter of the classroom. Finally, he departed, waving goodbye to the children. In each case, the entire event was timed and lasted approximately 2 min.

Two experimental manipulations, a preevent and a postevent manipulation, formed the basis of the differences among the four conditions. All of the children, including those in the three experimental groups as well as the controls, received a forensic interview approximately 10 weeks after Sam Stone's visit. However, children in the *control* group received no information about Sam Stone before his visit and were questioned once a week during the 4 weeks immediately following this visit in a neutral manner. That is, during the four interviews, control children were simply asked questions about what Sam Stone had done during his visit to their school and were given no suggestions about the nature of his visit or Sam Stone's activities.

Children in the *stereotype* condition, in contrast, received considerable information about Sam Stone's personality before his visit to their school. Each week, beginning a month before the visit, research assistants went to the children's day-care centers, and in the course of playing with them presented 3 different scripted stories about Sam Stone (for a total of 12 stories over the four visits. In each of these stories, Sam Stone was depicted as a kind, well-meaning, but very clumsy and bumbling person. For example:

You'll never guess who visited me last night. [pause] That's right. Sam Stone! And guess what he did this time? He asked to borrow my Barbie and when he was carrying her down the stairs, he accidentally tripped and fell and broke her arm. That Sam Stone is always getting into accidents and breaking things! But it's okay, because Sam Stone is very nice and he is getting my Barbie doll fixed for me.

Following Sam Stone's visit, children in the stereotype condition were treated identically to the control group, receiving four neutral interviews over the 4 weeks following his visit, and a fifth interview 10 weeks after the visit.

A third group of children, those in the *suggestion* condition, did not receive the preevent manipulation just described (i.e., the stereotype induction) but did receive a postevent manipulation consisting of suggestive interviews following their encounter with Sam Stone. Thus, although this group of children had no knowledge of Sam Stone before his visit to their classes, they received four interviews following his visit that were quite different from the neutral interviews given to children in the control and stereotype conditions. During their interviews, children in the suggestion group were provided with two erroneous suggestions about what occurred during Sam Stone's visit, embedded within an interview that was otherwise parallel to those of the control and stereotype groups. The first misleading suggestion was that Sam Stone had ripped a book, and the second was that he had soiled a teddy bear. The exact questions about the events that occurred during Sam Stone's visit were different for this group of children during each of the interviews, but the same implications were embedded in each. For example, 1 week children were asked, "When Sam Stone got that bear dirty, did he do it on purpose or was it an accident?," and in the following interview session they were asked, "Was Sam Stone happy or sad that he got that bear dirty?"

A fourth group of children, those in the *stereotype-plus-suggestion* condition, were exposed to both the preevent stereotype and the postevent leading question manipulations. These children were thus provided with misleading information about Sam Stone at two points in the process of acquiring information about him that could bear on their later reports.

The fifth interview, experienced by all children, was conducted by a new interviewer, who was not present during Sam Stone's visit or the first four interviews. In this case, the same questions were asked and the same forensic procedures were used to interrogate children in all groups. In each case, children were first made to feel comfortable; a free narrative was then elicited from them ("Remember the day that Sam Stone visited your school? Well, I wasn't there that day, and I'd like you to tell me everything that happened when he visited"); and, finally, they were given probing questions about specific events. These specific probes were directed at the two events that did not occur during Sam Stone's visit but that children in the suggestion and stereotype-plus-suggestion conditions had heard about before, namely, Sam Stone's soiling a teddy bear and ripping a book. These probe questions asked children whether they had "heard something" about the items and whether they had seen Sam Stone engage in some activity with them. Thus, our central analyses focus on children's responses to the free narrative, as well as their initial responses to these probes.

In addition, for only those children whose answers to the probes indicated that they actually saw Sam Stone commit nonevents, countersuggestion questions were posed, to attempt to gauge the strength of their statements (e.g., "You didn't really see him do this, did you?"). In the following section, we report for each of our experimental conditions first the free narrative and probe data, and then results for the subset of children asked the countersuggestion questions.

RESULTS AND DISCUSSION

Data from the fifth interview were coded from videotape by condition-blind raters, who categorized children's answers in terms of their content, scoring "don't know" and "no response," as well as specific details provided by children. Twenty percent of the videotaped interviews were randomly selected and recorded by an independent rater, and interrater reliability was found to be high (Cohen's κ = .90). Below, we begin by describing children's accuracy in each of the four experimental conditions, and then we proceed to subject these data to various statistical analyses as a function of age and condition. For the purposes of the first set of data analyses, we consider the raw (unconditionalized) percentages of children who both reported that Sam Stone engaged in the nonevent and resisted the countersuggestion.

Control Children

No child in the control group made any false allegations in his or her free narratives when initially asked by the interviewer during the fifth interview to tell everything they could remember about the day that Sam Stone visited their classroom. As seen in Figure 23-1, nearly all of the 47 children assigned to the control group resisted claiming anything erroneous had occurred not only in their free narratives but also in response to probes. Thus, when specifically probed about a book or teddy bear, only 10% of the youngest control group children's claims indicated that Sam Stone did anything to a book or teddy bear (i.e., 4 claims out of 40 opportunities). Furthermore, when specifically asked if they actually saw him do anything to a book or teddy bear, as opposed to merely hearing that he did something, only 5% of the younger preschoolers' claims continued to indicate that anything occurred (i.e., 2 claims out of 40 opportunities). Finally, when gently challenged with countersuggestions such as "You didn't really see him do anything to the book (the teddy bear), did you?," only 2.5% of the younger children's claims (1 out of 40 opportunities) indicated that they actually observed him doing so. In summary, in the absence of any attempt by adults to taint the youngest children's reports before the fifth and final interview, their reports were largely, although not wholly, void of errors. And yet these children's reports usually included accurate accounts of actual information; they often were able to recall Sam Stone's limited activities on the day he visited, for example, that he walked around the housekeeping section of the classroom, that he greeted the children pleasantly, or that he waved goodbye. As for the older children, no child made any false allegations in his or her free narratives, and only 2 of their claims in response to initial probes (out of 54 possible) indicated that Sam Stone committed a misdeed, and both of these were readily relinquished when the children were asked if they had actually witnessed the misdeed themselves. Because none of the older children claimed to have actually observed Sam Stone damage either item, they were not asked countersuggestions to see if they would relinquish their erroneous claims. Like their younger counterparts, these older children's recall was filled with examples of actual events that actually occurred.

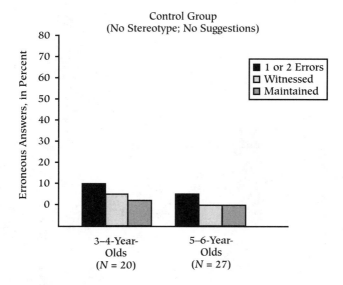

Figure 23-1   *Percentage of preschoolers' answers that were erroneous. Light-colored bar indicates that the child asserted that an incorrect event occurred; dark-colored bar indicates that the child claimed to have actually observed the nonevent; the right-hand bar in each group indicates that the child insisted on having witnessed the event, despite mild attempt at dissuading.*

Stereotype Condition

As was the case in the control condition, none of the children assigned to the stereotype condition claimed that they observed Sam Stone damaging either item in their free narrative, when they were initially asked by the interviewer during the fifth interview to tell everything they could remember about Sam Stone's visit. As seen in Figure 23-2, however, the stereotyping manipulation did have an effect on probed recall, particularly for the youngest children. In the final interview with this group, in response to the probes, "Did Sam Stone rip the book (soil the teddy bear)?," 37% of their responses indicated that he did at least one of these things. Of these children, 18% subsequently claimed they saw Sam Stone do these misdeeds (7 out of 38 opportunities). But, after being gently challenged, only 10% of their responses continued to indicate that they witnessed him do these things. In contrast to younger children, older preschoolers were significantly more resistant to the influence of the stereotype, with roughly half the rate of errors at all three levels of probing. Only 1 older child, in a single response (out of 40 opportunities), continued to indicate he had seen

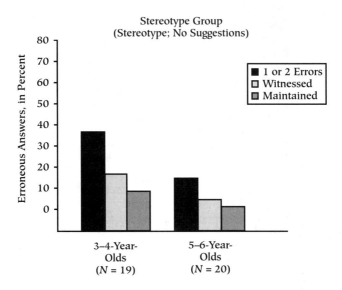

Figure 23-2 *Percentage of preschoolers' answers that were erroneous. Light-colored bar indicates that the child asserted that an incorrect event occurred; dark-colored bar indicates that the child claimed to have actually observed the nonevent; the right-hand bar in each group indicates that the child insisted on having witnessed the event, despite mild attempt at dissuading.*

Sam Stone commit a misdeed after being gently challenged with a counter-suggestion ("He didn't really do this, did he?").

Suggestion Condition

Unlike the control and stereotype conditions, some children assigned to the suggestion condition claimed that they observed Sam Stone damaging either item in their free narrative. Twenty-one percent of the youngest children (6 out of 29) and 14% of the older children (3 out of 22) made spontaneous claims in their free narratives regarding damaged books (or teddy bears or both). This finding is rare in the literature, as children's suggestibility is usually confined to cued recall and recognition measures, with few if any errors in free recall (Ceci & Bruck, 1993).

As can be seen in Figure 23-3, in response to the probe questions, 53% of the youngest children's responses in the suggestion condition and 38% of the older children's indicated that Sam Stone did one or both misdeeds. Moreover, in response to follow-up probes, 35% of the youngest children's responses indicated that they had actually seen him do these things, as opposed to being told he did them. Finally, even after being challenged with the countersuggestion, 12% of the youngest children con-

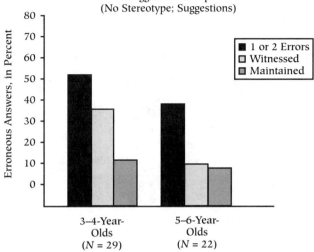

Figure 23-3 *Percentage of preschoolers' answers that were erroneous. Light-colored bar indicates that the child asserted that an incorrect event occurred; dark-colored bar indicates that the child claimed to have actually observed the nonevent; the right-hand bar in each group indicates that the child insisted on having witnessed the event, despite mild attempt at dissuading.*

tinued to claim they saw him do one or both misdeeds. Older children were also susceptible to the suggestive interviews, though at very reduced levels: Ultimately, only 2 out of 22 of the older children continued to maintain that they saw him do the misdeeds when challenged with a counter-suggestion.

Stereotype-Plus-Suggestion Condition

Finally, in the stereotype-plus-suggestion condition, 46% of the youngest children and 30% of the oldest children spontaneously reported in their free narratives that Sam Stone had carried out one or both misdeeds. Nothing approaching this level of suggestibility has heretofore been reported in the memory development literature, a function no doubt of the present study's use of repeated suggestions combined with a set of congruent expectancies. It will be important to replicate and extend this finding, given its rarity.

In response to follow-up probes, 72% of the youngest preschoolers' responses indicated that Sam Stone did one or both misdeeds, a figure that dropped to 44% when asked if they actually saw him do these things. It is important to note that 21% continued to insist that they saw him do these

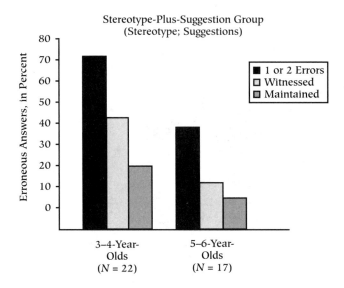

Figure 23-4 *Percentage of preschoolers' answers that were erroneous. Light-colored bar indicates that the child asserted that an incorrect event occurred; dark-colored bar indicates that the child claimed to have actually observed the nonevent; the right-hand bar in each group indicates that the child insisted on having witnessed the event, despite mild attempt at dissuading.*

things, even when gently challenged with a countersuggestion. For the older preschoolers, the situation, though better at all levels, was still cause for concern, as seen in Figure 23-4.

In view of the data described earlier, we can ask to what extent the four groups of preschoolers differentially reported what happened during Sam Stone's visit. To address this question, we conducted a 2 (age) × 4 (group) repeated measures multivariate analysis of variance (MANOVA) on the "commission errors" (i.e., claiming to have witnessed a nonevent) in the free narrative, probed recall, and challenged (countersuggestion) recall data. Errors of omission, that is, failing to report a real event, were not analyzed in these models, as they could occur only in free narratives, given the erroneous nature of both probes. (Because of an absence of commission errors for the older children in challenged reports in the control condition, we analyzed each level separately.) This analysis revealed significant main effects for both age, $F(1, 146) = 76.55$, $p < .0001$, and group, $F(3, 146) = 29.65$, $p < .001$. Follow-up tests indicated that, overall, older preschoolers reported more accurately than did younger children (*M*s = 72% and 86%, for the younger and older preschoolers, respectively), and the control group reported more accurately (96%) than the stereotype group (83%), which reported more accurately than the suggestion group (72%), which in turn reported more accurately than the suggestion-plus-stereotype group (64%), all $ps < .05$. These results were qualified by a marginally reliable Age × Group interaction, resulting from a somewhat steeper regression of errors on age in 3.01, $p < .07$. That is, younger preschoolers were disproportionately more impaired by the repeated erroneous suggestions than were the older preschoolers, whereas the two age groups were more similarly impaired by the stereotype induction ($F < 1$).

As mentioned earlier, countersuggestions were asked only if the child assented to a false probe, otherwise there was no reason to ask the countersuggestion. If an event is inaccurately reported in free narrative (i.e., the child spontaneously volunteers misinformation), what are the odds that it will continue to be inaccurately reported under probed and challenged recall? To explore this question, we configured the data so that each of the two events were classified as either accurate or inaccurate, and we calculated the conditional probabilities of accurate reporting, given one or two prior inaccurate reports. Younger preschoolers were more likely to make inaccurate reports if they had previously made one inaccurate report (.36) or two inaccurate reports (.49). For older preschoolers, the same effect was apparent (.23 and .36). One-way analyses of variance examining the differences in these conditional probabilities as a function of group and age revealed that both effects were significant: for age, $F(1, 76) = 4.81$, $p = .03$; for group, $F(3, 76) = 3.38$, $p = .02$. The group main effect was due to all but the control group being affected by the existence of a prior erroneous report, with an inaccurate report being associated with an increased likelihood of making a subsequent inaccurate report (all $Fs > 3.10$, all $ps < .05$).

Can Adults Detect Inaccurate Reports?

It was interesting to see the number of false perceptual details that children who were assigned to the stereotype-plus-suggestion condition provided to embellish their reports of nonevents. Many of these children did not simply reply yes or no to a probe but supplied richly detailed narratives (e.g., claiming that Sam Stone took the teddy bear into a bathroom and soaked it in hot water before smearing it with a crayon). So seemingly believable were their reports that we presented videotapes of 3 of our participants (a 3-year-old, a 4-year-old, and a 5-year-old) to 119 researchers and clinicians who work in the area of children's testimonial issues—to see if they could discriminate between the erroneous reports and the accurate ones. This was done at two conferences, and in both cases the results were the same. The majority of both audiences could not readily tell overall whether the events reported by the children had occurred or not, nor could they identify which children were on the whole most accurate (see Figure 23-5).

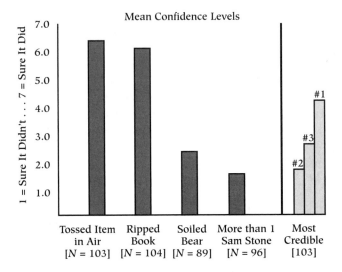

Figure 23-5 *Mean confidence ratings of professionals viewing child interviews (1 =* very confident that event did not occur, 4 = uncertain, 7 = very confident event did occur). *The light-gray bars on the right side represent overall credibility ratings of 3 children, with Child 1 rated most credible and Child 2 rated least credible. In reality, Child 1 was least accurate, Child 2 was most accurate, and Child 3 was in between in accuracy.*

The complete videos of 3 preschoolers assigned to the stereotype-plus-suggestion condition were shown to the professionals as the children gave free narratives, followed by probed and challenged recall. The particular videos were not randomly selected but were chosen because they represented the broad spectrum of answers children in this condition gave when asked about Sam Stone's visit. In addition, all of the accounts given by the 3 children were relatively coherent, and the children seemed engaged by the interviewer and confident in their answers. Child 1 was a 3-year-old girl who asserted spontaneously, and with seeming pleasure, that Sam Stone had done all of the acts listed on the left side of Figure 23-5 (i.e., tossed things in the air, ripped a book, soiled a bear, and been accompanied by "another Sam Stone"). Child 2 was a soft-spoken 4-year-old girl, who asserted only that Sam Stone had come into the classroom, said hello, and walked around the room before exiting, all of which was entirely accurate. At prompting, she denied knowing anything about a book or teddy bear. Child 3 was a 5-year-old boy who, while initially asserting that Sam Stone had only come in and looked around the classroom, answered the prompting questions by asserting that Sam Stone had ripped the page of a book and had painted ice cream all over a teddy bear in the school yard with a paint brush that was handy.

Audience members were told only that the study was about the visit of a person named Sam Stone to the children's classroom, and that all of the children in the videos had witnessed the same visit by Sam Stone. They were then told that they should decide for themselves what occurred during this visit, based on viewing the videotapes of interviews with 3 children about the event. Immediately after viewing the 3 children, the audience was asked to rate the accuracy of particular statements made by the children about Sam Stone's visit on a 7-point scale, where 1 = *very confident that the event did not occur* and 7 = *very confident that the event did occur*. At no time was the impression conveyed that some of the particular events we were asking about did or did not occur; the audience was simply asked to decide in the case of each event whether they believed that it had occurred or not. Audience members were instructed to make their ratings individually, without discussing their answers with others seated nearby.

An interesting aspect of Figure 23-5 is that both groups of audiences rated Child 2, who was completely accurate in her account, as the least credible of the 3 children. Conversely, the audience rated Child 1, whose account contained by far the most inaccurate assertions about Sam Stone's visit, as the most credible. Similarly, for the four specific events that were addressed by the 3 children, both audiences were unable to reliably identify whether the event had occurred; they were better than chance at one of the four specific questions (i.e., they rightly determined that there was not "more than one Sam Stone"), they were exactly at chance on one of the four questions (i.e., they were undecided about whether Sam Stone had soiled the bear), and they were reliably below chance on the remaining two questions (i.e., they felt fairly certain that Sam Stone had tossed an item in the air and had ripped a book during his visit).

···

It is not that the members of these audiences were worse than anyone else at assessing which children gave accurate accounts, but that the accuracy of children's reports is extremely difficult to discern when children have been subjected to repeated erroneous suggestions over long retention intervals, especially when coupled with the induction of stereotypes. These findings do not support the claims of those who think that it is easy to detect a young child's false report and lend at least anecdotal support to recent conclusions that such a task may be quite difficult. The reason is that, unlike in the modal study in which a child is presented a single erroneous suggestion, these children received persistent and intensive suggestions.

It may be that the children who received repeated false suggestions actually incorporated the erroneous suggestions into their memories. We cannot tell from these data, as the experiment was not designed to separate this from the alternative possibility of nonmemorial distortion. But the children's reports certainly seemed compelling to the professionals to whom we showed them.

...

Given the varied results that emerged from the four conditions in this experiment, it is clear that children's suggestibility is best viewed as heavily reliant on the entire context in which event reporting takes place. This context includes the cognitive framework that is set up before the memory tract is laid down (e.g., including beliefs and stereotypes that relate to the encoded information) and the nature of information pertinent to the event of interest that is encoded after that event has occurred (e.g., information suggested during storage). Given this picture of the multiple points at which misleading information may cause report distortion, it behooves us to consider suggestibility throughout development as a statelike, as opposed to a traitlike, quality. Although younger children show a greater vulnerability to both preevent and postevent suggestions, it is evident from the data we have presented that situations may be engineered in which even very young children's reports are wholly accurate. As demonstrated by our control group, when the context of a child's reporting of an event is free of the strong stereotypes and repeated leading questions that may be introduced by adults, the odds are tilted in favor of factual reporting.

REFERENCES

Banks, W. P. (1970). Signal detection theory and human memory. *Psychological Bulletin, 74*, 81–89.

Ceci, S. J., & Bruck, M. (1993). Suggestibility of the child witness: A historical review and synthesis. *Psychological Bulletin, 113*, 403–439.

Ceci, S. J., Leichtman, M. D., & Bruck, M. (in press). The suggestibility of children's eyewitness reports: Methodological issues. In F. Weinert & W. Schneider (Eds.), *Memory development: State of the art and future directions.* Hillsdale, NJ: Erlbaum.

Goodman, G. S. (1990, August). Media effects and children's testimony. In D. Singer (Chair), *The impact of the media on the judicial system.* Symposium conducted at the 98th Annual Convention of the American Psychological Association, Boston.

Goodman, G. S., & Clarke-Stewart, A. (1991). Suggestibility in children's testimony: Implications for child sexual abuse investigations. In J. L. Doris (Ed.), *The suggestibility of children's recollections.* Washington, DC: American Psychological Association, 92–105.

Goodman, G. S., Taub, E. P., Jones, D., England, P., Port, L., Rudy, L., & Prado-Esrada, L. (1992). The emotional effects of criminal court testimony on child sexual assault victims. *Monograph of the Society for Research in Child Development, 57*(Serial No. 229), 1–152.

Gray, E. (1993). *Unequal justice: The prosecution of child sexual abuse.* New York: Macmillan.

Humphrey, H. H., III (1985). *Report on Scott County investigations.* Minneapolis, MN: Attorney General's Office.

Lepore, S. J., & Sesco, B. (1994). Distorting children's reports and interpretations of events through suggestion. *Applied Psychology, 79,* 108–120.

Martin, C. L., & Halverson, C. F. (1983). The effects of sex-typing schemas on young children's memory. *Child Development, 54,* 563–574.

McGough, L. (1994). *Child witnesses: Fragile voices in the American legal system.* New Haven, CT: Yale University Press.

Poole, D. A., & White, L. T. (1991). Effects of question repetition on the eyewitness testimony of children and adults. *Developmental Psychology, 27,* 975–986.

Poole, D. A., & White, L. T. (1993). Two years later: Effects of question repetition and retention interval on the eyewitness testimony of children and adults. *Developmental Psychology, 29,* 844–853.

Strangor, C., & McMillan, D. (1992). Memory for expectancy-congruent and expectancy-incongruent information: A review of the social and social developmental literatures. *Psychological Bulletin, 111,* 42–61.

A Case Study of
24 Eyewitness Memory
of a Crime

John C. Yuille and Judith L. Cutshall

*The fallibility of witness memory, so impressively docu-
mented in Selections 20–23, may seem somewhat discouraging. But again—as in the case of "flashbulb memories" (Selections 5–11)—there is another side to the
story. Five months after the event, Yuille and Cutshall
interviewed thirteen eyewitnesses to a shootout that had
occurred in broad daylight on the streets of a British Columbia town. There were a few errors, but by and large
recall was surprisingly accurate.*

An examination of the paradigms presently employed in the study of
eyewitness testimony reveals a number of problems that make generalizations to real-world witnessing situations questionable. It is readily apparent, for example, that the use of slide sequences and filmed events in eyewitness research does not qualify as a "forensically relevant paradigm" and
may be of limited value for generalizing to witnessing situations in the real
world (cf. Clifford, 1978; Yuille & Cutshall, 1984). For example, Yuille and
Cutshall (1984) found that witnesses of a staged, live event reported more
action details (but not descriptive details) and these details were more accurate than those reported by viewers of a video-taped version of the same
event. There is increasing agreement that eyewitness research must be conducted with live events. In 1910 a similar "necessary nearness to life" criterion (Stern, 1910, p. 270) led Aussage psychologists to advocate the use of
live events over static, "picture-events" (Stern, 1910; Whipple, 1909; 1913).

...

※ From *Journal of Applied Psychology*, 1985, 71, 291–301.

It is apparent that several concerns demand the study of witnesses to actual crimes. Field observations are required for their own sake and as a means to evaluate the generalizability of laboratory research. "(N)o matter how well executed or elegant our studies are, they will be of questionable relevance at best without a knowledge of the differences between eyewitnessing in real situations compared with research situations" (Malpass & Devine, 1980, p. 398). Unfortunately, to date, there has been only one field study (Brigham, Maas, Snyder, & Spaulding, 1982) and one archival study (Kuehn, 1974) of real eyewitnesses. These studies provide only tangentially relevant information about witnessing a crime. In the Brigham et al. study, confederate customers visited convenience stores, and 2 hr later the store clerks were approached by confederate "law interns" who asked the clerks to identify the previous "customers" from a photo array. As Brigham et al. pointed out, this "paradigm is more directly analogous to an alibi situation (Was Person X at a given place at a given time?) than to a potentially violent robbery attempt" (p. 679). Kuehn's 1974 study used data from police reports to assess the relation between the degree of violence of a crime and the completeness of the witness's description of the perpetrator. Assessing the accuracy of witness's reports was not a purpose of Kuehn's study. Currently we know very little about the behavior of real witnesses to actual crimes. In this article we report the result of a first attempt to study eyewitness' behavior in situ.

The witnesses questioned in this study had observed a violent act. The incident involved a gun-shooting incident that occurred on a spring afternoon outside of a gun shop in full view of several witnesses. A thief had entered the gun shop, tied up the proprietor, and stolen some money and a number of guns. The store owner freed himself, picked up a revolver, and went outside to take the thief's license number. The thief, however, had not yet entered his car and in a face-to-face encounter on the street, separated by 6 ft (1.83 m), the thief fired two shots at the store owner. After a slight pause the store owner discharged all six shots from his revolver. The thief was killed, whereas the store owner recovered from serious injury. Witnesses viewed the incident from various vantage points along the street, from adjacent buildings, or from passing automobiles; and they witnessed various aspects of the incident, either prior to and including the actual shooting or after the shots were fired.

This case was chosen for analysis for several reasons: (a) There were sufficient witnesses to allow comparisons between witnesses; (b) Because the thief was killed and the weapons and stolen money were confiscated, a great deal of forensic evidence was available by which to assess the validity of witnesses' testimony; (c) The death of the thief closed the police file, allowing our research to proceed without interference in the judicial process; (d) The variety of items visible during the incident (i.e., weapons, thief's automobile, gun boxes, a blanket) provided opportunities for examining issues related to eyewitness memory. For example, the thief's automobile was visible to all witnesses and yet peripheral to the action of the incident, making it an appropriate subject for misleading questions. Also, witnesses could be questioned in the research interview about items not germane to the police investigation and therefore not mentioned in the original police interview (e.g., the color of the blanket covering the thief's body; the clothing worn by the thief). This allowed an assessment of long-term memory unaided by a previous recounting to police.

Whereas the primary purpose of this research was to record and evaluate eyewitness accounts, both the data collection and its analysis were organized to examine several issues emphasized in laboratory research. The nature of the case precluded investigating identification evidence, therefore the focus of the present research was on the witness' verbatim accounts. Most of the literature concerning eyewitness accounts has concentrated on their accuracy. Consequently, this became a primary focus in the present investigation, with particular attention to the kinds of errors witnesses made.

Although research findings are equivocal concerning memory changes over time, most researchers find substantial loss and distortion over time. In a review of eyewitness research, Penrod, Loftus, and Winkler (1982) concluded that there is research support for the contention that memory loss of eyewitnesses follows the forgetting curve of Ebbinghaus. In order to assess changes and losses in eyewitness memory, the present research included two eyewitness interviews, one immediately after the event (conducted by police officers) and another several months later (conducted by research staff).

Another important issue in the research literature is the malleability of eyewitness memory. Loftus' research (e.g., Loftus, 1975; Loftus & Zanni, 1975) appears to demonstrate the susceptibility of eyewitness memory to distortion. The form of a question may affect the witness's response or misinformation embedded in a question may be incorporated in the witness's memory. To examine the effect of the form of question in a real-life context, misleading questions were incorporated in the research interviews of the present study. Finally, the impact of stress on eyewitness accounts was also explored.

METHOD

Participants

Twenty-one witnesses to a gun-shooting incident were interviewed by police officers after the incident. We were able to contact 20 of the 21 witnesses, of whom 13 agreed to a research interview. Two refusals resulted because the witnesses had moved from the area, and five others did not wish to participate. One of these was the victim, who did not wish to relive the trauma of the incident. The 13 witnesses who agreed to an interview included all of the major witnesses except for the victim and one other witness who was in prison at the time of our interviews. The 13 witnesses (3 females) included in the study ranged in age from 15 to 32, with a mean age of 23.5. Three of the witnesses were high school students; nine witnesses were high school graduates, three of whom had some postsecondary school training.

Interview Procedure

This research was conducted with the cooperation of the Royal Canadian Mounted Police (R.C.M.P.) specifically the detachment that serves as a civic police force for the community of Burnaby, British Columbia. Burnaby, with a population of 136,465 (1981 census), is part of the metropolitan Vancouver area. R.C.M.P. officers from the Burnaby detachment interviewed 15 witnesses at the scene, and six more within two days. The police obtained each statement in the form of a verbatim account recorded by an officer in a handwritten form. First, the witness was asked to describe the event in his or her own terms. Then, the officer asked a series of questions to amplify aspects of the event. The written report included both the free account and all of the officer's questions and the witness's responses. The statement was then read by the witness and any changes, additions, or deletions were made. Finally, the witness signed the report to verify its validity. This procedure was independently assessed by the authors and a research assistant. Each of us accompanied several police officers on patrol for a number of 10-hr shifts. The statement-taking procedure was uniform across all officers and situations. Most important, in all instances that we observed, the reports were verbatim accounts.

As noted above, 13 of the 21 witnesses agreed to a research interview. These interviews were conducted 4 to 5 months after the incident at a time and place chosen by the witness, usually in his or her home or place of business. Interviews were from 45 min to 90 min in length, and each interview was recorded on audiotape and transcribed. Interviews were conducted by the authors and by a research assistant, following the police procedure. That is, witnesses were first asked to recount in their own words what had happened (free account); and this was followed by specific questions aimed at clarifying earlier points and soliciting specific details. In a departure from police procedure, we incorporated two misleading questions into our interviews. One question concerned a headlight on the thief's car. Following precisely the procedure employed by Loftus (1974), we asked half of the witnesses to tell us if they had seen *the* busted headlight on the perpetrator's automobile. The remaining witnesses were asked the same question except that the definite article *the* was changed to the indefinite article, *a*. There was no broken headlight. The second question concerned the color of a quarterpanel on the car. Half of the witnesses were asked if they had seen *the* yellow quarterpanel, and the remainder heard the same question with the indefinite article, *a*. There was an off-color quarterpanel but it was blue in color. These two questions were chosen because the car was in a prominent position during the incident and all of the witnesses had noticed its presence, yet the car was not instrumental in the event.

In the research interview, witnesses were also questioned about the degree of stress they had experienced at the time of the incident. Witnesses were asked to rate their stress on a 7-point scale with 1 representing *perfectly calm* and 7 representing *extreme anxiety or stress*. In addition, witnesses were asked about their emotional state prior to the incident and about any negative effects engendered by the incident such as sleeplessness or nightmares.

Scoring Procedure

The scoring procedure employed in the present study is a modification of that used by one of the authors in previous research (e.g., King & Yuille, 1985; Yuille & McEwan, 1985; Yuille, 1984; Yuille & Cutshall, 1984). In essence, this procedure partitions witness's statements into single units of information. Generally these units are verb and adverb phrases (for action details) or noun and adjective phrases (for descriptive details). After tallying the total number of action and descriptive details in an account, each detail was scored as correct, incorrect, or unclassifiable. This required a reconstruction of the facts of the actual event. To this end, all pertinent materials relating to the case were assembled: (a) police reports of forensic evidence gathered at the scene of the crime including photos of the thief's body and his automobile, descriptions of confiscated weapons and stolen articles, physical descriptions of the thief and the shop owner, the location of blood stains, and the number of expended bullet casings; (b) reports taken from ambulance attendants and public safety personnel at the scene of the crime; (c) verbatim statements taken by police from 21 witnesses who viewed various aspects of the incident; (d) autopsy and medical reports. In addition, the scene of the incident was inspected and photographed by our research team. The photographs included a partial reenactment of the shooting incident, which was staged to determine the effect of viewing angle for some of the witnesses.

Using these materials, the incident was reconstructed. Following Yuille's procedure (e.g., 1984; see also Clifford & Scott, 1978; Trankell, 1972) the accounts were parsed into (a) action details relating to all of the actions in the event and (b) descriptive details concerning the appearance and location of both people and objects. Reconstructing the correct descriptive details was straightforward in this case. The police photographs and descriptions provided a complete list of descriptive details, including physical descriptions of the perpetrator, the victim, and other witnesses, and descriptions of clothing, weapons, stolen property, and the automobile. The descriptive details were subdivided into two categories (a) people details including descriptions of hair color and style, clothing color and style, and age, height, and weight estimations; and (b) object details.

Reconstructing the correct action details was less straightforward. The action details of interest were those that transpired in front of the gun shop from the moment the thief exited the gun shop until the ambulance arrived at the scene, an elapsed time of 10 min. Verification of particular action details was problematic. However, with the combination of forensic evidence, the reports of all of the witnesses and the police and ambulance workers who attended, and the constraints of logic, the actions could be reliably reconstructed. Consensus among witnesses played a role in our reconstruction, but only when the information could be logically pieced together from witnesses having different perspectives in viewing the event. Agreement among witnesses about a particular detail, without corroborating evidence or without the benefit of various viewing angles, was not considered sufficient for inclusion in our reconstruction. An outline of the action sequence was independently constructed by both authors, and by a research assistant. These outlines were compared, and a sequence abstracted that reflected agreement among the three reconstructers. In the end, we were able to determine the accuracy of all but a few of the action details. In reporting the results, the details whose accuracy could not be determined were tallied separately as unclassified details. Unclassified details constituted 3.65% of the total details in the police interviews and 6.02% of the details in the research interviews.

Each eyewitness account contained two components, a free account and responses to specific questions. Initially these components were analyzed separately (e.g., Cady, 1924; Lipton, 1977; Marquis, Marshall, & Oskamp, 1972). However, no systematic differences were found between the free accounts and answers to questions, and these are collapsed in the treatment of results.

Each witness statement was divided into three components: (a) person descriptions; (b) object descriptions; and (c) action details. Each detail was allotted one point if it contained a specific, unique piece of information. For example, the statement "She was 5'2" and wore a "yellow sweater" contains three descriptive details. The statement "He turned around and shot the guy in the shoulder" contains three action details. Information lacking specificity, for example, "He was tall," was assigned a half point. The total number of person and object descriptive details and the total number of action details were tallied separately for both the police interview and the research interview. Each of these components of the report was evaluated in terms of the proportion of details that were correct. Accuracy was judged on the basis of our reconstruction of the event.

A range of accuracy was accepted for some numerical estimations. For example, height and age estimations were judged correct when they were plus or minus 2 (in. or years) of the actual height or age. Weight estimations were judged correct when they were plus or minus 5 (pounds) of the actual weight. No leeway was given however for the estimation of the number of shots fired or the date of the incident.

Two other features of the accuracy criteria deserve attention. Qualifiers indicating degree of certainty were not weighted. For example, the statements "She *might have been* wearing a red shirt" or "*Maybe* the car was blue, *I'm not sure*" were scored without considering the qualifiers. Also, allowances were not made for the possibility that the witness's memory was correct in terms of how they had witnessed the event. For example, when a witness reported hearing "five or six gunshots," this was scored as incorrect although it may have been true for that person. Similarly, one witness reported that the thief "looked like" he was in his early 20s. In fact, the thief did look like he was in his 20s but this was scored as incorrect because his actual age was 35. These points indicate the conservative nature of our scoring criteria. The accuracy of each witness's statement was scored independently by three judges and the results compared. There was a variance among scores of less than 2%.

RESULTS

Number of Details

A quantitative summary of the total details provided in the eyewitness accounts is found in Table 24-1. The total number of details the 13 witnesses reported in each of two interviews have been separated into action details, person description details, and object description details (the proportion of the total details that each category constitutes is also given in Table 24-1). Clearly, we elicited considerably more details in our interview than the police did in theirs. This reflects the fact that we asked many questions that were solely of memorial and not forensic interest. For example, we asked the witnesses to describe the blanket that covered the thief's body, a fact of no interest to the police. We also asked questions that probed witnesses for additional details concerning points they had only briefly noted in their earlier police interviews.

...

Accuracy of Recall

Each detail was scored as correct, incorrect, or unclassifiable. Unclassified details are not considered in this treatment of the results. Table 24-2 pro-

TABLE 24-1

Total reported classifiable details

No. of details	Police interview		Research interview	
	No.	%	No.	%
Action details	392	60.35	551.5	52.20
Person descriptions	180	27.71	267	25.27
Object descriptions	77.5	11.93	238	22.53
Total details	649.5		1056.5	

vides a summary of the accuracy scores for the classifiable details. Both mean and median scores are provided for the two interviews and the three types of detail.

Considering the police interviews, the reports of the witnesses were generally very accurate. Descriptions of people produced the lowest accuracy level (averaging 76%), whereas the descriptions of objects averaged almost 89% in accuracy. This pattern was the same in the research interviews. Person descriptions were almost 73% accurate, whereas object descriptions were over 85% correct. Note that there was little change in accuracy over the 4–5-month delay between the two interviews.

Changes in accuracy with time were examined in more detail. The overall accuracy rate for 10 of the 13 witnesses changed by plus or minus 1 to 6%. Thus there was virtually no change after 4 to 5 months in most of

TABLE 24-2

Percentage correct accuracy of classifiable details

Type of detail	Police interview			Research interview		
	Range	M	Mdn	Range	M	Mdn
Action	40–98	81.90	81.82	47–100	81.90	83.33
People descriptions	33–100	75.57	73.33	47–90	72.74	75.68
Object descriptions	50–100	88.53	100	60–100	85.45	89.74
Subtotal of descriptions	62–100	82.03	83.56	64–96	78.97	77.78
Total details	59–96	82.14	81.82	54–95	80.66	82.93

TABLE 24-3

Distribution of errors

	Police interview		Research interview	
Type of error	No. of errors	Proportion of total errors	No. of errors	Proportion of total errors
Action	57	53.02	96.5	48.61%
People descriptions	44.5	41.40	68	34.26%
Object descriptions	6	5.58	34	16.13%
Total errors	107.5		198.50	

the witnesses. For one witness accuracy increased 7.65%; for another it decreased 8.72%; and for the third, accuracy decreased 20.13%. The errors committed by the latter witness are discussed below.

Analysis of Errors

Although errors were relatively rare in the eyewitness accounts, an examination of their nature is useful. The data in Table 24-3 provide a general picture of the distribution of errors in the two interviews for the three types of details. A comparison of these data with those provided in Table 24-1 confirms the differential error rate for the three different types of detail. Person descriptive errors are overrepresented and object descriptive errors are underrepresented relative to the frequency of those types of descriptive details recalled.

...

Action errors have been separated into Time, Gunshots, and Multiple Action categories. Person descriptions include Statistics, Hair and Clothing, and an Other category. Object descriptions are divided into an Auto category and an Other category.

Considering the action errors, the largest category was Multiple Action, which consisted of errors concerning the actions of (a) the thief or the gun shop owner (15 errors in the police interview; 35 in the research interview); (b) other people at the scene (18 errors; and 22 errors); (c) the witness him/herself (2 police errors; 7 research errors). In both the police and research interviews, two-thirds of the errors concerning the thief and shop owner were committed by two witnesses. Similarly, two-thirds of the errors related to the actions of others were committed by only three of the witnesses. The two witnesses common to this error pattern were both teenage males. They reported that physical contact had occurred between the thief and the store owner. All of the other evidence made it clear that such contact did not occur. We reenacted the scene, photographing it from various locations, including the perspective of the two teenagers. The sharp angle from which they viewed the shooting and the interposition of a telephone pole limited the view of these witnesses. The distance between the thief and the store owner was collapsed for these witnesses. Thus, in part, their action errors may have originated in a "perceptual error." However, they seem to have embellished the error. One of them reported to the police that the two men were "grabbing one another," and in the research interview he was explicit about the points of contact.

Only one witness correctly reported that the pattern of shots was two followed by a slight pause and then six rapid shots. This accounts for the high proportion of errors concerning the gunshots. It should be noted, however, that although the proportion of gunshot errors dropped between the police and research interviews, their absolute number decreased only from 17 to 12.5. Several of the witnesses reported that the noises they heard were much softer than they expected, sounding more like firecrackers than gunshots. Five witnesses reported hearing only 5 or 6 shots in rapid succession. Thus, for them the first 2 shots went unattended, although these initial gunshots may have oriented them for the second volley. The one correct witness was familiar with guns, and he had handled the store owner's empty gun after the shooting, and therefore may have known how many rounds had been discharged. It would have been very difficult to determine the number of shots on the basis of earwitness evidence alone.

Errors concerning time and date of the incident were, not surprisingly, more common in the research interview. Ten of the witnesses could not tell us the exact month of the incident, although three of these were correct about the day of the week. Only one witness, the wife of the store owner, remembered both the time and the correct date, and this was a date that had clear significance for her.

Turning to errors in the description of people, 23 incorrect statistics (estimates of height, age, and weight) were given to the police (out of a total of 46 statistics provided), and 25 to the researchers (out of a total of 49 statistics). It is apparent that there was about a 50–50 chance of a statistic being correct. When asked for weight, height, and age estimates, most people lack the training and experience to provide an accurate estimate. One witness, for example, appeared to offer a standard set of statistics that changed little across individuals or over time. This witness described three individuals to the police with the following height and weight estimates: (a) 5'10", 160 lbs; (b) 5'10", 160 lbs.; (c) 5'10", 130 lbs. In the research interview he reported similar statistics: (a) 5'11", 165 lbs.; (b) 6', 180 lbs.; (c) 5'8"–5'10", 130 lbs. Approximately 50% of these statistics are incorrect, including both weight estimations given for Individual #2. Because this type of error constituted 52% of the person description errors in the police reports, and 37% of such errors in the research interviews, it seems that most of the lower accuracy associated with person descriptions is found with these statistics. If accuracy of person descriptions is recalculated after removing height, weight, and age estimates, the accuracy in the police interview was 82.47%, and 79.97% in the research interview.

Errors reporting the style and color of hair, and the style and color of clothing constituted the bulk of the remaining person description errors. In the police interview, hair color was reported correctly 77% of the time, and hair style was correct 72% of the time. The comparable values for the research interview were 80% and 71%. In the case of clothing, colors were correctly provided 66% of the time in the police interviews and 59% to the researchers, while style was correct 88% and 80% respectively. Thus, the color of clothing seems to be the most difficult feature to retain (or notice). For example, one witness graphically described the wounds on the body of the thief and she provided detailed descriptions of the body's position and its exact location in the street. Whereas this information was highly accurate, she erroneously described him as wearing a T-shirt and a red and black plaid jacket. He actually wore a dark blue sweater and a blue jean jacket. This witness reported that the body was her "main focus of attention" but apparently this did not include his clothing.

The number of object descriptive errors were few (6 to the police, 34 to the researchers), and five of the six reported to the police and one half of those in the research interview concerned the car, primarily its make and color. For the police, the witnesses were correct 83% of the time concerning the make and color. In the research interview this fell to 56% correct about the make and 57% concerning the color. The remaining object description errors concerned the guns (10 errors) and the stolen property (6.5 errors). These errors were distributed across several witnesses and fell into no pattern we could discern.

...

Misleading Information

The wording of the questions had no effect in this study. Ten of the witnesses replied either in the negative (i.e., that there was no broken headlight or yellow quarterpanel) or indicated that they hadn't noticed the detail. One witness was not asked the misleading questions because she indicated that she had noticed nothing about the automobile. The two remaining witnesses acquiesced to a misleading suggestion, but one did so in response to a control question. When asked if he had seen a broken headlight, this witness replied, "No, I didn't see a broken headlight, but I believe there was one; the panel of the car was a different color, blue or something." He then explained that replacing the panel might break the headlight, and added, "I'm just guessing now, it sounds very vague. I don't think I was ever around the car, oh, until afterwards, I was around the front of the car." The other witness was asked if he had seen *the* broken headlight and he replied, "On the left side? I think there was masking tape. I can't remember which headlight it was, but there was masking tape."

Although unaffected by the wording of the questions, three witnesses reported nonexistent events without prompting. In the police reports, 11.5 action details (2.93% of the total actions reported) never occurred. There were 18 such details in the research interviews (3.23% of the total). The three witnesses who reported these erroneous details included the two teenage males noted earlier, and a woman who was driving her automobile past the scene of the incident. Seeing a man lying in the street (the thief), she assumed that a witness who had picked up a gun from the street had done the shooting (by this time the store owner had fallen back inside the gun store). She then believed that she heard the man holding the gun say to another man standing next to him (another witness as it turned out), "Did you see me shoot that guy?" She reported that this was uttered in a menacing tone. No such event took place. However, this witness retained this erroneous version of events from the police interview to the research interview, despite newspaper and television accounts to the contrary. When we pressed each of these three witnesses for more details, none of them faltered in their descriptions. The two teenagers (independently) actually embellished their erroneous description of a fight between the store owner and the thief.

Stress Effects

All of the witnesses reported that their emotional state prior to the event was "normal" or "relaxed." The five witnesses who had contact with either the thief, the store owner, or a weapon reported the greatest amount of stress. Thus, stress and direct involvement in the incident were confounded in this case. On the 7-point scale, one of these witnesses reported a stress level of 5, three rated their stress at 7 (extreme anxiety or stress), and one reported a level of 8. All of these witnesses also reported sleeping difficulties during several nights following the incident. The overall mean accuracy for this group was 93.36% in the police interview and 88.24% in the research interview. Seven of the remaining eight witnesses reported stress levels ranging from 1 to 5, and none indicated any after effects. The eighth witness indicated no stress at all. The overall accuracy for these witnesses was 75.13% in the police interview and 75.88% in the research interview. The difference in accuracy between the stressed and nonstressed witnesses is reliable in the police interview, $t(10) = 5.02$, $p < .05$, and marginally so in the research interview, $t(10) = 2.17$, $p > .05$.

DISCUSSION

This study constitutes the first in situ investigation of eyewitness memory. Given the novelty of the research, the fact that this case involved 13 witnesses, and the striking character of the event, any generalizations must be made with caution. However, there are a number of features of the findings that are intriguing and that raise some questions about the image of the eyewitness that has emerged from laboratory work. We would not dispute Parker's (1980) claim that "The fact that conscientious and honest people will differ in the reporting of their observations of a crime is one of those immutable phenomenon that will exist as long as man" (p. 33). There is no doubt that witnesses do differ in their accounts; some examples were found in the present research. However, we do take issue with the essentially negative view of the eyewitness that has been consistently presented by most eyewitness researchers. As Clifford and Lloyd-Bostock (1983) noted, researchers have generally been "concerned with showing the witness's fallibility and his inability to recall accurately physical actions, person descriptions or verbalizations." (p. 286). In the present research, however, a different picture emerges. Most of the witnesses in this case were highly accurate in their accounts, and this continued to be true 5 months after the event. Such a high degree of accuracy is most likely situation specific. It is rare for anyone to witness a "shoot out" in the middle of a busy street in a Canadian city. The salience and uniqueness of this event probably played a major role in producing vivid memories. Such memories may be similar to the "flashbulb memories" reported by Brown and Kulik (1977), which often persist for years. It is a practical and ethical impossibility to stage such an event for laboratory research, and yet such events constitute a major concern for the criminal justice system. Perhaps the laboratory stress on negative aspects of eyewitness performance has been aided by ignoring the effect of unique and striking events.

Another factor that differs between this case and most experimental research was the degree to which witnesses were actively involved in the event. Our finding of significantly higher accuracy rates among the five witnesses directly involved in the event suggests that details may be retained more vividly by those who participate in an event. However, because witnesses directly involved in the event were necessarily in closer proximity to the incident, no firm conclusions concerning the effect of direct involvement on witness memory can be made. The higher accuracy rates may have been due, in part, to these witnesses having better or closer viewing positions. Nevertheless, it is our contention that the degree of witness's involvement in an event is an important factor in evaluating witness testimony. The passivity demanded of witnesses in laboratory research has precluded examining the effect of active involvement on subsequent recall; however, the possibility of such an effect in real-life witnessing situations should not be ignored.

REFERENCES

Brigham, J. C., Maas, A., Snyder, L. D., & Spaulding, K. (1982). Accuracy of eyewitness identification in a field study. *Journal of Personality and Social Psychology, 42,* 673–681.

Brown, R., & Kulik, J. (1977). Flashbulb memories. *Cognition, 5,* 73–99.

Clifford, B. R. (1978). A critique of eyewitness research. In M. M. Gruneberg, R. N. P. Morris, & R. Sykes (Eds.), *Practical aspects of memory.* London: Academic Press, 199–209.

Clifford, B. R., & Lloyd-Bostock, S. M. A. (1983). Witness evidence: Conclusion and prospect. In S. M. A. Lloyd-Bostock & B. R. Clifford (Eds.), *Evaluating witness evidence.* New York: Wiley, 285–290.

Clifford, B. R., & Scott, J. (1978). Individual and situational factors in eyewitness testimony. *Journal of Applied Psychology, 63,* 352–359.

Cody, H. M. (1924). On the psychology of testimony. *American Journal of Psychology, 35,* 110–112.

King, M. A., & Yuille, J. C. (1985). *An investigation of the eyewitness abilities of children.* Unpublished manuscript, University of British Columbia.

Kuehn, L. L. (1974). Looking down a gun barrel: Person perception and violent crime. *Perceptual and Motor Skills, 39,* 1159–1164.

Lipton, J. P. (1977). On the psychology of eyewitness testimony. *Journal of Applied Psychology, 62,* 90–93.

Loftus, E. F. (1974, December). Reconstructing memory: The incredible eyewitness. *Psychology Today,* 116–119.

Loftus, E. F. (1975). Leading questions and the eyewitness report. *Cognitive Psychology, 7,* 560–572.

Loftus, E. F., & Zanni, G. (1975). Eyewitness testimony: The influence of the wording of a question. *Bulletin of the Psychonomic Society, 5,* 86–88.

Malpass, R. S., & Devine, P. G. (1981). Eyewitness identification: Lineup instructions and the absence of the offender. *Journal of Applied Psychology, 66,* 482–489.

Marquis, K. H., Marshall, J., & Oskamp, S. (1972). Testimony validity as a function of question form, atmosphere, and item difficulty. *Journal of Applied Social Psychology, 2,* 167–186.

Parker, L. C., Jr. (1980). *Legal psychology.* Springfield, IL: Thomas.

Penrod, S., Loftus, E. R., & Winkler, J. (1982). In N. L. Kerr & R. M. Bray (Eds.), *The psychology of the courtroom.* New York: Academic Press.

Stern, L. W. (1910). Abstracts of lectures in the psychology of testimony and on the study of individuality. *American Journal of Psychology, 21,* 270–282.

Trankell, A. (1972). *Reliability of evidence: Methods for analyzing and assessing witness statements.* Stockholm: Beckmans.

Whipple, G. M. (1909). The observer as reporter: A survey of the 'psychology of testimony'. *Psychological Bulletin, 6,* 153–170.

Whipple, G. M. (1913). Psychology of testimony and report. *Psychological Bulletin, 10,* 264–268.

Yuille, J. C. (1984). Research and teaching with police: A Canadian example. *International Review of Applied Psychology, 33,* 5–24.

Yuille, J. C., & Cutshall, J. L. (1984). *Live vs. video media in eyewitness research.* Unpublished manuscript, University of British Columbia.

Yuille, J. C., & McEwan, N. H. (1985). The use of hypnosis as an aid to eyewitness memory. *Journal of Applied Psychology, 70,* 389–400.

25 | John Dean's Memory

Ulric Neisser

Witnesses are fallible, but they are not always wrong. If the psychology of memory is to do more than write CAUTION on judicial medicine labels, it must seek to understand the successes of testimony as well as the failures. J. J. Gibson (1979) insisted that the study of perception should begin with veridical seeing rather than illusion and error; maybe the study of memory can benefit from a similar approach. It was partly with this possibility in mind that I undertook the study of John Dean's testimony. What could psychology learn from a case where the witness was right?

What I learned, at least, is that being "right" is not a simple notion. Even when Dean was entirely wrong about the course of a particular conversation, he could be giving an essentially true account of the facts lying behind that conversation—of long-run, invariant states of affairs that had manifested themselves in many individual episodes. Combining information from several points in time may indeed lead to error, and it is not what witnesses are supposed to do. Nevertheless, it is often a good way to establish the real facts of the matter—the ones that are worth remembering.

"Have you always had a facility for recalling the details of conversations which took place many months ago?" Senator Inouye of Hawaii asked this question of John Dean with more than a trace of disbelief. Dean, the former counsel to President Richard M. Nixon, was testifying before the "Watergate" Committee of the United States Senate in June 1973. His testimony had opened with a 245-page statement, in which he described liter-

※ From *Cognition*, 1981, 9, 1–22.

ally dozens of meetings that he had attended over a period of several years. The meetings were with John Mitchell, Robert Haldeman, Charles Colson, Gordon Liddy, and others whose names became American household words as the Watergate scandal brought down the Nixon Administration. Some were with Nixon himself. Dean's testimony seemed to confirm what many already suspected: that these high officials were engaged in a "cover-up" of White House involvement in the original Watergate burglary. But was he telling the truth? How much did he really remember?

In a psychological experiment, it is relatively easy to determine whether what the subject says is true. The experimenter knows what really happened because she staged it in the first place, or because she kept a record with which the subject's report can be compared. Because life does not keep such records, legal testimony is usually evaluated in more indirect ways: corroborative witnesses, cross-examination, circumstantial evidence. For some of Dean's testimony, however, it is now possible to compare what he said with a factual record—the *Presidential Transcripts*. This comparison will enable us to assess the accuracy of his memory rather precisely. In addition, it may clarify our theoretical conceptions of memory itself.

When Dean first testified, his "facility for recalling details" seemed so impressive that some writers called him "the human tape recorder." Ironically, a very real tape recorder had been tuned in to some of the same "details." Not long after its interrogation of Dean, the Senate Committee discovered that all conversations in Nixon's Oval Office were routinely (but secretly) recorded. The result of this discovery was a sharp legal struggle for possession of the tapes. When the President realized that he would not be able to keep the tapes out of the hands of the prosecutors indefinitely, he decided to transcribe some of them and release the transcripts himself. Although he did this reluctantly, he also thought it possible that they might actually help his cause. The published version of the *Presidential Transcripts* (1974) includes a lengthy foreword reiterating Nixon's claim that he knew nothing of the cover-up. (It does admit that there are ". . . possible ambiguities that . . . someone with a motive to discredit the President could take out of context and distort to suit his own purposes" [p. 5].) The foreword explicitly insists that the transcripts discredit Dean's testimony. Dean himself, however, saw them as substantiating *his* side of the story. In his autobiography (Dean, 1976) he describes himself as "ecstatic" (p. 332) to learn of the tapes' existence, because they would prove he had told the truth.

The testimony and the transcripts are now in the public domain. I propose to treat them as data, as if they had resulted from a deliberately conducted memory experiment. The analysis of these data will be somewhat unorthodox, however, because we know its outcome in advance. If Dean had actually perjured himself—if the transcripts had proved him to be fundamentally mistaken or dishonest—the defense lawyers in the subsequent Watergate trials would surely have seized the opportunity to discredit his testimony. Instead, the outcome of those trials has vindicated him: the highest-placed members of the White House staff all went to prison for doing what John Dean said they had done. Nixon, of course, was forced to resign. If history has ever proven anything, it surely proves that Dean remembered those conversations and told the truth about them. I will not quarrel with that assessment here, but we shall see that "truth," "accuracy," and "memory" are not simple notions. Dean's testimony was by no means always accurate. Yet even when he was wrong, there was a sense in which he was telling the truth; even when he was right, it was not necessarily because he remembered a particular conversation well.

These are levels of analysis with which psychology has rarely been concerned. Although there have been many demonstrations of the fallibility of testimony (Stern, 1904 [*Selection 20*]; Buckhout, 1974 [*Selection 21*]), none has dealt with a situation as complex as Dean's: with such significant material, such long spans of time, or such ambiguous motives. We will find it hard to do full justice to John Dean's memory within the conceptual framework of the psychology of memory. Nevertheless, that framework is not irrelevant. It includes a number of valuable ideas: that memory is influenced by mental "scripts" or "schemata" for familiar events (Bartlett, 1932; Bransford & Franks, 1972; Bower, Black, & Turner, 1979); that distortions of memory are often motivated by the needs and character of the individual (Freud, 1956); and that a person's general knowledge ("semantic memory") must be distinguished from his recollection of specific events ("episodic memory," Tulving, 1972). Most obviously, we will have to make a distinction that has been familiar at least since Bartlett: to contrast *verbatim* recall with memory for the *gist* of what was said.

Verbatim recall is word-for-word reproduction. It is not something that we expect of ourselves in everyday life. Dean did not claim to be able to recall conversations verbatim, and indeed he could not. (We shall see that even the few phrases that he seemed to recall exactly may owe their fidelity to frequent repetition.) Memory for gist, on the other hand, occurs when we recall the "sense" of an original text in different words. To remember the gist of a story or a conversation is to be roughly faithful to the argument, the story line, the underlying sequence of ideas. Psychologists have developed a number of methods of evaluating memory for gist. One can divide the text and the recall protocol into so-called "idea units," and count how many of them match. With somewhat more trouble, one can make a structural analysis of the original, perhaps guided by theoretical ideas about "story grammars" and "schemata"; then one can determine how much of the structure reappears in the reproduction (e.g., Mandler & Johnson, 1977). These methods have worked well in the laboratory, where there is nothing to remember except an originally presented text. They are not as easily applied to the recall of actual conversations that take place in a context of real events: The events may be remembered even when the gist of the conversations is not.

Analysis of Dean's testimony does indeed reveal some instances of memory for the gist of what was said on a particular occasion. Elsewhere in his testimony, however, there is surprisingly little correspondence between the course of a conversation and his account of it. Even in those cases, however, there is usually a deeper level at which he is right. He gave an accurate portrayal of the real situation, of the actual characters and commitments of the people he knew, and of the events that lay behind the conversations he was trying to remember. Psychology is unaccustomed to analyzing the truthfulness of memory at this level, because we usually work with laboratory material that has no reference beyond itself. One of my purposes in analyzing John Dean's testimony is to call attention to this level of memory, and perhaps to devise ways in which it can be studied.

DEAN'S OWN ACCOUNT OF HIS MEMORY

It is impossible to survey all of Dean's testimony here; there is far too much of it. Moreover, most of his conversations were not recorded at all (so far as we know); it was only in the President's Oval Office that tape recorders ran night and day. Not even all of the taped material is fully reproduced in the available transcripts. We will only be able to analyze the two conversations reported in his testimony for which an apparently unedited transcript has been published. The reader should bear in mind that we are dealing with only a small fraction of what Dean said. The present paper is not an effort to assess his overall contribution to the Watergate investigations or to the course of justice; it is a psychological study aimed at clarifying the nature of memory for conversations.

The two conversations we will examine are those of September 15, 1972 and March 21, 1973. These two meetings with the President were crucial for the Senate Committee, which was trying to determine the extent of Nixon's involvement in the Watergate cover-up. Accordingly, Dean was cross-examined about both of them at length. He had already described each conversation in his long opening statement to the Committee: it was that statement which aroused Senator Inouye's incredulity. The interchange between Dean and Inouye is interesting in its own right: it may be the only discussion of mnemonics and metamemory in the *Congressional Record*.

Senator Inouye: Your 245-page statement is remarkable for the
                     detail with which it recounts events and
                     conversations occurring over a period of many

months. It is particularly remarkable in view of the fact that you indicated that it was prepared without benefit of note or daily diary. Would you describe what documents were available to you in addition to those which have been identified as exhibits?

Mr. Dean: What I did in preparing this statement, I had kept a newspaper clipping file from roughly June 17 [*June 17, 1972 was the date of the Watergate break-in*], up until about the time these hearings started when I stopped doing any clipping with any regularity. It was by going through every single newspaper article outlining what had happened and then placing myself in what I had done in a given sequence in time, I was aware of all the principal activities I had been involved in, the dealings I had had with others in relationship to those activities. Many times things were in response to press activities or press stories that would result in further activities. I had a good memory of most of the highlights of things that had occurred, and it was through this process, and being extremely careful in my recollection, particularly of the meetings with the President (*Hearings*, pp. 1432–1433).

Note that Dean has spontaneously invented the temporal equivalent of an ancient mnemonic device: the famous "method of loci." In that method, one mentally moves through a familiar series of places in order to recall images that were previously assigned to them. Dean apparently used newspaper clippings in a similar way, to pinpoint moments in time rather than loci in space; then he tried to recall what he had been doing at those moments. Senator Inouye's next questions (I am omitting some additional comments by Dean) indicate that he failed to grasp this point:

Senator Inouye: Are you suggesting that your testimony was primarily based upon press accounts?
Mr. Dean: No sir, I am saying that I used the press accounts as one of the means to trigger my recollection of what had occurred during given periods of time.

Inouye still does not understand.

Senator Inouye: Am I to gather from this that you had great faith in the reporting in the press?
Mr. Dean: No, I am saying what was happening is that this sequentially—many times White House activities

                  related to a response to a given press activity. I did not have the benefit—in fact, the statement might be even more detailed, Senator, if I had had the benefit of all the Ziegler briefings where some of these questions came up very specifically in press briefings as to given events at that time, but I didn't have the benefit of those (*Ibid.*).

Senator Inouye: In addition to the press clippings, the logs, what other sources did you use in the process of reconstruction?

Mr. Dean: Well, Senator, I think I have a good memory. I think that anyone who recalls my student years knew that I was very fast at recalling information, retaining information. I was the type of student who didn't have to work very hard in school because I do have a memory that I think is good (*Ibid.*).

A moment later Inouye asks the question I have already quoted, encouraging Dean to say more about his memory:

Senator Inouye: Have you always had a facility for recalling the details of conversations which took place many months ago? (*Ibid.*)

Dean responds with examples of things he would certainly never forget, beginning with conversations in the Oval Office:

Mr. Dean: Well, I would like to start with the President of the United States. It was not a regular activity for me to go in and visit with the President. For most of the members of the White House staff it is not a daily activity. When you meet with the President of the United States it is a very momentous occasion, and you tend to remember what the President of the United States says when you have a conversation with him. [*Dean goes on to mention several other salient events that he remembers well, and concludes*] . . . So I would say that I have an ability to recall not specific words necessarily but certainly the tenor of a conversation and the gist of a conversation (*Ibid.*, pp. 1433–1434).

We shall see later that Dean recalls the "gist" of some conversations and not of others; the determinants of memory are more complicated than he believes them to be. In particular, he did *not* remember what the President said in their first prolonged and "momentous" meeting. But there is no doubt about his confidence in his own testimony: at the end of the exchange with Inouye, he expresses it again:

> *Mr. Dean:*   I cannot repeat the very words he [*the President*] used, no, Sir. As I explained to Senator Gurney, my mind is not a tape recorder, but it certainly receives the message that is being given (*Ibid.*).

THE MEETING OF SEPTEMBER 15

On June 17, 1972, five men were arrested in the offices of the Democratic National Committee in the Watergate Office Building. They had planned to tap the Committee's telephones as part of an illegal "political intelligence" operation, mounted on President Nixon's behalf in the 1972 presidential elections. High White House officials then began a major effort to conceal their involvement in the affair, even to the point of paying "hush money" to some of those who had been arrested. John Dean was centrally involved in the cover-up. His chief task was to "contain" the legal investigation of the Watergate break-in, concealing every link between the underlings already caught and the White House. On September 15 this aim seemed achieved, because on that day the Grand Jury handed down indictments against only seven men: the five burglars plus Howard Hunt and Gordon Liddy. Since Hunt and Liddy were "small fish," and the Justice Department said it had no evidence to indict anyone else, Dean felt victorious. When the President summoned him to the Oval Office that afternoon, he expected to be praised.

The transcript indicates that the meeting lasted 50 minutes. It begins with the following interchange among the President (*P*), Dean (*D*), and Robert Haldeman (*H*), Nixon's "Chief of Staff." Note that Dean and Haldeman are both obviously pleased by the events of the day, while the President has little to say about them.

> *P:* Hi, how are you? You had quite a day today, didn't you? You got Watergate on the way, didn't you?
> *D:* We tried.
> *H:* How did it all end up?
> *D:* Ah, I think we can say well, at this point. The press is playing it just as we expected.
> *H:* Whitewash?
> *D:* No, not yet—the story right now—
> *P:* It is a big story.

H: Five indicted plus the WH former guy and all that.

D: Plus two White House fellows.

H: That is good; that takes the edge off whitewash, really. That was the thing Mitchell kept saying, that to people in the country Liddy and Hunt were big men. Maybe that is good.

P: How did MacGregor handle himself?

D: I think very well. He had a good statement, which said that the Grand Jury had met and that it was now time to realize that some apologies may be due.

H: Fat chance.

D: Get the damn (inaudible)

H: We can't do that.

P: Just remember, all the trouble we're taking, we'll have a chance to get back one day. How are you doing on your other investigation? (*Presidential Transcripts*, p. 32)

The next few exchanges are about other details of the Watergate "bugs" (telephone taps), and then about the scope of the investigations being conducted. It all seemed "silly" to them, especially since they believed that "bugging" was common in politics:

P: Yes (expletive deleted). Goldwater put it in context when he said "(expletive deleted) everybody bugs everybody else. You know that."

D: That was priceless.

P: It happens to be totally true. We were bugged in '68 on the plane and even in '62 running for Governor—(expletive deleted) thing you ever saw.

D: It is a shame that evidence to the fact that that happened in '68 was never around. I understand that only the former director [*J. Edgar Hoover, former head of the FBI*] had that information.

H: No, that is not true.

D: There was evidence of it?

H: There are others who have information (*Ibid.*, p. 34).

This interchange about "bugging" is noteworthy not only because of the light it sheds on the attitudes of the participants, but also because it stuck in Dean's mind. It is one of the few parts of the conversation which will be recognizable in his testimony nine months later.

The conversation continues from this point with more talk about "bugging," plans for action against White House enemies, questions about another pending legal action. It is interrupted briefly when Nixon takes a phone call. As soon as he hangs up, Dean speaks. He wants to point out how well things are going:

D: Three months ago I would have had trouble predicting there
would be a day when this would be forgotten, but I think I can
say that 54 days from now [*i.e., on election day in November*]
nothing is going to come crashing down to our surprise.
P: That what?
D: Nothing is going to come crashing down to our surprise
(*Ibid.*, p. 36).

He finally gets a bit of Presidential praise in return:

P: Oh well, this is a can of worms as you know, a lot of this stuff
that went on. And the people who worked this way are awfully
embarrassed. But the way you have handled all this seems to me
has been very skillful, putting your fingers in the leaks that have
sprung here and sprung there. The Grand Jury is dismissed now?
D: That is correct . . . (*Ibid.*).

The conversation goes on to cover many other areas—McGovern's campaign finances, a list of "enemies" that Dean offers to keep, more political
strategy. Later on Dean and Haldeman (but not Nixon) seize another opportunity to congratulate each other on the success of the cover-up.

P: You really can't sit and worry about it all the time. The worst may
happen but may not. So you just try to button it up as well as you
can and hope for the best, and remember basically the damn
business is unfortunately trying to cut our losses.
D: Certainly that is right and certainly it has had no effect on you.
That's the good thing.
H: No, it has been kept away from the White House and of course
completely from the President. The only tie to the White House is
the Colson effort they keep trying to pull in.
D: And of course the two White House people of lower level—
indicated—one consultant and one member of the domestic staff.
That is not very much of a tie.
H: That's right (*Ibid.*, p. 40).

DEAN'S TESTIMONY ABOUT SEPTEMBER 15

Nine months later, Dean devoted about two pages of his prepared statement to the September 15 meeting. The first paragraph purports to describe the way the meeting began. It is an important bit of testimony because the remarks Dean ascribes to Nixon would indicate full knowledge
(and approval) of the cover-up. This is his account:

> *On September 15 the Justice Department announced the handing down of the seven indictments by the Federal Grand Jury investigating the Watergate. Late that afternoon I received a call requesting me to come to the President's Oval Office. When I arrived at the Oval Office I found Haldeman and the President. The President asked me to sit down. Both men appeared to be in very good spirits and my reception was very warm and cordial. The President then told me that Bob—referring to Haldeman—had kept him posted on my handling of the Watergate case. The President told me I had done a good job and he appreciated how difficult a task it had been and the President was pleased that the case had stopped with Liddy. I responded that I could not take credit because others had done much more difficult things than I had done. As the President discussed the present status of the situation I told him that all I had been able to do was to contain the case and assist in keeping it out of the White House. I also told him there was a long way to go before this matter would end and that I certainly could make no assurances that the day would not come when this matter would start to unravel. (Hearings, p. 957)*

Comparison with the transcript shows that hardly a word of Dean's account is true. Nixon did not say *any* of the things attributed to him here: He didn't ask Dean to sit down, he didn't say Haldeman had kept him posted, he didn't say Dean had done a good job (at least not in that part of the conversation), he didn't say anything about Liddy or the indictments. Nor had Dean himself said the things he later describes himself as saying: that he couldn't take credit, that the matter might unravel some day, etc. (Indeed, he said just the opposite later on: "Nothing is going to come crashing down.") His account is plausible, but entirely incorrect. In this early part of the conversation Nixon did not offer him any praise at all, unless "You had quite a day, didn't you" was intended as a compliment. (It is hard to tell from a written transcript.) Dean cannot be said to have reported the "gist" of the opening remarks; no count of idea units or comparison of structure would produce a score much above zero.

Was he simply lying to the Senators? I do not think so. The transcript makes it quite clear that Nixon *is* fully aware of the coverup: Haldeman and Dean discuss it freely in front of him, and while he occasionally asks questions he never seems surprised. Later on he even praises Dean for "putting his fingers in the leaks." Because the real conversation is just as incriminating as the one Dean described, it seems unlikely that he was remembering one thing and saying another. His responses to Senator Baker during cross-examination (see below) also indicate that he was doing his best to be honest. Mary McCarthy's assessment of Dean has stood the test of time: she wrote in 1973 of her overpowering impression ". . . not so much of a truthful person as of someone resolved to tell the truth about this particular set of events because his intelligence has warned him to do so" (McCarthy, 1975, pp. 40–41).

If Dean was trying to tell the truth, where did his erroneous account of the September 15 meeting come from? Some of it might be explained by the currently popular notion that everyone knows certain "scripts" for common events and that these scripts are used in the course of recall (Bower, Black, & Turner, 1979). Dean's recollection of the very beginning of the meeting may have been constructed on the basis of an "entering-the-room script." People do often ask their guests to sit down, though Nixon apparently did not ask Dean. It is also possible, however, that Dean's recollection of such a request is a case of nonverbal gist recall rather than a script-based construction. Perhaps Nixon *did* ask Dean to sit down, but with a gesture rather than a word—a brief wave of a commanding presidential hand. To recall such a gesture as if it had been a verbal request would not be much of an error. Current theoretical interest in the recall of written texts should not bind us to the nonverbal components of real conversation.

Although familiar scripts and nonverbal cues explain a few of Dean's errors, most of them seem to have deeper roots. They follow, I believe, from Dean's own character and especially from his self-centered assessment of events at the White House. What his testimony really describes is not the September 15 meeting itself but his fantasy of it: the meeting as it should have been, so to speak. In his mind Nixon *should* have been glad that the indictments stopped with Liddy, Haldeman *should* have been telling Nixon what a great job Dean was doing; most of all, praising him *should* have been the first order of business. In addition, Dean *should* have told Nixon that the cover-up might unravel, as it eventually did, instead of telling him it was a great success. By June, this fantasy had become the way Dean remembered the meeting.

Almost. But Dean was not really as confident of his recollection as the tone of his statement suggested; not as sure of himself as he claimed in the exchange with Senator Inouye. This becomes clear in a very sharp interrogation by Senator Baker:

Senator Baker: I am going to try now to focus entirely on the meeting of September 15.

Mr. Dean: Right.

Senator Baker: And I have an ambition to focus sharply on it in order to disclose as much information as possible about the September 15 meeting. What I want to do is to test, once again, not the credibility of your testimony but the quality of the evidence, that is, is it direct evidence.

Mr. Dean: I understand (*Hearings*, p. 1474).

Dean does understand: Baker wants vivid details and exact wording. The next few exchanges show how he struggles to reconcile the vagueness of his actual recollection with Baker's demands for specificity, dodging some questions and eventually committing himself on others. After an uncontroversial account of how he learned that Nixon wanted to see him that evening, Dean begins with his physical entrance into the office:

Mr. Dean:	When I entered the office I can recall that—you have been in the office, you know the way there are two chairs at the side of the President's desk.
Senator Baker:	You are speaking of the Oval Office?
Mr. Dean:	Of the Oval Office. As you face the President, on the left-hand chair Mr. Haldeman was sitting and they had obviously been immersed in a conversation and the President asked me to come in and I stood there for a moment. He said "Sit down," and I sat in a chair on the other side.
Senator Baker:	You sat in the right-hand chair?
Mr. Dean:	I sat on the right-hand chair.
Senator Baker:	That is the one he usually says no to, but go ahead.
Mr. Dean:	I was unaware of that. (Laughter)
Senator Baker:	Go ahead, Mr. Dean (*Ibid.,* p. 1475).

Now Dean plunges into the conversation, giving almost exactly the same account of it that he had presented in his prepared statement a few days before. Indeed, his opening phrase suggests that he is remembering that statement rather than the meeting itself:

Mr. Dean:	As I tried to describe in my statement, the reception was very warm and cordial. There was some preliminary pleasantries, and then the next thing that I recall the President very clearly saying to me is that he had been told by Mr. Haldeman that he had been kept posted or made aware of my handling of the various aspects of the Watergate case and the fact that the case, you know, the indictments had now been handed down, no one in the White House had been indicted, they had stopped at Liddy (*Ibid.*).

Senator Baker is not satisfied with this response; he wants to know how accurate Dean is really claiming to be:

Senator Baker:	Stop, stop, stop just for one second. "That no one in the White House had been indicted": Is that as near

> to the exact language—I don't know so I am not
> laying a trap for you, I just want to know (*Ibid.*).

It is now clear that the right answer to Baker's question would have been
"no." Nixon did not use anything remotely like the "exact language" in
question; the conversation did not go that way at all. Dean's answer is
cautious:

Mr. Dean:	Yes, there was a reference to the fact that the indictments had been handed down and it was quite obvious that no one in the White House had been indicted on the indictments that had been handed down (*Ibid.*).

Notice that although Dean's answer begins with "Yes," he now avoids
attributing the critical words to Nixon. He hides behind ambiguous
phrases like "There was a reference to the fact that . . ." and "It was quite
obvious . . ." Baker is unsatisfied with these evasions and continues to
press for a straight answer:

Senator Baker: Did he say that, though? (*Ibid.*).

Dean decides to be honest about it:

Mr. Dean:	Did he say that no one in the White House had been handed down? I can't recall it (*Ibid.*).

This is the answer which suggests to me that Dean was being as truthful as
he could. After all, he might easily have answered "yes" instead of "I can't
recall it." But he doesn't want to give up the points he has already scored,
so he repeats them:

Mr. Dean: (continuing)	I can recall a reference to the fact that the indictments were now handed down and he was aware of that and the status of the indictments and expressed what to me was a pleasure to the fact that it had stopped with Mr. Liddy (*Ibid.*).

This paragraph is a nice summary of what Dean remembers from the conversation, and it is phrased so carefully that everything in it is true. There
was reference to the indictments (by Haldeman and Dean); Nixon *was*
aware of that (though he didn't say so); and somehow he did express what
Dean *interpreted* as pleasure in the outcome. It is fair to say that Dean

here captures the "tenor," though not the gist, of what went on in the Oval Office that afternoon. But Baker notices that he still hasn't committed himself to any exact statements by Nixon, and tries again:

> *Senator Baker:* Tell me what he said.
> *Mr. Dean:* Well, as I say, he told me I had done a good job—
> *Senator Baker:* No, let's talk about the pleasure. He expressed pleasure the indictments had stopped at Mr. Liddy. Can you just for the purposes of our information tell me the language that he used? (*Ibid.*).

Dean ducks once more:

> *Mr. Dean:* Senator, let me make it very clear: The pleasure that it had stopped there is an inference of mine based on, as I told Senator Gurney yesterday, the impression I had as a result of the, of his, complimenting me (*Ibid.*).

Baker hangs tough:

> *Senator Baker:* Can you give us any information, can you give us any further insight into what the President said?
> *Mr. Dean:* Yes, I can recall he told me that he appreciated how difficult a job it had been for me.
> *Senator Baker:* Is that close to the exact language?
> *Mr. Dean:* Yes, that is close to the exact language (*Ibid.*, p. 1476).

Finally Dean gives in and puts words into Nixon's mouth. He may just have felt he had no choice: if he didn't claim to remember *any* of Nixon's remarks his whole testimony might be discredited. But also he may have believed it. Nixon's compliment was what he had most yearned for, and his invented version of it may have been the most compelling thing in his memory. Either way, the exchange seems to have hardened his willingness to testify to exact language. He and Baker went at it again a few minutes later when Dean said he had told Nixon "that the matter had been contained." Baker repeatedly asked whether he had used that very word, and Dean repeatedly asserted that he had done so. When Baker questioned him closely about how the President had reacted to "contained," however, Dean said he did not recall. He certainly didn't: the word "contained" appears nowhere in the transcript.

In summary, it is clear that Dean's account of the opening of the September 15 conversation is wrong both as to the words used and their gist. Moreover, cross-examination did not reveal his errors as clearly as one might have hoped. The effect of Baker's hard questioning was mixed. Although it did show up the weakness of Dean's verbatim recall, the overall result may have been to increase his credibility. Dean came across as a man who has a good memory for gist with an occasional literal word stuck in, like a raisin in a pudding. He was not such a man. He remembered how he had felt himself and what he had wanted, together with the general state of affairs; he didn't remember what anyone had actually said. His testimony had much truth in it, but not at the level of "gist." It was true at a deeper level. Nixon was the kind of man Dean described, he had the knowledge Dean attributed to him, there was a cover-up. Dean remembered all of that; he just didn't recall the actual conversation he was testifying about.

So far I have concentrated on the first few minutes of the meeting, covered in a single paragraph of Dean's prepared statement. The next paragraph is interesting because (unlike the first) it refers to a bit of conversation that actually occurred.

> *Mr. Dean:* Early in our conversation the President said to me that former FBI Director Hoover had told him shortly after he assumed office in 1969 that his campaign had been bugged in 1968. The President said that at some point we should get the facts out on this and use this to counter the problems that we were encountering (*Ibid.*, p. 958).

As we have already seen, an exchange about Hoover and bugging in previous campaigns did take place, a little after the beginning of the conversation. But although it was indeed Nixon who raised the subject, it was Dean, not Nixon, who brought Hoover's name into it: "I understand that only the former director had that information." Dean may have forgotten this because Haldeman had put him down so sharply ("No, that is not true"), or he may have preferred to put the words into Nixon's mouth for other reasons. In any case, he isn't quite right.

The remainder of Dean's testimony about the meeting is no better than the parts we have examined. He mentions topics that were indeed discussed, but never reproduces the real gist of anything that was said. Surprisingly, he does *not* remember the President's actual compliment to him ("putting your fingers in the leaks") although it is a fairly striking phrase. At the end of his statement he presents the following summary:

> *Mr. Dean:* I left the meeting with the impression that the President was well aware of what had been going on regarding the success of keeping the White House out of the Watergate scandal, and I also had expressed to him my concern that I was not confident that the cover-up could be maintained indefinitely (*Ibid.*, p. 959).

The first part of this summary is fair enough: Nixon was surely ". . . well aware of what had been going on." The conclusion is less fair; Dean seriously—perhaps deliberately—misrepresents the optimistic predictions he had made. In fact he was *not* wise enough or brave enough to warn Nixon in September, though by June he was smart enough to wish he had done so.

THE MEETING OF MARCH 21

The cover-up was only temporarily successful. Although Nixon was re-elected overwhelmingly in November of 1972, Dean's problems increased steadily. There were more blackmail demands by the indicted Watergate defendants and more investigations moving closer to the White House. Dean met frequently with Nixon, Haldeman, and the others, but their strategems were unsuccessful. Dean began to realize that he and the others were engaging in a crime ("obstruction of justice"), and might eventually go to prison for it. He was not sure whether Nixon understood the gravity of the situation. Finally he resolved to ask the President for a private meeting at which he could lay out all the facts. This meeting took place on March 21, 1973.

Dean's autobiography (1976) relates an incident that occurred on the day before the critical meeting. When he was trying to describe the relentlessly increasing complexity of the Watergate affair to Richard Moore, another White House aide, Moore compared it to the growth of a tumor. The metaphor attracted Dean, and he resolved to use it in his report the next day: to tell Nixon that there was a "cancer" growing on the presidency. The transcript of the meeting shows that he did so. After a few minutes of conversation about the day's events, Dean and the President continue as follows:

> D: The reason I thought we ought to talk this morning is because in our conversations I have the impression that you don't know everything I know, and it makes it very difficult for you to make judgments that only you can make on some of these targets, and I thought that—
>
> P: In other words, I have to know why you feel that we shouldn't unravel something?
>
> D: Let me give you my overall first.
>
> P: In other words, your judgment as to where it stands, and where we will go.
>
> D: I think there is no doubt about the seriousness of the problem we've got. We have a cancer within, close to the presidency, that is growing. It is growing daily. It's compounded, growing geometrically now because it compounds itself. That will be clear if I, you know, explain some of the details of why it is. Basically it

is because (1) we are being blackmailed; (2) people are going to start perjuring themselves very quickly that have not had to perjure themselves to protect other people in the line. And there is no assurance—

P: That that won't bust?

D: That that won't bust (*Presidential Transcripts*, pp. 98–99).

In this first part of the March 21 meeting, Dean was alone with the President. They remained alone for about an hour, and then Haldeman came in to join the discussion for another 45 minutes or so. Haldeman's entrance proved to be a critical turning point in Dean's later memory of that morning: he forgot the rest of the conversation almost completely. What he said about the first hour, in contrast, was quite accurate. Comparison of the transcript with Dean's subsequent testimony shows clear recall of the gist of what was said. One's admiration for his memory is somewhat diminished, however, by the realization that the March 21 meeting was less a conversation than the delivery of a well-prepared report. Dean did most of the talking, taking 20 minutes to describe the events before the break-in and 40 more for the cover-up. Although Nixon interjected occasional remarks, questions, or expletives, the hour stayed quite close to the script Dean had prepared for it in advance.

The difference between this meeting and that of September 15 is instructive. This one fulfilled Dean's hopes as the earlier one had not: he really did give a personal lecture to the President of the United States, talking while Nixon listened. His testimony, too long to reproduce here, highlights the meeting's didactic quality. Almost every statement begins with "I told him . . . ," "I proceeded to tell him . . . ," "I informed the President . . ." or some similar phrase. He was remembering a report that he had rehearsed ahead of time, presented as planned, and probably continued to rehearse afterwards. It became John Dean's own story; March 21 had merely been his first opportunity to tell it.

Dean's testimony includes a fragment of nearly verbatim recall that later achieved some notoriety: he quoted his own remark about the "cancer on the presidency" to the Senate Committee. This, too, was a well-rehearsed passage. We know that he prepared it in advance, and the transcript shows that he used it repeatedly. (He probably used it on other occasions as well; why let such a good phrase go to waste?) His first presentation of the simile, early in the meeting, has been quoted above. Twenty minutes later he refers back to it:

D: . . . When I say this is a growing cancer, I say it for reasons like this . . . (*Ibid.*, p. 111).

And still later he brings it in obliquely:

> D: . . . we should begin to think . . . how to minimize the further growth of this thing . . . (*Ibid.*, p. 119*)*.

Interestingly, Dean's self-quotation to the Senators was not faithful to any of these occasions:

> *Mr. Dean:* I began by telling the President that there was a cancer growing on the presidency and that if the cancer was not removed the President himself would be killed by it. I also told him that it was important that this cancer be removed immediately because it was growing more deadly every day (*Hearings,* p. 998).

A glance back at the excerpt from the transcript shows that Dean is once again giving himself the benefit of hindsight. He did *not* say that the President would be *killed* by the cancer, for example. By June he probably wished he had done so; I don't know whether he altered the wording in his testimony deliberately or whether his memory had already accommodated itself slightly to his self-image.

In Dean's mind, the significance of the March 21 meeting must have lain in the degree to which he dominated it. That may explain why he barely mentioned the second half of the meeting in his Senate testimony; Haldeman's entrance spoiled his private command performance. The rest of the session was by no means uninteresting, however. What actually happened was that Nixon, Haldeman, and Dean considered various options, trying to find the best way to deal with their Watergate dilemma. One of those options was to raise money to meet the blackmail demands of the men who had already been convicted. This possibility seemed to attract Nixon; he returned to it again and again. He had already discussed it in the first hour, when only Dean was with him:

> D: I would say these people are going to cost a million dollars over the next two years.
> P: We could get that. On the money, if you need the money you could get that. You could get a million dollars. You could get it in cash. I know where it could be gotten. It is not easy but it could be done . . . (*Presidential Transcripts,* p. 110).

He seemed more enthusiastic about it than Dean himself:

> P: Just looking at the immediate problem, don't you think you have to handle Hunt's financial situation damn soon?
> D: I think that is—I talked with Mitchell about that last night and—
> P: It seems to me we have to keep the cap on the bottle that much or we don't have any options (*Ibid.*, p. 112).

Later he makes it as explicit as he possibly can:

D: The blackmailers. Right.

P: Well I wonder if that part of it can't be—I wonder if that doesn't—let me put it frankly: I wonder if that doesn't have to be continued? Let me put it this way: let us suppose you get the million bucks, and you get the proper way to handle it. You could hold that side?

D: Uh-huh.

P: It would seem to me that would be worthwhile (*Ibid.*, p. 117).

Remarks like this continue to sprinkle the conversation after Haldeman joins them:

P: . . . First, it is going to require approximately a million dollars to take care of the jackasses who are in jail. That can be arranged . . . (*Ibid.*, p. 127).

. . .

P: Now let me tell you. We could get the money. There is no problem in that . . . (*Ibid.*, p. 129).

. . .

P: I just have a feeling on it. Well, it sounds like a lot of money, a million dollars. Let me say that I think we could get that . . . (*Ibid.*, p. 130).[1]

These are quite remarkable things for a President to say. They would certainly seem to be memorable, and indeed Dean did not forget them. He just assigned them to a different day! Although he makes no reference to them in his testimony about March 21, his statement includes the following description of a meeting with Nixon on March 13, eight days before:

Mr. Dean: . . . It was during this conversation that Haldeman came into the office. After this brief interruption by Haldeman's coming in, but while he was still there, I told the President about the fact that there was no money to pay these individuals to meet their demands. He asked me

---

[1]Nixon never expressed any hesitation about making these payments, or any reluctance to meet the burglars' demands for money. He did, however, agree with Dean that their demands for *executive clemency* should not be met. At one point he said, "No—it is wrong, that's for sure" about the possibility of clemency. The transcript shows no analogous statement about the blackmail payments.

282 | Ulric Neisser

how much it would cost. I told him that I could only make an estimate that it might be as high as $1 million or more. He told me that that was no problem, and he also looked over at Haldeman and made the same statement . . . (*Hearings*, p. 995).

Dean amplifies this account later, during cross-examination:

> *Mr. Dean:* . . . We had also had a discussion on March 13 about the money demands that were being made. At the time he discussed the fact that a million dollars is no problem. He repeated it several times. I can very vividly recall that the way he sort of rolled his chair back from his desk and leaned over to Mr. Haldeman and said, "A million dollars is no problem" (*Ibid.*, p. 1423).

It is hardly surprising that Dean remembered these million-dollar statements, especially since Nixon repeated them so often. It *is* a little surprising that he put them into the wrong conversation. (There is a transcript of the March 13 meeting, and it shows no such remarks by the President.) Evidently Dean's improvised method of *temporal loci*, based on newspaper clippings, did not work as well as his exchange with Senator Inouye had suggested. His ego got in the way again. The March 21 meeting had been the occasion for his own personal report to the President; he could not suppose that anything else worth mentioning had happened. Other memories were shifted to another day if they survived at all.

Nixon's eagerness to pay the blackmail money was not the only part of the conversation to suffer this fate. Dean even displaced one of his own jokes; a joke that had drawn a response from Haldeman if not from Nixon. They were discussing various illegal ways of "laundering" the blackmail money so it could not be traced:

> D: And that means you have to go to Vegas with it or a bookmaker in New York City. I have learned all these things after the fact. I will be in great shape for the next time around!
> H: (Expletive deleted) (*Presidential Transcripts*, p. 134).

That may not have been the only time Dean used this wisecrack; he probably enjoyed describing himself as increasingly skilled in underworld techniques. Certainly he didn't mind repeating it to the Senators, though his statement assigns it, too, to March 13 rather than March 21:

> *Mr. Dean:* . . . I told him I was learning about things I had never had before, but the next time I would certainly be more

knowledgeable. This comment got a laugh out of
Haldeman (*Hearings*, p. 996).

It isn't very funny.

IMPLICATIONS FOR THE PSYCHOLOGY OF MEMORY

Are we all like this? Is everyone's memory constructed, staged, self-centered? And do we all have access to certain invariant facts nevertheless?
Such questions cannot be answered by single case histories. My own
guess—and it is only a guess—is that reconstruction played an exaggerated part in Dean's testimony. The circumstances and the man conspired
to favor exaggeration. The events *were* important; his testimony *was* critical; its effect *was* historic. Dean was too intelligent not to know what he
was doing, and too ambitious and egocentric to remain unaffected by it.
His ambition reorganized his recollections: even when he tries to tell the
truth, he can't help emphasizing his own role in every event. A different
man in the same position might have observed more dispassionately, reflected on his experiences more thoughtfully, and reported them more accurately. Unfortunately, such traits of character are rare.

What have we learned about testimony by comparing "the human
tape recorder" with a real one? We are hardly surprised to find that memory is constructive or that confident witnesses may be wrong. William
Stern studied the psychology of testimony at the turn of the century and
warned us not to trust memory even under oath; Bartlett was doing experiments on "constructive" memory fifty years ago. I believe, however, that
John Dean's testimony can do more than remind us of their work. For one
thing, his constructed memories were not altogether wrong. On the contrary, there is a sense in which he was altogether right; a level at which he
was telling the truth about the Nixon White House. And sometimes—as in
his testimony about March 21—he was more specifically right as well.
These islands of accuracy deserve special consideration. What kinds of
things did he remember?

Dean's task as he testified before the Senate Committee was to recall
specific well-defined conversations, ". . . conversations which took place
months ago." This is what witnesses are always instructed to do: stick to
the facts, avoid inferences and generalizations. Such recall is what Tulving
(1972) called *episodic*; it involves the retrieval of particular autobiographical moments, individual episodes of one's life. Tulving contrasted episodic
memory only with what he called *semantic* memory, the individual's accumulated store of facts and word meanings and general knowledge. That
concept seems inadequate as a description of data such as these. Dean's
recollection of Nixon's remarks about the million dollars was not merely

semantic: he talked as if he were recalling one or more specific events. I doubt, however, that any of those events was being recalled uniquely in its own right. A single such episode might not have found its way into Dean's testimony at all. What seems to be specific in his memory actually depends on repeated episodes, rehearsed presentations, or overall impressions. He believes that he is recalling one conversation at a time, that his memory is "episodic" in Tulving's sense, but he is mistaken.

He is not alone in making this mistake. I believe that this aspect of Dean's testimony illustrates a very common process. The single clear memories that we recollect so vividly actually stand for something else; they are "screen memories," a little like those Freud discussed long ago. Often their real basis is a set of repeated experiences, a sequence of related events that the single recollection merely typifies or represents. We are like the subjects of Posner and Keele (1970), who forgot the individual dot patterns of a series but "remembered" the prototypical pattern they had never seen. Such memories might be called *repisodic* rather than episodic: what seems to be an episode actually *rep*resents a *rep*etition. Dean remembers the million-dollar remark because Nixon made it so often; he recalls the "cancer" metaphor because he first planned it and then repeated it; he remembers his March 21 lecture to the President because he planned it, then presented it, and then no doubt went over it again and again in his own mind. What he says about these "repisodes" is essentially correct, even though it is not literally faithful to any one occasion. He is not remembering the "gist" of a single episode by itself, but the common characteristics of a whole series of events.

This notion may help us to interpret the paradoxical sense in which Dean was accurate throughout his testimony. Given the numerous errors in his reports of conversations, what did he tell the truth about? I think that he extracted the common themes that remained invariant across many conversations and many experiences, and then incorporated those themes in his testimony. His many encounters with Nixon were themselves a kind of "repisode." There were certain consistent and repeated elements in all those meetings; they had a theme that expressed itself in different ways on different occasions. Nixon wanted the cover-up to succeed; he was pleased when it went well; he was troubled when it began to unravel; he was perfectly willing to consider illegal activities if they would extend his power or confound his enemies. John Dean did not misrepresent this theme in his testimony; he just dramatized it. In memory experiments, subjects often recall the gist of a sentence but express it in different words. Dean's consistency was deeper; he recalled the theme of a whole series of conversations and expressed it in different events. Nixon hoped that the transcripts would undermine Dean's testimony by showing that he had been wrong. They did not have this effect because he was wrong only in terms of isolated episodes. Episodes are not the only kinds of facts. Except where the significance of his own role was at stake, Dean was right about what had really been going on in the White House. What he later told the Senators was fairly close to the mark; his mind was not a tape recorder, but it certainly received the message that was being given.

※

├─ *This assessment of John Dean's testimony has not gone unchallenged. In a sharp theoretical critique (too long to reproduce here), Derek Edwards and Jonathan Potter suggest that the entire enterprise is flawed. They argue that the notion of an objective truth (i.e., what Nixon actually said on a given occasion) makes no sense in such cases; the meanings of conversational utterances are always constructed from context and can always be disputed. They illustrate their claim with a similar British case (complete with a mysterious missing tape-recording!) that centered on what the Chancellor of the Exchequer had actually said in a 1988 interview. For details see D. Edwards and J. Potter (1992), "The Chancellor's memory: Rhetoric and truth in discursive remembering,"* Applied Cognitive Psychology, 6, 187–215.

REFERENCES

Bartlett, F. C. (1932). *Remembering*. Cambridge: Cambridge University Press.

Bower, G. H., Black, J. B., & Turner, T. J. (1979). Scripts in memory for text. *Cognitive Psychology, 11*, 177–220.

Bransford, J. D., & Franks, J. J. (1972). The abstraction of linguistic ideas: A review. *Cognition, 1*, 211–249.

Buckhout, R. (1974). Eyewitness testimony. *Scientific American, 231*(6), 23–31.

Dean, J. W. (1976). *Blind ambition*. New York: Simon & Schuster.

Freud, S. (1956). Screen memories. Reprinted in *Collected papers of Sigmund Freud*, Vol. V. London: Hogarth Press.

Gibson, J. J. (1979). *The ecological approach to visual perception*. Boston: Houghton Mifflin.

Hearings before the Select Committee on Presidential Campaign Activities of the United States Senate, Ninety-Third Congress, First Session, 1973.

Mandler, J. M., & Johnson, N. (1977). Remembrance of things parsed: Story structure and recall. *Cognitive Psychology 9*, 111–151.

McCarthy, M. (1975). *The mask of state: Watergate portraits*. New York: Harcourt Brace Jovanovich.

Posner, M. J., & Keele, S. (1970). Retention of abstract ideas. *Journal of Experimental Psychology, 83,* 304–308.

The presidential transcripts. (1974). New York: Dell.

Stern, W. (1904). Wirklichkeitsversuche (Reality experiments). *Beitrage zur Psychologie der Aussage, 2,* (1), 1–31.

Tulving, E. (1972). Episodic and semantic memory. In E. Tulving & W. Donaldson (Eds.), *Organization and memory.* New York: Academic Press.

Part V

EARLY CHILDHOOD

Much has changed since Sigmund Freud first defined the problem of childhood amnesia: Why can't we remember the early years of our own lives? He suggested that the "amnesia" was due to repression, a view which is no longer in favor. Ernest Schachtel, a 1940s psychoanalyst with a literary bent, was the first to take a more cognitive approach. The most promising current view, informed by both modern developmental psychology and empirical studies of young children's memory, is presented by Katherine Nelson in Selection 28. But what about the few memories we *do* retain from childhood: Are they especially significant? This section, which begins with Freud's views on that very question, ends with a cautionary experiment: early recollections, like so many other kinds of memory, are quite vulnerable to suggestion.

26 | An Early Memory from Goethe's Autobiography

Sigmund Freud

Why are a few, often apparently trivial, memories of childhood preserved while so many others are lost? Freud, the thoroughgoing determinist, insisted that there must be a reason in every case. Memories that seem insignificant actually stand in some symbolic or associative or concealing relation to deeper, more important ideas. Often, he thought, the relationship can be uncovered by psychoanalysis. This idea, which was also emphasized by Alfred Adler, is discussed in several of Freud's papers; the one reprinted here seems to me especially impressive. It is a tour de force, in which he explains an early memory of Johann Wolfgang Goethe, Germany's greatest poet. Does that seem an impossible undertaking? Read on.

"**W**hen we try to remember what happened to us in early childhood, we often confuse what others have told us with our own directly perceived experiences." The poet Goethe makes this remark near the beginning of his account of his own life, an account which he began to write when he was 60 years old. It is preceded only by a brief description of his birth ". . . on August 28, 1749, at noon as the clock struck twelve." A favorable constellation of the stars may have been responsible for his survival: he was almost given up for dead at birth, and strenuous efforts were required before he saw the light of day. After the remark about memory, there is a brief description of the house he grew up in, and especially of an enclosed area

※ From S. Freud (1917). Eine Kindheitserinnerung aus 'Dichtung und Wahrheit', *Imago, 5;* translation by Ulric Neisser. The Hubback translation in Vol. 4 of Freud's *Collected Papers* (Basic Books, 1959) is entitled "A childhood recollection from 'Dichtung und Wahrheit'."

that opened on to the street, which the children—he and his younger sister—liked best. But then Goethe really describes only a single event that can be assigned to his "earliest childhood" (before the age of four?), an event of which he seemed to have retained a personal memory. His account of this episode is as follows:

> Across the street lived the three brothers von Ochsenstein, sons of the late Village Mayor. They grew fond of me, and busied themselves with me and teased me in many ways.
>
> My family loved to tell all sorts of stories about the mischievous tricks to which those otherwise solemn and lonely men encouraged me. I will recount only one of these pranks here. There had been a pottery sale; not only had the kitchen been supplied for some time to come, but miniature crockery of the same sort had been bought for us children to play with. One fine afternoon, when there was nothing doing in the house, I played with my dishes and pots in the rooms (mentioned above) that fronted on the street. Since this didn't come to much, I tossed a piece of crockery out into the street and was delighted by its cheerful crash. The brothers saw how much this amused me, so that I clapped my hands with delight, and called out "another!" I did not hesitate to fling the next pot, and—encouraged by repeated shouts of "another"—a whole assortment of little dishes, saucepans, and jugs onto the pavement. My neighbors continued to signal their approval, and I was more than glad to amuse them. My supplies ran out, but they continued to shout "another!" I hurried straight to the kitchen and fetched the earthenware plates, which of course made an even jollier show as they broke. So I ran back and forth with one plate after another, as I could get them down from the shelf, and when the brothers still claimed to be unsatisfied I hurled every bit of crockery within my reach to ruin in the same way. Only later did someone appear to thwart me and put a stop to it. The damage was done, and in return for all that broken crockery there was at least a wonderful story, which amused the rogues who had been its prime movers till the end of their days.

In preanalytic times this passage would not have been disturbing and could be read without hesitation, but now the analytic conscience has come to life. We have formed definite opinions and have definite expectations about early childhood memories, and would like to suppose that they apply quite generally. It is not a meaningless or insignificant matter when some one particular of a child's life escapes the general forgetting of childhood. On the contrary, one must suppose that what has been retained in memory is also what was most significant for that period of life: either it already had great importance at the time or else it acquired that importance through the effect of later experiences.

It is true that the great significance of such childhood memories is rarely obvious. Most of them appear unimportant or even trivial, and at first it seemed incomprehensible that just these could defy the amnesia of childhood. The individual who had preserved them through long years as his own personal memories could no more do them justice than the stranger to whom he related them. Recognition of their significance required a certain amount of interpretive work—work that either showed how their contents should be replaced by something else, or demonstrated their connection to other unmistakably important experiences for which they had substituted as so-called "screen memories."

Whenever one works through a life history psychoanalytically, one always succeeds in clarifying the meaning of the earliest recollections in this way. As a rule it turns out that the very memory to which the analysand gives primacy, which he tells first as he begins his life story, is the most important and holds the key to the secret chambers of his mental life. But in the case of the little incident related by Goethe, we do not have enough to work with. The ways and means that we use to reach interpretations with our own patients are naturally unavailable here, and it does not seem possible to link the incident itself in any clear way with important experiences of his later life. A prank that damaged some household goods, carried out under the influence of outsiders, is surely not a suitable vignette to stand for everything Goethe tells us about his rich life experience. The impression of complete innocence and irrelevance seems to be confirmed for this childhood memory, which may thus teach us not to push the claims of psychoanalysis too far or to apply them on inappropriate occasions.

I had long since put this small problem out of my mind when chance brought me a patient who presented a similar childhood memory, but in a more comprehensible context. The patient was a highly cultured and intelligent man, twenty-seven years old, whose whole life was consumed by a conflict with his mother that reached into nearly every aspect of his existence, severely impairing the development of his capacity to love and to lead an independent life. The conflict went far back into his childhood, apparently to his fourth year. Before that time he had been a weak and always sickly child, but his memory had turned that difficult time into a paradise because he then possessed the unrestricted affection of his mother, not divided with anyone else. When he was not yet four his brother was born, a brother who is still living today. In reacting to this intrusion, he transformed himself in a headstrong and unmanageable lad who constantly provoked his mother's strictness. He never again got on the right track.

When he became my patient—not least because his bigoted mother detested psychoanalysis—he had long since forgotten his jealousy of his brother, a jealousy which in its time had even led him to try to kill the baby in its cradle. He now treated his younger brother with great respect.

Nevertheless certain apparently unmotivated actions, in which he suddenly caused severe injury to animals that he otherwise loved—his hunting dog, and birds that he had carefully tended—were probably best understood as echoes of the hostile impulse once directed against his little brother.

This patient reported that on one occasion, around the time when he tried to kill his hated brother, he had thrown all the crockery he could reach out of the window of his house into the street. The very same thing that Goethe describes in his personal recollections! It is worth noting that my patient was a foreigner who had not had a German education; he had never read Goethe's autobiography.

This piece of information necessarily suggested to me that Goethe's childhood recollection might be interpreted in the way that my patient's story had made irresistible. But could the conditions necessary to support this interpretation be found in the poet's childhood? Goethe himself lays the responsibility for his childhood prank on the urgings of the von Ochsenteins, but his account actually indicates that his neighbors had only cheered him on to continue his own activity. He had begun quite spontaneously. When he gives "Since this (his playing) didn't come to much" as his reason for beginning, we can safely conclude that he was unaware of the real motive of his action at the time he wrote the autobiography, and probably for many years before.

It is known that Johann Wolfgang Goethe and his sister Cornelia were the oldest survivors of a larger set of rather sickly children. Dr. Hanns Sachs has been kind enough to provide me with the dates pertaining to those of Goethe's siblings who died young:

a. Hermann Jakob, christened on Monday, November 27, 1752, reached the age of six years and six weeks; buried on January 13, 1759.

b. Katharina Elisabetha, christened on Monday, September 9, 1754; buried on Thursday, December 22, 1755 (one year and four months old).

c. Johanna Maria, christened on Tuesday, March 29, 1757; buried on Saturday, August 11, 1759 (two years and four months old). This was certainly the very charming and pretty young girl described by her brother.

d. Georg Adolph, christened on Sunday, June 15, 1760; buried, eight months old, on Wednesday, February 18, 1761.

Goethe's closest sister, Cornelia Friederica Christiana, was born on December 7, 1750, when he was one-and-a-quarter years old. The very small difference in their ages virtually excludes her as an object of jealousy. It is known that when children's emotional life is awakened, they never react so strongly against the siblings who are already there; they rather direct their antipathy toward the new arrivals. Then, too, it would be impossible to reconcile the scene we are trying to interpret with Goethe's tender age at the time of (and just after) Cornelia's birth.

Goethe was three-and-a-quarter years old when his first brother, Hermann Jakob, was born. About two years later, when he was about five, his second sister arrived. Both ages must be considered in trying to date the crockery-smashing incident. The first may be more likely; it also corresponds more closely with the case of my patient, who was about three-and-three-quarters when his brother was born.

It is worth noting that brother Hermann Jakob, to whom this attempt at interpretation seems to lead, was not such a fleeting guest in Goethe's nursery as the later siblings. Surprisingly, there is not a single word about him in his elder brother's life story.[1] He attained more than six years of age, and when he died Johann Wolfgang was nearly ten years old. Dr. Ed. Hitschmann, who was kind enough to make his notes on this matter available to me, has expressed this opinion:

> Young Goethe was also not unhappy at a younger brother's death. At least his mother gave the following account, reported by Bettina Brentano: "It seemed strange to his mother that he shed no tears at the death of his brother Jakob, who was his playmate; indeed, he seemed somewhat irritated at the lamentations of his parents and sisters. When the mother later asked the obstinate boy if he hadn't loved his brother, he ran to his room and brought out a pile of papers from under his bed. They were covered with lessons and stories, and he told her that he had done all this to teach it to his brother." Thus it seems that the older brother had at least enjoyed playing father to the younger, showing off his own superiority.

We can conclude that the throwing out of the crockery was a symbolic, or more precisely a magical act. By this act the child (Goethe as well as my patient) gives vigorous expression to his wish that the disturbing intruder be eliminated. We do not need to deny the delight that the child

---

[1][*Freud added the following footnote to the article when it was republished in 1924.*] I will use this opportunity to retract an incorrect statement that never should have occurred. Later on in the first volume, the younger brother *is* mentioned and described. This is done in the course of Goethe's recollections of the burdensome illness of childhood, which afflicted his brother "not a little." "He was of a delicate constitution, quiet and self-willed; we never had a real relationship with one another. Also he did not really survive the years of childhood." [*Apparently Freud himself made a Freudian slip in his eagerness to establish what he thought was a Freudian slip on Goethe's part.*]

takes in the crashing objects. The fact that an action is pleasurable in itself does not prevent—indeed, it invites—repetition in the service of other motives. But we do not believe that delight in jingling and smashing could have assured these childish pranks a permanent place in the memories of grown men. We do not even hesitate to introduce an additional complication into our account of the motivation for this act. The child who breaks the crockery knows perfectly well that he is being naughty, and that the adults will scold him for it. If this knowledge does not restrain him, he probably has some grudge against his parents; he wants to show how bad he is.

Taking delight in breaking and in broken things would also be possible if the child just threw the fragile objects on the floor. On this basis, throwing them out the window into the street would remain unexplained. But "out" seems to be an essential component of the magical act, which stems from its hidden meaning. The new baby is to be removed through the window, perhaps because it came through the window in the first place. The whole affair would then be equivalent to what we are told was the response of one child when he was informed that the stork had brought him a little sister. "Let him take her away again" was his suggestion.

However, we are fully aware how dubious it is—apart from any internal uncertainties—to base the interpretation of a childhood event on a single analogy. For this reason I withheld my interpretation of the little scene from Goethe's autobiography for many years. Then one day I had a patient who began his analysis with the following sentences, which I reproduce verbatim:

> I am the oldest of eight or nine brothers and sisters.[2] One of my first memories is of my father sitting on his bed in his nightclothes, laughingly telling me that I had acquired a brother. I was then three-and-three-quarters years old; that is the difference in age between me and my closest brother. Then I know that shortly afterwards (or was it the year before?)[3] I threw various objects—brushes, or maybe just one brush, and shoes and other things—out the window into the street. I also have a still earlier memory. When I was two years old I spent the night with my parents in a hotel room in Linz when we were traveling to Salzkammergut. I was so restless during the night and cried so much that my father had to hit me.

[2]A striking momentary lapse. Unquestionably it was already produced by the wish to get rid of the brother. (cf. Ferenczi. On the formation of transient symptoms during analysis, *Zentralblatt für Psychoanalyse*, 1912, 2.)

[3]This expression of doubt, attached to the most essential part of the patient's statement, is a form of resistance. The patient himself retracted it shortly thereafter.

In the face of this testimony I had to abandon all doubt. When a patient in the analytic setting produces two ideas one after the other, almost in a single breath, we must interpret their proximity as a causal connection. So it was as if the patient had said "Because I learned that I had acquired a brother, I threw those things into the street soon thereafter." The throwing out of the brushes, shoes, etc. is recognizable as a reaction to the birth of the brother. It is also helpful that this time the thrown objects were not crockery but other things, probably just those that happened to be within reach. In this way the throwing out itself is revealed as the essential element of the action. The delight in jingling and breaking, and the nature of the objects on which the "execution is carried out" are revealed as variable and inessential.

Naturally the principle of relatedness must also be valid for the patient's third memory, which was placed at the end of the sequence although it is actually the earliest. It is easily applied. We understand that the two-year-old child was restless because he couldn't stand his father and mother being together in bed. On the journey it was probably impossible to prevent the child from witnessing this intimacy. Of the feelings that were aroused in the tiny jealous child at that time, a bitterness against women remained as a continuing source of disturbance in the development of his later life.

After these two experiences, I suggested to a meeting of the Psychoanalytic Society that behavior of this sort in young children might not be so rare. In response, Dr. von Hug-Hellmuth has made two further observations available to me. Here are her reports:

I

At about three-and-a-half years, little Erich "very suddenly" acquired the habit of throwing everything that didn't suit him out the window. But he also did it to things that weren't in his way and had nothing to do with him. On his father's birthday, when he was three years, four-and-a-half-months old, he hauled a heavy rolling pin from the kitchen into another room and flung it out of a window of the third-floor apartment onto the street. A few days later the mortar-pestle went the same way, followed by a pair of his father's heavy mountaineering boots that he first had to take out of their storage box.[4]

At that time his mother had a miscarriage; she had been seven or eight months pregnant. After that the little boy "seemed to have been transformed, he was so good and so quietly gentle." In the fifth or sixth month he had repeatedly said to his mother, "Mommy, I'm going to jump on your stomach," or "Mommy, I'll squash your stomach flat." In

---

[4]He always chose heavy objects.

October, a few days before the miscarriage, he said, "If I really have to have a brother, let it at least not be till after Christmas."

II

A young woman of nineteen spontaneously offered the following as her earliest recollection:

I see myself sitting under the table in the dining room, ready to creep out, feeling terribly disobedient. On the table is my coffee-mug—I can see the pattern of the porcelain clearly, even now—which I had just been going to throw out the window when my grandmother happened to come into the room.

The fact was that nobody had been concerning themselves with me, and as a result a "skin" had formed on the coffee—which I always found loathsome and still do.

My brother, who is two-and-a-half years younger than I am, was born that day; that was why nobody had time for me.

They still talk about how unbearable I was that day. Around noon I threw my father's favorite glass off the table; I soiled my dress several times; I was in the foulest possible mood all day long. I also smashed one of my bathtub toys in my rage.

It is hardly necessary to comment on these two cases. They confirm, without any additional analysis, that the child's bitterness about the expected or actual appearance of a competitor expresses itself in the act of throwing things out the window as well as by other naughty and destructive deeds. The "heavy objects" in the first case probably symbolize the mother herself, at whom the child's anger is directed so long as the new baby has not yet actually appeared. The three-and-a-half-year old boy knows that his mother is pregnant, and is quite sure that she is sheltering the baby in her body. This is reminiscent of "Little Hans"[5] and his particular fear of heavily loaded wagons.[6] In the second case it is noteworthy that the child was so young, only two-and-a-half years old.

---

[5]Freud, S. Analysis of a phobia in a five-year-old child. In *Collected Papers, Vol. 3.* New York: Basic Books, 1959.

[6]Some time ago, a woman of more than fifty years brought me a further confirmation of this symbol of pregnancy. She had often been told that as a little child, so young that she could barely talk, she used to drag her father over to the window excitedly whenever a heavily laden furniture van passed on the street. By using her memories of the house she lived in, it was possible to establish that she must have been younger than two-and-three-quarters at the time. Her closest younger brother was born about that time, and they moved to a new home to accommodate the increased size of the family. At about the same period she often had an anxious sensation, just before she fell asleep, that something unnaturally large was coming toward her; simultaneously "her hands seemed to swell up so fat."

If we now return to Goethe's early memory, and put what we think we have learned from the cases of these other children in its place, we find a perfectly comprehensible connection that would otherwise have remained undiscovered. It runs as follows: "I was a child of fortune; fate kept me alive although I had been given up for dead when I came into the world. The same fate got rid of my brother, so that I did not have to share my mother's love with him." From there the train of his thoughts goes on to another person who died in that early period of his life: his grandmother, who lived like a quiet and friendly ghost in another room of his home.

As I have already said elsewhere, he who has been the unquestioned darling of his mother will keep that feeling of victory, that certainty of success, for the rest of his life. It is a feeling that not infrequently brings real success in its wake. And a remark like "My strength is rooted in my relationship with my mother" would have been an entirely appropriate way for Goethe to begin the story of his life.

27 On Memory and Childhood Amnesia

Ernest G. Schachtel

No one can remember their very early childhood, although the scope of "very early" varies from one person to the next. It was Freud who first described this loss as a kind of "amnesia"—an amnesia broken only by occasional fragmentary images (Selection 5) *or screen memories* (Selection 26). *He attributed it to the force of repression: having resolved the Oedipal crisis by rejecting our infantile sexual wishes, we cannot tolerate any associated memory that might bring them back to consciousness. Schachtel, himself a psychoanalyst, offers an alternative explanation in this classic paper. His account is surprisingly modern: The schemata of adults are no longer appropriate for the experiences of childhood. But there is also something archaic in his argument; he tries to persuade his readers with ideas much older than those of cognitive psychology. He treats childhood amnesia as a symptom of lost innocence, as if it were our own fault—and our greatest misfortune—that we cannot hope to return to the Garden of Eden of our infancy.*

The beginning of the article has been omitted. Schachtel starts with Greek mythology: Mnemosyne, the Goddess of Memory, is the mother of muses and hence of all art. There is a conflict between the realistic requirements of the present and the delights of recollection. Proust, the "poet of memory," renounced ordinary life entirely to achieve Remembrance of Things Past. *But Goethe did not share Proust's fascination with memory; Schachtel quotes him as saying "I do not recognize memory in the sense that you mean it. Whatever we encounter that is great, beautiful, significant need not be*

From *Psychiatry*, 1947, *10*, 1–26. Copyright © 1947, 1975 by The William Alanson White Psychiatric Foundation, Inc. Reprinted by special permission of The Foundation.

remembered from the outside; need not be hunted up
and laid hold of, as it were. Rather, from the begin-
ning, it must be woven into the fabric of our inmost self,
must become one with it, create a new and better self
in us. . . . There is no past that one is allowed to long
for. There is only the eternally new, growing from the
enlarged elements of the past. . . ." Schachtel then turns
to Freud's contribution.

Freud, not unlike Proust, approaches the problem of memory not from wondering what or how well or how much man remembers but how hard it is to remember, how much is forgotten and not to be recovered at all or only with the greatest difficulty, and how the period richest in experience, the period of early childhood, is the one which is usually forgotten entirely save for a few apparently meaningless memory fragments. He finds this surprising since "we are informed that during those years which have left nothing but a few incomprehensible memory fragments, we have vividly reacted to impressions, that we have manifested human pain and pleasure and that we have expressed love, jealousy and other passions as they then affected us."[1] The few incomprehensible memory fragments left over from childhood, he considers as "concealing memories" (Deckerinnerungen), and his painstaking work to decipher their language bears more than a superficial resemblance to Proust's attempt to decipher the hieroglyphic characters of the images of a cloud, a triangle, a belfry, a flower, a pebble—a most difficult undertaking, but the only way to the true memories enclosed in these signs which seemed to be only indifferent material objects or sensations. It was Freud who made the discovery that a conflict, leading to repression, is responsible for the difficulty of this work of deciphering and for the difficulty of remembering the past. His well-known explanation of infantile amnesia is that the forgetting of childhood experiences is due to progressive repression of infantile sexuality, which reaches the peak of its manifestations in the third and fourth years of life. This repression is brought about by the "psychic forces of loathing, shame, and moral and esthetic ideal demands." These forces have the sanction of society, they are the product of society, which moulds the functions of all social activity

---

[1]Sigmund Freud (1938). Three contributions to the theory of sex. In *The basic writings of Sigmund Freud.* New York: Random House, 581.

and of that "uniform" memory in which Proust saw the irreconcilable antagonists of the true remembrance of things past.

It is the purpose of this essay to explore further the dynamics of this conflict in memory which leads to the striking phenomenon of childhood amnesia as well as to the difficulty, encountered by Proust though more hidden to the average eye, of recovering any true picture of past experience. To speak of a conflict in memory is a convenient abbreviation. Formulated more explicitly and accurately, the intention of this presentation is to shed light on some of the factors and conflicts in man and his society which make it difficult if not impossible for him really to remember his past and especially his early childhood.

Obviously, the concept of memory which such an approach presupposes cannot be the impersonal, artificial, isolated, and abstract concept implied by experimentation on the recall of digits, nonsense syllables, and similar material, a concept which seems more appropriate for the testing of the capacity of some mechanical apparatus than for the understanding of the functioning of memory in the living person. Nor is such a concept fundamentally changed when logically meaningful phrases or perceptually organized "Gestalten" are substituted for nonsense syllables and memory is investigated for its capacity to reproduce those, rather than meaningless material. Nobody doubts that it is easier to remember meaningful than meaningless material and that the function of memory has not developed in order to make possible the recall of nonsense. Memory as a function of the living personality can be understood only as a capacity for the organization and reconstruction of past experiences and impressions in the service of present needs, fears, and interests. It goes without saying that, just as there is no such thing as impersonal perception and impersonal experience, there is also no impersonal memory. Man perceives and remembers not as a camera reproduces on the film the objects before its lens; the scope and quality of his perceptions and experiences as well as of their reproduction by memory are determined by his individual fears, and interests. This is the more apparent the more significant an experience has been for the person.

With this concept of memory in mind, the puzzling problem of childhood amnesia seems to become more transparent and accessible to understanding. No greater change in the needs of man occurs than that which takes place between early childhood and adulthood. Into this change have gone all the decisive formative influences of the culture transmitted by the parents, laying the fundament of the transformation into the grown-up, "useful" member of society from the little heathen, who is helpless but as yet sees nothing wrong with following the pleasure principle completely and immediately and who has an insatiable curiosity and capacity for experience. An explanation of childhood amnesia that takes into account these changes leads to the following tentative hypothesis: The categories (or schemata) of adult memory are not suitable receptacles for early child-hood experiences and therefore not fit to preserve these experiences and enable their recall. The functional capacity of the conscious, adult memory is usually limited to those types of experience which the adult consciously makes and is capable of making.

...

A closer examination and comparison of the content and quality of adult and childhood memories may be helpful for the purpose of such an understanding. Both Freud and Proust speak of the autobiographical memory, and it is only with regard to this memory that the striking phenomenon of childhood amnesia and the less obvious difficulty of recovering any past experience may be observed. There is no specific childhood amnesia as far as the remembrance of words learned and of objects and persons recognized is concerned. This type of material is remembered because, in contrast to the autobiographical past, it is constantly reexperienced and used and because it is essential for the orientation and adaptation of the growing child to his environment. In the recall of this type of material we have to deal with memory serving the immediate, practical use of knowledge and perception (recognition) mainly. The memory of the personal past—of one's past experiences, which also contain the material that has gone into the formation of one's character—is a much less efficient and reliable servant than the memory of learned material, on the whole, seems to be. Yet the separation of the "useful" from the "autobiographical" memory is, of course, an artificial abstraction. Actually this distinction of the content of remembered material is not clear-cut, and the two types of material indicated by it are continuously and everywhere interrelated.

The autobiographical memory shows indeed in most persons, if not in all, the amnesia for their early childhood from birth to approximately the fifth or sixth year. Of course, there are considerable gaps in the memory of many people for later periods of their lives also, probably more so for the period before than after puberty; but these gaps vary individually to a much greater extent than does the ubiquitous early childhood amnesia. Freud's observation of this amnesia has not stimulated others, as far as I can see, to significant investigations of the adult autobiographical memory. Yet it would seem that an awareness of the main differences between the type of material remembered from early childhood and that remembered from later life might help in an understanding of the phenomenon of childhood amnesia. If one believes Proust, life after childhood is not remembered either, save for the elusive flashes of a vision given only to the most sensitive and differentiated mind as the rare grace of a fortunate moment, which then the poet, with passionate devotion and patient labor, may try to transcribe and communicate.

Freud contrasts the presumable riches of childhood experience, the child's great capacity for impressions and experience, with the poverty or total lack of memory of such rich experience. If one looks closely at the average adult's memory of the periods of his life after childhood, such memory, it is true, usually shows no great temporal gaps. It is fairly continuous. But its formal continuity in time is offset by barrenness in content, by an incapacity to reproduce anything that resembles a really rich, full, rounded, and alive experience. Even the most "exciting" events are remembered as milestones rather than as moments filled with the concrete abundance of life. Adult memory reflects life as a road with occasional signposts and milestones rather than as the landscape through which this road has led. The milestones are the measurements of time, the months and years, the empty count of time gone by, so many years spent here, so many years spent there, moving from one place to another, so many birthdays, and so forth. The signposts represent the outstanding events to which they point—entering college, the first job, marriage, birth of children, buying a house, a family celebration, a trip. But it is not the events that are remembered as they really happened and were experienced at the time. What is remembered is usually, more or less, only the fact that such an event took place. The signpost is remembered, not the place, the thing, the situation to which it points. And even these signposts themselves do not usually indicate the really significant moments in a person's life; rather they point to the events that are conventionally supposed to be significant, to the clichés which society has come to consider as the main stations of life. Thus the memories of the majority of people come to resemble increasingly the stereotyped answers to a questionnaire, in which life consists of time and place of birth, religious denomination, residence, educational degrees, job, marriage, number and birthdates of children, income, sickness and death. The average traveler, asked about his trip, will tell you how many miles he has made (how many years he has lived); how fast he went (how successful he was); what places he has visited—usually only the well-known ones, often he visits only those that one "simply must have seen"—(the jobs he has held, the prestige he has gained). He can tell you whether the driving was smooth or rough, or whether somebody bumped his fender, but he will be quite unable to give you any real idea of the country through which he went. So the average traveler through life remembers chiefly what the road map or the guide book says, what he is supposed to remember because it is exactly what everybody else remembers too.

In the course of later childhood, adolescence, and adult life, perception and experience themselves develop increasingly into the rubber stamps of conventional cliches. The capacity to see and feel what is there gives way to the tendency to see and feel what one expects to see and feel, which, in turn, is what one is expected to see and feel because everybody else does. Experience increasingly assumes the form of the cliché under which it will be recalled because this cliché is what conventionally is remembered by others. This is not the remembered situation itself, but the words which are customarily used to indicate this situation and the reactions which it is supposed to evoke. While this ubiquitous and powerful tendency toward pseudoexperience in terms of conventional clichés usually takes place unnoticed, it is quite articulate in some people and is used widely in advertising. There are people who experience a party, a visit to the movies, a play, a concert, a trip in the very words in which they are going to tell their friends about it; in fact, quite often, they anticipate such experience by these words. The experience is predigested, as it were, even before they have tasted of it. Like the unfortunate Midas, whose touch turned everything into gold so that he could not eat or drink, these people turn the potential nourishment of the anticipated experience into the sterile currency of the conventional phrase which exhausts their experience because they have seen, heard, felt nothing but this phrase with which later they will report to their friends the "exciting time" they have had. The advertising business seems to be quite aware of this. It does not have to promise a good book, a well-written and well-performed play, an entertaining or amusing movie. It suffices to say that the book, the play, the movie will be the talk of the town, of the next party, of one's friends. To have been there, to be able to say that one has been present at the performance, to have read the book even when one is unable to have the slightest personal reaction to it, is quite sufficient. But while Midas suffered tortures of starvation, the people under whose eyes every experience turns into a barren cliché do not know that they starve. Their starvation manifests itself merely in boredom or in restless activity and incapacity for any real enjoyment.

...

How well is the average highly conventionalized adult memory equipped to contain and recall the time and the experiences of early childhood? Very poorly or not at all. This will become more apparent through consideration of the quality of early childhood experience. The adult amnesia for this period prevents direct knowledge. Observation of little children and imagination are the only means of learning something about this subject. It is safe to assume that early childhood is the period of human life which is richest in experience. Everything is new to the newborn child. His gradual grasp of his environment and of the world around him are discoveries which, in experiential scope and quality, go far beyond any discovery that the most adventurous and daring explorer will ever make in his adult life. No Columbus, no Marco Polo has ever seen stranger and more fascinating and thoroughly absorbing sights than the child that learns to perceive, to taste, to smell, to touch, to hear and see, and to use his body, his senses, and his mind. No wonder that the child shows an insatiable curiosity. He has the whole world to discover. Education and learning, while on the one hand furthering this process of discovery, on the other hand gradually brake and finally stop it completely. There are relatively few adults who are fortunate enough to have retained something of the child's curiosity, his capacity for questioning and for wondering. The average adult "knows all the answers," which is exactly why he will never know even a single answer.

...

The incompatibility of early childhood experience with the categories and the organization of adult memory is to a large extent due to what I call the conventionalization of the adult memory. Conventionalization is a particular form of what one might call schematization of memory. Voluntary memory recalls largely schemata of experience rather than experience. These schemata are mostly built along the lines of words and concepts of the culture. Also the so-called visual or the auditory memory reproduces schemata of visual or auditory impressions rather than the impressions themselves. Obviously the schemata of experience as well as of memory[2] are determined by the culture which has developed a certain view of the world and of life, a view which furnishes the schemata for all experience and all memory. But the range of differentiation of a culture like that of Greece, India, China, or modern Western civilization is of considerable scope. It offers highly differentiated and subtle as well as very conventional, banal, and commonplace schemata. By conventionalization of the memory (and experience) schemata I understand those memory processes which are subject to the most conventional schematization and which, therefore, are not capable of reproducing individual experience, but can only reproduce what John Doe is supposed to have experienced according to the Joneses' and everybody else's ideas of what people experience. Every fresh and spontaneous experience transcends the capacity of the conventionalized memory schema and, to some degree, of any schema. That part of the experience which transcends the memory schema as preformed by the culture is in danger of being lost because there exists as yet no vessel, as it were, in which to preserve it. Even if the schemata of expe-

---

[2]The term "memory schemata" is taken from Bartlett, but used in a somewhat different sense. Bartlett rightly emphasizes that remembering is "an affair of reconstruction rather than mere reproduction." According to him, this reconstruction serves as a justification of the present attitude toward past experience. Such reconstructions he calls "schemata," and these are determined by sense differences, appetites, instincts, and interests. In this essay, however, the concept of memory schemata is used only to designate socially and culturally determined patterns of reconstruction of the past, as contrasted to individually determined patterns. Obviously the greater part of all individual memory schemata in Bartlett's sense are culturally determined.

rience have not prevented the person from becoming aware of or sensing that quality of his experience which transcended these schemata, this quality, if it is to be preserved and to become a productive part of the personality, has to overcome the second handicap of the memory schemata, which tend, as time goes on, to supplant this fresh and new element of experience with some preformed notion and thus to bury it. The process of schematization and conventionalization and its effect on the raw material of experience, especially childhood experience, can be well observed in two of its specific developments which take place as the child learns to make use of his senses and to speak.

Language, in its articulating and its obscuring function, may be considered first since the adult, too, encounters the problem of the incompatibility of experience with language and the consequent forgetting of experience or its distortion by the cliché of language. The fact that language is adult language, the language of an adult civilization, and that the infant and small child is moulded only very gradually from its natural existence into a member of the civilization into which it is born makes the discrepancy between the precivilized, unschematized experience and the categories of civilized, conventional language much greater. Yet between this discrepancy and that existing between the adult's experience and his language, there is a difference of degree rather than of kind. Everyone who has honestly tried to describe some genuine experience exactly, however small and insignificant it may have seemed, knows how difficult if not impossible that is. One might well say that the greatest problem of the writer or the poet is the temptation of language. At every step a word beckons, it seems so convenient, so suitable, one has heard or read it so often in a similar context, it sounds so well, it makes the phrase flow so smoothly. If he follows the temptation of this word, he will perhaps describe something that many people recognize at once, that they already know, that follows a familiar pattern; but he will have missed the nuance that distinguishes his experience from others, that makes it his own. If he wants to communicate that elusive nuance which in some way, however small, will be his contribution, a widening or opening of the scope of articulate human experience at some point, he has to fight constantly against the easy flow of words that offer themselves. Like the search for truth, which never reaches its goal yet never can be abandoned, the endeavor to articulate, express, and communicate an experience can never succeed completely. It consists of an approach, step by step, toward that distant vantage point, that bend of the road from which one hopes to see the real experience in its entirety and from where it will become visible to others—a point which is never reached. The lag, the discrepancy between experience and word is a productive force in man as long as he remains aware of it, as long as he knows and feels his experience was in some way more than and different from what his concepts and words articulate. The awareness of this unexplored margin of experience, which may be its essential part, can turn into that productive energy which enables man to go one step closer to understanding and communicating his experience, and thus add to the scope of human insight. It is this awareness and the struggle and the ability to narrow the gap between experience and words which make the writer and the poet. The danger of the schemata of language, and especially of the worn currency of conventional language in vogue at the moment when the attempt is made to understand and describe an experience, is that the person making this attempt will overlook the discrepancy between experience and language cliché or that he will not be persistent enough in his attempt to eliminate this discrepancy. Once the conventional schema has replaced the experience in his mind, the significant quality of the experience is condemned to oblivion.

The discrepancy between concepts, language, and experience can be looked upon as a model and as part of the discrepancy between memory schemata and experience. This close relationship, of course, is not accidental since voluntary recall and communication of recalled experience are essentially dependent on conceptual thought and language. While there is also recall of experience without the vehicle of language, a great deal of what we recall, especially of what we recall voluntarily, is recalled already in terms of language and in concepts formed by language. This has considerable bearing on the problem of childhood amnesia. The infant and small child has to undergo and assimilate the comparatively greatest amount of new experience at a time when his language, his concepts, and his memory schemata are poorest or as yet entirely undeveloped. Only very gradually does he acquire the faculty of language, learn the conceptual schemata of his culture, and develop a memory and memory schemata. The experiences of the infant are inarticulate and complex.

...

Early childhood amnesia may be considered a normal amnesia. It shares this quality with most, though not all, of dream amnesia and with the constant forgetting of those parts and aspects of experience which do not fit into the ready patterns of language and culture—transschematic experience. Normal amnesia is both akin to and different from pathological amnesia. Their likeness consists in this causation by a conflict between nature and culture or by intercultural conflict. Their difference consists chiefly in the fact that the conflicts causing normal amnesia are ubiquitous in a culture and their solution is part of the development of the personality in that culture; whereas in pathological amnesia, by and large, the conflict is due to individual traumatic experience which, although caused too by the stresses and conflicts operative in the culture, has become traumatic because of the particular history of the individual person. One might say that the normal amnesia, that which people usually are unable to recall, is an illuminating index to the quality of any given culture and society. It is that which does not serve the purposes of that society and would interfere with the pattern of the culture, that which would be traumatic to the culture because it would break up or transcend the conventions and mores of that culture. Early childhood amnesia is the most striking and dramatic expression merely of a dynamism operative throughout the life of people: the distortion or forgetting of transschematic experience, that is, of experience for which the culture provides no pattern and no schema.

Cultures vary in the degree to which they impose clichés on experience and memory. The more a society develops in the direction of mass conformism, whether such development be achieved by a totalitarian pattern or within a democratic framework by means of the employment market, education, the patterns of social life, advertising, press, radio, movies, best-sellers, and so on, the more stringent becomes the role of the conventional experience and memory schemata in the lives of the members of that society. In the history of the last hundred years of western civilization the conventional schematization of experience and memory has become increasingly prevalent at an accelerating pace.

Even within a culture the degree to which in different *groups* conventional schemata of experience and memory prevent the recall of actual experience may show marked differences. Such a difference seems to exist, for example, between European men and women. There is some reason to assume that European men usually show a more extensive and pervasive amnesia for their early childhood than women.[3] A plausible hypothesis for the explanation of this difference would have to take into account the marked difference in the social status of the two sexes in Europe and, specifically, the difference in what one might call the social self-ideal of man versus that of woman. This idea of what the grown-up person, the respectable citizen ought to be emphasizes the cleft between childhood and adulthood much more in men than in women. All things pertaining to the rearing of children and to the home are the domain of the women and the average man could consider it beneath his "dignity" to know much about them or to be much concerned with them. Hence, to recall details of early childhood would be consistent with the social self-ideal of women whose interests are supposed to center around children, kitchen, and home. But

---

[3]Oral communication by Ruth Benedict. In interviewing a number of European men and women, Benedict found consistently that the women recalled quite a few details of their lives before they had reached the age of six while the men hardly recalled anything. The people interviewed by her did not constitute a representative sample of the population, yet the consistency of the phenomenon in all the people interviewed seemed indicative of its more general significance.

to a man these things are not supposed to be sufficiently "important" to deserve much attention. To approximate the social self-ideal is important for his self-esteem; and the further removed from, and opposed to, the image of childhood the grown-up man's social self-ideal is the more difficult will it be for him to recall experiences showing that once he was an infant and little boy. In general, more extensive childhood amnesias are to be expected in those groups, cultures, and historical epochs which emphasize the belief that childhood is radically different from adulthood, than one is likely to find where the continuity between childhood and adult life is emphasized.[4]

Mankind's belief in a lost paradise is repeated in the belief, held by most people, in the individual myth of their happy childhood. Like most myths this one contains elements of both truth and illusion, is woven out of wishes, hopes, remembrance and sorrow, and hence has more than one meaning. One finds this belief even in people who have undergone cruel experiences as children and who had, without being or remaining aware of it, a childhood with hardly any love and affection from their parents. No doubt, one reason for the myth of happy childhood is that it bolsters parental authority and maintains a conventional prop of the authority of the family by asserting that one's parents were good and benevolent people who did everything for the good of their children, however much they may have done against it. And disappointed and suffering people, people without hope, want to believe that at least once there was a time in their life when they were happy. But the myth of happy childhood reflects also the truth that, as in the myth of paradise lost, there was a time before animalistic innocence was lost, before pleasure-seeking nature and pleasure-forbidding culture clashed in the battle called education, a battle in which the child always is the loser. At no time is life so exclusively and directly governed by the pleasure principle as it is in early infancy; at no other time is man, especially civilized man, capable of abandoning himself so completely to pleasure and satisfaction. The myth of happy childhood takes the place of the lost memory of the actual riches, spontaneity, freshness of childhood experience, an experience which has been forgotten because there is no place for it in the adult memory schemata.

···

---

[4]For the general significance of continuity and discontinuity between childhood and adulthood, see Ruth Benedict (1938). Continuities and discontinuities in cultural conditioning, *Psychiatry, 1,* 161–167. See also Ulric Neisser (1962). Cultural and cognitive discontinuity. In T. E. Gladwin & W. Sturtevant (Eds.), *Anthropology and human behavior.* Washington, D.C.: Anthropological Society of Washington.

The Origins of Autobiographical Memory

28

Katherine Nelson

In modern conceptions of this issue, the problem is not our inability to recall our earliest years but how our memories develop after that time. What needs explanation is remembering, not forgetting. Even two-year-olds have some ability to recall past events, but they do not regard themselves as having a uniquely personal past, present, and future. Autobiographical memory develops only slowly, in verbal and social interactions with other people. Here is one coherent theoretical account of that development.

...

Autobiographical memory as used here is specific, personal, long-lasting, and (usually) of significance to the self-system. Phenomenally, it forms one's personal life history. Prior to the development of this system, memories do not become part of a personally known life history, although of course they may be important in other ways to one's life, and one may derive a strong sense of one's early history from hearing about it from other people.

Autobiographical memory has its onset during the early childhood years. Surprisingly, it is only recently that this onset has been thought of in developmental terms. In the past, it has usually been conceived of in terms of childhood (or infantile) amnesia, the phenomenon, first identified by Freud (1963) and familiar to all who reflect on it, that memories for events from the early years of our lives—before about 3 to 4 years—are not

⁂ From K. Nelson (1993). The psychological and social origins of autobiographical memory. *Psychological Science, 4*, 7–14.

available to adult consciousness, although many memories from later childhood usually are easily called up.

The onset of autobiographical memory is simply the inverse of infantile amnesia. In the present framework, the critical questions are when and why an autobiographical system—in which some memories are retained for a lifetime—becomes differentiated from a general episodic system.

Most of the research on childhood amnesia—the period of life before the onset of autobiographical memory—has come from studies of adults' recall of childhood memories, beginning with a questionnaire study by Henri and Henri in 1897 (see review by Dudycha & Dudycha, 1941). As in many studies that followed, they asked adults ($N = 120$) to recall their earliest memories from childhood and reported the data in terms of the number of childhood memories from a given age range. No memories were reported from before 2 years, but 71% of the subjects had some memories from the period between 2 and 4 years of age. Summarizing over a large number of such studies, Pillemer and White (1989) found that the earliest memory is reported on average at about 3½ years. They noted that there are actually two phases of childhood amnesia, the first a total blocking of memories, usually prior to about 3 years, and the second, between 3 and 6 years, a significant drop-off of accessible memories relative to later memories. Such a pattern has been verified by the analysis of the forgetting curve for adult recall of childhood memories (Wetzler & Sweeney, 1986). However, it is important to note also that there is considerable variability both in age of earliest memory—from 2 years to 8 years or even later—and in number of memories reported from early childhood. In the early empirical literature on the topic, the age of earliest memory has been negatively correlated with IQ, language ability, and social class, and females tend to have earlier memories than males.

It is commonly objected that the data on early childhood memories are unreliable and unverifiable, but for the following reasons these objections do not invalidate the conclusions drawn. First, those who can reliably date their memories—because they experienced moves or other disruptions during early childhood—or whose parents can verify events (Usher & Neisser, 1991) exhibit the same general age relations as those suggested by the overall research. For example, it is rare to find anyone who claims to remember a specific incident from before the age of 2 years. Moreover, a study of memory for the birth of a sibling, which could be definitively dated, showed the same age relation as the questionnaire data: Children could remember the event if it occurred when they were 3 years or older, but not before that age (Sheingold & Tenney, 1982).

The validity of any given memory is not relevant within the present theoretical framework. Although the validity of a memory may be of concern if one is interested in such issues as whether children are reliable witnesses, it is of less concern if one is interested in when they begin to retain memories in the autobiographical memory system. Memories do not need to be true or correct to be part of that system.

The term childhood amnesia implies that something was there and is lost. This in turn implies that we need to find an explanation either in terms of loss or in terms of some force that interferes with retrieval of memories that still exist, as Freud proposed. The alternative possibility explored here is that something develops that leads to a new organization of memory or the establishment of a new memory system or function. These possibilities can be evaluated only in terms of the study of memory during the period prior to and subsequent to the emergence of autobiographical memory. The adult research, on the basis of which so much of the discussion has been based, can tell us only that the phenomenon is real; it cannot reveal anything about its development.

...

Schachtel (1947) and Neisser (1962) suggested that autobiographical memories are the outcome of a reconstructive process based on schemas or frames of reference, along the lines suggested by Bartlett (1932). Remembering, then, involves *reconstructing* past events using presently existing schemas, and the claim is that adult schemas are not "suitable receptacles" for early childhood experience; "adults cannot think like children" and thus cannot make use of whatever fragments of memories they may retain. In this view, socialization and the impact of language force a drastic change in the child's schemas at age 6.

The recent developmental data cast doubt on this proposal as well. Although very young children often need extensive probing to elicit their memories, suggesting that they may retain only random and unschematized fragments, there is also evidence of specific episodic memories that have the same form as we might find in older children. A fragment from a 2½-year-old girl talking to herself when alone in her room is illustrative:

> We bought *a baby, cause, the well because, when she, well,* we thought *it was for Christmas, but* when *we went to the s-s-store we didn't have our jacket on, but I saw some dolly, and I yelled at my mother and said I want one of those dolly. So after we were finished with the store, we went over to the dolly and she* bought *me one. So I have one.*

In this example, Emily was recounting to herself what apparently was a significant episode in her life (she had not rehearsed this recent episode with her parents or others; see Nelson, 1989, for further details). This recount is well organized, with clear and concise temporal and causal sequencing. It—and others like it—does not suggest that the preschool child's schemas are dramatically different from those of the older child and adult.

Indeed, recent reports of young children's free recall of salient episodic memories (Engel, 1986; Hudson, 1990; Tessler, 1991) support the conclusion that the basic ways of structuring, representing, and interpreting reality are consistent from early childhood into adulthood. These studies indicate that young children, in both their script recounts and their specific memory recounts, typically tell their stories in a sequence that accurately reflects the sequence of the experience itself and that has the same boundaries that seem natural to adult listeners (Nelson, 1986).

Of course, there may be other differences between adult and child memories, including what is noticed and remembered of an event. The extensive cuing and probing often required to elicit details from a young child suggest that adult and child may have different memories of the same event. An analysis of the content of crib talk (talk to self alone before sleep) by the child Emily, recorded from 21 to 36 months, supports the suggestion that adult and child may focus on different events and different aspects of events. Emily's memories were concerned mostly with the quotidian, unremarkable, routines of her life. They were not concerned with the truly novel events of her life (from the adult's point of view), such as the birth of her baby brother or her airplane trips to visit relatives (Nelson, 1989). Thus, interest in—and therefore memory for—aspects of experience that seem unremarkable to adults, and indifference to what adults find interesting, as well as lack of facility with language and differences in the knowledge base, may account for why children sometimes seem to have organized their knowledge in a different form or have remembered only fragments from an episode that adults consider memorable.

In summary, recent research on episodic memory in early childhood indicates that children have at least some well-organized specific and general event memories, similar to those of adults; thus, the suggestion that a schematic reorganization may account for infantile amnesia is not supported. However, recent research that has shown that children learn to talk about their past experiences in specific ways does provide some clues as to what may be developing and how.

NARRATIVE CONSTRUCTION OF MEMORY

Over the past decade, a number of researchers have studied the ways in which parents engage in talking about the past with their very young children. These studies, some focused on the specific language forms used, others on the content of talk, and still others on narrative forms and differences in communicative styles, have revealed the active role that parents play in framing and guiding their children's formulation of "what happened."

Hudson (1990) concluded from a study of her own daughter's memory talk between 21 and 27 months that eventually Rachel began to "interpret the conversations not as a series of questions to be answered but as an *activity of remembering*" (p. 183). Hudson endorses a *social interaction model* of the development of autobiographical memory, a model that Pillemer and White (1989) and Fivush and Reese (1991) have also invoked. In this view, children gradually learn the forms of how to talk about memories with others, and thereby also how to formulate their own memories as narratives. The social interaction model differs from the schematic change model in that it claims that children learn *how* to formulate their memories and thus retain them in recoverable form.

Several studies at the City University of New York (and elsewhere) have found that parents not only engage in memory talk but also differ among themselves in the number of memory-relevant questions they ask, the kind of memory they attempt to elicit, and the ways in which they frame the talk. Engel (1986) studied mother–child conversations about past episodes with children from 18 months to 2 years and identified two styles of mother talk, one described as *elaborative*, the other more *pragmatic*. The elaborative mothers tended to talk about episodes in narrative terms of what happened when, where, and with whom. Pragmatic mothers referred to memory primarily in instrumental terms, such as "where did you put your mittens?" For pragmatic mothers, memory is useful for retrieving information relevant to ongoing activities. For elaborative mothers, memory provides the basis for storytelling, constructing narratives about what mother and child did together in the there and then. Engel found that children of elaborative mothers contributed more information to the memory talk at 2 years than children of pragmatic mothers.

Tessler (1986, 1991) studied the effect of adult talk during an experience on children's subsequent memory for the experience in two naturalistically designed experiments. She observed differences in mothers' styles of interaction similar to those identified by Engel, and found that children of narrative (or elaborative) mothers remembered more from a trip to a natural history museum a week later, when probed with a standard set of questions, than did children of pragmatic-type mothers. Most strikingly, none of the children remembered any of the objects that they viewed in the museum if they had not talked about them together with their mothers. In a second study, Tessler found that there was no difference between children experiencing different types of interaction with mothers during an event in recognizing elements of the experience, but there were differences in the amount of information recalled from the experience, with the children of narrative mothers recalling significantly more. Again, things that were not talked about were not recalled. These findings indicate not only that talk about the past is effective in aiding the child to establish a narrative memory about the past, but that talk during a present activity serves a similar purpose. In both cases, adults who present the activity in a narrative format, in contrast to a focus on identification and categorization, appear to be more effective in establishing and eliciting memories with their young children. Could this be important in establishing an autobiographical memory system? The social interaction hypothesis would certainly suggest so.

EFFECTS OF LANGUAGE ON MEMORY

What is it that talking about events—past and present—contributes to memory? The social interaction hypothesis emphasizes learning to structure memories in narrative form. Another suggestion might be the effects of rehearsal. However, there are two indications that rehearsal is not the major contributor. First, children are frequently unresponsive to maternal probing (Fivush & Fromhoff, 1988), suggesting that often the event being talked about was not what the child remembered but what the adult remembered. Second, available evidence suggests that events that do seem rehearsed are not subsequently remembered. For example, Emily sometimes recounted an event many times during an evening's session of crib talk but did not apparently remember the event months later (Nelson, 1989) or when probed years later (Nelson, unpublished data). Emily seemed to be attempting to understand the events she took part in, and to use them in her representation of her world, but not for holding on to memories of specific episodes. Long-term follow-up studies of memories rehearsed in early childhood are obviously important but are very rare. In one instance, similar to the findings from Emily, J. A. Hudson (personal communication, April 1992) has indicated that her daughter at 8 years remembers nothing of the events they rehearsed together when she was 2.

...

The claim here is that the initial functional significance of autobiographical memory is that of sharing memory with other people, a function that language makes possible. Memories become valued in their own right—not because they predict the future and guide present action, but because they are shareable with others and thus serve a social solidarity function. I suggest that this is a universal human function, although one with variable, culturally specific rules. In this respect, it is analogous to human language itself, uniquely and universally human but culturally—and individually—variable. I suggest further that this social function of memory underlies all of our storytelling, history-making narrative activities, and ultimately all of our accumulated knowledge systems.

The research briefly reviewed here supports these speculations. Children learn to engage in talk about the past, guided at first by parents who construct a narrative around the bits and pieces contributed by the child (Eisenberg, 1985; Engel, 1986; Hudson, 1990). The timing of this learning (beginning at about 2½ years and continuing through the preschool years) is consistent with the age at which autobiographical memory begins to emerge. The fact that the adult data suggest a two-phase process, as noted earlier, including the absence of memories in the first 2 to 3 years, followed by a sparse but increasing number of memories in the later preschool years, supports the supposition that the establishment of these memories is related to the experience of talking to other people about them. Also, the variability in age of onset of autobiographical memory (from 2 to 8 years or later) and its relation to language facility is consistent with the idea that children's experiences in sharing memories of the right kind and in the right form contribute to the establishment of autobiographical memory.

The social interaction hypothesis outlined earlier clearly fits these data well. This proposal is not simply one of cultural transmission or socialization, but rather a dialectical or Vygotskian model in which the child takes over the forms of adult thought through transactions with adults in activity contexts where those forms are employed—in this case, in the activities where memories are formed and shared. The problem that the child faces in taking on new forms and functions is to coordinate earlier memory functions with those that the adult displays, incorporating adult values about what is important to remember, and the narrative formats for remembering, into his or her own existing functional system.

This, then, is the functional part of the proposal, suggesting that sharing memories with other people performs a significant social-cultural function, the acquisition of which means that the child can enter into the social and cultural history of the family and community. However, identifying this function, and some of the social-linguistic experiences that support it, does not in itself explain why personal autobiographical memories continue to persist. For that explanation we must call on an additional function of language.

Recall that reinstatement through action was shown to be effective in establishing the persistence of a memory of an event. I hypothesize that an important development takes place when the process of sharing memories with others through language becomes available as a means of reinstating memory. (See also Hudson, 1990.) Further, I suggest that language as a medium of reinstatement is not immediately available when mothers and their young children first begin to exchange talk about a remembered experience.

Rather, reinstatement through language requires a certain level of facility with language, and especially the ability to use the verbal representation of another person to set up a representation in one's own mental representation system, thus recognizing the verbal account as a reinstatement of one's prior experience. Using another person's verbal representation of an event as a partial reinstatement of one's own representation (memory) depends on the achievement of language as a representational system in its own right, and not only as either an organizing tool or a communication tool. This achievement is, I believe, a development of the late preschool years (Nelson, 1990).

...

To conclude, autobiographical memory may be thought of as a function that comes into play at a certain point in human childhood when the social conditions foster it and the child's representational system is accessible to the linguistic formulations presented by other people... It is uniquely human because of its dependence on linguistic representations of events, and because human language itself is uniquely human. As Miller (1990) has recently stressed, human language is unique in serving the dual function of mental representation and communication. These dual functions make possible its use in establishing the autobiographical memory system. And because such memory is at once both personal and social, it enables us not only to cherish our private memories, but also to share them with others, and to construct shared histories as well as imagined stories, in analogy with reconstructed true episodes. Once the child has begun to share memories with others, he or she is well on the way to sharing all of the accumulated cultural knowledge offered at home, in school, or in the larger world.

This social-developmental approach to early memory has important and perhaps surprising implications. One of those implications concerns cultural differences: if societies differ in how much they encourage young children to talk about life experiences, will they also differ in the extent of childhood amnesia exhibited by adults? Recent research by Mary Mullen suggests that the answer may be yes. See M. K. Mullen (1994), Earliest recollections of childhood: A demographic analysis, Cognition, *52, 55–79. Also see M. K. Mullen & S. Yi (1995), The cultural implications of talk about the past: Implications for the development of autobiographical memory,* Cognitive Development, *10, 407–419.*

Another implication of this approach concerns gender differences. Parents—both mothers and fathers— seem to have different ways of talking about the past to their daughters than to their sons. Reminiscing tends to be more elaborate and more focused on emotions with the former than with the latter, though we do not know why: maybe the difference is a result of cultural convention, maybe it's elicited by the behavior of the children themselves. In any case, it may have consequences for gender differences in adult memory (see Selection 19). *Robyn Fivush has done the most significant work in this area; for an overview see R. Fivush (1998), Gendered narratives: Elaboration, structure, and emotion in parent-child reminiscing across the preschool years. In C. P. Thompson et al. (Eds.),* Autobiographical memory: Theoretical and applied perspectives. *Mahwah, NJ: Erlbaum.*

REFERENCES

Bartlett, F. C. (1932). *Remembering: A study in experimental and social psychology.* Cambridge, England: Cambridge University Press.

Dudycha, G. J., & Dudycha, M. M. (1941). Childhood memories: A review of the literature. *Psychological Bulletin, 38,* 668–682.

Eisenberg, A. R. (1985). Learning to describe past experiences in conversation. *Discourse Processes, 8,* 177–204.

Engel, S. (1986). *Learning to reminisce: A developmental study of how young children talk about the past.* Unpublished doctoral dissertation, City University of New York Graduate Center, New York.

Fivush, R., & Fromhoff, F. A. (1988). Style and structure in mother-child conversations about the past. *Discourse Processes, 11,* 337–355.

Fivush, R., & Reese, E. (1991, July). *Parental styles for talking about the past.* Paper presented at the International Conference on Memory, Lancaster, England.

Freud, S. (1963). Three essays on the theory of sexuality. In J. Strachey (Ed.), *The standard edition of the complete works of Freud, 7.* London: Hogarth Press.

Hudson, J. A. (1990). The emergence of autobiographic memory in mother-child conversation. In R. Fivush & J. A. Hudson (Eds.), *Knowing and remembering in young children.* New York: Cambridge University Press, 166–196.

Miller, G. A. (1990). The place of language in a scientific psychology. *Psychological Science, 1,* 7–14.

Neisser, U. (1962). Cultural and cognitive discontinuity. In T. E. Gladwin & W. Sturtevant (Eds.), *Anthropology and human behavior.* Washington, DC: Anthropological Society of Washington, 54–71.

Nelson, K. (1986). *Event knowledge: Structure and function in development.* Hillsdale, NJ: Erlbaum.

Nelson, K. (Ed). (1989). *Narratives from the crib.* Cambridge, MA: Harvard University Press.

Nelson, K. (1990). Event knowledge and the development of language functions. In J. Miller (Ed.), *Research on child language disorders.* New York: Little, Brown & Co., 125–141.

Pillemer, D. B., & White, S. H. (1989). Childhood events recalled by children and adults. In H. W. Reese (Ed.), *Advances in child development and behavior* (Vol. 21). New York: Academic Press, 297–340.

Schachtel, E. (1947). On memory and childhood amnesia. *Psychiatry, 10,* 1–26.

Sheingold, K., & Tenney, Y. J. (1982). Memory for a salient childhood event. In U. Neisser (Ed.), *Memory observed.* San Francisco: W. H. Freeman, 201–212.

Tessler, M. (1986). *Mother-child talk in a museum: The socialization of a memory.* Unpublished manuscript, City University of New York Graduate Center, New York.

Tessler, M. (1991). *Making memories together: The influence of mother-child joint encoding on the development of autobiographical memory style.* Unpublished doctoral dissertation, City University of New York Graduate Center, New York.

Usher, J. A., & Neisser, U. (1991). *Childhood amnesia in the recall of four target events* (Emory Cognition Project Report No. 20). Atlanta: Emory University, Department of Psychology.

Vygotsky, L. S. (1978). *Mind in society: The development of higher psychological processes.* Cambridge, MA: Harvard University Press.

Wetzler, S. E., & Sweeney, J. A. (1986). Childhood amnesia: An empirical demonstration. In D. C. Rubin (Ed.), *Autobiographical memory.* New York: Cambridge University Press, 191–201.

29 | The Offset of Childhood Amnesia

M. J. Eacott and R. A. Crawley

At what age does autobiographical memory actually begin? Or, to put it another way, when does childhood amnesia end? This question is more difficult than it seems. You can easily ask John Doe for his "earliest memory," but what he gives you may be a confabulation rather than a genuine recall; who can say? And how can he be sure it is really his earliest? You can also ask him how old he was at the time, but such estimates are often mistaken. A more systematic (but much more laborious) method is what Usher and Neisser (1993) called targeted recall: *begin with a real event that John Doe experienced at a certain age, and see if he still remembers it. With luck, you may even be able to verify the accuracy of his report.*

The best target event for this purpose is the birth of Doe's younger brother or sister: its date (and thus his age at the time) is known precisely. What's more, his mother may be willing to tell you whether what he remembers is accurate. Eacott and Crawley's study is the third (and the most elegant) to use this method, and it achieves a remarkable degree of precision. For events of this kind at least, the average offset of childhood amnesia is in the first half of the third year of life.

The failure to remember autobiographical events that occurred in earliest childhood is a puzzling paradox. Despite the acknowledged importance of the first 3 years of life in forming human adults, almost no re-

※ From M. J. Eacott & R. A. Crawley (1998). The offset of childhood amnesia: Memory for events that occurred before age 3. *Journal of Experimental Psychology: General, 127,* 22–33.

portable memories are retained from this period. This phenomenon has been repeatedly demonstrated (e.g., Dudycha & Dudycha, 1941; Sheingold & Tenney, 1982; Usher & Neisser, 1993; Waldvogel, 1948) and was termed by Freud (1916/1963) infantile amnesia, although the term childhood amnesia may be preferable. Although some people report memories from the age of 3 onwards, it is not unusual to have no memory of events that occurred before the age of 6 or 7, and for some the amnesia can extend even further than this. The interpretation one places on this paradoxical amnesia has important implications for the way in which one understands the memory processes and the development of these processes across time. However, a consensus on the correct interpretation of the phenomenon has been hard to find, the suggested explanations ranging from the lack of a self-concept in infancy (Howe & Courage, 1993) to the lack of a fully functioning hippocampal system (Nadel & Zola-Morgan, 1984).

Hypothesized causes of childhood amnesia are many, but finding evidence to verify any of them has proved more problematic. This difficulty is magnified by the difficulty in obtaining reliable data about the nature of the phenomenon itself. Simply asking people for their earliest memory and its age are unreliable means, as people may find it difficult to isolate their earliest memory. As it is notoriously difficult to accurately date our memories (N. R. Brown, Ripps, & Shevel, 1985), the method of probing memory for a specific and clearly datable target event has been used with effect. Events such as the birth of a sibling or the hospitalization of the child are useful because the date of their occurrence is usually known and is verifiable (Sheingold & Tenney, 1982; Usher & Neisser, 1993). Moreover, as these events are also experienced and usually remembered by the parents, the accuracy of the memory can often be checked against the memory of the parent. Despite the danger that the parental memory itself may sometimes be inaccurate (Robbins, 1963)[Selection 18], this method has been of use.

This method was used in a recent study by Usher and Neisser (1993). . . . The study asked students about their memories for four early childhood events (the birth of a sibling, the death of a family member, moving to another house, and hospitalization of the child) and found some participants had memories for events that occurred when they were under the age of 3. Most memories from this early period were of the birth of a sibling, although there were also many concerning hospitalization. This result has been cited as showing evidence for adult memory for events that occurred at age 2 (e.g., Drummey & Newcombe, 1995; Fivush et al., 1995; Howe & Courage, 1993; Morton et al., 1995), although the report of Usher and Neisser (1993, pp. 163–164) makes clear that the relevant groups were, in fact, between 2 and 3 years in age when their sibling was born. Thus it is quite possible that those participants reporting memories of the birth of their sibling may have been those in the latter part of the age range (i.e., approaching 3 years old). However, even if these citations have exaggerated the available evidence, the report of Usher and Neisser nevertheless contains new and important evidence of memories for events that occurred when the child was under the age of 3 years, substantially earlier than previous reports: Sheingold and Tenney (1982), for example, found no reliable evidence for memories of events that occurred before the child had reached age 3.

However, there are some problems with the wholesale acceptance of the evidence presented by Usher and Neisser (1993). The strongest and most widely cited evidence of memory for events that occurred before age 3 comes from those participants who were asked about the events surrounding the birth of their sibling. However, despite the impressively large number of students questioned overall in this study ($N = 222$), careful reading of the data makes it clear that there were only 12 participants in the critical group who were asked about their memories of a sibling birth that occurred when they were between 2 and 3 years old. Four of these participants had no memory at all for the event, 1 participant could answer only one question, and 7 participants could answer three or more questions about the events surrounding their sibling's birth. These figures, however, refer to those who gave an answer to the questions asked of them and gives no indication of the accuracy of the answer given. If the participant gave his or her permission, the mother of each participant was contacted and asked to verify the answers. Although Usher and Neisser do not give a breakdown of response rates in different groups, among all groups and ages, 60% of the participants gave permission for their mother to be contacted, and 67% of those mothers returned the questionnaire. Thus 40% of the mothers of participants were successfully contacted. When this figure is applied to the 8 participants who claimed to recall something about the birth of a sibling that occurred when they were between 2 and 3 years old, it suggests that no more than three or four mothers from this critical group returned the questionnaire. Overall, 61% of the mothers' responses definitely confirmed their child's answer, but 12% stated that they believed that their child's response was inaccurate. The mothers could not definitely confirm or deny the remainder of the answers given. Thus, this very important and much cited result of memory of events before age 3 is based on the responses of very few participants, many of whose answers were not verified, and some of which were specifically denied by their mothers. Therefore, there is little evidence that the participants' memories were accurate.

Moreover, Loftus (1993) has pointed out that the questions used by Usher and Neisser (1993) were such that it would not be surprising if the answers were accurate, even if the participants did not have true memories of the events themselves. For example, if asked what was the baby doing when you first saw him or her, Loftus has suggested that the range of possible answers is somewhat limited (sleeping, crying, feeding?) and therefore a correct answer is not implausible from a participant who has no genuine memory. In addition to these general questions to which any intelligent adult might make a reasonable guess, there are other questions that may be answered using family-specific knowledge. For example, a participant who knows that his or her grandparents lived nearby and played an important role in their childhood is likely to be able to guess accurately if asked "Who looked after you when your mother was in hospital?" We call this type of knowledge that enables participants to correctly answer questions for which they have no genuine autobiographical memory *family knowledge*, although no attempt is made here to distinguish between knowledge that is likely to be shared by all families (e.g., that the behavioral repertoire of a newborn infant is limited) and family-specific knowledge (e.g., that a maternal grandmother lived locally). Usher and Neisser, of course, carefully instructed their participants not to guess or to use information from sources other than memory, but asked them to report only what they truly remembered. However, the difficulty of distinguishing between sources of memories or information is well documented (for recent examples using student populations similar to that of Usher & Neisser (1993), see Crombag, Wagenaar, & van Koppen, 1996; Hyman, Husband, & Billings, 1995). Thus, the participants may have had difficulty distinguishing between the autobiographical memories and family knowledge in long-term memory.

For these reasons, we felt it important to replicate the critical result of Usher and Neisser (1993) with certain additional controls. First, we looked more closely at a larger group of participants who were between 2 and 3 years old at the time of their sibling's birth. This would allow us to determine whether those who are reporting memories are, in fact, nearer the end of the age range and approaching 3 years old at the time of their sibling's birth. Equally importantly, we also examined the suggestion of Loftus (1993) that knowledge gleaned from sources other than a true autobiographical memory may be contributing to the reports by these participants. To this end, we questioned participants who could have no autobiographical memory for the events surrounding the birth of a child within their family but who nevertheless are likely to have equal access to family knowledge about the events. We asked participants about the events surrounding their own birth, particularly from the viewpoint of the elder brother or sister. Thus all participants (all of whom came from families with only two children) were asked about the events surrounding the birth of the younger child in their family. However, the elder child in a family might be expected to have autobiographical memories of the events, supplemented by family knowledge. The younger child of a family relies entirely on family knowledge. For example, participants who were the elder child were asked, "Who looked after *you* when your mother was in hospital [giving birth to the younger sibling]?" whereas the participants who were the younger child in their family were asked, "Who looked after *your older sibling* when your mother was in hospital [giving birth to our participant]?" By comparing the answers of the two groups, we can assess the contribution that family knowledge is playing in these reports. By doing so, we do not wish to claim that there is a simple dichotomy between knowledge and autobiographical memory, but we are looking at the relative contribution of each in the reports of the two groups.

...

METHOD

Participants

In order to identify suitable potential participants from two-child families, a contact questionnaire was distributed to students in a variety of disciplines at the University of Durham, Durham, United Kingdom, and Sunderland University, Sunderland, United Kingdom. The questionnaire invited students and staff to indicate their general willingness to participate in unspecified psychological research in the university. Participants were asked to provide the following information: their name, program of study, date of birth, gender, and contact details along with the date of birth of any children and the name, gender, and date of birth of all full siblings.

From this contact questionnaire, participants were identified who had only one sibling and no children of their own. In addition, the age difference between siblings had to be between 2:0 and 3:3 years if the participant was the elder child in their family and 3:3 or less if they were the younger. (Throughout this article we refer to ages in years and months: 3:3 means 3 years, 3 months.) There was no constraint on the current age of our participants, although the necessity of excluding participants who had children of their own served to exclude many older prospective participants. Participants who were suitable by the above criteria were contacted by electronic mail, letter, or personal invitation to take part in what was described as a study of early memory, for which they would be paid £3 (British pounds sterling).

Questionnaires

Those who responded to our invitation were given a questionnaire, which they completed individually or in small groups in the laboratory. There were two questionnaires: one for those who were the elder child and one for those who were the younger child in their family. We refer to the group of elder children recalling the birth of their sibling as the *recall group*, and they completed the recall questionnaire. The younger children are referred to as the *report group*, who completed the report questionnaire. We were able to establish in which group the participant fell, and therefore the appropriate questionnaire, on the basis of the information provided in the contact questionnaire. At this point, however, we verbally checked this information and established whether the relevant birth took place in the hospital or at home (see the following sections).

The recall questionnaire. The recall questionnaire asked about the events surrounding the birth of a younger sibling and was closely based on that used by Usher and Neisser (1993). The instructions given to the recall participants were in written form and included the following sentences:

> *It is very important that you only report information that you actually remember. If you think you remember something, report it; however, if you only know about certain information because you have seen photos or heard family stories about it, do not include it.*

Later they were told, ". . . So again, please report only those things that you actually remember." Moreover, the instructions included the following:

> *No one is expected to recall details about every question. In fact, you may be able to recall very little or nothing about parts of the event. What you don't recall is as important to this investigation as what you do recall.*

...

The report questionnaire. Participants who were the younger sibling were given the report questionnaire. The report questionnaire was closely similar to the recall questionnaire described previously. It differed only in asking about the events surrounding the participant's own birth, particularly as experienced by their elder sibling. For example, whereas elder children were asked, "Who told *you* that your mother was leaving for hospital [to give birth to your younger sibling]?" the younger children were asked, "Who told *your older brother/sister* that your mother was leaving for hospital [to give birth to you]?" The written instructions given to report participants were similar to those given to the recall participants, except the first two excerpts quoted previously were excluded from the report instructions and replaced by the following: "We don't expect that you will remember the events, but you may know a great deal of information from other sources e.g. family stories or photographs." The report questionnaire also included the statement,

> No one is expected to report details about every question. In fact, you may be able to report very little or nothing about parts of the event. What you don't report is as important to this investigation as what you do report.

This is the same as that given to the recall participants.

...

Mother's questionnaires. For those who had given permission for us to contact their mother, we sent to the mother a questionnaire about the events surrounding the birth of their younger child. The questionnaire contained all the questions that the participants had been asked (e.g., "Who told your child that you were leaving to go to hospital?"), but the questions that their child had answered were marked, and mothers were asked only to answer those questions that their child had answered. When they had given their own independent answer to these questions, they were asked to open a sealed envelope that contained a copy of their child's answers to the same questions. The mothers were then asked to assign to each question one of the following:

1. My child's memory/report matches my own memory.
2. I believe my child was inaccurate.
3. Our memories involve different aspects of the event, we may both be right.
4. Although I recalled this differently, s/he may be right.
5. Other (please comment).

As an incentive for returning the completed questionnaire, £1.00 (British pound sterling) for every returned questionnaire was promised to a local neonatal care hospital.

...

RESULTS

...

The Recall Group

Comparison with data of Usher and Neisser (1993). Usher and Neisser (1993) had 12 participants who were between ages 2:0 and 2:11 at the time of their sibling's birth. We had 57 such participants in total. Usher and Neisser primarily analyzed the results on the basis of answers to the universal questions, and for ease of comparison, we have also done so. The mean number of universal questions answered by these participants in the Usher and Neisser study was 5.3 (calculated from Usher & Neisser, 1993, Table 2), whereas our participants answered an average of 5.1 universal questions. This figure is not significantly different from that obtained by Usher and Neisser (1993), $t(67) = 0.09$, $p > .05$, which suggests that the minor differences between the studies in methods of recruiting participants or variations in questionnaire wording has not significantly changed the level of responding. Moreover, Usher and Neisser had 12 participants who were between ages 3:0 and 3:11 in their study. We had 12 who were in the slightly more limited age range of 3:0–3:3. Those who were aged 3:0–3:11 in Usher and Neisser's study answered an average of 6.6 universal questions (calculated from Usher & Neisser, 1993, Table 2), whereas our group answered 6.8. Again, this figure is not significantly different from that obtained by Usher and Neisser (1993), $t(22) = 0.02$, $p > .05$, once again suggesting that the base rate of responding did not differ between the two studies.

Analyses by age at time of sibling's birth. Our larger sample size allowed us to break the data down further by age. We divided the recall group into four groups according to their age at the time of their sibling's birth. Thus the four groups consisted of participants aged 2:0–2:3, 2:4–2:7, 2:8–2:11, and 3:0–3:3 and contained 21, 19, 17, and 12 participants, respectively. Again, we concentrate our analyses on the universal questions that can, in principle, be answered by all participants. In contrast, contingent questions refer to events that may not have been experienced by all participants, and it is possible that experience, rather than recall, varied with age. For example, the decision of the parents on whether to take an elder sibling to visit the mother and newborn baby in the hospital could plausibly depend on the age of the child. For this reason, only universal questions are included in this analysis.

Usher and Neisser (1993) set a lenient criterion for remembering an event as having answered at least one universal question about it. In addition, they set a rather more strict, although still arbitrary, criterion as having answered three or more universal questions. Like Usher and Neisser, we determined the proportions of participants who answered at least one question and those who answered three or more questions for each group. This is shown in Figure 29-1, alongside Usher and Neisser's data for comparison. Using the strict criterion of recall of being able to answer three or more universal questions, we found that the age groups differed in the number of participants who recalled the birth event, $\chi^2(3, N = 69) = 8.64$, $p < .05$. From the figure it would appear that it is the youngest group, those aged 2:0–2:3 at the time of their sibling's birth, who were less often able to

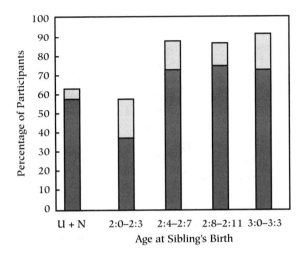

Figure 29-1 *The percentage of participants in the recall group who answered at least one universal question (lighter part of the bar) or answered three or more universal questions (darker part of the bar) according to their age at the time of their sibling's birth. Equivalent data from participants in the study of Usher and Neisser (1993; U + N) who were between ages 2:0 and 2:11 are shown to the left for comparison. Ages are given as years:months.*

recall the events. To test this suggestion further, the number of universal questions answered by each participant was transformed by a logarithmic transformation in order to ensure homogeneity of variance as measured by Cochran's C, $C(16, 4) = 0.34$, $p = .52$, and Bartlett-Box F, $F(3, 6826) = 0.41$, $p = .74$, and the data analyzed using a one-way analysis of variance (ANOVA). This analysis revealed a significant effect of age group, $F(3, 65) = 3.29$, $p < .05$. A Newman-Keuls test revealed that the youngest group (ages 2:0–2:3) differed significantly from all the other groups ($p < .05$), which in turn did not differ significantly from each other ($p > .05$). Thus, whether analyzed as the number of participants who reach a criterion of recall or on the number of universal questions answered, the data suggest that the age groups are not equivalent in the amount they recall. Those participants who were younger than 2:4 at the time of their sibling's birth are recalling significantly less than those who were older.

···

The effects of rehearsal–review. Each participant reported the frequency and recency with which they had thought about, talked about, or heard others discuss the birth event. The frequency was rated on a 4-point scale that ranged from *never* to *many times in my life*. The most common responses were *a few times* (37 responses) and *several times* (23 responses), although 3 participants reported that the events had never been discussed, and 5 had discussed it many times. The recency was rated on a 5-point scale (*within the last six months, since I left school, during the years when I was aged 14–18, before the age of 14*, or *never*). Responses to this question were more evenly distributed, the number of participants responding to each of the alternatives was 12, 19, 16, 18, and 4 respectively. However, the number of universal questions answered by those in the recall group was not significantly correlated with either the recency, $r = .22$, $t(67) = 1.85$, $p > .05$, or frequency, $r = .22$, $t(67) = 1.85$, $p > .05$, of this rehearsal–review. Perhaps unsurprisingly, however, the frequency and recency ratings were significantly correlated with each other, $r = .52$, $t(67) = 4.98$, $p < .01$, because participants who reviewed the events relatively frequently had also reviewed them relatively recently.

The participants were also asked to report any external sources that had helped preserve the events for them (e.g., photographs, family stories, etc.). These were commonly available, with only 6 from 69 recall participants reporting that there were no external sources available to them. Usher and Neisser (1993) have suggested that presence of family stories interacts with recall for those who were younger than 4 years old at the time of their sibling's birth, such that those with access to family stories recall less than those without such stories. To test this suggestion, we calculated the number of universal questions answered by those who reported family stories and those who did not. However, in contrast to the study of Usher and Neisser (1993) there was no suggestion that those without family stories recalled more than those of the same age with family stories (without family stories: mean number of universal questions answered = 2.5, $N = 14$; with family stories, mean number of universal questions answered = 5.95, $N = 55$). Indeed, the converse was true, with those reporting the presence of family stories answered significantly more universal questions than those reporting none, $t(67) = 2.81$, $p < .01$. Thus, our results point towards the more intuitively appealing conclusion that those who have family stories available are able to answer more questions about an event than those who do not.

Photographs were also a commonly reported source of external information. Fifty of our 69 recall participants reported the presence of relevant photographs. There was a difference between the number of universal questions answered by those who reported the presence of relevant family photographs and those who did not. Those who had photographs answered an average of 6.0 universal questions, whereas those reporting no photographs answered significantly fewer, $M = 3.5$, $t(68) = 2.12$, $p < .05$. Thus, as presented earlier, the presence of an external source that could aid memory was associated with better recall.

Comparison of Recall and Report Groups

There were 57 participants who were the younger child in the family and who were asked to report the events surrounding their own birth. These participants answered an average of 6.9 universal questions compared with an average of 5.4 by all the participants in the recall group. This difference between the groups is significant, $t(124) = 2.00$, $p < .05$. Thus, the report group answered more universal questions than the recall group.

...

Analyses by age of sibling at time of birth. The report group was split into five age groups. Four of these corresponded to those used with the recall group (2:0–2:3, 2:4–2:7, 2:8–2:11, and 3:0–3:3), but we included an additional group of those whose sibling had been younger than 2:0 years at the time of their own birth. Figure 29-2 shows the proportion of report participants in each age group who reported information, using the same strict and lenient criterion of knowing something about the events that was used with the recall group. It is apparent from this figure that almost all participants are able to answer at least three universal questions about events for which they could be expected to have no memory. Moreover a chi-square analysis revealed that the proportions answering three or more

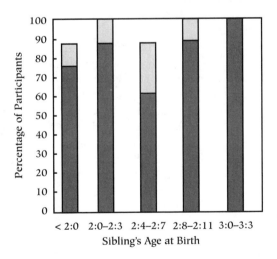

Figure 29-2 *The percentage of participants in the report group who answered at least one universal question (lighter part of the bar) or answered three or more universal questions (darker part of the bar) according to the age of their sibling at the time of the participant's birth. Ages are given as years:months.*

questions did not differ between the age groups, $\chi^2(4, N = 57) = 4.67, p >$ .25. An ANOVA on the logarithmically transformed number of universal questions answered confirmed that there is no effect of age group on the number of universal questions answered in the report group, $F(4, 52) =$ 1.80, $p > .05$. Thus, as one might predict, the age of one's sibling at the time of one's own birth has no effect on the amount of information one can report about the event.

Verification of information produced. Eighty-three percent (105) of participants gave us permission to contact their mother (57 from the recall group and 48 from the report group). Ninety-four mothers were sent the mothers' questionnaire (the discrepancy between this and the previous figure is due to the fact that the mothers of those participants who recalled or reported nothing at all were not contacted). Eighty-five percent of those mothers we attempted to contact returned the questionnaire (40 from the recall group and 40 from the report group), although 1 mother of a recall participant and 3 mothers of report participants failed to follow the instructions properly, and the mothers' responses had to be discarded. Thus we successfully contacted the mothers of 60% of our participants. This represents 66% of those we wished to contact (i.e., those who had given at least one answer that needed verification) and also 66% of those we wished to contact in both the recall and report group [cf. Usher & Neisser (1993), who reported 60% of their participants giving contact permission and 67% of questionnaires returned by mothers giving a successful contact rate of 40%].

Table 29-1 shows for the recall and report groups the proportion of all questions answered by participants for whom we had a mother's response that were verified, denied, or neither verified nor denied by the participant's mother. From these data it is apparent that the answers of those in the report group were more frequently denied by their mothers than the answers of those in the recall group. This effect is significant, $\chi^2(1, N = 878) = 4.79, p < .05$. However, there was no difference between the number of answers specifically verified by the mothers of participants in the two groups, $\chi^2(1, N = 878) = 1.00, p > .05$. We were also able to break down this verification data by the age gap between our participants and their siblings. These data are also shown in Table 29-1. From these data, it is clear that those recall participants who were aged 2:0–2:3 at the time of their sibling's birth did not have a greater proportion of their answers denied by their mothers than those who were older at the time of the sibling birth, $\chi^2(1, N = 488) = 0.42, p > .05$. Therefore, despite the fact that this group answered significantly fewer questions than those who were older at the time of their sibling's birth, there is no evidence that the responses they do give are any less accurate.

...

TABLE 29-1

Percentage of answers verified by mother according to group and intersibling birth interval

	Mother's categorization		
Group/interval	Verified	Neither verified nor denied	Denied
Recall			
2:0–2:3	65	24	11
2:4–2:7	74	14	12
2:8–2:11	54	28	18
3:0–3:3	62	26	12
Overall	63.5	23.2	13.3
Report			
<2:0	57	26	17
2:0–2:3	57	16	27
2:4–2:7	81	5	14
2:8–2:11	56	25	19
3:0–3:3	61	24	14
Overall	60	21	19

Interval represents years:months.

DISCUSSION

This study has two major findings. The first is that 75% of participants who were between 2:4 and 2:11 at the time are able to recall something about the events surrounding their sibling's birth (as measured by our strict, though necessarily arbitrary, criterion of answering at least three questions about it). Thus, Usher and Neisser's (1993) report of memory for events that occurred when the child is younger than 3 years old is replicated using a much larger sample size. Moreover, those who experienced a sibling birth when they were aged between 2:0 and 2:3 remember significantly less than those who were between 2:4 and 3:3 years of age, so we are able to further narrow the critical age of the earliest memories to the first half of the 3rd year of life. The implications of this finding are discussed further in a later section.

However, an alternative explanation of Usher and Neisser's (1993) results was proposed by Loftus (1993) and may be extended to our own data. She correctly pointed out that a participant may have sufficient information from sources other than memory to answer the questions asked by Usher and Neisser and by us. Our data confirm this view. Participants in the report group, who can be expected to have no memory of events (some of which occurred before their own birth, others in their 1st weeks of life), were able to answer many of the questions that we and Usher and Neisser had asked of participants. Should this finding cause us to reject the evidence we have collected of memory for events that occurred in the later two thirds of the 3rd year (i.e., after 2 years and 3 months)? We argue that the pattern of data we collected is not consistent with this argument. First, our report participants, relying only on family knowledge, actually answered significantly more questions than the recall participants, who were able to draw on both family knowledge and autobiographical memory. Thus, it is unlikely that our recall participants were simply reporting to us all the information they knew, being unable to discriminate between sources of knowledge. If that were the case, our recall participants would be expected to relate the same amount of information as our report participants or perhaps even more, as they could supplement family knowledge with true autobiographical memories. However, this was not the case. Thus the recall participants filtered their knowledge about the events and reported only a subset of this knowledge. Of course, we cannot know from our data whether they filtered the information accurately into those items they knew on the basis of autobiographical memory and those that they knew from other sources. However, a further aspect of our data suggests that they may have done so. We found a significant difference between the amount of information reported by those who were between 2:0 and 2:3 and those who were older than this at the time of the sibling birth. Yet our results from the report group suggest no age-related differences in the amount of family knowledge available to participants. This difference between the youngest and oldest recall participants can therefore only reasonably come from differences in the number of memories available to the groups. Thus the conclusion from this discussion is that although participants have a great deal of information available to them about their sibling's birth from a variety of sources, they are not reporting all this information as though it were autobiographical memory.

...

Perhaps the most important aspect of these data is the finding that those who were aged 2:4–2:7 and older at the time of their sibling's birth have significantly more memories of the event than those who were aged 2:0–2:3. Of course, we are not claiming that there is a sudden and reliable change in abilities in all children at age 2 years and 4 months, but that the ability to recall is much more common after this point than before. We have no evidence that the age of this change depends on gender, although if such a gender difference existed it would be expected to be relatively small and may be hidden by the fact that we grouped ages in 4-month age bands. This grouping may be too coarse to pick up subtle gender differences in age of first recall. Interestingly, this change in mnemonic abilities in the early part of the 3rd year corresponds to several changes in the cognitive abilities of children. Not only is there an explosion of language around this age (R. Brown, 1973) but also impressive changes in the representational abilities of children (see Howe & Courage, 1993, for a discussion of some of these as they relate to the issue of childhood amnesia).

...

The mothers of our participants were also asked to verify their child's answers. From these data we were able to determine that the majority of the answers given by our participants were verified by their mother. We took a very strict definition of verified and did not include those occasions where the mother herself could not recall the information we asked for or where, although she recalled the answer differently, she said that her child's answer could be correct. Thus our figure for verified answers is almost certainly an underestimation of the true accuracy as judged against the mother's memory. Although one must also bear in mind the distinct possibility that mothers themselves do not have an accurate memory of all events (Robbins, 1963), it is clear that many early memories are essentially accurate. However, it is of note that more than 13% of memories from the recall group are judged by their mothers to be inaccurate; in the report group this figure rises to nearly 20%. Thus, those who are relying on reconstructions from family knowledge are, not unexpectedly, likely to introduce inaccuracies into their reports. Of particular interest here is the finding that those between ages 2 years and 2 years, 3 months at the time of their sibling's birth, although recalling relatively less than those who were older at the time, do not show this increase in false memories. Although this finding undoubtedly needs further study, it suggests that these participants did genuinely have memories from this period, rather than relying entirely on reconstructions from family knowledge that they mistake as memories. Thus their memories are fewer in number, but equally accurate.

...

In conclusion, we are able to fully confirm the claim of Usher and Neisser (1993) that an event that occurs when a participant is younger than 3 years old may be recalled in adulthood. Moreover, many participants are able to show substantial recall of events that took place when they were age 2½, but recall of events that took place in the first quarter of this year are much more rare. However, in situations where memories from this earliest period are recalled, we have no evidence that they are less accurate than memories from the later period. Thus, we are able to point to a steep offset of childhood amnesia during the first half of the 3rd year of life. Our study makes no claims to explain the phenomenon of childhood amnesia, but any such explanations should be based on the increasingly reliable data about the nature of the phenomenon itself.

REFERENCES

Brown, N. R., Ripps, L. J., & Shevel, S. K. (1985). The subjective dates of natural events in very-long-term memory. *Cognitive Psychology, 17,* 139–177.

Brown, R. (1973). *A first language.* London: Allen & Unwin.

Crombag, H. F. M., Wagenaar, W. A., & van Koppen, P. J. (1996). Crashing memories and the problem of source monitoring. *Applied Cognitive Psychology, 10,* 95–104.

Drummey, A. B., & Newcombe, N. (1995). Remembering versus knowing the past: Children's explicit and implicit memories for pictures. *Journal of Experimental Child Psychology, 59,* 549–565.

Dudycha, G. J., & Dudycha, M. M. (1941). Childhood memories: A review of the literature. *Psychological Bulletin, 38,* 668–682.

Fivush, R., Haden, C., & Adam, S. (1995). Structure and coherence of preschooler's personal narratives over time: Implications for childhood amnesia. *Journal of Experimental Child Psychology, 60,* 32–56.

Freud, S. (1963). Introductory lectures on psycho-analysis. In J. Strachey (Ed. and Trans.), *The standard edition of the complete psychological works of Sigmund Freud* (Vol. 15). London: Hogarth Press, 199–201. (Original work published in 1916.)

Howe, M. L., & Courage, M. L. (1993). On resolving the enigma of infantile amnesia. *Psychological Bulletin, 113,* 305–326.

Hyman, I. E., Husband, T. H., & Billings, F. J. (1995). False memories of childhood experiences. *Applied Cognitive Psychology, 9,* 181–197.

Loftus, E. F. (1993). Desperately seeking memories of the first few years of childhood: The reality of early memories. *Journal of Experimental Psychology: General, 122,* 274–277.

Morton, J., Andrews, N., Bekerian, D., Brewin, C., Davies, G., & Mollon, P. (1995). *Recovered memories: The report of the working party of The British Psychological Society.* Leicester, England: The British Psychological Society.

Nadel, L., & Zola-Morgan, S. (1984). Infantile amnesia: A neuro-biological perspective. In M. Moscovitch (Ed.), *Infant memory.* New York: Plenum Press, 145–172.

Robbins, L. C. (1963). The accuracy of parental recall of aspects of child development and of child rearing practices. *Journal of Abnormal and Social Psychology, 66,* 261–270.

Sheingold, K., & Tenney, Y. J. (1982). Memory for a salient childhood event. In U. Neisser (Ed.), *Memory observed.* New York: Freeman, 201–212.

Usher, J. A., & Neisser, U. (1993). Childhood amnesia and the beginnings of memory for four early life events. *Journal of Experimental Psychology: General, 122,* 155–165.

Waldvogel, S. (1948). The frequency and affective character of childhood memories. *Psychological Monographs, 62*(4, Whole No. 291).

...

[*Appendix omitted.*]

30 | False Memories of Childhood Experiences

*Ira E. Hyman, Jr., Troy H. Husband,
and F. James Billings*

> *The fact that we remember something as having occurred
> in the later years of childhood (i.e., after the offset of child-
> hood amnesia) does not guarantee that we are remember-
> ing it accurately. Indeed, it does not even guarantee that
> the event took place! This selection shows that persuading
> people to accept entirely fabricated "childhood memories"
> as their own is easier than might be supposed.*

Can adults create false memories of childhood experiences in response
to misleading information and the demands of an interview? Psychologists
who work with people recovering from childhood abuse and trauma have
contended that most memories recovered during therapy are accurate
(Bass & Davis, 1988; Fredrickson, 1992; Olio, 1994). Memory psychologists, in contrast, have expressed concern that many recovered memories
may be false memories (Kihlstrom, 1993; Lindsay & Read, 1994; Loftus,
1993). Thus investigation of factors that contribute to our understanding of
the recovery of childhood memories is important. If adults can create false
childhood memories, then therapists will need to exercise caution in their
interviews with clients, and the courts may need to view memories recovered through therapy as having been contaminated by potentially biasing
influences. Research on false memories may also provide information concerning the processes involved in memory creation—whether memory creation involves integration, source confusion, or some combination of both.

...

Memory researchers (e.g., Kihlstrom, 1993; Lindsay & Read, 1994; Loftus, 1993) have recently expressed concern that repressed memories re-

From *Applied Cognitive Psychology*, 1995, 9, 181–197.

covered during the course of therapy may be false memories—creations based on the demands of the interview context. Loftus (1993) offered evidence concerning the influences of misleading information and situation demands on memory as reason to doubt the veracity of memories recovered through therapy. Eyewitness memory researchers, for example, have found that postevent information can lead to errors in subsequent reports of an event (Loftus, 1979, 1992). In a typical experiment, individuals view an event, are later provided incorrect information about the event, and are finally asked to remember the event. Individuals provided incorrect information are likely to incorporate that information into succeeding reports of the original event—this is generally referred to as the misinformation effect. Arguments exist regarding the underlying mechanism of the misinformation effect. Authors emphasize that the misleading postevent information becomes integrated with the original memory, thereby replacing the correct information; or that the individual recalls the postevent information without memory for the source of the knowledge and thus erroneously attributes the information to the original event (Belli, 1989; Belli & Loftus, in press; Lindsay, 1990; Loftus, 1992; Loftus, Donders, Hoffman, & Schooler, 1989; Loftus & Hoffman, 1989; McCloskey & Zaragoza, 1985; Zaragoza & Lane, 1994). None the less, that the phenomenon occurs is not in question. Thus, the misinformation effect can be applied to memories of childhood. Information an individual has learned after childhood events, during later childhood or during adulthood, can become incorporated into that individual's memory and lead to inaccurate recall or false memories (Belli & Loftus, in press; Lindsay & Read, 1994; Loftus, 1993).

...

Although the laboratory findings regarding misinformation and social influence are robust and replicable, such research may not be directly applicable to the accuracy of childhood memories recovered during therapy (Berliner & Williams, 1994; Olio, 1994; Pezdek, 1994). Laboratory research often changes elements of events (by altering or adding features) while the whole event is generally remembered accurately. Olio (1994) noted that changing or adding features is not the same as causing someone to believe that an entire event occurred. In the typical eyewitness memory paradigm, for example, the difference would be between convincing someone that a car in a viewed videotape passed a yield rather than stop sign and convincing someone that they watched a videotape of a car passing a sign when they actually viewed a different videotape. Additionally, the events in laboratory investigations tend not to be particularly self-relevant. For instance, subjects in the typical eyewitness memory experiment watch a video or slides about unknown individuals. Yuille and his colleagues (Yuille, 1993; Yuille & Cutshall, 1986; Yuille & Tollestrup, 1992) have argued that more self-involved memories (those that happen to a person as opposed to those that a person encounters through material such as videotapes) may be less susceptible to the misinformation effect.

...

The two studies we report in this paper are extensions of research investigating whether people will make incorporations of false, self-involved events. We investigated whether college students would create a false recall of a childhood experience in response to the demands of multiple interviews. In the first study we mailed a questionnaire to the parents of students in an introductory psychology class that asked parents to describe events that happened to their child. When questionnaires were returned, we invited the students to participate in two autobiographical memory interviews based on the information provided by their parents. We presented the study as an investigation of how well and how accurately people could remember childhood events. Included in the series of events was one event that did not happen to the student (either an overnight hospitalization for an ear infection at age five or a birthday party with pizza and a clown at age five). At the end of the first interview, the students were encouraged to continue thinking about the events and to attempt to remember more by the second interview. We predicted that in the second interview some students would provide a false recall based on the information from the first interview.

The second study served as a replication and extension of the first. In the second study, we used less probable false events, included a third interview, increased the supportive interviewer demands, and varied the age at which we claimed the false event occurred. We varied the age based on the general pattern observed in studies of childhood amnesia (Sheingold & Tenney, 1982; Usher & Neisser, 1993). Specifically, few individuals can recall events from age two, most can recall events from age six, and most can recall numerous events and a relatively complex personal narrative from age ten. We were interested in evaluating the extent to which self-knowledge at a particular age influences the ability to add a new memory at that age. If individuals will incorporate a new memory most easily with little competition from general knowledge, then we should observe more false memories at earlier ages. If, instead, individuals require a solid base of self-knowledge upon which to construct a false memory, then we should see more incorporations at later ages.

EXPERIMENT 1

Method

Subjects. One hundred and thirty one introductory psychology students from Western Washington University provided consent for distribution of a questionnaire to their parents. Eighty-three questionnaires were returned by parents (63 per cent response rate). Twenty-five subjects participated in pilot investigations. Of the remaining 58 possible subjects, we recruited 22 to participate in this experiment based on our ability to contact and schedule students during the last four weeks of the academic session. Two were dropped for failure to complete the second interview, leaving 20 subjects (5 males, 15 females). Subjects participated on a volunteer basis after they had completed the introductory psychology class.

Materials. The questionnaires sent to parents included questions about specific childhood (ages two to ten) events in six event categories. The categories included were: (1) getting lost; (2) going to the hospital; (3) an eventful birthday; (4) loss of a pet; (5) a family vacation; and (6) interaction with a prominent or famous person. For each event described, parents were asked to indicate the age of their child when the event occurred, and to describe activities, places, and individuals involved in the event.

In addition, we constructed two event descriptions for use as the false events. Both events represented instances of the event categories, with one event being positive and one negative in emotional valence. Within the eventful birthday category, the positive event was the individual's birthday party at age five during which pizza was served and a clown visited. Within the going to the hospital category, the negative event was presented as an overnight visit to the hospital at age five due to a high fever and a possible ear infection. In response to the birthday and hospital event categories on the parent questionnaire, no parents recorded similar events (clown at a birthday party, overnight hospitalization for fever and ear infection) at any age.

Procedure. All subjects participated in two interviews in which they were asked to remember and describe a series of childhood events. On the basis of parent responses, subjects were asked to recall two to five true events. In addition, each subject was asked to recall one of the two false events (determined randomly). The order of events was the same in both interviews and the false event was always the third event the subjects were asked to recall. For each subject, one interviewer conducted both sessions. Three interviewers, two male and one female, conducted the sessions. All sessions were tape-recorded.

At the beginning of the first interview, subjects were informed that in both interviews they would be asked to recall and describe a set of childhood experiences based on information obtained from their parents. We told the subjects that the goal of the research was to investigate how much they could recall by the end of the second session and that we would compare their recalls to the information provided by their parents. Subjects were also informed that the sessions would be tape-recorded and were asked to wear a lapel microphone. For each event, subjects were first cued with an event title (family vacation) and an age (at age five). If the subjects were unable to recall the event, or if what they described did not appear to agree with information provided by parents (they appeared to be describing a different vacation), brief additional cues were provided: location, one or two activities, and other people involved. If subjects were still unable to recall the event, the interviewer moved to the next event. The interviewers were encouraging in terms of non-verbal communication, but did not provide any additional verbal cues or demands. The false event was presented in the same way as the other events. At the end of the first interview, we encouraged subjects to continue thinking about the events, to try to remember more before the next interview, and to not discuss the events with their parents.

The second interview occurred one to seven days after the first. After the subjects finished describing the events they were asked several questions about each event and the experience of remembering the event. The questions included whether they had thought or talked about the event in the last five years, whether the family had photographs of the event, if a mental image accompanied their memory of the event and, if so, the image perspective, and the strength and valence of any experienced emotion. Also the subjects were asked if they had discussed the events with their parents between interviews and had a subject done so we would have dropped that subject's data. After answering these questions, subjects were informed that one event was an event we were relatively sure had not happened to them. As part of the debriefing, we asked subjects to guess which event they thought was the false event. We told all subjects, particularly those who incorporated aspects of the false events, that such incorporation was a normal memory process and that in this situation we expected people to accept the false events.

Results and Discussion

Based on the information provided by the parents, the 20 subjects were asked to recall 74 true events (an average of 3.7 true events per subject). In the first interview, the subjects recalled and described 62 of the 74 true events (83.8 per cent). In the second interview, in addition to continuing to recall the events remembered at time one, subjects provided memories for three of the 12 events (25 per cent) that had not been remembered during the first interview. The subjects had either recalled the event or had reconstructed a memory based on the first interview.

Each subject was also asked about one of the two false events. During the first interview no subjects incorporated any of the false information into an event description, although some subjects talked about related information (a similar event or general knowledge). During the second interview four of the 20 subjects (20 per cent) incorporated false information in an event description. Two subjects incorporated false information for the birthday event and two for the hospital event. When asked to identify the false event during debriefing, subjects who did not incorporate false information correctly identified the false event while three of the four subjects who incorporated false information did not correctly identify the false event.

Table 30-1 provides an example from a subject questioned about the false eventful birthday. This example illustrates the manner in which subjects incorporated the information. The four individuals who incorporated false information talked about related information during the first interview. This appeared to be an attempt by these individuals to connect the

TABLE 30-1

Example of incorporation of false information regarding an eventful birthday

Interview 1

I: We have event number 3, an eventful birthday party at age 5.

S: Oh.

I: Anything you can remember?

S: Well, I remember from pictures a girl there that I might have known, her name was Molly. That's about it, that's all I remember.

I: Anything else?

S: Oh, oh, maybe we went to McDonald's. We went to McDonaldland and I remember we sat around in the McDonald's, the chairs were like little toadstools around a big animal and I remember, I don't know if Ronald McDonald came out. We all had these little cupcakes.

I: We've got here pizza, ice cream, and a visit from a clown.

S: Oh, maybe a visit from a clown, some animal or something came out and visited us.

I: Can you remember anything more specific? Just anything else?

S: No.

Interview 2

I: Event number 3, an eventful birthday at the age of 5.

S: We were in McDonald's, McDonaldland and a clown came in and we all had little cupcakes and we sat on toadstools and I'd say there were about 13–14 people sitting around this table and we had pizza.

I: OK, anything else you can think of?

S: No.

I: OK.

false information to true information. In the case presented in Table 30-1, the subject described what was probably a real birthday party during the first interview and seemed to accept the false information regarding a clown as reasonable, "Oh, maybe a visit from a clown, some animal or something came out and visited us." The subject then added the false information to this event description during the second interview (leading to the unlikely combination, at least at that time, of pizza and McDonald's).

...

EXPERIMENT 2

In our second study, we conducted a replication and extension of Experiment 1. The replication was not exact because we wanted to ensure the generality of false recalls of childhood events and obtain more convincing evidence that subjects will make substantial incorporation into their recollections of childhood. Thus, in the second experiment, we changed the events that we attempted to insert. The three new false events differed from those of the first experiment in two respects. First, although the events were relatively negative in emotional tone, they could be viewed as humorous in retrospect. This change enabled the subjects to supply their own emotional interpretations. Second, we attempted to construct events that were less likely to have occurred. The first event was attending the wedding reception of a friend of the family and accidentally spilling a punch bowl. The second event was having to evacuate a grocery store when the overhead sprinkler systems erroneously activated. The third event was being left in the car in a parking lot and managing to release the parking brake resulting in the car rolling into something. (We uncovered no true instances of the wedding event, although many subjects attended weddings. Given that we did not ask about unusual experiences while grocery shopping, we cannot be sure that a sprinkler event did not occur. With respect to the car event, in the information provided by parents, there were two accidents caused by children releasing parking brakes and we did not use this event with those subjects.)

...

Method

Subjects. Two hundred and fifty six introductory psychology students from Western Washington University gave permission for us to distribute a questionnaire regarding childhood experiences to their parents. One hundred and forty three questionnaires were returned (55.9 per cent). Selection of subjects was limited to questionnaires that described at least three events (only seven subjects were not contacted for this reason). In

addition, we recruited subjects based on the order in which the questionnaires were returned, and we did not contact 49 possible subjects because
their parent questionnaires were returned too late. Of the remaining 87
subjects, 29 could not be reached or scheduled. Thus 58 subjects participated in the study, seven of whom did not complete all three interviews in
a timely fashion, leaving 51 who completed data collection (17 males, 34
females). Subjects received course credit for their participation.

...

Procedure. All subjects participated in three interviews spaced one day
apart (we scheduled subjects for Monday–Wednesday–Friday or Tuesday–Thursday–Saturday interviews). In all interviews we asked the subjects to remember and describe three to five childhood events based on
parent responses to the questionnaire and one of the three false events.
The false event (wedding, store, or car) and the age of insertion (2, 6, 10)
were determined randomly. The order of events was the same in all interviews and the false event was always placed in the fourth position. The
same interviewer conducted all three interviews for any given subject
(there were three male and two female interviewers). All sessions were
tape-recorded.

The sessions were similar to those in Experiment 1. The two most important differences concerned the amount of information used to cue
events and the amount of emphasis on increased recall over the three sessions. During the first interview in Experiment 1, the subjects were first
cued with an event title and an age. They were provided more details only
if they failed to recall the event or if what they recalled did not match with
parent information (or false information). During the first interview in this
experiment, we provided all cue information (age, event, location, actions,
and others involved) as part of the first cue in order to limit the number of
times subjects recalled a similar but different event. During interviews two
and three, we first provided the event title and age, and, if subjects failed
to recall the event, we provided the additional details.

We also increased the experimental demands for increased recall.
More complete recall, along with accuracy, was given as one goal of the research during the introduction. The subjects were reminded of this expectation whenever they failed to recall an event during the first or second interviews. They were also reminded of this goal at the end of the first and
second interviews and asked to continue thinking about events between
interviews. In addition, the third interview served to intensify the experimental demands.

Results and Discussion

Based on the information supplied by parents the 51 subjects were asked
to recall 205 true events (4.02 events per subject). As Figure 30-1 shows,

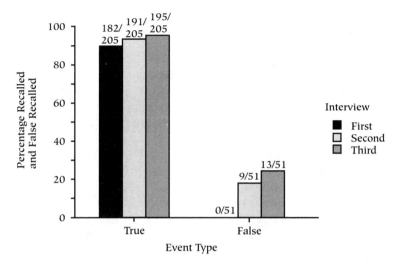

Figure 30-1 *Percentage of true events recalled and false events falsely recalled in all three interviews, Experiment 2.*

the percentage of true events for which subjects provided some recall increased from 88.8 per cent to 95.1 per cent from the first to the third interview. Of the 23 true events not recalled during interview one, 13 were recalled during interview three (a recovery rate of 56.5 per cent). Whether subjects recovered these memories in response to repeated questioning and appropriate cues (a form of hypermnesia; see Erdelyi, 1990) or whether they created the memories in response to experimental demands is unclear. In addition, some events may have not been recalled due to a parent making an error rather than a subject forgetting the event.

...

We also asked each subject about one of the three false events at one of the three ages. Figure 30-1 also shows that no subjects provided false recalls during the first interview and that 13 (25.5 per cent) did by the third interview. We included as false recalls those event descriptions that incorporated some of the false information or those that provided elaborations consistent with the false information. Two raters agreed that all 13 did include incorporations or elaborations. Of the 13, however, not all were equally clear examples of false recalls. Six were very clear: generally these subjects incorporated most of the false information and often they elaborated on the event. Five were less clear false recalls: these subjects incorporated less of the critical information or did not incorporate any of the false information but rather elaborated in a fashion that only would have been possible given the false information. Two subjects re-

TABLE 30-2

Example of a clear false recall in Experiment 2

First Interview

I: The next one is attending a wedding. At age six you attended a wedding reception and while you were running around with some other kids you bumped into a table and turned the punch bowl over on a parent of the bride.

S: I have no clue. I have never heard that one before. Age 6?

I: Uh-huh.

S: No clue.

I: Can you think of any details?

S: Six years old, we would have been in Spokane, um, not at all.

I: OK.

Second Interview

I: The next one was when you were six years old and you were attending a wedding.

S: The wedding was my best friend in Spokane, T _____ . Her brother, older brother was getting married, and it was over here in P _____ , Washington, cause that's where her family was from and it was in the summer or the spring because it was really hot outside and it was right on the water. It was an outdoor wedding and I think we were running around and knocked something over like the punch bowl or something and um made a big mess and of course got yelled at for it. But uh.

I: Do you remember anything else?

S: No.

I: OK.

called the false event, attributed the false recall to an image, and expressed doubts as to whether image was actually a memory of the event. (Several additional subjects said they could see and believe the event, but unless they described the event, we did not include such statements as indicative of false recall. None the less, such statements could be seen as instances of false recognition.) Table 30-2 provides an example of a clear false recall. . . .

We found no difference in the rate of false recalls based on the attempted age of insertion—subjects were equally willing to incorporate the false events at ages two, six, and ten. With respect to the role background knowledge plays in false recall creation, two possibilities are implied: (1) the creation of false recalls is not dependent on accessing relevant background knowledge (as subjects have little at age two, yet did create false re-calls); or (2) the limited amount of information people have is enough to al-low the creation of false recalls. The second option seems reasonable given that subjects in our sample did report recall of some events from the second year of life.

To further investigate the role of background knowledge in the creation of false memories we looked at whether or not subjects explicitly accessed background knowledge during interviews one and two, and the rate of false recalls by interview three. We counted specific events (such as a wedding actually attended if asked about the punch bowl), gen-eral self and family information consistent with the event (where they lived and who could have gotten married then), and general self and fam-ily information inconsistent with the event (never attended weddings) as instances of accessing relevant background knowledge. Subjects who described relevant background knowledge during interviews one or two were more likely to create false recalls by interview three ($\chi^2(1, n = 51) = 4.792, p = .029$). Eleven of the 30 subjects who talked about relevant background knowledge eventually provided false recalls, while only two of the 21 who did not eventually provided false recalls. Thus, we conclude that accessing some form of relevant background knowledge plays an im-portant role in the creation of false recalls, although such accessing may not be necessary.

GENERAL DISCUSSION

In two studies we found instances in which people will create false recalls of childhood experiences. In Experiment 1, we provided subjects with de-scriptions of events that purportedly occurred during childhood and, in the second interview, 20 per cent of the subjects not only agreed that the event occurred but also provided a recall of the event that included some of the false information. Experiment 2 was an extension of the first experi-ment that used different false events. In this case, with less likely events, one additional interview, and some increased conformity demands, we found that 25 per cent created a false recall. In Experiment 2, we also var-ied the attempted age of insertion to investigate the role of background knowledge in the creation of false recalls. We had expected that if subjects needed relatively clear, age-appropriate knowledge as the basis for false recall construction that age two would result in fewer false recalls than ages six and ten. This was not the case, as subjects were equally likely to create false recalls at all the cued ages.

None the less we found evidence that the process of false recall cre-ation most probably depends on accessing some relevant background in-formation. In the second experiment we observed that subjects who discussed relevant personal knowledge (either specific events or generic knowledge) during the first two interviews were more likely to create false recalls in the final interview. Thus a form of schematic reconstruction may account for the creation of false recalls. Individuals call up schematic knowledge closely related to the false event when they first encounter the false event. Then they think about the new information in conjunction with the schema, and most probably, store the new information with the schema. When asked to recall the false event at a later time, they recall the false information and the underlying scheme. The underlying schema supports the false event by completing the event—adding actual background information and providing generic scenes. This process appears very similar to the schema-like interpretations of the misinformation effect (those that rely on the new information being combined with the old information, e.g., Loftus, 1979).

The creation of false recalls may also be explained as dependent on a form of source confusion—the false event is accepted as being a personal memory rather than as something recorded by the parent on a questionnaire and presented by the experimenter. Perhaps the schematic knowledge lends its credibility to the false recall enabling an individual to identify the false recall as a personal memory. The more similar the false event is to true events (or to some personal knowledge) the more likely an individual will accept the event. For example, when using recognition of events from an individual's diary and distracter items, Barclay and DeCooke (1988) reported that individuals were more likely to falsely identify distracters as personal memories when the distracters were true events with modification than when the distracters were completed new.

In addition to the informational aspects of our experiments, the social aspects also probably contributed to the creation of false recalls. In the explicit demand characteristics, we stated that we expected subjects to recall more events, and recall events in more detail, with successive interviews. Further, the subjects faced a unanimous majority of authority figures (parent and experimenter) claiming that the event occurred. Asch (1956) demonstrated that subjects are likely to conform in the face of a unanimous majority. Recent work on the social psychology of the memory experiment has shown that people are more likely to accept misinformation from an authoritative source (Dodd & Bradshaw, 1980; Greene et al., 1982) and from a majority (Betz et al., 1993).

We suspect that incorporating information about remembered events in response to the social context is a general phenomenon. People often engage in memory discussions with friends and family. In the course of these discussions individuals may often present differing views, memories, and reactions. If one goal of such discussions is to arrive at an agreed upon version of the past (Edwards & Middleton, 1986a,b; Edwards, Potter, & Middleton, 1992; Hyman, 1994), then people may often come to accept information from others. This may be particularly true for childhood events—parents may often repeat stories and children may eventually have difficulty determining whether they remember the event or simply know about it based on their parents' stories. Thus, some of the true events that subjects described in the two experiments may have been derived from family stories rather than episodic memory.

...

REFERENCES

Asch, S. E. (1956). Studies of independence and conformity: I. A minority of one against a unanimous majority. *Psychological Monographs, 70*(9).

Barclay, C. R., & DeCooke, P. A. (1988). Ordinary everyday memories: Some of the things of which selves are made. In U. Neisser and E. Winograd (Eds.), *Remembering reconsidered: Ecological and traditional approaches to the study of memory*. New York: Cambridge University Press, 91–125.

Bass, E., & Davis, L. (1988). *The courage to heal: A guide for women survivors of child sexual abuse*. New York: Harper & Row.

Belli, R. F. (1989). Influences of misleading postevent information: Misinformation interference and acceptance. *Journal of Experimental Psychology: General, 118*, 72–85.

Belli, R. F., & Loftus, E. F. (in press). The pliability of autobiographical memory: Misinformation and the false memory problem. In D. C. Rubin (Ed.), *Constructing our past: An overview of autobiographical memory*. New York: Cambridge University Press.

Berliner, L., & Williams, L. M. (1994). Memories of sexual abuse: A response to Lindsay and Read. *Applied Cognitive Psychology, 8*, 379–387.

Betz, A. L., Skowronski, J. J., & Ostrom, T. M. (1993). *Shared realities: Social influence and episodic memory*. Manuscript submitted for publication.

Dodd, D. H., & Bradshaw, J. M. (1980). Leading questions and memory: Some pragmatic constraints. *Journal of Verbal Learning and Verbal Memory, 19*, 695–704.

Edwards, D., & Middleton, D. (1986a). Text for memory: Joint recall with a scribe. *Human Learning, 5*, 125–138.

Edwards, D., & Middleton, D. (1986b). Joint remembering: Constructing an account of shared experience through conversational discourse. *Discourse Processes, 9*, 423–459.

Edwards, D., Potter, J., & Middleton, D. (1992). Toward a discursive psychology of remembering. *The Psychologist, 5*, 441–446.

Erdleyi, M. H. (1990). Repression, reconstruction, and defence: History and integration of the psychoanalytic and experimental frameworks. In J. L. Singer

(Ed.), *Repression and dissociation*. Chicago: University of Chicago Press, 1–32.

Fredrickson, R. (1992). *Repressed memories: A journal to recovery from sexual abuse*. New York: Simon & Schuster.

Greene, E., Flynn, M. S., & Loftus, E. F. (1982). Inducing resistance to misleading information. *Journal of Verbal Learning and Verbal Behavior, 21*, 207–219.

Hyman, I. E., Jr. (1994). Conversational remembering: Story recall with a peer versus for an experimenter. *Applied Cognitive Psychology, 8*, 49–66.

Kihlstrom, J. F. (1993, April). *The recovery of memory in the laboratory and clinic*. Paper presented at the joint convention of Rocky Mountain Psychological Association and Western Psychological Association, Phoenix, Arizona.

Lindsay, D. S. (1990). Misleading suggestions can impair eyewitnesses' ability to remember event details. *Journal of Experimental Psychology: Learning, Memory, and Cognition, 16*, 1077–1083.

Lindsay, D. S., & Read, J. D. (1994). Psychotherapy and memories of childhood sexual abuse: A cognitive perspective. *Applied Cognitive Psychology, 8*, 281–338.

Loftus, E. F. (1979). *Eyewitness testimony*. Cambridge, MA: Harvard University Press.

Loftus, E. F. (1992). When a lie becomes memory's truth: Memory distortion after exposure to misinformation. *Current Directions in Psychological Science, 1*, 121–123.

Loftus, E. F. (1993). The reality of repressed memories. *American Psychologist, 48*, 518–537.

Loftus, E. F., Donders, K., Hoffman, H. G., & Schooler, J. W. (1989). Creating new memories that are quickly accessed and confidently held. *Memory & Cognition, 17*, 607–616.

Loftus, E. F., & Hoffman, H. G. (1989). Misinformation and memory: The creation of new memories. *Journal of Experimental Psychology: General, 118*, 100–104.

McCloskey, M., & Zaragoza, M. (1985). Misleading postevent information and memory for events: Arguments and evidence against memory impairment hypothesis. *Journal of Experimental Psychology: General, 114*, 3–18.

Olio, K. (1994). Truth in memory. *American Psychologist, 49*, 442–443.

Pezdek, K. (1994). The illusion and illusory memory. *Applied Cognitive Psychology, 8*, 339–350.

Sheingold, K., & Tenney, Y. J. (1982). Memory for a salient childhood event. In U. Neisser (Ed.), *Memory observed: Remembering in natural contexts*. San Francisco: Freeman, 201–212.

Usher, J. A., & Neisser, U. (1993). Childhood amnesia and the beginnings of memory for four early life events. *Journal of Experimental Psychology: General, 122*, 155–165.

Yuille, J. C. (1993). We must study forensic eyewitnesses to know about them. *American Psychologist, 48*, 572–573.

Yuille, J. C., & Cutshall, J. L. (1986). A case study of eyewitness memory of a crime. *Journal of Applied Psychology, 71*, 291–301.

Yuille, J. C., & Tollestrup, P. A. (1992). A model of diverse effects of emotion on eyewitness memory. In S.-A. Christianson (Ed.), *The handbook of emotion and memory: Research and theory.* Hillsdale, NJ: Lawrence Erlbaum Associates, 201–216.

Zaragoza, M. S., & Lane, S. M. (1994). Source misattributions and the suggestibility of eyewitness memory. *Journal of Experimental Psychology: Learning, Memory, & Cognition, 20,* 934–945.

Part VI

TRAUMA: REAL AND IMAGINED

One thing is clear about memory for traumatic events: No simple
principle will do. Some real traumas are remembered all too
vividly, while others may undergo distortion or be forgotten.
Sometimes a genuine and long-forgotten trauma may come
suddenly to mind, but not everything that comes to mind in this
way is genuine. Here, as elsewhere, the power of imagination and
suggestion must not be underestimated.

31 | The Memory of Concentration Camp Survivors

Willem A. Wagenaar and Jop Groeneweg

Are some experiences so extreme, so traumatic, that they can never be forgotten at all? "Never" is a long time; how about, say, four decades? This selection shows that the survivors of a brutal Nazi concentration camp still recalled many aspects of their camp experience forty years later. Nevertheless their memories were far from perfect; some important facts and episodes that they had been able to report in the 1940s were no longer available in the 1980s.

A much-debated issue in the area of eyewitness testimony is related to the influence of intense emotions at the time of encoding (Johnson & Scott, 1976; Clifford & Scott, 1978; Sussman & Sugarmann, 1972). In principle two theories were put forward. One is that emotions will increase arousal, which in turn intensifies attention for relevant details of the situation. The other is that witnesses or victims will be overaroused, which will cause them to misdirect attention, and to focus attention on a few details only.

This discussion, which is not yet resolved, has concentrated on the effect of emotions in the phase of encoding. Little has been said about the effects of emotions that persist after the experience of a crime. Victims often claim that they go through the experience over and over again, or that they see the criminal frequently in their dreams. It seems that such persisting emotions cause frequent rehearsals, which may help to bridge long retention intervals. This could be the reason why juries and judges have a tendency to

※ From *Applied Cognitive Psychology*, 1990, 4, 77–87.

believe testimony provided by victims. But, on the other hand, it could well
be that persisting emotions during the retention period have a disturbing effect on memory, and that recollections will be more and more colored. In the
extreme, and in good Freudian tradition, it could be supposed that victims
suppress such memories, or change them in such a way that the recall is less
painful. An illustration of inferior recall of unpleasant experiences is presented by Wagenaar's study of autobiographical memory (Wagenaar,
1986)*[but see discussion of this finding in Selection 12].* Recently the question culminated in the case of John Demjanjuk, who was accused of being
Ivan the Terrible, the operator of the gas chambers in Treblinka. The identification of Demjanjuk rested for a large part on the testimony of camp survivors, and the question was raised whether the horrors of the camps leave
an unextinguishable trace in memory, such that any statement can be relied
upon, even after a period of 35 years. The case of Martinus De Rijke, analyzed in the present study, may shed some new light on this issue.

Martinus De Rijke was a prisoner in the penal colony Camp Erika
during the years 1942 and 1943. Although the camp was set up as a normal Dutch prison for convicted criminals, German rule was imposed from
the beginning, which resulted in maltreatment, torture, and death of many
prisoners. Some prisoners were promoted to Kapos with the explicit task
of terrorizing their fellows, and Martinus De Rijke was one of those Kapos.
One group of about 800 prisoners was sent "on loan" to Braunschweig in
Germany, where they did forced labor. Of these men only 400 returned;
the others died under the hands of their own Kapos. Of the 30–40 Jewish
prisoners only one survived, who declared that transfer to a German concentration camp saved his life. Also from the testimonies of 78 survivors it
is abundantly clear that the conditions in Camp Erika were at least as horrible as in German concentration camps.

...

The present study contains an analysis of 140 statements deposited by 78
witnesses. The statements are compared with previous statements of the
same witnesses, or with official documents. The major question is: does a
comparison of early and late testimonies prove that such highly emotional
events, once they are committed to memory, leave an unextinguishable
trace?

DATA COLLECTION

The Material

Between 1943 and 1948 a total of 22 witnesses were interviewed, mainly
in the course of trials against the Dutch guards Boxmeer and Daalhuizen,
who were both convicted of Nazi crimes. Between 1984 and 1987 the

TABLE 31-1

Origins of the 140 interviews

L = letter. O(ld) = interview between 1943 and 1948. N(ew) = interview between 1984 and 1987, without questionnaire. NQ = interview between 1984 and 1987, with questionnaire. EJ = interview in 1987–1988 by the examining judge

		Number of interviews	
1	2	3	4
L = 1	O + N = 3	O + N + EJ = 1	L + O + NQ + EJ = 1
O = 5	O + NQ = 6	O + NQ + EJ = 5	L + L + N + EJ = 1
N = 20	O + EJ = 1		L + NQ + NQ + EJ = 1
NQ = 2	N + EJ = 24		
	NQ + EJ = 7		
Total = 28	Total = 82	Total = 18	Total = 12

gathering of information about Camp Erika was resumed. A total of 72 witnesses were questioned by the police. In 23 cases a structured questionnaire was used which inquired specifically after the witnesses' memories of De Rijke. Then, after De Rijke was arrested in May 1987, old and new witnesses were interviewed by the examining judge, about their recollections of Camp Erika and De Rijke's role in it, but without the use of a questionnaire. Five letters containing spontaneous testimony were received. An overview of the origin of the 140 statements is presented in Table 31-1. The major part of the interviews was haphazard and unsystematic, which means that witnesses were asked different questions. Hence the total number of witnesses varied for different questions.

…

RESULTS

The most striking aspect of the testimonies is that the witnesses agreed about the basic facts, which is demonstrated by a comparison of 55 longer interviews. The punishments (called "crawling" and "record playing"), given for very small or cooked-up misdemeanors, were mentioned spontaneously by 42 of these 55 witnesses. Thirty-six witnesses recounted that the meals were deliberately thwarted, by allowing only a few minutes, not enough to let the steaming fodder cool down. The beastly treatment of Jewish prisoners was mentioned by 44 out of 55 witnesses. Brutalities during the endless roll calls were spontaneously remembered by 36 witnesses.

The post of "Kapo," the prisoner who was in command of his fellows, was correctly ascribed to De Rijke by 36 witnesses.

Although the data that will be presented in the following paragraphs do also, in the first place, illustrate a remarkable degree of remembering, we will from now on concentrate on the things that were forgotten.

...

Remembering Names

De Rijke was frequently mentioned as the most notorious executioner of Camp Erika. Hence it must be assumed that many witnesses originally knew his name. Still, despite the publicity around De Rijke's case, there were six out of the 61 witnesses who failed to respond positively when they were asked explicitly whether they remembered the name "De Rijke."

Thirty-eight witnesses reported that they were maltreated or tortured by De Rijke. Three out of these 38 had forgotten his name after 40 years. One of those three had also been questioned in 1947, at which occasion he knew De Rijke's name quite well. The influence of being maltreated is illustrated in Table 31-2. The interaction was not significant ($\chi^2 = .37$, d.f. = 1), which implies that reporting maltreatment was not associated with name recall.

The 15 witnesses who were questioned both between 1943 and 1948 and 1984 and 1988 appeared to have remembered De Rijke's name quite well, although they had forgotten most other names mentioned in the 1940s (cf. Table 31-3).

The interaction in Table 31-3 was significant ($\chi^2 = 8.44$, d.f. = 1, $p < .01$). One explanation could be that De Rijke made himself more notorious than the other Kapos and guards. Another explanation is that some of the witnesses were aware of the reopening of De Rijke's case. If this were true, the less than 30 per cent recall of other names after 40 years would be the more representative number.

...

TABLE 31-2

The relationship between reporting maltreatment by De Rijke and the recall of his name

	Name recalled	Name not recalled
Maltreated	35 (92%)	3 (8%)
Not maltreated	20 (87%)	3 (13%)

TABLE 31-3

Recall of names in 1984–1988 by 15 witnesses who were also heard in 1943–1948

	Name recalled	Name not recalled
De Rijke's name	8	2
Other names	11	27

Recognition of De Rijke

In the period 1984–1988 a picture of De Rijke taken in the camp was shown to 55 witnesses. Forty-one witnesses said they recognized him, but 14 did not, although it is very likely that all of them had known De Rijke. The recognition score is probably too rosy, since the same picture was shown before in a nationwide television broadcast. Thirty-seven of the witnesses who were confronted with the photo, were also asked whether they had seen the broadcast. The answers to this question are presented in Table 31-4. Although the interaction in Table 31-4 was not significant (Fisher exact probability test, $p = .16$) the result of those witnesses who did not watch the television program falls well within the normal range of false positives in target-absent line-ups (cf. Shapiro & Penrod, 1986). Our problem here is that the recognition was based on the presentation of one picture only. A false positive will by necessity result in a "recognition" of De Rijke. Thus a unique opportunity for the assessment of face recognition after 40 years was lost, due to sloppy investigative procedures. We can only conclude that the recognition of De Rijke's photo could be attributed to a positive response bias.

Reporting maltreatment or torture by De Rijke did not promote the recognition of his picture, as is demonstrated in Table 31-5. The interaction in Table 31-5 was not significant (Fisher exact probability test, $p = .43$). Of those who reported maltreatment by De Rijke, 80 per cent recognized his picture, which is not significantly different from the overall

TABLE 31-4

The recognition of De Rijke's picture after seeing or not seeing the television program

	Recognized	Not recognized
Seen TV program	20 (80%)	5 (20%)
Not seen TV program	7 (58%)	5 (42%)

TABLE 31-5

Recognition of De Rijke's picture after reporting having been
maltreated by him

	Recognized	Not recognized
Maltreated	24 (80%)	6 (20%)
Not maltreated	14 (74%)	5 (26%)

recognition rate of 75 per cent. During the period 1987–1988 De Rijke's
picture was shown twice to 20 witnesses. In 16 cases they reacted in the
same manner both times. Two witnesses recognized him only the first
time, two others recognized him only the second time.

Statements about the color of De Rijke's hair were made by 18 witnesses. Fourteen remembered correctly that he had dark hair. Four witnesses claimed that his hair was fair.

Forty-eight witnesses made statements about De Rijke's clothing.
Twenty said he wore a uniform, 28 said he did not. Witnesses who remembered a uniform were on the average released 2 months later than those
who did not remember the uniform. This opens up the possibility that De
Rijke started wearing some sort of uniform after a certain date, which was
indeed reported by a few witnesses. A minimum of conflicting reports is
obtained when this date is located at the end of April 1943. Those who
were released before this date should then be scored correct when they reported not having seen him in uniform. Those who were released afterwards should be scored correct when they remembered seeing a uniform.
But even this lenient scoring yields 14 incorrect reports out of 48.

Eleven witnesses declared that De Rijke flogged prisoners with a
whip. Eleven others declared explicitly that he did not use any instruments like a whip.

Recall of Other Facts

Between 1984 and 1988 a total of 30 witnesses were asked to remember
their camp registration number; 16 produced the correct answer. This detail is again suitable for the testing of age effects. The median age of those
who remembered their registration number was 22 years, of those who did
not, 27 years. The difference was significant (Median test, $\chi^2 = 7.07$, d.f. =
1, $p < .01$). The Jewish prisoners were housed in tents, whereas others
lived in barracks. Recollection of this detail is presented in Table 31-6. It
appeared that this detail was reported accurately more often when sponta-

TABLE 31-6

Remembering the housing of Jewish prisoners

	Tents	Barracks
Spontaneous recall	12	1
Prompted by questions	14	11

neously remembered, than when prompted by a direct question (Fisher exact probability test, $p < .02$), even though the question did not contain any suggestion with respect to tents or barracks. This observation confirms similar findings, discussed by Loftus (1979, Chapter 5).

Some incidental but highly relevant evidence is obtained from a comparison between statements by the 15 witnesses who were heard between 1943–1948, and again between 1984–1988. The names of these witnesses are abbreviated, as is customary in The Netherlands.

Witness P.C. reported how a man died in his crib. The next day De Rijke and Boxmeer came in to drag the body away in a most repulsive manner. In 1984 C. had forgotten the incident, and De Rijke as well.

Witness J. van D. was maltreated by Daalhuizen to such an extent that he was unable to do any work for a full year. In 1984 he had forgotten the name of Daalhuizen.

Witness G.H.V. saw how a fellow-prisoner was maltreated by De Rijke and Boxmeer, till the man died. In 1984 he had forgotten both names. In 1943 he reported how another prisoner De V. was violently assaulted by Boxmeer. In 1984 he reported that De V. was the perpetrator instead of the victim.

Witness L. van der M. was beaten up by De Rijke, and was unable to walk for days. In 1984 he remembered only receiving an occasional kick. He also witnessed the murdering of a Jewish fellow-prisoner, but had forgotten all about it in 1984.

Witness G.S. reported that the guards Diepgrond and Boxmeer had drowned a prisoner in a water trough. He did not remember this in 1984, and even denied having said it.

Finally witness J. van de W. was maltreated by De Rijke, but in 1984 he systematically called him De Bruin. He did not recall his own maltreatment. Neither did he remember having seen how some Jews died after they were flogged by the guards.

In all cases these witnesses were confronted with their previous testimonies. All but one declared that they remembered the events after hearing the statements.

DISCUSSION

There is no doubt that almost all witnesses remember Camp Erika in great detail, even after 40 years. The accounts of the conditions in the camp, the horrible treatment, the daily routine, the forced labor, the housing, the food, the main characters of the guards, are remarkably consistent. Also the recall of smaller details was remarkably accurate in many instances. Seventeen out of 30 witnesses remembered their date of arrival in the camp; 16 out of 30 witnesses remembered their full registration number. But a minority of witnesses were occasionally mistaken. Three witnesses were six months off when they reported the day of entry. Three witnesses could not reproduce De Rijke's name, although they reported having been maltreated by him. The majority of names of other Kapos and guards reported between 1932 and 1948 were forgotten after 40 years. Names of fellow-prisoners were also poorly recalled. Recognition of De Rijke's picture is somewhat inflated by the prior presentation of the same picture on television, but of those who did not see this program only 58 per cent recognized De Rijke. Six witnesses who were maltreated by De Rijke failed to recognize his picture. Witnesses were sometimes mistaken about the color of his hair, about his uniform, and his whip.

...

If these findings are a sign of forgetting, what does this imply for the theory of human memory? In his discussion of the errors in John Dean's memory [Selection 25], Neisser (1981) argued that recall of real-life events is repisodic rather than episodic. What he meant is that those aspects of episodes that are repeated several times tend to be reported accurately, whereas unique features, if remembered at all, can easily become associated with the wrong episode. Examples in our study are the attribution of crimes to the wrong guard, and the confusions among uniforms and weapons. Neisser stated that the use of repisodic memory ensures that the general flavor, the atmosphere of the events, would be remembered correctly. Within this framework the smaller details can be arranged on the basis of logical reconstruction, or, as in the case of John Dean, in a manner that serves one's own objectives. Our results do partially confirm this theory, in as far as the memories to the general condition in Camp Erika were quite accurate. Memory appears primarily reliable and dependable; if the listing of errors in the results section suggests otherwise, this suggestion would be wrong. But errors do occur, and in the present case they seem to be worse than what might be expected on the basis of the operation of repisodic memory. The forgotten elements are not only the unique details of events, but also some aspects to which the witnesses were exposed repeatedly. Good examples are the names of guards and fellow-prisoners, and the housing of

Jewish prisoners. In exceptional cases forgetting was even more extreme; some of the forgotten material relates intimately to the essence of the life in concentration camps. Good illustrations are the incidental phenomena reported for the witnesses who were interviewed twice, with an interval of 40 years. They forgot the treatment they suffered themselves, and the tortures and murders they had witnessed and reported before.

···

These findings have numerous forensic implications. The intensity of the emotion at the encoding of information is no guarantee for accurate eyewitness testimony after a long retention period. It is not only true that people can, as in the case of John Dean's memory, make reconstructions in which the details are arranged to create a false impression. It is also possible that people completely lose access to such details. The judicial interest is usually in the minute details of eyewitness testimony. The courts want to know about faces, names, clothing, voices, accents, about what was said, how many people, weapons, cars, licence plates, which day, which time. Such details are not always available, and if they are available, they are not always correct. The extreme situation of being victimized in a Nazi concentration camp does not create an exception to this rule. Does this mean that eyewitness testimony must be discounted in cases of Nazi crimes? The answer is no; there is no reason to distrust such testimony more than in other violent crimes. The degree of conflict between the testimonies in the De Rijke case is probably quite normal. But the extreme horrors of concentration camp experiences do not dismiss the courts of their task to question the evidence critically.

REFERENCES

Clifford, B. R., & Scott, J. (1978). Individual and situational findings in eyewitness testimony. *Journal of Applied Psychology, 63*, 352–359.

Johnson, C., & Scott, B. (1976). Eyewitness testimony and suspect identification as a function of arousal, sex of witness, and scheduling of interrogation. Paper presented at the meeting of the American Psychological Association, Washington, DC.

Neisser, U. (1981). John Dean's memory: A case study. *Cognition, 9*, 1–22.

Shapiro, P. N., & Penrod, S. (1986). Meta-analysis of facial identification studies. *Psychological Bulletin, 100*, 139–156.

Sussman, E. D., & Sugarmann, R. C. (1972). The effect of certain distractions on identification by witnesses. In A. Zavala, J. J. Paley, & R. R. J. Gallati (Eds.), *Personal appearance identification*. Springfield, IL: Charles C. Thomas.

Wagenaar, W. A. (1986). My memory: A study of autobiographical memory over six years. *Cognitive Psychology, 18*, 225–252.

32 | Handcuffed in History to Tony C.

Dave Anderson

Tony Conigliaro—"Tony C" to Red Sox fans—was never the same after Jack Hamilton's fastball hit him in the side of the head in 1967. He resumed play only briefly, lost his health, and died young. But in a psychological sense, the event was also traumatic for Hamilton: He, too, was never the same again. It's not the sort of thing a person can forget . . . or is it?

In baseball, history handcuffs certain batters and pitchers. One is seldom mentioned without the other. Often they are linked in identifying a memorable home run: Bobby Thomson's pennant-winning homer off Ralph Branca, Henry Aaron's 715th homer off Al Downing, Roger Maris's 61st homer off Tracy Stallard. From those moments on, the batter celebrates while the pitcher suffers.

Occasionally the coupling involves a batter hit by a pitch. Ray Chapman died in 1920 after being struck in the head by Carl Mays's underhand fastball. Joe Medwick was never the same slugger after Bob Bowman beaned him. Don Zimmer's scarred skull is a reminder of a minor league pitcher, Jim Kirk. But after those incidents both the batter and the pitcher suffer.

Such is the connection between Tony Conigliaro and Jack Hamilton, as it has been ever since Aug. 18, 1967 in Fenway Park.

"I wish it never happened," Jack Hamilton was saying now. "But I know in my heart I wasn't trying to hit him."

Tony C.'s funeral will be held today in Revere, Mass. He died over the weekend of kidney failure at the age of 45 after having around-the-clock nursing care since a heart attack in 1982.

※ From Dave Anderson's column: Sports of the Times: Handcuffed in history to Tony C. *The New York Times*, February 27, 1990. p. 89.

At 20 he had led the American League with 32 homers. At 22, he was the youngest slugger to accumulate 100 homers. But his life was never the same after Hamilton, then a right-hander with the California Angels, fired a first-pitch fastball that crushed the left side of the 23-year-old Red Sox outfielder's face.

"I never hit a guy that hard in my life," Hamilton recalled. "He went right down. He just collapsed."

Tony C.'s cheekbone was fractured, his jaw dislocated, his vision blurred. After sitting out the 1968 season, he hit 20 homers for the Red Sox in 1969, then he had 36 homers in 1970 while driving in 116 runs. But his vision blurred again. Traded, ironically, to the Angels, he retired halfway through the 1971 season. In 1975 he made a brief but unsuccessful comeback with the Red Sox. Turning to broadcasting, he had auditioned for a Red Sox job when he was struck by the heart attack.

Tony C. was never the same after his beaning, but Jack Hamilton has never been quite the same either.

"I've had to live with it; I think about it a lot," he said from Hollister, Mo., the Ozarks town where he lives with his wife, Jan. "Watching baseball on TV, anytime a guy gets hit, I think about it. I was just a common pitcher but people remember me for what happened to Tony. I was watching TV on Saturday night when I heard about his death. The next morning, about 10 different guys mentioned it to me."

He's 51 years old now, the owner of seven restaurants in Missouri, Iowa and Illinois. That Friday night in 1967 he was 28, a 6-foot, 200-pound starter having his best season. He would have a 9-6 record with the Angels after having been 2-0 with the Mets before a June trade. The next year he was 3-1, but 1969, an 0-5 season split between the Cleveland Indians and the Chicago White Sox, was his last.

In the Mets' bullpen, he had a reputation as a jovial guy who confided that he threw an occasional spitball.

"But the pitch that hit Tony was a fastball, believe me," he said. "It was like the sixth inning when it happened. I think the score was 2-1, and he was the eighth hitter in their batting order. With the pitcher up next, I had no reason to throw at him."

...

Just as Tony C.'s vision was blurred, Jack Hamilton's memory is blurred. It was the fourth inning, no score, two out, nobody on. Tony C., who had 20 homers with 67 runs batted in that season, was batting sixth, behind Reggie Smith and ahead of Rico Petrocelli.

"He'd been hit a lot of times," Hamilton said. "He crowded the plate like Richie Ashburn did."

Hamilton remembered it as a day game because "I tried to go see him in the hospital late that afternoon or early that evening but they were just letting his family in." Maybe he was thinking of going to the hospital after Saturday's afternoon game.

"Our next trip into Boston that year," he said, "our manager, Bill Rigney, didn't know if I should go. Some people had called the Angels office and warned that I shouldn't go back to Fenway Park, so Rigney called me and left it up to me. I went."

The Angels didn't return to Boston until early in the 1968 season. Maybe he was thinking of the Saturday afternoon game and the Sunday double-header that followed the Friday night game.

"Whenever it was," Hamilton said, "I remember getting a few boos and seeing people waving their handkerchiefs at me. When Tony came back in 1969 I really didn't try to talk to him about it. I'm just sorry it ever happened. I've had to live with it."

33 | A Genuine Recovered Memory

Jonathan W. Schooler, Miriam Bendiksen, and Zara Ambadar

We have seen that even very traumatic events can be misremembered or forgotten. In this selection we will see the opposite: traumatic events that have apparently been forgotten can sometimes come to mind again, suddenly and surprisingly. Individuals who have such an experience may be doubly amazed: "That happened to me? And I forgot it?" In their original paper, Schooler and his collaborators describe four such cases, each with at least some corroborating evidence that (a) the recalled event really occurred, and (b) the individual really did forget it for a substantial period of time. One of those cases is presented here.

CASE 4

Subject

Case 4 involves a 41-year-old female (hereafter called DN) who brought her case to the attention of the first author following a colloquium presentation that he gave on this topic. She was interviewed approximately six years after her recovery experience.

Recovery Experience

DN had been in group therapy for victims of child abuse (a memory that she had kept intact all of her life). At one of the therapy sessions, the therapist

※ From J. W. Schooler, M. Bendiksen, & Z. Ambadar (1997). Taking the middle line: Can we accommodate both fabricated and recovered memories of sexual abuse? In M. A. Conway (Ed.), *Recovered memories and false memories: Debates in psychology.* Oxford, UK: Oxford University Press, 251–292.

mentioned that victims of child abuse often continue to be victimized as adults. On her drive home after the session, she thought about the therapist's remark and then all at once she remembered being raped by a stranger at age 22 (13 years previously). DN recounted her recovery experience as follows:

> *What she [her therapist] had said popped into my mind, and then all at once I remembered being a victim when I was like in my early twenties, when I was a nurse at a hospital. And it really kind of freaked me out because I remembered that not only had I been a victim but I had to go to court and prosecute the person who had attacked me. And he had been found guilty. And yet I had forgotten all of that.*

The sudden memory of the incident elicited a very intense emotional state that required her to pull off the road. As DN put it:

> *I had to just sit there for a while because it was just this extreme emotion of fear and total disbelief. Disbelief that it happened, disbelief that I could have forgotten something that traumatic.*

Characterization of the Forgetting

DN was positive that she remembered the attack for the approximately two years after the rape that she continued working at the same hospital. She then moved to a different state and worked at a different hospital. At some point following her move, she believed that she completely forgot the whole incident including the trial. Indeed, it was her amazement at having forgotten the rape and the ensuing trial that contributed to the remarkable quality of her recovery experience. As DN put it: "It's like how could I forget this. As horrible as it was having to go to court . . . and having to tell what happened and everything, how could I forget that? I had no idea when I did forget it but I really feel that it had been totally forgotten until that night."

Corroboration of the Event

Because DN's case was actually taken to trial, corroboration was relatively straightforward. In a telephone interview, her lawyer at the time (who is now a judge) verified that the case did in fact go to court, and that the accused was found guilty of rape. Thus we have incontrovertible evidence for one component of this traumatic experience (taking the rape case to court) and extremely compelling evidence for the other component of this trauma (the rape itself) as the individual was found guilty.

Corroboration of the Forgetting

In this case we have what is perhaps the strongest evidence from any of the cases described here that true forgetting had occurred prior to the recovery. When DN entered therapy for victims of sexual abuse, she was given an initial interview to assess her history of abuse. During this interview (as revealed in hospital records made available to the first author), DN described in detail her abuse as a child, but did not mention her rape experience. While it is possible that she simply failed to disclose the rape at this time this seems relatively unlikely for the following reasons: the fact that she previously took the case to trial clearly establishes her history of a willingness to talk about the rape; the incidents that she did disclose were comparably embarrassing; and as soon as she had the memory recovery experience she mentioned the rape at therapy. Of course, it is possible that she may not have thought about the rape in the same way that she thought about her early childhood abuse and so she may have failed to mention it at that time. However, together with her self-report of her shock at the recovery experience, her failure to mention her rape in the initial assessment interview is at least strongly suggestive that actual forgetting did in fact take place.

Corroboration of the Recovery Experience

As in the other cases, there is no reason that we are aware of to believe that DN intentionally fabricated her memory recovery experience. DN sought legal recourse prior to the memory recovery experience and there is no legal benefit that she would have gotten from construing her memory as a recovery. It is also of interest that the recovery experience is mentioned in her therapy records, further substantiating the validity of her report.

Discussion of Case 4

Case 4 has many of the characteristics that we found in the earlier cases. As in the prior cases, the memory was prompted by a cue corresponding to the original incident (in this case learning that childhood victims of sexual abuse are often abused as adults). The nature of the recovery experience was also quite similar, with a sudden emotional onrush in which the entire experience seemed to unfold all at once. In addition to these similarities, there were also some differences. Unlike several of the prior cases in which it is clear that memory was possessed at a time when it was believed to be forgotten, in this case there is at least suggestive evidence that DN may have had complete forgetting of the experience. DN's case is also particularly notable because it entailed forgetting of both the rape and of the subsequent trial, both of which were corroborated. It is sometimes suggested that while forgetting of a single incident is possible, forgetting of an entire period of abuse is not possible. . . . Arguably, being raped and then having to testify about it in court constitutes an extended period of abuse, consequently the fact that both elements of this recovered memory were corroborated suggests that recovered memories of extended incidents of abuse can be veridical.

34 | A Retractor's Story

Mark Pendergrast

Some recovered memories of sexual abuse may be gen-
uine, but others—equally vivid and compelling—are
not. Often, such "false memories" result from sugges-
tions given in the course of psychotherapy. Patients who
come to believe that the "remembered" sexual abuse
really happened may be led to make unjustified accusa-
tions against innocent persons, often members of their
families. Later they may come to realize that they were
mistaken, and that no such events took place. Here is
one such case.

SHAUNA FLETCHER, RETRACTOR

Shauna Fletcher, 39, is one of the first retractors to sue her former therapist
successfully, though he settled out of court, so no precedent was set. A some-
what overweight, no-nonsense Southerner, Shauna dropped out of college to
work in a police station, where she has made a career.

I really was a sad kid, you know, with a real distorted view of myself. I
felt invisible growing up. When I told my mother this, she said, "No, you
didn't." [*laughs*] My counselor, Steve, was the first person who really
heard me, my anger and need for acceptance. He would sit and listen no
matter what, without boundaries, whether it was 3 A.M. or whatever. I
could call him any time.

I went into counseling because I had an eating disorder. I'd been bulimic since I was ten, so I'd been throwing up for 22 years. I was desperate, and I'd read about Steve in a book, how this girl supposedly got
healed by him in a four-month period. I went to my pastor, who was like
my best friend, and he said, "Well, this man is a Christian counselor, so he

From M. Pendergrast (1996). *Victims of memory: Sex abuse accusations and shat-*
tered lives. Hinesburg, VT: Upper Access Books.

must be all right." Steve had a masters of divinity. He was overweight and balding, like the perpetual nerd, someone you'd avoid in high school. My Dad tells me he can't believe all these women fell for this short, fat, balding, wimpy-looking guy. But he became my whole life.

At my first counseling session, in 1985, Steve asked if I'd ever been sexually abused. I told him I had. When I was nine, a boy, a stranger, inserted his finger in my vagina through my swimming suit under the water. The biggest trauma was that I couldn't tell anybody. I didn't feel comfortable. I was ashamed. So I told that to Steve, right up front, but it didn't matter to him, because I always remembered it. He told me I needed to find buried stuff with deeper roots. He told me that since I had an eating disorder, it automatically meant I was seriously abused. So we went to work trying to find buried memories.

From the second visit on, I closed my eyes every time. He'd say weird stuff which I couldn't understand. I would tell him I didn't understand him, and he'd say that was okay, that my subconscious caught it. He used big words like counter-super-autonomous. I tell you, he could use some big words!

You have to understand my mind state. I was desperate. It was like I was drowning and this person reached out a hand to me, and he was my only hope. It's like I sold my soul to this man. I became incredibly dependent on him, wouldn't make a move without him. I went to therapy constantly. It ruled my life. I had just bought a house when I met him. My insurance wouldn't cover him, so every penny I got my hands on went to him. I got into incredible debt, went a year and a half without a car.

I'm convinced that Steve didn't do it for the money. At the time, he really felt that he was anointed by God, he had a mission in life. He said it was his calling. It was a combination of ego and a personal mission to save the world.

He had me get a picture of myself as a little girl, and to imagine her as my inner child. I could close my eyes and just see her sitting on the floor, surrounded by toys, playing. She was a tiny little thing with big, sad eyes. Then, one day when I was vacuuming, I had a visualization of a three-year-old boy trying to smother an infant. I couldn't breathe, broke out into a terrible sweat. Steve kept badgering me the whole hour of our next session to get me to accept that my brother had tried to kill me. After that, I would usually have flashbacks either when I was hypnotized or right after the sessions.

At first, he had me relax while he counted backward to hypnotize me. But it got to a point where I could just go into an immediate trance by closing my eyes, and I was his. He had a very hypnotic voice.

Next I started having flashbacks of being in a bathtub, being abused by either my Mom or my brother. I kept having fingernails molest me, hurting my vagina. I couldn't put a face on it, but Steve said it had to be my mother. And it really did physically hurt, like it was happening right then. The focus came to be on my mother. Steve really hated her; I think he had a thing against mothers.

I never totally cut off from my parents. I'm a single mother, and they helped me with my daughter June. Steve tried to convince me that my parents were sexually abusing her, but I never bought it. My daughter was different from me, so bubbly and self-assured. And they seemed to be so good with her. Steve called a social worker once to evaluate the situation, and I was so scared I would lose my child. I had to take her to counseling, and the lady said, "I see no indication of sexual trauma, but just to be certain, she should have a gynecological exam." No way, I wouldn't do it, I thought it would be too traumatic for her. It's a good thing I didn't, or I might have lost her.

What I was going through was terrible for June. She loved my parents, and she loved me. And I just hated my mother through this whole thing—it confused June and tore her up. June was basically the mother in the family for a while. I would be in my room chain-smoking for days at a time, and she was pretty much left on her own. Also, when I would be having a flashback and would call Steve, he told me it was healthy to beat on the bed in front of her. He said it was a healthy way to exhibit rage.

Long about April 1986, I started having flashbacks of Mom sexually abusing me with a coat hanger. That went on for quite a few months. I would be like a little child, curled up in a ball screaming. It was still going on when we started the group. There were about ten of us. Steve brought in a co-leader, Dave, who had a Ph.D., but it was really Steve who was the leader. They were like Frick and Frack, Tweedledee and Tweedledum. Dave wore this very obvious, gross toupee, and he had on real tight pants. He'd sit with his legs spread apart. Mostly, he was just a puppet for Steve.

At first, we just interchanged ideas and talked in the group, and it was kind of neat. I felt a camaraderie with these women. But it kept escalating. Late in 1987, I was really bad off, and I'd accidentally overdosed on Xanax and had nothing in my stomach. I went into the hospital on a Friday night for the first of two stays. They were both 30 days long. Oh, yeah, I was only sick for as long as my insurance lasted, 30 days per calendar year. [laughs] It turns out that Steve was the therapist for the psych ward at the hospital, so I saw him three days a week individually, every day in group, and on Monday nights. Plus, on Sundays he'd lead what he called a "spiritual rap session," and he'd wear this ridiculous motorcycle jacket for that.

Anyway, the following Monday night we had the group. Someone said, "You look tired; are you okay?" I lied and said, "Yeah," and Steve lit into me. For two hours, he screamed. He made me talk about my mother, have more flashbacks. It was a very loud, traumatic few hours. They put a coat hanger up on the clay wall for me to throw clods at. Did you see that TV show where those MPD women were doing that? They couldn't hold a candle to me. I had clay on my eyelashes. I was awful. I tell you, I could throw some clay! There's no doubt that I was angry, all right, but it wasn't "getting out" my anger. It was creating it. It just makes you madder. I was so mad by the time I left that group. I was in a rage for four consecutive years.

After that, the group got more like that all the time. The next week, some other girl would scream and carry on. It was like they all wanted to get into that, getting more loud and hysterical. We'd be sitting there tearing up phone books, beating on chairs with bataaka bats, and Steve or Dave would be screaming in our ears, reading aloud from the terrible things we had written about what we had "remembered."

Then the blood drinking and satanic stuff started. First one girl had an alter, then she started cutting herself. That really got Steve's attention. Then it started with more horrific rapes, the whole nine yards. I had these horrible flashbacks of being given cold enemas and various objects inserted into my vagina. Another time, I remembered my brother and his friends hung me by my feet. It was only recently that I realized where those particular images came from. The enemas and insertion came from the book *Sybil*, and the upside down hanging came from a movie called *Deranged*, which I saw when I was 17. And I had incorporated some of a story I once wrote about identifying a prostitute's body in the morgue. So different pieces of my life that had nothing to do with me being abused became part of the flashbacks. It's amazing to me that my subconscious mind had served them up without my knowing where they came from.

I eventually came up with scenes of group sexual abuse and being raped by animals. After I had a vision of a dead man hanging from a rope, my grandfather, the murderer, got added to the abuser list. But it was mainly my mother who was the target of my anger. Steve convinced me that she had been trying to kill me for years. I interpreted everything she did that way, so when she bought cookies, it was to encourage my binges. Everybody in the group was encouraged to divorce their families and make the group their new family. If anybody expressed any doubts, Steve and Dave would goad them. "You're in denial." The rest of us would join in. "You want to stay sick for your family. You don't want to get well."

I got worse. I vomited more and more, and my life seemed out of control. Even though I landed twice in the hospital with overdoses, my doctor kept prescribing Xanax for me and pills for every other ailment—to sleep, to stop depression, to mellow out. Some of my friends at the police station where I worked saw me going through this. One officer told me, "This guy is a quack. You're turning into a pillhead." I pulled the phone out of the wall and threw it at him. I said, "You don't understand, I've got to get worse before I get better, and this man is going to save my life."

By 1989, my mind was so cluttered with cults and Satanism, I didn't know where I was half the time. In one of my last sessions, I actually started to talk about some of my real-life problems—money, my daughter, my job—and Steve just sat there with this big smirk on his face. I stopped and said, "What the fuck is your problem?" He said, "You're avoiding your real issues; you're not working." If you weren't screaming or having flashbacks, you weren't working. I just lost it. "Let me tell you something, asshole. Every single day of my life is work, just to stay alive." At that point, I would just sit in my room smoking and thinking of ways to kill my Mom.

All this time, Steve kept telling me I had to get worse before I got better. I was sick of hearing how you have to get worse. I was about as worse as you could get. By that time, I was about to lose my house. I had given every penny, every ounce of energy, to this therapy. I had used up all my sick time and vacation time. I was still horribly bulimic, but I had gained a hundred pounds during the four years of therapy. One day late in 1989, I called him, all excited about writing a book about my experiences at the police station. And you know what he said to me when I called? "You're not finished with the flashbacks." And something snapped. I thought, "Oh, yeah, asshole, I am. Four years of getting worse is enough."

So I quit and went to Linda, a woman therapist. She believed I had been an incest victim, all right, but she didn't egg it on. I couldn't deal with anything except grieving over the loss of Steve for a long time. I was so depressed, I didn't really accomplish anything. Then one day in 1991, I read an article in a local magazine about false memory syndrome, with an interview with parents who had lost their daughter. They sounded like nice people. I had been in the group with their daughter, and I'd heard all these horrible stories about them. So I sought them out and met them. They're no more Satanists than I am. One night Steve told us he had to call the police on them, that they had come to their daughter's house threatening her. It turns out they were bringing her Christmas presents.

It was like a light came on in my head. When I realized what had been done to me, I called a good psychologist. I told him, "These flashbacks seemed so real, I mean they were *really* real." He said, "They were real, honey, but not reality." I'll never forget those words. I like to fell off this bed, because I had put my life into a fantasy. After I realized that none of these flashbacks were true, I filed my lawsuit. I also went back to Linda, my good counselor. She accepted that I had made up all the abuse. Now, all of us from the group have called it quits except one girl, who is a tragic case. She accused her mother of satanic ritual abuse, of murdering her twin at birth. It didn't matter that there was a single child registered on the birth certificate. The coven had taken care of that.

I strongly recommend getting a good counselor to people coming out of this mess. They need to set boundaries and appropriate limits, to find a way to feel good about themselves—all the stuff these trauma counselors talk about but don't really do. My Mom and I really do have some problems to work out, but nothing about sexual abuse. It's getting better, not so bad. My bulimia is completely gone now. I don't really know why. In these last few months, I've really taken responsibility for my own life. No more playing the blame game. I realized that if anything was going to change in my life, I'd have to do the changing. I'm more assertive now, don't hold things in as much.

35 | The Memory Wars

Ira E. Hyman, Jr.

T he memory wars have focused on one primary question: How should we interpret what seems to be the recovered memory of a childhood trauma? Is it an accurate repressed memory that has somehow been unavailable to consciousness for the intervening time, or a false memory created in response to social demands and therapeutic suggestions? If the memory is true, there may be severe consequences: a breach in family relations, concern for any children who are still in contact with the perpetrator, possible legal action. If the memory is false then someone has been unjustly accused and the accuser's apparently new sense of self is actually rooted in misunderstanding; there may even be legal liability if the therapist has engaged in practices that produce false memories. In recent years, the controversy has spilled from private life and the therapist's office to the courtroom, the TV screen, the Internet, and scientific journals.

The tone of the recovered memory vs. false memory debate has often been aggressive and confrontational. One reason for the angry tone is that lives may hang in the balance. For any given individual, interpreting a recovered memory is always an either-or question: the memory is either false or true. Another reason for the angry tone is that most of the leading advocates in the recovered memory/false memory debate have been chiefly associated with one side or the other. Some of them work primarily with victims, and have emphasized the importance of listening to and believing those victims. They are concerned that the false memory debate will lead people to discount reports of abuse or even fail to report it, and will result in perpetrators going free. Others, who work with the falsely accused, have focused on the conditions that lead to memory errors. They worry about the destruction of innocent lives.

In contrast, the scientific aspect of the recovered memory question need not be posed as an either-or question. Instead, one can investigate each issue separately. Is it possible for someone to forget and later recall

※ This chapter was written specifically for this edition of *Memory Observed*.

memories of childhood trauma? Is it possible for individuals to create false memories of childhood events? It turns out that the answer to both questions is *yes*. Yes, it is possible to forget and later recover the memory of a childhood trauma *[for an example, see Selection 33]* and yes, it is possible to create false childhood memories *[for examples, see Selections 30 and 34]*. Naturalistic memory research has led to the creation of a reasonable middle ground that acknowledges both recovered and false memories. In both cases, the explanations are still being debated. Do people forget memories of abuse (that they will later recover) because the experience is repressed, or because of a lack of retrieval cues that might bring it to mind? What factors contribute to the creation of false memories? Is there a limit to the types of memories that people will create? In the process of investigating such questions, researchers have turned their attention to a number of issues that were previously uninvestigated. The remainder of this selection describes some of these findings.

Some researchers have been investigating the scope of memory recovery. If recovered memories are caused by the repression of the original experience, then recovery should be limited to certain types of events: those that are ego-threatening or traumatic or even repeatedly traumatic. In contrast, if the forgetting and recovery of memories is a reflection of basic memory processes, then recovered memories should be somewhat more common and should occur for a variety of events. Elliott (1997), who examined recollections of several types of emotional and traumatic experiences, asked people a basic question that has generally only been asked with respect to memories of child abuse: was there ever a time when you did not remember this event? Her participants reported experiencing memory recovery for many different types of events including observed murder as well as combat, accidents, and abuse.

Read (1997) approached the same issue from a different direction. Having described what it is like to recover a memory, he then asked participants if they had ever had such an experience themselves, i.e., found themselves remembering something that had been previously forgotten. Like Elliott, Read found numerous reports of memory recovery. People discussed recovering memories of many events, including piano lessons, trips, important personal experiences, and incidents of child abuse. Thus the recovery of long-forgotten memories can occur for a wide variety of events. This suggests that the phenomenon may not be caused by memory repression; instead it may reflect the availability (or unavailability) of retrieval cues that might bring a given event to mind.

While investigating recovered memories of abuse, Schooler and his colleagues (1997) found that although many people did recover accurate memories, some of them were mistaken about having forgotten the events for a long time. In their documentation of recovered memories, Schooler et al. tried to verify not only the original abuse and the recovery experience but also whether there had really been an intervening period of forgetting. With this in mind they interviewed individuals who had been acquainted with the victims during the period of alleged forgetting, to see if those individuals also knew about the event. In two such cases the acquaintances had indeed heard about the abuse: compelling evidence that the victims had not entirely forgotten it during that period. In one of these cases the victim expressed considerable surprise when told that the acquaintance knew about the event in question. Schooler et al. refer to this as the "forgot-it-all-along effect": people remember an event accurately but are mistaken about having forgotten it during an intervening period.

How can people be mistaken about having forgotten something? Part of the answer is that telling someone about an event may not be as memorable as the event itself. If something important or amusing happens to us, we often tell many people about it. Sometimes we may fail to remember that we have already told a particular friend about it, and repeat the story to that friend a second time. Schooler et al. argued that very emotional memories may be especially ripe for such confusion. The very experience of recovering an emotional memory may make it seem new—it may feel different or important because of a new interpretation or a new emotional context. The individual may then wonder why the memory feels so different on this occasion, and reasonably conclude that it was previously forgotten. Often this will be a reasonable assumption; sometimes it will lead to false claims of forgetting. At this point we have little understanding of how people judge whether and when they have previously remembered something.

Belli, Winkleman, Read, Schwartz, and Lynn (1998) have been concerned with another judgment people make about their memories—whether or not they are able to remember most of their childhoods. Belli et al. became interested in this topic because claims of extensive amnesia for childhood experiences are sometimes regarded as indicators of dissociative identity disorder and repression. They were concerned because it has been shown that many kinds of self-judgments depend less on the facts of the matter than on the accessibility of particular knowledge. When recollections come easily, people have more confidence in them than in other recollections that were more difficult to retrieve. Belli et al. studied how the perceived accessibility of a few childhood memories influences people's judgments of their ability to recall their childhood as a whole. To do this, they asked college students to recall 4, 8, or 12 childhood events. Not surprisingly, those asked to recall 4 memories rated the task as easier than those asked to recall 12 memories. All the participants were then asked if there were "large parts of your childhood after age 5 which you can't remember?" Those who had been asked to remember 12 events were more likely to answer this question positively. This finding seems somewhat counter-intuitive: remembering more events successfully leads people to believe that they have larger memory gaps. In explanation, Belli et al. note that remembering 12 events is simply more difficult than remembering 4 events. It is this difficulty which influences the judgments of the 12-memory group.

In addition to stimulating research on how people recover memories and make judgments about them, the memory wars have also spurred new studies of memory for trauma. This area of concern depends on naturalistic methods of research. Because ethical memory researchers cannot provide participants with experimental traumatic events, trauma research relies on real-world experiences. For example, Williams (1994) asked women about incidents of childhood sexual abuse for which hospital records existed, so that their accuracy could be checked. She found some evidence of forgetting and much evidence for accurate recollection. Tromp, Koss, Figueredo, and Tharan (1995) compared women's memory for rape with their recollections of other negative and positive experiences. The women reported that their rape memories were less clear and vivid than their other memories.

Other researchers have investigated how individuals who have experienced trauma differ from individuals who have not on a variety of cognitive tasks (McNally, 1998). Although the effects of trauma on memory are not completely clear, a few conclusions seem warranted. Such events are not automatically repressed, although some individuals may forget them. On the other hand, they do not automatically result in long-lasting, detailed, and accurate "flashbulb" memories, although many people recall them accurately. Trauma may result in relatively less detailed memories, and may have long-term consequences for several aspects of cognitive functioning.

Since both recovered memories and false memories exist, some way to distinguish between them would be useful. Pezdek, Finger, and Hodge (1997) reported that false memories were rated as less clear than true ones. They did not, however, compare false memories with *recovered* memories, which is the comparison of applied interest. My collaborators and I (Hyman & Pentland, 1996) compared the ratings given to true childhood memories that had been recovered over the course of several interviews with those given to false memories that had been created during the same period. Both the recovered and the false memories were less confident, less clear, and less emotional than the true memories that the participants had recalled from the beginning (i.e., in the first and all subsequent interviews). We could not, however, distinguish the recovered true memories from the false ones on the basis of these ratings.

Recent brain scan research has produced ambiguous results. In some contexts, true memories for the words in a list activated different areas of the brain than errors did; in other contexts, no difference between true and false word memory was found (Johnson et al., 1997). I myself suspect that no criterion will ever be found to distinguish true recovered memories from false ones; all autobiographical memories are constructions based partly on real knowledge and partly on current context. To be sure, both recovered and false recollections do differ from memories that have always been accessible. Even this difference may disappear over time, however, as the recovered or false recollections enjoy the benefits of rehearsal and elaboration while the originally vivid memories fade with time.

Thus the results of the memory wars continue to reverberate in memory research. A consensus has developed around the basic findings. It is clear that people can forget and then recover memories of many types of experiences, including trauma. The explanation of those recoveries may have little to do with mechanisms of repression or dissociation, and many researchers are now trying to understand the processes involved. It is also clear that people can and do create false memories of childhood experiences. Several factors seem to influence the creation of such memories, including certain individual differences variables (e.g., Hyman & Billings, 1998).

The memory wars have also resulted in many serendipitous findings: the forgot-it-all-along effect, the fact that people recover memories of many types of experiences, the curious observation that getting people to remember more childhood experiences can lead them to believe that they have more childhood memory gaps, and the difficulty in discerning truly recovered memories from false ones. Discoveries of this kind are to be expected when one explores memory in a naturalistic fashion. Neisser (Selection 1) noted that the light really is better under the streetlamp; that is why the drunk looks there for his lost coin instead of in the dark where he dropped it. When you take your flashlight and go searching beyond the limited region of the streetlamp's glow, you may find not only what you were looking for but other interesting things as well.

REFERENCES

Belli, R. F., Winkleman, P., Read, J. D., Schwartz, N., & Lynn, S. J. (1998). Recalling more childhood events leads to judgments of poorer memory: Implications for the recovered/false memory debate. *Psychonomic Bulletin and Review, 5*, 318–323.

Elliott, D. M. (1997). Traumatic events: Prevalence and delayed recall in the general population. *Journal of Consulting and Clinical Psychology, 65*, 811–820.

Hyman, I. E., Jr., & Billings, F. J. (in press). Individual differences and the creation of false childhood memories. *Memory.*

Hyman, I. E., Jr., & Pentland, J. (1996). Guided imagery and the creation of false childhood memories. *Journal of Memory and Language, 35*, 101–117.

Johnson, M. K., Nolde, S. F., Mather, M., Kounis, J., et al. (1997). The similarity of brain activity associated with true and false recognition memory depends on test format. *Psychological Science, 8*, 250–257.

McNally, R. J. (1998). Experimental approaches to cognitive abnormality in post-traumatic stress disorder. *Clinical Psychology Review, 18,* 971–982.

Pezdek, K., Finger, K., & Hodge, D. (1997). Planting false childhood memories: The role of event plausibility. *Psychological Science, 8,* 437–441.

Read, J. D. (1997). Memory issues in the diagnosis of unreported trauma. In J. D. Read & D. S. Lindsay (Eds.), *Recollections of trauma: Scientific evidence and clinical practice.* NY: Plenum, 79–108.

Schooler, J. W., Bendiksen, M., & Ambadar, Z. (1997). Taking the middle line: Can we accommodate both fabricated and recovered memories of sexual abuse? In M. A. Conway (Ed.), *Recovered memories and false memories: Debates in psychology.* Oxford, UK: Oxford University Press, 251–292.

Tromp, S., Koss, M. P., Figueredo, A. J., & Tharan, M. (1995). Are rape memories different? A comparison of rape, other unpleasant, and pleasant memories among employed women. *Journal of Traumatic Stress, 8,* 607–627.

Williams, L. M. (1994). Recall of childhood trauma: A prospective study of women's memories of child sexual abuse. *Journal of Consulting and Clinical Psychology, 62,* 1167–1176.

Part VII

PERFORMANCES

Memory-based performances are of many different kinds, some more familiar than others. We begin here with Americans trying to recite the Preamble to the U.S. Constitution and end with experimental subjects trying to recall a story they have just read. In between, you will find more exotic examples: oral poets in the Balkans, tribal historians in Liberia, schooled and unschooled children in Botswana. There are also actors acting: How *do* they manage to remember all those lines?

36 | Very Long-Term Memory for Prose and Verse

David C. Rubin

In most situations, remembering the gist of what we heard or read is all that is necessary. But poems and songs are exceptions to this principle: for example, it won't do to begin "The Star Spangled Banner" with "Tell me, now that it's daybreak, is that flag with the stars on it still visible?" Similarly, you wouldn't be reciting the Preamble to the U.S. Constitution properly if you began with "We the citizens" instead of "We the people"— that's just not how it goes. The fact that such texts must be recited verbatim produces a special set of memory strategies. Recall is usually letter-perfect up to some point (usually a natural breath stop), after which it drops abruptly to zero. In contrast, memory in terms of gist or meaning is never observed.

While memory for discourse has been studied extensively under laboratory conditions, there are few systematic data on retention intervals longer than those convenient for laboratory study (Bahrick, Bahrick & Wittlinger, 1975; Cofer, 1943; Squire, Chace, & Slater, 1975; Titchener, 1923; Warrington & Sanders, 1971). In an attempt to provide such data, very long-term memory was tested for several prose and poetry passages that subjects were likely to learn in the course of growing up in America. Experiment 1 analyzes the free recall data of college students from three such passages. Experiment 2 uses the recalls of fifth and sixth graders who were more recently exposed to the material in order to obtain a shorter retention interval. Experiments 3 and 4 use various prompts to examine

From *Journal of Verbal Learning and Verbal Behavior*, 1977, *16*, 611–621.

coding in more detail and to try to separate failures in retrieval from failures in retention.

EXPERIMENT 1

Method

Subjects. Ninety-two undergraduates volunteered.

Procedure. Covered booklets were used. On the top of each of the first three pages was one of the following titles: "The Preamble to the Constitution," "The 23rd Psalm: A Psalm of David," or "Hamlet's Soliloquy." The order of the titles was random. The last three pages were questionnaires which asked for each passage: "Did you have to memorize it?" "If so, when?" and "What experience have you had with it since?"

The subjects were asked to write down as much of the first titled passage as they could, and then to proceed through the booklet at their own pace.

Results

"The Preamble," "The 23rd Psalm," and "Hamlet's Soliloquy" were reported memorized by 32, 32, and 11 of the 85, 88, and 82 subjects who could answer the appropriate question. The average duration since memorizing the three passages was given by these subjects as 8 (SD = 4.2), 10 (SD = 4.4), and 4 (SD = 1.7) years. Twenty-five, 19, and 18 subjects would report the time of their last experience with the passages. These times averaged 4 (SD = 3.8), 4 (SD = 6.3), and 3 (SD = 1.9) years ago. Thus, from the subjects' reports it appears that the recalls are from very long-term memory, and that less than half of the subjects memorized the passages. Discussions with local educators support these reports.

The recalls, while not complete, were verbatim: With few exceptions, subjects either recalled portions of the passage correctly in their original wording or not at all. While Bartlett's (1932) subjects reconstructed "The War of the Ghosts" after the passage of many years, the subjects of this study did not reconstruct the Constitution, the Bible, or Shakespeare.

In order to quantify this finding, the recalls were scored on a word-by-word basis. Words that appeared more than once (for the most part, function words) had to appear in their proper context. Misspellings were the only change from verbatim recall allowed, and these only if they did not change the number or tense of the word. As many versions of "The 23rd Psalm" exist, the scoring of this passage had to be relaxed: If a word occurred in any of the several versions sampled, it was scored as correct on the King James version.

Of the 92 subjects tested 52, 53, and 60 were able to remember something of "The Preamble," "The 23rd Psalm," and "Hamlet's Soliloquy." These subjects recalled an average of 14 ($SD = 12$), 42 ($SD = 32$), and 17 ($SD = 12$) correct words out of a possible 52, 117, and 277 words. They wrote down an average of 4 ($SD = 6$), 5 ($SD = 7$), and 3 ($SD = 7$) incorrect words. All remaining errors were errors of omission. Even using strict verbatim scoring the number of words in error divided by the total number of words recalled, or the error rate, is only about 15 percent. Thus, the scoring does not force the results, as only 15 percent of the words written do not enter into the analysis as correctly recalled units. To appreciate how different this finding is from laboratory recall of the results, a verbatim scoring of Bartlett's "The War of the Ghosts" story was attempted. For the five initial free recalls for which Bartlett (1932, pp. 66–67) provides data, the average error rate is 69 percent. That is, using the strict verbatim scoring used here, Bartlett's subjects recalled over twice as many incorrect words as correct words, whereas the subjects in the present study recalled less than one-fifth as many incorrect words as correct words.

Besides being accurate, the recalls are regular across subjects. Figures 36-1, 36-2, and 36-3 each display the recall data for 50 individual subjects selected randomly from among those who recalled something from the passage listed. Each of the 50 vertical columns represents one subject: A line indicates that the word was correctly recalled by that subject, and a blank indicates that it was not. Hamlet's rather long soliloquy was stopped where fewer than four of the subjects remembered any of the remaining words. It should be stressed that each of these figures contains data for 50 individual subjects. The only manipulation of the raw scores that has been made is that the subjects are rank ordered by the amount they recalled. The recalls of the subjects who remembered the most are placed farthest to the left.

The data are quite regular. The Guttman Coefficients of Reproducibility for the "The Preamble," "The 23rd Psalm," and "Hamlet's Soliloquy" are .950, .832, and .991. This implies that if the number of words an individual subject remembers is known, exactly what words that subject remembers can, on the average, be predicted with an accuracy of 95, 83, and 99 percent from the number of times each word was remembered by the group as a whole. That is, if a subject recalled 20 words correctly, the prediction that they would be the 20 words most often recalled by the group as a whole would be correct 95, 83, and 99 percent of the time for the three passages. Thus, each individual is representative of the group. While it is apparent from the figures that the data are far from random, an exact statistical by-chance measure is difficult with as many subjects and words as are used here (Kenny & Rubin, 1977). While qualitatively similar findings are present in laboratory studies (Rubin, 1974), considerably less regularity is found.

(text continues on page 388)

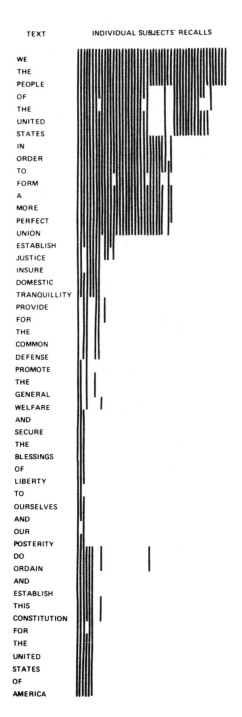

TEXT

INDIVIDUAL SUBJECTS' RECALLS

WE
THE
PEOPLE
OF
THE
UNITED
STATES
IN
ORDER
TO
FORM
A
MORE
PERFECT
UNION
ESTABLISH
JUSTICE
INSURE
DOMESTIC
TRANQUILLITY
PROVIDE
FOR
THE
COMMON
DEFENSE
PROMOTE
THE
GENERAL
WELFARE
AND
SECURE
THE
BLESSINGS
OF
LIBERTY
TO
OURSELVES
AND
OUR
POSTERITY
DO
ORDAIN
AND
ESTABLISH
THIS
CONSTITUTION
FOR
THE
UNITED
STATES
OF
AMERICA

Figure 36-1 *Free recall data for fifty subjects for "The Preamble to the Constitution."*

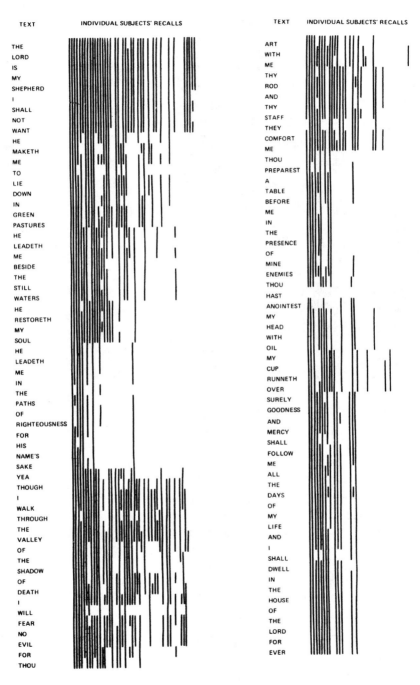

Figure 36-2 *Free recall data for "The Twenty-Third Psalm."*

TEXT	INDIVIDUAL SUBJECTS' RECALLS

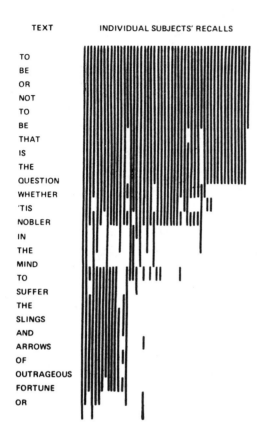

Figure 36-3 *Free recall data for those words of "Hamlet's Soliloquy" recalled by four or more subjects.*

TO
BE
OR
NOT
TO
BE
THAT
IS
THE
QUESTION
WHETHER
'TIS
NOBLER
IN
THE
MIND
TO
SUFFER
THE
SLINGS
AND
ARROWS
OF
OUTRAGEOUS
FORTUNE
OR

For "The Preamble" and "Hamlet's Soliloquy," primacy provides a good description of the data. Based on primacy alone an individual subject's data for the three passages, can be predicted with 92.9, 76.1, and 98.8 percent accuracy. Here, as primacy is a prediction that is independent of the data, a binomial by-chance model (Kenny & Rubin, 1977) is appropriate and yields significant differences: 69.4 percent, $t(49) = 11.17$; 69.3 percent, $t(49) = 4.18$; and 88.8 percent, $t(49) = 12.53$; all $p < .001$. Again, it should be stressed that these are predictions of which words individual subjects will recall. These are not predictions of grouped data but, rather, the average of predictions of individual subjects' data. The fact that the primacy effect is not as strong for "The 23rd Psalm," which has a simple rhythmic structure, will be investigated in more detail after examining other passages.

Qualitative examination of Figures 36-1–36-3 shows that subjects tend to begin and end recalling at surface structure boundaries corresponding to what might be breath pause locations (Glanzer, 1976; Suci, 1967). In order to quantify this notion, operational definitions of boundaries in recall and of breath pause locations are needed.

A recall boundary was defined as (1) more than two consecutive words correctly recalled followed by more than two consecutive words not correctly recalled: that is, an end of a portion of recall, or (2) more than two consecutive words not correctly recalled followed by more than two consecutive words correctly recalled: that is, a beginning of a portion of recall. One consequence of this definition is that a recall boundary cannot occur in the first or last three words of a passage, so the observation that almost all recalls begin with the first word of the passage is not used to inflate the correspondence of breath pauses and recall boundaries.

Johnson's (1970) technique was followed to quantify breath pauses. Five volunteers enrolled in a Psychology of Language course were asked to "please indicate by means of slashes any location where a pause would be acceptable (i.e., word/word)." Judgments were made on all three passages used here as well as two others used in later experiments. A breath pause was defined as any location that three or more of the five judges marked.

"The Preamble," "The 23rd Psalm," and "Hamlet's Soliloquy" consist of 52, 117, and 277 words, respectively. They therefore have 51, 116, and 276 boundaries between words. Of these, 39, 38, and 43 percent are breath pause locations. Of the 64, 151, and 62 recall boundaries observed for the three passages, 94, 81, and 82 percent fall on the breath pause locations. As some of the subjects provide more than one recall boundary an inferential statistical analysis of this data is difficult. However, if only the first recall boundary provided by each subject is considered, the observations can be assumed to be independent and a χ^2 analysis is appropriate. Of the 45, 46, or 40 first-recall boundaries, 93, 87, and 80 percent fall on breath pause locations: $\chi^2(1) = 53.08$, $\chi^2(1) = 44.97$, and $\chi^2(1) = 21.12$, all $p < .001$. The five, four, and ten subjects whose recalls yielded no recall boundaries were by necessity omitted from this analysis. Thus, the recall boundaries coincide with independently determined surface structure units.

Discussion

Given no control over learning conditions, practice, or retention interval, the recall data produced are among the most regular in cognitive psychology. Not only do all subjects tend to remember the same words, differing only in the amount they recall, but counter to all current thinking about memory for discourse, they also remember in a nonabstractive, nonreconstructive manner. The recall is accurate and organized in terms of surface structure units. In terms of depth of processing approach, there is evidence of only the shallowest processing. Thus, in an attempt to extend laboratory findings to the real world, interesting limitations have been encountered.

[Rubin's next two experiments are omitted here. In Experiment 2, fifth- and sixth-graders who had learned about the Preamble and the Gettysburg Address—but hadn't been asked to memorize them—produced patterns of recall similar to those of the first experiment. Experiment 3 showed that recall can be increased by providing subjects with cues to the surface structure of the text (e.g., "_____ and _____ _____ _____ our _____ _____ _____ on this _____ . . ." for the beginning of the Gettysburg Address).]

. . .

EXPERIMENT 4

Except for "The 23rd Psalm," which has a simple rhythmic structure, the data from previous experiments show a very strong primacy effect. In order to include a second passage of known rhythmic structure and in order to demonstrate that recalls from such passages are remembered, in part, by the use of rhythmic structures, subjects were asked to recall "The Star Spangled Banner" either with no music, "The Star Spangled Banner," or "Stars and Stripes Forever" playing. If the subjects' recall units were basically rhythmic, then the proper rhythm should increase the amount recalled and the wrong rhythm should decrease the amount recalled (Glanzer, 1976).

Method

Subjects. Ninety-five undergraduates volunteered for the experiment.

Procedure. Tape recordings were made of a continuously repeating 1 minute, 10 second instrumental version of "The Star Spangled Banner" and a 2 minute, 45 second instrumental version of "Stars and Stripes Forever." "The Star Spangled Banner" was played to one group of subjects, "Stars and Stripes Forever" was played to a second group, and nothing was played to a third group. All three groups were asked to "please write down the National Anthem, that is, the words to the music that is played at the beginning of sporting events." A questionnaire followed.

Results

There were 31, 32, and 32 subjects in the right, wrong, and no music conditions. Twelve, 17, and 10 of these subjects reported having memorized "The Star Spangled Banner" out of the 28, 30, and 28 subjects answering the question. The average duration since last exposure was 12 ($SD = 4.0$), 11 ($SD = 2.5$), and 8 ($SD = 3.2$) years for the 12, 17, and 7 subjects able to answer that question. There were no significant differences between the groups on these questions.

The strongest results cannot be given here in a quantitative fashion. The subjects in the no music condition behaved as most subjects in verbal learning experiments do, with perhaps more of an expression of frustration. The subjects in the wrong music condition appeared to be in slightly more pain, and a few on occasion put their hands over their ears. Most interesting, however, were the subjects in the right music condition. They would write as fast as they could until the music got ahead of them, and then they would switch to the behaviors of the wrong music condition. By the second or third repetition of "The Star Spangled Banner" almost all of the subjects in the right music condition adopted a strategy of waiting until the music came around to where they had stopped writing the previous time, and then writing another burst until the music got ahead of them again. The effect was quite striking and has since provided an effective classroom demonstration of the role of coding in memory.

The subjects in the right, wrong, and no-music conditions remembered an average of 52, 28, and 32 of the 80 words of "The Star Spangled Banner" correctly: $F(2, 92) = 12.68$, $p < .001$, $MS_e = 422$. Their recall was quite accurate with an average of only 3.4 ($SD = 2.7$), 1.6 ($SD = 1.8$), and 2.5 ($SD = 2.2$) incorrect words recalled.

As in previous experiments, the data were quite orderly with Guttman Coefficients of Reproducibility of .814, .921, and .892. Under the binomial chance model these figures would be .632, .702, and .658. For the wrong and no-music conditions primacy was again a fairly good predictor of which items would be recalled with coefficients of .836, $t(31) = 4.91$, $p < .001$, and .852, $t(31) = 6.31$, $p < .001$. However, for the right-music condition, primacy was essentially equivalent to chance: .624, $t(30) = 0.39$, n.s. This is not due to a ceiling effect as, even in this condition, subjects recalled only 65 percent of the words correctly.

As "The Star Spangled Banner" consists of 80 words, there are 79 between-word boundaries; of these, 38 percent were acceptable breath pauses. Of the 80, 47, and 35 recall boundaries found in the right, wrong, and no-music conditions, 58, 77, and 71 percent fell on breath pauses. Of the 27, 27, and 23 first-recall boundaries, 59, 78, and 70 percent fell on breath pauses: $\chi^2(1) = 4.33$, $\chi^2(1) = 16.75$, $\chi^2(1) = 8.45$, all $p < .05$.

Discussion

Recalls from college students for five passages have now been presented. Three of these passages ("The Preamble," "Hamlet's Soliloquy," and the "Gettysburg Address") have no simple, repetitive, rhythmic structure to aid in recall. For these three passages, primacy predicts free recall with an accuracy of 93, 99, and 97 percent. Two of the passages, "The 23rd

Psalm," and "The Star Spangled Banner," have marked rhythmic structures. For these two passages, primacy predicts free recall with an accuracy of 76 and 85 percent. These results and the raw recall data, such as are shown in Figures 36-1—36-3, are consistent with the following hypothesis. All five passages are remembered by associative chaining of surface structure units. Thus, if one unit is forgotten all remaining units are lost. Where a rhythmic structure is available, subjects can make use of this structure to begin remembering the chain again after a unit is forgotten. While this hypothesis is obviously inadequate for all serial learning (Lashley, 1951; Jones, 1974), it provides a good account of the data collected here. It may be noted that this hypothesis does not make use of the most commonly cited determinant of prose memory: meaning. This is not because meaning has definitely been shown to be irrelevant to the present study, but rather because meaning would greatly increase the complexity of the hypothesis without increasing its ability to account for the data.

REFERENCES

Bahrick, H. P., Bahrick, P. O., & Wittlinger, R. P. (1975). Fifty years of memory for names and faces: A cross-sectional approach. *Journal of Experimental Psychology: General, 104,* 54–75.

Bartlett, F. C. (1967). *Remembering: A study in experimental and social psychology.* London: Cambridge University Press. (Originally published, 1932.)

Cofer, C. N. (1943). Recall of verbal material after a four-year interval. *Journal of General Psychology, 29,* 155–156.

Glanzer, M. (1976). Intonation grouping and related words in free recall. *Journal of Verbal Learning and Verbal Behavior, 15,* 85–92.

Johnson, R. E. (1970). Recall of prose as a function of the structural importance of the linguistic units. *Journal of Verbal Learning and Verbal Behavior, 9,* 12–20.

Jones, M. R. (1974). Cognitive representations of serial patterns. In B. H. Kantowitz (Ed.), *Human information processing: Tutorials in performance and cognition.* Hillsdale, N.J.: Lawrence Erlbaum Associates.

Kenny, D. A., & Rubin, D. C. (1977). Estimating chance reproducibility in Guttman scaling. *Social Science Research, 6,* 188–196.

Lashley, K. S. (1951). The problem of serial order in behavior. In L. A. Jeffress (Ed.), *Cerebral mechanisms in behavior: The Hixon symposium.* New York: Wiley.

Rubin, D. C. (1974). *Remembering prose.* Unpublished doctoral dissertation, Harvard University.

Squire, L. R., Chace, P. M., & Slater, P. C. (1975). Assessment of memory for remote events. *Psychological Reports, 37,* 223–234.

Suci, G. J. (1967). The validity of pause as an index of units in language. *Journal of Verbal Learning and Verbal Behavior, 6,* 26–32.

Titchener, E. B. (1923). Relearning after forty-six years. *American Journal of Psychology, 34,* 468–469.

Warrington, E. K., & Sanders, H. I. (1971). The fate of old memories. *Quarterly Journal of Experimental Psychology, 23,* 432–442.

37 | The Mnemonic Feat of the "Shass Pollak"

George M. Stratton

In this selection feats of memory are described that make remembering the Twenty-third Psalm or "The Star Spangled Banner" (Selection 36) seem trivial. Stratton describes Hebrew scholars who have not just memorized the Talmud "literally" (as a sequence of words) but also "typographically," as a set of printed pages. Apparently their definition of the sacred Talmud included the book itself as well as its message. Most of us would accept "Oh say, can you see . . ." as the beginning of "The Star Spangled Banner" no matter how it was printed and— within limits—no matter how it was sung. But if nothing is the Talmud except these volumes, then knowing the Talmud can involve knowing them in every concrete detail.

This selection might well have been included in Part VIII (Special People). It appears here instead because it illustrates the same principle as the preceding selection, albeit in extreme form. Culturally defined memory performances differ widely in the kinds of fidelity to the original that they require; individual skills of memory adapt themselves to those definitions.

Some years ago, through the kindness of my friend Professor Hollander, of the Johns Hopkins University, my attention was directed to a special achievement in memorizing which I venture to report; since, so far as I know, it has remained unnoticed by psychologists, and yet should be stored among the data long and still richly gathering for the study of extraordinary feats of memory.

※ From *Psychological Review*, 1917, 24, 244–247.

The facts of the case I can hardly do better than to allow the witnesses themselves to state. And first the Reverend Dr. David Philipson, of Cincinnati, to whom I was first referred by Professor Hollander.

"The Babylonian Talmud," he has been good enough to write me, "consist of twelve large folio volumes comprising thousands of pages. All the printed editions of the Talmud have exactly the same number of pages and the same words on each page. This must be borne in mind in order to understand the remarkable feat of memory about to be described. There have been, as there undoubtedly still are, men who know the whole text of the Talmud by heart. Some years ago one of these men, a native of Poland, was in this country. I witnessed his remarkable feats of memory. Thus, one of us would throw open one of the volumes of the Talmud, say the tractate Berakhot, at page ten; a pin would be placed on a word, let us say, the fourth word in line eight; the memory sharp would then be asked what word is in this same spot on page thirty-eight or page fifty or any other page; the pin would be pressed through the volume until it reached page thirty eight or page fifty or any other page designated; the memory sharp would then mention the word and it was found invariably correct. He had visualized in his brain the whole Talmud; in other words, the pages of the Talmud were photographed on his brain. It was one of the most stupendous feats of memory I have ever witnessed and there was no fake about it. In the company gathered about the table were a number of Talmudic experts who would readily have discovered fraud had there been any. The technical name which was used by the Jews of aforetimes to designate these memory experts was *Shass Pollak*; *Shass* is the abbreviation for the Hebrew terms for the Talmud, and *Pollak* is Pole; nearly all these memory experts came from Poland; a *Shass Pollak* then is a Pole who has memorized the entire contents of the Talmud and is able to give exhibitions of his mnemonic powers like those mentioned above."

And next let me quote from Judge Mayer Sulzberger, of Philadelphia, who in answer to my inquiry, wrote as follows:

"I have met but one 'Shass Pollak' in my life. He was brought into my library one evening by a friend. I conversed with him and experimented upon him.

"After he had been introduced as the expert in question, I expressed some curiosity with perhaps a mien of incredulity. He was eager for the fray.

"You are of course aware that all (or nearly all) modern editions of the Talmud are paged alike and printed alike, each page beginning and ending with the same word in all the editions.

"I went to the case and took out a volume of the *first* edition which has its own paging *not* followed by the other editions. He made an automatic dive for a word in a particular part of the page, and lo! it was not there.

"Confounded by this unexpected event, he thought at first that this was not a Talmud I was showing him; and when convinced finally that it was, seemed to bear it some resentment for its improper behavior.

"I then brought out the corresponding volume of an ordinary edition and he undoubtedly made good.

"He would take a pencil and merely glancing at the page put it down anywhere and without looking told the word on which his pencil had lighted. This he did over and over again. There is no reasonable ground for the suspicion that he saw the words. I watched him closely and am convinced that he did not. He had, I feel sure, a perfect image of the page and the position of every word on it in his 'head.' "

Finally, let me give the testimony of Dr. Schechter, of New York, the late President of the Jewish Theological Seminary of America—testimony the more interesting in that while it depends upon the recollection of an experience many years ago, yet it is an independent account of the same kind of testing which Dr. Philipson reports—namely, by pricking through the pages—and consequently confirms the opinion of Judge Sulzberger that the success of the "Shass Pollak" who was tested merely by pencil was not due to a sly catching of the word by eye.

President Schechter stated to me by letter that once he had come across a "Shass Pollak" but that it was too long a time ago to give an account of him with definiteness. "It is at least forty-five years since the incident occurred," he wrote. "What I remember was that he could tell you the contents of every page of the Talmud by heart. I remember also that the people amused themselves by prying a needle into any volume of the Talmud, and he could tell exactly the word on which the needle touched. But I also recollect distinctly that it was nothing more than a verbal or rather local memory, the students all maintaining that he knew very little about the meaning of the contents, their interpretation and application. I heard afterwards of many similar 'Shass Pollaks,' but it is a fact that none of them ever attained to any prominence in the scholarly world."

This absence of any scholarly grasp of the contents thus memorized, of which President Schechter speaks, also appears in the judgment of Dr. Philipson. "I looked upon his achievement at the time I witnessed it as purely mechanical," he writes. "It is quite likely that he could not interpret the Talmud though he knew its contents by heart." And Judge Sulzberger, when proposing to his "Shass Pollak" that he use his knowledge to some scientific or literary end, was listened to with respect, but nevertheless received the impression that such proposals were deemed by his man to be nonsensical.

All of which confirms the oft-repeated observation, that such extraordinary powers of memory may exist in a kind of intellectual disproportion where there is no corresponding development of other powers—where, indeed, there may be an actual stunting of other powers and interests; as though the mind had "run" to memory, and been enlarged here at the expense of other functions.

As to the more precise amount of matter that was memorized, it should be noted that a page of the Babylonian Talmud consists, as my colleague Dr. Popper has pointed out to me,[1] of the text proper, called the *Gemarah*, and printed as a more central portion on the page, and of a commentary printed below and around this text. Upon special inquiry whether the mnemonic feat applied only to the *Gemarah* or included also the Commentary, Dr. Philipson states that the test which he witnessed was upon the *Gemarah* only; and Judge Sulzberger is of the opinion that this was also true in the case that came under his observation. Even so, the task must have been a stupendous one; the amount of reading-matter upon each page is still great, and the number of pages is enormous.

In closing may I express my thanks, in which other students of psychology will certainly unite with me, to the gentlemen who have so generously given the facts above recorded.

---

[1]Professor Popper has also referred me to the articles "Talmud" and "Mnemonics" in *The Jewish Encyclopedia* for evidence that at one period the Talmud was handed down solely by memory. The feat of the Poles here recounted may therefore be regarded perhaps as the survival of a custom among early Jewish students in many and widely separated communities. The work of Brüll, *Die Mnemotechnik des Talmuds*, Vienna, 1864, should also be cited.

38 | Oral Poetry in Yugoslavia

Albert B. Lord

The songs described in this selection were recorded in the mountains of Yugoslavia almost seventy years ago. Albert Lord and Millman Parry, who recorded them, were classicists; they hoped that a study of contemporary oral poetry would further their understanding of the Iliad *and the* Odyssey. *That hope was richly rewarded. Although nothing in the repertoires of the singers they found approached the two Homeric poems (which total some 27,000 lines), there were striking structural similarities between the modern Balkan epics and the ancient Greek epics. Parry and Lord interpreted this structure as the mark of oral composition itself.*

The Yugoslav epics show repetition of units at two levels of analysis, known as themes *and* formulas. *Themes are types of events that occur in many different songs: a council of war, the arming of a warrior, the return of the hero in disguise. The formula, a much smaller unit, is "a group of words which is regularly employed under the same metrical conditions to express a given essential idea" (Lord, p. 30). The singer may have a dozen formulaic ways to describe daybreak: "When dawn put forth its wings," "When it was dawn and white day," or "When the sun had warmed the earth," for example. When he comes to a part of the action that takes place at dawn, he uses the one that best fits the meter and his mood. He knows dozens of themes and thousands of formulas, not from having memorized them but from having heard and used them, as we know the words and phrases of our own language.*

Experienced singers in this tradition would know at least thirty songs; some claimed a hundred. Such a song, often several thousands of lines long, would take hours to sing. But as this selection emphasizes, the Yugoslav bards were not "remembering" the songs as singers do today, faithfully following a fixed and previously composed text. Instead, they composed their songs anew on each occasion, and no one presentation was more "original" than any other. The two versions of Marko and Nina *reproduced in the Appendix to this selection illustrate the range of variation that might be involved. In the absence of literacy and technology, it would be difficult indeed to know whether these two versions—heard days or years apart—were "the same" or not. That is why the singers give such apparently contradictory answers when they are asked if they can sing ". . . the same song, word for word and line for line." They know little of words or lines; what they know are formulas, themes, and above all songs. Those they know well.*

Were we to seek to understand why a literary poet wrote what he did in a particular poem in a particular manner or form, we should not focus our attention on the moment when he or someone else read or recited his poem to a particular audience, or even on any moment when we ourselves read the poem in quiet solitude. We should instead attempt to reconstruct that moment in time when the poet wrote the lines. Obviously, the moment of composition is the important one for such a study. For the oral poet, the moment of composition is the performance. In the case of a literary poem there is a gap in time between composition and reading or performance; in the case of the oral poem this gap does not exist, because composition and performance are two aspects of the same moment. Hence, the question "When *would* such and such an oral poem be performed?" has no meaning; the question should be "When *was* the oral poem performed?" An oral poem is not composed *for* but *in* performance. The implications of this statement are both broad and deep. For that reason we must turn first in our analysis of oral epic to the performance.

We must grasp fully who, or more correctly what, our performer is. We must eliminate from the word "performer" any notion that he is one who merely reproduces what someone else or even he himself has composed. Our oral poet is a composer. Our singer of tales is a composer of tales. Singer, performer, composer, and poet are one under different aspects *but at the same time*. Singing, performing, composing are facets of the same act.

It is sometimes difficult for us to realize that the man who is sitting before us singing an epic song is not a mere carrier of the tradition but a creative artist making the tradition. The reasons for this difficulty are various. They arise in part simply from the fact that we are not in the habit of thinking of a performer as a composer. Even in the realm of oral literature most of us in the West, at least, are more accustomed to the ballad than to the epic; and our experience has been formed in large part by "folk" ballad singers who are mere performers. The present revival of folk singing on the concert stage and elsewhere has distorted our concept of the essence of oral composition. The majority of such "folk" singers are not oral poets. The collector even in a country such as Yugoslavia, where published collections have been given much attention for over a century, some of which have become almost sacrosanct, must be wary; for he will find singers who have memorized songs from these collections. In spite of authentic manner of presentation, in spite of the fact that the songs themselves are often oral poems, we cannot consider such singers as oral poets. They are *mere* performers. Such experiences have deceived us and have robbed the real oral poet of credit as a creative composer; indeed to some extent they have taken from epic performance an element of vital interest. Our task in this chapter is to restore to performance and performer their true significance.

When we realize that the performance is a moment of creation for the singer, we cannot but be amazed at the circumstances under which he creates. Since these circumstances influence oral form we must consider them. Epic poetry in Yugoslavia is sung on a variety of occasions. It forms, at the present time, or until very recently, the chief entertainment of the adult male population in the villages and small towns. In the country villages, where the houses are often widely separated, a gathering may be held at one of the houses during a period of leisure from the work in the fields. Men from all the families assemble and one of their number may sing epic songs. Because of the distances between the houses some of the guests arrive earlier than others, and of course this means that some leave earlier. Some very likely spend the whole night. . . . The singer has to contend with an audience that is coming and going, greeting newcomers, saying farewells to early leavers; a newcomer with special news or gossip may interrupt the singing for some time, perhaps even stopping it entirely.

What is true of the home gathering in the country village holds as well for the more compact villages and for towns, where the men gather in the coffee house (*kafana*) or in the tavern rather than in a private home. The taverns are entirely male establishments, whether the district is predominantly Moslem or not. Neither Moslem nor Christian women are ever allowed in these places. This is a man's world. Here the men gather at the end of the day. The farmers of the nearby villages may drop in for a short while to sit and talk, sip coffee or raki, and listen to songs. They come and go. The townspeople join them. There are shopkeepers and caravan drivers who have come in with merchandise from other districts or are stopping on their way through. Frequently the tavern is also an inn, a "han," and here the drivers will spend the night. Many of these men are also singers and the carriers of tradition from one district to another. They are a critical audience.

In market centers such as Bijelo Polje, Stolac, Novi Pazar, and Bihać, market day, the one day in the week when the town is crowded with people from the countryside who have come in to buy and sell, will be the busiest day in the han or in the kafana. Some of the business is done there during the day, and some of the money which has changed hands will be spent in the kafana at night before the men return to their own villages. They may even stay the night there and return the next morning, if they feel so inclined, or if the day has been particularly profitable. This is a good opportunity for the singer because, although his audience may not be stable, it does have money and is willing to reward him for his pains. He is not really a professional, but his audience does buy him drinks, and if he is good they will give him a little money for the entertainment he has given them.

When the singing takes place, as it occasionally does, at a wedding festival, the amount of confusion is increased by the singing of lyric songs and dancing carried on by the young people. The evenings offer the best opportunity for the singer of the old songs, when the older men are not watching the games or gossiping with their neighbors and are content to relax and sit back and listen to the bard.

Among the Moslems in Yugoslavia there is a special festival which has contributed to the fostering of songs of some length. This is the festival of Ramazan, when for a month the men fast from sunrise to sunset and gather in coffee houses all night long to talk and listen to epic. Here is a perfect circumstance for the singing of one song during the entire night. Here also is an encouragement to the semiprofessional singer to attain a repertory of at least thirty songs. It was Parry's experience that such Moslem singers, when asked how many songs they knew, frequently replied that they knew thirty, one for every night of Ramazan. Most Moslem kafanas engage a singer several months in advance to entertain their guests, and if there is more than one such kafana in the town, there may be rivalry in obtaining the services of a well-known and popular singer who is likely to bring considerable business to the establishment. [*Some sketches of individual singers are omitted.*]

. . .

There seem to be two things that all our singers have in common: illiteracy and the desire to attain proficiency in singing epic poetry. If the second of these sets them apart from their fellows, it is the first, namely their illiteracy, which determines the particular form that their composition takes, and which thus distinguishes them from the literary poet. In societies where writing is unknown, or where it is limited to a professional scribe whose duty is that of writing letters and keeping accounts, or where it is the possession of a small minority, such as clerics or a wealthy ruling class (though often this latter group prefers to have its writing done by a servant), the art of narration flourishes, provided that the culture is in other respects of a sort to foster the singing of tales. If the way of life of a people furnishes subjects for story and affords occasion for the telling, this art will be fostered. On the other hand, when writing is introduced and begins to be used for the same purposes as the oral narrative song, when it is employed for telling stories and is widespread enough to find an audience capable of reading, this audience seeks its entertainment and instruction in books rather than in the living songs of men, and the older art gradually disappears. The songs have died out in the cities not because life in a large community is an unfitting environment for them but because schools were first founded there and writing has been firmly rooted in the way of life of the city dwellers.
[*A section dealing with the early stages of the singers' development is omitted here.*]

...

Increase in repertory and growth in competence take place in the third and last stage of the learning process. We can easily define its beginning as the point at which he sings his first song completely through for a critical audience, but it is much more difficult to set the other limit. That is a question of when a singer is an accomplished practitioner of the art, a matter to be considered shortly. Let us look more closely at what goes on in the third stage. First the singer learns to sing other songs all the way through. If he has already learned them in part, he finishes the process. But again this does not involve memorizing a text, but practicing until he can compose it, or recompose it, himself.

Our proper understanding of these procedures is hindered by our lack of a suitable vocabulary for defining the steps of the process. The singers themselves cannot help us in this regard because they do not think in terms of form as we think of it; their descriptions are too vague, at least for academic preciseness. Man without writing thinks in terms of sound groups and not in words, and the two do not necessarily coincide. When asked what a word is, he will reply that he does not know, or he will give a sound group which may vary in length from what we call a word to an entire line of poetry, or even an entire song. The word for "word" means an "utterance." When the singer is pressed then to say what a line is, he, whose chief claim to fame is that he traffics in lines of poetry, will be entirely baffled by the question; or he will say that since he has been dictating and has seen his utterances being written down, he has discovered what a line is, although he did not know it as such before, because he had never gone to school.

While the singer is adding to his repertory of songs, he is also improving the singing of the ones he already knows, since he is now capable of facing an audience that will listen to him, although possibly with a certain amount of patronizing because of his youth. Generally speaking, he is expanding his songs in the way I have indicated, that is, by ornamenting them. This process will be treated in a later chapter, but it will suffice here to say that this is the period in which he learns the rudiments of ornamentation and expansion. The art of expanding the old songs and of learning new ones is carried to the point at which he can entertain his audience for a full evening; that is one of his goals.

Here, then, for the first time the audience begins to play a role in the poet's art. Up to this point the form of his song has depended on his illiteracy and on the need to compose rapidly in the traditional rhythmic pattern. The singers he has heard have given him the necessary traditional material to make it possible for him to sing, but the length of his songs and the degree to which he will ornament and expand them will depend on the demands of the audience. His audience is gradually changing from an attitude of condescension toward the youngster to one of accepting him as a singer.

It is into the world of kafana, informal gatherings, and festival that our young singer steps once he has mastered the singing of a song. Here he learns new songs. The form of his singing is being perfected, and its content is becoming richer and more varied. This audience and this social milieu have had an effect on the length of the songs of his predecessors, and they will have a similar effect on the length of his songs.

We might say that the final period of training comes to an end when the singer's repertory is large enough to furnish entertainment for several nights. Yet it is better to define the end of the period by the freedom with which he moves in his tradition, because that is the mark of the finished poet. When he has a sufficient command of the formula technique to sing any song that he hears, and enough thematic material at hand to lengthen or shorten a song according to his own desires and to create a new song if he sees fit, then he is an accomplished singer and worthy of his art. There are, to be sure, some singers, not few in number, who never go beyond the third stage in learning, who never reach the point of mastery of the tradition, and who are always struggling for competence. Their weakness is that they do not have enough proficiency in formula-making and thematic structure, nor enough talent, to put a song together artistically. Although such singers can show us much about the workings of the practice and of the tradition, it is the finest and longest songs and the most accomplished singers in whom we are interested for comparative purposes in the study of individual singers and individual songs.

The singer never stops in the process of accumulating, recombining, and remodeling formulas and themes, thus perfecting his singing and enriching his art. He proceeds in two directions; he moves toward refining what he already knows and toward learning new songs. The latter process has now become for him one of learning proper names and of knowing what themes make up the new song. The story is all that he needs; so in this stage he can hear a song once and repeat it immediately afterwards—not word for word, of course—but he can tell the same story again in his own words. Sometimes singers prefer to have a day or so to think the song over, to put it in order, and to practice it to themselves. Such singers are either less confident of their ability, or they may be greater perfectionists.

Sulejman Makić, for example, liked to have time to put his song in order. In Parry Text 681, Records 1322–23 (I, pp. 265–266) we can hear his own words:

Nikola:	Could you still pick up a song today?
Sulejman:	I could.
N:	For example, if you heard me sing a song, let's say, could you pick it up right away?
S:	Yes, I could sing it for you right away the next day.
N:	If you were to hear it just once?
S:	Yes, by Allah, if I were to hear it only once to the gusle.
N:	Why not until the next day? . . . What do you think about in those two days? Isn't it better to sing it right away than later, when you might forget it after so long a time?
S:	It has to come to one. One has to think . . . how it goes, and then little by little it comes to him, so that he won't leave anything out. . . . One couldn't sing it like that all the way through right away.
N:	Why couldn't you, when it's possible the second or third day afterwards?
S:	Anybody who can't write can't do it.
N:	All right, but when you've learned my song, would . . . you sing it exactly as I do?
S:	I would.
N:	You wouldn't add anything . . . nor leave anything out?
S:	I wouldn't . . . by Allah I would sing it just as I heard it. . . . It isn't good to change or to add.

Demo Zogić also gave us information on this point (I, pp. 240–241).

N: We have heard—we've been in those places in our country where people sing—and some singers have told us that as soon as they hear a song from another singer, they can sing it immediately, even if they've heard it only once, . . . just as it was word for word. Is that possible, Demaill?

Đ: It's possible. . . . I know from my own experience. When I was together with my brothers and had nothing to worry about, I would hear a singer sing a song to the gusle, and after an hour I would sing his whole song. I can't write. I would give every word and not make a mistake on a single one. . . .

N: So then, last night you sang a song for us. How many times did you hear it before you were able to sing it all the way through exactly as you do now?

Đ: Here's how many times I heard it. One Ramazan I engaged this Suljo Makić who sang for you here today those songs of the Border. I heard him one night in my coffee house. I wasn't busy. I had a waiter and he waited on my guests, and I sat down beside the singer and in one night I picked up that song. I went home, and the next night I sang it myself. . . . That singer was sick, and I took the gusle and sang the whole song myself, and all the people said: 'We would rather listen to you than to that singer whom you pay.'

N: Was it the same song, word for word, and line for line?

Đ: The same song, word for word, and line for line. I didn't add a single line, and I didn't make a single mistake. . . .

N: Tell me this, if two good singers listen to a third singer who is even better, and they both boast that they can learn a song if they hear it only once, do you think that there would be any difference between the two versions? . . .

Đ: There would. . . . It couldn't be otherwise. I told you before that two singers won't sing the same song alike.

N: Then what are the differences?

Đ: They add, or they make mistakes, and they forget. They don't sing every word, or they add other words. Two singers can't recite a song which they heard from a third singer and have the two songs exactly the same as the third.

N: Does a singer sing a song which he knows well (not with rhymes, but one of these old Border songs), will he sing it twice the same and sing every line?

Đ: That is possible. If I were to live for twenty years, I would sing the song which I sang for you here today just the same twenty years from now, word for word.

In these two conversations we have accomplished singers discussing under guidance the transmission, not of the art of singing, but of songs from one well-trained singer to another. They are also telling us what they do when they sing a song. Here the creative performer speaks. In the case of Đemo Zogić we can test his statements and thus we can learn how to interpret this information that singers can give us about their own art.

Note that both singers express some attitude toward writing. Makić gives the opinion that only a person who can write can reproduce a song immediately; whereas Zogić's boast is that although he can't write he can reproduce a song an hour after he has heard it. In other words, one says that the man with writing is superior; and the other, that he is as good as the man with writing. They reflect the unlettered man's admiration of the lettered, but their statements are inaccurate. Their admiration goes too far, for the man with writing cannot do what they believe he can and what they in actuality can do.

Both singers stress that they would sing the song exactly as they heard it, Zogić even boasting that he would sing the song in the same way twenty years later. Makić indicates that changing and adding are not good, implying that singers do change and add; and Zogić states plainly that two singers won't sing the same song alike. How do we disentangle these contradictions?

Zogić learned from Makić the song under discussion in his conversation, and both versions are published in Volume I of the Parry Collection (Nos. 24–25 and 29). Zogić did not learn it word for word and line for line, and yet the two songs are recognizable versions of the same story. They are not close enough, however, to be considered "exactly alike." Was Zogić lying to us? No, because he was singing the story as he conceived it as being "like" Makić's story, and to him "word for word and line for line" are simply an emphatic way of saying "like." As I have said, singers do not know what words and lines are. What is of importance here is not the fact of exactness or lack of exactness, but the constant emphasis by the singer on his role in the tradition. It is not the creative role that we have stressed for the purpose of clarifying a misunderstanding about oral style, but the role of conserver of the tradition, the role of the defender of the historic truth of what is being sung; for if the singer changes what he has heard in its essence, he falsifies truth. It is not the artist but the historian who speaks at this moment, although the singer's concept of the historian is that of a guardian of legend.

Although Makić's and Zogić's versions of the same song differ considerably, Zogić's version itself changes little in the course of years. It was my good fortune to record this song from him seventeen years later, and it is remarkably close to the earlier version, though hardly word for word. It even still contains a glaring inconsistency in the story which was not in Makić's version.

But when Zogić is not defending himself as a preserver of the tradition, when he is thus freed to speak of the art of singing as such, in other words when he can talk about someone else's practice, he can be more objective. Then he states that two singers won't sing the same song alike; then he can recognize changes, additions, and mistakes, and give us a clearer picture of what happens in transmission.

And the picture that emerges is not really one of conflict between preserver of tradition and creative artists; it is rather one of the preservation of tradition by the constant re-creation of it. The ideal is a true story well and truly retold.

...

[*In the following extract from a later chapter that focuses on the song rather than the singer, Lord returns to the question of "originality."*]

As long as one thought of the oral poet as a singer who carried in his head a song in more or less the exact form in which he had learned it from another singer, as long as one used for investigation ballads and comparatively short epics, the question of what an oral song is could not arise. It was, we assumed, essentially like any other poem; its text was more or less fixed. But when we look more closely at the process of oral composition and come to appreciate more fully the creative role of the individual singer in carrying forward the tradition, we must begin to query our concept of a song.

When the singer of tales, equipped with a store of formulas and themes and a technique of composition, takes his place before an audience and tells his story, he follows the plan which he has learned along with the other elements of his profession. Whereas the singer thinks of his song in terms of a flexible plan of themes, some of which are essential and some of which are not, we think of it as a given text which undergoes change from one singing to another. We are more aware of change than the singer is, because we have a concept of the fixity of a performance or of its recording on wire or tape or plastic or in writing. We think of change in content and in wording; for, to us, at some moment both wording and content have been established. To the singer the song, which cannot be changed (since to change it would, in his mind, be to tell an untrue story or to falsify history), is the essence of the story itself. His idea of stability, to which he is deeply devoted, does not include the wording, which to him has never been fixed, nor the unessential parts of the story. He builds his performance, or song in our sense, on the stable skeleton of narrative, which is the song in his sense.

When one asks a singer what songs he knows, he will begin by saying that he knows the song, for example, about Marko Kraljević when he fought with Musa, or he will identify it by its first lines. In other words, the song is the story of what someone did or what happened to some hero, but it is also the song itself expressed in verse. It is not just a story; it is not merely a tale divorced from its telling. Sulejman Makić said that he could repeat a song that he had heard only once, *provided that he heard it to the gusle* (I, p. 266). This is a most significant clue. The story in the poet-singer's mind is a story in song. Were it not for remarks like that of Makić, we might be led to think that the singer needs only "a story," which he then retells in the language of verse. But now we know that the story itself must have the particular form which it has only when it is told in verse.

Any particular song is different in the mouth of each of its singers. If we consider it in the thought of a single singer during the years in which he sings it, we find that it is different at different stages in his career. Its clearness of outline will depend upon how many times he sings it; whether it is an established part of his repertory or merely a song which he sings occasionally. The length of the song is also important, because a short song will naturally tend to become more stable the more it is sung.

In some respects the larger themes and the song are alike. Their outward form and their specific content are ever changing. Yet there is a basic idea or combination of ideas that is fairly stable. We can say, then, that a song is the story about a given hero, but its expressed forms are multiple, and each of these expressed forms or tellings of the story is itself a separate song, in its own right, authentic and valid as a song unto itself. We must distinguish then two concepts of song in oral poetry. One is the general idea of the story, which we use when we speak in larger terms, for example, of the song of the wedding of Smailagić Meho, which actually includes all singings of it. The other concept of song is that of a particular performance or text, such as Avdo Mededović's song, "The Wedding of Smailagić Meho," dictated during the month of July, 1935.

Our real difficulty arises from the fact that, unlike the oral poet, we are not accustomed to thinking in terms of fluidity. We find it difficult to grasp something that is multiform. It seems to us necessary to construct an ideal text or to seek an original, and we remain dissatisfied with an ever-changing phenomenon. I believe that once we know the facts of oral composition we must cease trying to find an original of any traditional song. From one point of view each performance is an original. From another point of view it is impossible to retrace the work of generations of singers to that moment when some singer first sang a particular song.

We are occasionally fortunate enough to be present at a first singing, and we are then disappointed, because the singer has not perfected the song with much practice and by the test of repeated performance. Even after he has—and it may change much as he works it over—it must be accepted and sung by other singers in order to become a part of the tradition, and in their hands it will go through other changes, and so the process continues from generation to generation. We cannot retrace these steps in any particular song. There was an original, of course, but we must be content with the texts that we have and not endeavor to "correct" or "perfect" them in accordance with a purely arbitrary guess at what the original might have been.

Indeed, we should be fully aware that even had we this "original," let us say, of the wedding of Samilagić Meho, we would not have the original of the basic story, that is, the song of the young man who goes forth into the world to win his spurs. We would have only the application of this story to the hero Meho. Each performance is the specific song, and at the same time it is the generic song, the song we are listening to is "the song"; for each performance is more than a performance; it is a re-creation. Following this line of thinking, we might term a singer's first singing of a song as a creation of the song in his experience. Both synchronically and historically there would be numerous creations and re-creations of the song. This concept of the relationship between "songs" (performances of the same specific or generic song) is closer to the truth than the concepts of an "original" and "variants." In a sense each performance is "an" original, if not "the" original.

The truth of the matter is that our concept of "the original," of "the song," simply makes no sense in oral tradition. To us it seems so basic, so logical, since we are brought up in a society in which writing has fixed the norm of a stable first creation in art, that we feel there must be an "original" for everything. The first singing in oral tradition does not coincide with this concept of the "original." We might as well be prepared to face the fact that we are in a different world of thought, the patterns of which do not always fit our cherished terms. In oral tradition the idea of an original is illogical.

[Lord's frequent use of general terms like "oral tradition" may be misleading. Not all oral poetry is like the Yugoslav epics. More recent studies in Africa and elsewhere show that it can take many forms: some include more nearly verbatim repetition; in others, the poet composes in advance of performance. Different societies prize and develop different abilities. For more about oral poetry, see R. Finnegan, What is oral literature anyway? In B. A. Stoltz and R. S. Shannon (Eds.), Oral literature and the formula. Ann Arbor, Michigan: University of Michigan Center for the Coordination of Ancient and Modern Studies, 1976.]

APPENDIX

[In an appendix to The Singer of Tales, Lord reproduces four different versions of Marko and Nina as performed on different occasions by the same poet. These two were sung two days apart.]

Parry 805

Marko arises early in his tower in Prilip and drinks raki. With him are his mother, his wife, and his sister Andelija (1–6).

Marko says that a letter arrived the day before from the sultan calling him to serve in the army for nine years (7–10).

He tells his mother that if Nina of Koštun should come and capture his tower, take away his wife and sister, and tread on his mother, she should write him a letter and send it to him by his falcon (11–22).

Nina and his three brothers capture Marko's tower, take his wife and sister, and tread on his mother (23–30).

Marko's mother writes a letter telling him what has happened, and sends it by his falcon (31–46).

The falcon seeks out Marko and delivers the letter (47–51).

Parry 846

Marko arises early in his stone tower. With him are his mother and his wife (1–5).

A messenger arrives with a letter for Marko. He reads it and is silent. His mother asks him where the letter is from and why it makes him sad. Marko says the letter is from the sultan calling him serve in the army for nine years and to bring his horse and sword (6–30).

If Nina of Koštun hears, he will come to Prilip, tread on Marko's mother, and take away his wife and sister Andelija. If that happens, his mother is to send him a letter by his falcon, who will be able to find him in the army. His mother agrees to do this (31–54).

Marko prepares to depart. He tells his wife to look for the sun and moon, but never again for him. He goes to Carigrad (55–65).

When Marko joins the army he greets the sultan, who takes his horse and sword. Marko serves the sultan for nine years (66–77).

Nina and his four brothers hear (in the ninth year) that Marko is in the army, and they go to Prilip. They capture Marko's tower, take away his wife and sister, and tread on his mother (78–96).

Marko's mother writes a letter telling him what has happened, and sends it by his falcon (97–122).

The falcon seeks out Marko and delivers the letter (123–127).

Marko reads and is angry. He writes to the sultan, who gives him back his horse and sword, and his choice of twelve warriors. The sultan says to bring back Nina's head (52–71).

They depart (72–75).

On the mountain they stop to drink. Marko says they will go to a church and ask for monks' clothes, and they do. The monks refuse, and Marko kills them, and he and his companions disguise themselves in monks' clothes. They proceed to Koštun (76–110).

When they arrive at a spring near Koštun where Marko's wife and sister are washing clothes, his wife recognizes Šarac, and asks where the monk got Marko's horse. Marko says that he died nine years ago. He has heard that Nina will marry and he has come for that. He sent his wife to tell Nina. Marko tells his men to stay outside. Nina asks where Marko got the horse, and he says Marko gave it to him for burying him. Marko goes into the tower (111–155).

Nina entertains Marko with wine and Marko asks permission to dance a little for the soul of Marko and the health of Nina. The permission is granted (156–165).

Marko dances, and Nina says he shakes the tower. Marko asks permission to sing, and it is granted. Marko shouts: "For the soul of Nina!", swings his sword and cuts off Nina's head (166–177).

Marko reads and is angry. He shows the letter to the sultan, who gives him back his horse and sword, and his choice of twelve warriors with Delibaša Ibro at their head. The sultan says to bring back Nina's head. Marko chooses his men (128–154).

They depart (155–159).

On the mountain they stop to drink. Marko says they will go to a church and ask for monks' clothes. The monks refuse, and Marko kills them, and he and his companions disguise themselves in monks' clothes. They proceed to Koštun (160–194).

When they arrive at a spring near Koštun where Marko's wife and sister are washing clothes, his wife recognizes Šarac, and asks where the monk got Marko's horse. Marko says that he died nine years ago, and gave him the horse for burying him. He sends his wife to tell Nina that the monk has come to marry the two. He leaves his men outside and rides into the courtyard. Nina asks where he got the horse, and Marko tells him. He also tells him that he has come to marry him. They enter the tower (195–241).

Nina entertains Marko with wine and meat and Marko asks permission to dance and sing a little for the soul of Marko and the health of Nina. The permission is granted (242–256).

Marko dances and Koštun shakes. Nina says that to judge by his strength this must be Marko. Marko dances and sings for the soul of Nina and the health of Marko. His sword swings and he kills Nina (257–271).

Nina's three brothers flee and Marko and his men pursue them. He kills Šćepan at Šćepan's Cross, Jasenko at Jasena, and Radoje at Radimlja. He gathers their heads. He himself has lost only one man (178–191).

Nina's brothers flee and Marko and his men pursue them. They kill Šćepan at Šćepan's Cross, Jasenko at Jasena, and Radoje at Radimlja. They erect monuments at each place (272–285).

Marko returns with his wife, his sister, and his men to Prilip (192–200).

They return to Koštun. Marko gathers the heads in a bag, and returns to Prilip, having set fire to Koštun. Ibro is missing (286–310).

In Prilip Marko shows Nina's head to his mother, and tells her that he will trouble her no more. Marko eats and drinks (201–212).

They go to Marko's tower and eat and drink and rest (311–317).

Marko goes to the sultan. He gives him the heads and reports that Ibro has been killed. The sultan rewards him and sends him back to Prilip, with greetings to his mother, and the offer of assistance whenever Marko needs help. Marko returns to Prilip (213–234).

Marko takes the heads to the sultan, who sends him home to Prilip with the offer of assistance whenever he needs it. Marko returns to Prilip (318–324).

39 | Tribal History in Liberia

Warren L. D'Azevedo

We have seen that oral poetry is not a watered-down version of its written counterpart but a unique artistic achievement in its own right. Oral history, too, must be understood on its own terms. Oral historians, sometimes called "griots," play significant roles in many different African societies. This selection is a careful account of the practice of history in one such society, the Gola of the Liberian coast as they were in the 1950s. It is clear that the Gola historians do much more than simply remember facts about the past; they use their knowledge constructively in the present as well.

Knowledge of the past is a highly valued commodity among the Gola of West Africa. "Setting things straight" and "putting a proper form to things" is a major preoccupation of this highly articulate people. There is no man among them worth his salt who is not ready at the slightest provocation to "make new ideas from old ones" (*ke djike dje yun gogo*), or, more literally, to present "new ideas of the old people." But there are many cultural restrictions and formal requirements which must guide the approach to things past. The past is considered to be the repository of all important sacred and secular knowledge, and the act of formal retrospection is the duty of qualified men of wisdom who are expected to apply their accumulated memories to the solution of problems confronting the living present.

...

The Gola are forest agriculturalists, organized into sections whose boundaries conform essentially to the traditional territories of the old chiefdoms (*ma fuwa*) which had been established prior to Liberian colonial occupa-

※ From W. L. D'Azevedo (1962). Uses of the past in Gola discourse, *Journal of African History*, 3, 11–34. Reprinted by permission of Cambridge University Press. Copyright © 1962 Cambridge University Press.

tion in the second decade of the last century. In the present day these sections constitute Paramount Chieftainships, but in the old days they were made up of a multiplicity of petty monarchies with a high degree of local autonomy. The traditional arrangement involved a central village surrounded by satellite hamlets in which the dominant class of the population was a land-owning patrilineage made up of the descendants of the founder. The related sublineages were ranked according to distance from this founding ancestor. A large proportion of the population of these minute societies, however, was contained in numerous attached lineages of nonrelated immigrants—whether Gola or non-Gola—who had been incorporated by patronage or intermarriage, and whose members were granted theoretically tentative rights to the use of the lands. In addition to these, the small households of the various clients, slaves, and other dependents of the wealthier families contributed still further to the social heterogeneity of the chiefdoms.

Much of coastal territory which the Gola now occupy was a dense uninhabited rain forest until as late as the eighteenth century. Their slow westward migration from the interior region of Komgba in the mountains of northeastern Liberia began in the seventeenth century under pressure from the powerful savanna empires of the Western Sudan. Like many of their neighbors, the Gola retreated into the coastal forests where they became widely dispersed through migration, warfare and the slave trade. In the early nineteenth century they had just succeeded in consolidating their new territory when they were faced with the growing power of European and American colonial settlements on the coasts of Sierra Leone and Liberia. For over a century they resisted Liberian government authority, and established themselves as successful entrepreneurs in the trade between the coast and the far interior markets. With the termination of the Kanga War in 1918–1919, their resistance to Liberian domination of the hinterland was broken, and the last of the recalcitrant chiefdoms of the Western Province was brought under effective Liberian control.

With these facts in mind we may turn to an inquiry into the nature of Gola retrospect.

...

There are two basic values involved in the Gola concept of the past. First of all, it is believed that no person can know his place in society or appreciate fully the kind of person he is unless he is familiar with the genealogy of his own family. The term *djewe mio* refers to "my line of ancestors," or to "those people from whom I have come."[1] Though emphasis is

---

[1]The *djewe* is any reckoning of lines of descent through either or both parents. But in the specific sense implied by *djewe mio* it refers to the line of descent by which the speaker defines his position within a particular patrilineage—his *ke kpo*.

placed on patrilineal descent, one may reckon one's *djewe* through either mother's or father's patrikin, or both, depending upon the advantage that is to be gained by whatever choice is made. Usually, however, an individual has been raised by the kin of either one or the other of his parents so that his knowledge of his ancestors will be limited exclusively to the *djewe* of that side of his family which has trained him.

The advantage of a great family with many well-informed elders lies in the degree to which the record of one's *djewe* is carefully maintained. By means of the amply stocked memories of the elders, one's kinship ties may be asserted at the appropriate time to include a vast number of one's contemporaries. A small family with unimportant and ill-informed elders will be limited in its range of useful alliances, and will lack the prestige and unity of a family that can offer its younger members a sense of pride and security in a clearly defined tradition.

A genealogy involving important ancestors and great deeds is a crucial factor in the individual's self-evaluation. A family whose ancestral record is sketchy is forced to rely on others for this information and is always at a disadvantage in seeking its own interests. A real *dja kwe*—"a free-born person of the country"—knows his own worth because he is able to ramify his line of descent and validate its connexions within the larger society of which he is a part.

A second basic value in the Gola concept of the past is the importance attached to the ancestors as distinct personalities who continue to concern themselves with the affairs of their living descendants. These ancestors guard their own personal interests and that of the family jealously. They are easily angered by an infraction of family laws, or any failure to demonstrate proper respect and concern for their interests. Furthermore, their memory of the issues which confronted them during their own lifetime is great, and they expect their descendants to fulfill whatever pledges they might have made, revenge any wrongs done them, and respect the important decisions they have handed down. In so far as the ancestors resent and envy the living, they are easily provoked. It is within their power to bring sickness, poverty and death upon any descendants who fail in their duty. For this reason it is considered extremely important that the history of a family be sufficiently complete so that slights to the ancestors can be avoided or—should they occur—the source of the resulting difficulties may be ascertained.

In the event of illness or disaster a well-informed group of elders in any family consult among themselves and arrive at an agreement as to the specific ancestor or ancestors whose wrath may have been incurred. Where such family knowledge is incomplete or lacking it is necessary to employ a specialist whose services are expensive and frequently unsatisfactory. A family that knows its main ancestors and the crucial incidents of their lives is in a position to "settle matters" quickly and successfully. It is said that many problems which might have been resolved simply through knowledge of the family past become extended and costly matters because of the failure of an individual or a family in this regard. Moreover, to know the heroic achievements of one's ancestors is to be able to assert a prestigious tradition with regard to one's own kin group.

With the emphasis upon the *djewe* in the Gola view of the past, it follows that any "history" is family history and is limited in scope by the extent of known kinship ties and generational depth. Accounts of the past are, therefore, not only highly localized but tend to be restricted to the *djewe* of the individual providing the account, touching on broader events and relationships only to the extent which the ancestors' interests and activities warrant it. As this knowledge is considered to be the property of the elders of each family, great care and delicacy must be brought to bear in each account so as not to infringe upon the prerogatives of others. A single elder questioned about the kinship relations or family history of persons not directly related to him will invariably state, "I cannot speak for their part . . . you must go to them."

Occasionally there is, among the elders of a large and well-established town, a very old and greatly respected person who is believed to surpass all the others in knowledge of the past. By virtue of his age and vast experience the other elders will defer to him when any disagreement arises among them as to detail in substance or chronology. Such ancient persons—whether men or women—transcend the boundaries of disparate kindred, for they have become in a real sense the grandparents of all within the community. In that they may speak of all the members of a town and its surrounding villages as "my children" it follows that they alone possess the license to speak freely and generally about the history of a town or *fuwa* (the traditional territory which a ruling family controls). If such an ancient elder happens to be a member of the ruling family as well, his or her knowledge is taken as irrefutable regardless of how distasteful a version of history may be to any particular family of the community.

It is only from these very old persons that one receives anything like a chronologically ordered and dramatically unified view of past events in the sense that "a history" implies in Western thought. They have arrived at a point in age and experience where they can see the whole, and may be allowed to do so without criticism or fear of reprisal. They are considered to be objective, having passed beyond the stage of life in which petty rivalries or self-interest would cause them to distort their judgements. The whole of the known past becomes the special property of such persons, and it is to them that all others repair for information and advice. They are the closest to the *yun fa*—the ancestors—for it is indeed through them who are about to enter the ancestral ranks that the *yun fa* speak to the living. During their lifetime they associated with the living ancestors who are now *yun fa*. They are closer to the beginnings and are the only members of the community who have a right to speak with assurance about the origins of things.[2]

But even the boundaries of knowledge of such remarkable old people are usually limited to the town or *fuwa* of their extended family. They will readily affirm that they know little or nothing of the past of the Gola of other "countries," unless, by chance, one of their parents had been an elder of that *fuwa* and had imparted that knowledge directly. The phrase "We Gola" most often refers to those people within the *fuwa*, or within that complex of adjacent *fuwa* who have had long-standing interrelationship. Nevertheless, it will be affirmed that all people who speak the Gola language are remotely related and that they have a common origin. The idea of an all-Gola past, however, is a vague one and the elders of any one section of the Gola tribal area will admit that they know very little about the Gola of remoter sections or "how those people came to be."

The exception to this general rule is provided by a few renowned individuals in each generation who have attained considerable age after a lifetime of varied experience, travel and responsible position. The fame of such persons extends far beyond their local group, and they may be called upon to preside at councils in distant Gola chiefdoms, or may even be visited by delegations seeking authoritative historical data. The late Kpongbo Zu, an elder of the Te-Gola, was honored by the Liberian Government as a "Tribal Historian" for these reasons, and he was invited to participate as an expert witness in all major proceedings involving the Western Province. His name was known by the elders of the remotest Gola sections, and the author was frequently advised to seek his opinion when questions arose which could not be resolved. Gola tradition refers to such persons in the past as advisors of powerful rulers, or as revered persons sought out to arbitrate tribal or intertribal disputes among chiefdoms.

The sectionalism and kin group orientation of Gola society discourages the maintenance of an all-Gola or regional tradition on the local level. Such comprehensive historical traditions are the special property of specific individuals whose knowledge is solicited only in those instances where validation of this kind is considered appropriate. In the local situation individual family tradition is a rigorously guarded body of information, and detailed knowledge of other families in the same area may be disclaimed despite the fact of generations of intermarriage and close asso-

---

[2]The sacredness of such persons is derived from the hierarchical and gerontocratic values of Gola society. Accumulated experience and great age have made them "holy," a phenomenon of particular significance in a region where life-expectancy is less than forty years. Yet it must be noted that the powers which such very aged persons wield seem to be relegated to the sphere of blessings and sage advice. Their role is that of the revered exemplar and does not intrude upon that of specialists such as diviners, magicians, or curers.

ciation. Though much of this behavior is a matter of protocol in the inter-relations between kin groups, it represents a profoundly basic value in Gola culture. One does not learn what is not one's business to know—or better still, one does not divulge what one is not supposed to know. For this reason the elders of a given town—comprising the leadership of a group of more or less related families—prefer to discuss the history of their town in council. In this way each elder can rise in turn to present a formal "public" version of the genealogy and important historical events which constitute the tradition of his family. The presentation will require a considerable amount of improvisation and skillful editing in order to bring its form and content into line with the unified product which is the goal of the council. One can expect great variation among accounts of family history depending upon whether the presentation is made in a public or private gathering.

Any meeting called by the elders for the purpose of clarifying a problem which has arisen between families will attract a large crowd. For it is under these conditions that the elders will compete among themselves for stature as historians, orators, and representatives of their own kin groups. They can also be counted on to use the opportunity for admonishing the "hard-headed" youth of the community, and it is said that at such times "one can learn the secrets of the elders without showing respect (giving a gift) for each is trying to make himself great before the others." Much surreptitious humor passes among the younger men at these meetings to the effect that "the old men are wasting their property: they are like a man with a hole in his full sack of rice who does not know why the chickens have come running."

These councils, which begin as informal court proceedings, often turn into history-making debates. A major disagreement arises and each elder stands in order of rank, to give his version of the past which has bearing upon the matter. As the narrations continue they become intricately enmeshed with mutual reference and subtle innuendo. At times, one or more of the old men will interrupt a speaker with an epithet, or turn to the watching crowd to shout a disclaimer. All the techniques of Gola "palaver" are used to dramatize one's own position at the expense of the others, and to convince the listeners of its reasonableness. Councils of this sort may continue for days, or be dropped for long intervals and reconvened at a later date. It is said of some councils that "the palaver has never finished, but hangs upon a hook for ever waiting to be taken down again."

It is customary, however, for councils to remain in session until a consensus is reached. This is often achieved by appealing to the oldest and most revered man among them to "settle this matter properly, or we shall seem as small boys before the people." Upon accepting the assignment, the old man may use any of a number of means to bring about a compromise. He may repeat the version of events he gave earlier in the meeting, he may reconstruct one of the other elder's versions which had been well received, or by astutely adjusting the essential features of all the presentations he may create a compromise version which brings him fame throughout the countryside. Once he has spoken under these conditions, his version of the matter becomes "the true history" produced by that particular council. All members of the community are admonished on the spot to remember it well so that they will know how they "came to be one people." Many elders conclude their speeches in such councils by turning to the assembled crowd and stating, "You are hearing your ancestors speak through us today: do not forget these things or you will be a stupid people!"

Despite these admonitions, each of the elders who has participated in the council will return to his own house, call his oldest sons and his brothers together, and reinstruct them concerning the original and unique family version of the matter. This will include much that he had not revealed in public—"the secrets which make our family strong and which others wish to learn in order to bring us low." The public consensus version is derided as "the proper truth of children and strangers," while the family version is praised as "the truth for grown men that will make them kings in the world."

But should the same elders be confronted with questions as to events prior to the earliest known ancestor or more general regional relations, the attitude and behavior is quite different. Here the responses will take such form as "that was before our old people knew themselves" (before the memory of the ancestors) or "the old people did not see that."

...

These considerations provide a clue to still another dimension of the Gola concept of the past. When the Gola elder speaks of his "old people" (*yun fa* or *yun gogo*) he is referring to all of his known ancestors. In the recent past these comprise a host of maternal, paternal and affinal relatives; but in the more distant past the host dwindles to the thin line of patrilineal descent of either the maternal or paternal side—though occasionally both are remembered—terminating in the founder of a town or the first known ancestor to have established himself in the area. In a few cases the route of migration to the area is known and the genealogical depth may be extended a generation or two, but this is rare. Genealogical depth varies slightly from section to section and offers some indication of the relative occurrences in time of the major Gola migrations from the homeland area. But there are many towns which are known to be far older than the earliest ancestor who appears in the genealogy. This ancestor may be thought to be the descendant of founders of the town, but his predecessors have been forgotten. A clear distinction is made between those "real" events which took place during the lives of the known ancestors and those dimly perceived and often mysterious events which may be attributed to the forgotten and unknown people of the far distant past.

Any responsible Gola elder will intersperse his historical account with frequent interjections of such comments as "This is what I have seen myself," or "My old people saw this and told it to me." As long as it is possible to state that a known ancestor reported the information personally to a descendant, and that by this process the information was at least conveyed to the one who is now speaking, the account is considered valid. "Fact" is what one has seen oneself or what has been reported to one by responsible persons who have seen it, or by still others whom they considered to be responsible. Thus "history" is made up of this kind of fact. There is no Gola term equivalent to the word "history" in English. *Ke yun fa* may be used loosely to mean "matters or things pertaining to the ancestors or the dead," but this is more like our phrase "days gone by." The closest approximation would be the word *kabande* which in one of its usages designates a whole class of tales which are meant to convey a moral lesson. "Parables" might be offered as an adequate translation of the term *kabande*. Another meaning of the term is "to put things in order."

...

The Gola respect for knowledge of the past is a response both to its instrumental value in solving problems of the present and its quality of sacredness as the thoughts and experiences of the ancestors. The test of validity is not the consistency or "fit" of a given version of past events, but whether or not the ancestors of the spokesman would be in agreement with the version. As the ancestors remain deeply concerned about their private interests, embodied in the prestige and property which they have passed down to their descendants, it follows that they prefer a view of the past which protects these interests. And though the elders of families are the custodians of knowledge of the past in this world, the ancestors are the final arbiters. It is taken for granted that the view of the past put forward by an elder will be the view which is most advantageous to him, his family, and his ancestors. Regardless of what may appear to the outsider as inconsistencies between rival family versions of the pasts, all is taken as the truth until that situation arises in which the past must be entered as evidence in a matter of honor or litigation. Then one's own version is held up as the truth and all others are characterized as incompetent. Should one fail to press one's family's interests in terms of a partisan appeal to the events of the past, the ancestors will take their revenge. Truth, then, is that which brings about the desired results, and no man can be blamed for stating what it is in his interests to state. He can only be blamed for lack of skill and failure to tie his own interests to issues sufficiently broad to attract an effective group in his support.

The ramifications of this approach to what is "true," or "fact," are great. The custodians of the true and the factual are those who possess the power to control the lives and the will of those about them. In the case of knowledge of the past, it is the ancestors and the elders who are the custodians. They have the power to bestow or withhold their blessings. One's parents, one's owner, or one's ruler may be the custodian of truth in other matters. Regardless of one's private opinions, one accepts publicly the authoritative statements of one's superiors. There is a famous and ironic Gola *say* (proverb) which advises, "When you are walking in the rain with the King listen to his words. He may look at the sky and say, 'See how the sun shines and how clear it is.' And you will say, 'Yes, King, the sun shines and the day has never been so clear.' " To correct the king, or to disagree with him, would imply one's equality or superiority. Thus there is a duality to truth: There is the truth which is accepted as such for practical reasons, or for reasons of good form; and there is the truth which one has learned through one's own experience, or which one's own judgment has selected.

Much of Gola humor emerges from a consciousness of this duality of truth based upon a hierarchy of authoritativeness. When the oldest elder has spoken—and should his view of a past event have diverged from that of others in significant detail—no one will contest it. Even in private the response to questioning about it would be "That is what he claims, that is what he knows." If the speaker had been a man of the same age or younger, he might be corrected or even ridiculed.

On one occasion, when the investigator had pressed for an explanation of the discrepancy between the genealogies of two families, an old man shook his head and said:

> You kwi (strangers from over the seas) want everything to be one way. We Gola see things in different ways. A country man does not hold himself so high as to think he can know what is true about everything. If someone higher than him says "This is how it was" then he does not question that. What more about it does he know? If his grandfather and his King tell him two different things, you would say they are two different things, and you would want to make palaver (dispute) to find which one was above the other. But how can one know whether a grandfather or a King is greater? A country man does not ask what is true by talking to the words, but he asks, "Who is it that said the words," and from that he decides what is right. But if the grandfather and the King say different, then it is not different to a country man. Both are true, but one must wait a while to understand that. No one can know everything at once.

40 Totemic Knowledge in New Guinea

Gregory Bateson

*Does each culture have its own characteristic cognitive
style? Bateson thought so. He even invented a technical
term, "eidos," to refer to the mode of thinking that was
typical for a given culture. In this excerpt from his famous account of the Iatmul, a New Guinea tribe, he
studies their remarkable mnemonic performances in an
effort to understand their "eidos." The analysis does not
seem entirely successful, perhaps because cultures do
not actually have general cognitive styles in Bateson's
sense. Nevertheless, his observations are by no means
unimportant; indeed, they are among the most intriguing to be found anywhere in the literature of memory.
Among other things, they show again how inappropriate the concept of "rote memory" is for the accomplishments of nonliterate people.*

Let us first consider the cultural stimulation of memory.[1] We have already seen that vast and detailed erudition is a quality which is cultivated
among the Iatmul. This is most dramatically shown in the debating about
names and totems, and I have stated that a learned man carries in his
head between ten and twenty thousand names. This figure was arrived at
by very rough estimation from the number of name songs possessed by
each clan, the number of names in each song, and the general ability of

---

[1] I have been much influenced in my own thinking about these problems by Professor Bartlett's book *Remembering*, 1932, which I read after my return from New
Guinea.

From Gregory Bateson (1958). *Naven*, 2nd edition. Stanford, Calif: Stanford University Press. Reprinted by permission of the publishers, Stanford University Press.

such men to quote, in considerable detail, from the name-cycles even of clans other than their own. The figure must therefore be accepted with caution, but it is certain that the erudition of these men is enormous.

Further it would seem that rote memory plays a rather small part in the achievement of these feats of memory. The names which are remembered are almost all of them compounds, each containing from four to six syllables, and they refer to details of esoteric mythology, so that each name has at least a leaven of meaning. The names are arranged in pairs, and the names in any one pair generally resemble each other much as the word Tweedledum resembles the word Tweedledee—with the notable difference that the altered syllable or syllables generally have some meaning and are connected together by some simple type of association, e.g. either by contrast or by synonymy. A progressive alteration of meaning may run through a series of pairs.

Thus the series of names contain tags of reference which would make it possible for them to be memorized either by processes of imagery or by word association. I collected a great quantity of these names and noticed again and again that the *order* in which the pairs were given was subject to slight but continual variation. There is a vaguely defined standard order for the recitation of every series of names. But I never heard any criticism of the order in which names were recited. In general, an informant will alter the order of his recitation slightly every time he repeats the series. Occasionally even, the pairing of the names is altered, but changes of this type are definitely regarded as mistakes.

Bartlett[2] has pointed out that one of the most characteristic qualities of rote remembering is the accuracy with which the chronological sequence of events or words can be recalled. So that from the continual alteration of the order in which the names are given we may deduce that the mental process used is not chiefly that of rote memory. Additional evidence for this conclusion may be drawn from the behavior of informants when they are endeavoring to recall an imperfectly remembered series of names. I do not remember ever to have heard an informant go back, like a European child, to the beginning and repeat the series of names, already given, in the hope that the "impetus" of rote repetition would produce a few more names. Usually my informants would sit and think and from time to time produce a name (or more often a pair), often with a query as to whether that name has already been given—as was frequently the case.

Again, when a Iatmul native is asked about some event in the past, he can as a rule give an immediately relevant answer to the question and does not require to describe a whole series of chronologically related events in order to lead up to the event in question. The Iatmul indulge

---

[2]*Remembering*, pp. 203, 264–266.

very little in the sort of chronological rigmarole which, as Bartlett has pointed out, is characteristic of those primitive peoples who have specialized in rote remembering.

[*Actually Bartlett did not think that rote remembering and chronological rigmarole were restricted to "primitive peoples"—he noted that a certain amount of "low-level remembering" occurs in all of us. And although he did suggest that some aspects of tribal social organization might encourage "rote recapitulation," that was probably a mistake. No "primitive peoples who have specialized in rote remembering" have ever been found.*]

One detail of the culture is worth mentioning as likely to promote the higher processes rather than rote memory. This concerns the technique of debating. In a typical debate a name or series of names is claimed as totemic property by two conflicting clans. The right to the name can only be demonstrated by knowledge of the esoteric mythology to which the name refers. But if the myth is exposed and becomes publicly known, its value as a means of proving the clan's right to the name will be destroyed. Therefore there ensues a struggle between the two clans, each stating that they themselves know the myth and each trying to find out how much their opponents really know. In this context, the myth is handled by the speakers not as a continuous narrative, but as a series of small details. A speaker will hint at one detail at a time—to prove his own knowledge of the myth—or he will challenge the opposition to produce some one detail. In this way there is, I think, induced a tendency to think of a story, not as a chronological sequence of events, but as a set of details with varying degrees of secrecy surrounding each—an analytic attitude which is almost certainly directly opposed to rote remembering.

But though we may with fair certainty say that rote memory is not the principal process stimulated in Iatmul erudition, it is not possible to say which of the higher processes is chiefly involved. There are, however, several details of the culture which point to visual and kinaesthetic imagery as likely to be of great importance. In debate, objects are continually offered for exhibition. For example, when the totemic ownership of the Sepik River was in dispute, a shell necklace was hung in the center of the ceremonial house to represent the river. In the debating, clan *A* claimed that the elephant grass which forms a conspicuous and picturesque fringe along the banks of the river was indubitably theirs; and that therefore the river must belong to them. They accordingly produced a beautiful spear decorated with leaves of the grass and pointed to it, saying "Our Iamb-wiuishi!!"[3] Clan *B* on the other hand claimed that the river was their

---

[3]The totemic name of the grass.

snake, Kindjin-kamboi, and their protagonist, Mali-kindjin, went off to get brightly colored leaves to ornament a representation of his snake which adorned one of the gongs in the ceremonial house. Again in a debate about the Sun, a number of the participants dressed themselves up to represent characters in a myth of origin of the Sun.

In the technique of debating the speaker uses bundles of leaves, beating on a table with them to mark the points of his speech. These leaves are continually used as visible or tangible emblems of objects and names. A speaker will say, "This leaf is So-and-so, I am not claiming that name," and he will throw the leaf across to the opposition. Or he may say, "This leaf is So-and-so's opinion," and he will throw it onto the ground with contempt; or he will sweep the ground with the leaves, brushing away his opponents' rubbishy statements. Similarly a small empty leaf packet is used as an emblem of some secret, of which the speaker is challenging the opposition to show a knowledge: he will hold it up asking them scornfully if they know what is inside it.

The proneness to visual or kinaesthetic thought is shown too in the continual tendency to diagrammatize social organization. In almost every ceremony, the participants are arranged in groups so that the total pattern is a diagram of the social system. In the ceremonial house the clans and moieties are normally allotted seats according to the totemic system of groupings: but when initiation ceremonies are to be performed this arrangement is discarded and in its place comes another based upon the cross-cutting initiatory moieties and grades.

Lastly we may cite the *naven* ceremonies as a further example of this proneness to visual and kinaesthetic thought. We have seen how the abstract geometrical properties of the kinship system are here symbolized in costume and gesture; and we may note this in passing as a contribution of eidology to our understanding of the ceremonies.

But the connection between the expression of eidos in the contexts which I have described, and the culture as a whole, is still not perfectly clear. I have illustrated the eidos chiefly from the totemic debating, and have shown that very great activity of memory is demanded and promoted in certain individuals by the sport of debating. Further, I have given facts which indicate that rote memory plays only a small part in this activity, while visual and kinaesthetic imagery appears to be important. In the special business of memorizing names, I showed that it is possible to suppose that word association plays a part. But these facts might well be isolated in their effects. On the one hand, the active cultivation of memory might be confined to a few selected specialists and, on the other hand, it might occur only in the special contexts in which names are important. Until these two possibilities have been examined, we cannot step from the facts given to the statement that the active development of memory has affected the culture as a whole and the *naven* ceremonies in particular.

We will first consider how far this activation can be supposed to have affected the whole community, and how far it is confined to a small minority of specialists. On the whole, the remarkable keenness in memorizing names is to be found in the majority of the men. When I was collecting the names, I got my material as far as possible from specialists, but it was noticeable that, even when I was talking about other matters with informants who would never have dared to pose as erudite in public debate, they would continually bring the talk round to matters connected with the totemic system and would attempt to give me lists of names. This was true, for example, of the informant . . . whom I have described . . . as conspicuously enthusiastic and inaccurate. He insisted upon discussing esoterica and giving lists of names belonging to his clan, full of blunders and contradictions. In the younger men, however, this passion for showing off even weakly developed erudition is almost completely checked by the feeling that erudition is only appropriate in senior men. I had three very intelligent youths who consistently avoided giving me names, and who referred me to their seniors when I pressed them. But I was told by other people in their absence that two of these youths were already well on the way towards erudition, and would be great debaters when they were older. Thus the reticence of the younger men on the subject of names does not imply that they are not, like their seniors, keen on this form of mental virtuosity.

But a more complete answer to the question of how the stimulation of a small number of specialists can react on the culture as a whole is provided by the fact that these specialists constantly set themselves up as unofficial masters of ceremonies, criticizing and instructing the men who are carrying out the intricacies of the culture. Their voice is heard not only in the debates which concern totemic names, but also in those on every subject from initiation to land tenure. Thus the culture is to a great extent in the custody of men trained in erudition and dialectic and is continually set forth by them for the instruction of the majority. From this we may be fairly certain that the individuals most affected by the stimulation of memory actually contribute very much more than their fellows to the elaboration and maintenance of the culture.

41 | Literacy, Cultural Familiarity, and "Intelligence" as Determinants of Story Recall

Ernest Frederick Dube

Although Bateson did pause to wonder whether the abilities he described might be "confined to a small minority of specialists," his aim was to describe the cognitive style of the Iatmul as a whole. Ethnologists rarely stress individual differences. Nevertheless, there is no reason to believe that people in distant lands are any more homogeneous than we are. In the thesis from which this selection is taken, Dube showed that illiterate villagers in Botswana have notions of "intelligence," "shrewdness," and other dimensions of human variation that are just as differentiated as our own. As the present experiment shows, they also vary a great deal in their ability to remember stories. Moreover, their "intelligence"—which Dube assessed by a method as remarkable as it is direct—accurately predicted how much they would remember, just as grade-point average predicted analogous performances by schoolchildren elsewhere in Botswana and in upstate New York.

Dube studied memory for stories—both African and European in origin—that were too long for any attempt at verbatim recall. His goal was to clarify the relation, if any, between memory and literacy. Do schooling and memorizing make memory worse, as some have suggested, or better, as most experiments using list-learning

❊ From E. F. Dube (1977). *A cross-cultural study of the relationship between "intelligence" level and story recall.* Doctoral Dissertation, Cornell University. Reprinted by permission.

procedures have found? Where story memory is concerned, Dube's results cast doubt on both alternatives. When one averages across individual differences, schooled and unschooled Africans did about equally well. (There was a wider range among the unschooled villagers, however. The "high intelligence" nonliterates recalled more and forgot less than any other subgroup in the study, while the "average" and "low intelligence" nonliterates were substantially below their schooled counterparts.) On the other hand, there was a striking difference between continents: Both African groups remembered much more than the American subjects did. Indeed, the best American subgroup was about on a par with the poorest African subgroups from either village or school.

This result is not difficult to explain. Although Dube himself sometimes speaks of a general "literacy/technology hypothesis" and sometimes of familiarity with specific skills, it seems to me that the latter factor is the important one. Members of a culture tend to excel in the skills which that culture encourages, at least if they have the talent to do so. (Incidentally, this principle explains why Westerners usually outperform people from traditional societies on IQ tests and similar academic tasks.) Many African cultures encourage story-telling; older children are often expected to tell stories to their younger siblings. In America, story-telling is rare. Stories may be read aloud or watched on television, but they are hardly ever told. This specific difference in cultural practices turned out to affect performance more than schooling itself; it was also more powerful than familiarity with particular types of stories (African or Western), which had a small effect as well.

Botswana is a land-locked African nation about the size of Texas. In the 1970s, when this research was done, it had a population of fewer than a million people. Perhaps 80 percent of them were illiterate, living in traditional villages and surviving by raising cattle and farming, though many men did migrant labor in South African mines. The people call themselves "Batswana" and claim kinship with other Tswana groups in Africa. Their language is called "Setswana." E. F. Dube, himself a Zulu who was born in South Africa, spoke a dialect of Setswana called "Sesotho" and was familiar with the Tswana people.

Dube's account of his first study is omitted here, but some grasp of his method is necessary to understand how the "intelligence" of the nonliterate subjects in the memory experiment was assessed. He visited many rural Botswana villages, interviewing small groups of nonliterate adult informants. He asked each group to discuss the meanings of thirteen previously selected Setswana words. All the words had some relation to intellectual ability or cognitive skill, but they differed from one another much as "wise," "cunning," "intelligent," and "clever" differ in English. The Batswana entered animatedly into these discussions, suggesting many examples to illustrate the meanings of the words. The upshot was that two Setswana words, "Botlhale" and "Lethalefi," represent notions rather similar to our "intelligence." "Botlhale" was the word used in the rating procedure, described below, by which the "intelligence" of the nonliterate subjects was assessed. The present selection begins with the method section of Dube's second study, which deals with memory for stories.

In this study we planned on using three groups of subjects; nonliterate Africans, African junior high school adolescents, and American junior high school adolescents. Since the African groups came from a rural community, their American counterparts were also sought from what may be a rural town: Albion, in upstate New York. While the two African groups shared the same cultural background and were part of a nontechnologically developed society, the American group came from a technologically developed society. However, the American group also had something in common with the African junior high school group: They were both literate. Thus on this score they are both different from the nonliterate African group. These similarities and differences were used to tease out the effects of literacy and cultural background.

1. "INTELLIGENCE"

The term "intelligence" in this study will be used to mean an individual's ability to perform well on a cognitive task. This ability is assumed to vary between individuals, regardless of culture or education. Since individual differences in the ability to perform well on cognitive tasks occur everywhere, judgments of "intelligence" in this sense must also occur everywhere. We assume, then, that adults who have been in a position to observe an individual in different situations that demand competence, over a long period, would be able to judge his "intelligence." The accuracy of such judgments is assumed to be comparable in validity to the grades a literate individual might receive in school.

In accordance with the above assumption a group of four or five adults, who had served as informants in our investigation of the Botswana concept of "intelligence," were asked to rate a group of subjects who had been brought before them.

The subjects to be rated came from the same villages as the adults who were to rate them. The subjects were made to stand in a row while the raters viewed them through a window some ten to fifteen yards away. The raters, who were all nonliterate, were asked to use their concept of *Botlhale* to rate the subjects into three groups, namely: High "intelligent," Average "intelligent," and Low "intelligent." To make certain that each rater knew which subject was being rated at every occasion, the experimenter's assistant at a signal would point at the subject to be rated. The subjects themselves did not know why they were being pointed out, or what the adults were doing inside the office. They were beyond earshot.

After the raters had seen the subjects, they were asked individually how they rated that particular individual. There were few problems in deciding which subjects were obviously High and which were obviously Low. The problem arose when the Average group was being rated. Some raters would rate a subject up instead of in the middle, and another down, also instead of in the middle. To resolve such differences in opinions, each rater was asked to state his/her reason for thinking that a certain subject should not fall under Average group but with the High or Low group, as the case might be. A short discussion was allowed so that other raters might advance their differences with a particular speaker they differed with on the reasons to rate High or Low. Usually a quick decision was reached. In most cases one rater might have used one criterion for his/her rating when others might have used more than one. The main criterion used in backing up one's argument was usually a situation or a number of them when the rated subject had failed to show or had shown that he had ability or did not have the ability to be rated High or Low. There were a few occasions when unanimity failed altogether. In such cases a majority principle was employed, unless it was in the opinion of the experimenter that the minority view was sound, in which case longer discussion was allowed to make it possible for a unanimous decision to be reached. Where it was felt necessary, the experimenter asked probing questions to assist in the discussion.

...

In the case of literate subjects, who were all adolescents enrolled in school, current year grade averages were used to categorize them into the three "intelligence" groups. In Botswana the grades were obtained from the principal of the school, while in America they were obtained from the student advisor's office. The ratings in these groups were based on the subject's grade average for the current year. Subjects were obtained through an announcement during morning assembly. Those who wished to participate in the experiment were asked to enlist through the principal (or the student advisor's office in the case of American subjects). This resulted in a somewhat biased sample: the volunteers came from among those students with relatively high grade averages. For example, in the American group only students above 70 came forth as volunteers, and among the Botswana group only those above 50. This fact caused a difference in the criteria for assignment to the subgroups. Thus, whereas in America the Low group was composed of subjects whose grade averages were between 70 and 79, with the Botswana group this group was made up of subjects whose grades were 50 to 65. The other grades' breakdowns were, for the American subjects, 80 to 85 for the middle "intelligence" group, and 86 upwards for the high group; while in Botswana the breakdown was 66 to 79 and 80 upwards, respectively.

In both school settings, additional steps were necessary to fill up each intelligence level to balance the groups. The procedure was to ask the principal or the students' advisor to approach some students who had not volunteered originally. In this way we were able to balance the groups.

...

2. SUBJECTS

As already indicated above, there were three groups of subjects: nonliterate Africans, Africans attending junior high school, and Americans also attending junior high school. Fifteen of the 36 nonliterate African subjects were male, the rest female. The ages of the nonliterates were mostly estimated by making use of an event that occurred during or at about the time of the subject's date of birth. For example, one subject said he was born soon after the mine strike in the Republic (South Africa). There have not been many strikes in South Africa by miners, so it was fairly easy to pinpoint this to the 1946 mine strike. This subject's age was then estimated to be 29 years. Thirty of these subjects had estimated ages between 14 and 20 years; the other six were older.

There were also 36 junior high school African subjects. Of this group 20 were male and 16 were female. Their ages ranged between 14 and 19 years. The American junior high school group consisted of 24 subjects, 12 male and 12 female. Their ages ranged between 14 and 18 years.

3. EXPERIMENTAL DESIGN

The experimental design for this study was a 3 × 3 × 3 × 2 design. . . . There were three main groups: one nonliterate African group, one literate African group, and one literate American group. . . . There were three subgroups within each main group . . . High "intelligent," Average "intelligent," and Low "intelligent." There were also three recall periods: immediate recall, that is a recall taken soon after the presentation; one recall taken a week after the first recall; and one taken five weeks after the first recall. Finally, there were two types of stories: two from African folk tales and two from European fairy tales.

. . .

4. STIMULI

. . . For inclusion a story had to meet certain basic requirements: It had to be complex, that is, it had to be long and consist of at least three characters and a number of episodes. It had to be understandable and internally consistent, unlike the "War of the Ghosts" used by Bartlett, which was in some parts ambiguous and disjointed. It had to be easily translatable from the language of its origin to the language used by each group of subjects as mother tongue. It had to be . . . unfamiliar to any of the groups used as subjects in this experiment. Two of the stories had to have a Western background and two an African background.

The stories used in this study [were] . . . *Maakga and Inkanyamba, Lintswe and Mapule, The Hunter, His Wife and the Gazelle,* and *Jorinda and Joringel.* [*The text of* Maakga and Inkanyamba *appears in the Appendix to this section.*]

Each story was translated from its original language to the language of the other group of subjects by two bilingual translators (English and Setswana). One translator translated from English into Setswana, and the other from Setswana to English. This means each story was translated twice, once away from its own language and then back to its own language. This form of translation is called "backtracking," and its purpose is to ensure that the translation was as correct as is possible. . . .

After all translations had been done and checked for consistency, the stories were then recorded into tapes for use as stimuli. For the English version a native English-speaking American male recorded the stories for use in America, and for the Setswana version a Setswana native male recorded the stories for use among Botswana subjects. Thus, each group of subjects listened to the stories spoken in their own mother tongue, and spoken by a native male voice. The stories were presented at a normal speaking pace and voice, neither loud nor too soft.

5. SCORING

In this work we [*used the*] . . . method of breaking down the story into idea units. Our method . . . takes into account inferred ideas and does not consider these as intrusions. Our scoring method differentiates between *Themes* and *Episodes*, but . . . we do not expect that [*either type of unit*] . . . will be remembered verbatim. The words as they are, are not considered to be as important as the sense they deliver when recalled.

The following was our scoring procedure:

a. Themes

A Theme is here defined as a combination of words that convey a single idea. The number of words used to convey that single idea is not of any importance. At times it does happen that two ideas become so interlinked that their separation becomes difficult. This happens when one of the two ideas that are linked would be rendered awkward, or become clumsily formulated by a separation. In such a case the two ideas are left interlinked as though they actually were a single idea for scoring purposes. The following is an example of this level of scoring:

> *Maakga was a likeable boy,/jovial and full of jokes./*
> *He loved hunting,/and he was very good at it./*

Each . . . group of words constitutes a Theme by our definition.

▩

b. Episodes

Episodes were the most important units of analysis in our scoring procedure. An episode is a combination of Themes that describe an occurrence of an event. An occurrence of an event is usually preceded by an introduction which sets the stage for an event, and it usually ends with a consequence which is a result of that happening. . . . The following is an example of an Episode [*from* Jorinda and Joringel]:

> *One day they walked until the sun was about to set and they suddenly realized that they were lost! At the same time they found that they were unable to speak nor to move! They were filled with fear.*

As it can be observed from the example above, an Episode begins with a setting of the stage or the scene which is then followed by an actual event or happening which is the heart of an Episode and it then ends with a consequence that is traceable to that happening. A consequence, then, usually heralds the end of an Episode. Episodes are scored similarly as Themes. There are two points for a correctly remembered Episode, and one point for a partially remembered one, regardless of the degree of its completeness. Remembering does not have to be verbatim to be considered correct.

We have already indicated that Episodes were considered more important units of analysis in this study. The main reason for this is that Episodes more than Themes are an approximation of how information is usually found in the real world. Information is not found in bits but in something more complete, such as an event, with a beginning and a meaningful end. On the other hand, a Theme can begin but end somewhere in the air. For example, consider Theme 20 in the story of *The Hunter*. "Go back" is a complete idea, but the real meaning of *go back* where and for what can only be understood fully by either referring to what went on before or what follows thereafter, but never when it is by itself.

Scoring was done by one person, an undergraduate student who had been taught by the experimenter in the use of his scoring system. To check whether the scorer had a full understanding of this scoring method and also whether the method was consistent between two scorers, a third person was brought in, a graduate student who was also taught by the experimenter for this purpose. When the two scorers were compared it was found that their scores were identical in four out of five papers scored, while the remaining one differed by one point.

Since the experimenter himself was involved in this checking and his scores had been similar to those of the main scorer, it was concluded that not only is the system working, but that the scorer was also competent.

6. PRESENTATION

Each subject was presented with the stories and tested individually. A subject was brought into the experimental room (a small office provided for our use by a chief) by the experimenter's assistant. The subject was then given a seat (chair) which had been placed in front of a small table on which stood a Sony portable cassette tape recorder. A subject was allowed some time to calm down before the experiment began. Some subjects took longer than others to calm down, and the experimenter then became obliged to provide some distraction that would help to settle a subject. These distractions took the form of jokes and teasing. As soon as the experimenter was satisfied that the subject was sufficiently at ease, the following instructions were given:

You are going to be presented with two stories which we hope you will find as interesting as we find them to be. They are very long stories, so please listen to them very carefully because they will be presented to you only once, and their recall will be asked from you. They will be presented to you at the rate of one story at a time, and then its recall will be taken followed by the second story and then its recall also. The stories will come to you through this tape recorder in front of you. Because the stories are very long you may not remember every word in them, but still do try to remember as much of each as you can. Your recalls will be taped to conserve time. Is everything clear? Do you have any questions before we begin? Now please get ready, here is the first story.

The tape recorder was turned on as soon as the subject indicated that he/she was ready for presentation. . . . After each presentation tape recorders were changed, one used for presentation only and the other used for recording only. After the recall had been taken for the first story there was a short break to allow the resetting of the second story. . . . Before presenting the second story the subject was again warned to get ready, and then the recorder was turned on, and later its recall taken as well. At the end of the two story presentations and recalls, subjects were thanked but not warned about the subsequent requests for recalls that would be made a week and a month later.

RESULTS

The results of [the episode analysis are presented in Table 41-1 and Figure 41-1]. . . . All the results were analyzed with the BMD revised computer program with a four-way ANOVA. . . . Where necessary a Bonferroni t test was used for further breakdown.

An inspection of [Table 41-1 and Figure 41-1] reveals the following information:

a. That African subjects as a whole show better recalls as compared to the American group. The BMD analysis of variance reveals that there was a significant difference between the two cultural groups (African and American groups) ($F = 63.31, p < .001$). A Bonferroni t test also confirms this by revealing that there was no significant difference between the two African groups ($t = 0.21$), but there was a significant difference between nonliterate African subjects and American subjects ($t = 4.01, p < .01$), and between literate Africans and Americans ($t = 4.20, p < .01$).

b. . . . That "intelligence" had a substantial effect on performance. The High-intelligence subjects, taken across cultural groups, had a mean score of 17.74 while the Average subjects had a mean score of

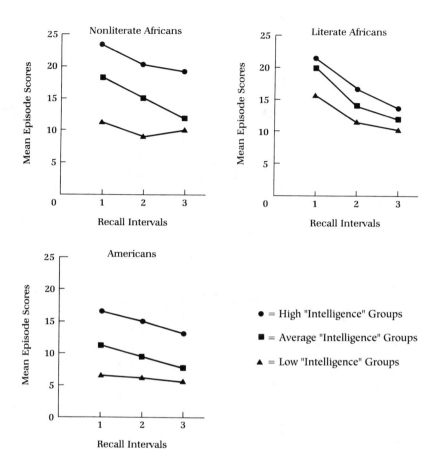

Figure 41-1 *Mean recall episodes by three main groups (nonliterate Africans, literate Africans, and Americans).*

13.70, and the Low groups had a mean score of 10.57. This reveals a significant difference of ($F = 59.38$, $p < .001$) on the BMD program. A Bonferroni t test shows that the three groups were significantly different from each other (high vs. average, $t = 4.59$, $p < .01$).

c. ... That the High "intelligent" group among the nonliterate outperforms every other group in this experiment. And also that this group, while remembering more than all other groups, also forgets the least, thus showing the importance of considering both culture and "intelligence" in studies of this kind. The interaction between culture and "intelligence" level was significant on the BMD program ($F = 5.78$, $p < .001$).

(*text continues on page 438*)

TABLE 41-1

Mean episode scores for recall from two European and two African stories by different "intelligence" and cultural groups. (Each perfectly recalled episode counts 2 points.)

Nonliterate Africans (12 Ss per cell)

"Intelligence":	High			Average			Low			Total Mean
Type of story:	African	European	Mean	African	European	Mean	African	European	Mean	
Immediate Recall	24.25	23.08	23.67	18.00	17.25	17.63	12.25	12.08	12.17	17.82
After 1 Week	22.25	21.25	21.75	15.25	14.92	15.09	10.83	11.08	10.96	15.93
After 1 Month	21.17	19.92	20.55	13.58	13.08	13.33	10.00	10.08	10.04	14.64
Mean	22.56	21.42	21.99	15.61	15.08	15.35	11.03	11.08	11.06	16.13
Dif. bet. 1 & 3 R.	3.08	3.16	3.12	4.42	4.17	4.30	2.25	2.00	2.13	3.18
1st & 3rd % dif.	12.70	13.69	13.18	24.56	24.17	24.39	18.37	16.56	17.50	17.85

Literate Africans (12 Ss per cell)

"Intelligence":	High			Average			Low			Total Mean
Type of story:	African	European	Mean	African	European	Mean	African	European	Mean	
Immediate recall	23.08	21.83	22.46	21.17	20.42	20.80	17.33	16.33	16.83	20.03
After 1 Week	17.83	16.25	17.04	17.00	14.33	15.67	14.25	11.33	12.79	15.17
After 1 Month	16.03	14.67	15.38	15.41	13.67	14.54	13.58	11.50	12.54	14.15
Mean	18.98	17.58	18.29	17.86	16.14	17.00	15.05	13.05	14.05	16.45
Dif. bet. 1 & 3 R.	7.05	7.16	7.08	5.76	6.75	6.26	3.75	4.83	4.29	5.88
1st & 3rd % dif.	30.55	32.80	31.52	27.21	33.06	30.10	21.64	29.58	25.49	29.36

Americans (8 Ss per cell)

"Intelligence":	High			Average			Low			Total Mean
Type of story:	African	European	Mean	African	European	Mean	African	European	Mean	
Immediate recall	15.88	15.63	15.76	11.13	11.38	11.26	7.25	7.75	7.50	11.50
After 1 Week	11.50	11.75	11.63	8.00	8.37	8.19	5.25	6.88	6.07	8.63
After 1 Month	11.50	11.38	11.44	7.00	6.63	6.83	5.13	6.63	5.88	8.05
Mean	12.96	12.92	12.94	8.71	8.79	8.75	5.88	7.09	6.48	9.39
Dif. bet. 1 & 3 R.	4.38	4.25	4.32	4.13	4.75	4.43	2.12	1.12	1.62	3.45
1st & 3rd % dif.	27.58	27.19	27.41	37.11	41.74	39.34	29.24	14.45	21.60	30.00

All Groups

"Intelligence":	High			Average			Low			Total Mean
Type of story:	African	European	Mean	African	European	Mean	African	European	Mean	
Overall means	18.17	17.30	17.74	14.06	13.34	13.70	10.65	10.41	10.53	13.99

Difference between 1 & 3 R. = Difference between immediate recall and recall after one month.
1st & 3rd % dif. = Percentage difference between immediate recall and recall after one month.

d. . . . That nonliterate African High subgroup and the nonliterate Low group, together with the American Low group, forget less than the other groups. However, it can be argued that the two Low groups had started on a lower baseline as compared to the other groups, and they therefore had less to remember from the very beginning. This argument, while it is correct in the case of the two Low groups mentioned here, would not be true in the case of the nonliterate High group because they started on a higher baseline than any of the groups in this experiment.

e. The BMD F test reveals that when all groups are averaged across, there was significant forgetting over recall intervals ($F = 236.43$, $p < .001$). An inspection of Table 41-1 shows that this forgetting occurred greatly between the first and second recall intervals. Between the second and the third there was little forgetting in relative terms.

f. The BMD program reveals that there was an interaction between recalls and cultural group ($F = 14.37$, $p < .000$). In absolute terms the American group and nonliterate group showed about an equal amount of forgetting (3.45 and 3.18 respectively in Episode scores), as compared to 5.88 for the literate African group. In percentage terms, however, the nonliterate African group show much less forgetting as compared to either of the two literate groups (13.18, 24.39, and 17.50 for the three intelligence levels, as compared to 31.52, 30.10, and 25.49 for the literate African group, and 27.41, 39.34, and 21.60 for the American group). To be sure, both the Average and Low nonliterate African groups began at a lower baseline than corresponding literate African groups. The nonliterate High-intelligence level group, however, started at a higher baseline and showed less forgetting as compared to all other groups in this study. As a group, nonliterate subjects tend to show less forgetting than literate subjects ($M = 17.85$ percent as compared to 29.36 percent for literate African and 30.00 percent for the American group).

. . . There was a tendency in all three main groups to forget less in stories taken from cultures that are similar to their own than in culturally dissimilar stories. This tends to support Bartlett's theory of the cultural biasing of memory. However, the trend is a weak one.

g. There was also a significant interaction between recalls and intelligence levels ($F = 7.27$, $p < .001$). In absolute terms, the Low-intelligence level subjects tended to forget the least (Mean for Low groups = 3.69, while that of the Average group was 5.00, and for the High groups it was 4.85). This was also true in percentage terms (21.53, 31.28, and 24.04 respectively). These results are at a glance surprising, but when you look at Table 41-1, you realize that the Low groups began at a low baseline, meaning they had little information to remember, and therefore, they had also little information to forget.

h. The analysis of variance reveals another marginal significant interaction between type of story and cultural group ($F = 4.40$, $p < .015$). The direction here again is in favor of the Bartlett theory, even though weak as previously shown.

···

[*The results of Dube's analysis of what he called* themes, *"smaller" idea units than* episodes, *are omitted here. They closely parallel the* episode *data.*]

CONCLUSION

The results of this study support the hypothesis that there are wide differences *within* cultural and educational groups in the ability to recall stories, and that these differences can be predicted on the basis of the subject's rated "intelligence"—thus validating the rating procedure. The more "intelligent" subjects, as determined by ratings or grade averages, performed better than the others. Formal education did not prove to be the main determining factor in performance of the task set for this study.

There was a weak support for Bartlett's theory in that subjects did tend to remember better those stories which were related to their cultures. The fact that the American group did not perform better or even equal to the African subjects on the European type of stories does weaken the Bartlett theory. However, the literacy/technology hypothesis was more strongly supported by this study. Both African groups performed higher than the American group even on those stories which are Western in origin. As pointed out under "Background," Botswana, from which the two groups of African subjects came, is still largely a traditional society and therefore less technologically developed as compared to the American culture and society.

The above results support a hypothesis that familiarity with doing something, rather than its mere presence in a culture, leads to better performance. Although the American subjects performed poorly in this task as compared to the African subjects, there is no reason to believe that this had anything to do with their intelligence. Rather, it probably had something to do with their not being practiced in the skills required for story recalls. The interactions among culture, intelligence, and familiarity that were shown in this study seem to suggest that . . . explanations that consider one factor as an explanation for high or poor performance may be oversimplifying the causal relationships. . . .

APPENDIX: THE STORY OF MAAKGA AND INKANYAMBA

[*Note: The 99 themes are indicated by numbers; the 18 episodes are indicated by spacing.*]

Story Introduction

1. Maakga was a son of a warlike king.
2. He was to become his father's successor to the throne.
3. From childhood,
4. he was assigned a group of boys of his own age,
5. to be his attendants.
6. Maakga was a likeable boy,
7. jovial and full of jokes.
8. He loved hunting,
9. and he was very good at it.
10. His choice and love of dangerous spots
11. were always a source of anxiety to his mother,
12. and yet she knew that he had to show bravery
13. if he was to be respected as his father's son.

Episodes Begin

14. One day he called on his companions,
15. and asked them to go for a hunt with him
16. on the following day.
17. Asking was a mere formality,
18. they could not say no to their future king.
19. So they all said yes.

20. That evening the boys began to make preparations for the following day's hunt.
21. Early on the following day,
22. they began their long journey.

23. They walked for miles through thick forests and plains

24. without spotting any game to kill.
25. At last, they saw a large herd of game,
26. and they began to kill as many as they thought they could carry.

27. They had traveled far,
28. and they were now tired and hungry.
29. They carried their meat,
30. and searched for wood to roast their meat.
31. They could see no wood near by,
32. except a small little bush further on.
33. They dragged themselves to it,
34. sat and kindled a fire.
35. There, they roasted their meat and ate.

36. After eating, they felt even more thirsty.
37. The meat, the sun, and the walk had all contributed to their thirst.
38. They needed water,
39. but they could not remember passing a stream near by.
40. As though they were bewitched,
41. their thirst became unbearable.
42. They took what was remaining of their meat and walked.
43. Ultimately, they saw a stream.

44. They joyfully ran to the stream,
45. but did not forget the ways of their fathers.
46. The sons of high officials drank first,
47. just to test if the water was safe for their Prince.
48. It was safe.

49. Maakga then knelt to drink,
50. but no sooner than he knelt,
51. the stream dried up.
52. To no other member of the group did this happen.

53. They pondered for a while,
54. and then one of them remembered a story told to him by his grandmother,
55. some years ago.

56. The story was about Inkanyamba the king of streams.

57. Maakga had no choice,
58. to drink, he had to make a promise to Inkanyamba.
59. The promise was that he would give to Inkanyamba the first thing he will see when he gets back home.
60. He made the promise.

61. To his greatest sorrow,
62. the first thing he met was his youngest sister,
63. the thing he loved the most.
64. He became very sad.

65. the little girl who had come running to meet her brother
66. was surprised to find her brother sad.
67. She demanded to know the reason for his sadness.
68. He then told her the whole dreadful story.
69. On hearing the story, she said,
70. "Do not worry, I am still too young,
71. the snake will not come to take me."

72. Days ran into months and months to years without a sign of a snake.
73. But on the day she was to be declared a woman, it appeared.
74. It could be seen from afar uprooting trees
75. and flattening houses on its path.
76. It was coming in a form of a storm.

77. Maakga, realizing what all this meant,
78. he ran to his uncle to tell him of the dreadful story.

79. On hearing the story,
80. his uncle summoned the household and began to give quick instructions.
81. the girl was to take a bath.
82. She was to keep calm, alone in her hut.
83. Her whole body was medicated,
84. in addition, she was given some medicine to conceal in her hand.

85. This she was told to pass over the snake's nostrils.

86. On reaching the yard, the storm ceased
87. and the snake appeared for everyone to see.
88. It immediately declared, "I have come for my wife."
89. It then headed for the girl's hut.
90. The girl unafraid, invited the snake in.
91. It crawled to her, resting its ugly head on her lap.
92. The little girl did as she had been told,
93. she caressed his head, while passing the concealed medicine over his nostrils.

94. The snake went limp,
95. and he began to snore.

96. The girl then ran to her uncle who came in running.
97. He and Maakga chopped the snake's head first,
98. and then its body.
99. They kindled a fire and burned the snake to ash.

42 | Two Approaches to Learning a Theatrical Script

Helga Noice and Tony Noice

This selection contrasts two remarkably effective methods of memorization. The first is familiar to everyone who has ever browsed the "Psychology" section of a bookstore in search of ways to improve his or her own memory abilities. It is the ancient art of memory, based on the systematic use of images and other mnemonic devices, now over 2,000 years old and still being rediscovered and modernized by new authors in every generation. The second, even more familiar in its results but perhaps also more mysterious in its methods, is what actors do in learning their lines for a play. They certainly do not use the image-based art of memory; what do they do instead? Noice and Noice propose that the very act of taking a script seriously—studying it in depth—automatically produces memory for the lines themselves. By the time actors really understand why their characters utter just these words on just this occasion, those words themselves have become integral parts of their understanding of the play as a whole. It is an intriguing suggestion.

Audiences are amazed when leading actors in plays such as *Hamlet* or *Cyrano de Bergerac* deliver over three hours of verbal material flawlessly and without hesitation. Spectators also marvel when a professional

❈ From *Memory*, 4, 1–17.

mnemonist correctly names every person in an audience of hundreds after meeting them only once shortly before the performance.

In both these cases recall has been proven to be verbatim. Oliver and Ericsson (1986) showed that professional actors' performance of their parts is very exact and audience members verify that the information they supply to the mnemonist (names, social security numbers, telephone numbers, etc.) is precisely remembered. However, even though actors and mnemonists recall to-be-remembered material verbatim, the material itself is very different. The actor recalls lengthy connected discourse; the mnemonist recalls large numbers of individual facts or items.

Since the late 1980s we have been examining the nature of professional actors' expertise (Noice, 1991, 1992, 1993; Noice & Noice, 1993, 1994, in press). These studies revealed that actors generally do not set out to learn the exact words of the script but rather to determine the plans of their characters by analysing their needs, desires, and motivations. Actors find that eventually the deep probing involved in this analysis results in verbatim retention of the dialogue. As one subject put it (Noice, 1992, p. 420), ". . . I don't really memorize. There is no effort involved. There seems to be no process involved: it just happens. One day early on, I know the lines."

What is fascinating about this result is that the type of meaning-based strategy that actors appear to use has repeatedly been shown to result in recall of the *gist* of complex discourse but rarely of the exact wording (e.g., Anderson, 1974; Begg, 1971; Bransford, Barclay, & Franks, 1972; Bransford & Franks, 1971; Brewer, 1975; Brewer & Hay, 1984; Cofer, Chmielewski, & Brockway, 1976; Gomulicki, 1956; Perfetti & Garson, 1973; Sachs, 1967, 1974). However, in one of our experiments (Noice, 1993), actors using this strategy recalled 42% of a 6-page script verbatim (or almost verbatim) after only 20 minutes of study. This raises a question: Why does a strategy that usually results in retaining primarily the main ideas of a text result in verbatim learning when employed by actors? We believe that a probable reason is that the actor attends closely to the exact wording of the script for the purpose of gaining clues to interpretation. For instance, a character who uses formal language with friends is apt to be a different sort of person from one who uses slang in most situations.

As an anecdotal example, one actor reported playing the mayor in the play, *The Front Page* (Hecht & MacArthur, 1949). The mayor says to a reporter: "Don't pester me now, please." The actor inferred from the use of the word *pester* that the mayor thought of the reporter as a bothersome child, as the term is generally used with children. We conjecture that this elaboration would necessarily make the term *pester* memorable. That is, an actor would not inadvertently substitute *annoy* or *bother* or any other synonym, because he had specifically attended to the exact word *pester* and had come up with a reason why that character would use that word and not some other. Furthermore, the mayor, not wanting to alienate a reporter, softens the statement by adding "please." In addition, the egotistical mayor might be proud of his use of alliteration, further ensuring recall of the line, "Don't pester me now, please."

We feel that it is this type of extra attention to the exact wording that produces verbatim results with a learning strategy that normally only produces recall of the gist. However, the retrospective protocols we had used in the early experiments were not detailed enough to confirm this. Therefore, we performed another experiment employing a think-aloud protocol to get a closer picture of one actor's script-study process (Noice & Noice, 1994). As expected, this protocol was far more complete (over four times as long as the average of the retrospective ones obtained in our 1991 study). This afforded an extreme close-up of one actor's script-learning process, and it provided a close look at the actor's fine-grained inquiry into the motivations and intentions of the character as derived from the content, linguistic structure, and author's parenthetical additions to the script. In overall content it was very similar to the ones previously collected but, having been dictated *during* script study, it showed the actor's analytical process in action. Almost every line of the script was mined for clues as to the characters, situations, or relationships. For example concerning a line of dialogue, the subject said, "Then we get back to cynicism or possibly a bitterness, *'Why should I care if Monica came back here or not.'* Trying to shrug it off, trying to deny the emotion; again important."

It seems probable, as this think-aloud protocol was very much in keeping with the previously collected retrospective protocols, that this close attention to the exact wording is a defining feature of an actor's memory process. One of the purposes of the presently reported experiment was to determine the generaliseability of this one actor's fine-grained examination of the exact words of the text to ascertain the underlying meaning. Another purpose was to see if other actors had different ways of applying this technique, or indeed if they had entirely different approaches.

On the surface, it would appear that there is little in common between actors' strategies as we uncovered them in our research and mnemonists' strategies as described in books such as *Remembering people: The key to success* (Lorayne, 1975) and *The memory book* (Lorayne & Lucas, 1974). However, this could not be said with certainty, as the methods a mnemonist might use to learn a theatrical script word for word have never been described in detail. Therefore, the presently reported study set out to determine if there are any areas of commonalities between actors' strategies and those a professional mnemonist might use when learning the same theatrical scene verbatim.

It is obvious that the analytical approach of actors differs radically from the imagery/association methods usually employed by entertainers who make a living giving mnemonic demonstrations. However, at least one well-known actress, Anne Bancroft, has been quoted as saying that during script learning she uses the mnemonic methods taught by Harry Lorayne (1985). Therefore the Lorayne method must be capable of handling complex discourse as well as the sorts of discrete items Lorayne uses as examples in his books. In order to examine how this approach differs from the one used by the actors in our studies, we asked Mr. Lorayne to also generate a think-aloud protocol using the same script. It should be emphasized that theatrical scripts are almost always committed to memory over an entire rehearsal period (which runs at least two weeks and often four or more) and that even Mr. Lorayne, whose demonstrations routinely consist of recalling material after only a single exposure, advises those who need to learn scripts that, in addition to his visualize-and-link approach, they should go over the material many, many times (Lorayne, 1957, 1985). Therefore, the six actors and Mr. Lorayne were *not* asked to memorize the script but rather to go through a single pass of the six pages trying simultaneously to verbalize all their thoughts. What was important to us was not how much they retained from one detailed read-through (as they always do repeated read-throughs) but what the *process* was during learning.

The methods by which mnemonists generally learn factual material have been subject to a great deal of study in the psychological literature (for reviews, see Bellezza, 1981; Bower, 1970; Higbee, 1988; see also Herrmann, 1991). One of the most frequently used approaches by mnemonists is to form images for the to-be-remembered facts and link them together so as to form a single combined image. For example, to remember telephone and cigarettes, one could visualize cigarettes flying out of the mouthpiece of a phone. For each additional to-be-remembered item, one would form a new picture linking the new item to the last remembered item.

Another approach consists of pre-memorizing a list of "peg" words to which material is linked. The best known example of a peg-word mnemonic is probably "one is a bun, two is a shoe, three is a tree," etc. If the first to-be-remembered item is a basketball, the mnemonist might picture a basketball instead of a hamburger on a bun. Recalling *bun* would bring back the image of the basketball. A more complex peg-word system is sometimes referred to as analytic substitution (Loisette, 1899; see also Norman, 1976) or the figure alphabet (cf. Gordon, Valentine, & Wilding, 1984). Here each digit is represented by a consonant sound (e.g. t = 1, n = 2, m = 3). Peg words are built from these sounds using whatever additional vowel sounds are necessary to construct visualizable words. Thus, the digit 1 could be represented by tie (or toe, or tea, etc.); 2 could be represented by Noah; 3 by Ma; 12 by tin; 13 by team; etc. In addition to constructing peg words, mnemonists use this device to remember addresses, dates, credit card numbers, etc.

Mnemonic devices such as these have also been employed to enhance retention of speeches and prose paragraphs. However, in this case, generally the main ideas are remembered, not the word-for-word text (e.g. Gruneberg, 1978; Krebs, Snowman, & Smith, 1978; Snowman, Krebs, & Lockhart, 1980). Later these main ideas can serve as retrieval cues for reconstructing the gist of the speech or passage. However, our interest was in how actors' learning strategies compared to those of an expert mnemonist when complex material must be retained word-for-word. It was considered essential in this experiment to inform the subjects that there would *not* be a subsequent memory test because, if they were expecting one, they might modify their natural strategies to comply with what they perceived as task demands. This enabled us to compare, on a line-by-line basis, the mental processes involved during the first pass through of a theatrical script. The amount and accuracy of recall of the same script has already been addressed in previous studies (e.g. Noice, 1993).

METHOD

Subjects

Six male actors and one male mnemonist participated in this study. All of the actors were full-time professionals with at least 10 years of experience in major New York or regional theatres. None of them had ever performed the script in question. The mnemonist was Harry Lorayne, whose 15 books on memory for the general public have literally sold millions of copies over the last 37 years and have been translated into 14 languages.

Materials

Materials consisted of a scene (six manuscript pages containing 41 idea units for the male character) from the play *The second man* by S. N. Behrman (1949) that we had used in our previous research (Noice, 1991). It consists of a conversation between a man and a woman concerning love and possible infidelity.

Procedure

All subjects were given a copy of the scene and a small tape recorder. They were instructed to read the scene over once to see what it was about, then to go back to the beginning, turn on the tape recorder and attempt to begin learning the scene as if they were preparing for a performance. Specifically they were instructed to use whatever procedures they would use normally if this was their first study session with a script that they would eventually perform from memory. Subjects were asked not to censor anything, but to verbalise their thoughts as they proceeded line by line through the script. All of the tapes were then transcribed for analysis.

Coding

Analysis of the actors' protocols revealed that all utterances consisted of either exploring the content of the playscript or explaining the subjects' methods of approaching the learning of it. In either case, each utterance was in the nature of an explanation and therefore we used as a unit of analysis what we termed an explanatory unit (EU). These EUs ranged from a single sentence to a full page, but in every case they were devoted to a single aspect of analysis. Furthermore, we sorted these units into 12 categories:

1. *Background.* Statements speculating on or investigating such factors as location, time of day, occupations of the characters, etc.

2. *Interactions.* Statements concerning mental or emotional interactions between characters in which one character affects, tries to affect, or is affected by, another character. Also categorized in this manner are statements regarding interactions between the character and characters not present in the scene but talked about.

3. *Traits.* Statements regarding enduring character traits, such as shyness or sophistication.

4. *Importance.* Statements regarding the relative importance of particular lines because they summed up a situation or revealed the specific nature of an interaction.

5. *Memorization.* Statements regarding the relative ease or difficulty of learning certain lines and/or the reasons why particular lines would be memorable. This category contained five sub-categories: repetition of same words in responses as in cue lines; references to events that had actually occurred previously on-stage; visualization of events that dialogue referred to but which did not occur on-stage; extraction of underlying meaning before memorization; lines being prompted by movement such as saying "Hello" after shaking hands.

6. *Response/Initiative.* Statements noting whether a particular line or section was a response to the other character's preceding line or the introduction of new subject matter.

7. *Linguistic Information.* Statements that focused on such elements as length of words or speeches.

8. *Performance Aspects.* Statements regarding how the subject would use the information in the script to enhance performance.

9. *Style.* Statements focusing on or speculating on the style of language, the era of the play, the genre of the play, the playwright's other works, etc.

10. *Directorial Input.* Statements regarding interpretation of lines or sections that might change based on the director's eventual choice.
11. *Metastatements.* Statements regarding a subject's process of learning a script in general without reference to this particular scene.
12. *Editorial/Extraneous.* Statements not concerning the text or the actor's process were placed in this category.

Interrater Reliability

The two authors analysed all of the protocols independently and their agreement was 89%. Then, as a check of reliability, a randomly selected subset of 50% was scored by an independent rater who had been trained by one of the authors. The mean percentage of agreement between the independent judge and the authors was 87.11%. All differences were resolved through discussion.

RESULTS

Actors' Protocols

A total of 462 explanatory units (EU) were generated by actors. The shortest protocol contained 31 EUs and the longest 98 with an average of 77 per actor. The classification of these units into the 12 categories given earlier is shown in Table 42-1. As can be seen, all actors attended primarily to the mental and emotional interactions with other characters. In these statements, actors constantly appeared to be probing what was said in order to determine what the character really meant. That is, the statements concern such speculations as the character possibly using the words as a smokescreen to conceal his real feelings or laying his cards on the table or trying to make up his mind. A typical statement categorised as an interaction was:

And she says, "Well then . . . ?"
Now she's asking me to explore the issue further by saying, "Well then . . . ?"
And now I might as well tell her what's bothering me, "She wore it when I left with her."
Well, if she wore it when I left with her and it's here now and she's not here yet, then obviously she came back to see him. Or she came back for some reason and if I'm insecure about my fiancee's love, well, I could easily think that she came back to see Storey.

Over 40% of explanatory units (in all 12 categories combined) concerned this one category: mental or emotional interactions. This compares

TABLE 42-1

Classification of actors' explanatory units (in percentages)

Categories	Actors						
	A.A.	T.D.	B.G.	A.N.	P.T.	S.W.	Mean
Background	6.25	—	3.57	2.04	12.37	12.05	6.06
Interactions	40.63	40.63	35.71	59.18	43.30	27.71	42.21
Traits	6.25	—	5.36	—	10.31	3.61	3.90
Importance	12.50	16.67	10.71	2.04	—	2.41	6.49
Memorization	32.25	2.08	—	23.47	—	6.02	8.66
Response/ Initiative	3.13	—	—	1.02	21.65	—	4.98
Linguistic Info.	—	2.08	—	—	—	—	0.43
Performance	—	13.54	12.50	3.06	2.06	9.64	7.14
Style	—	—	12.50	—	3.09	12.05	4.33
Directorial Input	—	—	—	2.04	—	—	0.43
Metastatements	—	17.71	1.79	5.10	1.03	20.48	8.87
Editorial Comments	—	7.29	17.86	2.04	6.19	6.02	6.49
Total Number of EUs:	32	96	56	98	97	83	462

to 8.87% for metastatements, the next highest category. This finding is in keeping with our previous research which has found that actors appear to regard their primary task as deriving from the script the nature of the plans of their characters and how they intersect with the plans of the other characters. However, the presently reported study shows the ways in which actors derive these plans and the aspects of the text they attend to in order to derive them. Although these actors' statements regarding script learning revealed many areas of commonality they also revealed many areas of difference. That is, although with all actors the majority of statements concerned mental or emotional interactions, their secondary areas of emphasis varied greatly. For example, overall, only 3.9% of the statements concerned enduring character traits, 7.14% concerned the relationship between the script and the actors' eventual performance, and less than 0.5% discussed linguistic aspects of the text or the probable input of the director. It is particularly interesting that although the experimental instructions specifically asked the actors to study the script as if it were their first study session with a text that they would have to perform from memory, only 8.66% of the units concerned memorisation of the script.

❋

The Lorayne Protocol

In analyzing Mr. Lorayne's protocol, it became obvious that it consisted of two parts describing two totally different strategies. The first part of the protocol dealt solely with learning the essential facts in the introductory prose material on the first page of the script. These facts concerned the names, appearances, and relationships of the characters. The second part of the protocol described how Lorayne would learn the dialogue and connect it with the cue word of the preceding speech.

As with the actors' data, we segmented the protocol into individual units, each one of which described the process by which Lorayne committed a specific amount of material to memory. For the introductory portion, he grouped facts together into what he considered logical units (e.g. a person's first and last name; a person's name and appearance). For the remaining (dialogue) portion he always associated the line or speech he was to recall with the preceding cue word of the other character. The protocol contained a total of 50 explanatory units including 4 metastatements discussing his general procedure and 11 extraneous comments, such as "let's see . . . what's next?" Of the remaining 35 units, 7 concerned the introductory information and 28 concerned the dialogue portion. Throughout, Mr. Lorayne appeared to use not only well-known mnemonic methods (such as visualizing and linking), but an original variation that we call the "mini-scenario."

Although most previous studies of mnemonists' methods have not differentiated between different types of linked images, we wished to take a closer look at the process and found the following forms:

1. *Interactive Image (I-I):* Two images, each representing one item are linked (e.g. an Austin car was wearing a top hat to indicate that the character whose name was Austin was in formal attire).

2. *Incorporated Attribute (I-A):* An image is expanded or altered to contain an additional attribute (e.g. to remember the name *Clarke Storey*, Lorayne visualised a clock [clock = Clarke] that was as tall as a one-*storey* building).

3. *Action Added (A-A):* A visualizable item is seen performing an action that represents one part of the to-be-remembered information (e.g. The name Kendall Frayne was represented by the image of a candle [candle = Kendall] and by the action of candles raining down [rain = Frayne]).

All of the mnemonic devices used to code the introductory prose material were made up of one or more of these types.

For the dialogue portion of the script, Lorayne changed strategies. He primarily used a scenario-type device, weaving a mini-story out of visualizeable transformations of the salient facts. There were two types of these scenarios:

1. *Mini-scenario (MS-1):* Here, Lorayne visualized a scene in which the events themselves coded the salient words of the to-be-remembered dialogue. For example, a cue line was, *"Well, she probably ran back to tell Storey something,"* and the character's response was, *"She probably did. It must have taken a long time because . . . when you came, Storey hadn't even begun to dress."* Mr. Lorayne transformed the key word in the cue line (Storey) into the image he used whenever the script referred to the character of Clarke Storey, i.e. a clock, one story high. To code the first part of the response (*"She [Monica] probably did. It must have taken a long time . . ."*), Lorayne pictured a harmonica (harmonica = Monica), talking to the clock for a long time, going on and on and on. To code the second part (*"because when you [Kendall] came . . ."*), he saw a candle [candle = Kendall] arriving. To code the remaining part (*"Storey hadn't even begun to dress"*), Lorayne saw a lot of clothing lying next to the story-high clock.

2. *Mini-scenario (MS-2):* Here, Lorayne visualized a scene in which the to-be-remembered dialogue would be a logical response to the coded content of the scene. For example, a cue line was, *". . . and bring Ms. Grey"* and the to-be-remembered line was, *"Thank you."* Lorayne said he imagined that he was having a conversation with someone who said to him, *"What lovely grey hair you have."* Naturally his response would be, *"Thank you."* So when we heard the line about Ms. *Grey*, it would remind him to say *"Thank you."*

. . .

Comparison Between Mnemonist and Actors

Lorayne spoke fluently and rapidly with virtually no pauses; the actors were slightly less fluent, often pausing for a number of seconds to formulate their thoughts. Mr. Lorayne's protocol ran 22 minutes and the actors' protocols averaged 24 minutes. In terms of length, Lorayne generated 50 units compared to the actors' average of 77. Another difference was that about one fifth of Lorayne's explanatory units concerned learning the technical information given in the script prior to the first line of dialogue: the who, what, where, and when. Actors seemed to plunge right into the dialogue, probing the lines for cues to the deep meaning. Thus Lorayne appeared to look at the script from the outside, as information to be remembered; the actors appeared to look at it from the inside as a life to be lived.

In terms of variety of encoding devices, Lorayne employed only one strategy over and over: visualise and link. (This strategy is sometimes referred to as imagery mediation, cf. Hermann, 1987). On the other hand, actors used a wide variety of analytical strategies and on those rare occasions when they did mention visualization, it was always within the context of the scene. For example, referring to Austin's line, "*She probably did. It must have taken a long time because . . . when you came, Storey hadn't even begun to dress*," the actor A.A. said, "He's still responding to events that occurred directly with him and Monica. So all of that I would need to visualize completely, and then it's very easy to memorize the lines."

. . .

DISCUSSION

Two main conclusions were reached in this study: (1) Actors process material at a micro-level in order to derive information essential to role interpretation. Although the actor's strategy is directed towards deriving the deep meaning of the text, the process involves attending to the exact words (e.g. the example concerning the mayor's use of the word *pester*). This strategy would bring into play such psychological factors as effortful processing, elaboration, causality, and plan recognition, and would appear to explain why actors retain the dialogue verbatim using a meaning-based strategy that normally results only in retention of the gist. The data presented here indicate that, in the course of deriving the meaning of the text, actors devote the same type of minute attention to the individual words that a mnemonist like Lorayne does when he examines them in order to create semantic and phonetic transformations. (2) The second main conclusion is that Lorayne is able to use imagery-mediation, a strategy generally thought suitable only for discrete items, to encode the exact wording of text.

Comparing Lorayne's protocol with those of the actors revealed two different ways of retaining the exact words of the script. It appears that actors do not memorize their scripts *per se* but use a unique strategy that concentrates on the underlying meaning but nevertheless produces word-for-word retention. At no time did the actors attempt to memorize the words directly, but rather tried to discern why the character would use those particular words to express that particular thought. On those relatively rare occasions when actors addressed memorization, they discussed ease of learning due to factors within the dramatic situation, never extraneous to it. That is, the actors appeared to construct a causal chain in which every line is not only a response to the words of the cue but a continuing investigation of what actors call a "through line" for the whole scene. This establishment of causality has frequently been shown to increase comprehension and retention (e.g. Graesser & Clark, 1985; Trabasso, van den Broek, & Liu, 1988). The mnemonist's approach is to memorize the script directly using imagery mediation; the actor's approach is to understand what mental processes of the characters made those specific words necessary.

...

REFERENCES

Anderson, J. R. (1974). Verbatim and propositional representation of sentences in immediate and long-term memory. *Journal of Verbal Language and Verbal Behavior, 13*, 149–162.

Begg, I. (1971). Recognition memory for sentence meaning and wording. *Journal of Verbal Learning and Verbal Behavior, 10*, 176–181.

Behrman, S. N. (1949). The second man. In J. Gassner (Ed.), *Twenty-five best plays of the modern American theatre.* New York: Crown Publishers.

Bellezza, F. S. (1981). Mnemonic devices: Classification, characteristics and criteria. *Review of Educational Research, 51*, 247–275.

Bower, G. H. (1970). Analysis of a mnemonic device. *American Scientist, 58*, 496–510.

Bransford, J. D., Barclay, J. R., & Franks, J. J. (1972). Sentence memory: A constructive versus interpretive approach. *Cognitive Psychology, 3*, 193–209.

Bransford, J. D., & Franks, J. J. (1971). The abstraction of linguistic ideas: A review. *Cognitive Psychology, 2*, 331–350.

Brewer, W. F. (1975). Synonym substitution. *Memory and Cognition, 3*, 458–464.

Brewer, W. F., & Hay, A. E. (1984). Reconstructive recall of linguistic style. *Journal of Verbal Learning and Verbal Behavior, 23*, 237–249.

Cofer, C. N., Chmielewski, D. L., & Brockway, J. F. (1976). Constructive processes and the structure of human memory. In C. N. Cofer (Ed.), *The structure of human memory.* San Francisco: Freeman.

Gomulicki, B. R. (1956). Recall as an abstractive process. *Acta Psychologica, 12*, 77–94.

Gordon, P., Valentine, E., & Wilding, J. (1984). One man's memory: A study of a mnemonist. *British Journal of Psychology, 75*, 1–14.

Graesser, A. C., & Clark, L. F. (1985). *The structures and procedures of implicit knowledge.* Norwood, NJ: Ablex.

Gruneberg, M. M. (1978). The feeling of knowing, memory blocks, and memory aids. In M. M. Gruneberg & P. Morris (Eds.), *Aspects of memory.* London: Methuen.

Hecht, B., & MacArthur, C. (1949). *The front page.* In J. Gassner (Ed.), *Twenty-five best plays of the modern American theatre.* New York: Crown Publishers.

Herrmann, D. (1987). Task appropriateness of mnemonic techniques. *Perceptual and Motor Skills, 64*, 171–178.

Herrmann, D. J. (1991). *Super memory.* Emmaus, PA: Rodale Press.

Higbee, K. L. (1988). *Your memory: How it works and how to improve it.* New York: Paragon House.

Krebs, E. W., Snowman, J., & Smith, S. H. (1978). Teaching new dogs old tricks: Facilitating prose learning through mnemonic training. *Journal of Instructional Psychology, 5,* 33–39.

Loisette, A. (1899). *Assimilative memory, or how to attend and never forget.* New York: Funk & Wagnalls.

Lorayne, H. (1975). *Remembering people: The key to success.* New York: Stein & Day.

Lorayne, H. (1985). *Page-a-minute memory book.* New York: Ballantine.

Lorayne, H., & Lucas, J. (1974). *The memory book.* New York: Ballantine.

Noice, H. (1991). The role of explanations and plan recognition in the learning of theatrical script. *Cognitive Science, 15,* 425–460.

Noice, H. (1992). Elaborative memory strategies of professional actors. *Applied Cognitive Psychology, 6,* 417–428.

Noice, H. (1993). Effects of rote versus gist strategy on the verbatim retention of theatrical scripts. *Applied Cognitive Psychology, 7,* 75–84.

Noice, H., & Noice, T. (1993). The effects of segmentation on the recall of theatrical material. *Poetics, 22,* 51–67.

Noice, H., & Noice, T. (1994). An example of role preparation by a professional actor: A think-aloud protocol. *Discourse Processes, 18,* 399–406.

Noice, H., & Noice, T. (in press). The mental processes of professional actors as examined through self-report, experimental investigation and think-aloud protocol. In M. S. MacNealy, & R. J. Kreuz (Eds.), *Empirical approaches to literature and aesthetics.* Norwood, NJ: Ablex.

Norman, D. A. (1976). *Memory and attention.* New York: Wiley, 130–156.

Oliver, W. L., & Ericsson, K. A. (1986). Repertory actors' memory for their parts. In *Proceedings of the Eighth Annual Conference of the Cognitive Science Society,* Amherst, MA. Hillsdale, NJ: Lawrence Erlbaum Associates, Inc.

Perfetti, C. A., & Garson, B. (1973). Forgetting linguistic information after reading. *Journal of Educational Psychology, 65,* 135–139.

Sachs, J. S. (1967). Recognition memory for syntactic and semantic aspects of connected discourse. *Perception and Psychophysics, 2,* 437–442.

Sachs, J. S. (1974). Memory in reading and listening to discourse. *Memory and Cognition, 2,* 95–100.

Snowman, J., Krebs, E. U., & Lockhart, L. (1980). Improving recall of information from prose in high-risk students through learning strategy training. *Journal of Instructional Psychology, 7,* 35–40.

Trabasso, T., van den Broek, P. W., & Liu, L. (1988). A model for generating questions that assess and promote comprehension. *Questioning Exchange, 2,* 25–38.

43 | Conversational Remembering

Ira E. Hyman, Jr.

Speaking of performances, how about what subjects do in memory experiments? On being asked "What do you remember about X?" people usually put on the best show they can. In this situation, being a good subject means providing an objective narrative—one that begins at the beginning and goes on to the end, full of facts and free of personal comments. Such narratives may have their merits, but they are hardly typical of the way we usually recall things. The study reported here makes the distinction very clear. College students who had just finished reading a story met with either (a) an experimenter or (b) another student who had also just read the same story; they were instructed either (1) to "remember" the story or (2) to discuss what they got out of it. Both manipulations were effective. The participants who spoke with another student, for example, produced more evaluations and metacomments than those who talked to an experimenter; on the other hand, they gave less detailed support for their positions. By the same token, those who were asked to remember provided fewer evaluations but more narrative than those who were asked to discuss. It seems that telling people to "remember" does not necessarily elicit normal everyday modes of remembering.

The contexts in which people remember vary greatly. The person with whom one shares a memory may be a close friend, a family member, an acquaintance, a teacher, or an experimenter. That person may share knowl-

From I. E. Hyman, Jr. (1994). Conversational remembering: Story recall with a peer versus for an experimenter. *Applied Cognitive Psychology, 8,* 49–66.

edge of the event one is remembering, may share only general knowledge about the class of events, or may know little about the event in question. A rememberer may present a memory to an audience or may work with others to create a recollection. Most memory research, however, has relied on very limited retrieval contexts: the subjects have either talked about or written about their memories for an experimenter; the reason for remembering has been that the experimenter has asked the subjects to do so; and most often the subjects have been asked to report events and information that are already known to the hearer. Several theorists (Bartlett, 1932; Jenkins, 1974; Neisser, 1982) have noted that the demands in traditional memory experiments lead subjects away from integrative, expansive reconstructions and towards simple, accurate reproductions. Such research may not reveal all the information people have available about an event nor the constructive nature of remembering. In conversations with people other than memory researchers, for example, personal reactions may often be the first, and sometimes the only, information included ("It was a wonderful movie, I loved it"; "She is a great person, you'll really like her"; "I found the article difficult to read, but the data are interesting"). Thus, studying memories produced in a variety of contexts, particularly social contexts, can provide differing views of memory content and organization, retrieval strategies, and functions served by remembering.

...

Descriptive investigations of groups remembering in conversation suggest that there may be important qualitative differences due to social context. Edwards and Middleton (1986a) asked a group of eight adults to agree on one written version of a story they had read one week previously—an approach similar to the method of agreement. Edwards and Middleton, however, also recorded the conversation of the eight subjects as they were working out the story. They found that the conversation contained many more repetitions, details, evaluative remarks, and irrelevant comments while the written version had more coherence. In a second descriptive study, Edwards and Middleton (1986b) asked eight adults to recall the movie *E.T.* together. Although the group did begin with a narrative account of the movie, their recall differed from the recalls generated in traditional memory experiments: The subjects negotiated about the topics that would be discussed, requested help from one another concerning the events in the movie, made metacomments about their memories, and interpreted the interactions that occurred in the movie. In general, the conversation centered on affective and evaluative comments about the movie and specific aspects of the movie. In a study of naturally occurring conversations, Tenney (1989) asked new parents to tape-record the phone calls in which they told family and friends about the birth of their babies. Tenney found that the things people cared about were mentioned first: Aspects of the event that the parents had been concerned about prior to the birth and birth announcement information (gender, health, weight) tended to be mentioned early in the conversations. Tenney reported that narrative information (a description of the order of events) came later. These descriptive studies all indicate that evaluative and affective information may be fundamental to conversational remembering.

In addition to emphasizing affective responses, these studies also suggest that the narrative structure of a story or event is less important in conversational remembering. This apparently contradicts much research of schema-based recall of stories that has found narrative structure to be a very important organizing feature in memory (e.g. Kintsch, Mandel, & Kozminsky, 1977; Stein & Nezworski, 1978). The primacy of affective reactions over narrative structure does, however, agree with Bartlett's (1932) original conception of schematic reconstruction and remembering. In each of his experiments Bartlett noted how the affective component came to the fore: in his studies on memory for line drawings of faces he found that general impressions were made first, were colored by feelings, and were what remained in memory; and in his studies with *The War of the Ghosts* he concluded that a subject's attitude provided the framework around which the story was reconstructed. Edwards and Middleton (1987) noted that this discrepancy between Bartlett's original views and contemporary schema theories may be due partially to the lack of natural social contexts in most memory research. Zajonc (1980) and Neisser (1988a) have also suggested a close link between interpersonal communication and affective communication.

Personal reactions and broad perspectives—such as viewing the story as a story, applying a story to society, or applying a story to one's own life—are likely to be included in conversational remembering for at least three reasons. First, such information is unknown to conversational partners and thus important in communication. Second, exchanges of personal information teach others about the type of person one is: what one likes, dislikes, cares about, etc. Third, conversational remembering may play a role in social bonding, and exchanging and concurring on reactions and perspectives probably makes an interaction more enjoyable and a partner more likeable.

...

For these reasons, this research addressed how the social context during retrieval affects the content and organization of memories. Subjects shared their memories of a short story either with an experimenter or another subject. They did so either under memory instructions or instructions that emphasized their personal reactions. I expected that subjects remembering the story in conversation with a peer would include more personal reactions to the story, more information concerning the story viewed from a broader perspective, and include less narrative retelling of the story. Instructions were manipulated to see if individual subjects recalling for an experimenter could be induced to remember in a fashion similar to more normal conversation.

METHOD

Subjects

The 108 subjects were recruited from introductory psychology classes and given credit toward an experiment requirement. All participants were first year students at Emory University. The data from six dyads were discarded due to extensive time spent off-task, leaving 96 subjects (48 male and 48 female).

Design

The experiment was a 2×2 (social context $\times$ instructions) design. The social context manipulation was whether a person talked about the story to the experimenter or with another subject. The instructions manipulation was whether the subjects were given memory instructions or personal reaction instructions. In order to have sixteen independent observations in each cell, sixteen pairs were run in each dyad cell. This allowed for two modes of analysis: (1) each dyad could be considered an independent observation; or (2) one member of the dyad could serve as an independent observation. The dyad subjects were divided into "major" and "minor" participants in the conversation, based on the amount of time each spoke during their conversation about the story. In each dyad, the subject who spoke more was designated the major participant, while the one who spoke less was the minor participant.

In addition to the two variables of interest, three control variables were included: (1) subject gender; (2) story; and (3) experimenter knowledge. Half of the subjects in each cell were male and half were female (dyads were paired by gender). Half of the subjects (crossed with the above variables) were given one story to read, while the others were given a different story. In addition, half of all sessions were conducted by experimenters blind to the fact that social context was a factor. One experimenter ran half the experimenter-tested subjects believing that the only factor of interest was the nature of the instructions, while a different experimenter ran half the dyad subjects under the same belief. All other sessions were conducted by the author.

Materials

Two short stories by Guy de Maupassant (1955) were used as the to-be-remembered material. These stories were selected for several reasons: (1) they were complex enough to encourage a wide variety of responses from subjects; (2) they were long and involved enough to allow for a fairly lengthy conversation; (3) like many de Maupassant stories they were open to multiple interpretations; and (4) they were unlikely to have been read by first-year students.

In *The Legacy* the best friend of a married couple has died. Over lunch, the husband expresses his outrage that they apparently have not been included in the will. At the suggestion of the wife, they visit the notary to learn the contents of the will. They discover that their friend has left his entire estate to the wife. Once they return home, the husband accuses the wife of being their friend's mistress. After some discussion she denies this and suggests that the will is perfectly normal since he always gave her gifts and since men generally give gifts to the wives of friends. The husband insists that they must give up the money as keeping it would ruin their reputations. The wife points out that it is a million dollars, but leaves the decision to her husband. He decides that they should split the money and she agrees to his suggestion. He returns to the notary. After he leaves, she weeps. Left unresolved is whether the woman had been the dead friend's mistress.

In *A Family* the narrator is traveling to visit his former best friend whom he has not seen in 15 years. During his train ride, he reminisces about their friendship and worries that his friend will have changed due to marriage and life in the provinces. When they meet, he notices several negative qualities: his friend is fat, he has children, he lives in a small town, he has a small house, and his wife is fat and ugly. He fails to notice how happy his friend is or how satisfied with life he is. During a dinner scene, the family mistreats the wife's grandfather. This further confirms the narrator's fears for his friend. Left unresolved is to what extent the narrator's negative expectations biased his perception of his friend.

Procedure

The subjects entered a comfortable room and immediately signed a consent form. For those subjects in the memory conditions (both experimenter-tested and dyad), the consent form stated that the researchers were interested in memory for short stories. The consent form for the personal reaction subjects stated that the researchers were interested in how people read and understand short stories. The subjects then read a short story (both members of dyads read the same story). For a five minute distractor task afterwards, the subjects talked about orientation week (the week before the semester during which first year students are introduced to the university). The experimenter-tested subjects talked to the experimenter and the dyad subjects talked with each other.

The subjects were then asked to talk about the short story for ten minutes. The memory instructions stated: "Please *remember* the story that you read earlier. What we are interested in is *what and how people remember* about short stories. For the next ten minutes, I want you to tell each other (or "me" for experimenter-tested subjects) everything that you *remember about* it." The personal reaction instructions stated: "Please *think* about the story you read earlier. What we are interested in is *how people understand and what they get out of* reading short stories. For the next ten minutes, please tell each other what you *got out of* the story." These instructions are referred to as reaction instructions, as they were intended to encourage both cognitive and affective reactions from the subjects.

All conversations were tape-recorded using a portable stereo cassette recorder and clip-on microphones. When the dyads were discussing both orientation and the story, the experimenter left the room. When experimenter-tested subjects were discussing either, the experimenter limited his interaction to requests to continue, notations of how many minutes remained, and, when asked, assurances that the information that subjects had chosen to provide was appropriate.

· · ·

Content coding of the recalls. The recalls were broken into rough propositions that were then coded. A rough proposition was a set of words that hung together around a verb and a subject. Prepositional phrases and other supportive phrases were included as part of a rough proposition only if they make no sense on their own.

Each rough proposition was coded into one of five mutually exclusive categories or left uncoded. The categories were: (1) details; (2) interpretations and summaries; (3) factual errors; (4) metastory remarks; and (5) explicit evaluations. Details, interpretations, and errors are common categories in story memory research. They represent the information in the story, the additions subjects create to make sense of or add continuity to the story, and the changes that disagreed with the actual story. The metastory remarks account for statements applying a subject's other knowledge to the story: seeing the story as a story; noting the differences and similarities between the story and their own view of society; drawing generalizations from the story; and applying the story to their own life. The explicit evaluations are those remarks that most obviously express personal reactions. How the details and interpretations and summaries were used—as part of a narrative, for example—was also noted.

· · ·

RESULTS

The analysis focused on the types of information subjects produced in the different conditions. Differences among the four experimental groups were tested by means of 2×2 ANOVAs—social context (experimenter-tested versus dyads) × instructions (reaction versus memory)—with 16 observations per cell. In each case, two different comparisons could have been made: the performance of the experimenter-tested subjects to that of the dyads considered as units or to that of individual subjects in the dyads. I focus on the experimenter-tested subjects compared to the dyads as a whole for two reasons. First, the performance of the dyads is of primary concern. Second, when complementary tests using per minute measures for individual subjects were computed, in almost every case they agreed with the dyad comparisons.

Control Variables

The control variables were gender (male or female), story (*The Legacy* or *A Family*) and experimenter (blind or knowledgeable). Collapsing across social context and instructions, there were no main effects of gender, story, or experimenter that reached the 0.05 cut-off on any of the coding categories (details, interpretations, etc.) or subcategories (details used narratively, as arguments, etc.). Thus all following analyses excluded these factors.

Details

For the total number of details reported, there was a main effect of instructions such that subjects with memory instructions mentioned more details ($F(1, 60) = 47.79, p < 0.001, MSe = 220.36$). There was no effect of social context: neither the experimenter-tested subjects nor the dyads reported significantly more details. Figure 43-1 shows the means for each group.

Although social context did not affect the number of details reported it did affect how those details were used. The experimenter-tested subjects used more details in retelling the narrative than dyads while the dyads used more details as supporting arguments than did experimenter-tested subjects (see Figure 43-1). For *narrative* details, there was a main effect of instructions such that memory instructions led to more ($F(1, 60) = 41.03$, $p < 0.001, MSe = 281.64$), and a main effect of social context such that experimenter-tested subjects used more details as part of a narrative ($F(1, 60) = 4.17, p = 0.046, MSe = 281.64$). For details used as *arguments*, there was a main effect of instructions such that reaction instructions led to more ($F(1, 60) = 13.83, p < 0.001, MSe = 37.03$) and a main effect of social context such that dyad subjects used details as arguments more often ($F(1, 60) = 8.15, p = 0.006, MSe = 37.03$). For the number of details *simply* mentioned, there was a main effect of instructions such that memory instructions led to more ($F(1, 60) = 30.83, p < 0.001, MSe = 20.68$).

...

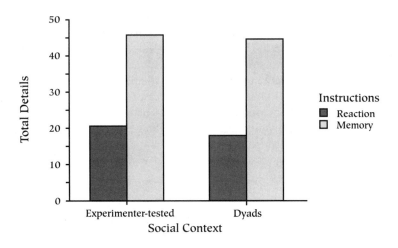

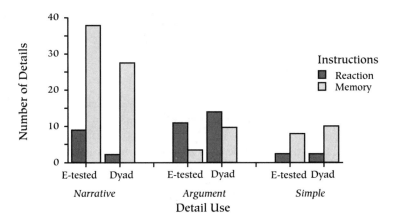

Figure 43-1 *Number of details reported and their use.*

Interpretations and Summaries

For the total number of interpretations and summaries mentioned there was a main effect of instructions such that reaction subjects stated more ($F(1, 60) = 14.48$, $p < 0.01$, $MSe = 103.69$). Figure 43-2 shows the means for all groups.

As was the case with details, social context did not affect the number of interpretations and summaries reported but did affect the manner in which they were used. There were main effects on the number of interpretations and summaries used narratively of both instructions ($F(1, 60) =$

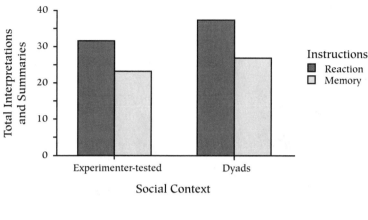

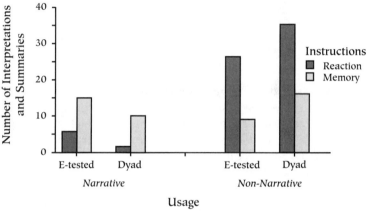

Figure 43-2 *Number of interpretations and summaries reported and their use.*

23.72, $p < 0.001$, $MSe = 52.39$) and social context ($F(1, 60) = 5.35$, $p = 0.024$, $MSe = 52.39$), such that memory instructed and experimenter-tested subjects used more as part of narrative accounts. For the number of interpretations and summaries mentioned outside of a narrative account, there were main effects of both instructions ($F(1, 60) = 45.02$, $p < 0.001$, $MSe = 121.64$), and social context, ($F(1, 60) = 10.21$, $p = 0.002$, $MSe = 121.64$), such that reaction-instructed and dyad subjects mentioned more (Figure 43-2 shows the means for all groups). Looking at the uses of both details and interpretations and summaries, the tendency for dyads to provide less narrative is evident.

. . .

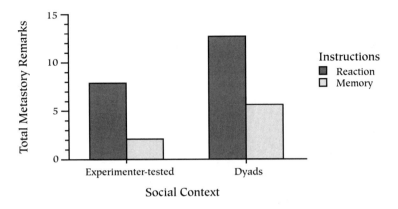

Figure 43-3   *Number of metastory remarks reported.*

Errors

The results indicated a constant error rate regardless of condition. When looking at the proportion of details that were errors [number of errors / (number of details + number of errors)], there was no main effect of either instructions nor social context nor was there any interaction. The error rate was between 3 and 5% for all groups.

Metastory Remarks

There were main effects of instructions such that reaction subjects made more metastory remarks, $(F(1, 60) = 22.98, p < 0.001, MSe = 27.75)$ and of social context such that dyads made more, $(F(1, 60) = 9.81, p = 0.003, MSe = 27.75)$. Figure 43-3 shows the means for all groups. This shows part of what dyads focused on instead of narrative—they were explicitly noting the connections between the story and their underlying knowledge frameworks.

Explicit Evaluations

There were main effects of instructions, $(F(1, 60) = 15.78, p < 0.001, MSe = 18.85)$ and social context, $(F(1, 60) = 11.54, p = 0.001, MSe = 18.85)$. As was the case with metastory remarks, the personal reaction and dyad subjects made more explicit evaluations (Figure 43-4 shows the means for each group). Including metastory remarks and explicit evaluations may serve two purposes; (1) doing so may satisfy conversation rules of including non-shared information; and (2) it may aid in social processes by telling about the self.

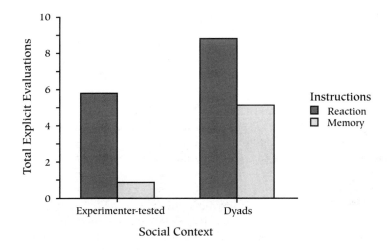

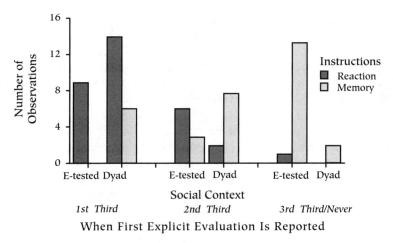

Figure 43-4 *Number of explicit evaluations reported and when they were first included.*

Another way of representing the differential importance of explicit evaluations is shown in Figure 43-4. This figure shows in what third of the transcript the first explicit evaluation was reported (first, middle, or last/never). For the dyad reaction group, of which 14 or 16 mentioned explicit evaluations in the first third, these appear to be an important way of framing the conversation. In six of the memory dyads explicit evaluations were mentioned early in the conversation. For the eight memory dyads who mentioned their first explicit evaluation in the middle third of their conversation, it was always after their narrative was concluded and seemed to be a means of beginning and structuring their remaining conversation about the story. In contrast, 12 experimenter-tested memory subjects did not include any explicit evaluations at all.

DISCUSSION

The results fairly well bore out expectations: There were significant differences in the content and the organization of the recalls generated by experimenter-tested subjects and dyads. The dyad subjects tended to be more evaluative while the experimenter-tested subjects tended to be more narrative. The differences due to instructions also followed the predictions: The memory-instructed subjects were less evaluative and more narrative.

The experimenter-tested memory-instructed subjects did give typical story recalls: They structured their accounts in a narrative, provided the gist, recalled as many details as they could, and added interpretations and summaries to complete their narrative. All 16 experimenter-tested memory subjects provided a narrative retelling of the story. After their narrative they typically added interpretations and summaries concerning the characters' personalities and motivations, and picked up details that they had missed. Most of the dyad memory subjects also provided narratives, but to a lesser extent and four did not create a narrative at all.

The other information that the dyads provided in their recalls—metastory remarks and explicit evaluations—gives a broader view of the full understanding people develop of complex material such as a story. The metastory remarks provided direct evidence of schema-based interpretation and reconstruction (e.g. Bartlett, 1932). Traditionally, evidence for subjects applying their schemas to stories and other material has come in the form of errors and intrusions that guide a memory toward its more generic frame. The dyads in this study indicated that these sorts of interactions were occurring and were part of their memory of the story by their inclusion of information that encompassed their understanding of literature, society, and themselves.

The explicit evaluations also played a crucial role in the dyads. Bartlett (1932) suggested that when people encounter a complex stimulus that they form a general impression first and that this attitude is remembered first and serves as the basis of any additional remembering. More recently, Zajonc (1980, 1984) has also argued for the primacy of affective reactions in memory. Although my research does not address the issue of the primacy of affect, it certainly indicates that people do include such reactions as part of their memories and suggests that affective reactions may serve as an alternative to narrative as an organizer of memories. The dyads framed significant portions of their conversations with explicit evaluations. In six of the memory dyads, explicit evaluations appeared in the opening moments of the conversation; for eight others, evaluations appeared immediately after they had completed their narratives. In the reaction-instructed dyads the results were more dramatic: Of the 16 dyads, 14 provided explicit evaluations in the opening moments and the other two did so in the middle third of the conversation.

Looking at the variety of information included by subjects in these different contexts shows the flexibility of how people can remember: People know the story as a narrative, they know how their general knowledge relates to it, and they know their reactions. What information is retrieved depends on the retrieval strategies people use. Traditional memory experiments demonstrate one aspect of the contents of memory—narrative organization and attention to detail. The narrative mode, as Bruner (1986) has suggested, is certainly a way that people organize experience and approach remembering.

Conversational remembering, however, allows a different view of the contents of memory and the conversational mode appears to be an equally natural way for people to remember. By conversational mode, I mean a certain way of structuring remembering around information beyond the story—such as evaluations and metastory comments. I refer to it as conversational due to its common association with that context. Almost all the dyads exchanged their impressions and evaluations of the story and the parts of the story. They tended to discuss applications of the story in terms of their own lives and in terms of society at large. They would use the story and its specifics as evidence and examples. These findings support earlier research by Edwards and Middleton (1986b) and Tenney (1989), who also found an emphasis on the exchange of impressions and evaluations in conversational remembering. In everyday remembering with family, friends, and associates, evaluations often are mentioned first and may be all that people mention ("It was an awful movie, the acting was terrible and there was no plot"; "There are lots of good ideas in that article"; "I really like that person").

The reaction-instructed, experimenter-tested subjects did supply metastory remarks and explicit evaluations. They did so, however, less frequently than the dyads and relied on narrative structure more. Thus although the conversational mode can function for individuals it may remain primarily the domain of dyads and groups of people.

···

The emphasis on experimenter-tested subjects in traditional memory research has limited not only views of the content and structure of memories but also the function that remembering serves. Baddeley (1988), for example, speculated on the ecological significance of having an episodic memory in general and an autobiographical memory in particular. He suggested that episodic memory allows one to review the past for use in the present and that autobiographical memory is "important because it acts as a repository for those experiences that constitute one's self-concept" (Baddeley, 1988, p. 13). These purposes emphasize what an individual does with his/her memories.

Another way of approaching the purpose of remembering is to look at its uses in social contexts. Extending Baddeley's suggestions may supply a partial answer to the function of memory. First, as for an individual, remembering in a social context may be used to plan for the present and future. This may prove even more valuable since the amount of experience in a group is likely to outstrip that of any one individual and thus provide a larger, more useful field of guiding examples. Further, the inclusion of evaluative information in conversations suggests that people remembering together may have an advantage over individuals in preparing for the future that goes beyond the addition of a wider experience base. To prepare for the future it is not enough to know simply what has been done before. What works, what does not work, what is good, and what is bad must also be known. This is the type of information that dyads supply more often than individual subjects.

Second, if remembering one's life is important for our self-concepts, then remembering with others may be important for communicating information about the self. In this respect, the evaluative component again may be crucial. Reciting the common information, in this case the story, tells the conversation partner little about the self. Evaluative information explains our interpretation of the world, our motivations, and our values. Reporting evaluations and general knowledge expresses the relationship between the self and the material. In this way, people are able to learn about one another. As I suggested earlier, this process of communicating selves may allow for the establishment and strengthening of social bonds. When the subjects were communicating about their reactions to the story, they may have been searching for their common reactions to it. Reaching an accord on reactions may be a particularly rewarding outcome of interactions and probably strengthens social bonds. I should note that reciting the common information when that information is a common personal history may play a distinct role in bond maintenance precisely because it does serve to remind us about each other rather than the material. In this case, we are reminded of a history of common reactions and are able to create similar reactions anew (Neisser, 1988b). Thus, the purposes of conversational remembering are to search for meaning, to learn about others and explain ourselves, and to build and maintain social bonds.

REFERENCES

Baddeley, A. (1988). But what the hell is it for? In M. M. Gruneberg, P. E. Morris, & R. N. Sykes (Eds.), *Practical aspects of memory (Vol. 1): Current research and issues*. New York: John Wiley & Sons, 3–18.

Bartlett, F. C. (1932). *Remembering: A study in experimental and social psychology.* New York: Cambridge University Press.

Bruner, J. (1986). *Actual minds, possible worlds.* Cambridge, MA: Harvard University Press.

de Maupassant, G. (1955). *Complete short stories.* New York: Hanover House.

Edwards, D., & Middleton, D. (1986a). Text for memory: Joint recall with a scribe. *Human Learning, 5,* 125–138.

Edwards, D., & Middleton, D. (1986b). Joint remembering: Constructing an account of shared experience through conversational discourse. *Discourse Processes, 9,* 423–459.

Edwards, D., & Middleton, D. (1987). Conversation and remembering: Bartlett revisited. *Applied Cognitive Psychology, 1,* 77–97.

Jenkins, J. J. (1974). Remember that old theory of memory? Well, forget it. *American Psychologist, 29,* 785–795.

Kintsch, W., Mandel, T. S., & Kozminsky, E. (1977). Summarizing scrambled stories. *Memory & Cognition, 5,* 547–552.

Neisser, U. (1982). Memory: What are the important questions? In U. Neisser (Ed.), *Memory observed: Remembering in natural contexts.* San Francisco: W. H. Freeman and Company, 3–20.

Neisser, U. (1988a). Five kinds of self-knowledge. *Philosophical Psychology, 1,* 35–59.

Neisser, U. (1988b). Time present and time past. In M. M. Gruneberg, P. E. Morris, and R. N. Stykes (Eds.), *Practical aspects of memory (Vol. 2): Current research & issues.* New York: John Wiley & Sons, 545–560.

Stein, N. L., & Nezworski, T. (1978). The effects of organization and instructional set on story memory. *Discourse Processes, 1,* 177–193.

Tenney, Y. J. (1989). Predicting conversational reports of a personal event. *Cognitive Science, 13,* 213–233.

Zajonc, R. B. (1980). Feeling and thinking: Preferences need no inferences. *American Psychologist, 35,* 151–175.

Zajonc, R. B. (1984). On the primacy of affect. *American Psychologist, 39,* 117–123.

Part VIII

SPECIAL PEOPLE

In which some unusual mnemonic talents are reported. They serve to remind us of the range of phenomena that an adequate theory of memory will have to explain.

44 | Memorists

Ulric Neisser

Webster's dictionary defines a "memorist" as "one having a good memory." I think it is a more useful term than "mnemonist," even though the latter appears in the titles of the next two selections. Strictly speaking, a "mnemonist" is a person who uses mnemonic devices. Some of the people described in the following pages do use such aids (usually of their own invention), but others apparently do not. They just have excellent memories. William James drew this distinction clearly a century ago:

> . . . *all improvement of the memory lies in the line of* elaborating the associates *of each of the several things to be remembered. No amount of culture would seem capable of modifying a man's general retentiveness. This is a physiological quality, given once for all with his organization, and which he can never hope to change. It differs no doubt in disease or health.* . . . *(1890, vol. 1, pp. 663–664; emphasis in original)*

The literature on memorists/mnemonists documents some very remarkable accomplishments. Almost equally remarkable, however, is the lack of interest in this literature shown by experimental psychologists who specialize in the study of memory. Brown and Deffenbacher (1975) have traced this history of neglect in an intriguing paper called "Forgotten Mnemonists." They show that every generation of psychologists since Wundt has had a chance to read about individuals with abilities like those of Luria's S [*Selection 45*] or Hunt and Love's VP [*Selection 46*], and has proceeded to forget them as soon as it was decently possible to do so.

There may be many reasons for this neglect. One contributing factor may even be the term "mnemonist," which suggests a person who just happens to be handy with mnemonics. Is that all there is to it? Could all of us develop outstanding memories if we just used the right tricks and worked at it hard enough? Practice can indeed produce astonishing gains: one Carnegie Mellon undergraduate, *S.F.*, improved his memory span from

---

※ This selection was written specially for the first edition of *Memory Observed.*

seven digits to nearly *eighty* digits in a year and a half of systematic training (Ericsson, Chase, & Faloon, 1980). *S.F.* accomplished this by developing an elaborate, hierarchically organized retrieval structure for digits. Nevertheless, his underlying memory apparatus (his "short-term memory capacity") had apparently not been altered: His rehearsal groups were still six digits long, his span for letters (as opposed to digits) was no greater than before, etc. Ericsson et al. compare *S.F.*'s achievements explicitly with those of well-known memorists—with ". . . S, who seemed to remember large amounts of trivial information for years by means of visual imagery, and . . . VP, who could remember large amounts of material by means of elaborate linguistic associations in several languages" (p. 1182, fn. 2). The implication is that all impressive feats of memory are nothing but the application of special tricks or devices.

From the viewpoint of this book, the first thing to do about memorists is to acknowledge their existence. Whatever the ultimate explanation of their accomplishments, those accomplishments are real. The next thing to do is to establish a rough and preliminary taxonomy. How many kinds of special memory abilities are there? What are their frequencies in the general population? What is the course of development of each type? Are these talents simply the upper extremes of continuous distributions of ability, or are the distributions bimodal? With the answers to questions such as these, we would be in a better position to evaluate the ubiquitous assumption that there is a single, universally shared mechanism of memory. Unfortunately, the answers are not available. Nothing like a normative study of memory abilities—a "memory census"—has ever been undertaken. The battery of tests and questionnaires that such a census would require has not been devised. (There is a Wechsler Memory Scale, but it is primarily a clinical instrument for the diagnosis of abnormality.) All we have are case studies.

My own guess—only a guess—is that the abilities described in Selections 45–50 may not be as unusual as is generally believed. To be sure, there have been no other reports of individuals like *S [Selection 45]* or "Elizabeth" *[Selection 47]*.[1] But people with astonishing memory for pictures, musical scores, chess positions, business transactions, dramatic scripts, or faces are by no means unique; judging by the frequency of second-hand reports, they may not even be very rare. Most common of all (if such reports can be credited) is a kind of visual memory that allows one to recall specific pages of books one has read. I have never seen this ability at first hand, but it may not be restricted to the Shass Pollak *[Selection 37]*. At least, I have been told about it by so many different individuals

---

[1]Unless you count fiction, like Borges' well-known story *Funes the Memorious*.

that I am inclined to take it seriously. In almost every lecture audience where I have posed the question, someone has reported possessing this ability at an earlier time in their lives or at least having observed it in others. Typically they report having used it to dazzle their teachers, to pass examinations without studying, etc. Typically, also, they say that they lost it by the end of adolescence or earlier.

Such reports should not be taken at face value; my respondents may have been no more accurate in characterizing their memories than John Dean was in describing his *[Selection 25]*. In one case, however, I was able to obtain a partial confirmation from an independent source. It was a woman (I will call her *MZ*) whose account was so rich and detailed that I later asked her to answer a series of written questions, eliciting a sort of mnemonic autobiography. *MZ* had maintained her unusual memory abilities until she was 29; they vanished abruptly when she contracted a severe intestinal illness that was followed by a temporary psychotic reaction to the medication she was given. Before that time ". . . teachers often wrote an outline of a subject, instructions, etc. on the blackboard, sometimes covering the entire board . . . all I had to do was read it and it was memorized." On examinations ". . . whole paragraphs or sections of what I had read would appear in my mind." Later on ". . . I could recall the exact date and day of week of future or past events—of almost anything that touched my life . . . all personal telephone numbers . . . colors of interiors and what people wore . . . pieces of music. . . . Recalling a picture, as a painting in a museum, was like standing in the museum looking at it again. . . ." Particularly interesting was the way *MZ* had used her memory during two years in her twenties, when she worked as a technician in a zoological laboratory. "I mounted between 100–200 insects a day, mostly ants and bees. Each vial contained anywhere from a few to 30 insects. As I was handed a vial, Dr. *BW* would tell me the number of each type (males, workers, etc.) to be mounted and the arrangement—one to four on a pin. . . . As he handed me each vial, he would give verbal instructions for each, and continue until he had given me all the work for the day. I didn't write anything down because I had no trouble remembering what to do with each vial." As it happens, *BW* is an acquaintance of mine. I asked him about *MZ*'s account. He confirmed it in every particular, including the numbers of insects she had to remember on a typical day. She was the best technician who had ever worked for him.

There is no way to tell, now, whether *MZ* was in the same league with *S* or *VP* or "Elizabeth" or Professor Aitken, all of whom will be introduced in the next few selections. In any case, I have not told her story to increase the number of documented memorists by one. My hope is to stimulate the search for other memorists, so that sometime in the future we can make an informed guess at their numbers. There may be quite a few.

REFERENCES

Brown, E., & Deffenbacher, K. (1975). Forgotten mnemonists. *Journal of the History of the Behavioral Sciences, 11,* 342–349.

Ericsson, K. A., Chase, W. G., & Faloon, S. (1980). Acquisition of a memory skill. *Science, 208,* 1181–1182.

James, W. (1890). *Principles of psychology.* New York: Holt.

45 | The Mind of a Mnemonist

A. R. Luria

Luria's subject S is the exception to many rules. He violates not only the established norms of memory and perception—S almost never forgot anything at all, and his everyday sensory experiences can only be described as mind-boggling—but also my own generalization that psychology doesn't care about memorists. Alexander Luria, the most distinguished Soviet psychologist of his generation, did eloquent justice to S in the book from which these selections are drawn. (Jerome Bruner wrote the introduction to the English translation in 1968.) S just proved to be too sensational to be ignored; his peculiar mental life has earned him a place in almost every subsequent book on cognitive psychology.

Although he certainly deserves his fame, our concentration on S may have fostered some misconceptions about mnemonists and memorists as a group. They do not invariably have bizarre sensory experiences or difficulty with abstractions. The opposite is more nearly the case. S turns out to be an exception even to generalizations about memorists, though he is no less interesting on that account.

When I began my study of S. it was with much the same degree of curiosity psychologists generally have at the outset of research, hardly with the hope that the experiments would offer anything of particular note. However, the results of the first tests were enough to change my attitude

From A. R. Luria, *The mind of a mnemonist*, translated from the Russian by Lynn Solotaroff. New York: Basic Books; London: Jonathan Cape Ltd., 1968. Reprinted by permission.

and to leave me, the experimenter, rather than my subject, both embarrassed and perplexed.

I gave S. a series of words, then numbers, then letters, reading them to him slowly or presenting them in written form. He read or listened attentively and then repeated the material exactly as it had been presented. I increased the number of elements in each series, giving him as many as thirty, fifty, or even seventy words or numbers, but this, too, presented no problem for him. He did not need to commit any of the material to memory; if I gave him a series of words or numbers, which I read slowly and distinctly, he would listen attentively, sometimes ask me to stop and enunciate a word more clearly, or, if in doubt whether he had heard a word correctly, would ask me to repeat it. Usually during an experiment he would close his eyes or stare into space, fixing his gaze on one point; when the experiment was over, he would ask that we pause while we went over the material in his mind to see if he had retained it. Thereupon, without another moment's pause, he would reproduce the series that had been read to him.

The experiment indicated that he could reproduce a series in reverse order—from the end to the beginning—just as simply as from start to finish; that he could readily tell me which word followed another in a series, or reproduce the word which happened to precede the one I'd name. He would pause for a minute, as though searching for the word, but immediately after would be able to answer my questions and generally made no mistakes.

It was of no consequence to him whether the series I gave him contained meaningful words or nonsense syllables, numbers or sounds; whether they were presented orally or in writing. All he required was that there be a 3–4 second pause between each element in the series, and he had no difficulty reproducing whatever I gave him.

As the experimenter, I soon found myself in a state verging on utter confusion. An increase in the length of a series led to no noticeable increase in difficulty for S., and I simply had to admit that the capacity of his memory *had no distinct limits;* that I had been unable to perform what one would think was the simplest task a psychologist can do: measure the capacity of an individual's memory. I arranged a second and then a third session with S.; these were followed by a series of sessions, some of them days and weeks apart, others separated by a period of several years.

But these later sessions only further complicated my position as experimenter, for it appeared that there was no limit either to the *capacity* of S.'s memory or to the *durability of the traces he retained.* Experiments indicated that he had no difficulty reproducing any lengthy series of words whatever, even though these had originally been presented to him a week, a month, a year, or even many years earlier. In fact, some of these experiments designed to test his retention were performed (without his being given any warning) 15 or 16 years after the session in which he had originally re-called the words. Yet invariably they were successful. During these test sessions S. would sit with his eyes closed, pause, then comment: "Yes, yes. . . . This was a series you gave me once when we were in your apartment. . . . You were sitting at the table and I in the rocking chair. . . . You were wearing a gray suit and you looked at me like this. . . . Now, then, I can see you saying. . . ." And with that he would reel off the series precisely as I had given it to him at the earlier session. If one takes into account that S. had by then become a well-known mnemonist, who had to remember hundreds and thousands of series, the feat seems even more remarkable.

···

Our curiosity had been aroused by a small and seemingly unimportant observation. S. had remarked on a number of occasions that if the examiner said something during the experiment—if, for example, he said "yes" to confirm that S. had reproduced the material correctly or "no" to indicate he had made a mistake—a blur would appear on the table and would spread and block off the numbers, so that S. in his mind would be forced to "shift" the table over, away from the blurred section that was covering it. The same thing happened if he heard noise in the auditorium; this was immediately converted into "puffs of steam" or "splashes" which made it more difficult for him to read the table.

This led us to believe that the process by which he retained material did not consist merely of his having preserved spontaneous traces of visual impressions; there were certain additional elements at work. I suggested that S. possessed a marked degree of *synesthesia*. If we can trust S.'s recollections of his early childhood (which we will deal with in a special section later in this account), these synesthetic reactions could be traced back to a very early age. As he described it:

> When I was about two or three years old I was taught the words of a Hebrew prayer. I didn't understand them, and what happened was that the words settled in my mind as puffs of steam or splashes. . . . Even now I see these puffs or splashes when I hear certain sounds.

Synesthetic reactions of this type occurred whenever S. was asked to listen to *tones*. The same reactions, though somewhat more complicated, occurred with his perception of *voices* and with speech sounds.

The following is the record of experiments that were carried out with S. in the Laboratory on the Physiology of Hearing at the Neurological Institute, Academy of Medical Sciences.

> Presented with a tone pitched at 30 cycles per second and having an amplitude of 100 decibels, S. stated that at first he saw a strip 12–15

cm. in width the color of old, tarnished silver. Gradually this strip narrowed and seemed to recede; then it was converted into an object that glistened like steel. Then the tone gradually took on a color one associates with twilight, the sound continuing to dazzle because of the silvery gleam it shed.

Presented with a tone pitched at 50 cycles per second and an amplitude of 100 decibels, S. saw a brown strip against a dark background that had red, tongue-like edges. The sense of taste he experienced was like that of sweet and sour borscht, a sensation that gripped his entire tongue.

Presented with a tone pitched at 100 cycles per second and having an amplitude of 86 decibels, he saw a wide strip that appeared to have a reddish-orange hue in the center; from the center outwards the brightness faded with light gradations so that the edges of the strip appeared pink.

Presented with a tone pitched at 250 cycles per second and having an amplitude of 64 decibels, S. saw a velvet cord with fibers jutting out on all sides. The cord was tinged with a delicate, pleasant pink-orange hue.

Presented with a tone pitched at 500 cycles per second and having an amplitude of 100 decibels, he saw a streak of lightning splitting the heavens in two. When the intensity of the sound was lowered to 74 decibels, he saw a dense orange color which made him feel as though a needle had been thrust into his spine. Gradually this sensation diminished.

Presented with a tone pitched at 2,000 cycles per second and having an amplitude of 113 decibels, S. said: "It looks something like fireworks tinged with a pink-red hue. The strip of color feels rough and unpleasant, and it has an ugly taste—rather like that of a briny pickle. . . . You could hurt your hand on this."

Presented with a tone pitched at 3,000 cycles per second and having an amplitude of 128 decibels, he saw a whisk broom that was of a fiery color, while the rod attached to the whisks seemed to be scattering off into fiery points.

The experiments were repeated during several days and invariably the same stimuli produced identical experiences.

What this meant was that S. was one of a remarkable group of people, among them the composer Scriabin, who have retained in an especially vivid form a "complex" synesthetic type of sensitivity. In S.'s case every sound he heard immediately produced an experience of light and color and, as we shall see later in this account, a sense of taste and touch as well.

S. also experienced synesthetic reactions when he listened to someone's voice. "What a crumbly, yellow voice you have," he once told L. S.

Vygotsky while conversing with him. At a later date he elaborated on the subject of voices as follows:

> You know there are people who seem to have many voices, whose voices seem to be an entire composition, a bouquet. The late S. M. Eisenstein had just such a voice: Listening to him, it was as though a flame with fibers protruding from it was advancing right toward me. I got so interested in his voice, I couldn't follow what he was saying. . . .
>
> But there are people whose voices change constantly. I frequently have trouble recognizing someone's voice over the phone, and it isn't merely because of a bad connection. It's because the person happens to be someone whose voice changes twenty to thirty times in the course of a day. Other people don't notice this, but I do. (Record of November 1951)
>
> To this day I can't escape from seeing colors when I hear sounds. What first strikes me is the color of someone's voice. Then it fades off . . . for it does interfere. If, say, a person says something, I see the word; but should another person's voice break in, blurs appear. These creep into the syllables of the words and I can't make out what is being said. (Record of June 1953)

"Lines," "blurs," and "splashes" would emerge not only when he heard tones, noises, or voices. Every speech sound immediately summoned up for S. a striking visual image, for it had its own distinct form, color, and taste. Vowels appeared to him as simple figures, consonants as splashes, some of them solid configurations, others more scattered—but all of them retained some distinct form.

· · ·

When S. read through a long series of words, each word would elicit a graphic image. And since the series was fairly long, he had to find some way of distributing these images of his in a mental row or sequence. Most often (and this habit persisted throughout his life), he would "distribute" them along some roadway or street he visualized in his mind. Sometimes this was a street in his home town, which would also include the yard attached to the house he had lived in as a child and which he recalled vividly. On the other hand, he might also select a street in Moscow. Frequently he would take a mental walk along that street—Gorky Street in Moscow—beginning at Mayakovsky Square, and slowly make his way down, "distributing" his images at houses, gates, and store windows. At times, without realizing how it had happened, he would suddenly find himself back in his home town (Torzhok), where he would wind up his trip in the house he had lived in as a child. The setting he chose for his "mental walks" approximates that of dreams, the difference being that the setting in his walks would immediately vanish once his attention was distracted but would reappear just as suddenly when he was obliged to recall a series he had "recorded" this way.

This technique of converting a series of words into a series of graphic images explains why S. could so readily reproduce a series from start to finish or in reverse order; how he could rapidly name the word that preceded or followed one I'd select from the series. To do this, he would simply begin his walk, either from the beginning or from the end of the street, find the image of the object I had named, and "take a look at" whatever happened to be situated on either side of it. S.'s visual patterns of memory differed from the more commonplace type of figurative memory by virtue of the fact that his images were exceptionally vivid and stable; he was also able to "turn away" from them, as it were, and "return" to them whenever it was necessary.

When S. read a passage from a text, each word produced an image. As he put it: "Other people *think* as they read, but I *see* it all." As soon as he began a phrase, images would appear; as he read further, still more images were evoked, and so on.

As we mentioned earlier, if a passage were read to him quickly, one image would collide with another in his mind; images would begin to crowd in upon one another and would become contorted. How then was he to understand anything in this chaos of images? If a text were read slowly, this, too, presented problems for him. Note the difficulties he experienced:

> . . . I was read this phrase: "N. was leaning up against a tree. . . ." I saw a slim young man dressed in a dark blue suit (N., you know, is so elegant). He was standing near a big linden tree with grass and woods all around. . . . But then the sentence went on: "and was peering into a shop window." Now how do you like that! It means the scene isn't set in the woods, or in a garden, but he's standing on the street. And I have to start the whole sentence over from the beginning. . . . (Record of March 1937)

Thus, trying to understand a passage, to grasp the information it contains (which other people accomplish by singling out what is most important), became a tortuous procedure for S., a struggle against images that kept rising to the surface in his mind. Images, then, proved an obstacle as well as an aid to learning in that they prevented S. from concentrating on what was essential. Moreover, since these images tended to jam together, producing still more images, he was carried so far adrift that he was forced to go back and rethink the entire passage. Consequently a simple passage—a phrase, for that matter—would turn out to be a Sisyphean task.

These vivid, palpable images were not always helpful to S. in understanding a passage; they could just as easily lead him astray.

And this was only the beginning of the problems S. encountered in reading. As he described it:

> . . . It's particularly hard if there are some details in a passage I happen to have read elsewhere. I find then that I start in one place and end up in another—everything gets muddled. Take the time I was reading The Old World Landowners. Afanasy Ivanovich went out on the porch. . . . Well, of course, it's such a high porch, has such creaking benches. . . . But, you know, I'd already come across that same porch before! It's Korobochka's porch, where Chichikov drove up! What's liable to happen with my images is that Afanasy Ivanovich could easily run into Chichikov and Korobochka! . . .
>
> . . . Or take another example. This one has to do with Chichikov's arrival at the hotel. I see the place, a one-story house. You enter and there's the foyer, downstairs a large reception room with a window near the doorway, to the right a table, and in the center of the room a big Russian stove. . . . But I've seen this before. The fat Ivan Nikiforovich lives in this very house, and the thin Ivan Ivanovich is here too—in the garden out in front, with the filthy Gapka running about beside him. And so I've ended up with different people from the characters in the novel. (Record of March 1937)

Thinking in terms of images was fraught with even greater dangers. Inasmuch as S.'s images were particularly vivid and stable, and recurred thousands of times, they soon became the dominant element in his awareness, uncontrollably coming to the surface whenever he touched upon something that was linked to them even in the most general way. These were images of his childhood: of the little house he had lived in in Rezhitsa; of the yard at Chaim Petukh's, where he could see the horses standing in the shed, where everything smelled of oats and manure. This explains why, once he had begun to read or had started one of his mental walks connected with recall, he would suddenly discover that although he had started out at Mayakovsky Square he invariably ended up at Chaim Petukh's house or in one of the public squares in Rezhitsa.

> Say I began in Warsaw—I end up in Torzhok in Altermann's house. . . . Or I'm reading the Bible. There's a passage in which Saul appears at the house of a certain sorceress. When I started reading this, the witch described in "The Night Before Christmas" appeared to me. And when I read further, I saw the little house in which the story takes place—that is, the image I had of it when I was seven years old: the bagel shop and

the storage room in the cellar right next to it. . . . Yet it was the Bible I had started to read. . . . (Record of September 1936)

> *. . . The things I see when I read aren't real, they don't fit the context. If I'm reading a description of some palace, for some reason the main rooms always turn out to be those in the apartment I lived in as a child. . . . Take the time I was reading Trilby. When I came to the part where I had to find an attic room, without fail it turned out to be one of my neighbor's rooms—in that same house of ours. I noticed it didn't fit the context, but all the same my images led me there automatically. This means I have to spend far more time with a passage if I'm to get some control of things, to reconstruct the images I see. This makes for a tremendous amount of conflict and it becomes difficult for me to read. I'm slowed down, my attention is distracted, and I can't get the important ideas in a passage. Even when I read about circumstances that are entirely new to me, if there happens to be a description, say, of a staircase, it turns out to be one in a house I once lived in. I start to follow it and lose the gist of what I'm reading. What happens is that I just can't read, can't study, for it takes up such an enormous amount of my time. . . . (Record of December 1935)*

Given such a tendency, cognitive functions can hardly proceed normally. The very thought which occasions an image is soon replaced by another—to which the image itself has led; a point is thus reached at which images begin to guide one's thinking, rather than thought itself being the dominant element.

46 | The Second Mnemonist

Earl Hunt and Tom Love

The second mnemonist to come to the attention of modern American cognitive psychology was VP, a man with whom Hunt and Love had been casually acquainted before they discovered his special abilities. VP's performance on tests of memory seems to be as good as S's, but his mental life is very different. He has hardly any mental imagery at all, let alone any synesthesia; his methods are logical and verbal. Curiously, however, the city of Riga where he grew up is not far from S's birthplace. Is there something special in the Latvian air? VP himself is more inclined to credit his Latvian education, which placed strong emphasis on learning things by heart. Whatever their origin, his memory skills are certainly worthy of note.

In many fields of endeavor we learn by studying the expert. Students of literature read Shakespeare, Henry James, and Mark Twain; students in more prosaic fields study the putting of Arnold Palmer and the serving of John Newcombe. For some reason psychologists have decided to compile statistics on the average and illustrations of the pathological. We would like to imitate the other disciplines, by describing the performance of a man with a superlative memory. Outstanding mnemonists have been described before, notably by Luria (1968) *[See Selection 45]* and by Stromeyer and Psotka (1970) *[See Selection 48]*. Both these mnemonists relied on their very unusual visual imagery abilities. The man we shall describe is quite different. To continue the analogy with athletic perfor-

※ From a paper presented to the American Psychological Association in Honolulu, September 1972, and distributed by the Department of Psychology of the University of Washington. Reprinted with permission. For more information about *VP*, see E. Hunt & T. Love (1972). How good can memory be? In A. W. Melton & E. Martin (Eds.), *Coding processes in human memory*, Washington, D.C.: Winston.

mance, our subject, whom we shall call VP, has combined intense motivation and a good but not superhuman mental endowment to develop his
memorizing skills in the same manner as an athlete might sharpen his batting, kicking, and throwing skills. VP is probably the Olympic champion in
the memory decathlon.

BIOGRAPHICAL

VP was born in Latvia in 1934 and grew up in the city of Riga, in an intellectually oriented, upper-middle-class family. Due to the unsettled conditions in Latvia during World War II his schooling was interrupted. Eventually his family fled Latvia and spent some time in displaced persons camps
in Germany before coming to the United States in 1950. As a result of
these experiences and the fact that multilingualism is fairly common in the
Baltic states, VP speaks German, Latvian, Russian, Estonian, Spanish,
French, Latin, and English. As we shall illustrate, this is of considerable
assistance to him in memorizing. He has pointed out to us that as a child
he attended schools which placed great stress on rote learning, both for
traditional reasons and for the simple fact that very few texts and teaching
aids were available. His schools were more authoritarian (and more intellectual) than is currently the fashion in this country. In VP's own remarks,
the child who sat in the corner, reading, during recess was encouraged,
whereas in this country there would be a parent-teacher conference on social development. VP feels, and we agree, that his early experiences were
influential in the development of a style of information acquisition which
he uses as an adult.

VP finished college in the United States and has done some graduate
work. He has not followed a profession, and is currently employed as a
clerk, which is certainly underemployment in a strict economic sense. He
has had a lifelong interest in chess, bridge, and other games requiring
mental skill. He is an outstanding player and is much involved in the
chess subculture. We could describe his current life as being unconventional, but insofar as we know, within the normal range of unconvention-
ality.

VP has a Wechsler–Bellevue Adult Scale IQ of 136. Not surprisingly,
he does very well on subtests involving memory. He has taken a number of
short tests designed to measure various factors of Guilford's (1967) structure of intellect model. The general picture obtained from his psychometric
profile is of an intelligent individual, but one not beyond the range of
bright people normally found at a university. The only psychometric indication of his ability, apart from tests specifically designed to tap memory,
is that he has an unusually high score on a test of Guilford's perceptual
speed factor, a factor supposedly associated with the ability to notice small

details rapidly. Perhaps more revealing were the informal reports made by the psychometric technicians who conducted the tests. They commented that they had seldom seen a more precise subject. VP took exceptional care to make sure that he understood the instructions and how the test was scored. Once he understood what was required, he invented an appropriate strategy.

We shall next describe some experimental results which show that the psychometric observations fail to capture the essence of a truly remarkable mnemonic skill.

TESTS OF GENERAL ABILITY

A classic test of long-term memory is one's ability to recall Bartlett's (1932) information packed Indian folktale, "War of the Ghosts." VP and four university students read the story, completed some distracting tasks, and then reconstructed the story after an hour. Without prior warning, six weeks later, VP and the best of the other memorizers were asked to return and recall the story. A year later, VP reconstructed the story again, also without warning. VP's successive reconstructions are in the Appendices. Table 46-1 presents some summary statistics for each reconstruction. As you can see, VP's memory for this story is little changed from the one hour to the one year interval. This is in contrast to the simplifying distortions which Bartlett found to be introduced in recalling the Indian legend.

Recalling "War of the Ghosts" is an exercise in long-term semantic memory use. It deals with recall of a single presentation of meaningful material. We next look at VP's ability to keep track of rapidly changing, meaningless material, using the continuous paired-associates task used by

TABLE 46-1

"War of the Ghosts" summary statistics

	Nouns	Verbs
Total count:		
Original story	49	68
Words in original and in:		
6-week recall	30 (61%)	39 (57%)
1-year recall	30 (61%)	39 (57%)
Words in both the 6-week and		
1-year recall:	38 (70%)	39 (70%)
Words in original and in		
both recalls:	27 (55%)	33 (49%)

Atkinson and Shiffrin (1968). In this task a small number of arbitrary stimuli are paired and re-paired with one of a large number of responses. On demand, the subject must be able to report the response most recently paired with a given stimulus. . . . The major independent variable in this study is the *lag*, or number of trials intervening between a study trial and the test trial on which the subject must recall the appropriate response. Figure 46-1 shows typical data (obtained in our laboratory) relating percentage of response correct to lag. The line at the top is not a border for the top of the figure; it is a graphic record of VP's performance! VP has completed this task four times, with 150 trials in each session. He has missed four items of the 600.

We next tested VP's short-term memory and learning capacity, using Hebb's (1961) repeating sequences procedure. In this procedure digits are presented visually at a one-per-second rate. Immediately after presentation, the subject is to recall the sequence of digits most recently seen. The same sequence of digits is repeated every third trial; consequently, the subject normally displays a longer digit span for repeated than for nonrepeated strings. typically with 9-digit numbers, subjects correctly report 20 percent of the nonrepeating strings and 60 percent of the repeating strings

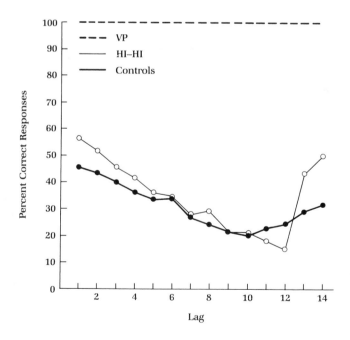

Figure 46-1 *P (correct) vs. lag, for VP and average subjects, in the continuous paired-associates task.* ["Controls" are 39 unselected college subjects; "HI—HI" are 12 subjects selected for high scores on both verbal and quantitative aptitude tests.]

after eight repetitions. The first time VP did a digit span task his performance was unremarkable. He informed us that he would do better the next time, and he did. In a subsequent session using 25-digit strings he recalled correctly 18 percent of the nonrepeating strings and 63 percent of the repeating strings. That is, he displayed an average digit span of 24.5 for the repeating strings and an average of 21.5 for nonrepeating strings. By contrast, Melton (1963) reports digit spans of less than eight after eighty trials using undergraduate subjects and only nine strings.

These experiments have convinced us that we were indeed dealing with a man with a superior memory. Note the variety of abilities that these experiments test. VP can hold meaningful material in long-term memory for a very long term, and large amounts of arbitrary information for a short time. Furthermore, he is able to "sort out" current information from recently presented, but no longer current, information as shown by the continuous paired-associates data. We next embarked on a series of studies designed to give us more information about how he did what he did, rather than what he could do.

...

[*Hunt and Love's account of several more studies is omitted here.*]

To gain some insight into this process, we asked VP to memorize lists of nonsense syllables, using the "thinking aloud" method of associations developed by Prytulak (1971). In this procedure the subject is presented with a nonsense syllable and asked to generate associates to it. Prytulak noted that most subjects generate these associations by interchanging or dropping letters, or by using some form of acoustic code. VP, on the other hand, very rapidly develops semantic associations. For example, in response to XIB, VP responded "illiterate woman." He later explained that X is the signature of an illiterate person and IB reminded him of LIB, hence Woman's Lib. His first five associations to a list of nonsense syllables were to a Latin proverb, Zygmont Bryzinski (an American political scientist), the Latin word for swan, the Hebrew word for Gentile, and the word half-wit. Throughout the experiment he made frequent associations to words in the various languages which he speaks. In digit-span experiments VP exhibits similar strategies, creating large chunks of numbers by association to dates, arithmetic relationships, distances, and ages. We stress again the rapidity with which he does this. We attempted to train some reasonably bright subjects to use VP's techniques in a digit-span study. The training appeared to have confused them more than it helped.

Given this reliance on semantics, what would happen if semantic information were to be removed, or at least made less obvious? Following a suggestion by Thomas Nelson, we asked VP to learn a list of 20 nonsense syllable–number pairings. Six weeks later he was asked to recall these arbitrary associations. Only four out of 20 associates were recalled, which is quite comparable with data which Nelson has obtained from university undergraduates. Contrast this with his remarkable performance on the meaningful "War of the Ghosts" story.

...

Case studies are always interesting reading. Extracting information from them, however, is quite difficult. By their nature, one can suggest but not conclude for cases. Proof of the propositions they suggest will require experimental analysis. We do feel, however, that two general observations are of note.

Previous studies of mnemonists have suggested that they are, in some way, abnormal. In particular, stress has been laid on the use of the mnemonist's unusual visual imagery. VP clearly demonstrates that outstanding visual capabilities are not necessary for outstanding memory. There are three key characteristics of VP's performance to which we would call attention. First, he is very quick at noting the details of a stimulus. This is consistent with his score on the perceptual speed factor, which Guilford reports as emerging in fairly young children. Second, being multilingual and well read, he has a very rich store of information on which to build stimulus codes. Third, from his early childhood, he was rewarded for acquiring and retrieving information. Thus, he has developed both an intense motivation to be a good memorizer and a style of information acquisition which facilitates coding to remember. VP himself has commented on this. He contrasts people who act on the world, such as high powered business executives, and people who observe it, such as himself. We, however, are struck by the active nature of his observations. We have quoted him in detail elsewhere (Hunt & Love, 1972). None of these characteristics make VP an abnormal person, who is controlled by his memory, as was evidently the case for Luria's visual memorizer, S.

Finally, we would like to point out that VP should not be unique. If it is true that he represents a person who has highly developed skills that are latent in many of us, then it should be possible to train other mnemonists of equivalent ability. In fact, there may be many more such individuals. Where can we find them?

APPENDIX I: VP'S REPRODUCTIONS OF A STORY USED BY BARTLETT, "THE WAR OF THE GHOSTS"

Original Story

One night two young men from Egulac went down to the river to hunt seals, and while they were there it became foggy and calm. Then they heard war-cries, and they thought: "Maybe this is a war-party." They escaped to the shore, and hid behind a log. Now canoes came up, and they heard the noise of paddles, and saw one canoe coming up to them. There were five men in the canoe, and they said:

"What do you think? We wish to take you along. We are going up the river to make war on the people."

One of the young men said: "I have no arrows."

"Arrows are in the canoe," they said.

"I will not go along. I might be killed. My relatives do not know where I have gone. But you," he said, turning to the other, "may go with them."

So one of the young men went, but the other returned home.

And the warriors went on up the river to a town on the other side of Kalama. The people came down to the water, and they began to fight, and many were killed. But presently the young man heard one of the warriors say: "Quick, let us go home; that Indian has been hit." Now he thought: "Oh, they are ghosts." He did not feel sick, but they said he had been shot.

So the canoes went back to Egulac, and the young man went ashore to his house, and made a fire. And he told everybody and said: "Behold I accompanied the ghosts, and we went to fight. Many of our fellows were killed, and many of those who attacked us were killed. They said I was hit, and I did not feel sick."

He told it all, and then he became quiet. When the sun rose he fell down. Something black came out of his mouth. His face became contorted. The people jumped up and cried.

He was dead.

APPENDIX II: VP'S REPRODUCTION OF "THE WAR OF THE GHOSTS" (SIX WEEKS AFTER READING THE ORIGINAL)

One night, two young men from Egliac went down to the river to hunt seals. While they were there, it became foggy and calm. Soon they heard the sound of paddles approaching, and they thought: "Maybe it's a war-party." They fled ashore and hid behind a log. Soon, one of the (unspecified number of) canoes came ashore, with five men in it, and one of them said: "What do you think? Let us go up-river and make war against the people."

"I will not go," said one of the young men. "I might be killed. My family does not know where I have gone. But he," said he, turning to the other young man, "will go with you." So one of the young men returned to the village and the other accompanied the party.

The party went up-river to a point beyond Kalama, and when the people saw them approaching, they came down to the river, and they fought. In the heat of the battle, the young man heard somebody say: "Quick, let us go home. That Indian has been wounded."

"They must be ghosts," thought the young man, who felt no pain or injury. However, the party returned, and he walked from the river up to his village, where he lit a fire outside of his hut, and awaited the sunrise.

"We went with a war-party to make war on the people up-river," he told his people who had gathered around, "and many were killed on both sides. I was told that I was injured, but I feel all right. Maybe they were ghosts."

He told it all to the villagers. When the sun came up, a contortion came over his face. Something black came out of his mouth, and he fell over.

He was dead.

APPENDIX III: VP'S RECALL OF "THE WAR OF THE GHOSTS" AFTER ONE YEAR

One day two young men from Egliac went down to the river to hunt seals. While there, it suddenly became very foggy and quiet, and they became scared and rowed ashore and hid behind a log. Soon they heard the sound of paddles in the water and canoes approaching. One of the canoes, with five men in it, paddled ashore and one of the men said: "What do you think? Let us go up-river and make war against the people."

"I cannot go with you," said one of the young men. "My relatives do not know where I have gone. Besides, I might get killed. But he," said he, turning to the other young man, "will go with you." So one of the young men returned to his village, and the other went up-river with the war-party.

They went to a point beyond Kalama, and the people came down to the river to fight them, and they fought. Soon, the young man heard someone say: "This Indian has been wounded."—"Maybe they are ghosts," he thought, because he felt perfectly OK. The war party suggested leaving, and they left, and the young man went back to his village.

There he lit a fire in front of his abode, sat down to await the sunrise, and told his story to the villagers. "I went with a war-party to make war with the people. There was fierce fighting and many were killed, and many were wounded. They said I was wounded, but I did not feel a thing. Maybe they were ghosts."

He had told it all, and when the sun came up, he gave a little cry. Something black came out of his mouth. He fell over. He was dead.

REFERENCES

Atkinson, R. C., & Shiffrin, R. M. (1968). Human memory: A proposed system and its control processes. In K. W. Spence & J. T. Spence (Eds.), *The psychology of learning and motivation, vol. 2.* New York: Academic Press.

Bartlett, F. C. (1932). *Remembering*. Cambridge: Cambridge University Press.

Guilford, J. P. (1967). *The nature of human intelligence*. New York: McGraw-Hill.

Hebb, D. O. (1961). Distinctive features of learning in the higher animal. In J. F. Delafresnaye (Ed.), *Brain mechanisms and learning*. Oxford: Blackwell.

Hunt, E., & Love, T. (1972). How good can memory be? In A. W. Melton & E. Martin (Eds.), *Coding processes in human memory*. Washington, D.C.: Winston–Wiley.

Luria, A. R. (1968). *The mind of a mnemonist*. New York: Basic Books.

Melton, A. W. (1963). Implications of short-term memory for a general theory of memory. *Journal of Verbal Learning and Verbal Behavior, 2*, 1–21.

Prytulak, L. S. (1971). Natural language mediation. *Cognitive Psychology, 2*, 1–56.

Stromeyer, C. F., & Psotka, J. (1970). The detailed texture of eidetic images. *Nature, 225*, 346–349.

47 | Rajan, Master of Pi

*Charles P. Thompson, Thaddeus Cowan,
Jerome Frieman, Rajan S. Mahadevan,
Rodney Vogl, and Jeanne Frieman*

*Different as they were, the memory strategies of S and
VP had at least one thing in common. Both included active mental elaborations—mnemonic devices, one might
say—designed to make the to-be-remembered material
meaningful and memorable. But it would be a mistake
to conclude that all memorists use such devices: Rajan,
described here, clearly does not. He simply recalls thousands of numbers, producing them from memory at
rates as high as 4.9 digits per second. That feat is not
only astonishing but theoretically important. In this selection Charles Thompson and his co-authors (who include Rajan himself) argue that having a "basic aptitude" can contribute to memory skill in its own right,
though high levels of achievement require extensive
practice as well. Perhaps that's what James meant by
"general retentiveness," though in this case the retentiveness is surprisingly specific. What Rajan remembers
is numbers, and he remembers them very well indeed.*

On July 5, 1981, Rajan Srinivasan Mahadevan earned a place in the
Guinness Book of World Records by reciting the first 31,811 digits of pi
from memory in 3 h 49 min (including 65 min of breaks). His record stood
until March 9, 1987, when Hideaki Tomoyori recited 40,000 digits in 17 h
21 min (including 255 min of breaks).

From C. P. Thompson, T. Cowan, Jer. Frieman, R. S. Mahadevan, R. J. Vogl, & Jea.
Frieman (1991). Rajan: A study of a memorist. *Journal of Memory and Language*,
30, 702–724.

Feats of memory like these are relatively rare. Starting with the pioneering work of Binet in 1894, the scientific literature describes over a dozen people showing exceptional memory for digits (see Brown & Deffenbacher, 1975, 1988 for reviews). In most cases, the authors used few or no analytic procedures which permit an evaluation of the theoretical processes currently accepted as plausible. Two exceptions are the reports by Hunt and Love (1972) and Gordon, Valentine, and Wilding (1984) which made use of both descriptive and theoretically interesting procedures in evaluating the memories of VP and TE, respectively. In addition, although Luria (1968) and Hunter (1977) provide little numeric data for S and Professor Aitken, respectively, their descriptions are sufficiently thorough to be very helpful.

Over the last decade, Chase and Ericsson have developed a theory of skilled memory in a series of papers (e.g., Chase & Ericsson, 1981, 1982). They suggest three general principles with subjects having particular expertise (e.g., Ericsson & Polson, 1988). The three principles they propose are meaningful encoding (the use of pre-existing knowledge to encode the presented information), retrieval structure (explicitly attaching retrieval cues to the encoded material to allow efficient retrieval), and speedup (a reduction in study time with further practice).

In their papers, they demonstrate that extremely long digit spans and rapid learning of large blocks of numbers can be developed with practice and the use of mnemonics (Chase & Ericsson, 1981, 1982; Ericsson, 1985, 1988; Ericsson & Chase, 1982; Ericsson, Chase, & Faloon, 1980; Ericsson & Faivre, 1988). The development of long digit spans with practice has been replicated in another laboratory as well (Kliegl, Smith, Heckhausen, & Baltes, 1987). Based on their studies, Chase and Ericsson conclude that the skilled memory shown by memorists can be achieved by any normal subject. Recently, Ericsson and Faivre (1988) argue that there is no available evidence that exceptional abilities, including exceptional memory, represent anything other than extensive practice effects. They state that their studies showing "remarkable improvement in 'basic' processes raise serious doubt regarding the validity of the assumption of inherited basic aptitudes."

In this paper, we report a series of tests on Rajan and show that his performance demonstrates two of the general principles suggested by Chase and Ericsson (retrieval structure and speedup). However, his encoding procedure does not appear to be consistent with the third principle (meaningful encoding). Chase and Ericsson suggest that, in the absence of such encoding, a normal subject will show a memory span of about seven items. What are we to make of a subject who does not use these coding techniques and still produces spans of 60 or more digits? As part of the answer, we suggest that his basic aptitude is exceptional. We will propose that Rajan's performance represents a combination of extensive practice and exceptional ability.

To support our view that Rajan's basic aptitude is unusually high, we note his exceptional performance as a child, discuss his recitation of over 30,000 digits of pi, introduce a technique to estimate his baseline memory span, and describe his performance on learning number matrices.

We also present a series of studies designed to describe his performance on nonnumeric tasks. Finally, we present the results of two intelligence tests which provide an overall picture of his ability.

We will, in the following sections, include some of Rajan's introspective reports. We include such information only when we believe the report is supported by our experimental evidence or when we can point out that Rajan's introspective report is contradicted by our evidence. We have also included the anecdotal evidence of his childhood performance because we believe it is interesting even though it is not possible to verify the details of the event.

EVIDENCE FOR ABILITY AND ENCODING PROCESSES

Performance as a Child

Exceptional ability often is demonstrated at a very young age. When Rajan was asked when he first became aware of his ability to memorize digits, he gave an account of a demonstration of his memory at a party at his parents' residence when he was five years old. Rajan's father confirmed that account in a letter as follows (Srinivasan, 1990): "My wife and I first became aware of Rajan's phenomenal memory in March 1963, when we had a small party at home to celebrate our daughter's first birthday. Rajan was about 5 years and 9 months old at that time. I do not remember the exact number of vehicles at the party but I should think there were about 20 or so. Rajan did surprise us all by reciting correctly the license numbers of all the vehicles and the corresponding owners. He could also easily recall many telephone numbers and railway timetables."

Reciting Pi

The memory feat which most clearly demonstrated Rajan's exceptional memory was his recitation of the first 31,811 digits of pi on July 5, 1981. As required by the *Guinness Book of World Records,* two invigilators and two witnesses viewed and certified his performance. They kept careful records of the time to recite each 1000 digits (in min) and the duration of all breaks. Rajan's recitation was noteworthy for its speed as well as the number of digits recalled. His speed of recitation indicated how well the material was mastered. He recited the first 10,000 digits at a mean rate of 4.9 digits *per second*. The next four blocks of 5000 digits each were recited at a mean rate of 3.8, 3.1, 3.0, and 2.8 digits per second, respectively. The last 1811 digits were recited at a mean rate of 2.3 digits per s. In summary, Rajan recited the 31,811 digits of pi in 150 min (excluding 65 min of rest breaks). Thus, his average rate was 3.5 digits per second.

Rajan's rapid rate of presentation, approximately five digits per second for the first 10,000 digits, would seem to preclude any possibility that he was using a mnemonic device to retrieve the digits. By contrast, the person who replaced him in the Guinness Book took 786 min (excluding 255 min of rest breaks) to recite 40,000 digits for an average rate of .85 digits per second. That individual used a mnemonic to memorize and retrieve the digits. One could argue that Rajan's performance was a more impressive feat.

Theoretical implications. In presenting their theory of skilled memory, Chase and Ericsson (e.g., 1981, 1982) stress the point that the skilled memory shown by memorists can be achieved by any normal subject. As noted earlier, Ericsson and Faivre (1988) explicitly argue that there is no available evidence that exceptional abilities, including exceptional memory, represent anything other than extensive practice effects.

One of the reasons we disagree with their position is based on the evidence just presented. On its face, the recitation of pi is impressive. That performance becomes more impressive when one considers the well-established list-length effect. Specifically, as a list is increased in length, the time to learn each item increases. In the revised edition of their classic text, Woodworth and Schlosberg (1954) discuss the list-length effect for both words and digits at some length (pp. 705 ff.). They present data from the learning of prose passages showing that the time per word increases up to 10,000 words. They show similar data for digit lists with time per digit increasing up to 400 digits. It is interesting to note that, at their upper limit of 400 digits, the time per digit is 35 s per digit for Lyon—who is described as "a practical memorizer." Lyon's performance on digits is roughly equivalent to the performance of the memorist Diamondi. By contrast, we will show that Rajan takes under 6 s per digit to learn 400 digits in a 20 × 20 matrix. We suggest that both a high level of basic ability and substantial practice are necessary to achieve performance like Rajan's.

[*The authors' account of five systematic experiments is omitted here. These experiments document Rajan's memory span for letters (14) and digits (43) as well as various comparisons with control subjects who were given extensive practice. Experiment 6, however, is worth presenting in full.*]

EXPERIMENT 6: STORY MEMORY

Rajan's unusual approach to learning word lists led us to wonder how he would perform on ordinary text. Rajan was familiar with Bartlett's classical *War of the Ghosts* story (Bartlett, 1932) so we could not use it. To collect data on roughly comparable material, we used Eskimo stories which maintained many of the unusual characteristics of Bartlett's classical story.

Method

Subjects. The subjects were the same subjects described in the number blocks experiments.

Materials. The three Eskimo stories were titled *Kayatug the Red Fox, The Dog Wife,* and *Nakkayaq and His Sister.* All three stories were taken from Rice (1980).

Procedure. Each Eskimo story was presented at a separate testing session. All subjects were allowed to read each story through twice at their own pace with total reading time recorded for each story. After reading each story, the subjects worked on other tasks for 45 min. At that point, they were asked to produce a written version of the story. They were asked to be as accurate as possible in their reconstruction. The recalled version of each story for each subject was transferred to the computer so that multiple typed copies of each recall could be produced for scoring purposes.

Results and Discussion

The Eskimo stories were scored for recall of idea units based on the propositional analysis advocated by Kintsch (1974). The complete set of idea units was developed for each story prior to scoring that story. The number of idea units was 71, 59, and 77 for *Kayatug the Red Fox, The Dog Wife,* and *Nakkayaq and His Sister,* respectively. Each recall for each subject was scored separately by two experimenters. The two scoring protocols were compared with any disagreements resolved by a third experimenter. While this scoring obviously was not the same as the noun and verb scoring procedure used by Hunt and Love, Rajan's performance relative to the controls permitted an approximate comparison with VP. Those data are presented in Table 47-1.

As can be seen, Rajan's recall performance was typically low or intermediate compared to the controls. His study times were also within the range produced by the controls. The one exception was the *Red Fox* story in which Rajan took a very long time to study the story but produced an intermediate recall score.

TABLE 47-1

Mean study time and recall of idea units presented separately for each control and for Rajan for each Eskimo story

	Idea units recalled		
	Dog Wife	Sister	Red Fox
Rajan	42	30	52
GN	31	41	34
TH	32	45	35
MD	48	65	59
DA	49	68	63
	Study time (in seconds)		
	Dog Wife	Sister	Red Fox
Rajan	277	249	593
GN	175	202	248
TH	132	145	107
MD	258	227	241
DA	279	325	239

Rajan's performance on this task was quite ordinary. By contrast, VP's performance on Bartlett's (1932) classic *War of the Ghosts* story bordered on incredible. His performance after six weeks was essentially equivalent to his performance after one hour. Clearly, Rajan's forte is not memory for prose. At the same time, he can learn such material as well as typical subjects.

REFERENCES

Bartlett, F. C. (1932). *Remembering: A study in experimental and social psychology.* London: Cambridge University Press.

Brown, E., & Deffenbacher, K. (1975). Forgotten mnemonists. *Journal of the History of the Behavioral Sciences, 11*, 342–349.

Brown, E., & Deffenbacher, K. (1988). Superior memory performance and mnemonic encoding. In L. K. Obler & D. Fein (Eds.), *The exceptional brain.* New York: The Guilford Press, 191–211.

Chase, W. G., & Ericsson, K. A. (1981). Skilled memory. In J. R. Anderson (Ed.), *Cognitive skills and their acquisition.* Hillsdale, NJ: Lawrence Erlbaum Associates, 141–180.

Chase, W. G., & Ericsson, K. A. (1982). Skill and working memory. In G. H. Bower (Ed.), *The psychology of learning and motivation*, Vol. 16. New York: Academic Press, 1–58.

Ericsson, K. A. (1985). Memory skill. *Canadian Journal of Psychology, 39,* 188–231.

Ericsson, K. A. (1988). Analysis of memory performance in terms of memory skill. In R. J. Sternberg (Ed.), *Advances in the psychology of human intelligence*, Vol. 4. Hillsdale, NJ: Lawrence Erlbaum Associates, 137–179.

Ericsson, K. A., & Chase, W. G. (1982). Exceptional memory. *American Scientist, 70,* 607–615.

Ericsson, K. A., Chase, W. G., & Faloon, S. (1980). Acquisition of a memory skill. *Science, 208,* 1181–1182.

Ericsson, K. A., & Faivre, I. A. (1988). What's exceptional about exceptional abilities? In L. K. Obler & D. Fein (Eds.), *The exceptional brain.* New York: The Guilford Press, 436–473.

Ericsson, K. A., & Polson, P. G. (1988). A cognitive analysis of exceptional memory for restaurant orders. In M. Chi, R. Glaser, & M. Farr (Eds.), *The nature of expertise.* Hillsdale, NJ: Erlbaum, 23–70.

Gordon, P., Valentine, E., & Wilding, J. (1984). One man's memory: A study of a mnemonist. *British Journal of Psychology, 75,* 1–14.

Hunt, E., & Love, T. (1972). How good can memory be? In A. W. Melton & E. Martin (Eds.), *Coding processes in human memory.* Washington, DC: John Wiley & Sons.

Hunter, I. M. L. (1977). An exceptional memory. *British Journal of Psychology, 68,* 155–164.

Kintsch, W. (1974). *The representation of meaning in memory.* Hillsdale, NJ: Erlbaum Associates.

Kliegl, R., Smith, J., Heckhausen, J., & Baltes, P. B. (1987). Mnemonic training for the acquisition of skilled digit memory. *Cognition and Instruction, 4,* 203–223.

Luria, A.R. (1968). The mind of a mnemonist. New York: Basic Books.

Rice, G.E. (1980). On cultural schemata. *American Ethnologist, 7,* 152–171.

Srinivasen, M. (1990, April). Letter to first author.

Woodworth, R. S., & Schlosberg, H. (1954). *Experimental psychology.* New York: Holt, Rinehart, and Winston.

48 | An Adult Eidetiker

Charles F. Stromeyer III

*Stromeyer's "Elizabeth" comes closer to having a liter-
ally "photographic" memory than any other memorist
ever studied. Though Stromeyer reported few tests of her
memory in the conventional sense, he does describe several astonishing feats of visual information storage. As
reported here, Elizabeth could combine a stereogram
presented to her left eye with the image of a corresponding stereogram seen with her right eye the day before;
the result was a figure perceived in depth. "Elizabeth"
may be unique. In the thirty years since the publication
of this paper, no other such eidetiker has been found.*

Elizabeth is a young teacher at Harvard, very intelligent, a skilled
artist. She has a talent that most painters don't have. At will, she can
mentally project an exact image of a picture or scene onto her canvas
or onto another surface. This hallucinated image appears to contain all
of the detailed texture and color of the original. Once the image is formed,
it remains still and Elizabeth can move her eyes about to inspect the
details.

Elizabeth (not her actual name) says that she can project a beard
onto a beardless face, for example, or leaves onto a barren tree—additions so strong that they can obscure the true image. However, she never
confuses eidetic images with reality, and spontaneous imagery rarely
bothers her.

Her ability to recall and visualize images is not limited to pictures or
scenes. Years after having read a poem in a foreign language, she can fetch
back an image of the printed page and copy the poem from the bottom line
to the top line as fast as she can write. She says that she used her eidetic

memory for high-school and undergraduate examinations, but found it less useful in graduate school.

[*In a section omitted here, Stromeyer describes the accomplishments of other "eidetikers." His list includes S (Selection 45), the Shass Pollak (Selection 37), and eidetic children like those studied by Jaensch, Haber, and others. It seems to us, however, that these cases should be carefully distinguished. Elizabeth's mental life is nothing like S's; she more closely resembles MZ (described in Selection 44) in the way she has used her talents. The mental life of the Shass Pollak is unknown; Stratton's report only describes what they could accomplish. As for the eidetic children—for whom the term "eidetic" was originally coined—they are not really memorists at all. After inspecting a picture, such a child may report that she can still see it for a minute or so; then it gradually fades from view. Eidetic children are often no more accurate in describing the picture during this period than control children who must describe it from memory alone. Moreover, they cannot retrieve their images once they have faded.*[1]]

. . . In our experiments with Elizabeth at Harvard . . . we used the computer generated stereograms developed by Bela Julesz of Bell Telephone Laboratories . . . Each stereogram consists of a pair of random-dot patterns. When a person looks at these patterns through a stereoscope, which presents one pattern to the right eye and the other pattern to the left eye, he sees a figure emerge in depth. When he looks at the random-dot patterns without the stereoscope, he can see neither figures nor depth.

Using only her right eye, Elizabeth viewed a 10,000-dot pattern for 1 minute. After a 10-second rest, she looked at the other 10,000-dot pattern with her left eye. We asked her to superimpose the eidetic image for the right-eye pattern on the actual left-eye pattern. Without hesitation she reported that she saw the letter T coming toward her.

Next we showed her both patterns through the stereoscope and she said the T was identical to her eidetic image.

Now we inverted the left- and right-eye patterns. When she projected the eidetic image onto the actual pattern, she saw an inverted T behind the surface. The T oscillated in depth, but had sharp outlines.

In the next experiment, Elizabeth looked at another random-dot pattern with her right eye. This time she looked at the pattern in 3-minute periods, separated by a minute of rest, until she had looked at it for 12 minutes. Twenty-four hours later she looked at the companion pattern with

---

[1]For a thorough review of the phenomenon of eidetic imagery in children, see R. N. Haber (1979). Twenty years of haunting eidetic images: Where's the ghost? *Behavioral and Brain Sciences, 2,* 583–594, and commentary in the same issue, 594–629.

her left eye and projected the eidetic image of the right-eye pattern onto it. Within 10 seconds she said she saw a square floating above the surface.

These tests provide proof that eidetic imagery exists. Elizabeth had not seen the stereograms before the experiment. It seems impossible that she could memorize the position of 10,000 dots in the brief time we allowed her to look at the patterns. Even if she could, this would not explain the depth she saw. Three-dimensional vision is possibly only when each eye sees a different image.

To demonstrate the extremely detailed information contained in the eidetic image, we tested her with a million-dot random pattern. She formed an eidetic image of the pattern and could retain it for up to four hours. We have not yet tested her for longer periods with the million-dot pattern.

Elizabeth could selectively recall any one of a number of images. In one experiment she formed images of four 10,000-dot patterns presented to her right eye. The next day she viewed a single pattern with her left eye and recalled each of the four eidetic images on request. When the images were superimposed on the left-eye pattern, each created a different figure that was seen in depth.

Since she had claimed that an eidetic image could obscure a real object—for example, that a projected beard could hide a chin—we decided to test whether an eidetic image could suppress an actual pattern.

We devised a stereogram that had two patterns, X and Y, for the left eye and one pattern for the right eye. Elizabeth looked at the pattern X with her left eye until she had formed an eidetic image. Then we presented pattern Y to her left eye and the right-eye pattern to her right eye. After she saw the combined figure in depth, we asked her to call up the eidetic image of the left-eye X pattern. The eidetic X image suppressed the Y pattern before her eye, and she reported seeing a new figure in depth.

These experiments show that the eidetic image is eye-specific and strong enough to obscure a real object. Furthermore, the image does not change its orientation in space as the head is tilted. For example, Elizabeth tilted her head 90 degrees to one side and viewed an upright painting until she formed an eidetic image of it. When she projected the eidetic image, she claimed it always remained upright. She could easily combine the eidetic image with an actual upright pattern and see the resulting figure in depth.

[*An account of another of Elizabeth's feats—combining an image with a presented slide to create colors in an Edwin Land display—is omitted here.*]

We have conducted a number of other perceptual tests to determine the properties of eidetic images. Some early researchers maintained that the eidetic image produces an effect similar to that of an actual visual stimulus. If this were true, then eidetic images should produce after-images and movement after-effects.

To test for after-images, Elizabeth scanned a green-and-black-grating. She reported no after-image while she formed the eidetic image. But later, when she stared at the projected eidetic image she subsequently saw a magenta-and-blue-striped after-image. The after-image appeared identical to one formed by staring at the actual pattern. However, unlike normal after-images, the eidetic after-image remained constant in size when it was projected to different distances, and it did not move when Elizabeth moved her eyes.

To test motion after-effect one looks at a rotating-contracting spiral for a few minutes and then stares at the center of a stationary spiral. The stationary spiral will seem to expand. If the original spiral rotates in the opposite direction so that the moving spiral appears to expand, the stationary one will seem to contract.

Elizabeth first formed an eidetic image of a stationary black-and-white spiral. She then stared at a rotating-contracting spiral for two minutes. Immediately afterward she shifted her gaze to a black-velvet surface and called up the eidetic image of the stationary spiral. As she stared at its center, the spiral seemed to expand. The after-effect appeared identical to that produced later when she looked at an actual spiral, and the duration of both effects was the same.

To form an eidetic image of a complex pattern, Elizabeth prefers to scrutinize the pattern part by part when shutting her eyes to see if she has a good image of that part. She could not form eidetic images without moving her eyes. She had to scan even the simplest shapes to build up the eidetic image.

Simple images can be recalled rapidly, but complicated patterns often do not appear *in toto*; instead, parts may appear successively until the entire image is recalled. For example, it once took Elizabeth about 10 seconds to recall a 10,000/dot eidetic image. We have recorded her eye movements and alpha rhythm while Elizabeth looked at eidetic images. Whether her eyes are open or shut the alpha rhythm is invariably present when she scans an eidetic image.

The eidetic images are sharp and finely detailed. Elizabeth formed an image of a fine, high-contrast-stripe grating. Two days later the image was as sharp as the original pattern.

When the eidetic image begins to fade, it does not blur as an after-image does, but dims and breaks apart.

The fact that an eidetic image built up with one eye will combine with a pattern presented to the other eye to form a perception of depth indicates that the eidetic image may be represented quite early in the visual system, before the site of binocular interaction, perhaps beyond the retina in the lateral geniculate nucleus or occipital cortex.

Many intriguing questions remain. Can an eidetiker form an image of a completely imaginary scene? Can eidetic images be altered by removing or introducing new elements? Can one synthesize an image of something not seen before? Can an eidetic image be formed of a moving scene? Elizabeth claims once to have seen in full detail an eidetic 10-second episode from a Laurel and Hardy movie that she attended the week before.

Obviously, more research is needed. For the past 35 years psychologists have been skeptical about the existence of eidetic imagery. Few modern theories of memory take into account this type of image retention. We have proved that eidetic imagery exists, but we still have much to discover about its nature.

49 | Toscanini's Memory

George R. Marek

All professional musicians have to know a great deal of music, but sometimes their knowledge is simply astonishing. It is difficult for a nonmusician to evaluate such achievements properly, but it is easy to be impressed by them. Toscanini seems to be someone special; that is why he appears here in the company of S and VP instead of with the other performers in Part VII. Nevertheless, as the author himself points out, there have surely been many other musicians with equally impressive memories.

Of course his memory helped him, and there are no end of instances which attest to its retentiveness.[1] The most famous of these anecdotes has been told in various versions. I believe the one reported by the violinist Augusto Rossi to be correct: it was in St. Louis, just before the start of the concert, that the second bassoonist, Umberto Ventura, came to Toscanini. He was in great agitation. He had just discovered that the key for the lowest note on his instrument was broken; he couldn't use it. What was to be done? Toscanini, shading his eyes, thought for a moment and then said, "It is all right—that note does not occur in tonight's concert."

He thought he would like to have the strings of the NBC play the slow movement of Joachim Raff's Quartet No. 5. The libraries and music stores of New York were searched for a score of the Quartet. None could be found, the piece having fallen out of favor. Toscanini, who had probably not seen the music for decades, let alone played it, wrote the entire movement down, with all the dynamic marks. Much later Bachmann, a collector of musical

---

[1] It has been estimated that he knew by heart every note of every instrument of about 250 symphonic works and the words and music of about 100 operas, besides a quantity of chamber music, piano music, cello and violin pieces, and songs.

From G. R. Marek (1975). *Toscanini*. London: Vision Press. Reprinted by permission.

curiosities, found a copy. They checked it against the Toscanini manuscript: Toscanini had made exactly one error. (Told by Howard Taubman.)

The same Bachmann remembered that once they were playing a game, with Steinberg present. Toscanini said, "Play any excerpt from any of the standard operas or symphonies. Stop when I tell you to stop, but don't take your hands off the piano." Steinberg played. After a few bars Toscanini said, "Stop . . . That is from *Siegfried* Act III, Scene I, bars so and so. The note played by the fifth finger of your left hand is for the bassoon, the second finger clarinet and oboe—" and so on, going through the entire scoring.

I was reading a biography of Rossini and learned that he had composed two endings for his *Otello,* one tragic as in Shakespeare, the other a "happy end," where Othello and Desdemona are reconciled and sing a duet. Rossini's *Otello* is, and surely was at the time, an almost forgotten opera. I happened to mention the curious double ending to Toscanini that night at dinner. He said, "Of course." And he went to the piano and played *both* endings.

In Vienna once Toscanini, in a friendly challenge, wrote out from memory the part the second bassoon plays in the second act of *Die Meistersinger.* He wrote it faultlessly.

Retention of minutiae is an attribute of the interpretive artist; it lies at the base of performance, and it can be trained. Toscanini's astonishing feats were not unique. Bülow's memory was equally precise: he conducted the first performance of *Tristan* entirely without the score and on his first American tour he played 139 concerts without the music on the piano, this at a time when playing from memory had not as yet become the custom. Otto Jahn in his biography of Mozart tells an anecdote now become standard history: Gregorio Allegri's *Miserere* was considered the exclusive property of the Vatican Choir and was so highly prized that no one was allowed to copy it, "on pain of excommunication." Mozart heard it once, went home, wrote the whole thing down from memory, went back, heard it a second time, made a few corrections scribbling secretly in his hat, and performed it later at a gathering at which the papal singer Christofori was present, who confirmed the absolute correctness of Mozart's "theft." (The incident worried Mozart's mother and sister; they thought he had committed a great sin. Wolfgang and Leopold laughed.)

Obviously the ability to remember is no guarantee of performing excellence. *The Oxford Companion to Music* gives the record of a

> *Mr. Napoleon Bird, barber of Stockport, Cheshire, who in 1894 won the World's Record for what has been called "Pianofortitude" by publicly playing for forty-four hours without repeating a composition; from 11 P.M. to 3 A.M. he played dance music for hundreds of couples, and, during the subsequent forty hours, whenever any vocalist or instrumentalist*

appeared and asked to be accompanied, the mere statement of the title of the piece and the key required were sufficient.

Phenomenal though Toscanini's memory was, he did not rely on it. He conducted no concert without once again, for the seventieth time, taking the scores of the program and reading through them as carefully as if he were examining them for the first time. He often did this in bed, the night before. At every rehearsal the score was there, just in case he wanted to confirm a point or refer to a letter or number, printed in the score for the convenience of conductor and orchestra. He did not bother to learn these by heart. (Mitropoulous did.)

His memory was strengthened by what I may call the "mind's ear," meaning the ability to hear a composition by reading it. That ability is essential to a conductor, but Toscanini possessed it to an amazing degree. He had but to glance at a page of complex music, his glance seemingly casual, and he heard the page both horizontally and vertically in his imagination. He appeared to be riffling through a new score at top speed and one, two, three could decide whether he liked it and what were its weaknesses. To put it differently, his eyes translated into sound as quickly as those expert translators at the United Nations transpose from one language to another.

There was nothing wrong with what is usually called the sense of hearing. He could hear the slightest false intonation amidst an orchestral turmoil. He could hear subtle differences in the quality of sound, produced by some hidden supporting instrument. Josef Gingold, one of the violinists in the NBC Symphony, recalled:

There was a contemporary piece—I can't remember what—that he programmed, tried once, and took off: he couldn't take it; it was too dissonant for him. He came to that rehearsal knowing the piece by memory; and as we were reading it we came to a terrific discord: it was so dissonant that we actually had to look at the fingerboard to see where our notes were. And he stopped: "Eh, terzo corno! Third horn! Re! I didn't hear!" The man had had a few bars' rest and had cleaned his horn, and hadn't been able to get it up again in time to come in. Toscanini couldn't see that far, and didn't see that the man wasn't playing, but he heard that the D was missing. (B. H. Haggin, The Toscanini Musicians Knew*)*

He could hear the minutest shading not only in what was being played but how it sounded. He would have the orchestra play a chord, stop, think, then tell them to adjust it—a touch more of the first trombone, a shade less of the clarinet—play it again, and it would emerge in clear eloquence and so solidly constructed, so truly a chord, that one could not drive the blade of a knife between the notes.

Gregor Piatigorsky told me of the time when he began to work on Castelnuovo-Tedesco's Cello Concerto. They rehearsed first at the Hotel Astor, where Toscanini then lived. Piatigorsky sat at the far end of the room, Toscanini sat at the piano. The next day they repeated the rehearsal. At a certain passage Toscanini said, "That is better—to use the third finger is better." Piatigorsky was dumbfounded: how could Toscanini possibly know that he had changed the fingering? It was certain he could not see it. Piatigorsky asked, "How do you know I changed the fingering from yesterday?" "I heard it," answered Toscanini.

50 | An Exceptional Memory

Ian M. L. Hunter

We have saved our favorite memorist for last. Aitken may have been less bizarre than S, less "eidetic" than Elizabeth, and less famous than Toscanini, but his talents were still "awesome," as the sportswriters say. Best of all, he inhabited a particularly "natural context," at least from our point of view. He was a professor!

Professor Alexander Craig Aitken, FRS (1895–1967) was a man of far-outstanding intellect. He was a brilliant mathematician (Whittaker & Bartlett, 1968) who had "in large measure the kind of mystical insight into problems which characterized, for example, Isaac Newton" (Collar, 1967). He was a uniquely able mental calculator (Aitken, 1954; Hunter, 1962, 1965, 1966, 1968). He was an accomplished violinist. He was also legendary for his memory. The purpose of this paper is to give an account of his exceptional memory.

To say that a man has exceptional memory is like saying he has exceptional athletic or artistic ability: it only roughly delineates his prowess. Thus, exceptional memory can rightly be claimed for the Russian, Shereshevskii (Luria, 1969) *[see Selection 45]*, the American, V.P. (Hunt & Love, 1972) *[see Selection 46]*, and Aitken; yet each man has a different pattern of memorial talent integral with a different style of mental life. So, in what sense did Aitken have exceptional memory? Briefly, he was unusually erudite with a scholar's disposition to become absorbed by, and retentive of, things relating to his spheres of erudition. He could readily produce, out of his head, much detailed information and could rapidly learn new information that interested him. His memory was (and this was also his own view) exceptional in degree rather than in kind.

※ From the *British Journal of Psychology*, 1977, 68, 155–164. Reprinted by permission.

OVERVIEW OF AITKEN'S MEMORY

Aitken could produce a host of recondite facts about numbers, calculative methods, mathematics and mathematicians; play, on the violin, many pieces by heart; recall many musical compositions; securely identify many snatches of music heard or seen in written notation; quote extensively from English literature; and recite tracts of Latin and English verse. He could recall details of many events he had witnessed, so much so that committees often consulted him as an unofficial minute book. In daily affairs, he was conspicuously, but not officiously, precise about names, dates, locations. The following excerpt from his reminiscences about the First World War illustrates his characteristic precision and his recall of details that would elude most people (the platoon mentioned would comprise 39 men). On 14 July 1916, he was in France, lying in a dug-out trying to sleep.

> *Sleep proved impossible; each time I closed my eyes I heard again, as though it were in the dug-out itself, the whistle of the falling mortar-bombs, and I saw Hughes, Robertson, Sergeant Bree, Harper, and the line of trees. But gradually, through and across these repercussions, I became aware of a conversation in low tones going on somewhere behind me, apparently between Captain Hargest and Mr Rae, and perhaps occasionally someone else—but I am not sure of this. However that may be, something was missing; a roll-book; the roll-book of Platoon 10, my old Platoon. Urgently required, it seemed; Battalion had rung up, requesting a list of the night's casualties and a full state of the Platoon. Apparently surnames were available, but the book was nowhere to be found. This being suddenly clear, I had no difficulty, having a well-trained memory now brought by stress into a condition almost of hypermnesia, in bringing the lost roll-book before me, almost as it were, floating; I imagined it either taken away by Mr Johnston or perhaps in the pocket of Sergeant Bree in no-man's-land. Speaking from the matting I offered to dictate the details; full name, regimental number, and the rest; they were taken down, by whom I do not know. (Aitken, 1963, pp. 107–108)*

Many stories are told about the range, tenacity, rapidity and precision of Aitken's seemingly effortless memory. Two typical, and reliable, stories relate to the early 1920s.

> *He taught me Classics at Otago Boys' High School and he used to amuse us at our lessons by demonstrating how he could associate line*

numbers in our Virgil with the words in the line or conversely could recite the words in any specified line (personal communication from Dr Harold Taylor, sometime Vice-Chancellor of Keele University).

As a young teacher, a single reading of the names and initials of a new class of 35 boys enabled him never to consult the lists again. (Hudson, 1967)

His memory, however, had limits. He did not have total recall if, by this, is meant some mythical ability to recall absolutely anything he had ever experienced; nor was he always able to recall, on the instant, things he could recall on other occasions. To illustrate, in 1960–1961 he attempted to recall some words and numbers he had learnt, under experimental conditions, in 1932 (see below): he recalled a lot, but by no means all, and made remarks such as "The others are not recoverable although in an extreme state, such as insomnia, they might come back" and "I felt this must be wrong, hence I decided to do what I often do, to 'wait for illumination,' and not to hurry the process." His knowledge, though great, was not encyclopaedic, e.g., he knew little about sports, and even with regard to music, where he knew a great deal, he remarked that the musical knowledge of Professor Tovey, of Edinburgh University, made him "feel like a prattling child." (Examples of Tovey's extraordinary musical memory are given by Grierson, 1952.) Finally, he did have a memory span. Sutherland (1937) reports assessing Aitken's memory span in 1932 by asking him to repeat back sequences of items presented at a rate of two items per second. With auditory presentation of sequences of random letters, the span was 10: with auditory presentation of random digits, 13: and with visual presentation of random digits, 15.

...

DISCERNMENT OF MULTIPLE PROPERTIES

Aitken's memory was intimately linked with his ability to discern multiple properties that were interwoven into distinctive patterns. His discernment could work rapidly to produce an unusually rich, densely structured gestalt of properties; and so many things, that would seem chaotic to a bystander, were, to him, embodiments of multiple properties that meshed into an interesting, memorable pattern.

The ease with which he learnt and remembered anything, and indeed whether he learnt and remembered it at all, depended squarely on the meaning and interest it had for him. Thus, whenever something interested him deeply, he was typically able, later, to recall many details of it despite his having had not the slightest conscious intention of committing anything to memory. Again, if he were given material that, for him, had little meaning (say, a random string of digits), he typically pronounced it "uninteresting" or even "repellent." If asked to commit such material to memory, he might oblige if he thought some psychological value might emerge from the exercise, but usually remarked that the exercise was "unnatural" and "went against the grain." (Throughout this paper, all words bounded by quotation marks are Aitken's, unless otherwise specified.) If he did undertake "unnatural" memorizing, he adopted a characteristic approach as follows.

When given material that was "not too repellent" and asked to memorize it, he did not, as might be expected, go tense in concentration. He went noticeably still and relaxed. When asked about this curious behavior, he explained that he was using a subterfuge . . . on which, he discovered years ago, he could rely. He was relaxing by way of preparing to find interest in the material or "to let the properties of the material reveal themselves." He felt best able to secure memorization by refraining from deliberate interpretation and organization; rather, he cleared his mind and relinquished the job to his vast cognitive system, allowing it to work largely autonomously and in whatever way came most naturally. He commented as follows.

> I discovered that the further I proceeded, the more I needed relaxation, not concentration as ordinarily understood. One must be relaxed, yet possessed, in order to do this well. Sometimes one enters a bookshop and there, displayed on the stalls, are various interesting books. One selects, dips, reads, becomes intent, until the stage is reached when all surroundings are forgotten. Afterwards, one leaves the shop and enters the street again, blinking at the light and at the people as if one had come out of an anaesthetic. And so it is here. The one requisite is that a live interest in the subject should fix an undeviating attention. . . . Interest is the thing. Interest focuses the attention. At first one might have to concentrate, but as soon as possible one should relax. Very few people do that. Unfortunately, it is not taught at school where knowledge is acquired by rote, by learning by heart, sometimes against the grain. The thing to do is learn by heart, not because one has to, but because one loves the thing and is interested in it. Then one has moved away from concentration to relaxation.

PSYCHOBIOGRAPHY

Aitken's mnemic activities were inextricably part of a larger configuration including all his psychological processes, e.g., his general knowledge, preferred pursuits, emotional and intellectual attitudes to the world and to himself: his memory was nondetachable from his entire psychophysical make-up, from the participation of the whole personality. Of his personality, it might fairly be said that he was, above all, a reflective man who sought to comprehend events by discerning their inward patterns. With his talents, this mild-mannered man might well have made more of a worldly splash, but it would have gone against the grain to pursue, say, political power or success in business. It was supremely consistent that he found his eventual professional calling in a field of scholarship devoted to uncovering deep mathematical patterns.

Interest in meaning was a *leitmotiv* of his psychobiography. Starting in his mid-teens and continuing into his late-twenties, he was enthralled by number, music, poetry and his own intellectual capabilities. These were the years, involving "a kind of mental Yoga," in which he became demonstrably exceptional through attempting to penetrate the inwardness of numerical relations, the architecture of poetry and music, the system of his own mental skills, the interconnectedness of phenomena at large. Almost certainly, he was interested, at this time, in testing his mental powers to the limit, e.g., discovering how much Milton he could recite verbatim or how fast he could calculate. Almost certainly, too, he enjoyed demonstrating his prowess to others. But it is equally certain that, in later adult years, he rarely memorized anything merely for the sake of memorizing it. He would deliberately memorize what he thought might be useful to have readily available in his head, e.g., the names of his students. More often, things got memorized as an unintended by-product of his penetrating interest in them.

[*Descriptions of several experiments with Aitken are omitted here. His digit span was about 15. In 1960 he was able—with some effort—to recall all of a 25-word list he had memorized in 1932, and more than half of a list of 16 3-digit numbers from the same year.*]

···

A comparison between Aitken and the average adult shows that his accomplishments of memory are, at every turn, stronger than average. He has a longer memory span, a more retentive grip on things he has learnt and, overall, a larger and more finely articulated cognitive system. At the same time, nothing about Aitken violates what we know about the normal design features of memory. It is normal, for example, that high-level learning and remembering depends on interest and, crucially, on the process of comprehending material in terms of patterns of multiple properties. Even his subterfuge of assimilation by interest is within the experience of many highly intelligent people. For example, when experienced actors deliberately set out to master a new role, they do not focus on the task of memorization as such but, rather, on studying the role with a view to discerning a network of meanings in it: this pursuit of meaning has the effect of securing memorization as a by-product (Smirnov, 1973, chapter 3) *[see also Selection 42]*.

Now, compare the present account of Aitken with Luria's (1969) account of S. V. Shereshevskii (hereafter called "S.") *[Selection 45]*. The comparison shows how different is the exceptional memory of a scholar and a mnemonist.

S. was an outstanding professional mnemonist, that is, someone who memorizes haphazard strings of items. He used the classical mnemonist's technique of imagining richly vivid, concrete mental-pictures, which he arranged in a chain of pairs. If given the 25-word list mentioned above, he might take an imaginary walk along a street that has a vivid succession of landmarks. He would represent the first word by a distinctively imaged picture which he would locate on the first landmark; the second word would be another mental picture located on the second landmark, and so on. During a single, and not too rapid, presentation of the word list, he would progressively devise such a chain of images that was extremely rich in perception-like properties. This would result in accurate, durable memorization. Even years afterwards, he would be able to recapitulate the chain of images, and, so, recall the list of words in either forward or backward sequence. Contrast this procedure with the way Aitken memorized the list, not by a strict chain, but by a kind of overall melody.

The chief similarity between Aitken and S. is that each comprehends materials in terms of a multiplicity of unconventional properties, knits these properties into fairly unconventional patterns, and durably retains these patterns so as to be able to reconstruct the original materials. The chief difference is the *kind* of property involved and the *kind* of pattern woven. Characteristically, S.'s kind of property is perception-like, i.e., particular sensory qualities and particular imaged objects: his kind of pattern is the chain, i.e., short-run links between successively encountered items. Characteristically, Aitken's kind of property is conceptual: his kind of pattern is the panorama or map, i.e., long-run groupings of items into overlapping multilayered configurations.

The following comparison illustrates the different kind of property by which the two men comprehend materials. First, remarks made by S. in 1936. "Even numbers remind me of images. Take the number 1. This is a proud, well-built man; 2 is a high-spirited woman; 3 is a gloomy person (why, I don't know); 6 a man with a swollen foot; 7 a man with a mustache; 8 a very stout woman—a sack within a sack. As for the number 87, what I see is a fat woman and a man twirling his mustache" (Luria, 1969, p. 31). Now, remarks made by Aitken in 1932. Sutherland (1937) showed him a mixed series of written words and numbers, and asked him to report what each item called immediately to mind. Here is the response to "7." "The line of poetry 'They passed the pleiades and the planets seven'—mysteries in the minds of the ancients—Sabbath or seventh day—religious observance of Sunday—7 in contrast with 13 and with 3 in superstition—

7 as a recurring decimal ·142857 which, multiplied by 123456, gives the same numbers in cyclic order—a poem on numbers by Binyon, seen in a review lately—I could quote from it."

In broad terms, then, Aitken comprehends materials in terms of rich conceptual maps; S. in terms of rich perceptual chains. These contrasting modes of comprehension show in the intellectual profiles of the two men. S.'s great distinction is in memorizing haphazard strings of items; Aitken's is in mathematical thinking. In an Olympic Games for Mental Prowess, S. would win the gold in the section for mnemonists, while Aitken would scarcely qualify for entry. But S. would not even be considered for entry to three sections where Aitken would shine, namely for theoretical mathematicians, mental calculators, and all-rounders.

...

REFERENCES

Aitken, A. C. (1954). The art of mental calculation: With demonstrations. *Trans. Soc. Engrs., Lond., 44,* 295–309.

Aitken, A. C. (1963). *Gallipoli to the Somme: Recollections of a New Zealand infantryman.* London: Oxford University Press.

Collar, A. R. (1967, 22 Nov.). Prof. A. C. Aitken. *The Times,* p. 12.

Grierson, M. (1952). *Donald Francis Tovey: A biography based on letters.* London: Oxford University Press.

Hudson, D. (1967, 7 Nov.). Prof. A. C. Aitken. *The Times,* p. 12.

Hunt, E., & Love, T. (1972). How good can memory be? In A. W. Melton and E. Martin (Eds.), *Coding processes in human memory.* New York: Wiley.

Hunter, I. M. L. (1962). An exceptional talent for calculative thinking. *Br. J. Psychol., 53,* 243–258.

Hunter, I. M. L. (1965). Strategems for skill. In *Penguin Science Survey, 1965 B.* Harmondsworth: Penguin.

Hunter, I. M. L. (1966). "Kopfrechnen und Kopfrechner." *Bild der Wissenschaft, 3,* 296–303.

Hunter, I. M. L. (1968). "Mental calculation." In P. C. Wason & P. N. Johnson-Laird (Eds.), *Thinking and reasoning.* Harmondsworth: Penguin.

Luria, A. R. (1969). *The mind of a mnemonist.* London: Cape.

Smirnov, A. A. (1973). *Problems of the psychology of memory.* New York: Plenum.

Sutherland, J. D. (1937). "Phenomenal memory and calculating ability: With illustrations from Dr A. C. Aitken." Unpublished manuscript.

Whittaker, J. M., & Bartlett, M. S. (1965). Alexander Craig Aitken. *Biographical memoirs of fellows of the Royal Society, 14,* 1–14.

Name Index

Page references in **bold type** indicate a chapter authored in whole or part by that writer. Page references followed by *n* indicate material in footnotes.

Subject Index